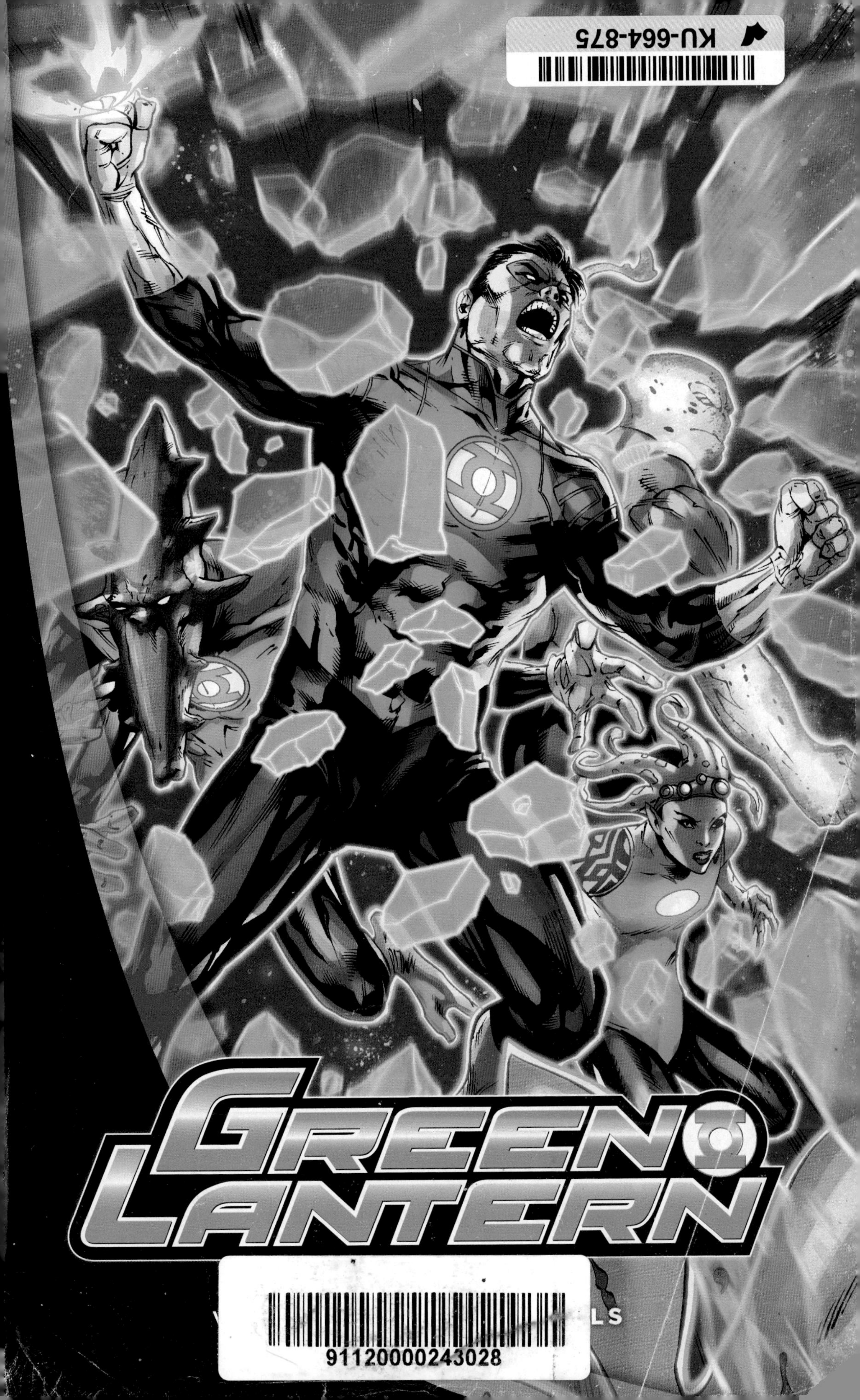

GREEN LANTERN

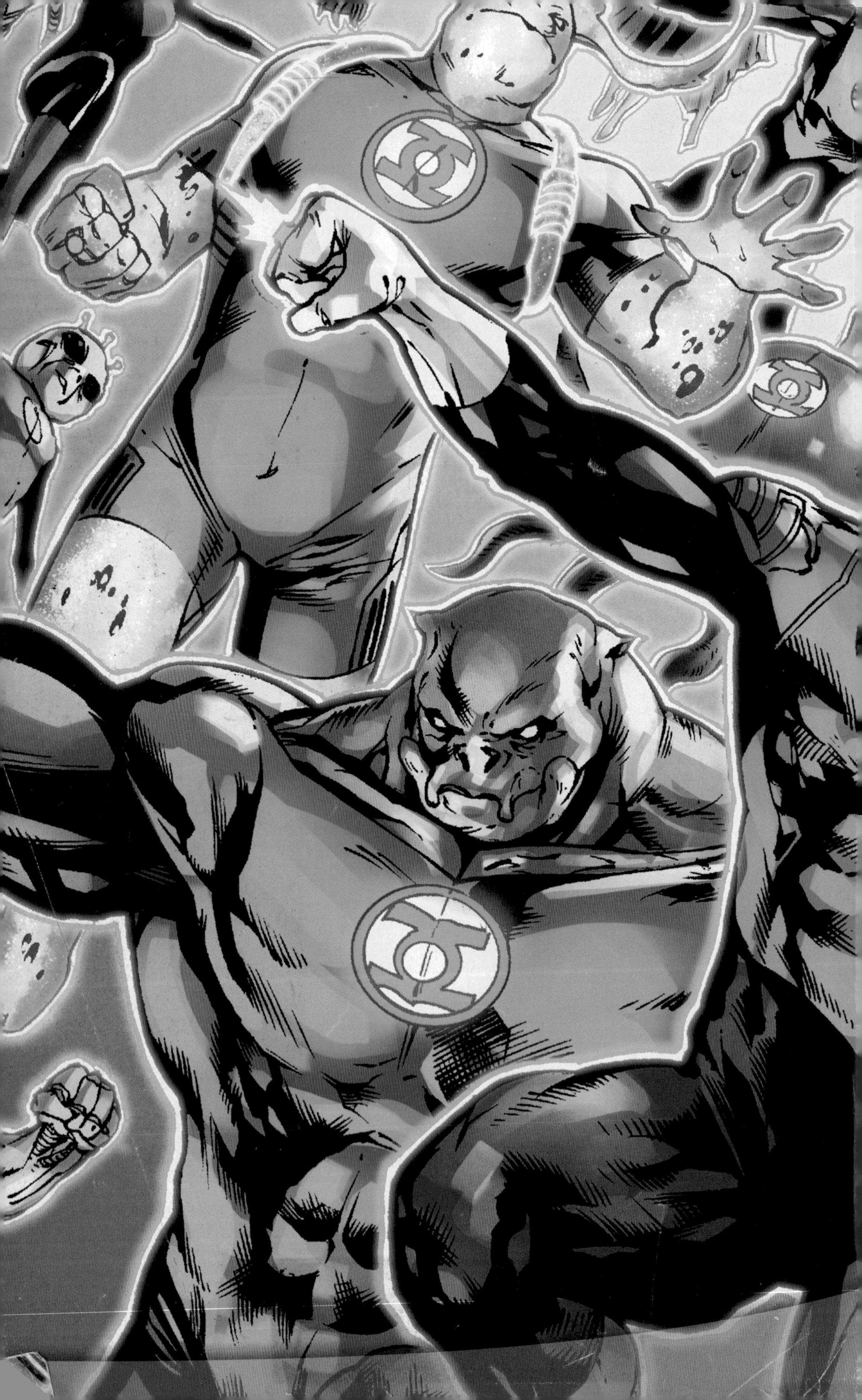

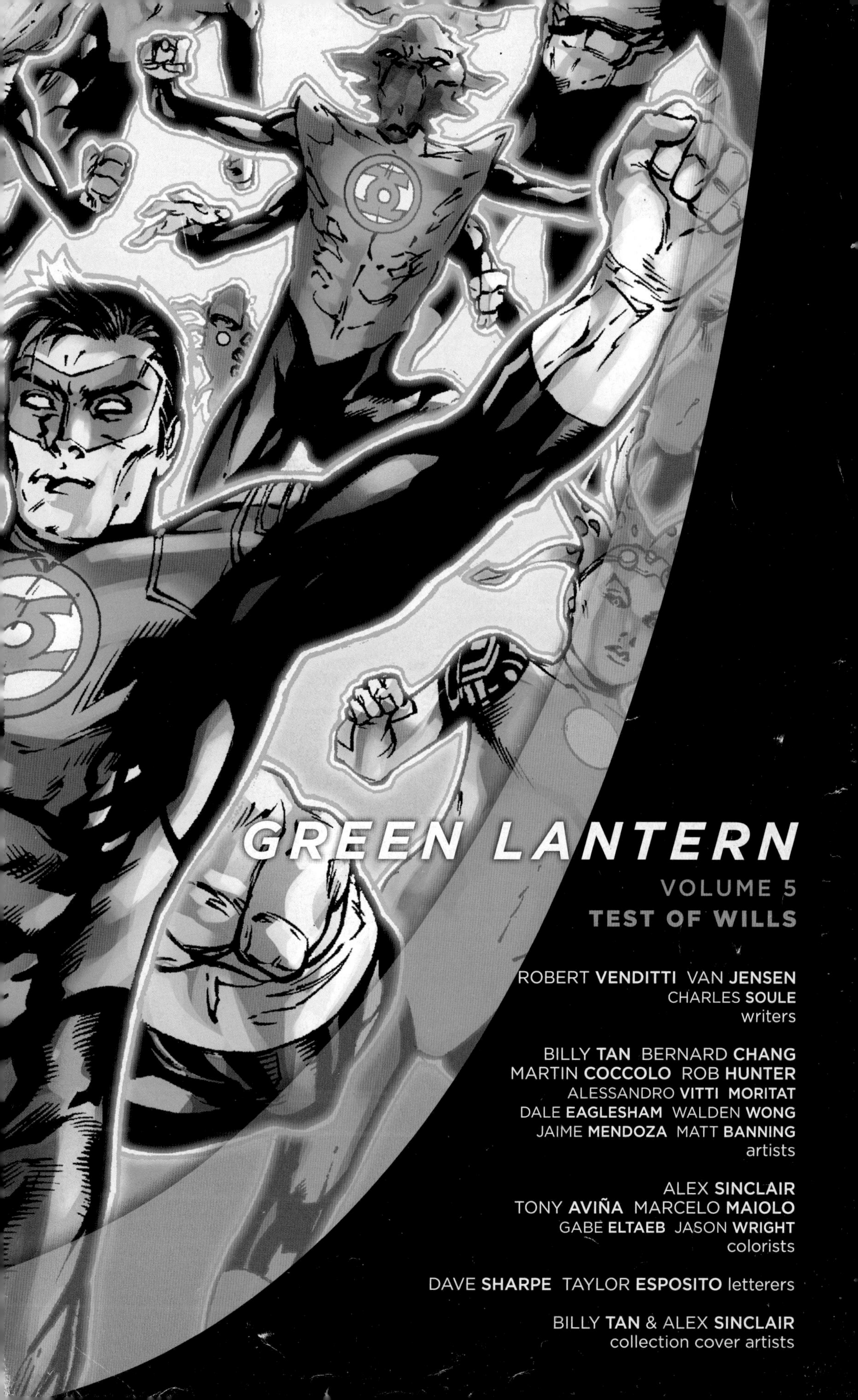

GREEN LANTERN

VOLUME 5
TEST OF WILLS

ROBERT **VENDITTI** VAN **JENSEN**
CHARLES **SOULE**
writers

BILLY **TAN** BERNARD **CHANG**
MARTIN **COCCOLO** ROB **HUNTER**
ALESSANDRO **VITTI** **MORITAT**
DALE **EAGLESHAM** WALDEN **WONG**
JAIME **MENDOZA** MATT **BANNING**
artists

ALEX **SINCLAIR**
TONY **AVIÑA** MARCELO **MAIOLO**
GABE **ELTAEB** JASON **WRIGHT**
colorists

DAVE **SHARPE** TAYLOR **ESPOSITO** letterers

BILLY **TAN** & ALEX **SINCLAIR**
collection cover artists

GREEN LANTERN VOLUME 5: TEST OF WILLS

Published by DC Comics. Compilation Copyright © 2015 DC Comics. All Rights Reserved.

Originally published in single magazine form in GREEN LANTERN 27-34, GREEN LANTERN CORPS 31-33, and RED LANTERNS 28.
Copyright © 2014 DC Comics. All Rights Reserved. All characters, their distinctive likenesses and related elements featured
in this publication are trademarks of DC Comics. The stories, characters and incidents featured in this publication are entirely fictional.
DC Comics does not read or accept unsolicited ideas, stories or artwork.

DC Comics, 4000 Warner Blvd., Burbank, CA 91522
A Warner Bros. Entertainment Company.
Printed by RR Donnelley, Salem, VA, USA. 4/10/15. First Printing.

ISBN: 978-1-4012-5416-2

SUSTAINABLE
FORESTRY
INITIATIVE

Certified Chain of Custody
20% Certified Forest Content,
80% Certified Sourcing
www.sfiprogram.org
SFI-01042
APPLIES TO TEXT STOCK ONLY

Library of Congress Cataloging-in-Publication Data

Venditti, Robert, author.
Green Lantern. Volume 5, Test of wills / Robert Venditti, writer ; Billy Tan, artist.
pages cm. — (The New 52!)
ISBN 978-1-4012-5089-8 (hardback)
1. Graphic novels. I. Tan, Billy, illustrator. II. Title. III. Title: Test of wills.

PN6728.G74V47 2014
741.5'973—dc23

2014027842

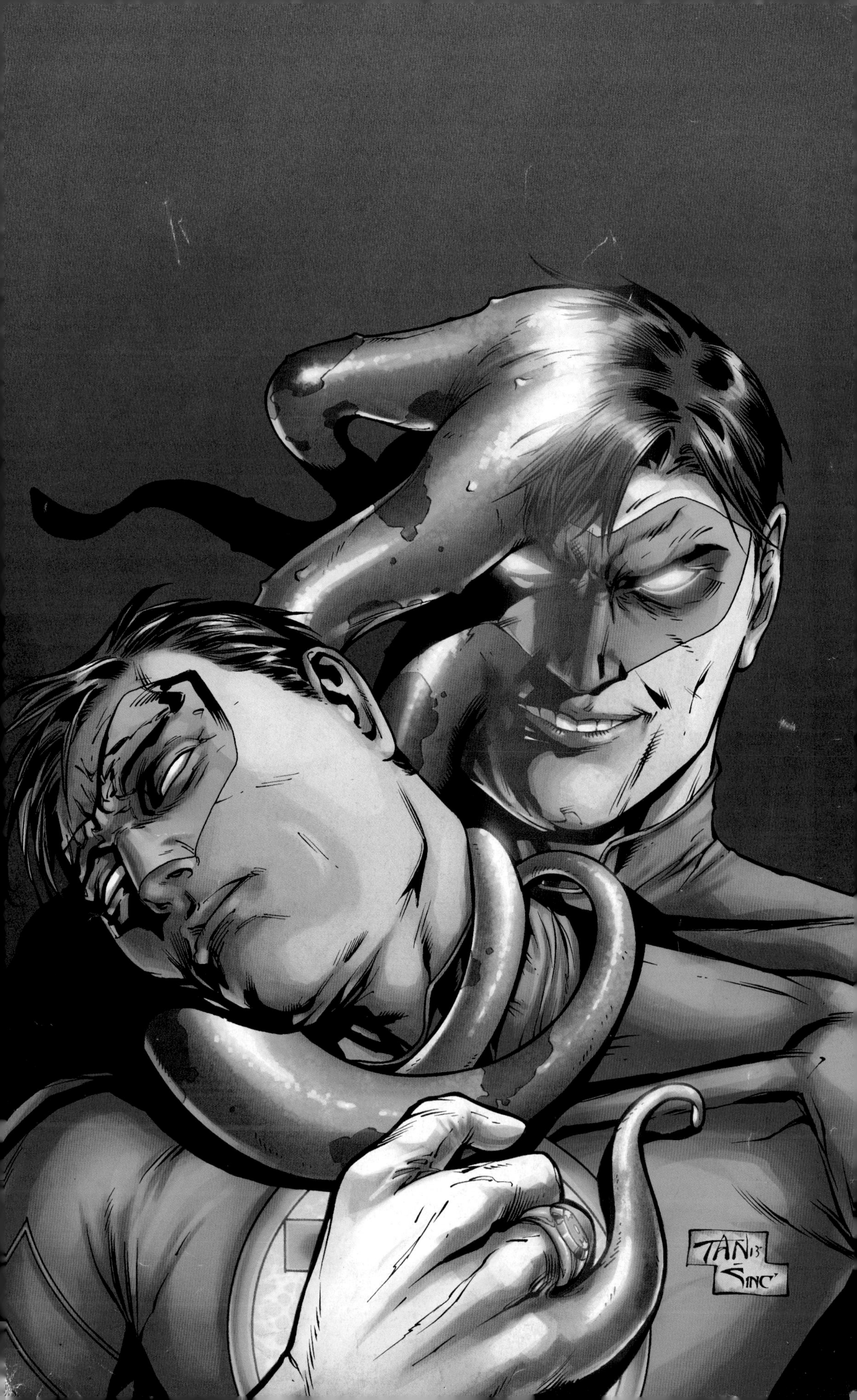

HARSH REALITIES

ROBERT VENDITTI writer DALE EAGLESHAM artist JASON WRIGHT colorist
cover art by BILLY TAN & ALEX SINCLAIR SCRIBBLENAUTS variant cover by JOHN KATZ after NEAL ADAMS

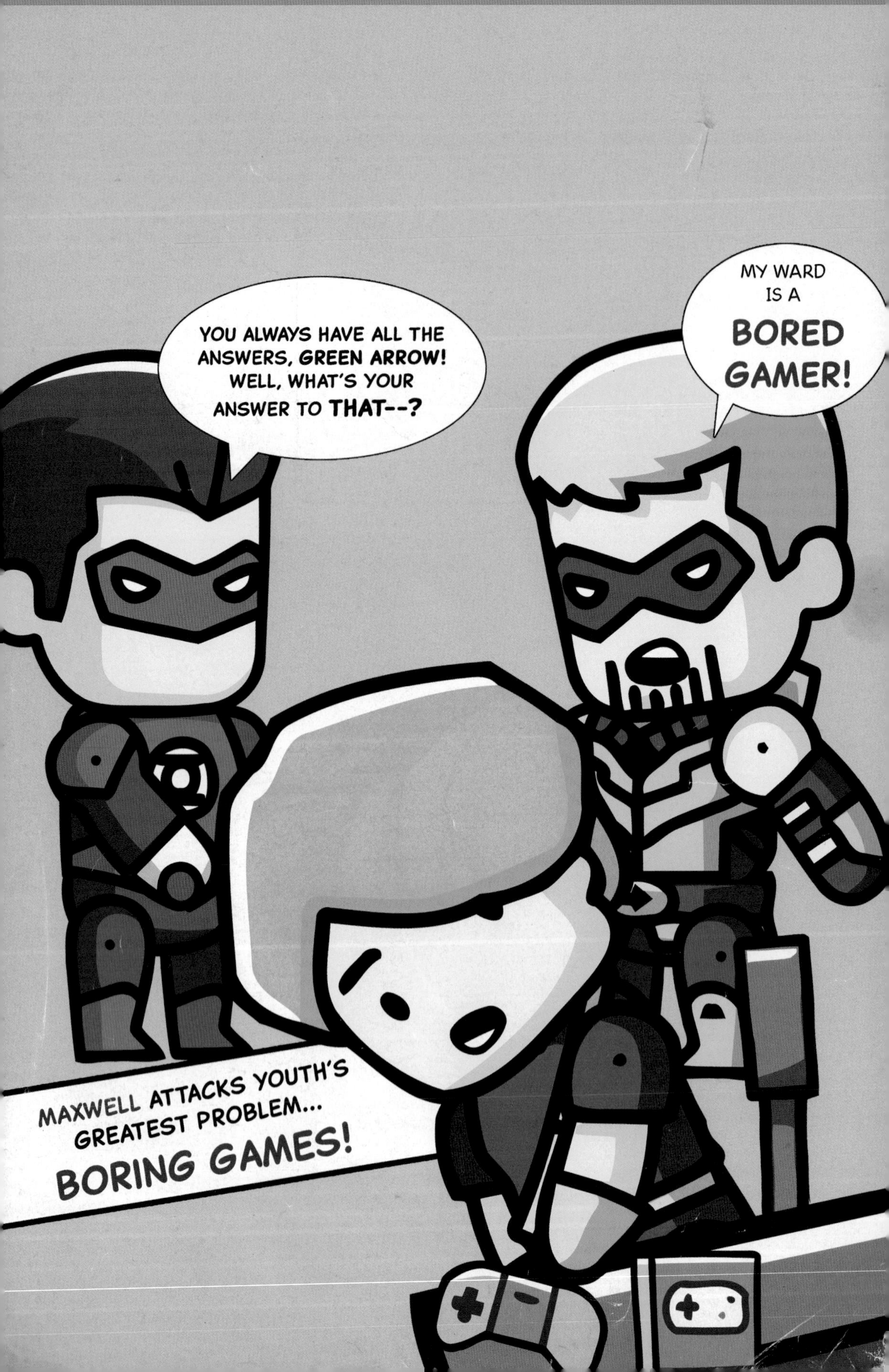
YOU ALWAYS HAVE ALL THE ANSWERS, GREEN ARROW! WELL, WHAT'S YOUR ANSWER TO THAT--?
MY WARD IS A BORED GAMER!
MAXWELL ATTACKS YOUTH'S GREATEST PROBLEM... BORING GAMES!

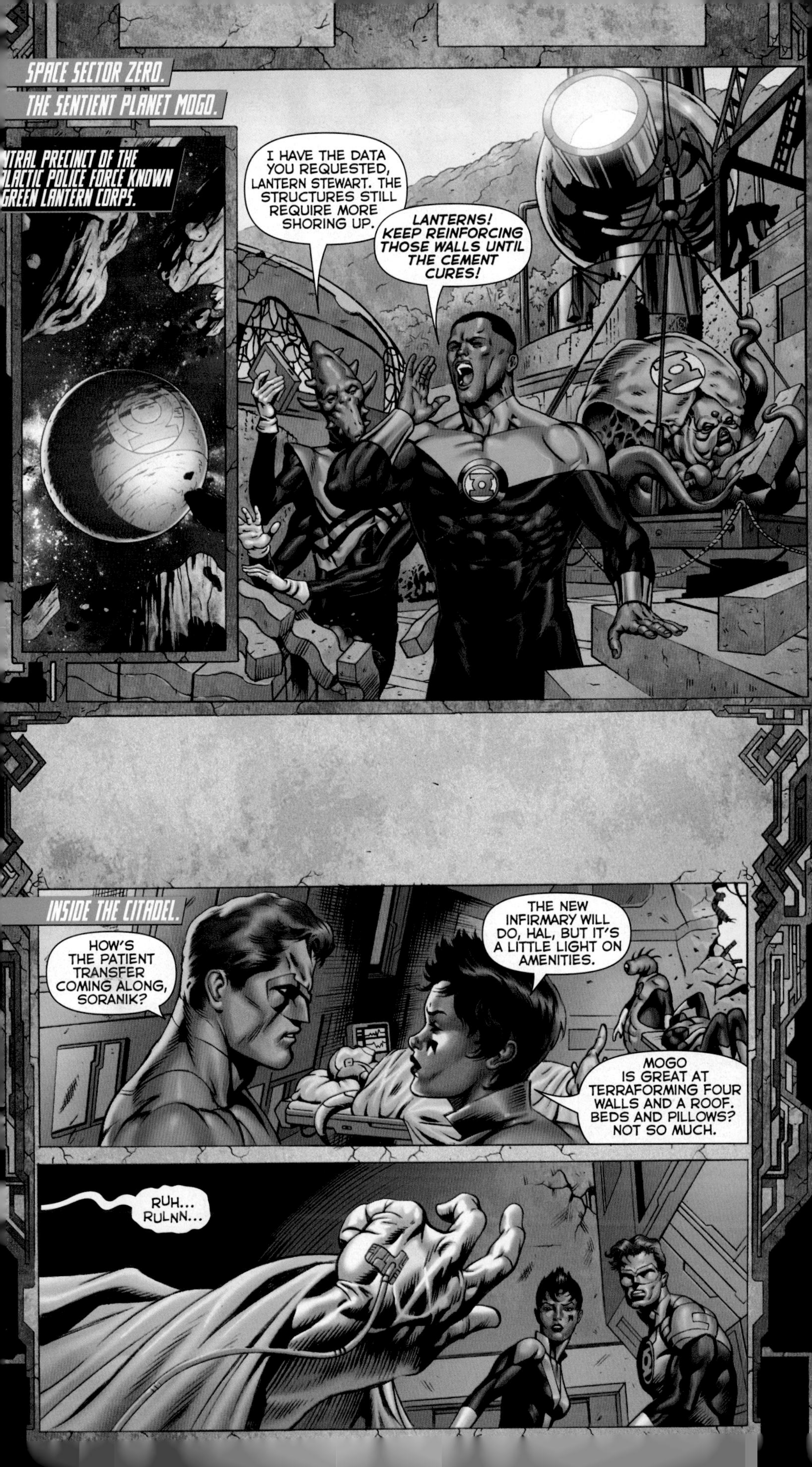
SPACE SECTOR ZERO.
THE SENTIENT PLANET MOGO.
NTRAL PRECINCT OF THE
LACTIC POLICE FORCE KNOWN
GREEN LANTERN CORPS.
I HAVE THE DATA YOU REQUESTED, LANTERN STEWART. THE STRUCTURES STILL REQUIRE MORE SHORING UP.
LANTERNS! KEEP REINFORCING THOSE WALLS UNTIL THE CEMENT CURES!
INSIDE THE CITADEL.
HOW'S THE PATIENT TRANSFER COMING ALONG, SORANIK?
THE NEW INFIRMARY WILL DO, HAL, BUT IT'S A LITTLE LIGHT ON AMENITIES.
MOGO IS GREAT AT TERRAFORMING FOUR WALLS AND A ROOF. BEDS AND PILLOWS? NOT SO MUCH.
RUH... RULNN...

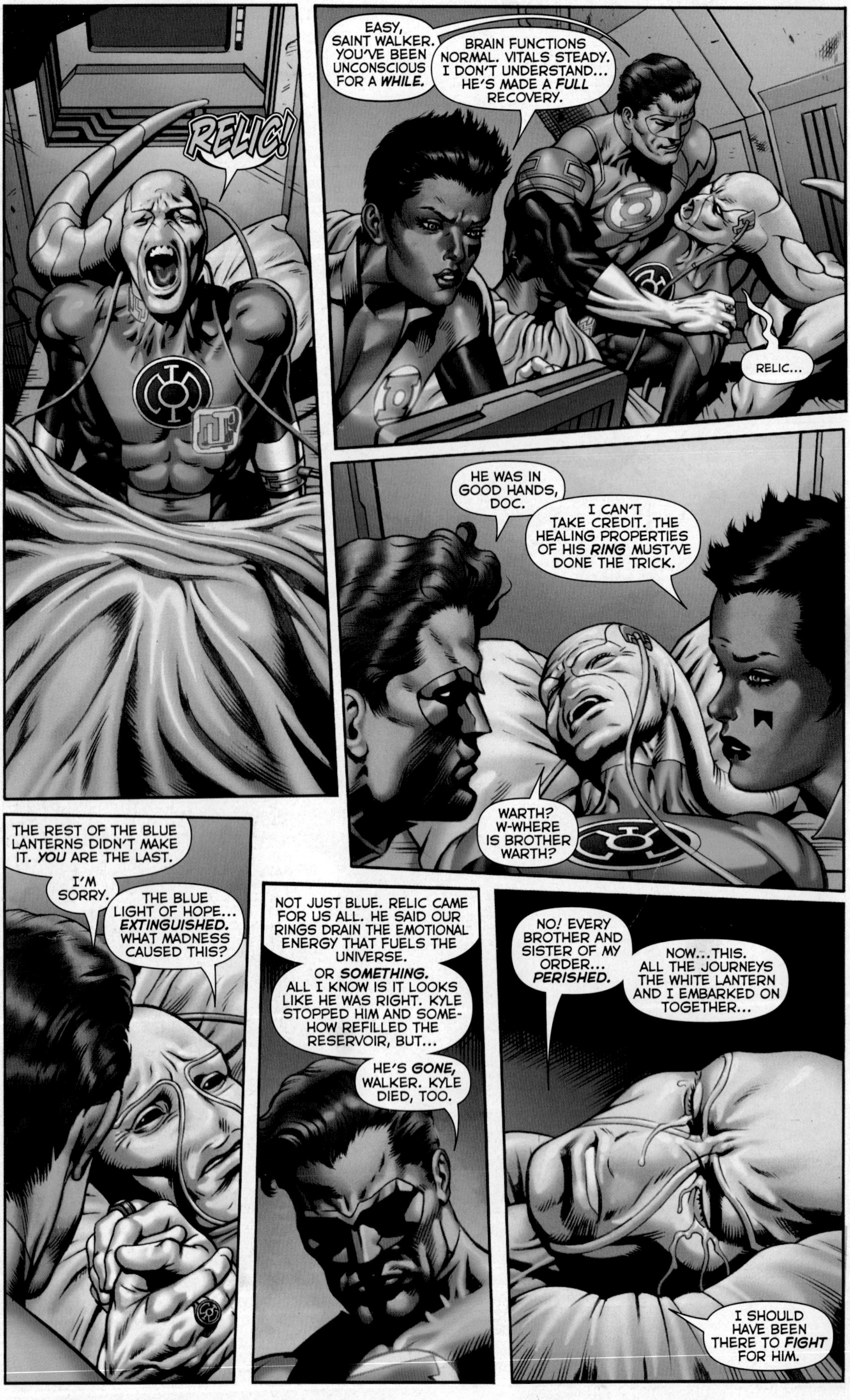
RELIC!
EASY, SAINT WALKER. YOU'VE BEEN UNCONSCIOUS FOR A WHILE.
BRAIN FUNCTIONS NORMAL. VITALS STEADY. I DON'T UNDERSTAND... HE'S MADE A FULL RECOVERY.
RELIC...
HE WAS IN GOOD HANDS, DOC.
I CAN'T TAKE CREDIT. THE HEALING PROPERTIES OF HIS RING MUST'VE DONE THE TRICK.
WARTH? W-WHERE IS BROTHER WARTH?
THE REST OF THE BLUE LANTERNS DIDN'T MAKE IT. YOU ARE THE LAST.
I'M SORRY.
THE BLUE LIGHT OF HOPE... EXTINGUISHED. WHAT MADNESS CAUSED THIS?
NOT JUST BLUE. RELIC CAME FOR US ALL. HE SAID OUR RINGS DRAIN THE EMOTIONAL ENERGY THAT FUELS THE UNIVERSE.
OR SOMETHING. ALL I KNOW IS IT LOOKS LIKE HE WAS RIGHT. KYLE STOPPED HIM AND SOMEHOW REFILLED THE RESERVOIR, BUT...
HE'S GONE, WALKER. KYLE DIED, TOO.
NO! EVERY BROTHER AND SISTER OF MY ORDER... PERISHED.
NOW...THIS. ALL THE JOURNEYS THE WHITE LANTERN AND I EMBARKED ON TOGETHER...
I SHOULD HAVE BEEN THERE TO FIGHT FOR HIM.

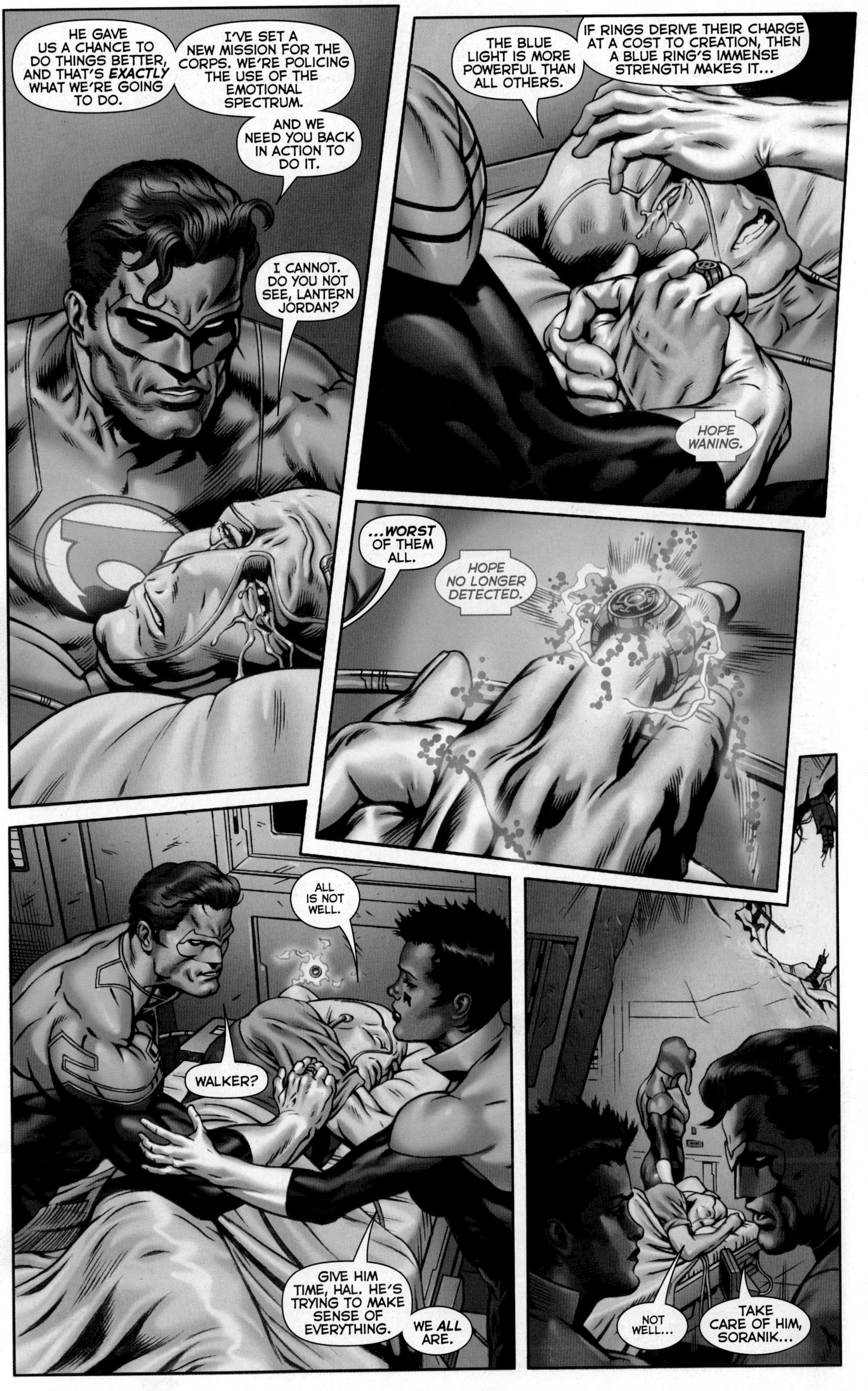
HE GAVE US A CHANCE TO DO THINGS BETTER, AND THAT'S *EXACTLY* WHAT WE'RE GOING TO DO.
I'VE SET A NEW MISSION FOR THE CORPS. WE'RE POLICING THE USE OF THE EMOTIONAL SPECTRUM.
AND WE NEED YOU BACK IN ACTION TO DO IT.
I CANNOT. DO YOU NOT SEE, LANTERN JORDAN?
THE BLUE LIGHT IS MORE POWERFUL THAN ALL OTHERS.
IF RINGS DERIVE THEIR CHARGE AT A COST TO CREATION, THEN A BLUE RING'S IMMENSE STRENGTH MAKES IT...
HOPE WANING.
...*WORST* OF THEM ALL.
HOPE NO LONGER DETECTED.
ALL IS NOT WELL.
WALKER?
GIVE HIM TIME, HAL. HE'S TRYING TO MAKE SENSE OF EVERYTHING.
WE *ALL* ARE.
NOT WELL...
TAKE CARE OF HIM, SORANIK...

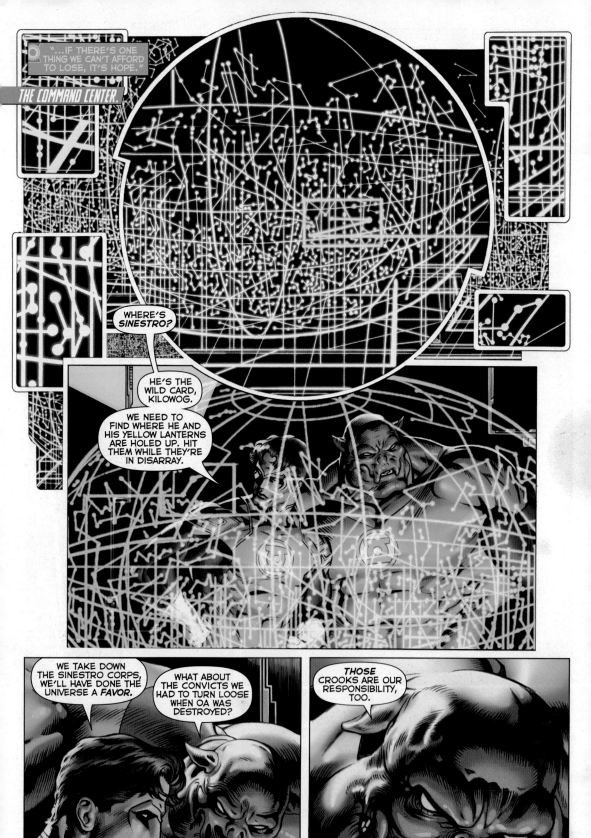

"...IF THERE'S ONE THING WE CAN'T AFFORD TO LOSE, IT'S HOPE."

THE COMMAND CENTER.

WHERE'S SINESTRO?

HE'S THE WILD CARD, KILOWOG.

WE NEED TO FIND WHERE HE AND HIS YELLOW LANTERNS ARE HOLED UP. HIT THEM WHILE THEY'RE IN DISARRAY.

WE TAKE DOWN THE SINESTRO CORPS, WE'LL HAVE DONE THE UNIVERSE A *FAVOR.*

WHAT ABOUT THE CONVICTS WE HAD TO TURN LOOSE WHEN OA WAS DESTROYED?

THOSE CROOKS ARE OUR RESPONSIBILITY, TOO.

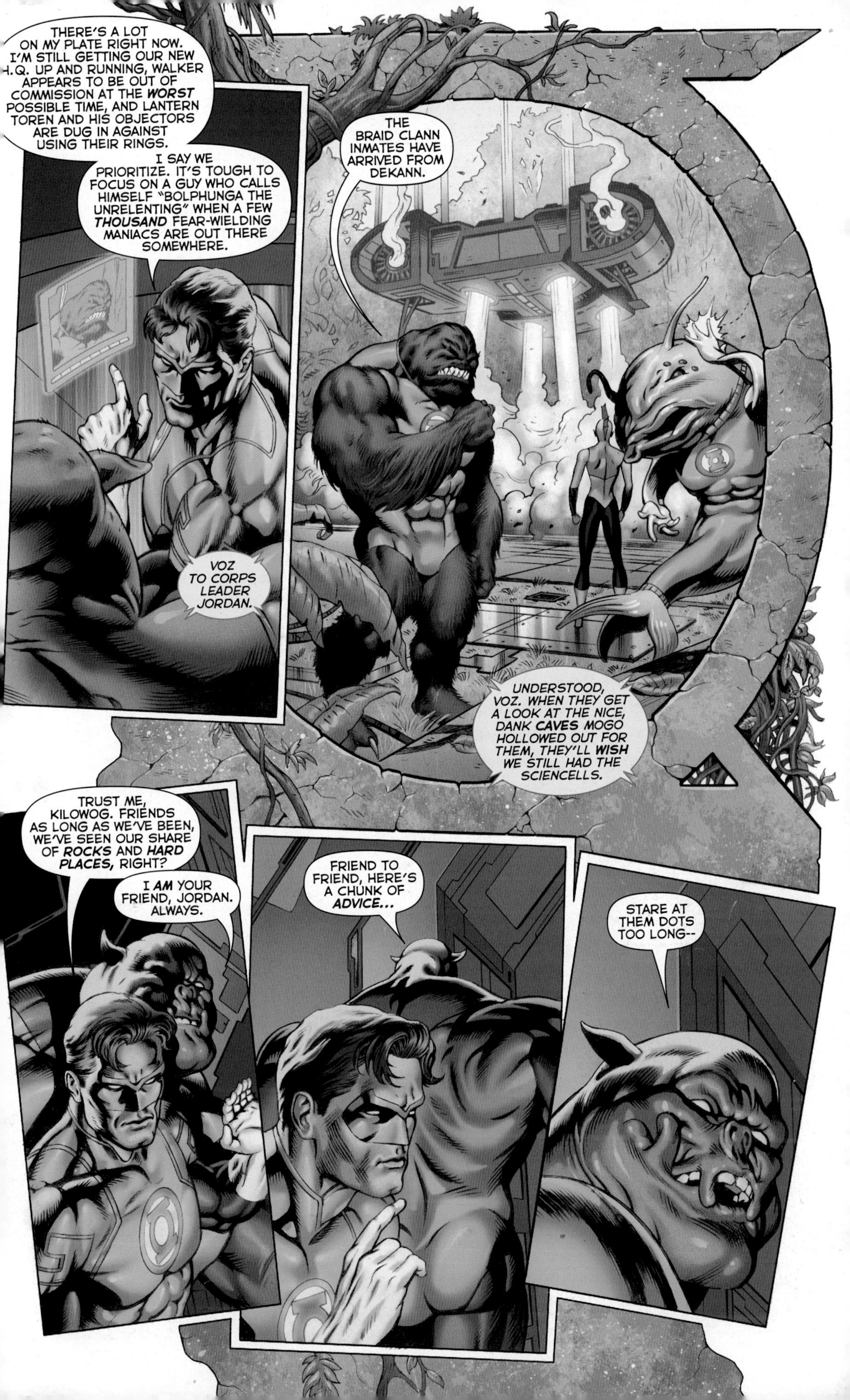
THERE'S A LOT ON MY PLATE RIGHT NOW. I'M STILL GETTING OUR NEW H.Q. UP AND RUNNING, WALKER APPEARS TO BE OUT OF COMMISSION AT THE WORST POSSIBLE TIME, AND LANTERN TOREN AND HIS OBJECTORS ARE DUG IN AGAINST USING THEIR RINGS.
I SAY WE PRIORITIZE. IT'S TOUGH TO FOCUS ON A GUY WHO CALLS HIMSELF "BOLPHUNGA THE UNRELENTING" WHEN A FEW THOUSAND FEAR-WIELDING MANIACS ARE OUT THERE SOMEWHERE.
VOZ TO CORPS LEADER JORDAN.
THE BRAID CLANN INMATES HAVE ARRIVED FROM DEKANN.
UNDERSTOOD, VOZ. WHEN THEY GET A LOOK AT THE NICE, DANK CAVES MOGO HOLLOWED OUT FOR THEM, THEY'LL WISH WE STILL HAD THE SCIENCELLS.
TRUST ME, KILOWOG. FRIENDS AS LONG AS WE'VE BEEN, WE'VE SEEN OUR SHARE OF ROCKS AND HARD PLACES, RIGHT?
I AM YOUR FRIEND, JORDAN. ALWAYS.
FRIEND TO FRIEND, HERE'S A CHUNK OF ADVICE...
STARE AT THEM DOTS TOO LONG--

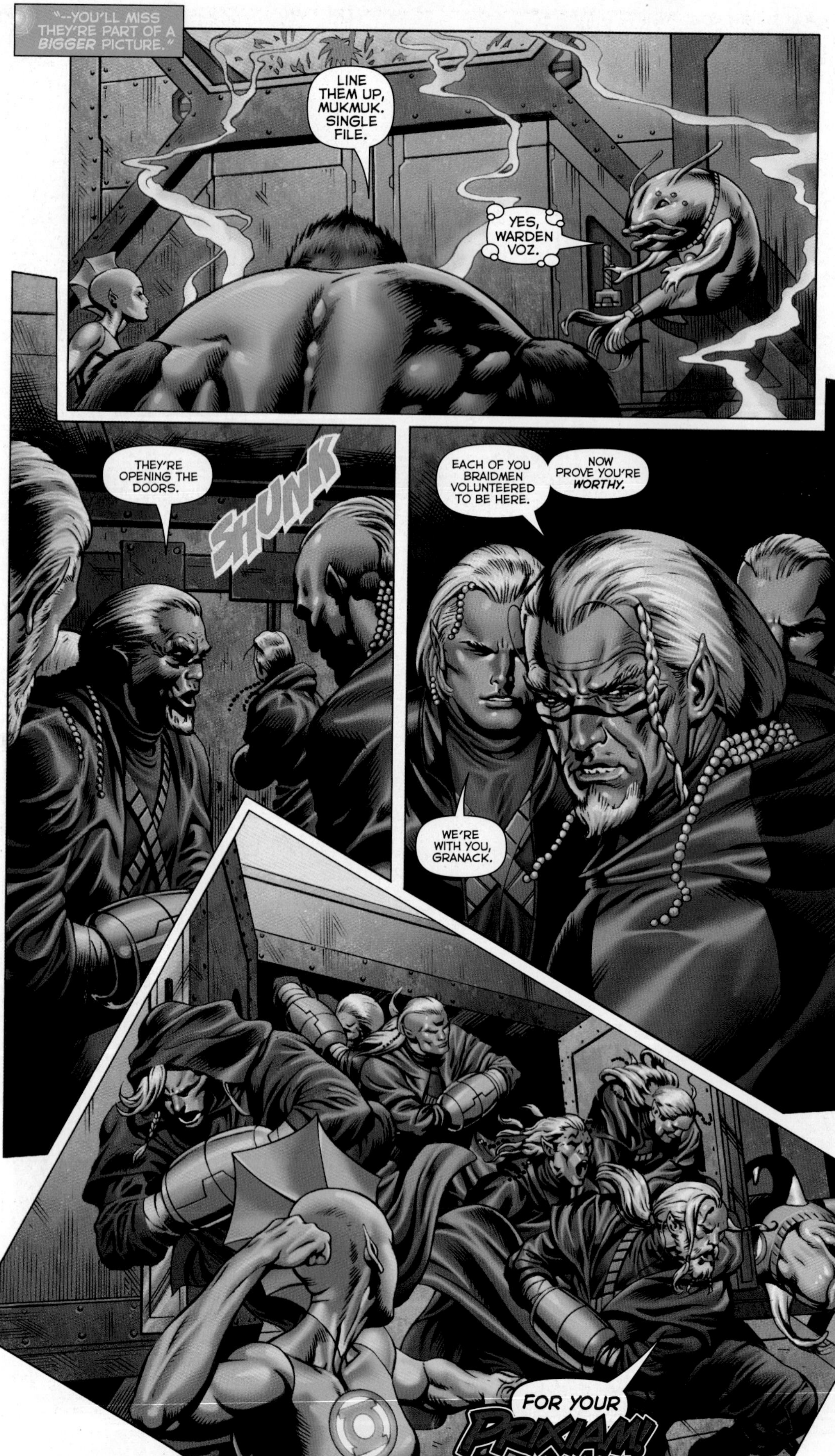
"--YOU'LL MISS THEY'RE PART OF A BIGGER PICTURE."
LINE THEM UP, MUKMUK. SINGLE FILE.
YES, WARDEN VOZ.
THEY'RE OPENING THE DOORS.
SHUNK
EACH OF YOU BRAIDMEN VOLUNTEERED TO BE HERE.
NOW PROVE YOU'RE WORTHY.
WE'RE WITH YOU, GRANACK.
FOR YOUR PRIXIAM!

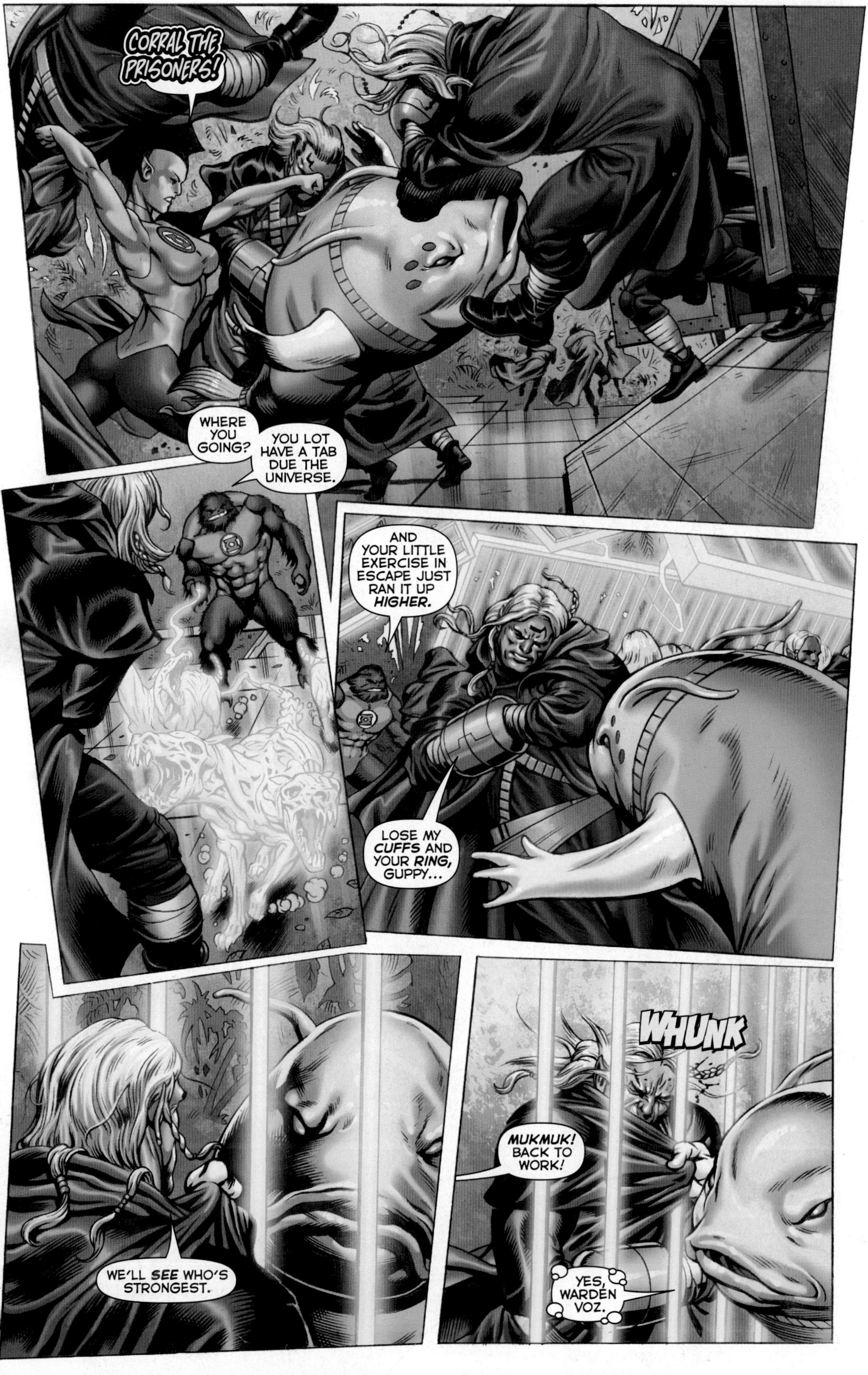
CORRAL THE PRISONERS!
WHERE YOU GOING?
YOU LOT HAVE A TAB DUE THE UNIVERSE.
AND YOUR LITTLE EXERCISE IN ESCAPE JUST RAN IT UP HIGHER.
LOSE MY CUFFS AND YOUR RING, GUPPY...
WE'LL SEE WHO'S STRONGEST.
WHUNK
MUKMUK! BACK TO WORK!
YES, WARDEN VOZ.

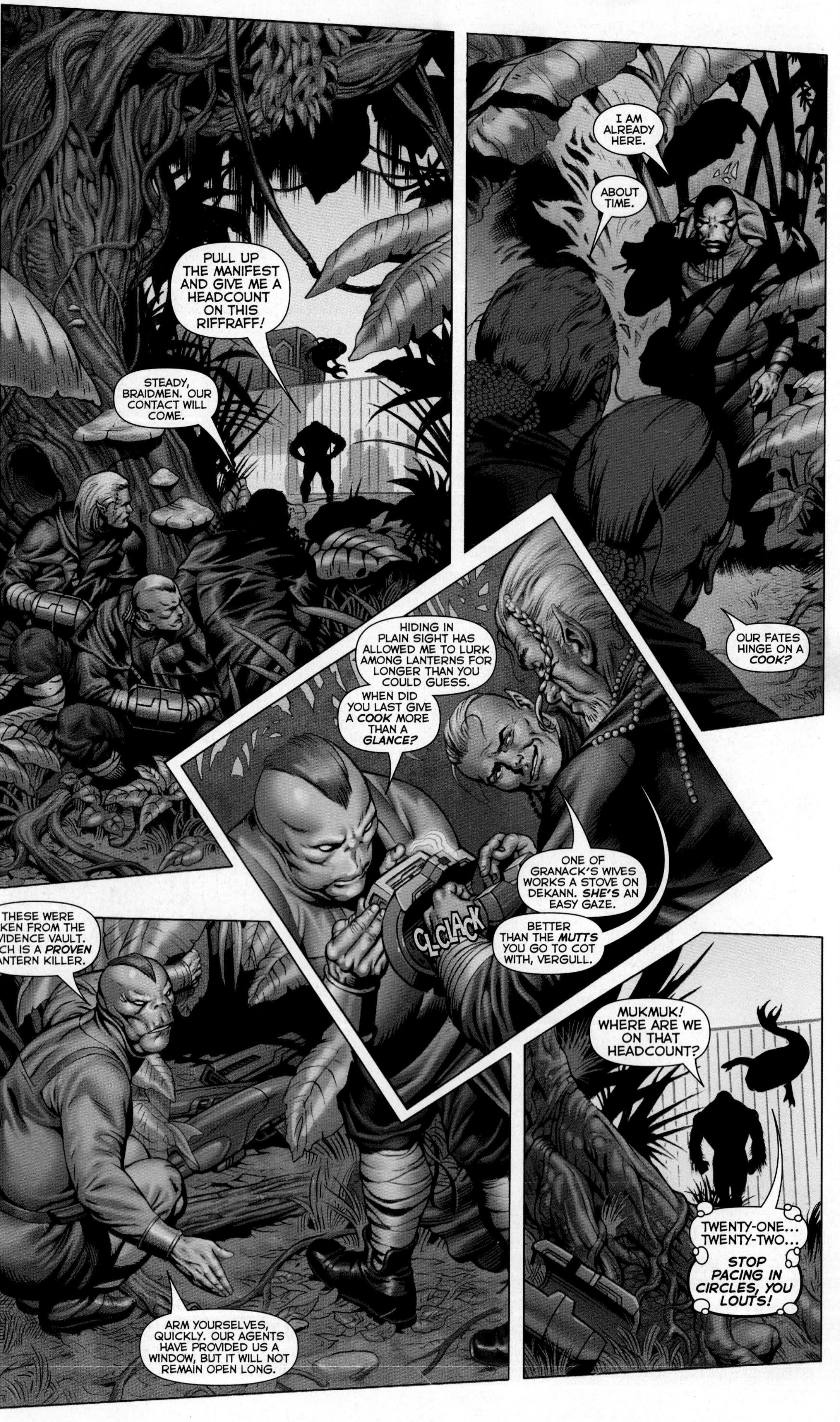

PULL UP THE MANIFEST AND GIVE ME A HEADCOUNT ON THIS RIFFRAFF!
STEADY, BRAIDMEN. OUR CONTACT WILL COME.
I AM ALREADY HERE.
ABOUT TIME.
OUR FATES HINGE ON A COOK?
HIDING IN PLAIN SIGHT HAS ALLOWED ME TO LURK AMONG LANTERNS FOR LONGER THAN YOU COULD GUESS.
WHEN DID YOU LAST GIVE A COOK MORE THAN A GLANCE?
ONE OF GRANACK'S WIVES WORKS A STOVE ON DEKANN. SHE'S AN EASY GAZE.
CL-CLACK
BETTER THAN THE MUTTS YOU GO TO COT WITH, VERGULL.
THESE WERE TAKEN FROM THE EVIDENCE VAULT. EACH IS A PROVEN LANTERN KILLER.
ARM YOURSELVES, QUICKLY. OUR AGENTS HAVE PROVIDED US A WINDOW, BUT IT WILL NOT REMAIN OPEN LONG.
MUKMUK! WHERE ARE WE ON THAT HEADCOUNT?
TWENTY-ONE... TWENTY-TWO...
STOP PACING IN CIRCLES, YOU LOUTS!

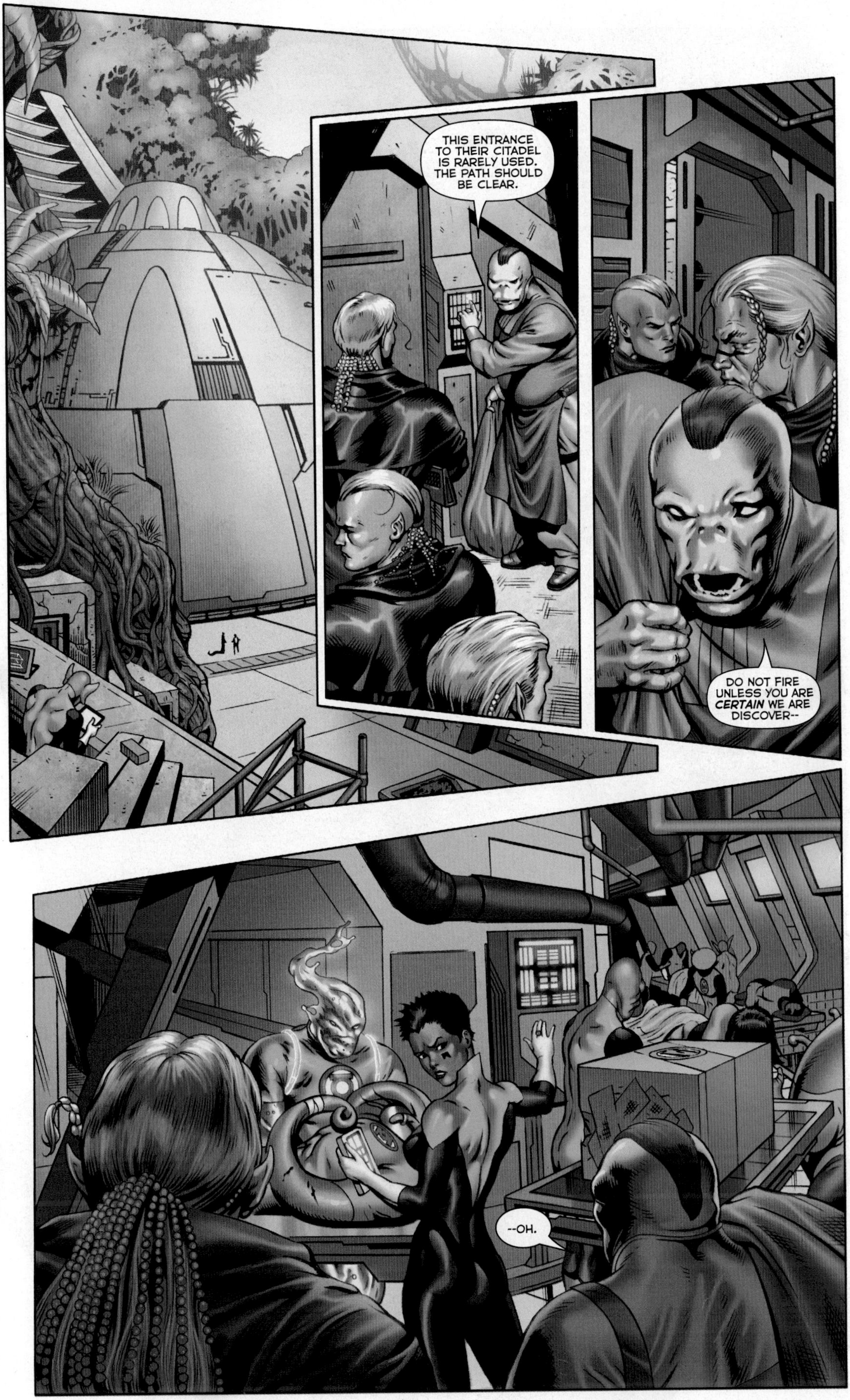
THIS ENTRANCE TO THEIR CITADEL IS RARELY USED. THE PATH SHOULD BE CLEAR.
DO NOT FIRE UNLESS YOU ARE CERTAIN WE ARE DISCOVER--
--OH.

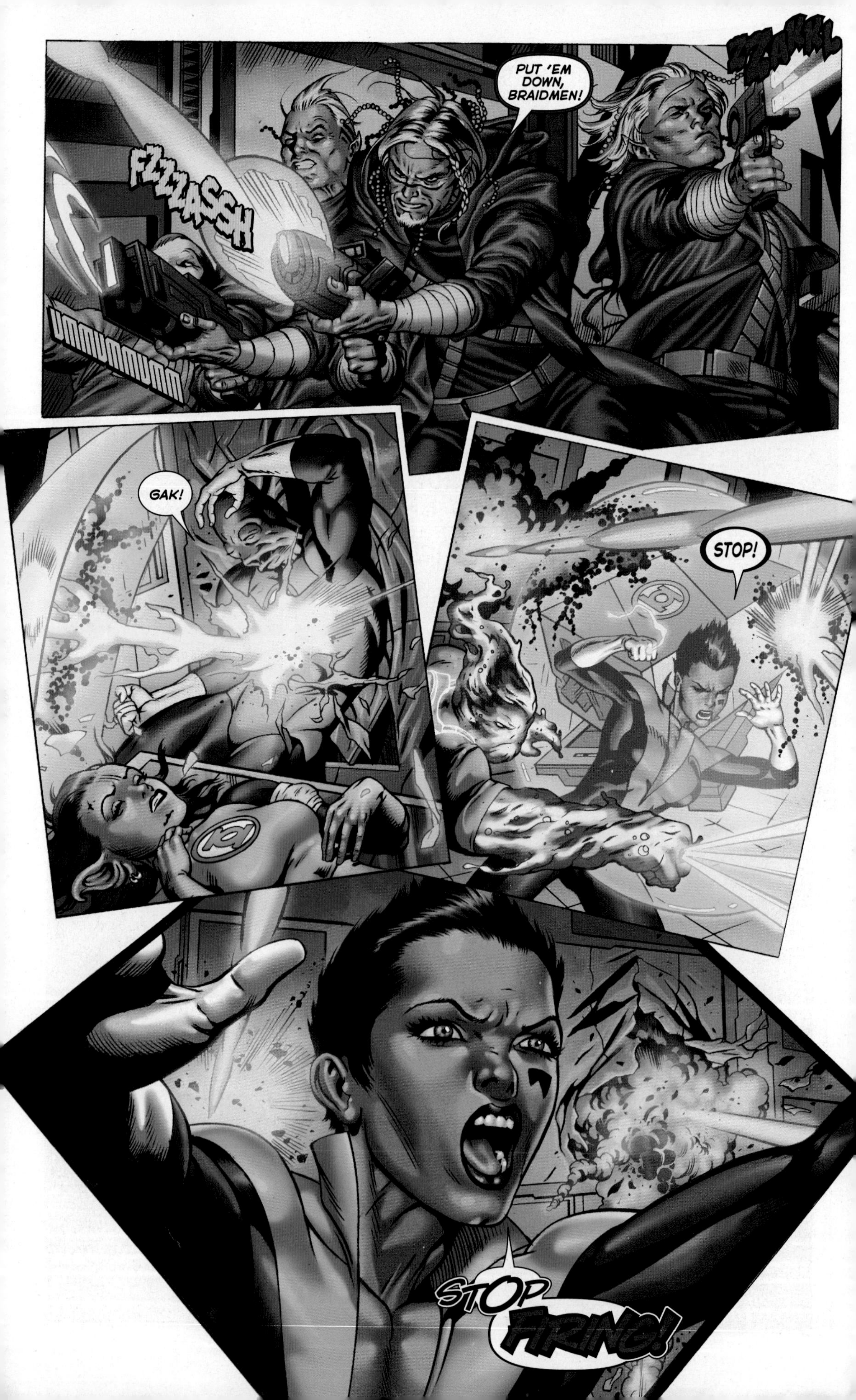
ZZAKK
PUT 'EM DOWN, BRAIDMEN!
FZZZASSH
UMMMUMMMUMM
GAK!
STOP!
STOP FIRING!

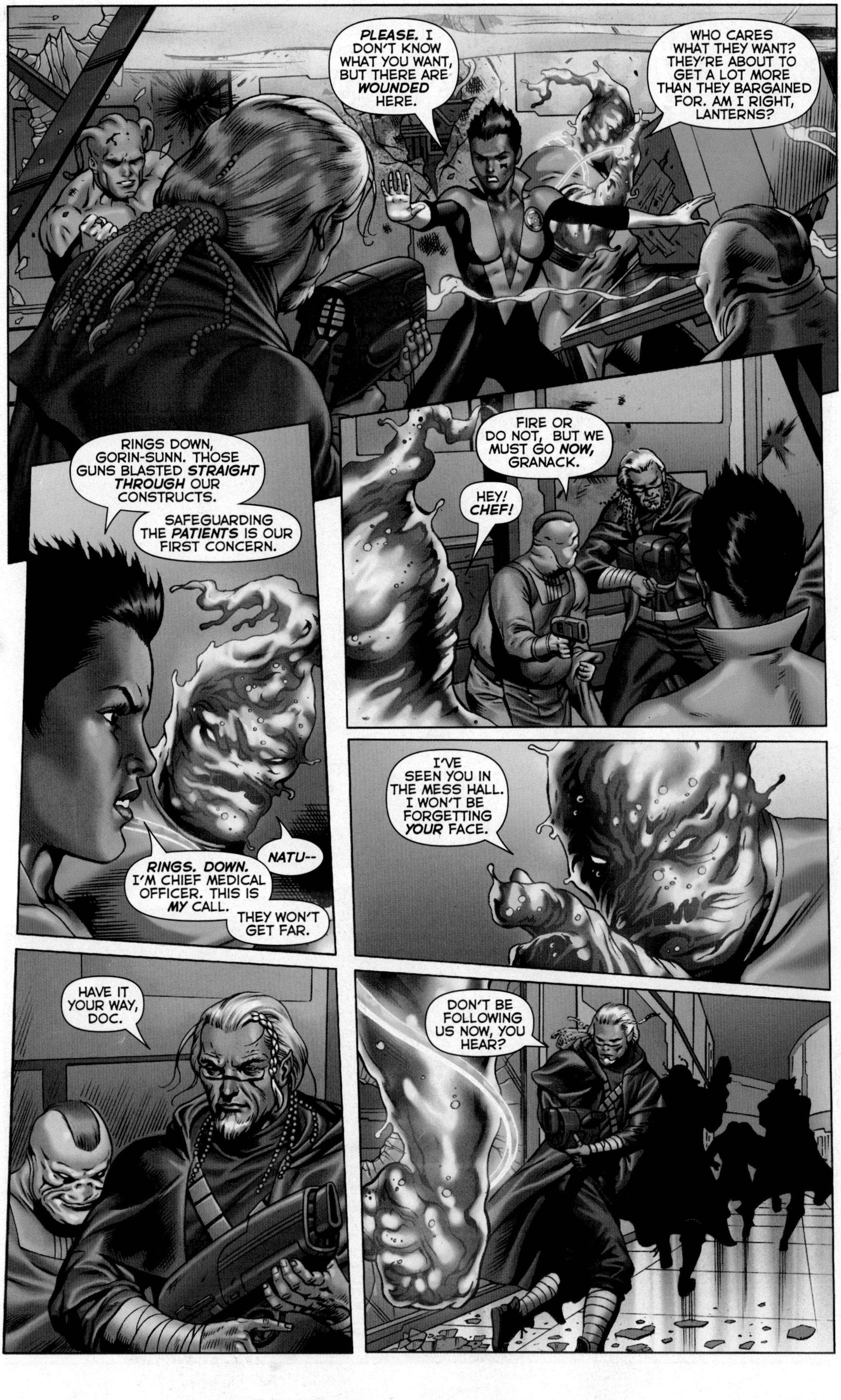
PLEASE. I DON'T KNOW WHAT YOU WANT, BUT THERE ARE WOUNDED HERE.
WHO CARES WHAT THEY WANT? THEY'RE ABOUT TO GET A LOT MORE THAN THEY BARGAINED FOR. AM I RIGHT, LANTERNS?
RINGS DOWN, GORIN-SUNN. THOSE GUNS BLASTED STRAIGHT THROUGH OUR CONSTRUCTS.
SAFEGUARDING THE PATIENTS IS OUR FIRST CONCERN.
NATU--
RINGS. DOWN. I'M CHIEF MEDICAL OFFICER. THIS IS MY CALL.
THEY WON'T GET FAR.
FIRE OR DO NOT, BUT WE MUST GO NOW, GRANACK.
HEY! CHEF!
I'VE SEEN YOU IN THE MESS HALL. I WON'T BE FORGETTING YOUR FACE.
HAVE IT YOUR WAY, DOC.
DON'T BE FOLLOWING US NOW, YOU HEAR?

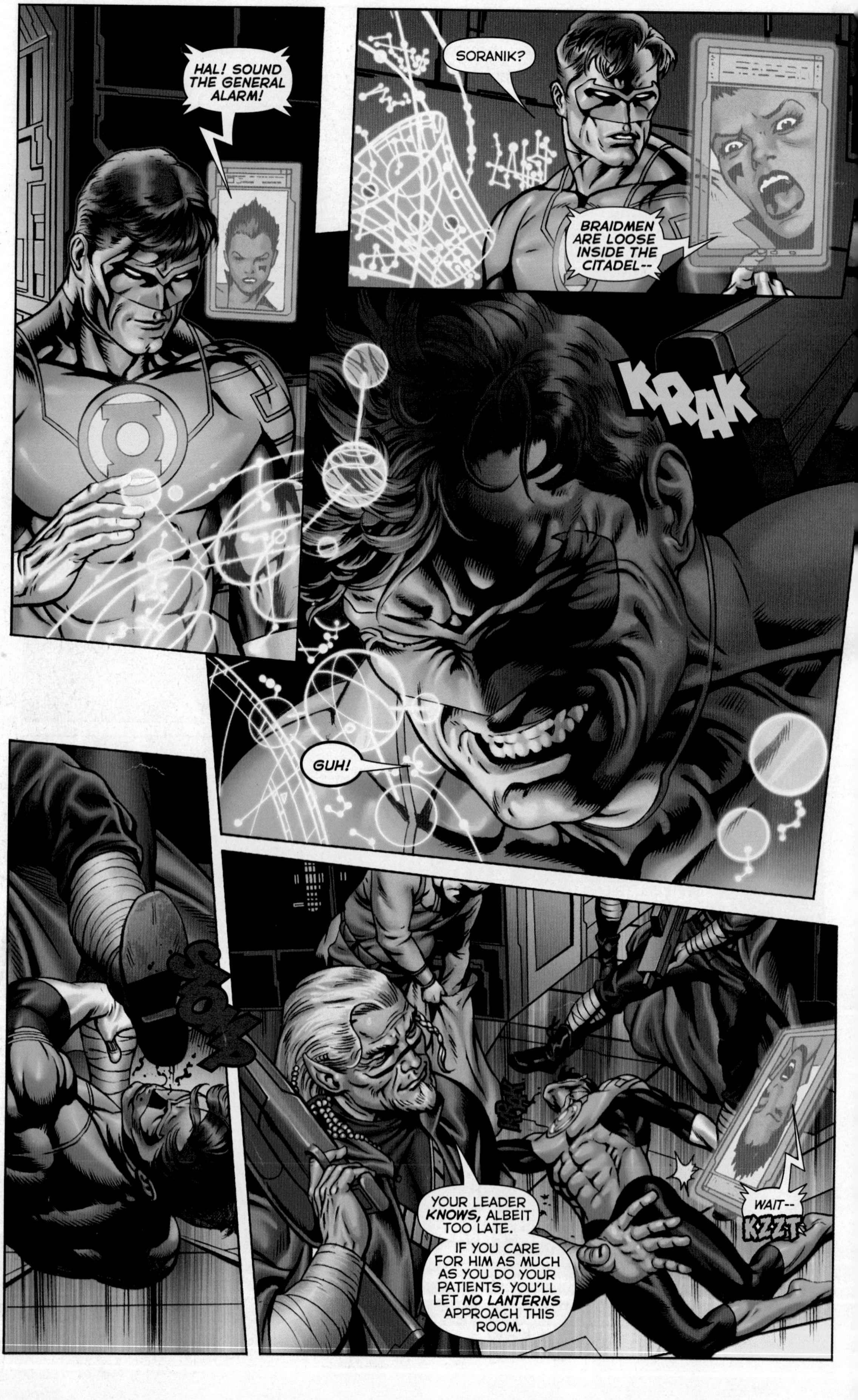
HAL! SOUND THE GENERAL ALARM!
SORANIK?
BRAIDMEN ARE LOOSE INSIDE THE CITADEL--
KRAK
GUH!
YOUR LEADER KNOWS, ALBEIT TOO LATE.
IF YOU CARE FOR HIM AS MUCH AS YOU DO YOUR PATIENTS, YOU'LL LET NO LANTERNS APPROACH THIS ROOM.
WAIT--
KZZT

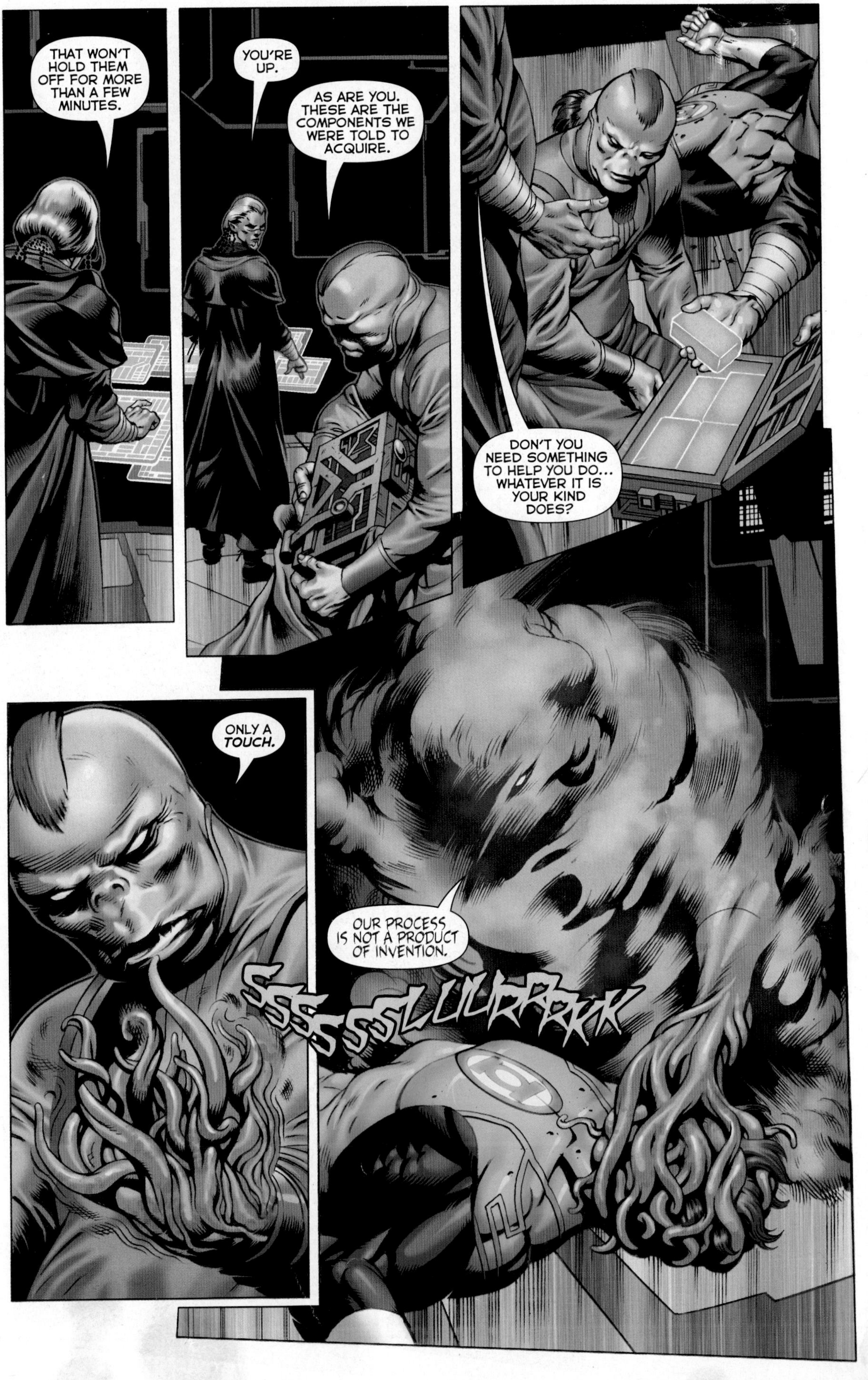

THAT WON'T HOLD THEM OFF FOR MORE THAN A FEW MINUTES.
YOU'RE UP.
AS ARE YOU. THESE ARE THE COMPONENTS WE WERE TOLD TO ACQUIRE.
DON'T YOU NEED SOMETHING TO HELP YOU DO... WHATEVER IT IS YOUR KIND DOES?
ONLY A *TOUCH.*
OUR PROCESS IS NOT A PRODUCT OF INVENTION.
SSSSSSLUURRRKK

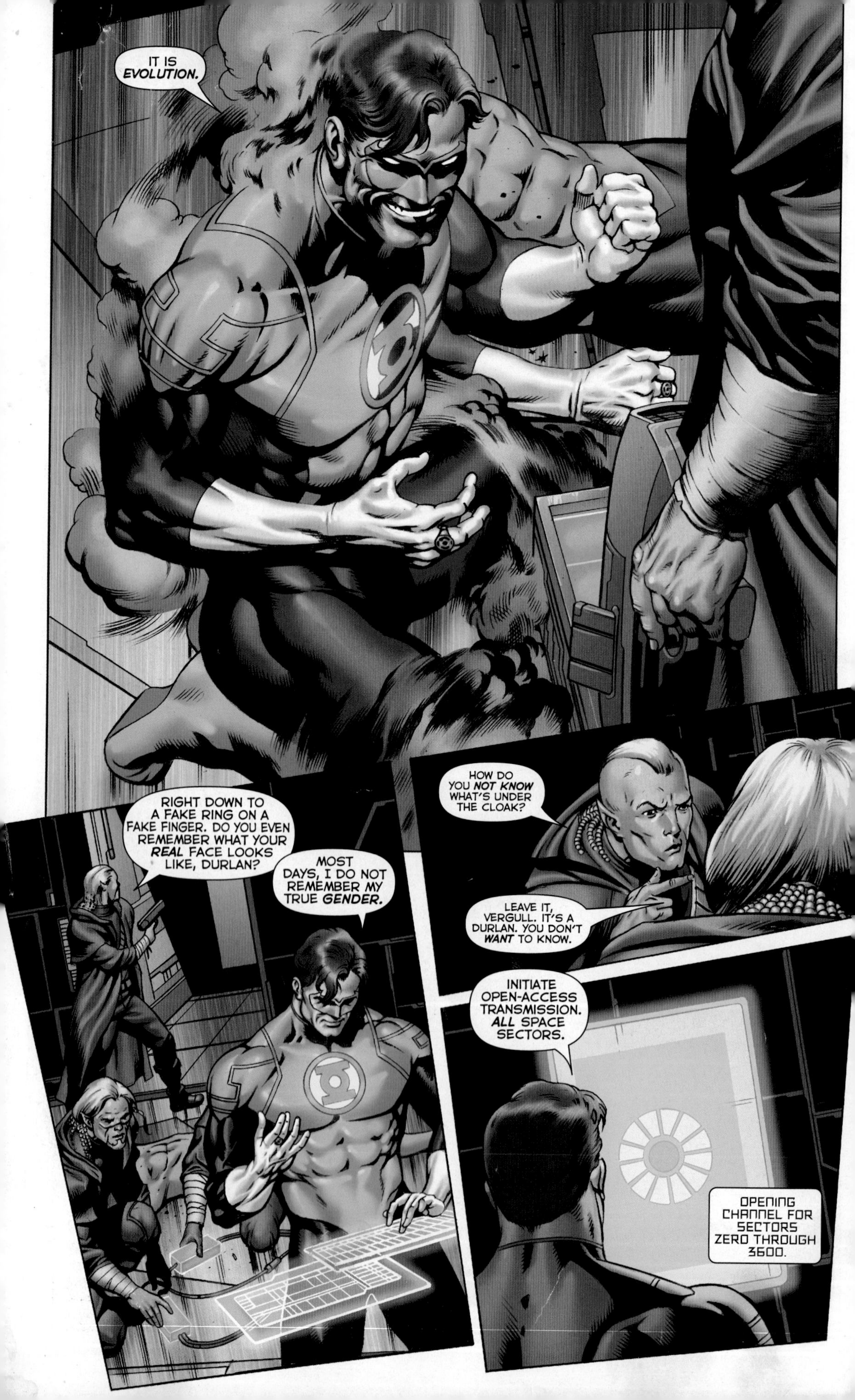
IT IS *EVOLUTION.*
RIGHT DOWN TO A FAKE RING ON A FAKE FINGER. DO YOU EVEN REMEMBER WHAT YOUR *REAL* FACE LOOKS LIKE, DURLAN?
MOST DAYS, I DO NOT REMEMBER MY TRUE *GENDER.*
HOW DO YOU *NOT KNOW* WHAT'S UNDER THE CLOAK?
LEAVE IT, VERGULL. IT'S A DURLAN. YOU DON'T *WANT* TO KNOW.
INITIATE OPEN-ACCESS TRANSMISSION. *ALL* SPACE SECTORS.
OPENING CHANNEL FOR SECTORS ZERO THROUGH 3600.

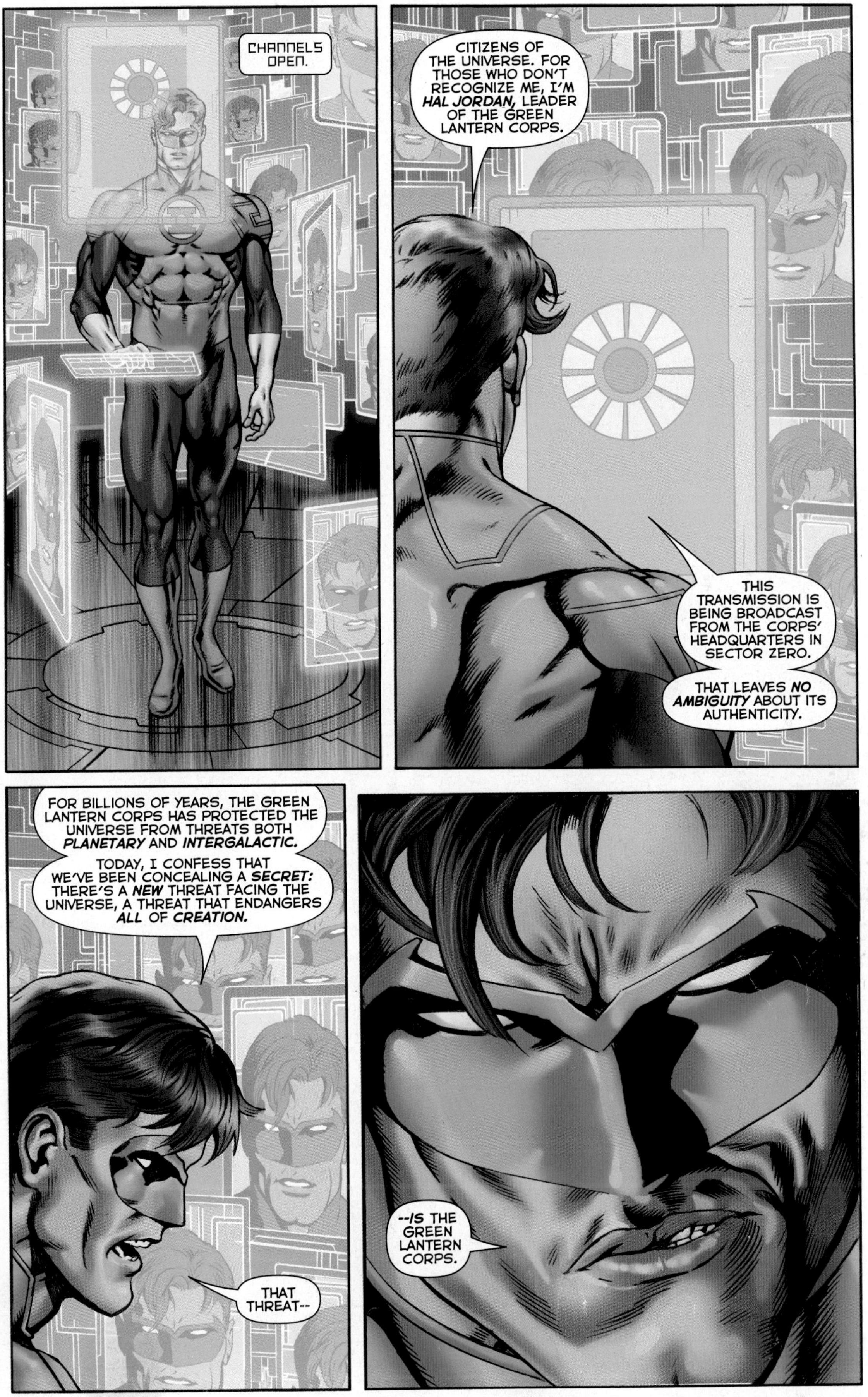
CHANNELS OPEN.
CITIZENS OF THE UNIVERSE. FOR THOSE WHO DON'T RECOGNIZE ME, I'M HAL JORDAN, LEADER OF THE GREEN LANTERN CORPS.
THIS TRANSMISSION IS BEING BROADCAST FROM THE CORPS' HEADQUARTERS IN SECTOR ZERO.
THAT LEAVES NO AMBIGUITY ABOUT ITS AUTHENTICITY.
FOR BILLIONS OF YEARS, THE GREEN LANTERN CORPS HAS PROTECTED THE UNIVERSE FROM THREATS BOTH PLANETARY AND INTERGALACTIC.
TODAY, I CONFESS THAT WE'VE BEEN CONCEALING A SECRET: THERE'S A NEW THREAT FACING THE UNIVERSE, A THREAT THAT ENDANGERS ALL OF CREATION.
THAT THREAT--
--IS THE GREEN LANTERN CORPS.

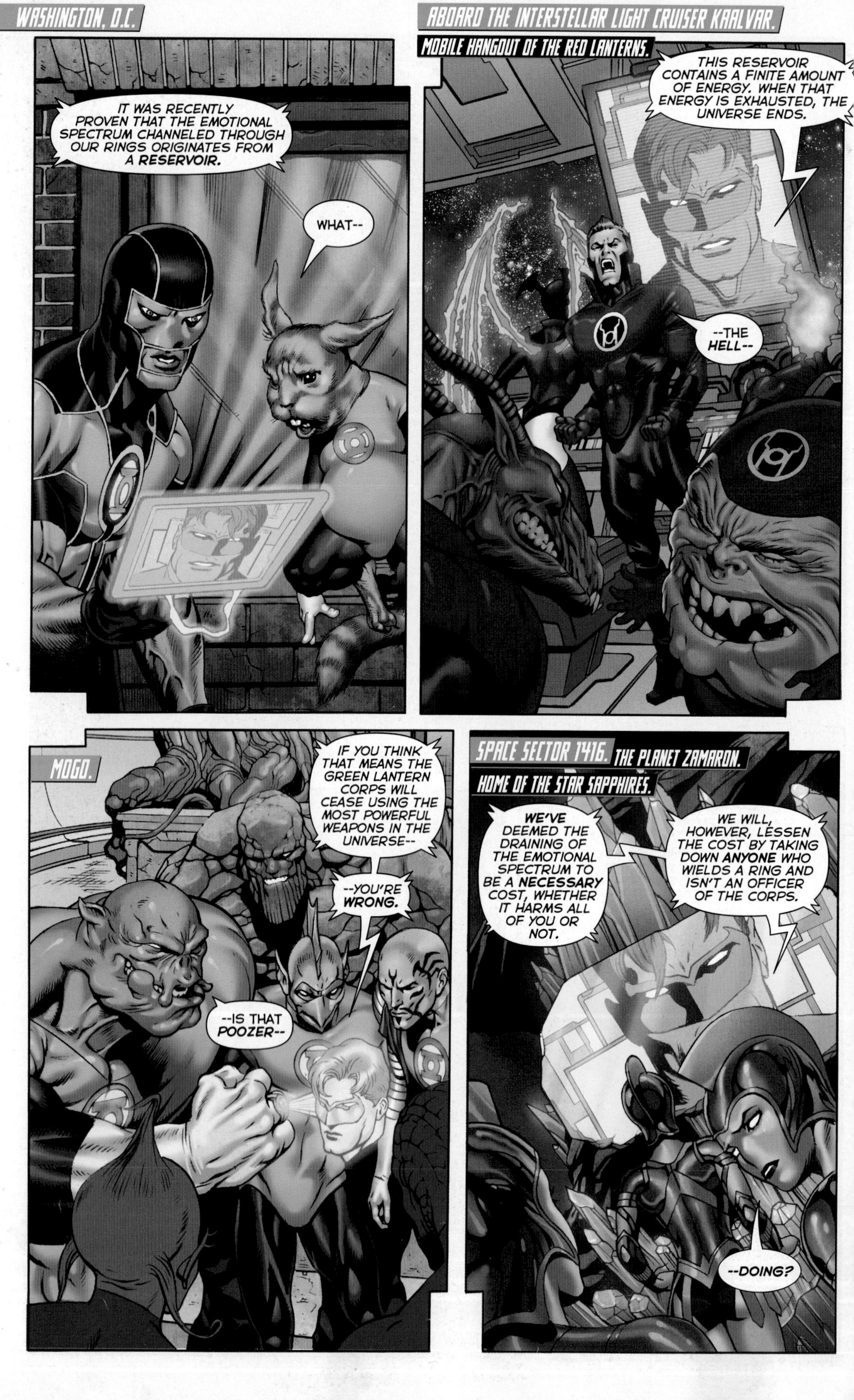
WASHINGTON, D.C.
IT WAS RECENTLY PROVEN THAT THE EMOTIONAL SPECTRUM CHANNELED THROUGH OUR RINGS ORIGINATES FROM A RESERVOIR.
WHAT--
ABOARD THE INTERSTELLAR LIGHT CRUISER KAALVAR.
MOBILE HANGOUT OF THE RED LANTERNS.
THIS RESERVOIR CONTAINS A FINITE AMOUNT OF ENERGY. WHEN THAT ENERGY IS EXHAUSTED, THE UNIVERSE ENDS.
--THE HELL--
MOGO.
IF YOU THINK THAT MEANS THE GREEN LANTERN CORPS WILL CEASE USING THE MOST POWERFUL WEAPONS IN THE UNIVERSE--
--YOU'RE WRONG.
--IS THAT POOZER--
SPACE SECTOR 1416. THE PLANET ZAMARON.
HOME OF THE STAR SAPPHIRES.
WE'VE DEEMED THE DRAINING OF THE EMOTIONAL SPECTRUM TO BE A NECESSARY COST, WHETHER IT HARMS ALL OF YOU OR NOT.
WE WILL, HOWEVER, LESSEN THE COST BY TAKING DOWN ANYONE WHO WIELDS A RING AND ISN'T AN OFFICER OF THE CORPS.
--DOING?

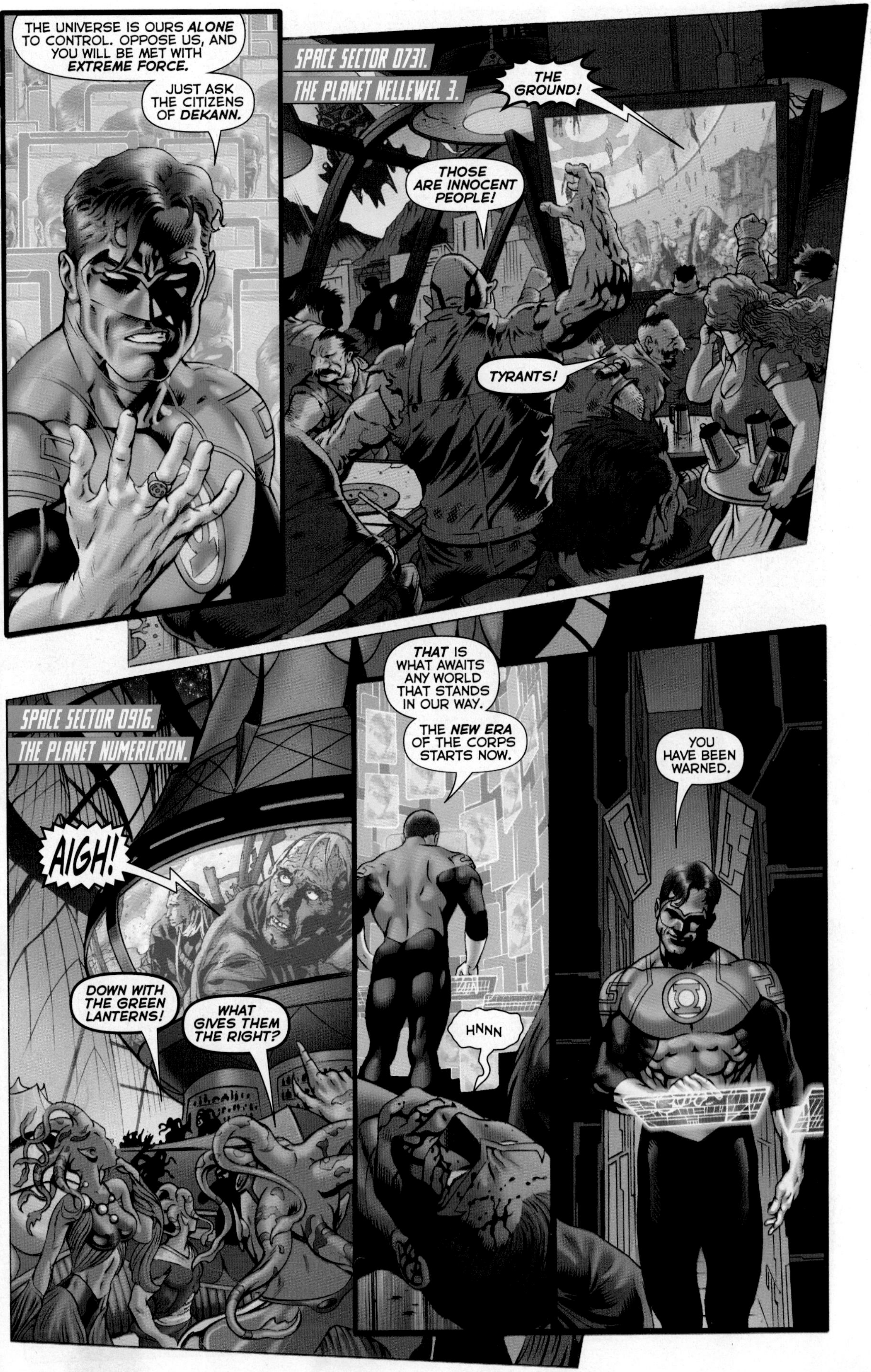
THE UNIVERSE IS OURS ALONE TO CONTROL. OPPOSE US, AND YOU WILL BE MET WITH EXTREME FORCE.
JUST ASK THE CITIZENS OF DEKANN.
SPACE SECTOR 0731.
THE PLANET NELLEWEL 3.
THE GROUND!
THOSE ARE INNOCENT PEOPLE!
TYRANTS!
SPACE SECTOR 0916.
THE PLANET NUMERICRON.
AIGH!
DOWN WITH THE GREEN LANTERNS!
WHAT GIVES THEM THE RIGHT?
THAT IS WHAT AWAITS ANY WORLD THAT STANDS IN OUR WAY.
THE NEW ERA OF THE CORPS STARTS NOW.
HNNN
YOU HAVE BEEN WARNED.

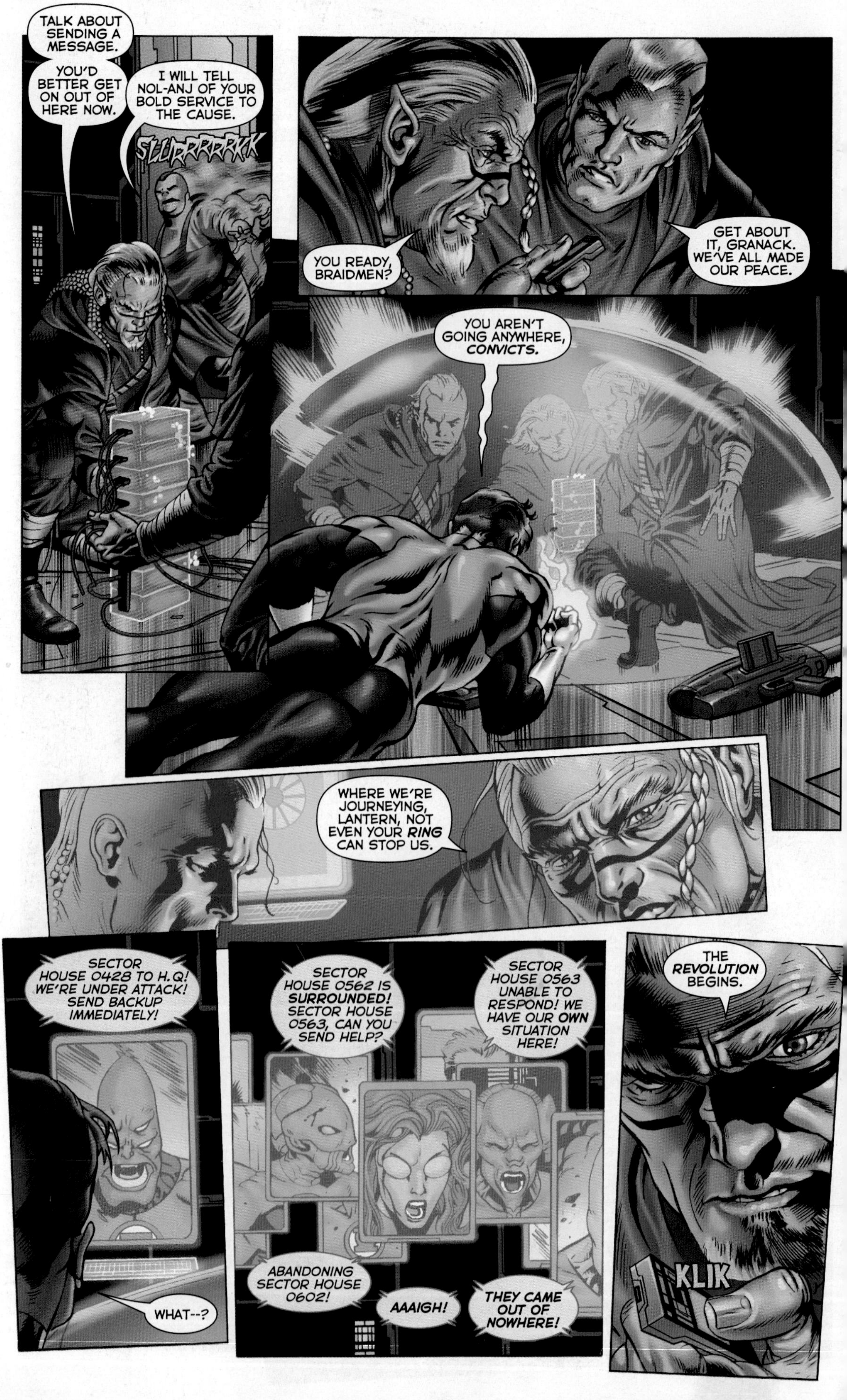
TALK ABOUT SENDING A MESSAGE.
YOU'D BETTER GET ON OUT OF HERE NOW.
I WILL TELL NOL-ANJ OF YOUR BOLD SERVICE TO THE CAUSE.
SLURRRRRKK
YOU READY, BRAIDMEN?
GET ABOUT IT, GRANACK. WE'VE ALL MADE OUR PEACE.
YOU AREN'T GOING ANYWHERE, CONVICTS.
WHERE WE'RE JOURNEYING, LANTERN, NOT EVEN YOUR RING CAN STOP US.
SECTOR HOUSE 0428 TO H.Q! WE'RE UNDER ATTACK! SEND BACKUP IMMEDIATELY!
WHAT--?
SECTOR HOUSE 0562 IS SURROUNDED! SECTOR HOUSE 0563, CAN YOU SEND HELP?
SECTOR HOUSE 0563 UNABLE TO RESPOND! WE HAVE OUR OWN SITUATION HERE!
ABANDONING SECTOR HOUSE 0602!
AAAIGH!
THEY CAME OUT OF NOWHERE!
THE REVOLUTION BEGINS.
KLIK

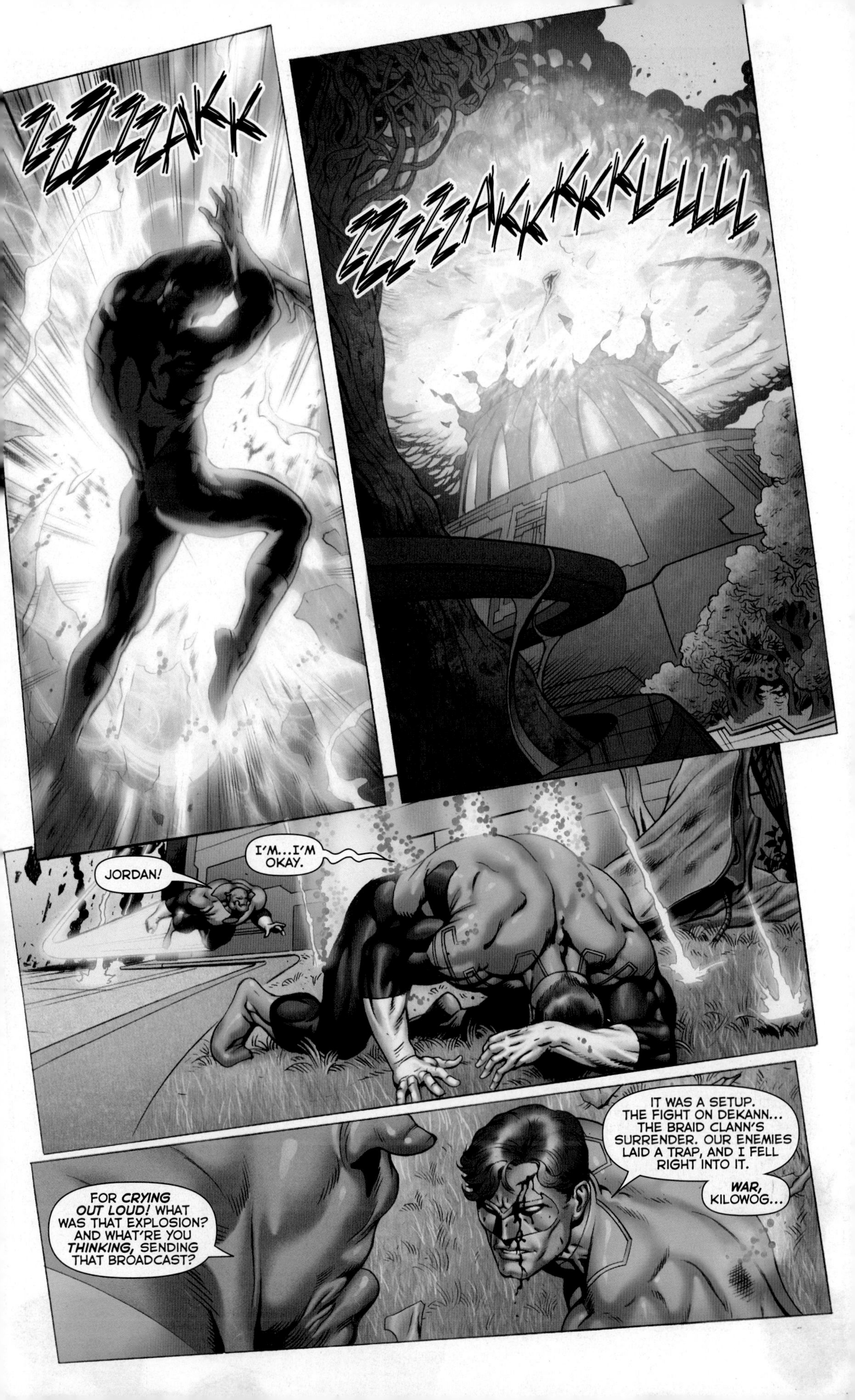
ZZZZZAKK
ZZZZZAKKKKKLLLLLL
JORDAN!
I'M...I'M OKAY.
IT WAS A SETUP. THE FIGHT ON DEKANN... THE BRAID CLANN'S SURRENDER. OUR ENEMIES LAID A TRAP, AND I FELL RIGHT INTO IT.
FOR CRYING OUT LOUD! WHAT WAS THAT EXPLOSION? AND WHAT'RE YOU THINKING, SENDING THAT BROADCAST?
WAR, KILOWOG...

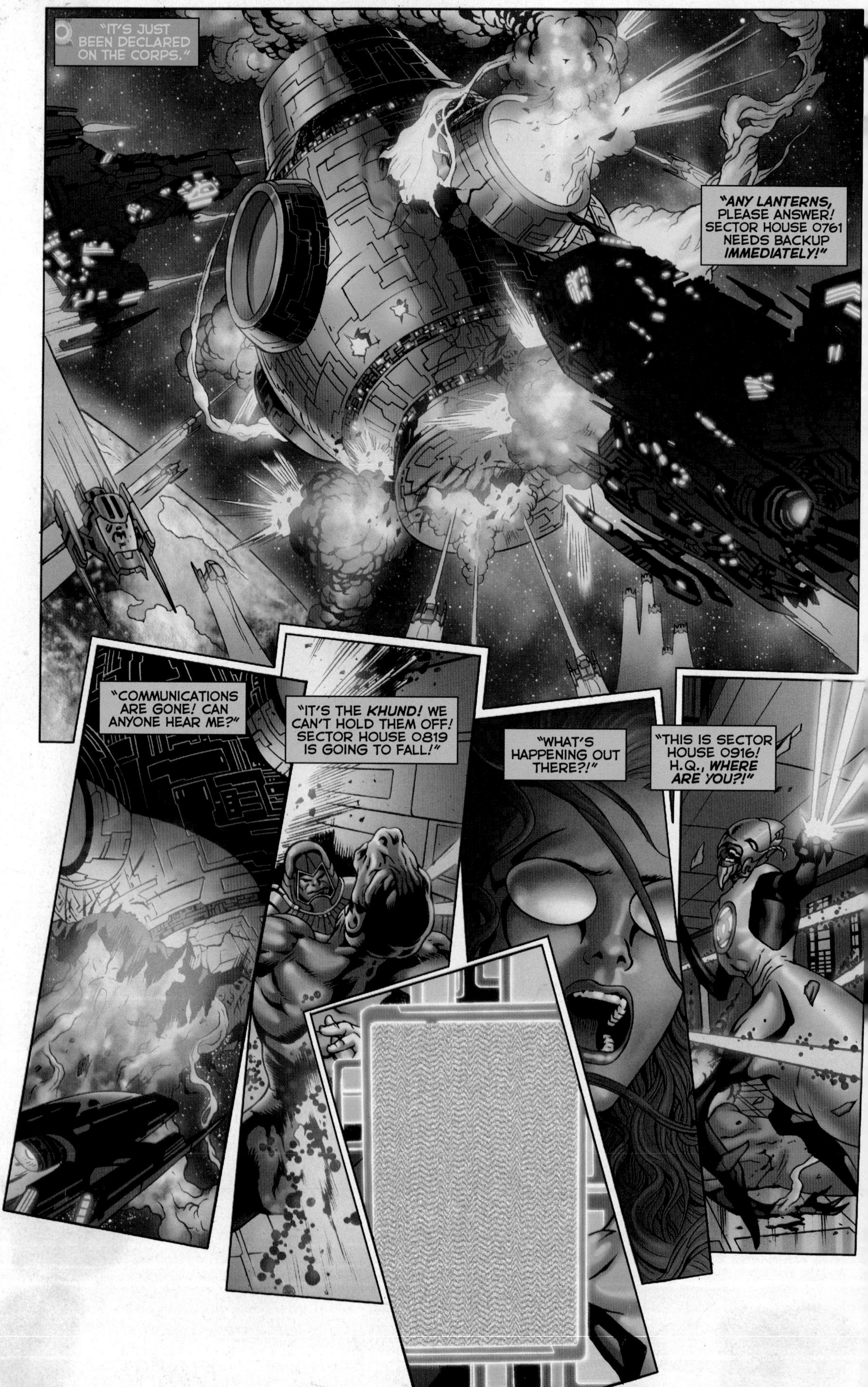
"IT'S JUST BEEN DECLARED ON THE CORPS."
"ANY LANTERNS, PLEASE ANSWER! SECTOR HOUSE 0761 NEEDS BACKUP IMMEDIATELY!"
"COMMUNICATIONS ARE GONE! CAN ANYONE HEAR ME?"
"IT'S THE KHUND! WE CAN'T HOLD THEM OFF! SECTOR HOUSE 0819 IS GOING TO FALL!"
"WHAT'S HAPPENING OUT THERE?!"
"THIS IS SECTOR HOUSE 0916! H.Q., WHERE ARE YOU?!"

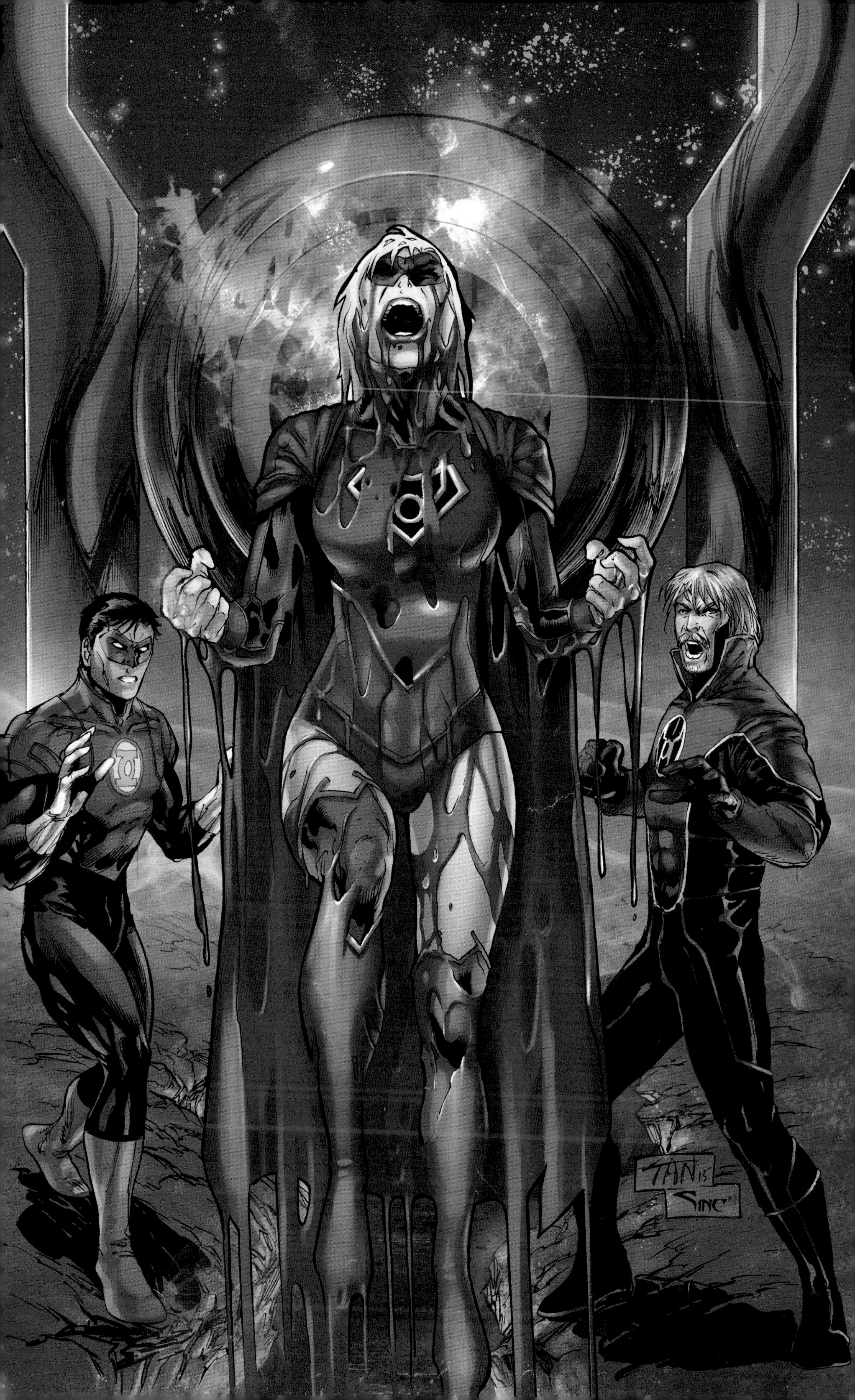

RED ALERT PART 1

ROBERT VENDITTI writer **BILLY TAN** penciller **ROB HUNTER** inker **ALEX SINCLAIR** colorist
cover art by **BILLY TAN & ALEX SINCLAIR**

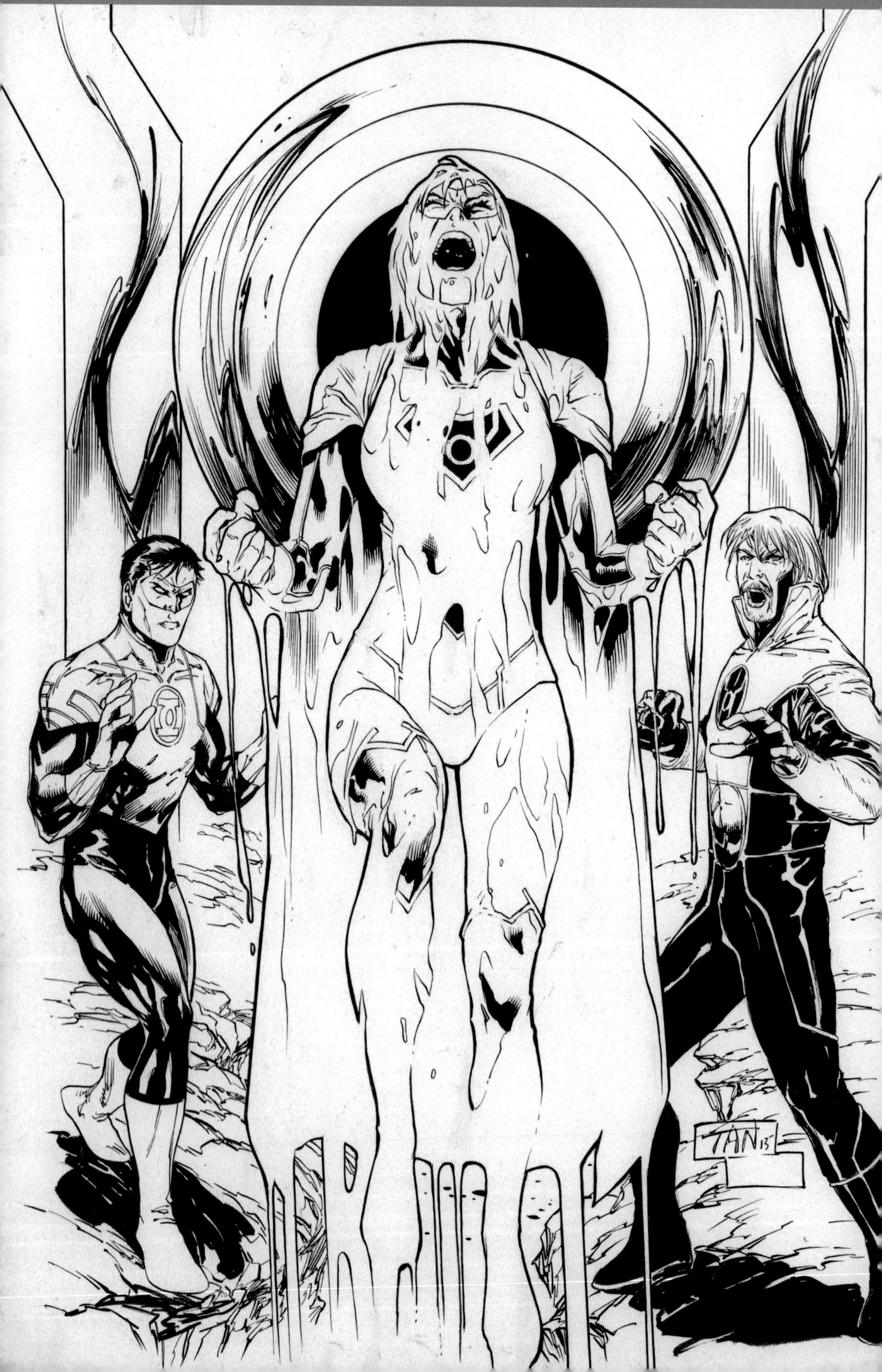

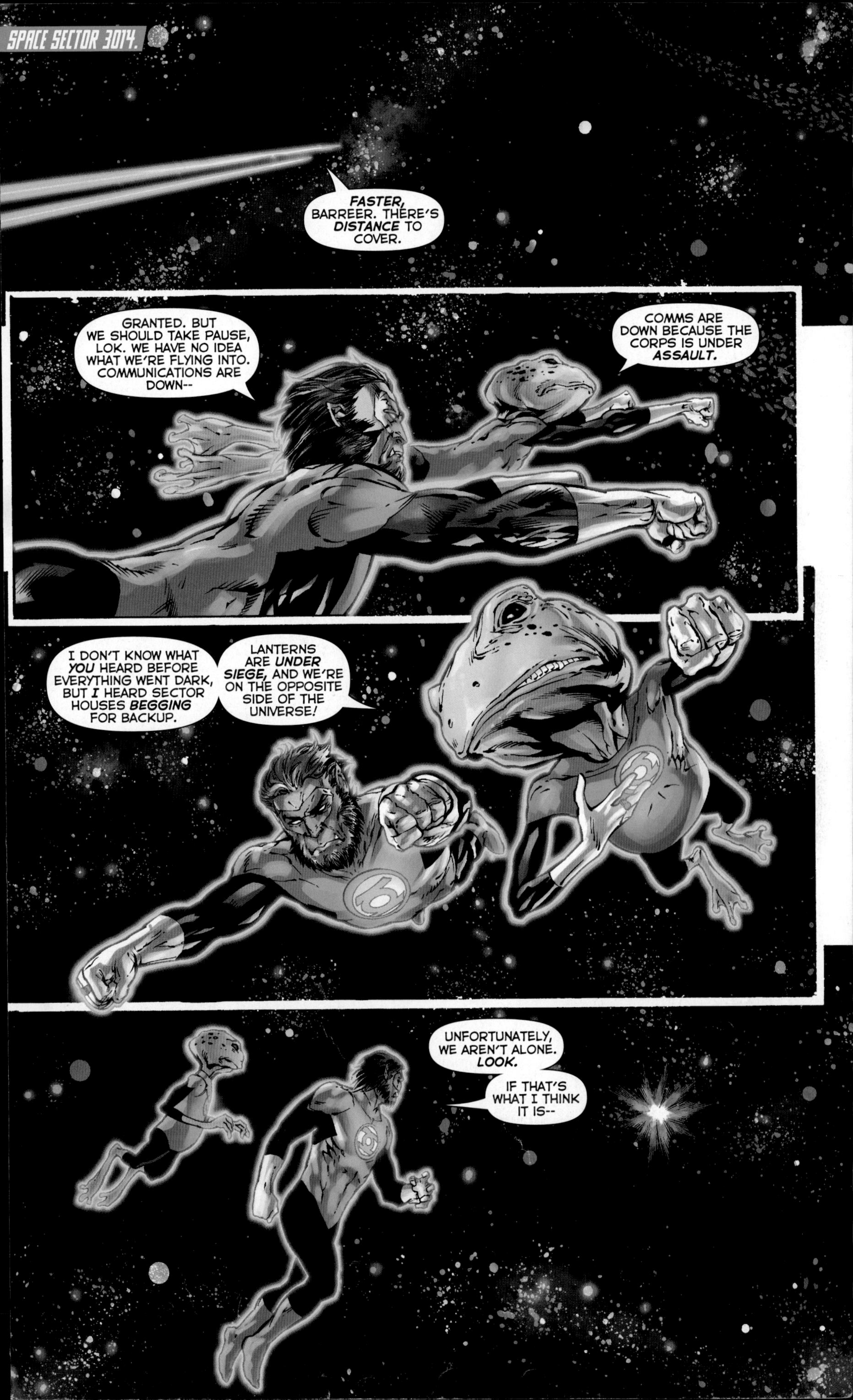
SPACE SECTOR 3014.
FASTER, BARREER. THERE'S DISTANCE TO COVER.
GRANTED. BUT WE SHOULD TAKE PAUSE, LOK. WE HAVE NO IDEA WHAT WE'RE FLYING INTO. COMMUNICATIONS ARE DOWN--
COMMS ARE DOWN BECAUSE THE CORPS IS UNDER ASSAULT.
I DON'T KNOW WHAT YOU HEARD BEFORE EVERYTHING WENT DARK, BUT I HEARD SECTOR HOUSES BEGGING FOR BACKUP.
LANTERNS ARE UNDER SIEGE, AND WE'RE ON THE OPPOSITE SIDE OF THE UNIVERSE!
UNFORTUNATELY, WE AREN'T ALONE. LOOK.
IF THAT'S WHAT I THINK IT IS--

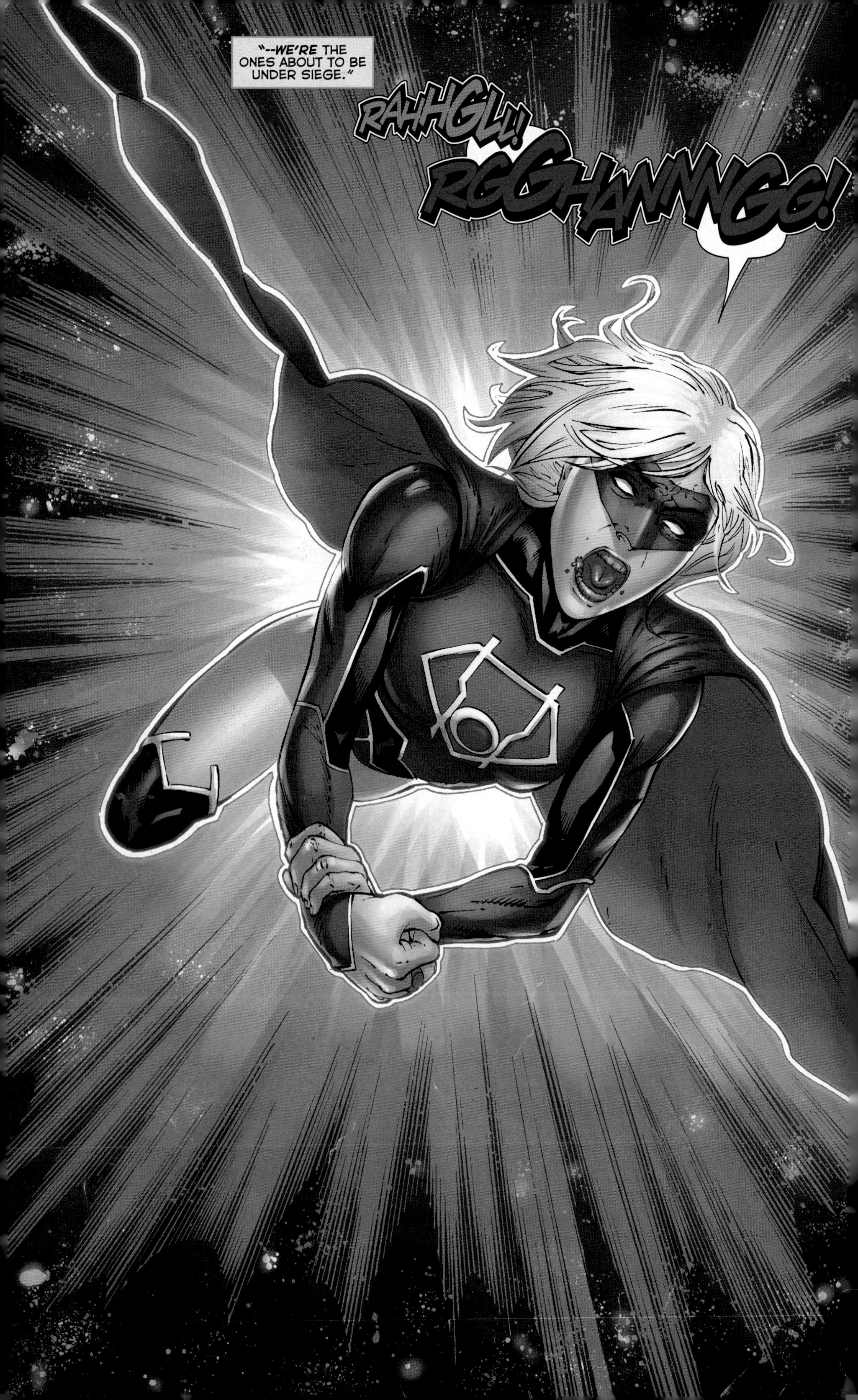
"--WE'RE THE ONES ABOUT TO BE UNDER SIEGE."
RAHHGLL! RGGHANNNGG!

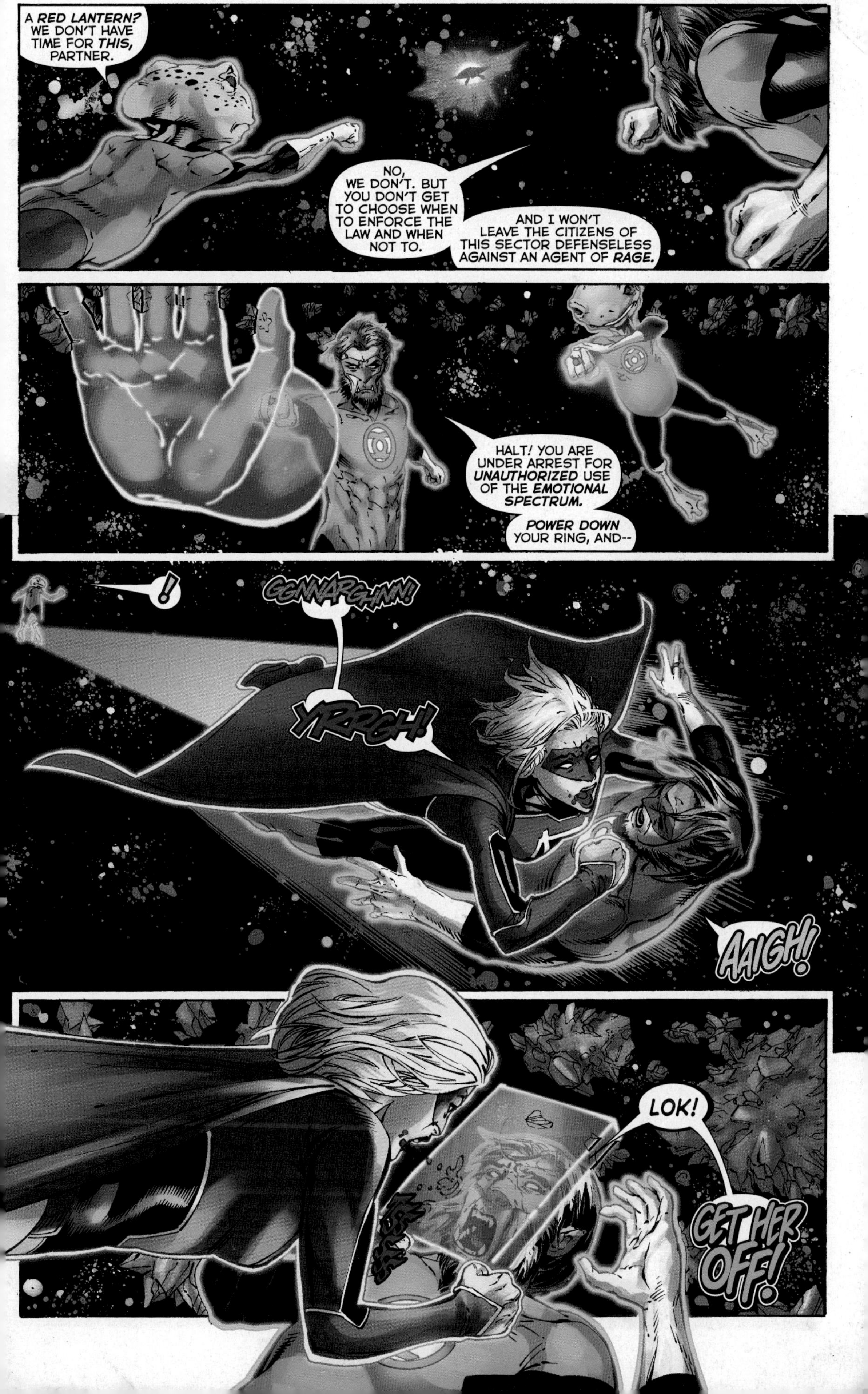
A RED LANTERN? WE DON'T HAVE TIME FOR THIS, PARTNER.
NO, WE DON'T. BUT YOU DON'T GET TO CHOOSE WHEN TO ENFORCE THE LAW AND WHEN NOT TO.
AND I WON'T LEAVE THE CITIZENS OF THIS SECTOR DEFENSELESS AGAINST AN AGENT OF RAGE.
HALT! YOU ARE UNDER ARREST FOR UNAUTHORIZED USE OF THE EMOTIONAL SPECTRUM.
POWER DOWN YOUR RING, AND--
!
GGNNARGHNN!
YRRGH!
AAIGH!
LOK!
GET HER OFF!

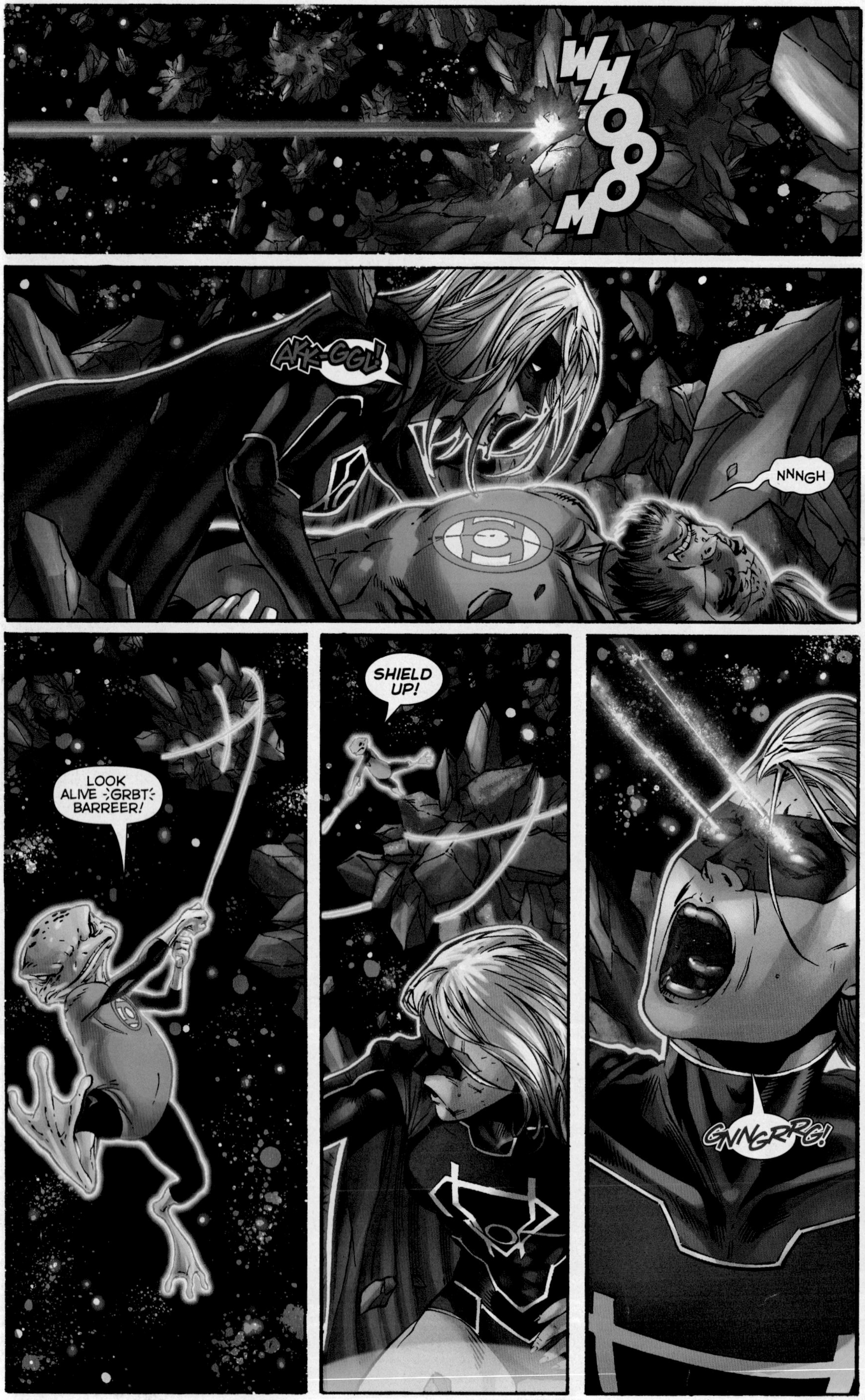
WHOOOOM
AKK-GGL!
NNNGH
LOOK ALIVE -GRBT- BARREER!
SHIELD UP!
GNNGRRRG!

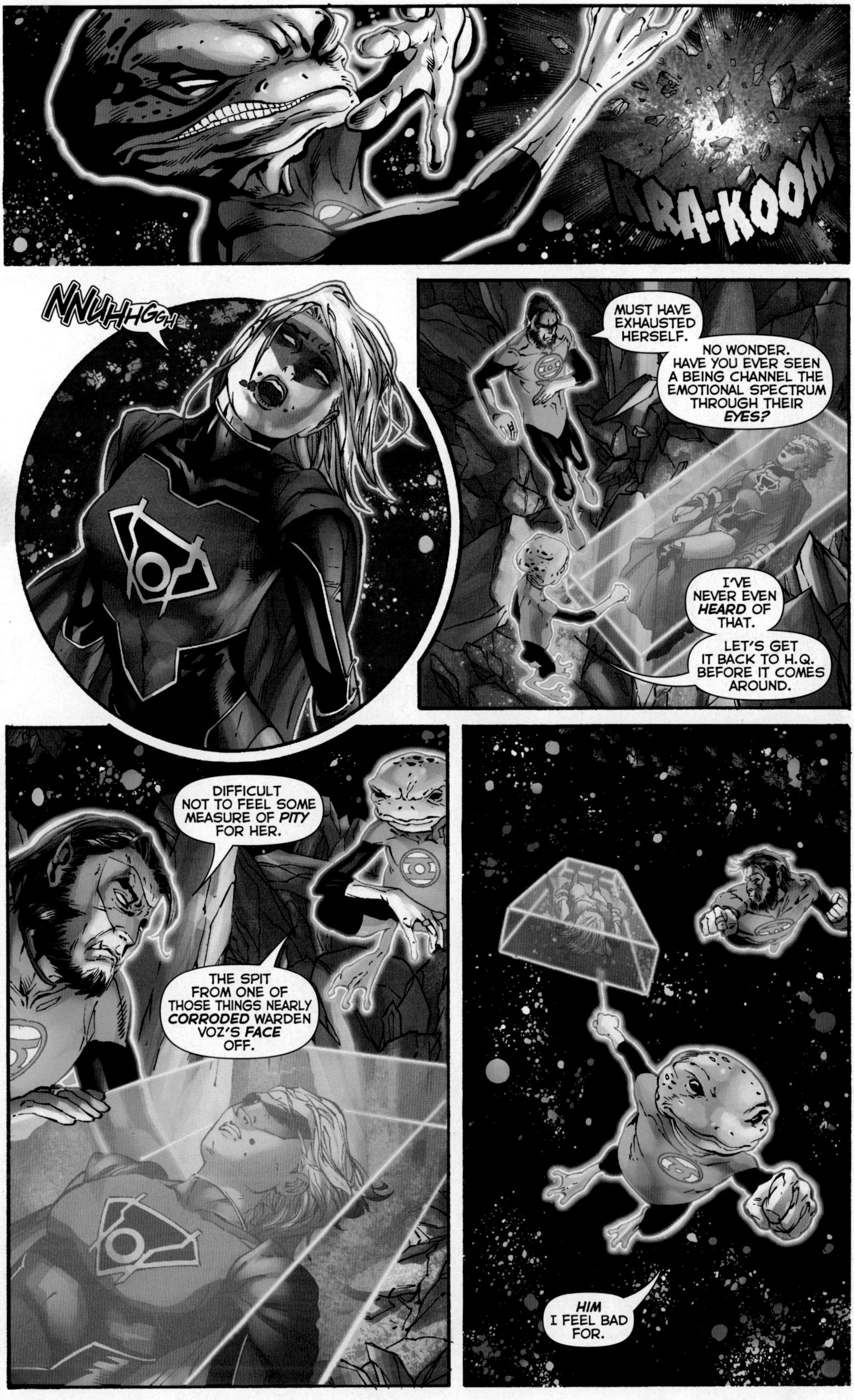
BRA-KOOM
NNUHHGGH
MUST HAVE EXHAUSTED HERSELF.
NO WONDER. HAVE YOU EVER SEEN A BEING CHANNEL THE EMOTIONAL SPECTRUM THROUGH THEIR EYES?
I'VE NEVER EVEN HEARD OF THAT.
LET'S GET IT BACK TO H.Q. BEFORE IT COMES AROUND.
DIFFICULT NOT TO FEEL SOME MEASURE OF PITY FOR HER.
THE SPIT FROM ONE OF THOSE THINGS NEARLY CORRODED WARDEN VOZ'S FACE OFF.
HIM I FEEL BAD FOR.

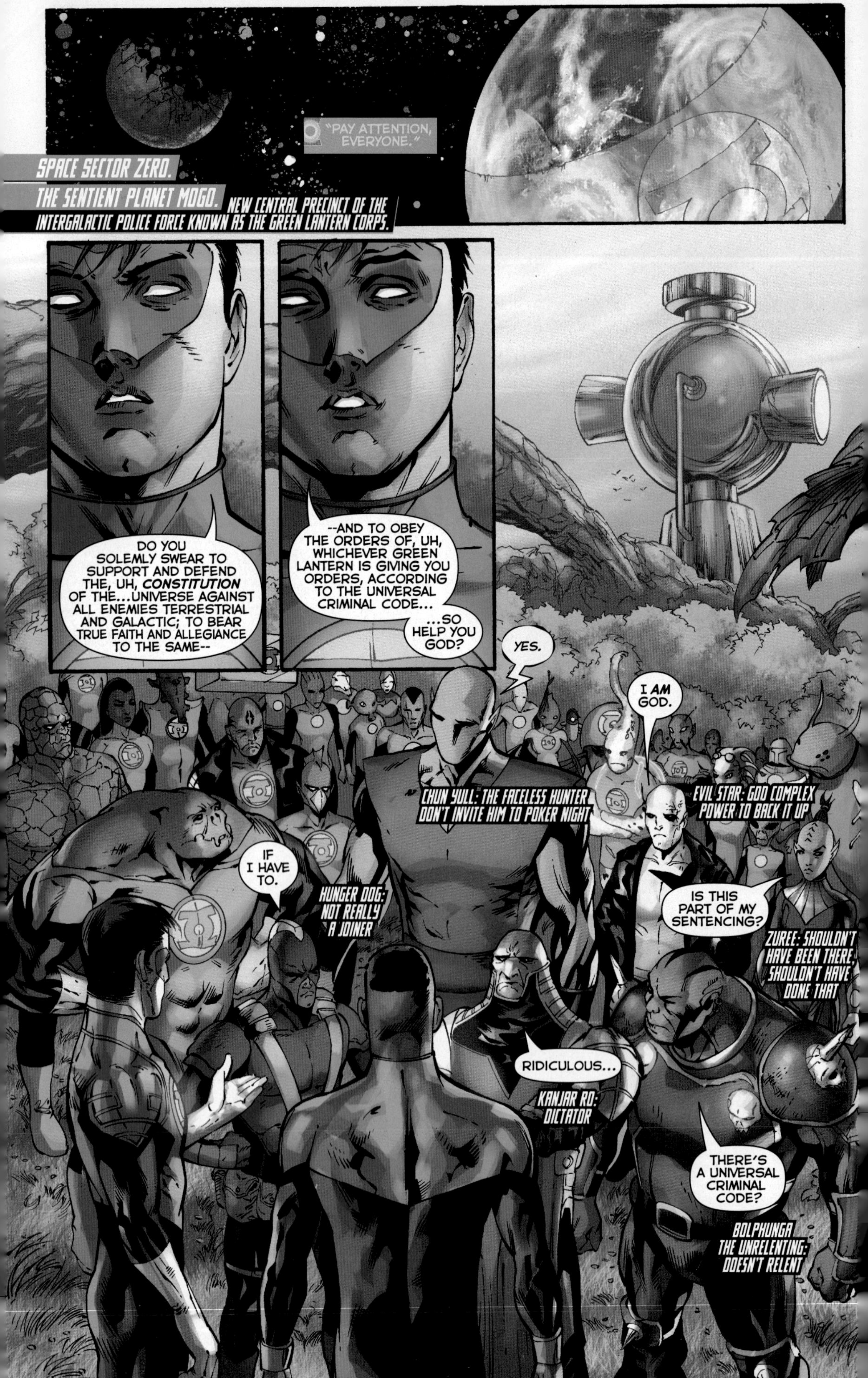

SPACE SECTOR ZERO.
THE SENTIENT PLANET MOGO.
NEW CENTRAL PRECINCT OF THE INTERGALACTIC POLICE FORCE KNOWN AS THE GREEN LANTERN CORPS.
"PAY ATTENTION, EVERYONE."
DO YOU SOLEMLY SWEAR TO SUPPORT AND DEFEND THE, UH, CONSTITUTION OF THE...UNIVERSE AGAINST ALL ENEMIES TERRESTRIAL AND GALACTIC; TO BEAR TRUE FAITH AND ALLEGIANCE TO THE SAME--
--AND TO OBEY THE ORDERS OF, UH, WHICHEVER GREEN LANTERN IS GIVING YOU ORDERS, ACCORDING TO THE UNIVERSAL CRIMINAL CODE...
...SO HELP YOU GOD?
YES.
I AM GOD.
CHUN YULL: THE FACELESS HUNTER DON'T INVITE HIM TO POKER NIGHT
EVIL STAR: GOD COMPLEX POWER TO BACK IT UP
IF I HAVE TO.
HUNGER DOG: NOT REALLY A JOINER
IS THIS PART OF MY SENTENCING?
ZUREE: SHOULDN'T HAVE BEEN THERE, SHOULDN'T HAVE DONE THAT
RIDICULOUS...
KANJAR RO: DICTATOR
THERE'S A UNIVERSAL CRIMINAL CODE?
BOLPHUNGA THE UNRELENTING: DOESN'T RELENT

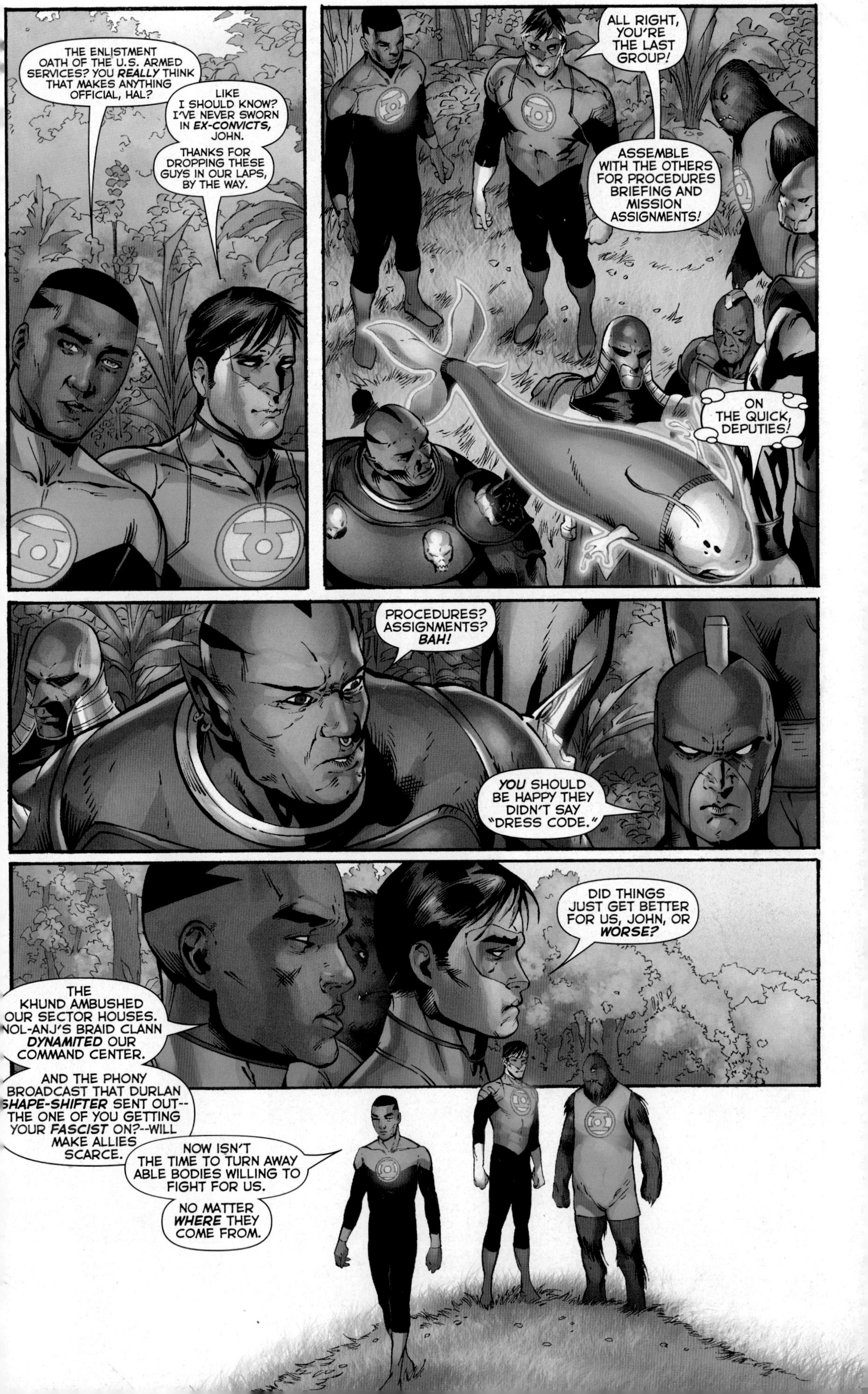
THE ENLISTMENT OATH OF THE U.S. ARMED SERVICES? YOU REALLY THINK THAT MAKES ANYTHING OFFICIAL, HAL?
LIKE I SHOULD KNOW? I'VE NEVER SWORN IN EX-CONVICTS, JOHN.
THANKS FOR DROPPING THESE GUYS IN OUR LAPS, BY THE WAY.
ALL RIGHT, YOU'RE THE LAST GROUP!
ASSEMBLE WITH THE OTHERS FOR PROCEDURES BRIEFING AND MISSION ASSIGNMENTS!
ON THE QUICK, DEPUTIES!
PROCEDURES? ASSIGNMENTS? BAH!
YOU SHOULD BE HAPPY THEY DIDN'T SAY "DRESS CODE."
DID THINGS JUST GET BETTER FOR US, JOHN, OR WORSE?
THE KHUND AMBUSHED OUR SECTOR HOUSES. NOL-ANJ'S BRAID CLANN DYNAMITED OUR COMMAND CENTER.
AND THE PHONY BROADCAST THAT DURLAN SHAPE-SHIFTER SENT OUT--THE ONE OF YOU GETTING YOUR FASCIST ON?--WILL MAKE ALLIES SCARCE.
NOW ISN'T THE TIME TO TURN AWAY ABLE BODIES WILLING TO FIGHT FOR US.
NO MATTER WHERE THEY COME FROM.

IT'S A **WRONG** DAY WHEN WE CAN COUNT ON **FELONS** OVER FELLOW LANTERNS, **EH, GRAF?**

MEANING **WHAT, VATH?** SPEAK YOUR MIND.

WHAT LITTLE THERE IS OF IT.

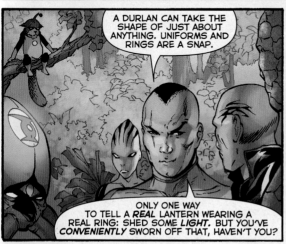

A **DURLAN** CAN TAKE THE SHAPE OF JUST ABOUT ANYTHING. UNIFORMS AND RINGS ARE A SNAP.

ONLY ONE WAY TO TELL A **REAL** LANTERN WEARING A REAL RING: SHED SOME **LIGHT.** BUT YOU'VE **CONVENIENTLY** SWORN OFF THAT, HAVEN'T YOU?

OUR RINGS DRAIN THE RESERVOIR OF THE EMOTIONAL SPECTRUM. I DON'T WIELD LIGHT ON **PRINCIPLE.**

SO YOU AND YOUR OBJECTORS SAY. OR MAYBE THAT'S JUST YOUR **COVER.**

ONE SPARK. GIMME JUST **ONE.**

IF YOU CAN.

WHOM

AW, C'MON! SEE HOW **EASY** THAT WAS?

CURSE YOU, VATH.

THE DURLANS ARE RIGHT WHERE THEY WANT TO BE-- INSIDE OUR HEADS.

VATH HAS A POINT. ROUND UP THE CIVILIAN SUPPORT STAFF, VOZ.

NO WAY THE DURLANS COULD'VE SET UP SUCH A COORDINATED STRIKE UNLESS THEY HAD AGENTS KEEPING TABS ON US.

UNTIL WE KNOW FOR SURE WHO'S WHO, ANYONE WHO CAN'T USE A RING CAN'T BE TRUSTED AS FAR AS WE CAN--

RSSSTLE

RSSSTLE

...THROW THEM?

YEALLGH!

THE HELL?

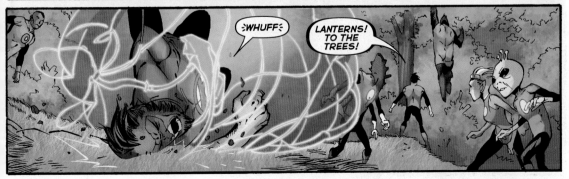

:WHUFF:

LANTERNS! TO THE TREES!

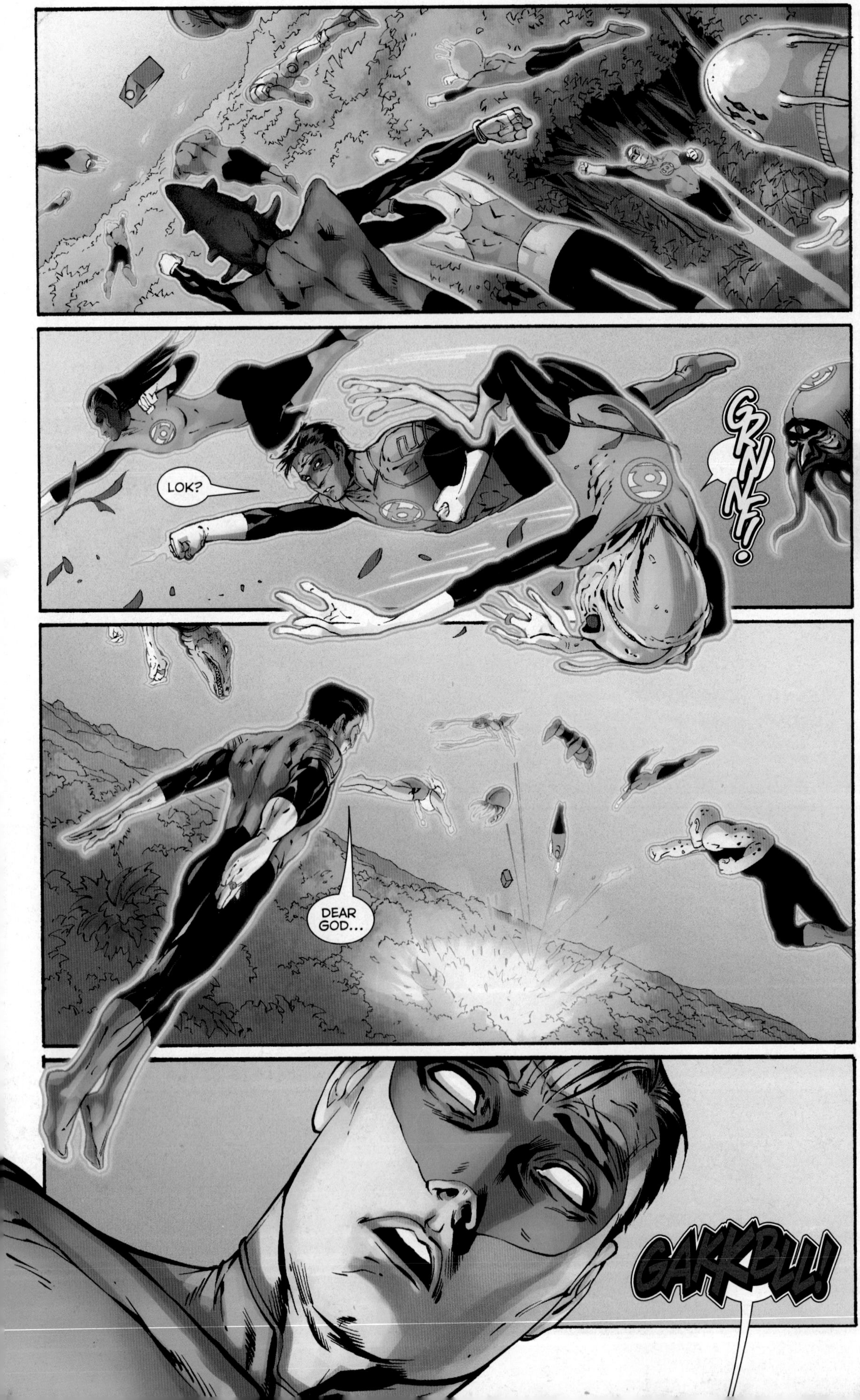
LOK?
GRNNF!
DEAR GOD...
GAKKBLL!

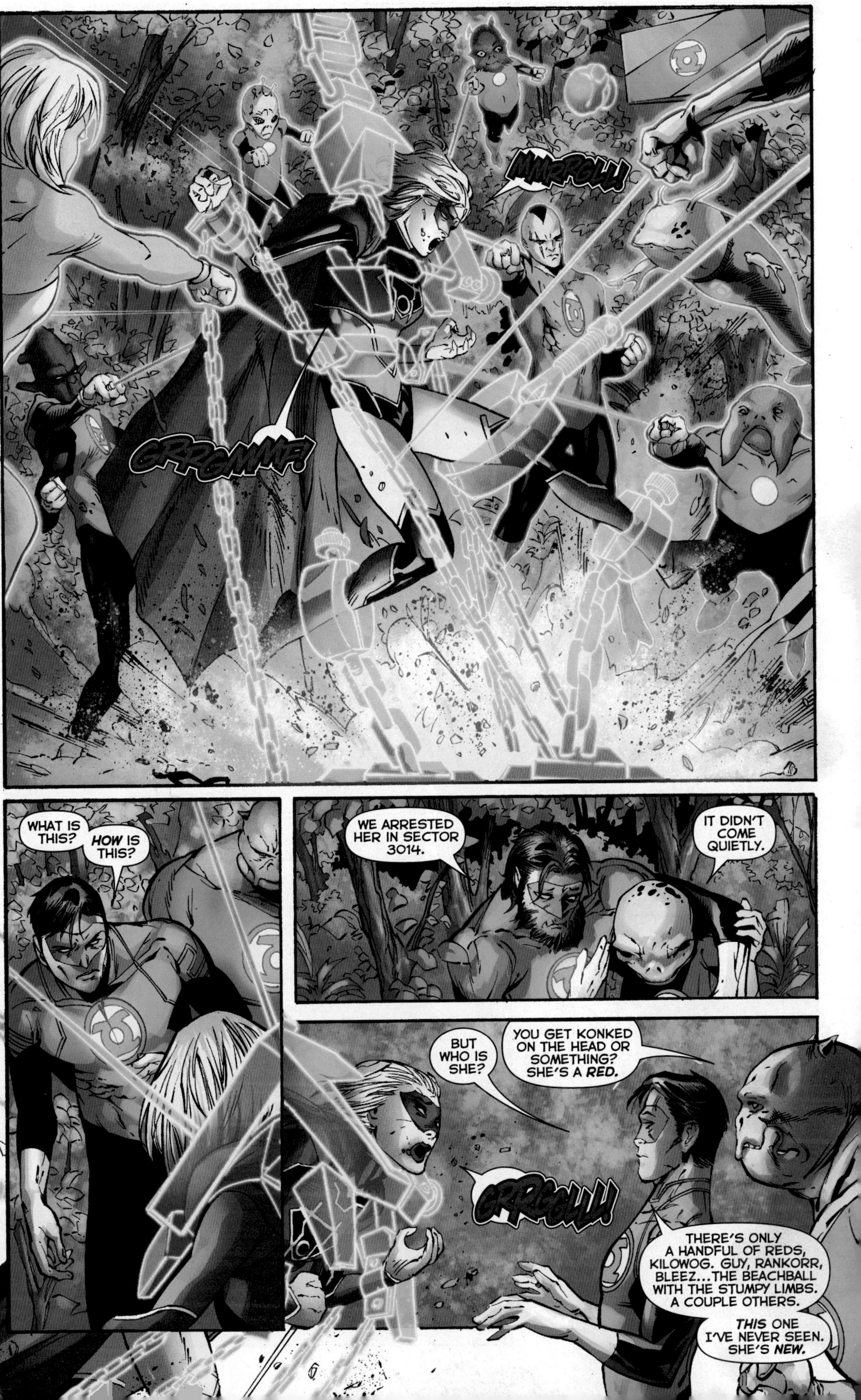
MMRFGLL!
GRRGMMMF!
WHAT IS THIS? HOW IS THIS?
WE ARRESTED HER IN SECTOR 3014.
IT DIDN'T COME QUIETLY.
BUT WHO IS SHE?
YOU GET KONKED ON THE HEAD OR SOMETHING? SHE'S A RED.
GRRGGLL!
THERE'S ONLY A HANDFUL OF REDS, KILOWOG. GUY, RANKORR, BLEEZ...THE BEACHBALL WITH THE STUMPY LIMBS. A COUPLE OTHERS.
THIS ONE I'VE NEVER SEEN. SHE'S NEW.

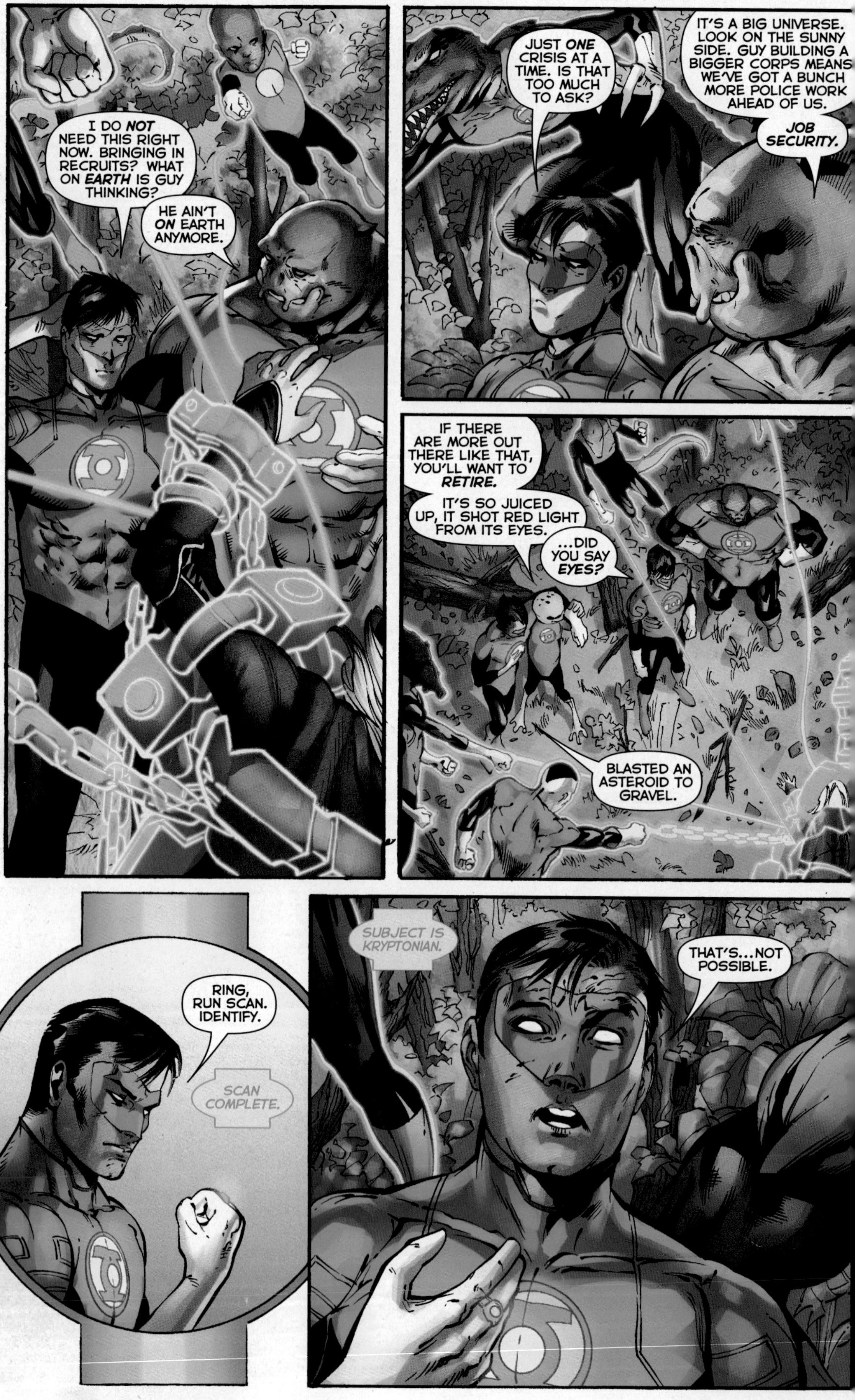
I DO NOT NEED THIS RIGHT NOW. BRINGING IN RECRUITS? WHAT ON EARTH IS GUY THINKING?
HE AIN'T ON EARTH ANYMORE.
JUST ONE CRISIS AT A TIME. IS THAT TOO MUCH TO ASK?
IT'S A BIG UNIVERSE. LOOK ON THE SUNNY SIDE. GUY BUILDING A BIGGER CORPS MEANS WE'VE GOT A BUNCH MORE POLICE WORK AHEAD OF US.
JOB SECURITY.
IF THERE ARE MORE OUT THERE LIKE THAT, YOU'LL WANT TO RETIRE.
IT'S SO JUICED UP, IT SHOT RED LIGHT FROM ITS EYES.
...DID YOU SAY EYES?
BLASTED AN ASTEROID TO GRAVEL.
RING, RUN SCAN. IDENTIFY.
SCAN COMPLETE.
SUBJECT IS KRYPTONIAN.
THAT'S...NOT POSSIBLE.

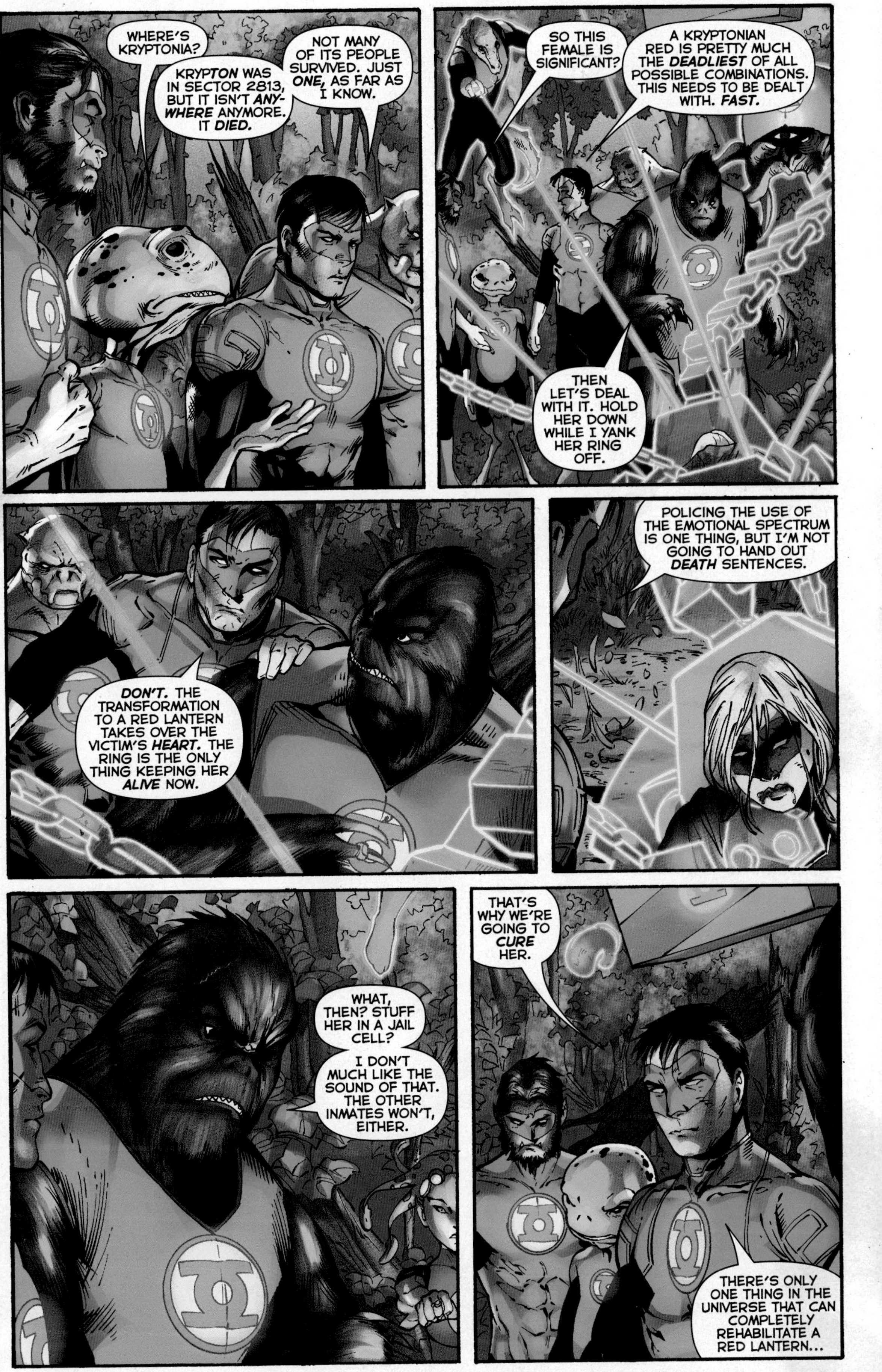
WHERE'S KRYPTONIA?
KRYPTON WAS IN SECTOR 2813, BUT IT ISN'T ANYWHERE ANYMORE. IT DIED.
NOT MANY OF ITS PEOPLE SURVIVED. JUST ONE, AS FAR AS I KNOW.
SO THIS FEMALE IS SIGNIFICANT?
A KRYPTONIAN RED IS PRETTY MUCH THE DEADLIEST OF ALL POSSIBLE COMBINATIONS. THIS NEEDS TO BE DEALT WITH. FAST.
THEN LET'S DEAL WITH IT. HOLD HER DOWN WHILE I YANK HER RING OFF.
DON'T. THE TRANSFORMATION TO A RED LANTERN TAKES OVER THE VICTIM'S HEART. THE RING IS THE ONLY THING KEEPING HER ALIVE NOW.
POLICING THE USE OF THE EMOTIONAL SPECTRUM IS ONE THING, BUT I'M NOT GOING TO HAND OUT DEATH SENTENCES.
WHAT, THEN? STUFF HER IN A JAIL CELL?
I DON'T MUCH LIKE THE SOUND OF THAT. THE OTHER INMATES WON'T, EITHER.
THAT'S WHY WE'RE GOING TO CURE HER.
THERE'S ONLY ONE THING IN THE UNIVERSE THAT CAN COMPLETELY REHABILITATE A RED LANTERN...

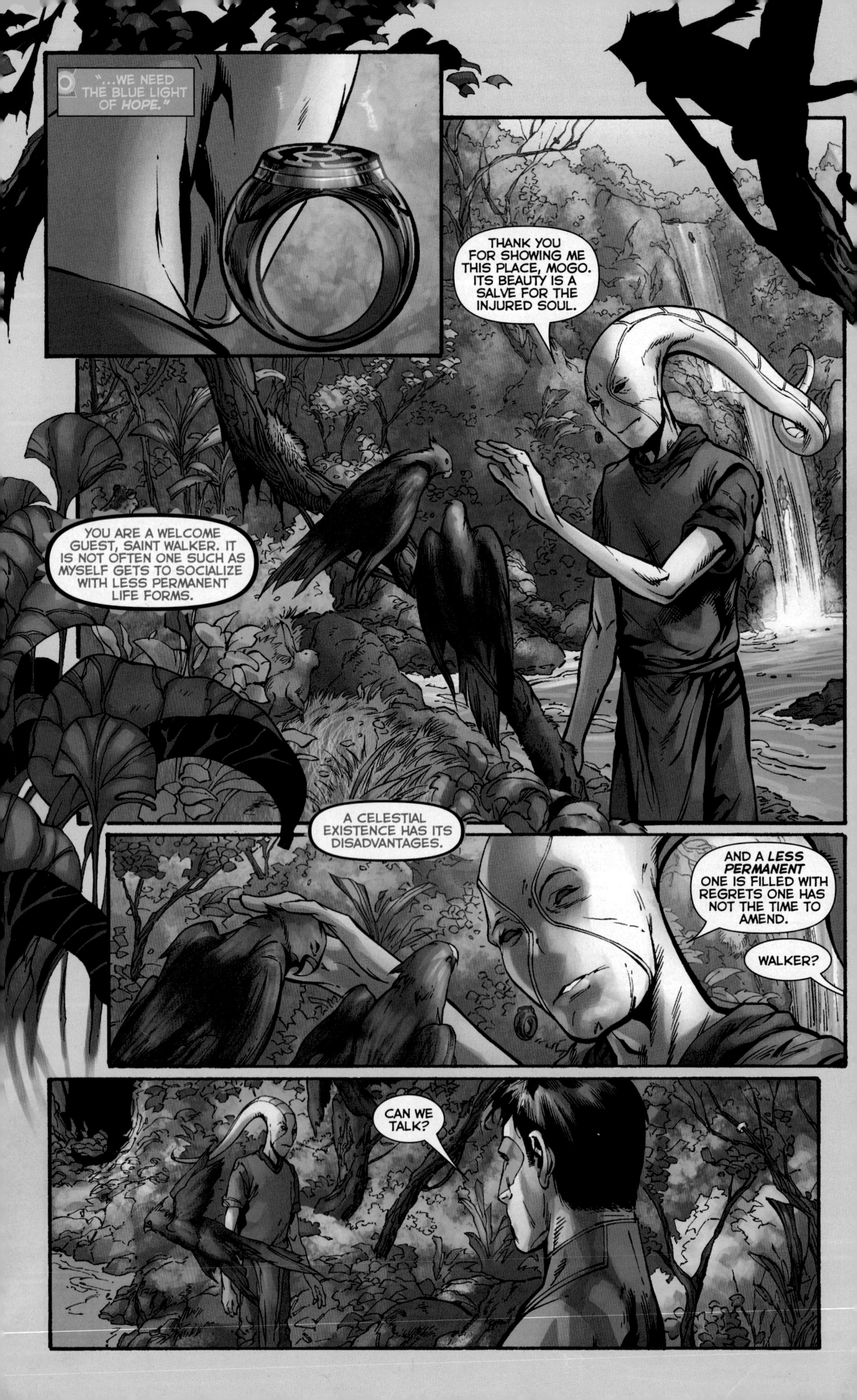
"...WE NEED THE BLUE LIGHT OF *HOPE.*"
THANK YOU FOR SHOWING ME THIS PLACE, MOGO. ITS BEAUTY IS A SALVE FOR THE INJURED SOUL.
YOU ARE A WELCOME GUEST, SAINT WALKER. IT IS NOT OFTEN ONE SUCH AS MYSELF GETS TO SOCIALIZE WITH LESS PERMANENT LIFE FORMS.
A CELESTIAL EXISTENCE HAS ITS DISADVANTAGES.
AND A *LESS PERMANENT* ONE IS FILLED WITH REGRETS ONE HAS NOT THE TIME TO AMEND.
WALKER?
CAN WE TALK?

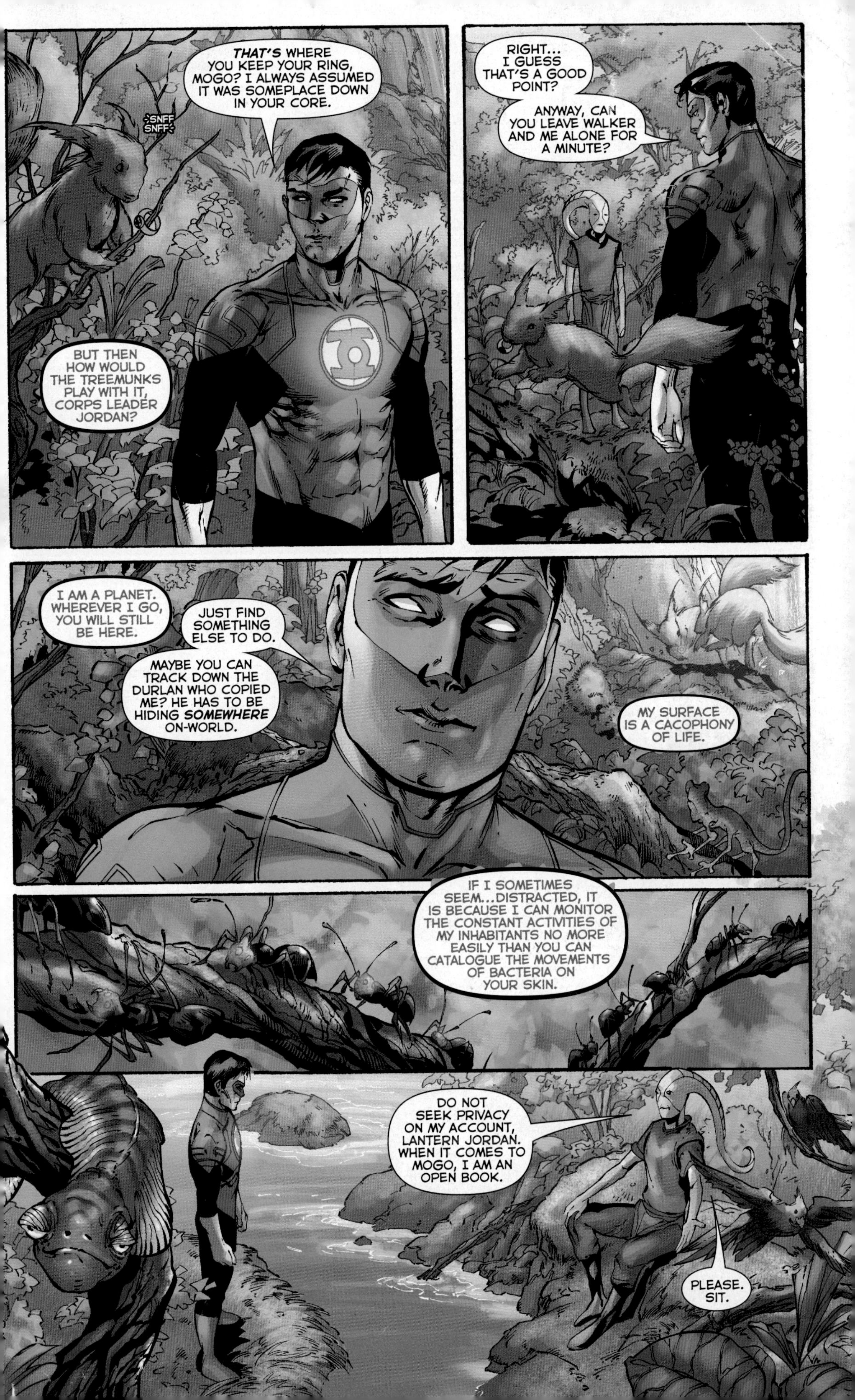
THAT'S WHERE YOU KEEP YOUR RING, MOGO? I ALWAYS ASSUMED IT WAS SOMEPLACE DOWN IN YOUR CORE.
SNFF SNFF
BUT THEN HOW WOULD THE TREEMUNKS PLAY WITH IT, CORPS LEADER JORDAN?
RIGHT... I GUESS THAT'S A GOOD POINT?
ANYWAY, CAN YOU LEAVE WALKER AND ME ALONE FOR A MINUTE?
I AM A PLANET. WHEREVER I GO, YOU WILL STILL BE HERE.
JUST FIND SOMETHING ELSE TO DO.
MAYBE YOU CAN TRACK DOWN THE DURLAN WHO COPIED ME? HE HAS TO BE HIDING SOMEWHERE ON-WORLD.
MY SURFACE IS A CACOPHONY OF LIFE.
IF I SOMETIMES SEEM...DISTRACTED, IT IS BECAUSE I CAN MONITOR THE CONSTANT ACTIVITIES OF MY INHABITANTS NO MORE EASILY THAN YOU CAN CATALOGUE THE MOVEMENTS OF BACTERIA ON YOUR SKIN.
DO NOT SEEK PRIVACY ON MY ACCOUNT, LANTERN JORDAN. WHEN IT COMES TO MOGO, I AM AN OPEN BOOK.
PLEASE. SIT.

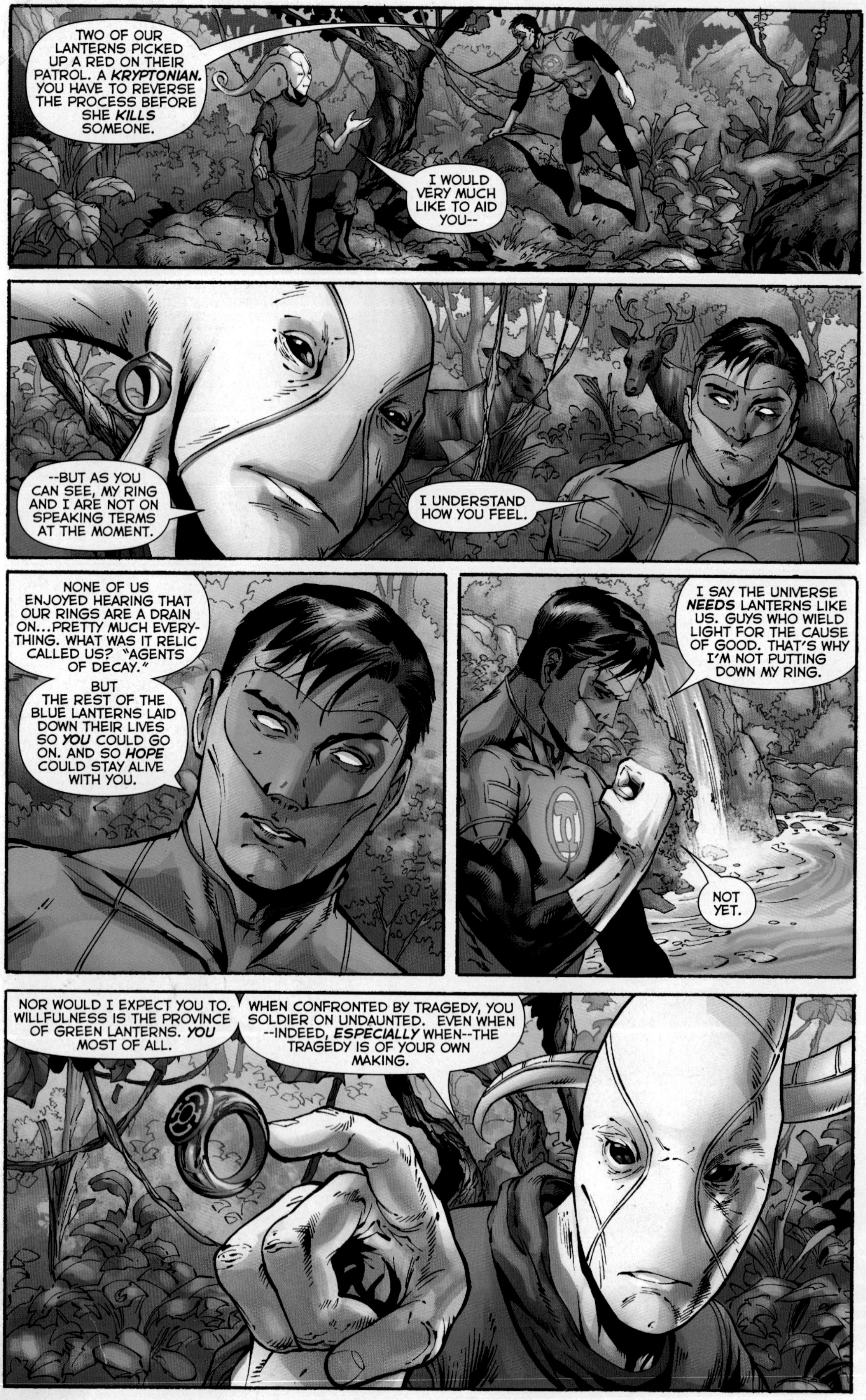
TWO OF OUR LANTERNS PICKED UP A RED ON THEIR PATROL. A KRYPTONIAN. YOU HAVE TO REVERSE THE PROCESS BEFORE SHE KILLS SOMEONE.
I WOULD VERY MUCH LIKE TO AID YOU--
--BUT AS YOU CAN SEE, MY RING AND I ARE NOT ON SPEAKING TERMS AT THE MOMENT.
I UNDERSTAND HOW YOU FEEL.
NONE OF US ENJOYED HEARING THAT OUR RINGS ARE A DRAIN ON...PRETTY MUCH EVERY-THING. WHAT WAS IT RELIC CALLED US? "AGENTS OF DECAY."
BUT THE REST OF THE BLUE LANTERNS LAID DOWN THEIR LIVES SO YOU COULD GO ON. AND SO HOPE COULD STAY ALIVE WITH YOU.
I SAY THE UNIVERSE NEEDS LANTERNS LIKE US. GUYS WHO WIELD LIGHT FOR THE CAUSE OF GOOD. THAT'S WHY I'M NOT PUTTING DOWN MY RING.
NOT YET.
NOR WOULD I EXPECT YOU TO. WILLFULNESS IS THE PROVINCE OF GREEN LANTERNS. YOU MOST OF ALL.
WHEN CONFRONTED BY TRAGEDY, YOU SOLDIER ON UNDAUNTED. EVEN WHEN --INDEED, ESPECIALLY WHEN--THE TRAGEDY IS OF YOUR OWN MAKING.

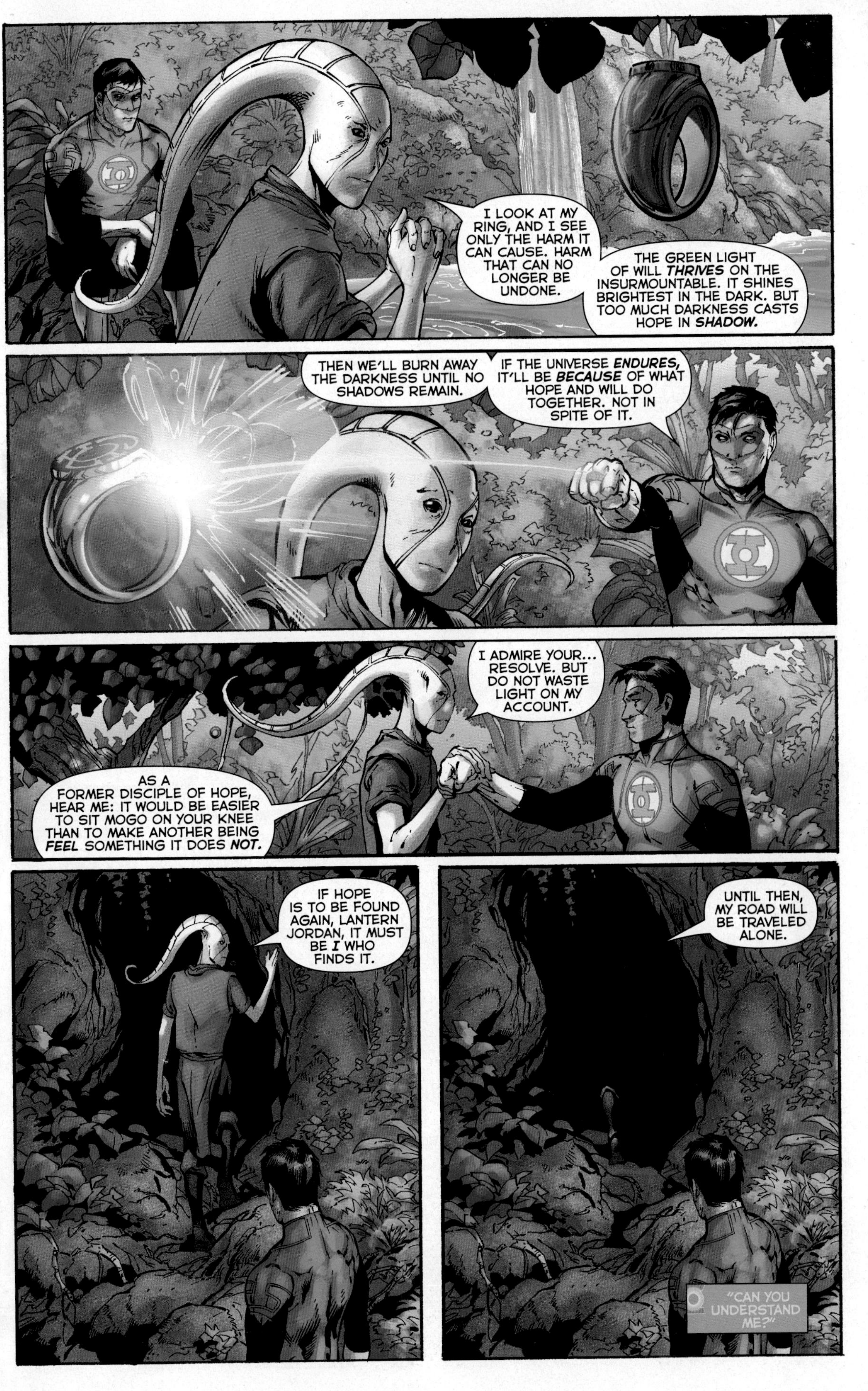
I LOOK AT MY RING, AND I SEE ONLY THE HARM IT CAN CAUSE. HARM THAT CAN NO LONGER BE UNDONE.
THE GREEN LIGHT OF WILL THRIVES ON THE INSURMOUNTABLE. IT SHINES BRIGHTEST IN THE DARK. BUT TOO MUCH DARKNESS CASTS HOPE IN SHADOW.
THEN WE'LL BURN AWAY THE DARKNESS UNTIL NO SHADOWS REMAIN.
IF THE UNIVERSE ENDURES, IT'LL BE BECAUSE OF WHAT HOPE AND WILL DO TOGETHER. NOT IN SPITE OF IT.
I ADMIRE YOUR... RESOLVE. BUT DO NOT WASTE LIGHT ON MY ACCOUNT.
AS A FORMER DISCIPLE OF HOPE, HEAR ME: IT WOULD BE EASIER TO SIT MOGO ON YOUR KNEE THAN TO MAKE ANOTHER BEING FEEL SOMETHING IT DOES NOT.
IF HOPE IS TO BE FOUND AGAIN, LANTERN JORDAN, IT MUST BE I WHO FINDS IT.
UNTIL THEN, MY ROAD WILL BE TRAVELED ALONE.
"CAN YOU UNDERSTAND ME?"

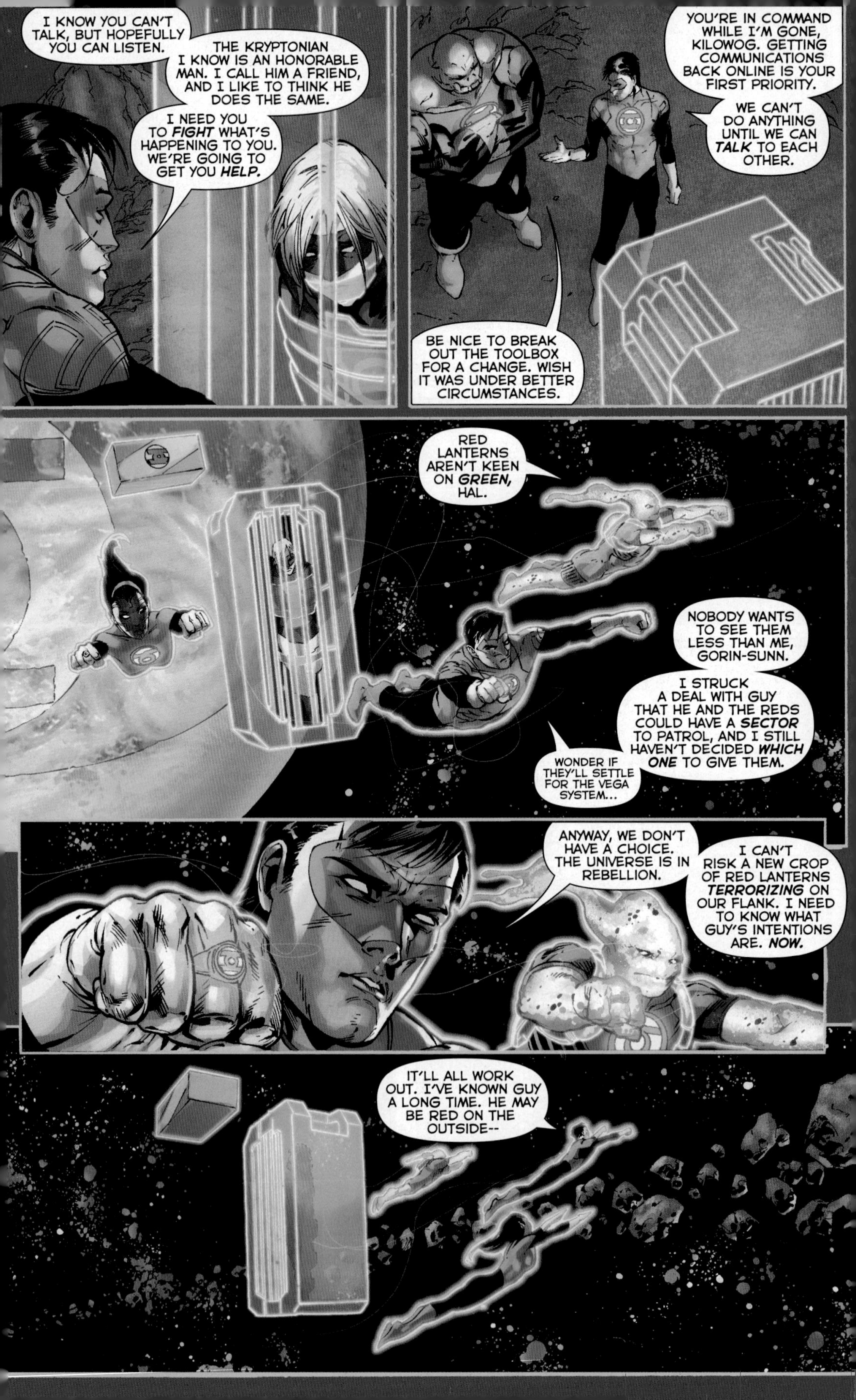
I KNOW YOU CAN'T TALK, BUT HOPEFULLY YOU CAN LISTEN.
THE KRYPTONIAN I KNOW IS AN HONORABLE MAN. I CALL HIM A FRIEND, AND I LIKE TO THINK HE DOES THE SAME.
I NEED YOU TO FIGHT WHAT'S HAPPENING TO YOU. WE'RE GOING TO GET YOU HELP.
YOU'RE IN COMMAND WHILE I'M GONE, KILOWOG. GETTING COMMUNICATIONS BACK ONLINE IS YOUR FIRST PRIORITY.
WE CAN'T DO ANYTHING UNTIL WE CAN TALK TO EACH OTHER.
BE NICE TO BREAK OUT THE TOOLBOX FOR A CHANGE. WISH IT WAS UNDER BETTER CIRCUMSTANCES.
RED LANTERNS AREN'T KEEN ON GREEN, HAL.
NOBODY WANTS TO SEE THEM LESS THAN ME, GORIN-SUNN.
I STRUCK A DEAL WITH GUY THAT HE AND THE REDS COULD HAVE A SECTOR TO PATROL, AND I STILL HAVEN'T DECIDED WHICH ONE TO GIVE THEM.
WONDER IF THEY'LL SETTLE FOR THE VEGA SYSTEM...
ANYWAY, WE DON'T HAVE A CHOICE. THE UNIVERSE IS IN REBELLION.
I CAN'T RISK A NEW CROP OF RED LANTERNS TERRORIZING ON OUR FLANK. I NEED TO KNOW WHAT GUY'S INTENTIONS ARE. NOW.
IT'LL ALL WORK OUT. I'VE KNOWN GUY A LONG TIME. HE MAY BE RED ON THE OUTSIDE--

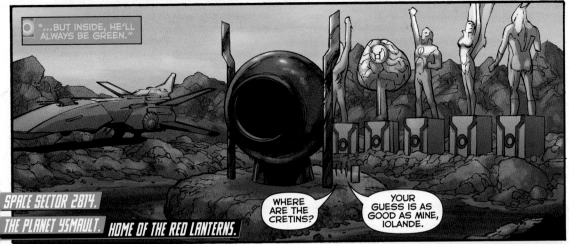

"...BUT INSIDE, HE'LL ALWAYS BE GREEN."

SPACE SECTOR 2814.
THE PLANET YSMAULT. HOME OF THE RED LANTERNS.

WHERE ARE THE CRETINS?

YOUR GUESS IS AS GOOD AS MINE, IOLANDE.

I'VE NEVER BEEN HERE WHEN THEY WEREN'T STANDING AROUND THEIR BATTERY. IT'S KIND OF WHAT THEY DO.

BUT IT'S NICE TO SEE GUY'S NEW ROLE HASN'T CHANGED HIS TENDENCY TO OVER-COMPENSATE...

SUCH *PUTREFACTION.* NOTHING LIKE THE SEA OF GENERATIONS MY KIND RESIDES IN.

STRANGE...

...THEIR *SHIP* IS JUST SITTING OUT IN THE OPEN.

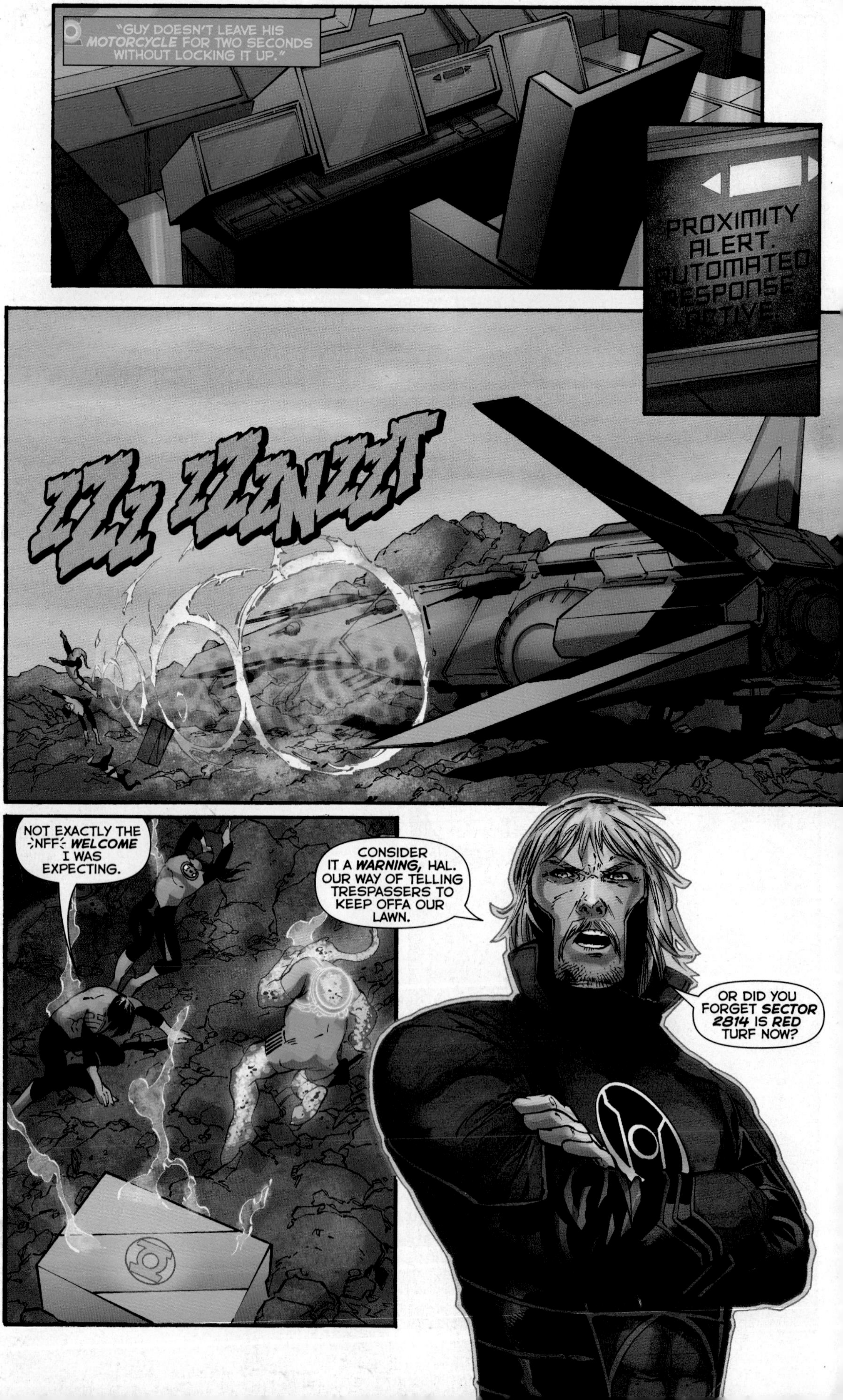
"GUY DOESN'T LEAVE HIS *MOTORCYCLE* FOR TWO SECONDS WITHOUT LOCKING IT UP."
PROXIMITY ALERT. AUTOMATED RESPONSE ACTIVE.
ZZZ ZZZNZZT
NOT EXACTLY THE NFF *WELCOME* I WAS EXPECTING.
CONSIDER IT A *WARNING,* HAL. OUR WAY OF TELLING TRESPASSERS TO KEEP OFFA OUR LAWN.
OR DID YOU FORGET *SECTOR 2814* IS *RED* TURF NOW?

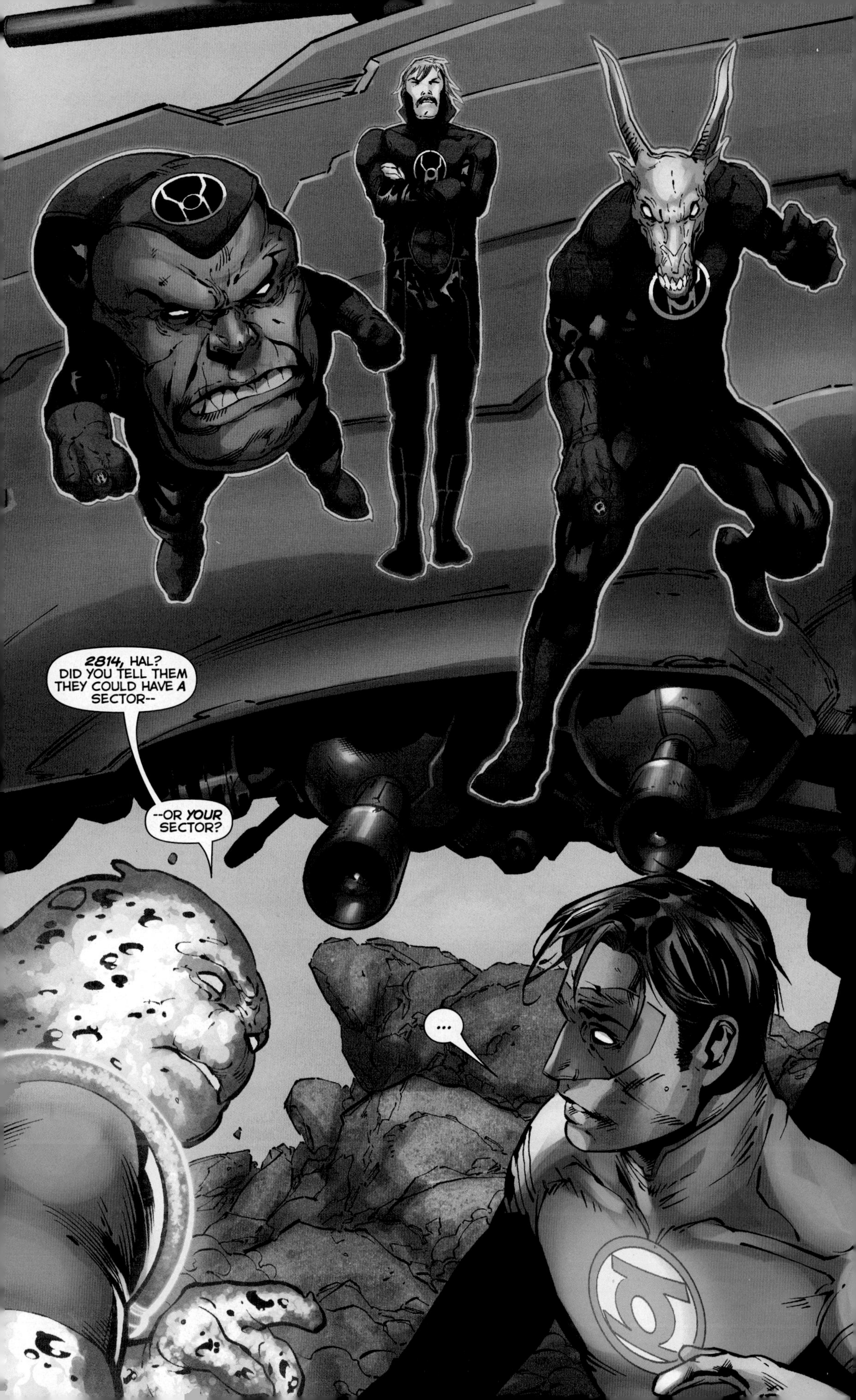
2814, HAL? DID YOU TELL THEM THEY COULD HAVE A SECTOR--
--OR YOUR SECTOR?
...

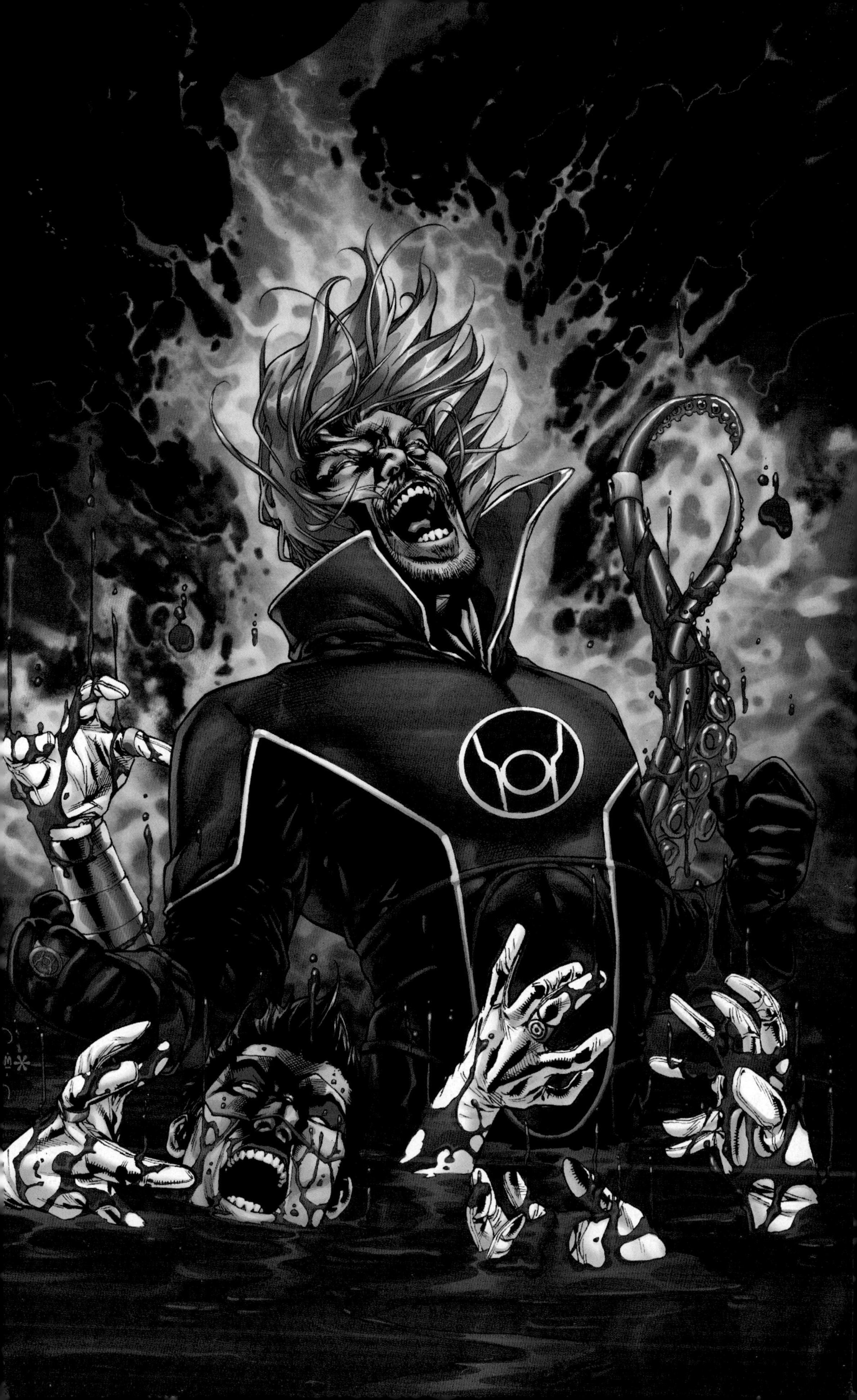

RED ALERT PART 2

CHARLES SOULE writer ALESSANDRO VITTI artist GABE ELTAEB colorist
cover art by STEPHEN SEGOVIA & HI-FI

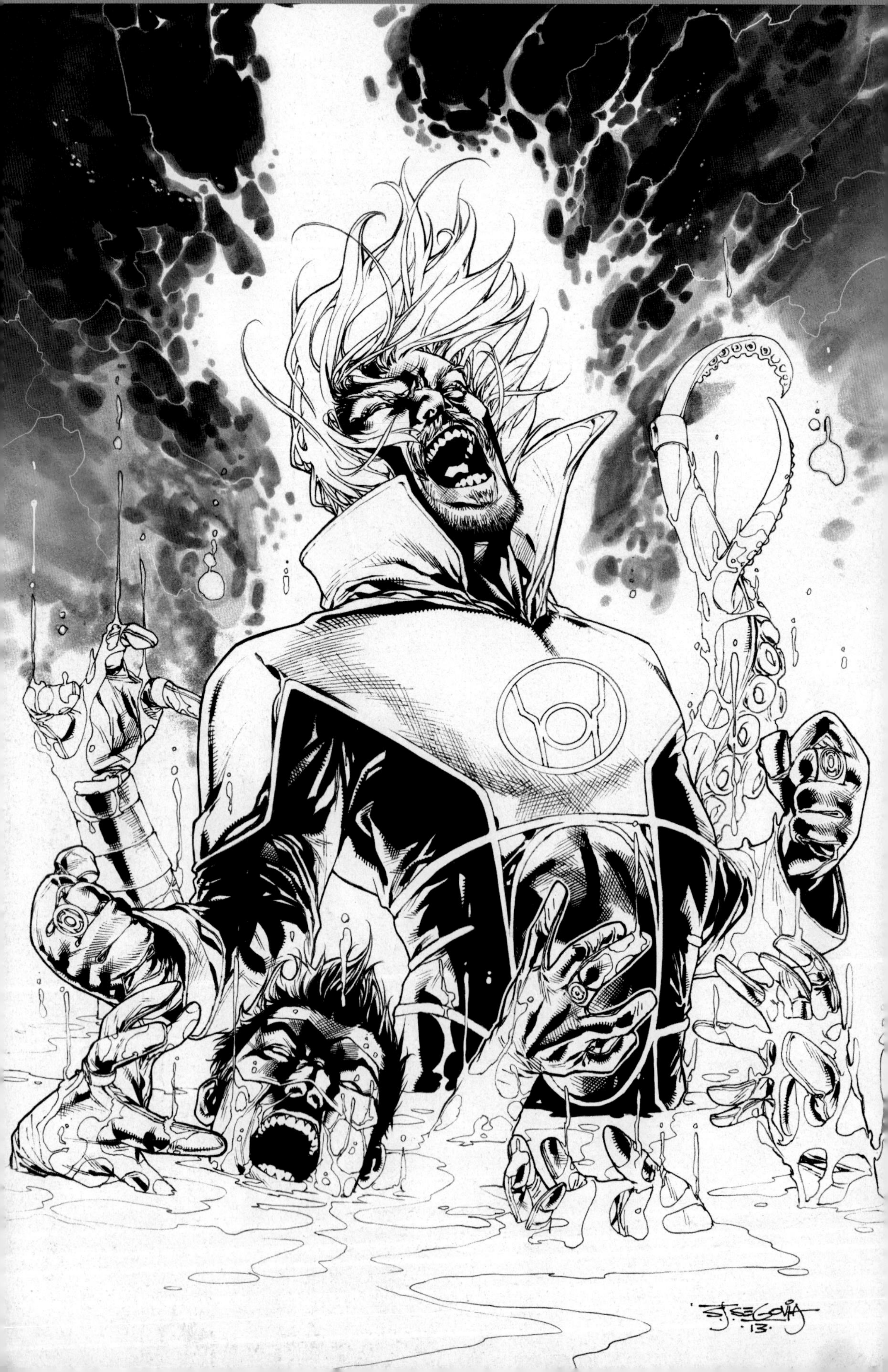
ST SEGOVIA
·13·

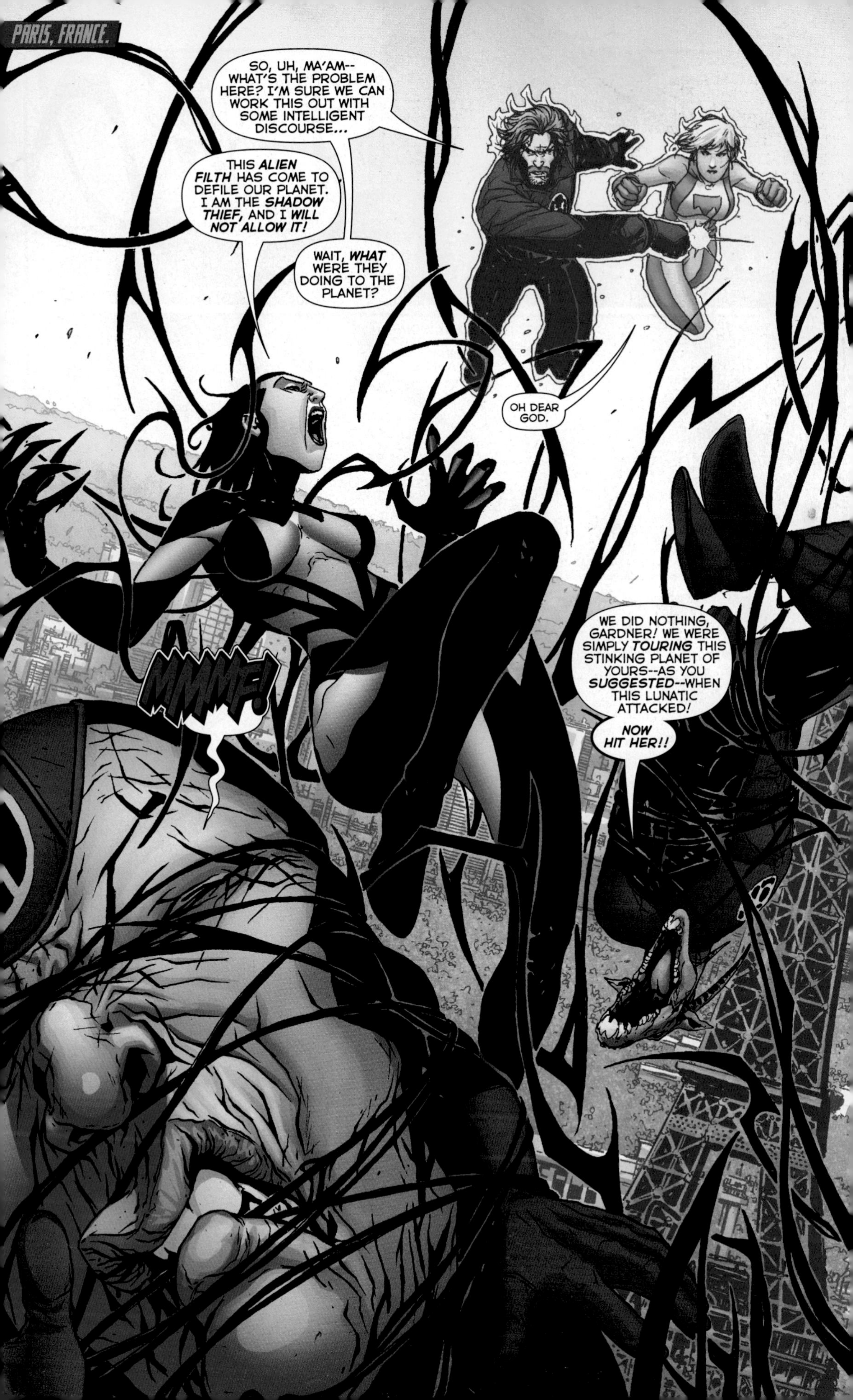

PARIS, FRANCE.
SO, UH, MA'AM-- WHAT'S THE PROBLEM HERE? I'M SURE WE CAN WORK THIS OUT WITH SOME INTELLIGENT DISCOURSE...
THIS ALIEN FILTH HAS COME TO DEFILE OUR PLANET. I AM THE SHADOW THIEF, AND I WILL NOT ALLOW IT!
WAIT, WHAT WERE THEY DOING TO THE PLANET?
OH DEAR GOD.
MMMF!
WE DID NOTHING, GARDNER! WE WERE SIMPLY TOURING THIS STINKING PLANET OF YOURS--AS YOU SUGGESTED--WHEN THIS LUNATIC ATTACKED!
NOW HIT HER!!

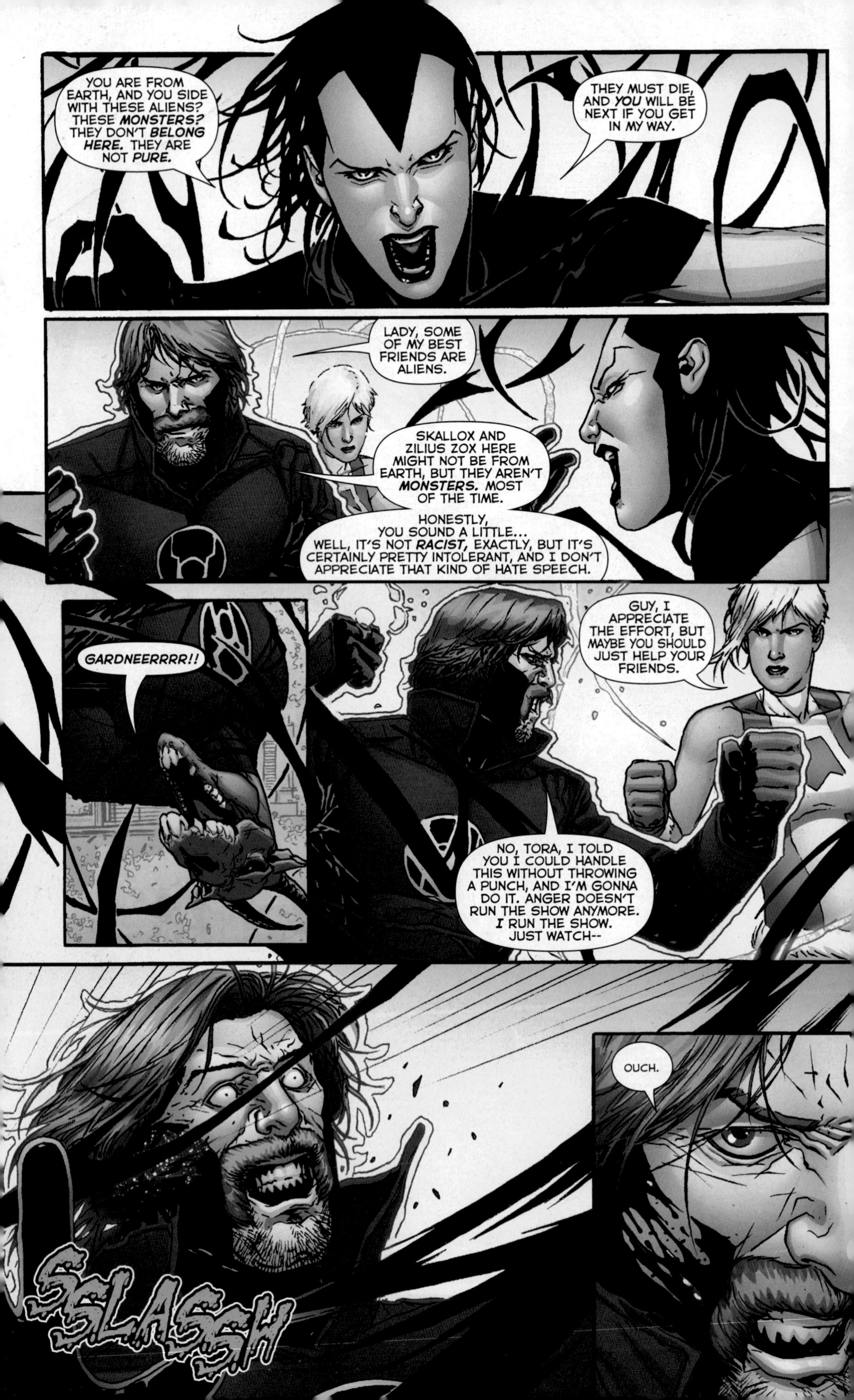
YOU ARE FROM EARTH, AND YOU SIDE WITH THESE ALIENS? THESE MONSTERS? THEY DON'T BELONG HERE. THEY ARE NOT PURE.
THEY MUST DIE, AND YOU WILL BE NEXT IF YOU GET IN MY WAY.
LADY, SOME OF MY BEST FRIENDS ARE ALIENS.
SKALLOX AND ZILIUS ZOX HERE MIGHT NOT BE FROM EARTH, BUT THEY AREN'T MONSTERS. MOST OF THE TIME.
HONESTLY, YOU SOUND A LITTLE... WELL, IT'S NOT RACIST, EXACTLY, BUT IT'S CERTAINLY PRETTY INTOLERANT, AND I DON'T APPRECIATE THAT KIND OF HATE SPEECH.
GARDNEERRRR!!
GUY, I APPRECIATE THE EFFORT, BUT MAYBE YOU SHOULD JUST HELP YOUR FRIENDS.
NO, TORA, I TOLD YOU I COULD HANDLE THIS WITHOUT THROWING A PUNCH, AND I'M GONNA DO IT. ANGER DOESN'T RUN THE SHOW ANYMORE. I RUN THE SHOW. JUST WATCH--
OUCH.
SSLASSH

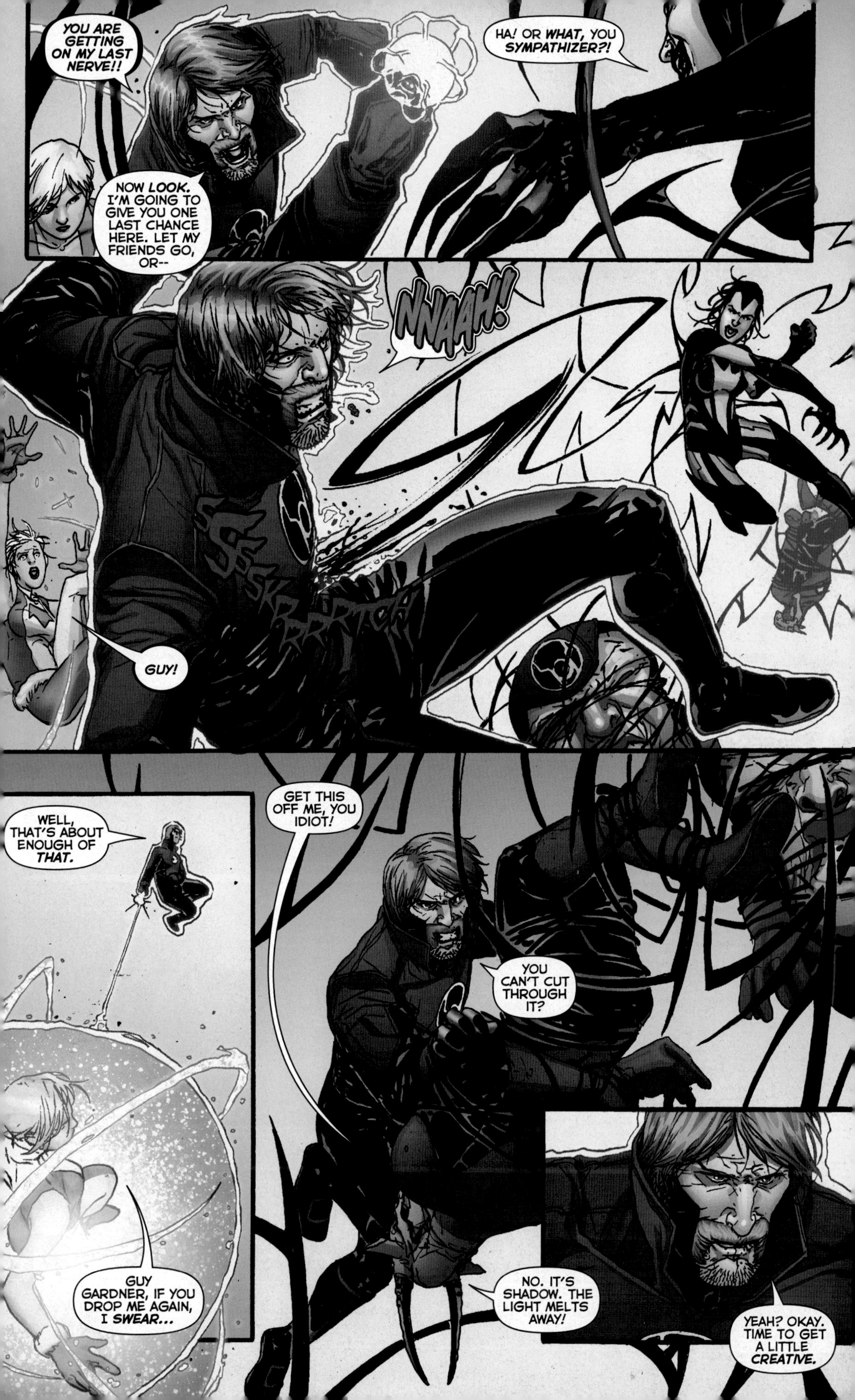
YOU ARE GETTING ON MY LAST NERVE!!
HA! OR WHAT, YOU SYMPATHIZER?!
NOW LOOK. I'M GOING TO GIVE YOU ONE LAST CHANCE HERE. LET MY FRIENDS GO, OR--
NNAAH!
GUY!
WELL, THAT'S ABOUT ENOUGH OF THAT.
GUY GARDNER, IF YOU DROP ME AGAIN, I SWEAR...
GET THIS OFF ME, YOU IDIOT!
YOU CAN'T CUT THROUGH IT?
NO. IT'S SHADOW. THE LIGHT MELTS AWAY!
YEAH? OKAY. TIME TO GET A LITTLE CREATIVE.

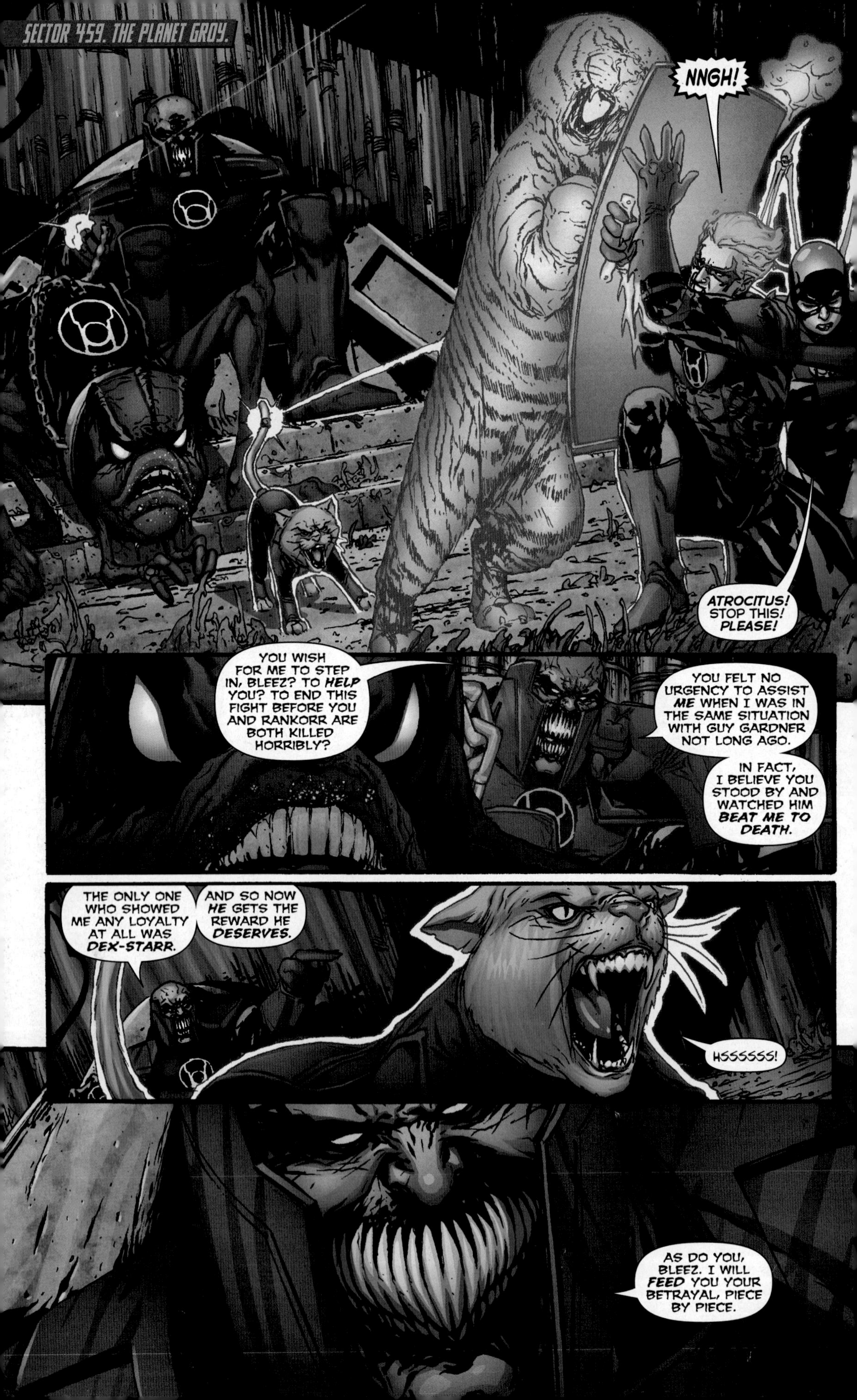
SECTOR 459. THE PLANET GROY.
NNGH!
ATROCITUS! STOP THIS! PLEASE!
YOU WISH FOR ME TO STEP IN, BLEEZ? TO HELP YOU? TO END THIS FIGHT BEFORE YOU AND RANKORR ARE BOTH KILLED HORRIBLY?
YOU FELT NO URGENCY TO ASSIST ME WHEN I WAS IN THE SAME SITUATION WITH GUY GARDNER NOT LONG AGO.
IN FACT, I BELIEVE YOU STOOD BY AND WATCHED HIM BEAT ME TO DEATH.
THE ONLY ONE WHO SHOWED ME ANY LOYALTY AT ALL WAS DEX-STARR.
AND SO NOW HE GETS THE REWARD HE DESERVES.
HSSSSSS!
AS DO YOU, BLEEZ. I WILL FEED YOU YOUR BETRAYAL, PIECE BY PIECE.

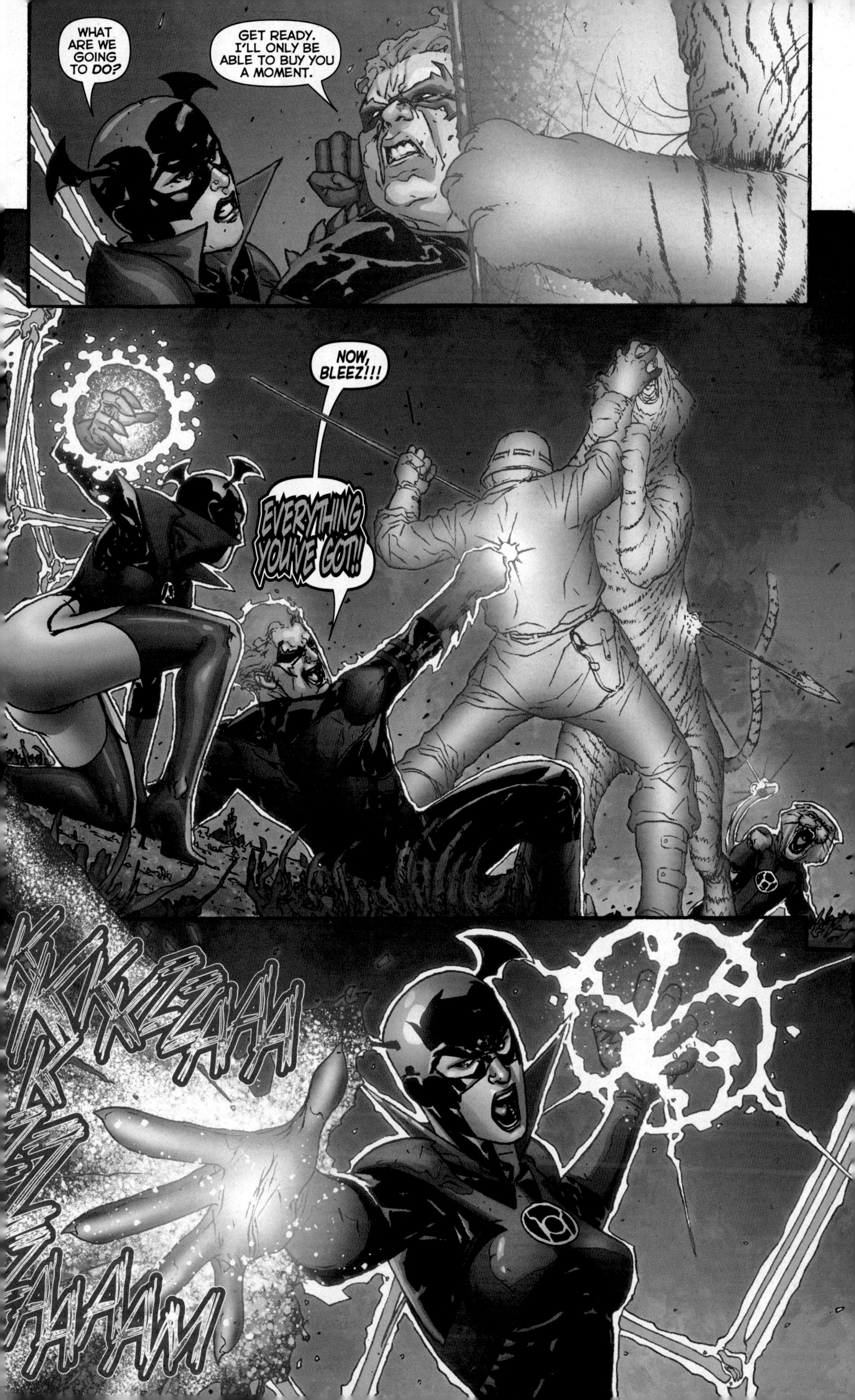

WHAT ARE WE GOING TO DO?
GET READY. I'LL ONLY BE ABLE TO BUY YOU A MOMENT.
NOW, BLEEZ!!!
EVERYTHING YOU'VE GOT!!

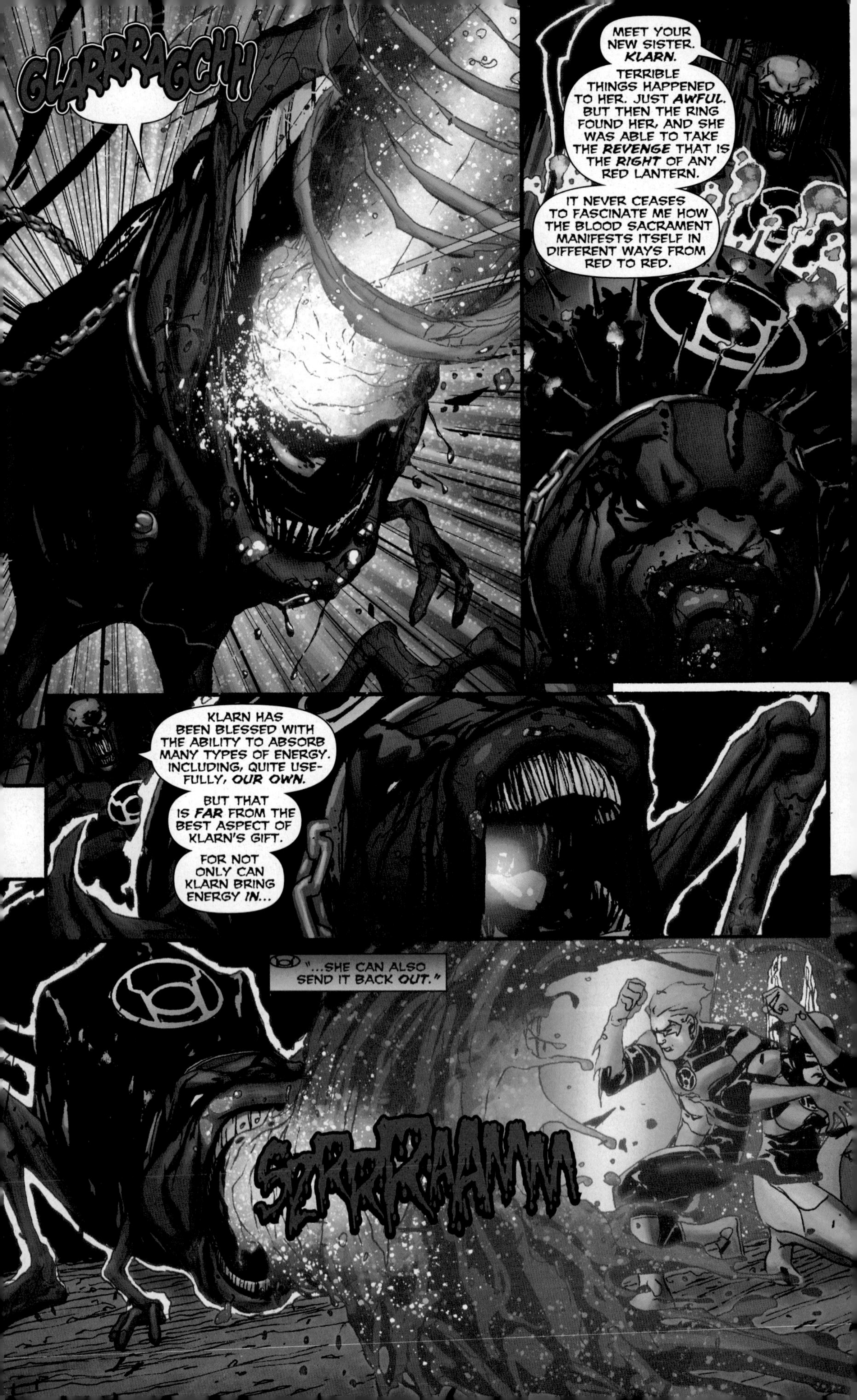
GLARRRAGCHH
MEET YOUR NEW SISTER. KLARN.
TERRIBLE THINGS HAPPENED TO HER. JUST AWFUL. BUT THEN THE RING FOUND HER, AND SHE WAS ABLE TO TAKE THE REVENGE THAT IS THE RIGHT OF ANY RED LANTERN.
IT NEVER CEASES TO FASCINATE ME HOW THE BLOOD SACRAMENT MANIFESTS ITSELF IN DIFFERENT WAYS FROM RED TO RED.
KLARN HAS BEEN BLESSED WITH THE ABILITY TO ABSORB MANY TYPES OF ENERGY. INCLUDING, QUITE USE-FULLY, OUR OWN.
BUT THAT IS FAR FROM THE BEST ASPECT OF KLARN'S GIFT.
FOR NOT ONLY CAN KLARN BRING ENERGY IN...
"...SHE CAN ALSO SEND IT BACK OUT."

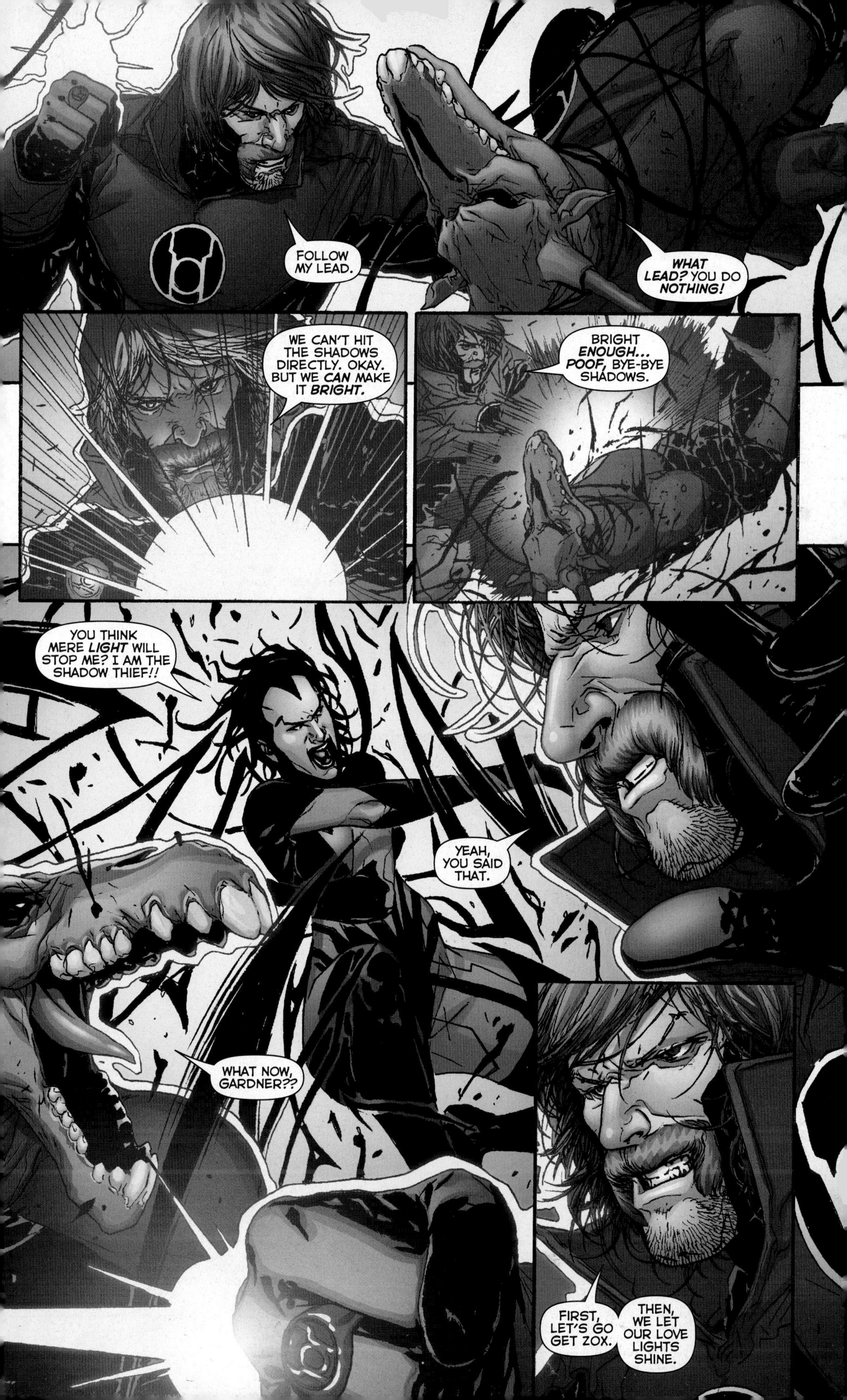
FOLLOW MY LEAD.
WHAT LEAD? YOU DO NOTHING!
WE CAN'T HIT THE SHADOWS DIRECTLY. OKAY. BUT WE CAN MAKE IT BRIGHT.
BRIGHT ENOUGH... POOF, BYE-BYE SHADOWS.
YOU THINK MERE LIGHT WILL STOP ME? I AM THE SHADOW THIEF!!
YEAH, YOU SAID THAT.
WHAT NOW, GARDNER??
FIRST, LET'S GO GET ZOX.
THEN, WE LET OUR LOVE LIGHTS SHINE.

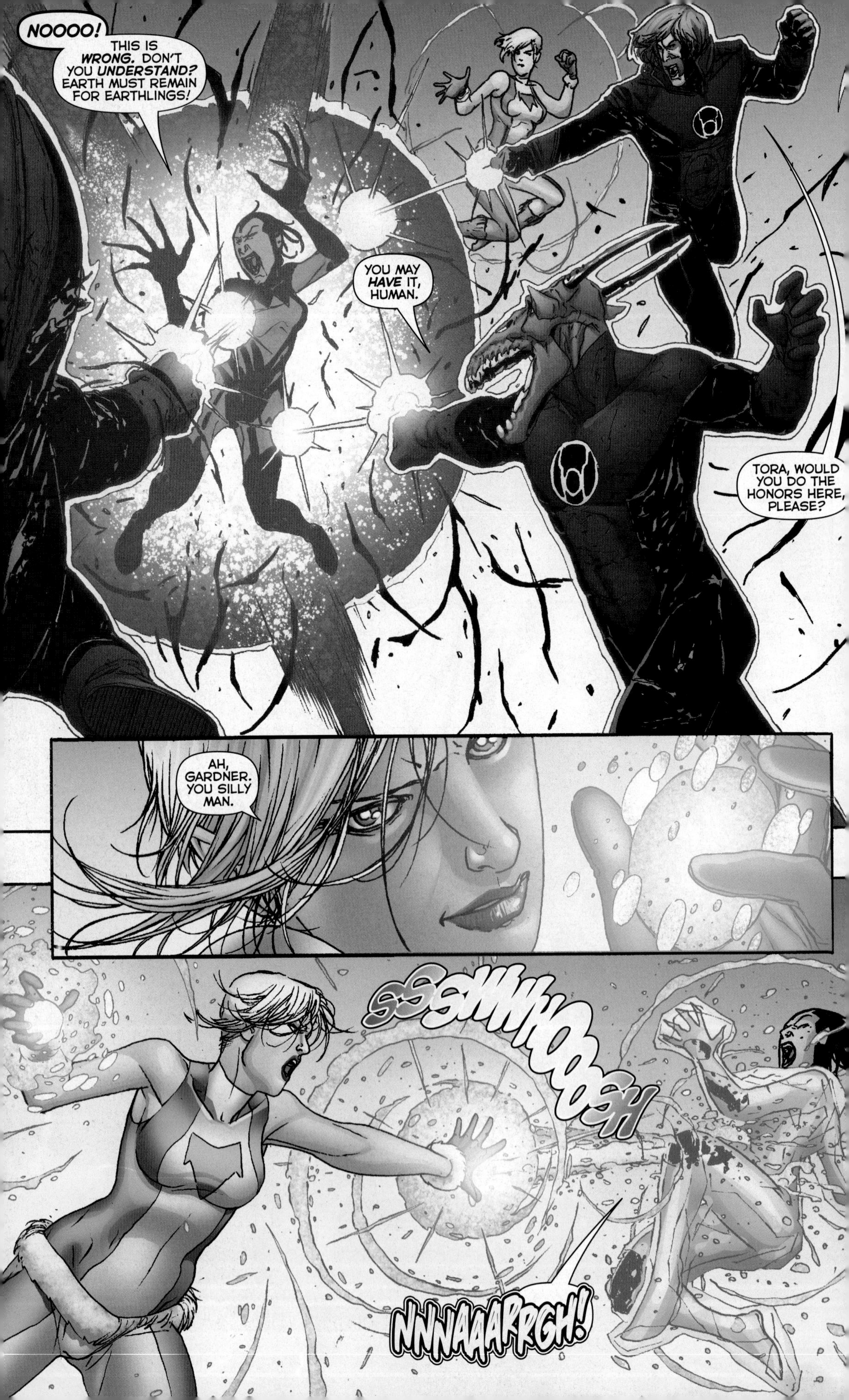
NOOOO!
THIS IS WRONG. DON'T YOU UNDERSTAND? EARTH MUST REMAIN FOR EARTHLINGS!
YOU MAY HAVE IT, HUMAN.
TORA, WOULD YOU DO THE HONORS HERE, PLEASE?
AH, GARDNER. YOU SILLY MAN.
SSSHWHOOOSH
NNNAAARRGH!

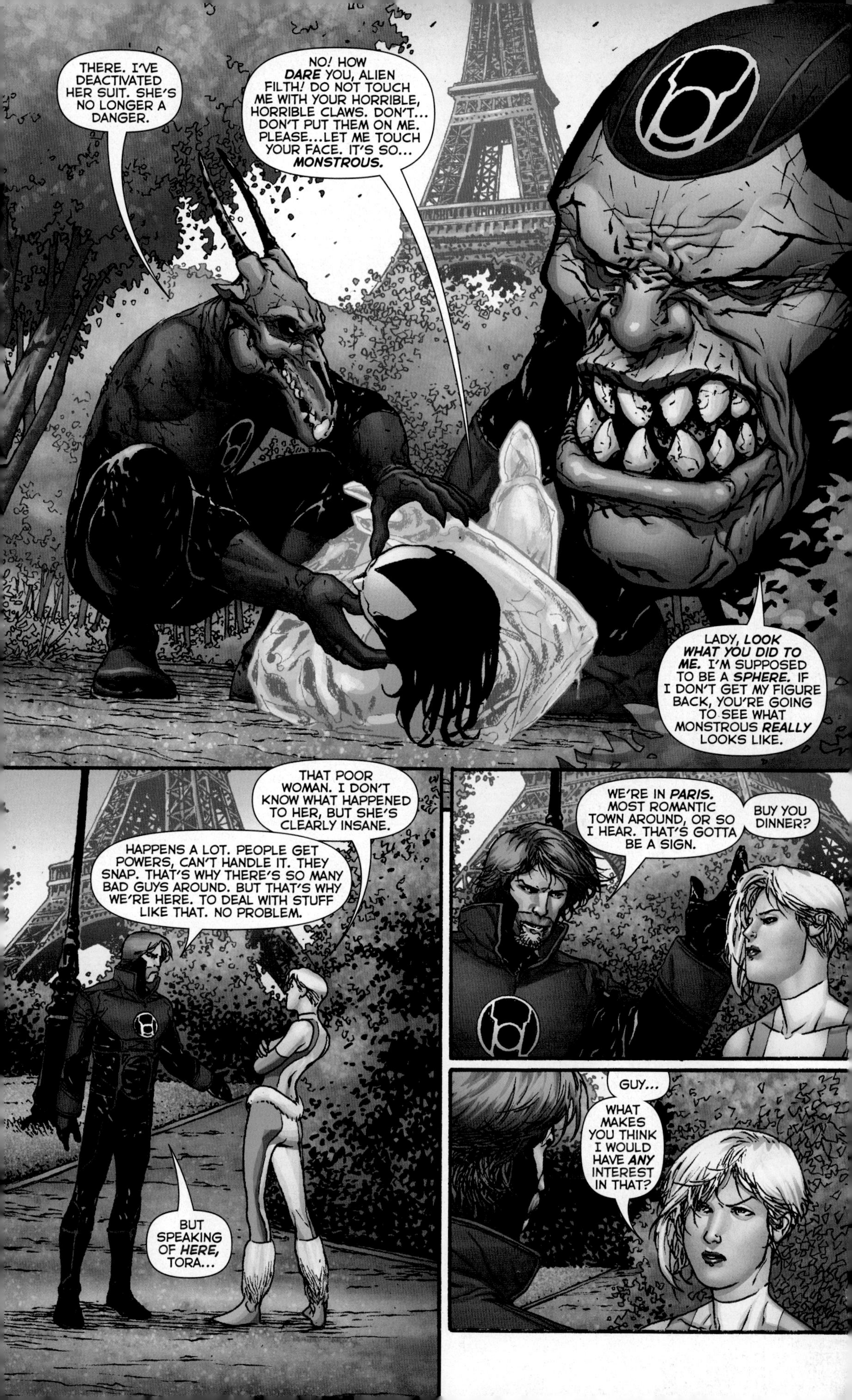
THERE. I'VE DEACTIVATED HER SUIT. SHE'S NO LONGER A DANGER.
NO! HOW DARE YOU, ALIEN FILTH! DO NOT TOUCH ME WITH YOUR HORRIBLE, HORRIBLE CLAWS. DON'T... DON'T PUT THEM ON ME. PLEASE...LET ME TOUCH YOUR FACE. IT'S SO... MONSTROUS.
LADY, LOOK WHAT YOU DID TO ME. I'M SUPPOSED TO BE A SPHERE. IF I DON'T GET MY FIGURE BACK, YOU'RE GOING TO SEE WHAT MONSTROUS REALLY LOOKS LIKE.
THAT POOR WOMAN. I DON'T KNOW WHAT HAPPENED TO HER, BUT SHE'S CLEARLY INSANE.
HAPPENS A LOT. PEOPLE GET POWERS, CAN'T HANDLE IT. THEY SNAP. THAT'S WHY THERE'S SO MANY BAD GUYS AROUND. BUT THAT'S WHY WE'RE HERE. TO DEAL WITH STUFF LIKE THAT. NO PROBLEM.
BUT SPEAKING OF HERE, TORA...
WE'RE IN PARIS. MOST ROMANTIC TOWN AROUND, OR SO I HEAR. THAT'S GOTTA BE A SIGN.
BUY YOU DINNER?
GUY...
WHAT MAKES YOU THINK I WOULD HAVE ANY INTEREST IN THAT?

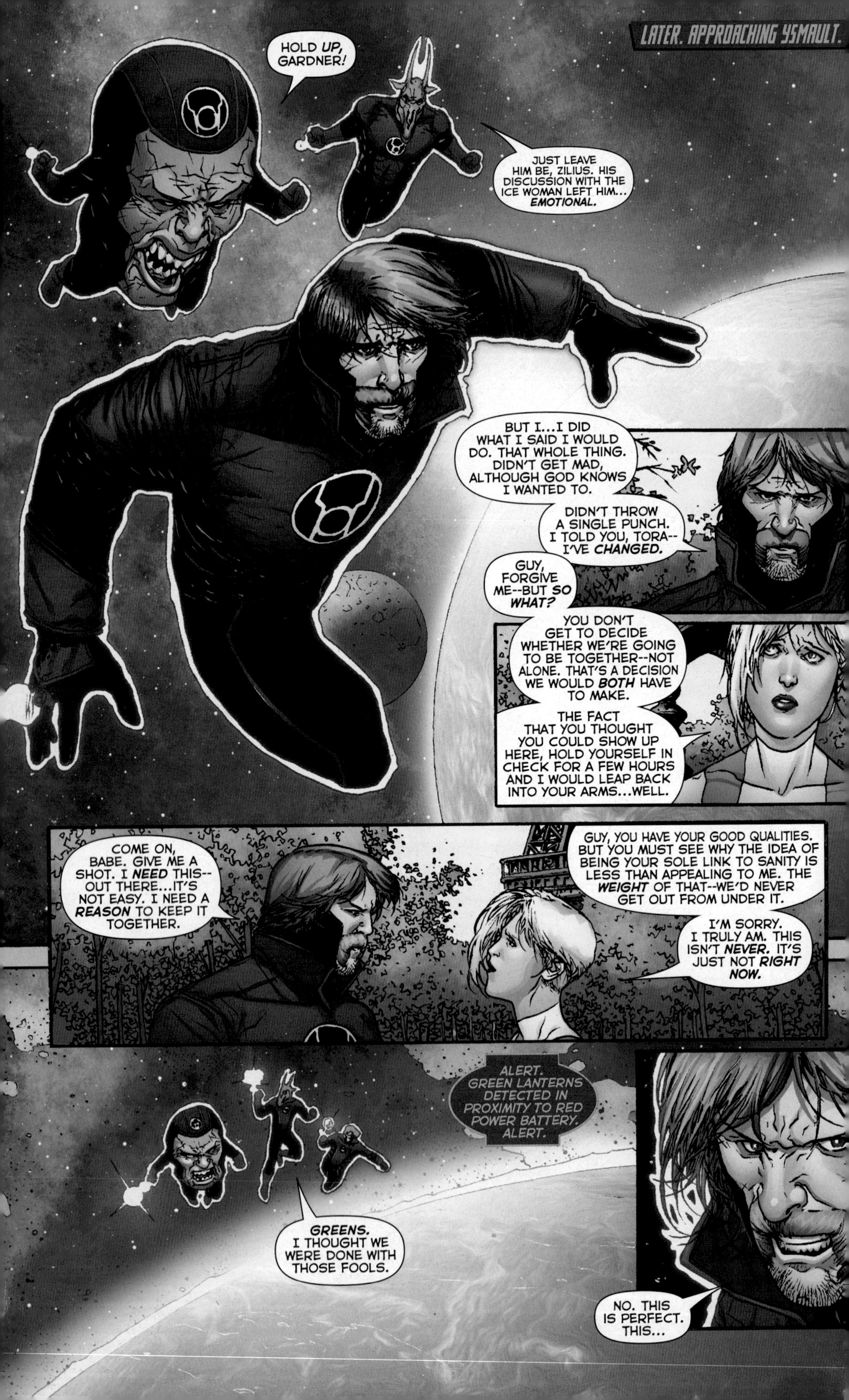
LATER. APPROACHING YSMAULT.
HOLD UP, GARDNER!
JUST LEAVE HIM BE, ZILIUS. HIS DISCUSSION WITH THE ICE WOMAN LEFT HIM... EMOTIONAL.
BUT I...I DID WHAT I SAID I WOULD DO. THAT WHOLE THING. DIDN'T GET MAD, ALTHOUGH GOD KNOWS I WANTED TO.
DIDN'T THROW A SINGLE PUNCH. I TOLD YOU, TORA-- I'VE CHANGED.
GUY, FORGIVE ME--BUT SO WHAT?
YOU DON'T GET TO DECIDE WHETHER WE'RE GOING TO BE TOGETHER--NOT ALONE. THAT'S A DECISION WE WOULD BOTH HAVE TO MAKE.
THE FACT THAT YOU THOUGHT YOU COULD SHOW UP HERE, HOLD YOURSELF IN CHECK FOR A FEW HOURS AND I WOULD LEAP BACK INTO YOUR ARMS...WELL.
COME ON, BABE. GIVE ME A SHOT. I NEED THIS-- OUT THERE...IT'S NOT EASY. I NEED A REASON TO KEEP IT TOGETHER.
GUY, YOU HAVE YOUR GOOD QUALITIES. BUT YOU MUST SEE WHY THE IDEA OF BEING YOUR SOLE LINK TO SANITY IS LESS THAN APPEALING TO ME. THE WEIGHT OF THAT--WE'D NEVER GET OUT FROM UNDER IT.
I'M SORRY. I TRULY AM. THIS ISN'T NEVER. IT'S JUST NOT RIGHT NOW.
ALERT. GREEN LANTERNS DETECTED IN PROXIMITY TO RED POWER BATTERY. ALERT.
GREENS. I THOUGHT WE WERE DONE WITH THOSE FOOLS.
NO. THIS IS PERFECT. THIS...

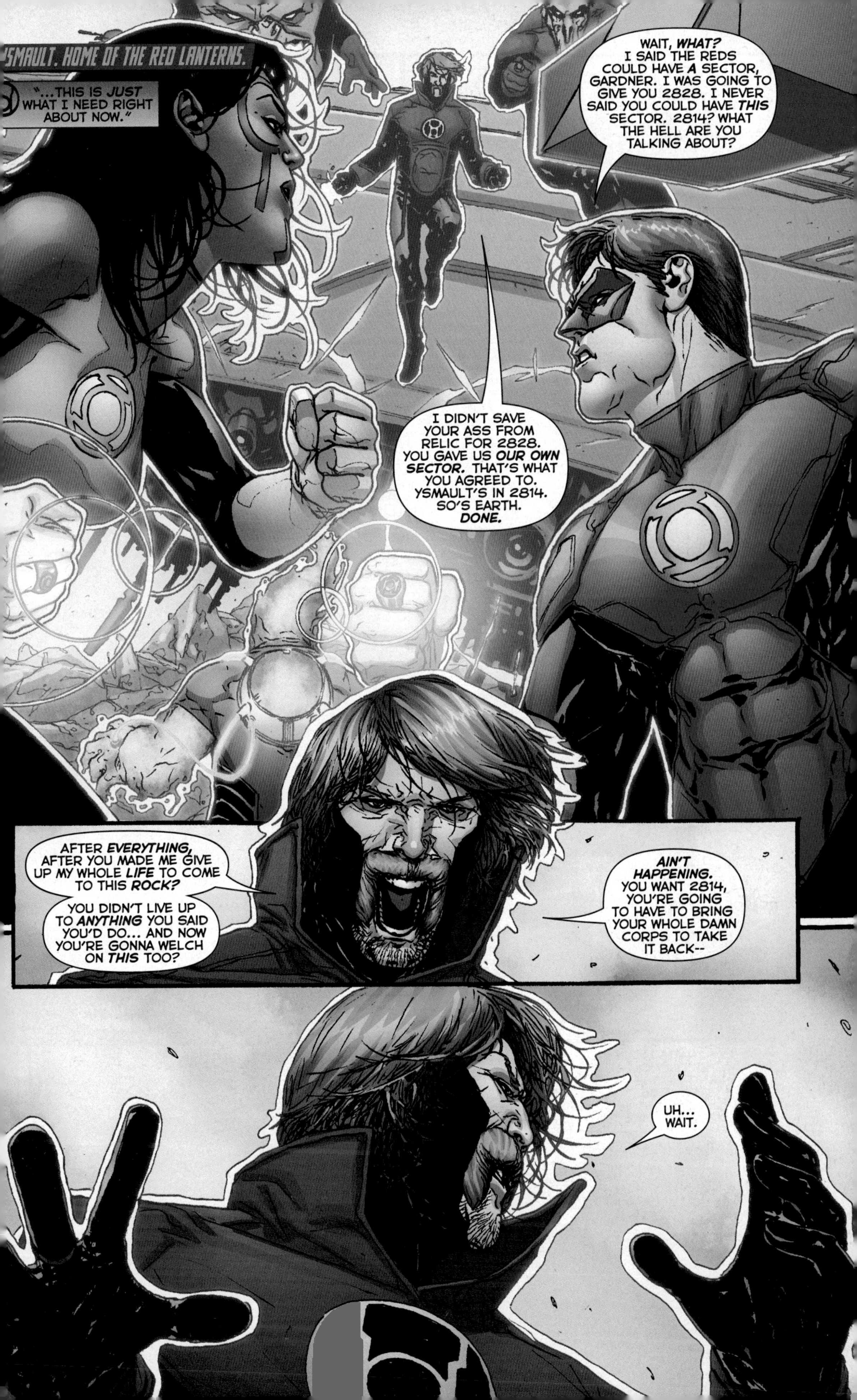
YSMAULT. HOME OF THE RED LANTERNS.
"...THIS IS JUST WHAT I NEED RIGHT ABOUT NOW."
WAIT, WHAT? I SAID THE REDS COULD HAVE A SECTOR, GARDNER. I WAS GOING TO GIVE YOU 2828. I NEVER SAID YOU COULD HAVE THIS SECTOR. 2814? WHAT THE HELL ARE YOU TALKING ABOUT?
I DIDN'T SAVE YOUR ASS FROM RELIC FOR 2828. YOU GAVE US OUR OWN SECTOR. THAT'S WHAT YOU AGREED TO. YSMAULT'S IN 2814. SO'S EARTH. DONE.
AFTER EVERYTHING, AFTER YOU MADE ME GIVE UP MY WHOLE LIFE TO COME TO THIS ROCK?
YOU DIDN'T LIVE UP TO ANYTHING YOU SAID YOU'D DO... AND NOW YOU'RE GONNA WELCH ON THIS TOO?
AIN'T HAPPENING. YOU WANT 2814, YOU'RE GOING TO HAVE TO BRING YOUR WHOLE DAMN CORPS TO TAKE IT BACK--
UH... WAIT.

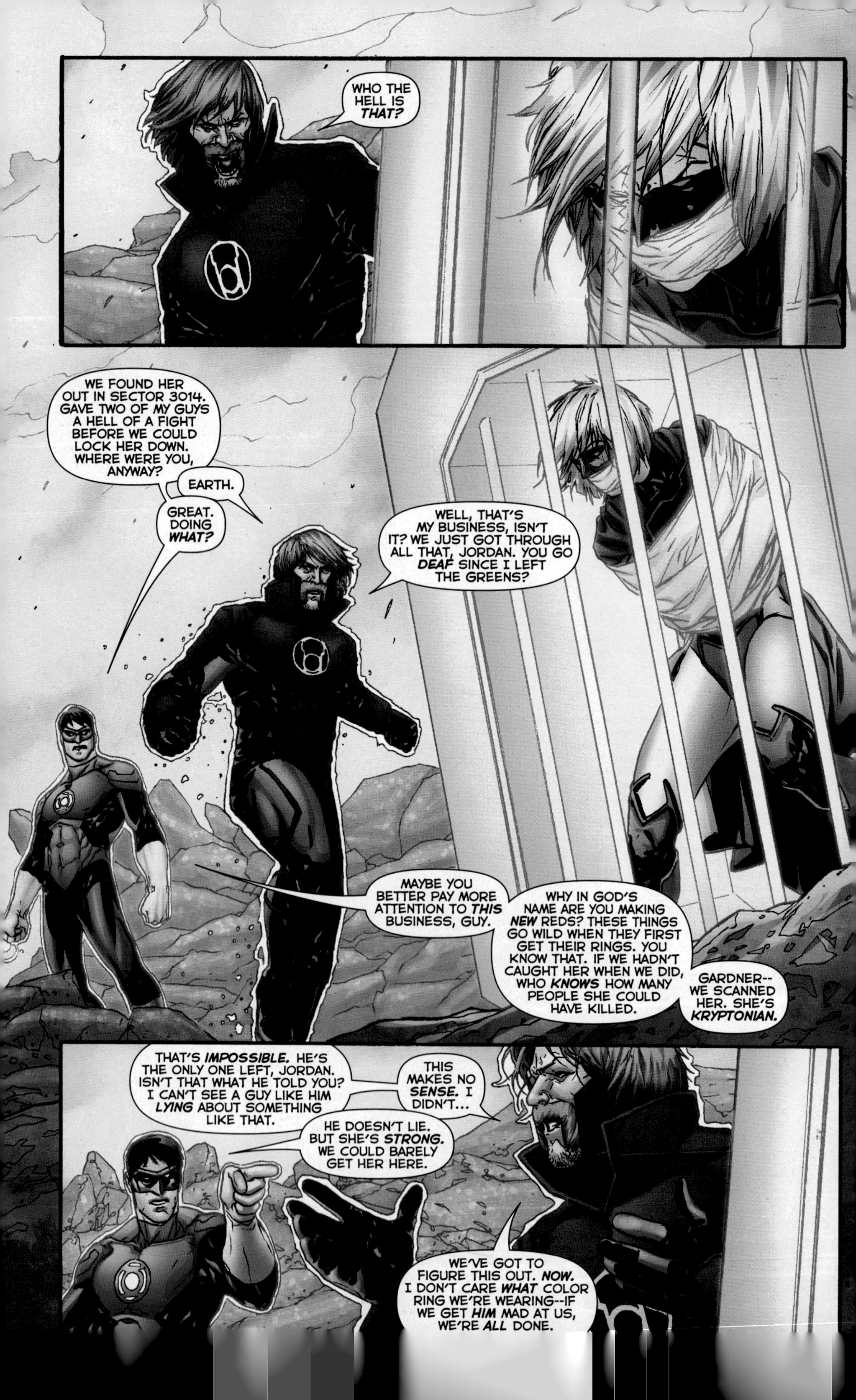
WHO THE HELL IS *THAT?*
WE FOUND HER OUT IN SECTOR 3014. GAVE TWO OF MY GUYS A HELL OF A FIGHT BEFORE WE COULD LOCK HER DOWN. WHERE WERE YOU, ANYWAY?
EARTH.
GREAT. DOING *WHAT?*
WELL, THAT'S MY BUSINESS, ISN'T IT? WE JUST GOT THROUGH ALL THAT, JORDAN. YOU GO *DEAF* SINCE I LEFT THE GREENS?
MAYBE YOU BETTER PAY MORE ATTENTION TO *THIS* BUSINESS, GUY.
WHY IN GOD'S NAME ARE YOU MAKING *NEW* REDS? THESE THINGS GO WILD WHEN THEY FIRST GET THEIR RINGS. YOU KNOW THAT. IF WE HADN'T CAUGHT HER WHEN WE DID, WHO *KNOWS* HOW MANY PEOPLE SHE COULD HAVE KILLED.
GARDNER-- WE SCANNED HER. SHE'S *KRYPTONIAN.*
THAT'S *IMPOSSIBLE.* HE'S THE ONLY ONE LEFT, JORDAN. ISN'T THAT WHAT HE TOLD YOU? I CAN'T SEE A GUY LIKE HIM *LYING* ABOUT SOMETHING LIKE THAT.
THIS MAKES NO *SENSE.* I DIDN'T...
HE DOESN'T LIE. BUT SHE'S *STRONG.* WE COULD BARELY GET HER HERE.
WE'VE GOT TO FIGURE THIS OUT. *NOW.* I DON'T CARE *WHAT* COLOR RING WE'RE WEARING--IF WE GET *HIM* MAD AT US, WE'RE *ALL* DONE.

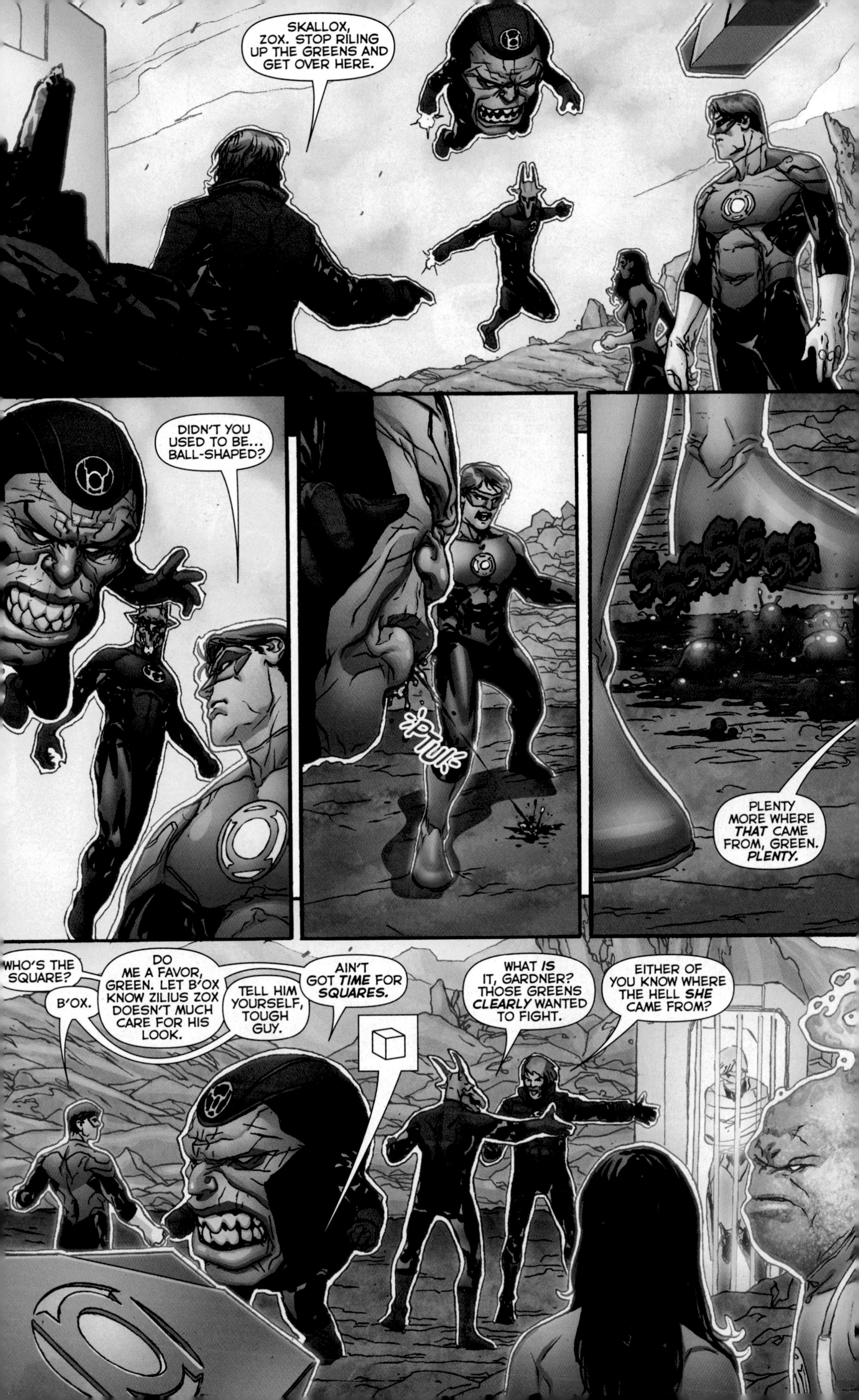
SKALLOX, ZOX. STOP RILING UP THE GREENS AND GET OVER HERE.
DIDN'T YOU USED TO BE... BALL-SHAPED?
PTUI
SSSSSSS
PLENTY MORE WHERE THAT CAME FROM, GREEN. PLENTY.
WHO'S THE SQUARE?
B'OX.
DO ME A FAVOR, GREEN. LET B'OX KNOW ZILIUS ZOX DOESN'T MUCH CARE FOR HIS LOOK.
TELL HIM YOURSELF, TOUGH GUY.
AIN'T GOT TIME FOR SQUARES.
WHAT IS IT, GARDNER? THOSE GREENS CLEARLY WANTED TO FIGHT.
EITHER OF YOU KNOW WHERE THE HELL SHE CAME FROM?

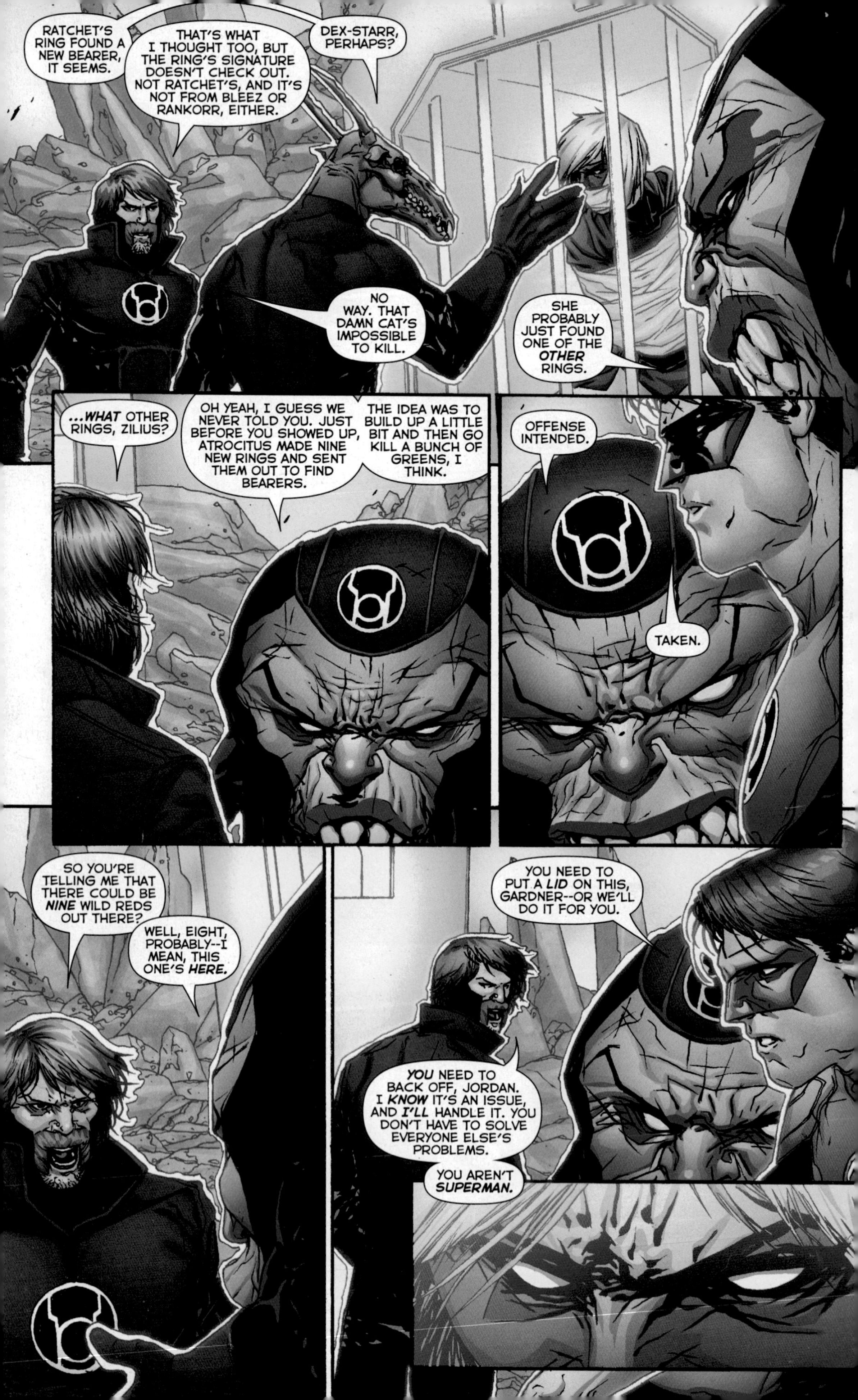
RATCHET'S RING FOUND A NEW BEARER, IT SEEMS.
THAT'S WHAT I THOUGHT TOO, BUT THE RING'S SIGNATURE DOESN'T CHECK OUT. NOT RATCHET'S, AND IT'S NOT FROM BLEEZ OR RANKORR, EITHER.
DEX-STARR, PERHAPS?
NO WAY. THAT DAMN CAT'S IMPOSSIBLE TO KILL.
SHE PROBABLY JUST FOUND ONE OF THE *OTHER* RINGS.
...*WHAT* OTHER RINGS, ZILIUS?
OH YEAH, I GUESS WE NEVER TOLD YOU. JUST BEFORE YOU SHOWED UP, ATROCITUS MADE NINE NEW RINGS AND SENT THEM OUT TO FIND BEARERS.
THE IDEA WAS TO BUILD UP A LITTLE BIT AND THEN GO KILL A BUNCH OF GREENS, I THINK.
OFFENSE INTENDED.
TAKEN.
SO YOU'RE TELLING ME THAT THERE COULD BE *NINE* WILD REDS OUT THERE?
WELL, EIGHT, PROBABLY--I MEAN, THIS ONE'S *HERE.*
YOU NEED TO PUT A *LID* ON THIS, GARDNER--OR WE'LL DO IT FOR YOU.
YOU NEED TO BACK OFF, JORDAN. I *KNOW* IT'S AN ISSUE, AND *I'LL* HANDLE IT. YOU DON'T HAVE TO SOLVE EVERYONE ELSE'S PROBLEMS.
YOU AREN'T *SUPERMAN.*

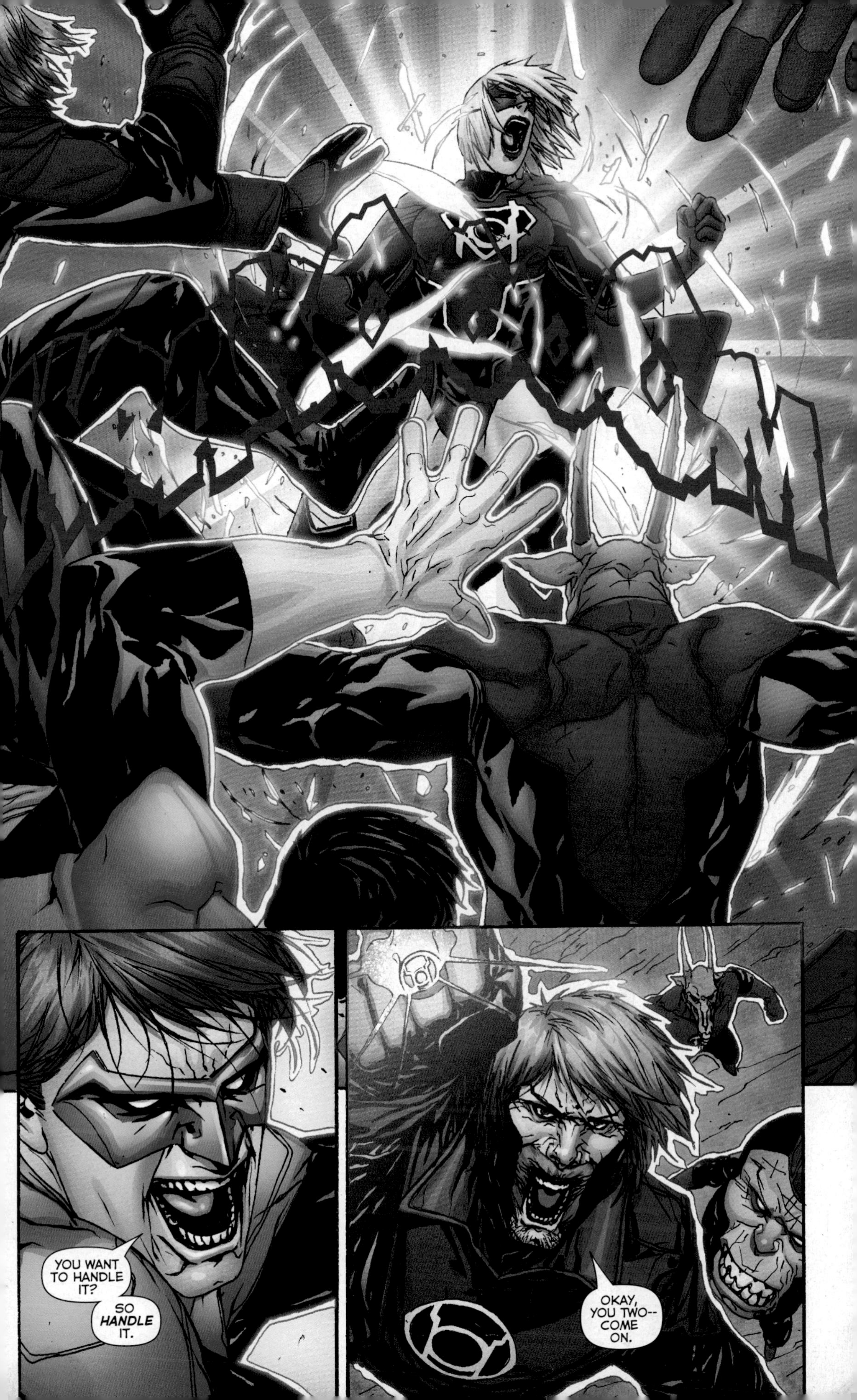
YOU WANT TO HANDLE IT?
SO HANDLE IT.
OKAY, YOU TWO-- COME ON.

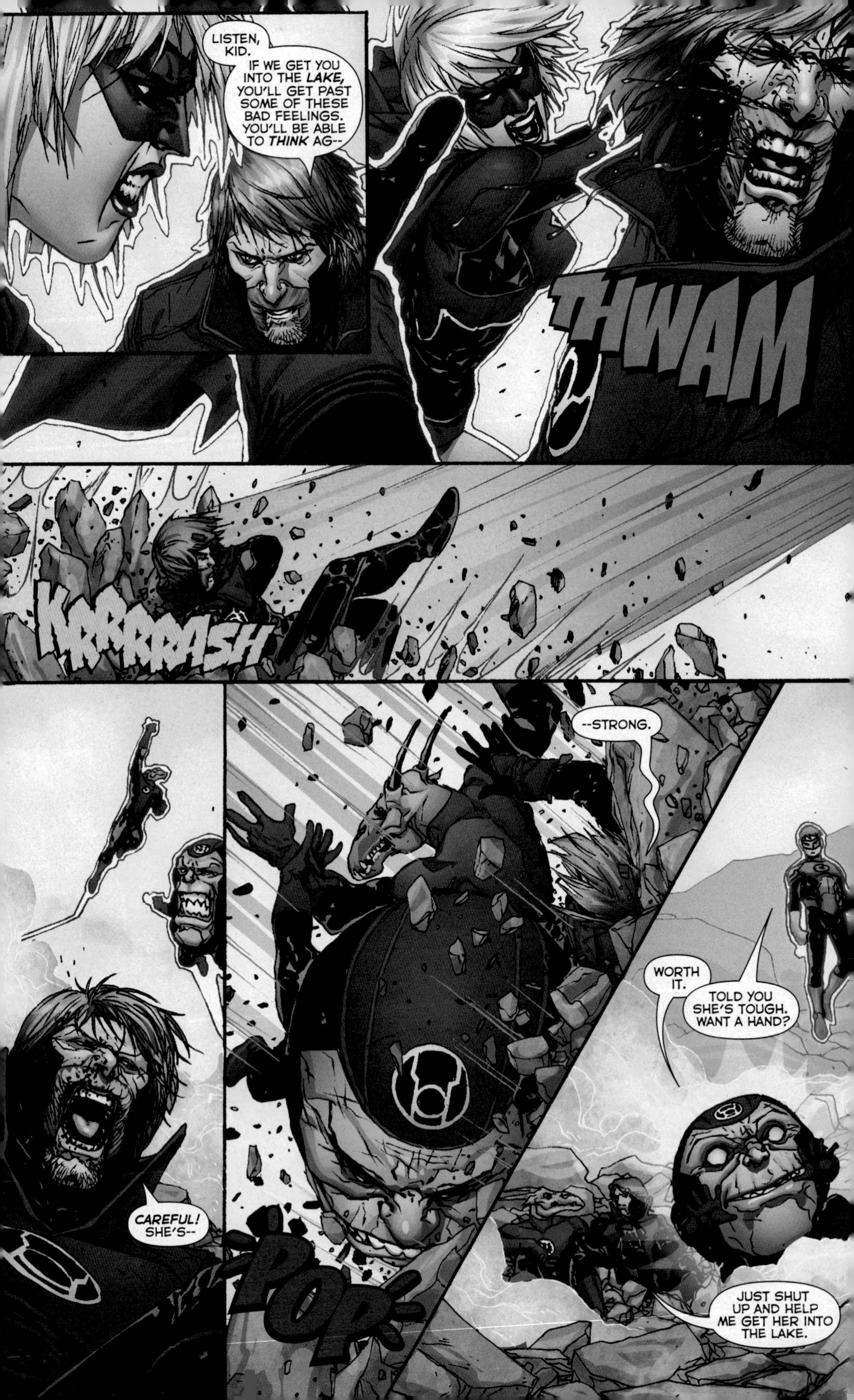
LISTEN, KID.
IF WE GET YOU INTO THE LAKE, YOU'LL GET PAST SOME OF THESE BAD FEELINGS. YOU'LL BE ABLE TO THINK AG--
THWAM
KRRRRASH
CAREFUL! SHE'S--
--STRONG.
POP
WORTH IT.
TOLD YOU SHE'S TOUGH. WANT A HAND?
JUST SHUT UP AND HELP ME GET HER INTO THE LAKE.

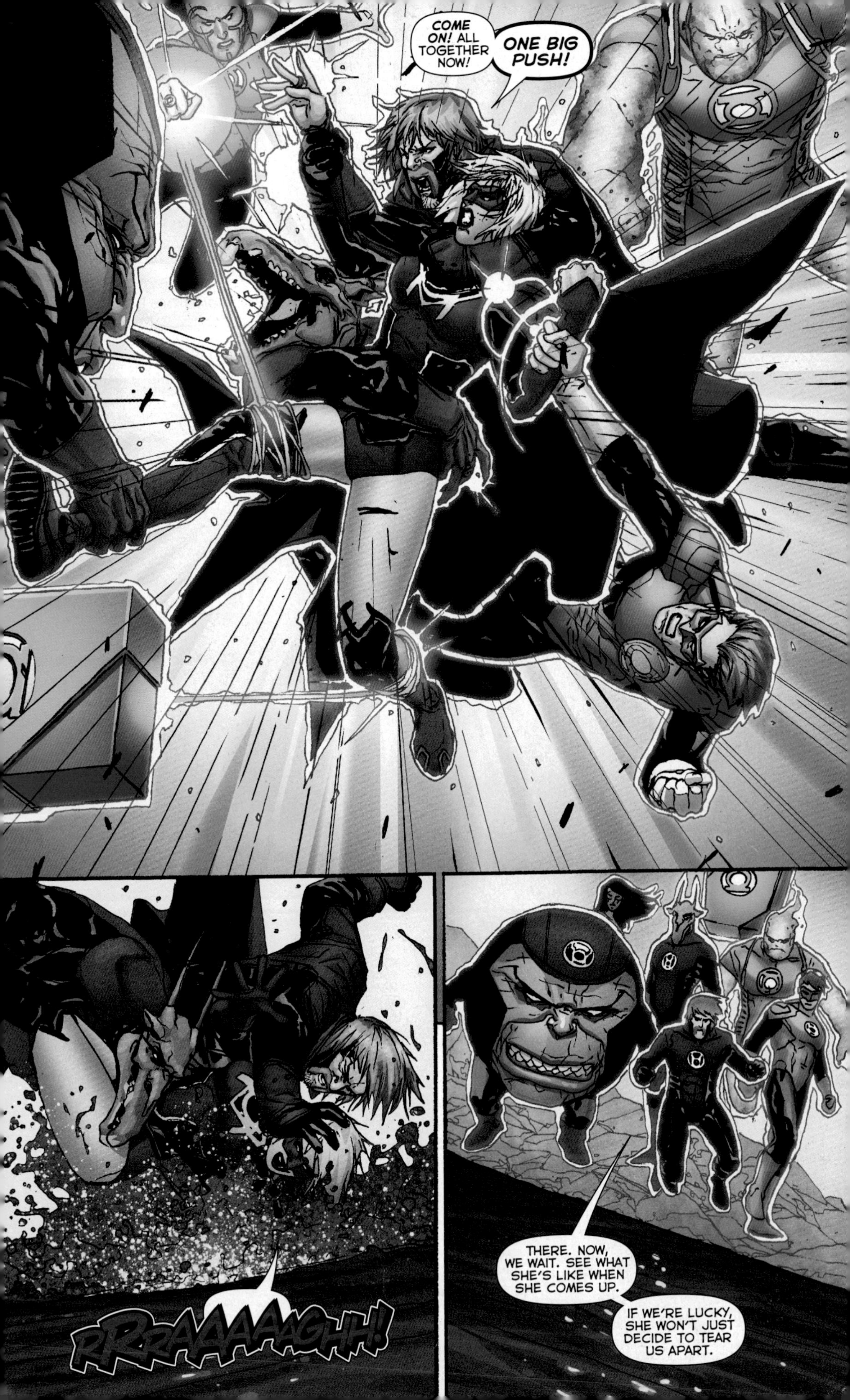
COME ON! ALL TOGETHER NOW!
ONE BIG PUSH!
RRRAAAAAGHH!
THERE. NOW, WE WAIT. SEE WHAT SHE'S LIKE WHEN SHE COMES UP.
IF WE'RE LUCKY, SHE WON'T JUST DECIDE TO TEAR US APART.

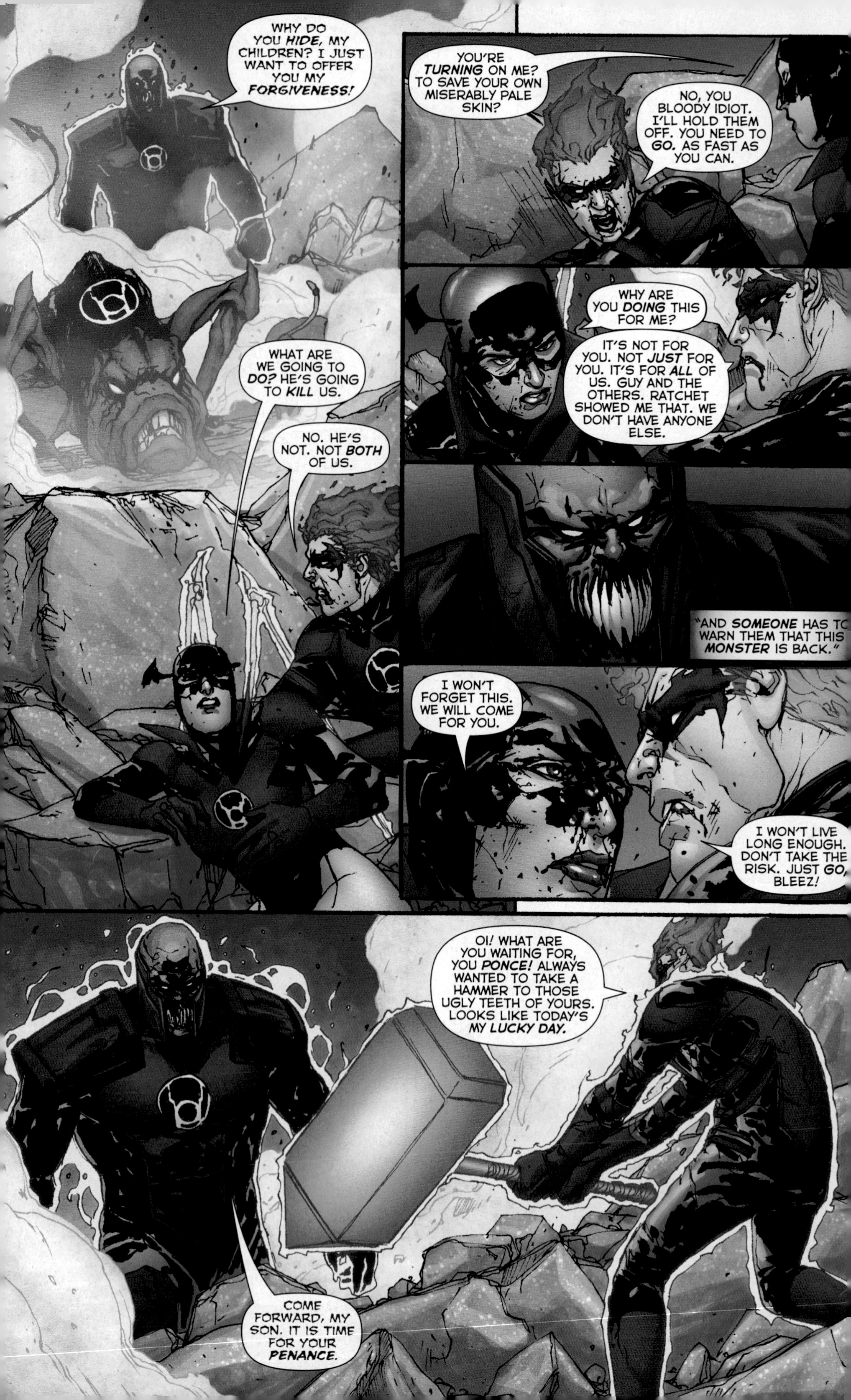
WHY DO YOU HIDE, MY CHILDREN? I JUST WANT TO OFFER YOU MY FORGIVENESS!
WHAT ARE WE GOING TO DO? HE'S GOING TO KILL US.
NO. HE'S NOT. NOT BOTH OF US.
YOU'RE TURNING ON ME? TO SAVE YOUR OWN MISERABLY PALE SKIN?
NO, YOU BLOODY IDIOT. I'LL HOLD THEM OFF. YOU NEED TO GO. AS FAST AS YOU CAN.
WHY ARE YOU DOING THIS FOR ME?
IT'S NOT FOR YOU. NOT JUST FOR YOU. IT'S FOR ALL OF US. GUY AND THE OTHERS. RATCHET SHOWED ME THAT. WE DON'T HAVE ANYONE ELSE.
"AND SOMEONE HAS TO WARN THEM THAT THIS MONSTER IS BACK."
I WON'T FORGET THIS. WE WILL COME FOR YOU.
I WON'T LIVE LONG ENOUGH. DON'T TAKE THE RISK. JUST GO, BLEEZ!
OI! WHAT ARE YOU WAITING FOR, YOU PONCE! ALWAYS WANTED TO TAKE A HAMMER TO THOSE UGLY TEETH OF YOURS. LOOKS LIKE TODAY'S MY LUCKY DAY.
COME FORWARD, MY SON. IT IS TIME FOR YOUR PENANCE.

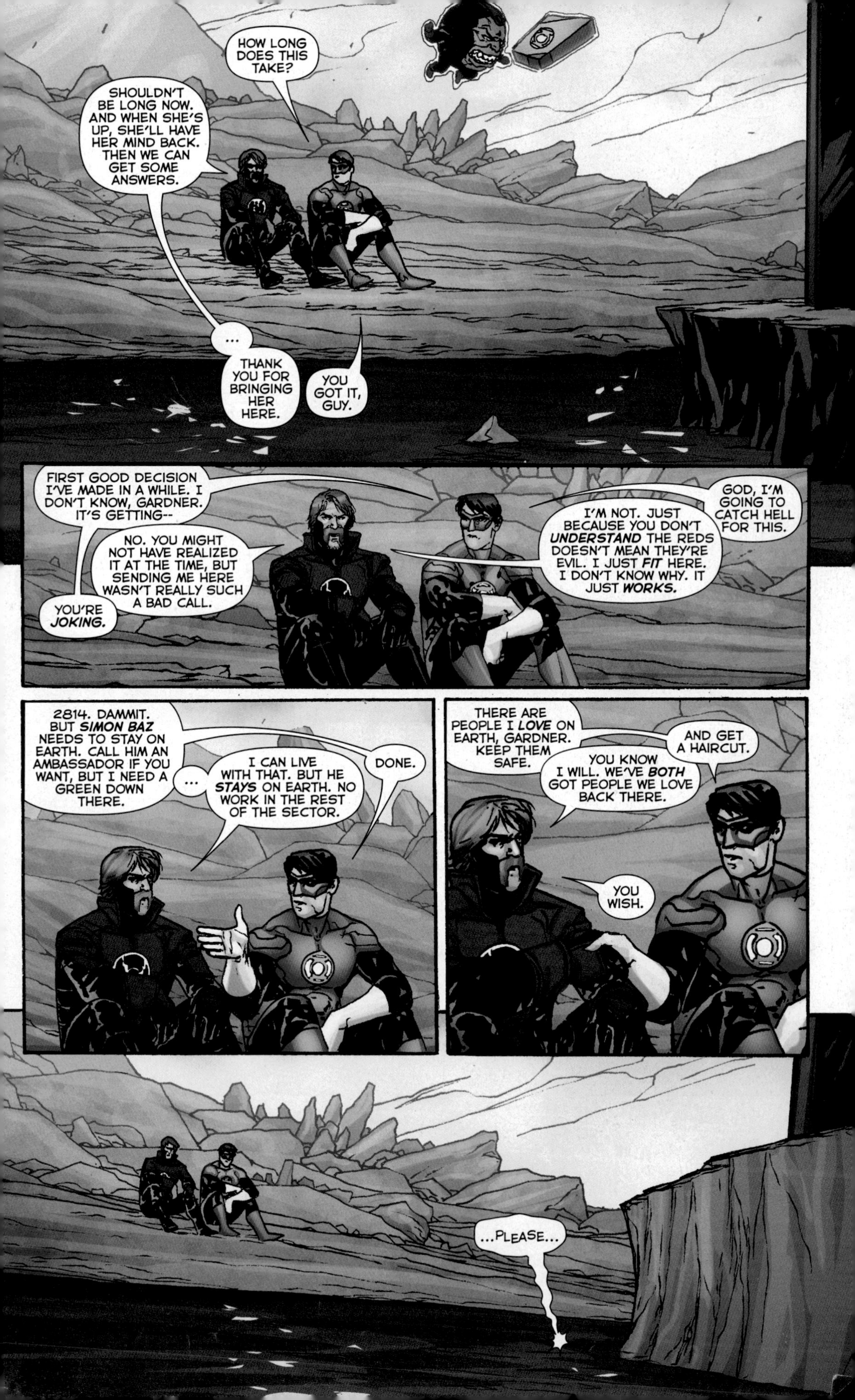
HOW LONG DOES THIS TAKE?
SHOULDN'T BE LONG NOW. AND WHEN SHE'S UP, SHE'LL HAVE HER MIND BACK. THEN WE CAN GET SOME ANSWERS.
...
THANK YOU FOR BRINGING HER HERE.
YOU GOT IT, GUY.
FIRST GOOD DECISION I'VE MADE IN A WHILE. I DON'T KNOW, GARDNER. IT'S GETTING--
NO. YOU MIGHT NOT HAVE REALIZED IT AT THE TIME, BUT SENDING ME HERE WASN'T REALLY SUCH A BAD CALL.
YOU'RE JOKING.
I'M NOT. JUST BECAUSE YOU DON'T UNDERSTAND THE REDS DOESN'T MEAN THEY'RE EVIL. I JUST FIT HERE. I DON'T KNOW WHY. IT JUST WORKS.
GOD, I'M GOING TO CATCH HELL FOR THIS.
2814. DAMMIT. BUT SIMON BAZ NEEDS TO STAY ON EARTH. CALL HIM AN AMBASSADOR IF YOU WANT, BUT I NEED A GREEN DOWN THERE.
...
I CAN LIVE WITH THAT. BUT HE STAYS ON EARTH. NO WORK IN THE REST OF THE SECTOR.
DONE.
THERE ARE PEOPLE I LOVE ON EARTH, GARDNER. KEEP THEM SAFE.
YOU KNOW I WILL. WE'VE BOTH GOT PEOPLE WE LOVE BACK THERE.
AND GET A HAIRCUT.
YOU WISH.
...PLEASE...

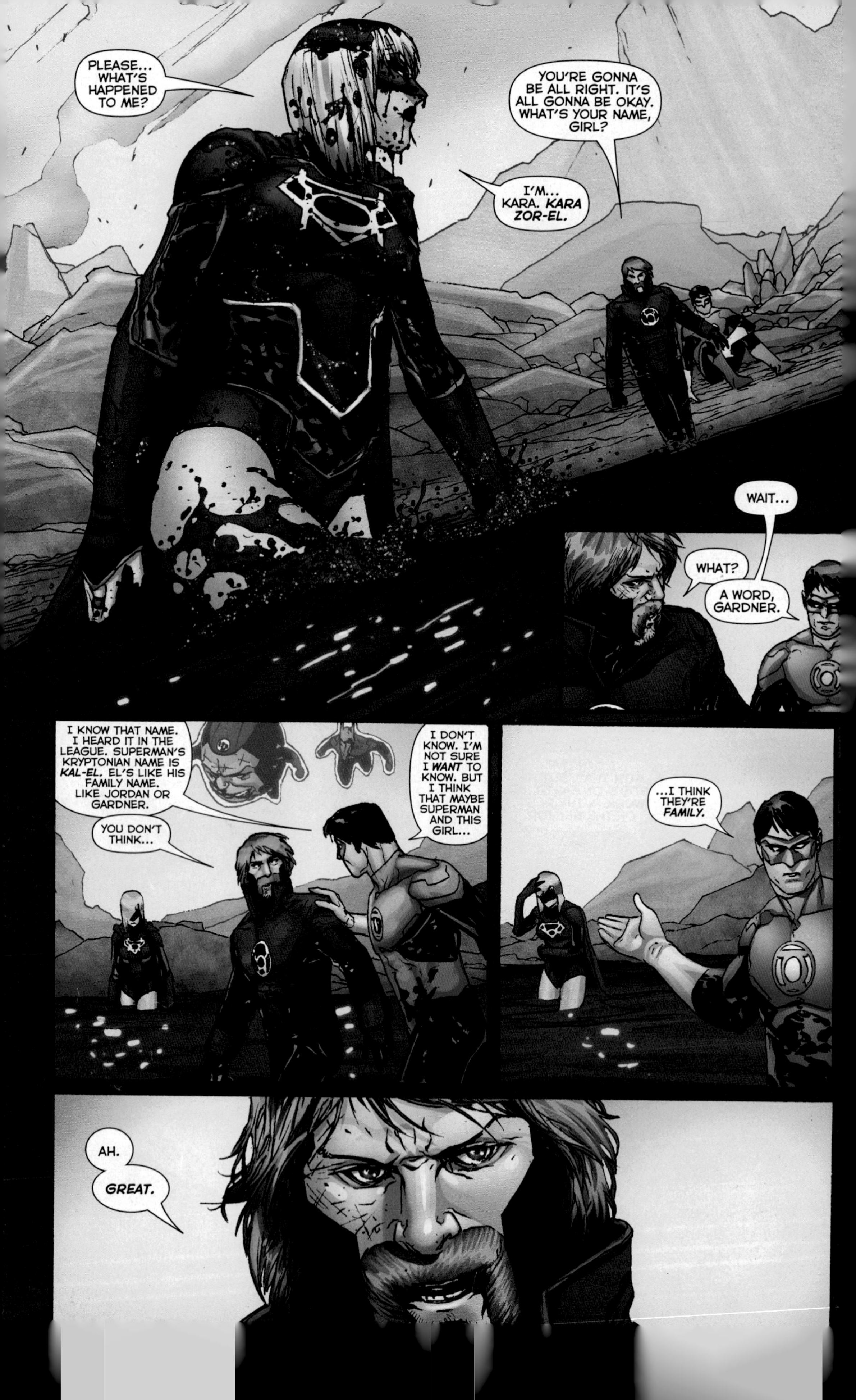
PLEASE... WHAT'S HAPPENED TO ME?
YOU'RE GONNA BE ALL RIGHT. IT'S ALL GONNA BE OKAY. WHAT'S YOUR NAME, GIRL?
I'M... KARA. KARA ZOR-EL.
WAIT...
WHAT?
A WORD, GARDNER.
I KNOW THAT NAME. I HEARD IT IN THE LEAGUE. SUPERMAN'S KRYPTONIAN NAME IS KAL-EL. EL'S LIKE HIS FAMILY NAME. LIKE JORDAN OR GARDNER.
YOU DON'T THINK...
I DON'T KNOW. I'M NOT SURE I WANT TO KNOW. BUT I THINK THAT MAYBE SUPERMAN AND THIS GIRL...
...I THINK THEY'RE FAMILY.
AH.
GREAT.

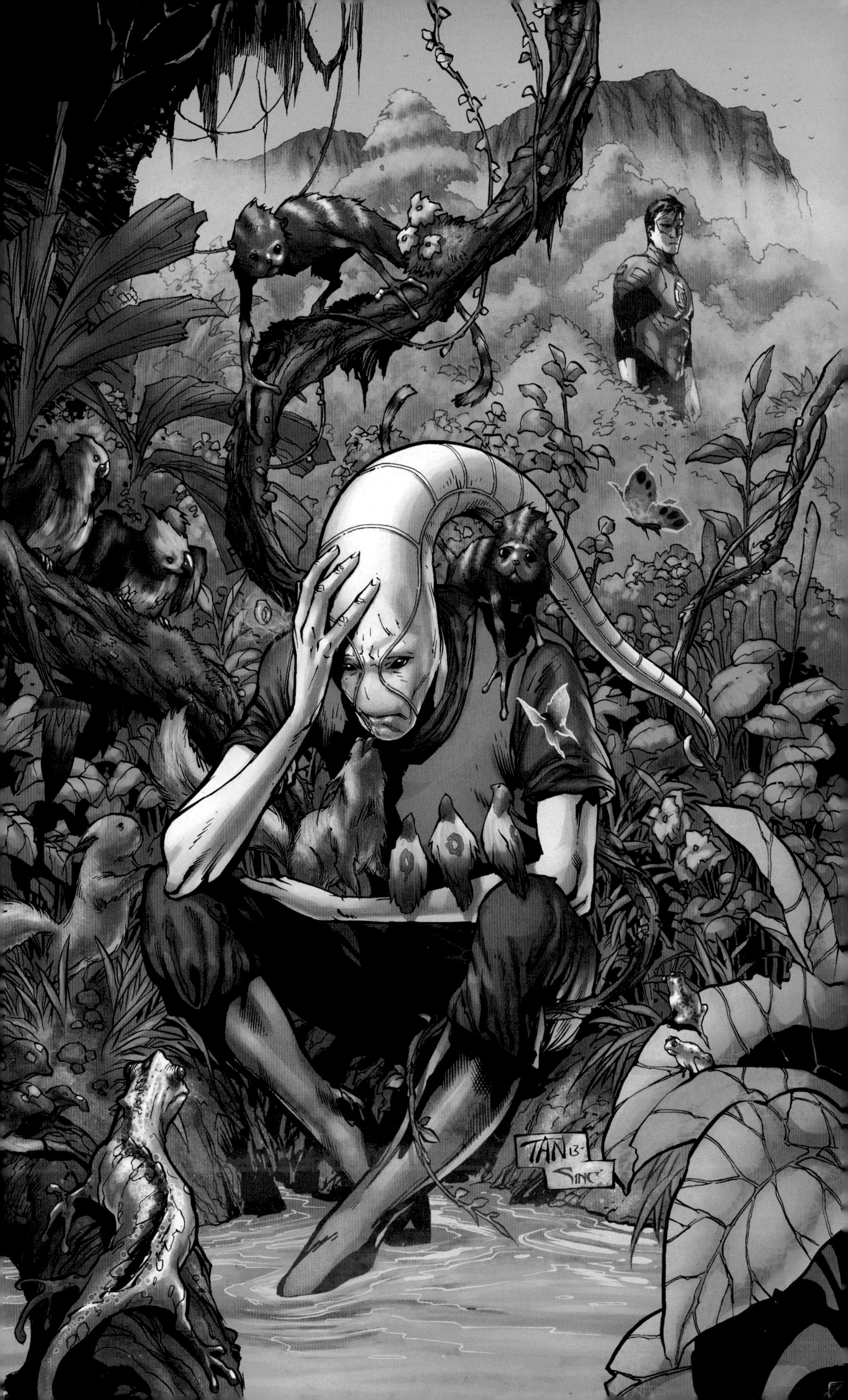
TAN 13
SINC

SHIPPING OUT

ROBERT VENDITTI writer BILLY TAN & MARTIN COCCOLO pencillers ROB HUNTER & WALDEN WONG inkers
TONY AVIÑA & ALEX SINCLAIR colorists cover art by BILLY TAN & ALEX SINCLAIR ROBOT CHICKEN variant cover by RC STOODIOS

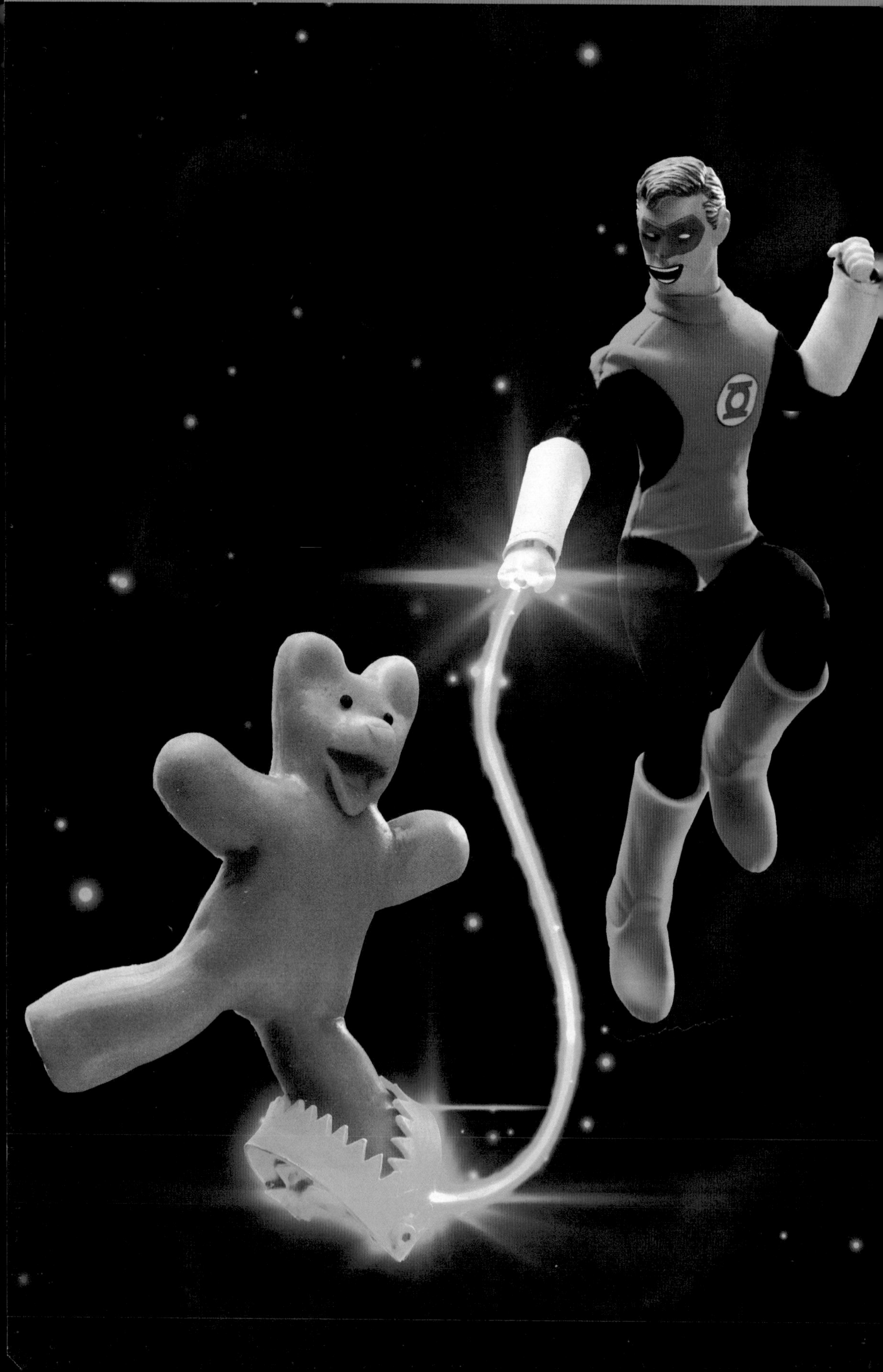

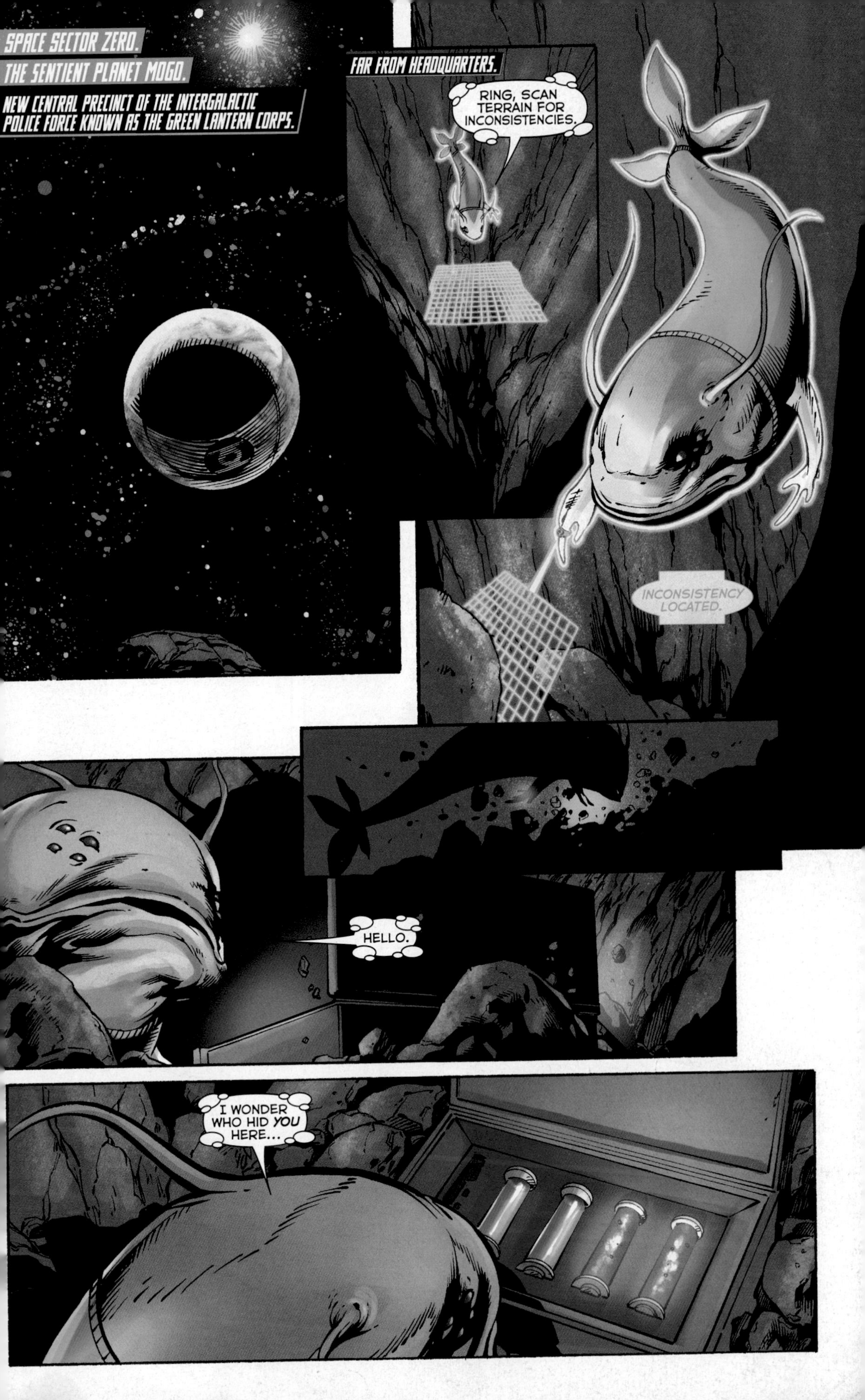
SPACE SECTOR ZERO.
THE SENTIENT PLANET MOGO.
NEW CENTRAL PRECINCT OF THE INTERGALACTIC POLICE FORCE KNOWN AS THE GREEN LANTERN CORPS.
FAR FROM HEADQUARTERS.
RING, SCAN TERRAIN FOR INCONSISTENCIES.
INCONSISTENCY LOCATED.
HELLO.
I WONDER WHO HID YOU HERE...

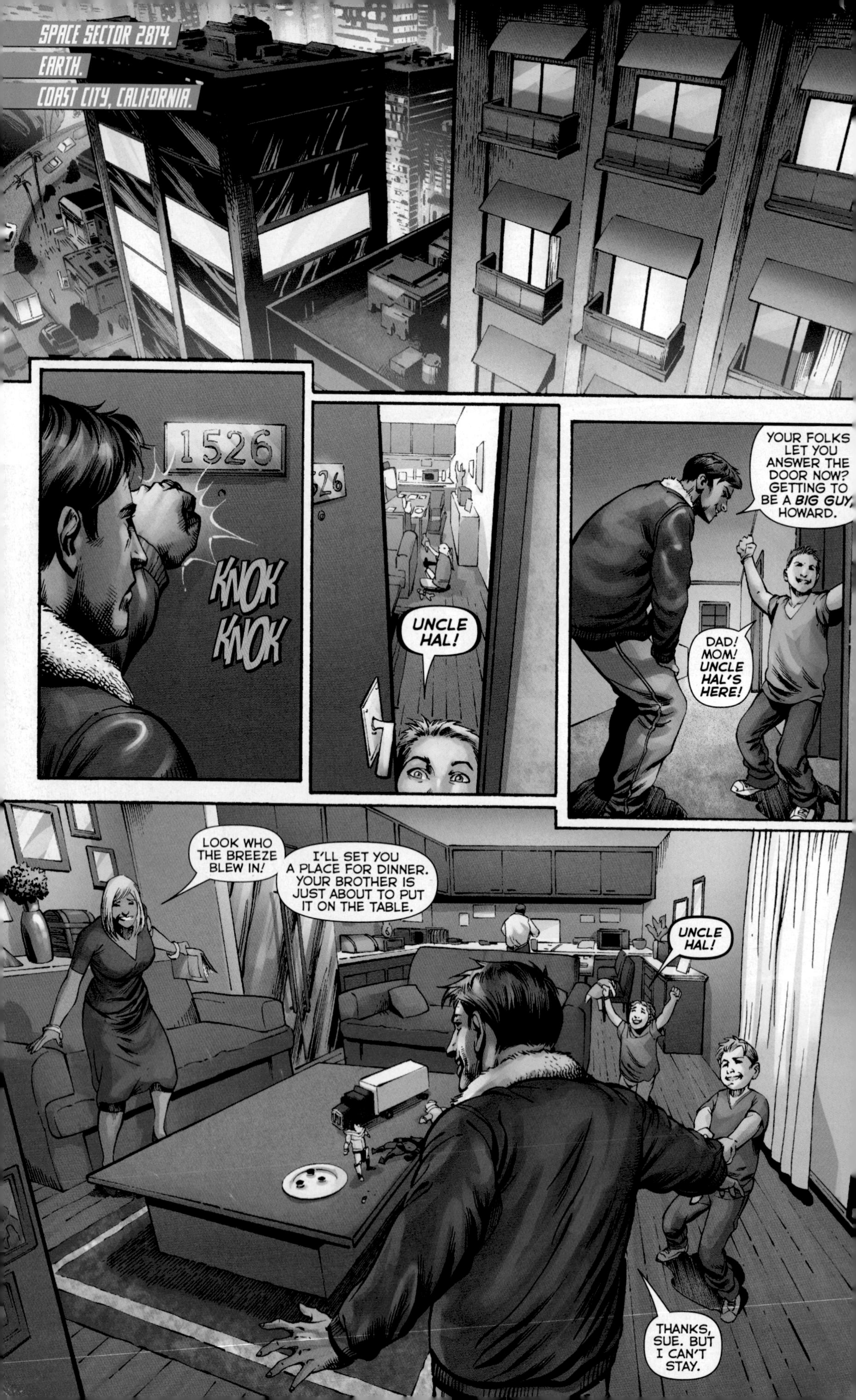
SPACE SECTOR 2814.
EARTH.
COAST CITY, CALIFORNIA.
1526
KNOK KNOK
526
UNCLE HAL!
YOUR FOLKS LET YOU ANSWER THE DOOR NOW? GETTING TO BE A *BIG GUY*, HOWARD.
DAD! MOM! UNCLE HAL'S HERE!
LOOK WHO THE BREEZE BLEW IN!
I'LL SET YOU A PLACE FOR DINNER. YOUR BROTHER IS JUST ABOUT TO PUT IT ON THE TABLE.
UNCLE HAL!
THANKS, SUE. BUT I CAN'T STAY.

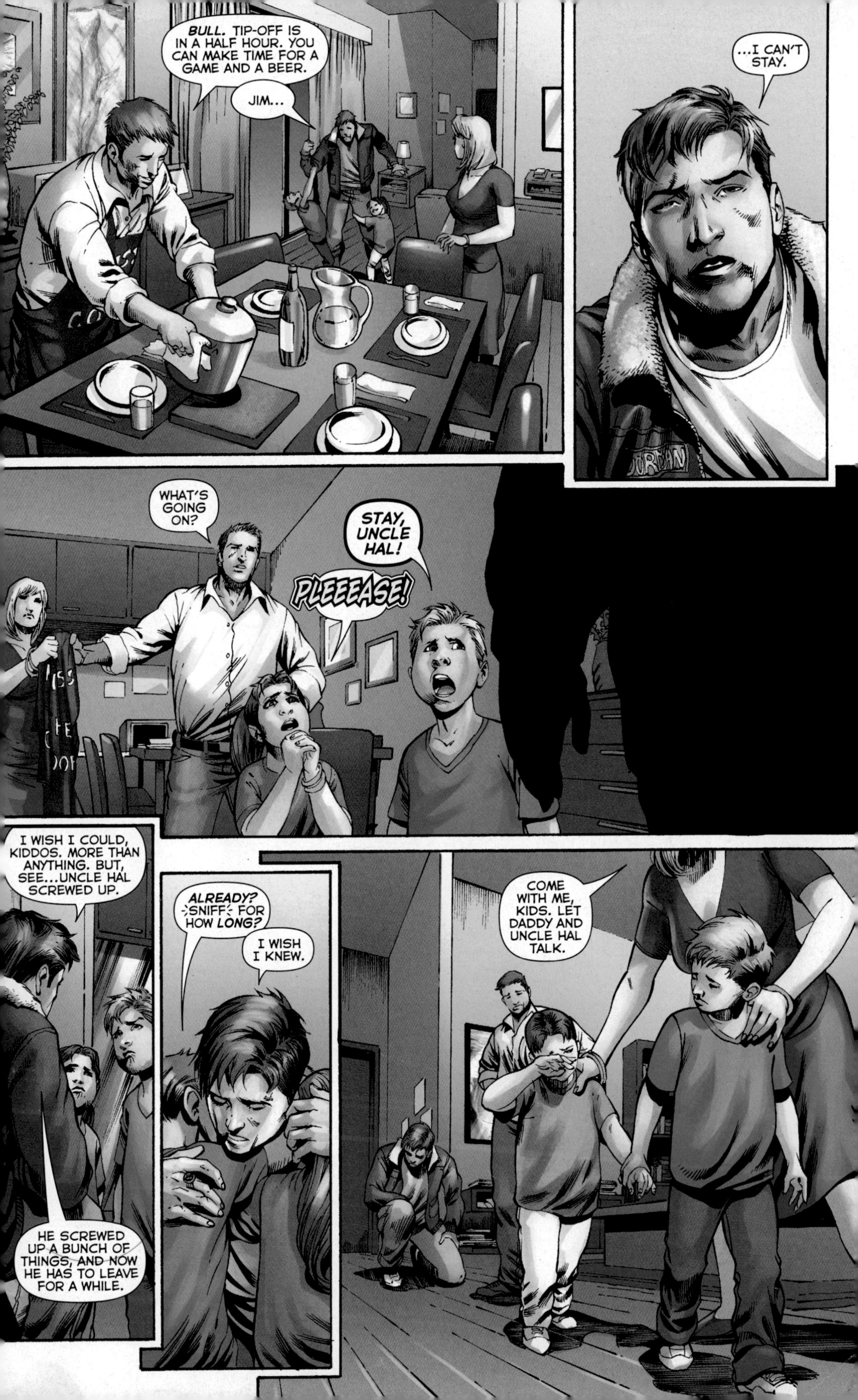

BULL. TIP-OFF IS IN A HALF HOUR. YOU CAN MAKE TIME FOR A GAME AND A BEER.
JIM...
...I CAN'T STAY.
WHAT'S GOING ON?
STAY, UNCLE HAL!
PLEEEASE!
I WISH I COULD, KIDDOS. MORE THAN ANYTHING. BUT, SEE...UNCLE HAL SCREWED UP.
HE SCREWED UP A BUNCH OF THINGS, AND NOW HE HAS TO LEAVE FOR A WHILE.
ALREADY? *SNIFF* FOR HOW *LONG?*
I WISH I KNEW.
COME WITH ME, KIDS. LET DADDY AND UNCLE HAL TALK.

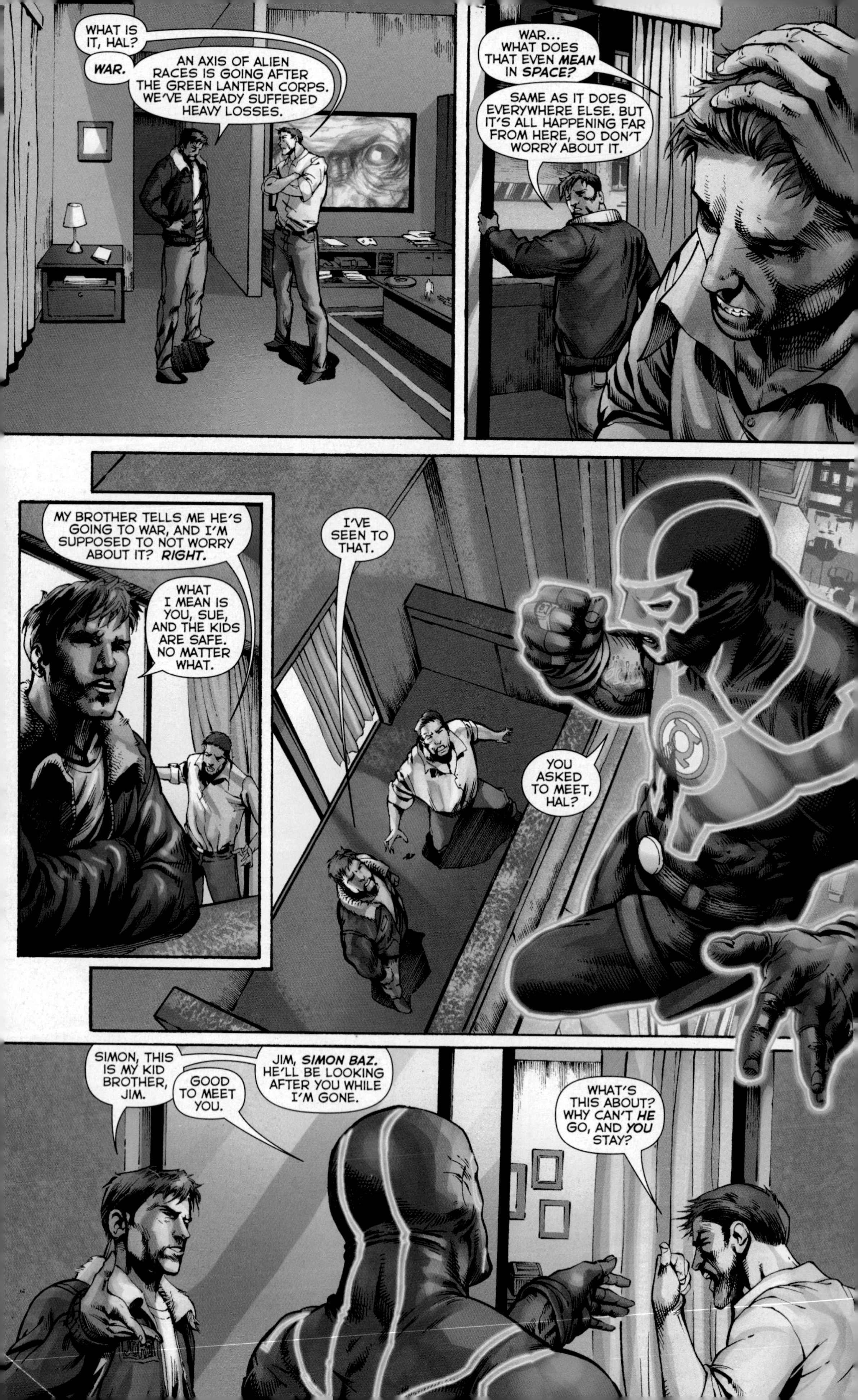

WHAT IS IT, HAL?
WAR.
AN AXIS OF ALIEN RACES IS GOING AFTER THE GREEN LANTERN CORPS. WE'VE ALREADY SUFFERED HEAVY LOSSES.
WAR... WHAT DOES THAT EVEN MEAN IN SPACE?
SAME AS IT DOES EVERYWHERE ELSE. BUT IT'S ALL HAPPENING FAR FROM HERE, SO DON'T WORRY ABOUT IT.
MY BROTHER TELLS ME HE'S GOING TO WAR, AND I'M SUPPOSED TO NOT WORRY ABOUT IT? RIGHT.
WHAT I MEAN IS YOU, SUE, AND THE KIDS ARE SAFE. NO MATTER WHAT.
I'VE SEEN TO THAT.
YOU ASKED TO MEET, HAL?
SIMON, THIS IS MY KID BROTHER, JIM.
GOOD TO MEET YOU.
JIM, SIMON BAZ. HE'LL BE LOOKING AFTER YOU WHILE I'M GONE.
WHAT'S THIS ABOUT? WHY CAN'T HE GO, AND YOU STAY?

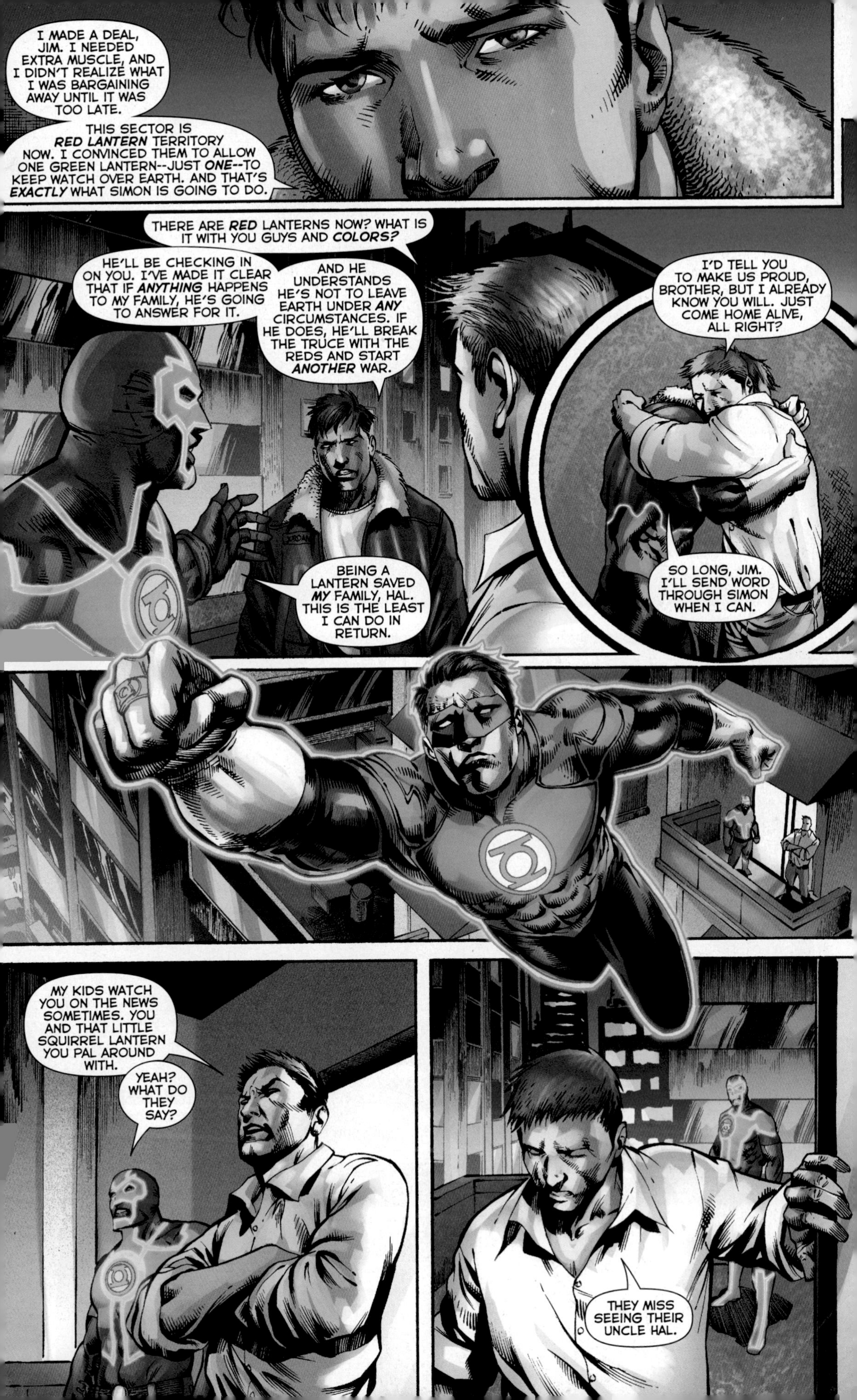
I MADE A DEAL, JIM. I NEEDED EXTRA MUSCLE, AND I DIDN'T REALIZE WHAT I WAS BARGAINING AWAY UNTIL IT WAS TOO LATE.
THIS SECTOR IS RED LANTERN TERRITORY NOW. I CONVINCED THEM TO ALLOW ONE GREEN LANTERN--JUST ONE--TO KEEP WATCH OVER EARTH. AND THAT'S EXACTLY WHAT SIMON IS GOING TO DO.
THERE ARE RED LANTERNS NOW? WHAT IS IT WITH YOU GUYS AND COLORS?
HE'LL BE CHECKING IN ON YOU. I'VE MADE IT CLEAR THAT IF ANYTHING HAPPENS TO MY FAMILY, HE'S GOING TO ANSWER FOR IT.
AND HE UNDERSTANDS HE'S NOT TO LEAVE EARTH UNDER ANY CIRCUMSTANCES. IF HE DOES, HE'LL BREAK THE TRUCE WITH THE REDS AND START ANOTHER WAR.
BEING A LANTERN SAVED MY FAMILY, HAL. THIS IS THE LEAST I CAN DO IN RETURN.
I'D TELL YOU TO MAKE US PROUD, BROTHER, BUT I ALREADY KNOW YOU WILL. JUST COME HOME ALIVE, ALL RIGHT?
SO LONG, JIM. I'LL SEND WORD THROUGH SIMON WHEN I CAN.
MY KIDS WATCH YOU ON THE NEWS SOMETIMES. YOU AND THAT LITTLE SQUIRREL LANTERN YOU PAL AROUND WITH.
YEAH? WHAT DO THEY SAY?
THEY MISS SEEING THEIR UNCLE HAL.

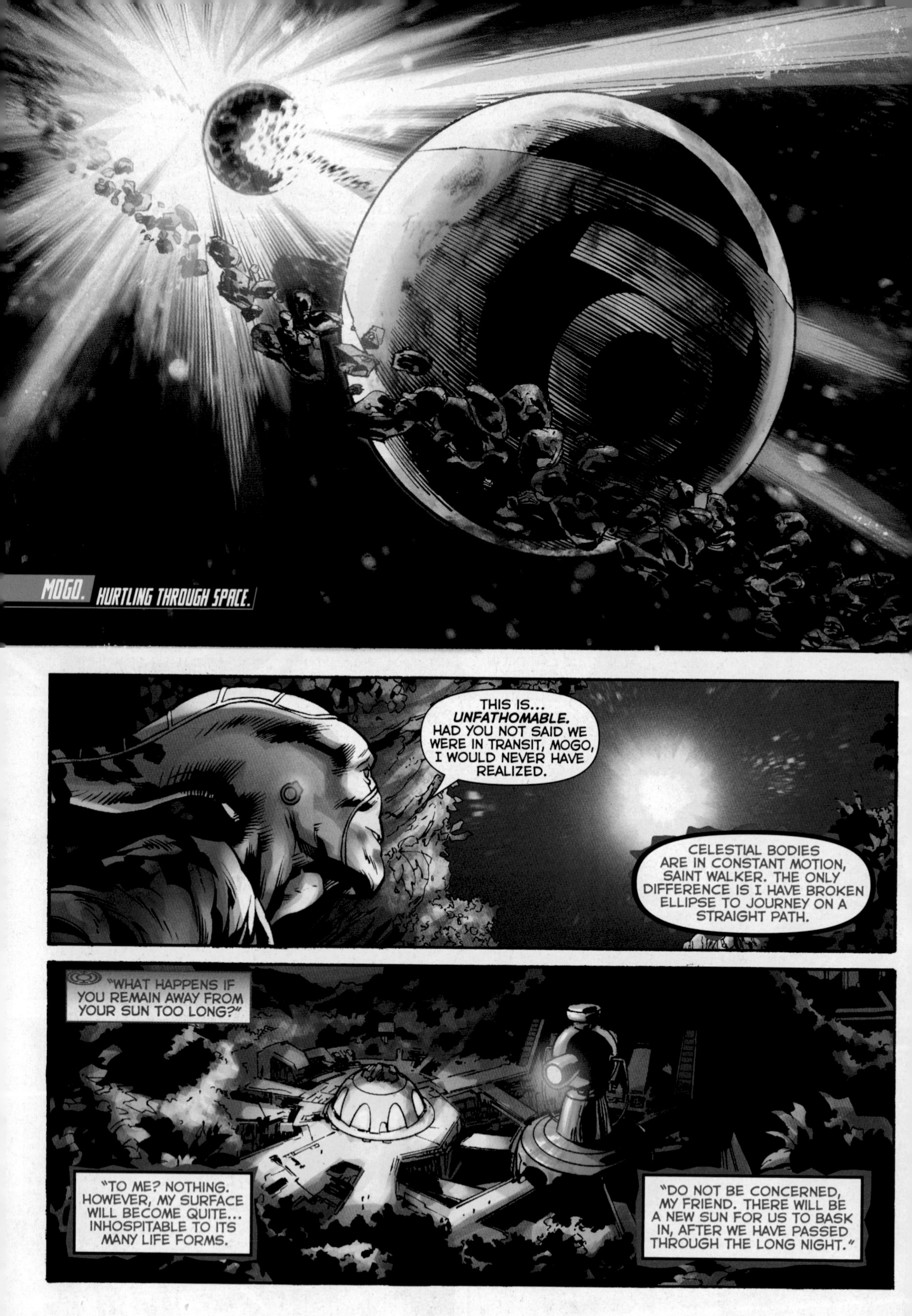
MOGO. HURTLING THROUGH SPACE.
THIS IS... UNFATHOMABLE. HAD YOU NOT SAID WE WERE IN TRANSIT, MOGO, I WOULD NEVER HAVE REALIZED.
CELESTIAL BODIES ARE IN CONSTANT MOTION, SAINT WALKER. THE ONLY DIFFERENCE IS I HAVE BROKEN ELLIPSE TO JOURNEY ON A STRAIGHT PATH.
"WHAT HAPPENS IF YOU REMAIN AWAY FROM YOUR SUN TOO LONG?"
"TO ME? NOTHING. HOWEVER, MY SURFACE WILL BECOME QUITE... INHOSPITABLE TO ITS MANY LIFE FORMS.
"DO NOT BE CONCERNED, MY FRIEND. THERE WILL BE A NEW SUN FOR US TO BASK IN, AFTER WE HAVE PASSED THROUGH THE LONG NIGHT."

YOU MAKE IT SOUND A TRIVIAL THING. *RELOCATING* TO A *WAR ZONE*.

THE STRATEGY IS NOT WITHOUT MERIT. DO YOU NOT AGREE?

AS FIRST OF THE BLUE LANTERNS, I WAS A CHAMPION OF *HOPE* AND *PEACE*. WAR HAS NEVER BEEN MY SPECIALTY.

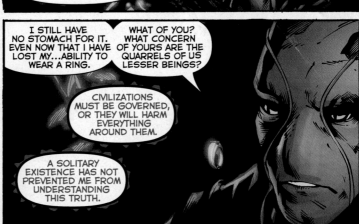

I STILL HAVE NO STOMACH FOR IT. EVEN NOW THAT I HAVE LOST MY...ABILITY TO WEAR A RING.

WHAT OF YOU? WHAT CONCERN OF YOURS ARE THE QUARRELS OF US LESSER BEINGS?

CIVILIZATIONS MUST BE GOVERNED, OR THEY WILL HARM EVERYTHING AROUND THEM.

CORPS LEADER JORDAN BELIEVES WE WILL BE BETTER ABLE TO QUELL THE UPRISING IF WE ARE POSITIONED CLOSE TO THE COMBAT.

A SOLITARY EXISTENCE HAS NOT PREVENTED ME FROM UNDERSTANDING THIS TRUTH.

THE CORPS' MISSION IS NOBLE IN CONCEPT, IF NOT ALWAYS EXECUTION. BUT FAILURE IS THE FERTILE SOIL OF SUCCESS. IN TIME, THE JUST WILL PREVAIL.

"ALL WILL BE WELL"? I HAVE SEEN TOO MUCH TO SHARE YOUR OPTIMISM.

WITHOUT OPTIMISM, WE MAY AS WELL ALL GO BACK TO SLEEP.

EVERY LANTERN I SHEPHERDED... I TAUGHT THEM TO WIELD THE LIGHT, AND UNKNOWINGLY MADE THEM DETRIMENTS TO CREATION.

BROTHER WARTH, SISTER SERCY, *LANTERN RAYNER*...THEY ALL LOST THEIR LIVES BECAUSE OF ME.

THERE IS HOPE WITHIN YOU YET, SAINT WALKER, EVEN IF YOU DO NOT ACKNOWLEDGE IT.

I AM A SAINT NO MORE.

I AM ONLY A WALKER.

INSIDE THE COMMAND CENTER.

WISHFUL THINKING, EH, SALAAK...?

HOPING ALL RELIC'S *LIGHT-DRAINING* TECH GOT DESTROYED WITH HIM.

WE KNOW AT LEAST ONE *DURLAN* CONCEALED ITSELF AMONG THE SUPPORT STAFF I EVACUATED FROM OA...

DIRTY *SHAPE-SHIFTER* COULDA LAID TENTACLES ON A DRAINER, EASY.

WHO DO YOU FIGURE DID THE MODS TO THIS ONE? WE FOUND IT IN A SECTOR HOUSE ATTACKED BY THE *KHUND*, BUT THIS AIN'T THEIR WORK.

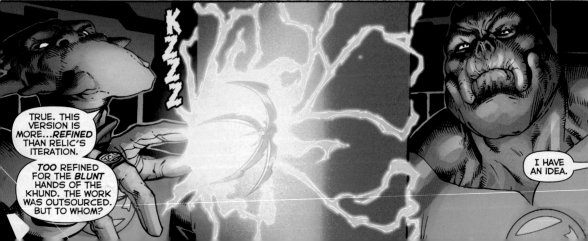

KZZZZ

TRUE. THIS VERSION IS MORE...*REFINED* THAN RELIC'S ITERATION.

TOO REFINED FOR THE *BLUNT* HANDS OF THE KHUND. THE WORK WAS OUTSOURCED. BUT TO WHOM?

I HAVE AN IDEA.

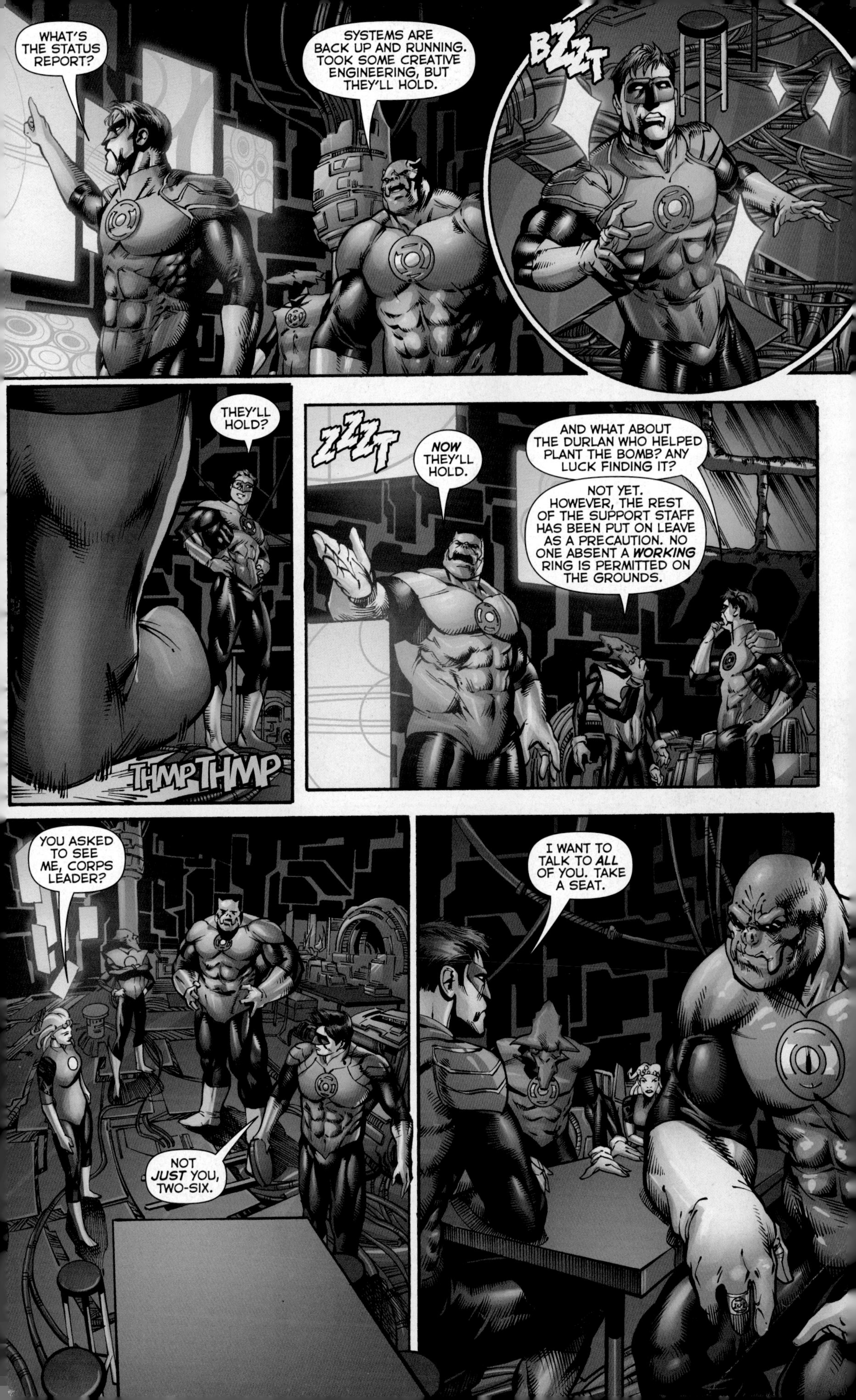
WHAT'S THE STATUS REPORT?
SYSTEMS ARE BACK UP AND RUNNING. TOOK SOME CREATIVE ENGINEERING, BUT THEY'LL HOLD.
BZZZT
THEY'LL HOLD?
THMP THMP
ZZZT
NOW THEY'LL HOLD.
AND WHAT ABOUT THE DURLAN WHO HELPED PLANT THE BOMB? ANY LUCK FINDING IT?
NOT YET. HOWEVER, THE REST OF THE SUPPORT STAFF HAS BEEN PUT ON LEAVE AS A PRECAUTION. NO ONE ABSENT A WORKING RING IS PERMITTED ON THE GROUNDS.
YOU ASKED TO SEE ME, CORPS LEADER?
NOT JUST YOU, TWO-SIX.
I WANT TO TALK TO ALL OF YOU. TAKE A SEAT.

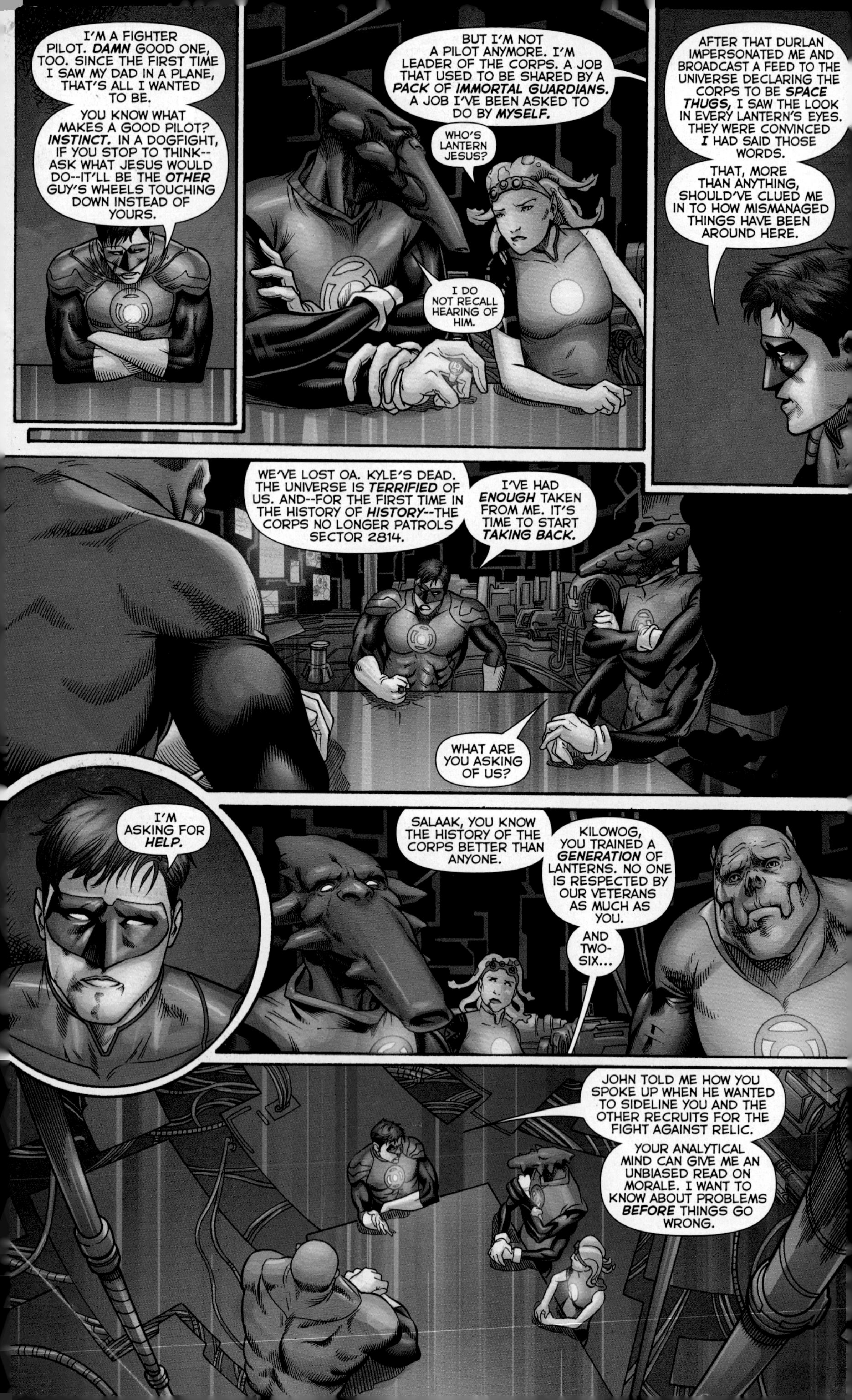
I'M A FIGHTER PILOT. DAMN GOOD ONE, TOO. SINCE THE FIRST TIME I SAW MY DAD IN A PLANE, THAT'S ALL I WANTED TO BE.
YOU KNOW WHAT MAKES A GOOD PILOT? INSTINCT. IN A DOGFIGHT, IF YOU STOP TO THINK--ASK WHAT JESUS WOULD DO--IT'LL BE THE OTHER GUY'S WHEELS TOUCHING DOWN INSTEAD OF YOURS.
BUT I'M NOT A PILOT ANYMORE. I'M LEADER OF THE CORPS. A JOB THAT USED TO BE SHARED BY A PACK OF IMMORTAL GUARDIANS. A JOB I'VE BEEN ASKED TO DO BY MYSELF.
WHO'S LANTERN JESUS?
I DO NOT RECALL HEARING OF HIM.
AFTER THAT DURLAN IMPERSONATED ME AND BROADCAST A FEED TO THE UNIVERSE DECLARING THE CORPS TO BE SPACE THUGS, I SAW THE LOOK IN EVERY LANTERN'S EYES. THEY WERE CONVINCED I HAD SAID THOSE WORDS.
THAT, MORE THAN ANYTHING, SHOULD'VE CLUED ME IN TO HOW MISMANAGED THINGS HAVE BEEN AROUND HERE.
WE'VE LOST OA. KYLE'S DEAD. THE UNIVERSE IS TERRIFIED OF US. AND--FOR THE FIRST TIME IN THE HISTORY OF HISTORY--THE CORPS NO LONGER PATROLS SECTOR 2814.
I'VE HAD ENOUGH TAKEN FROM ME. IT'S TIME TO START TAKING BACK.
WHAT ARE YOU ASKING OF US?
I'M ASKING FOR HELP.
SALAAK, YOU KNOW THE HISTORY OF THE CORPS BETTER THAN ANYONE.
KILOWOG, YOU TRAINED A GENERATION OF LANTERNS. NO ONE IS RESPECTED BY OUR VETERANS AS MUCH AS YOU.
AND TWO-SIX...
JOHN TOLD ME HOW YOU SPOKE UP WHEN HE WANTED TO SIDELINE YOU AND THE OTHER RECRUITS FOR THE FIGHT AGAINST RELIC.
YOUR ANALYTICAL MIND CAN GIVE ME AN UNBIASED READ ON MORALE. I WANT TO KNOW ABOUT PROBLEMS BEFORE THINGS GO WRONG.

THAT'S RIGHT, I'M THINKING *AHEAD.* NO ONE IS MORE SHOCKED THAN ME.

SO, HOW ABOUT IT?

I ACCEPT.

YOU HAD ME AT "ANALYTICAL."

YOU KNOW YOU DON'T GOTTA ASK, PAL.

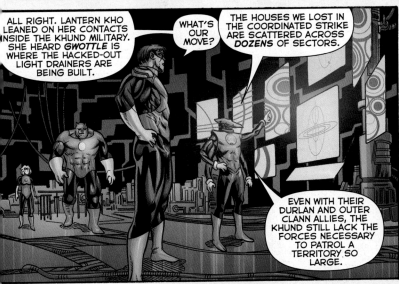

ALL RIGHT. LANTERN KHO LEANED ON HER CONTACTS INSIDE THE KHUND MILITARY. SHE HEARD *GWOTTLE* IS WHERE THE HACKED-OUT LIGHT DRAINERS ARE BEING BUILT.

WHAT'S OUR MOVE?

THE HOUSES WE LOST IN THE COORDINATED STRIKE ARE SCATTERED ACROSS *DOZENS* OF SECTORS.

EVEN WITH THEIR DURLAN AND OUTER CLANN ALLIES, THE KHUND STILL LACK THE FORCES NECESSARY TO PATROL A TERRITORY SO LARGE.

THEY'LL EXPECT US TO HIT 'EM AT THE EDGES, BUT I SAY WE POSITION MOGO *DEAD CENTER.*

SEE HOW *THEY* LIKE BEING INVADED. BESIDES, WE POKE OUR FINGER IN THEIR EYE, THEY'LL BE LESS LIKELY TO SET THEIR SIGHTS ON *CIVILIAN* WORLDS.

AND IF GWOTTLE IS THE SPOT, OUR FIRST MOVE IS TO BREAK THE SUPPLY CHAIN. CAN'T HAVE THE ENEMY ARMING THEMSELVES WITH *ANTI-LIGHT* TECH.

I LIKE IT. KILOWOG, PUT TOGETHER A TEAM. SALAAK, BRIEF THEM ON GWOTTLE.

AS SOON AS MOGO DROPS ANCHOR, I'M GOING IN.

DON'T SUPPOSE YOU'D LEAD FROM H.Q., AND LET THE *TROOPS* DO THE FIGHTING?

BABY STEPS, KILOWOG.

LET'S GET TO IT, LANTERNS.

WE'VE GOT GROUND TO MAKE UP.

GWOTTLE POPULATION: 453 MILLION

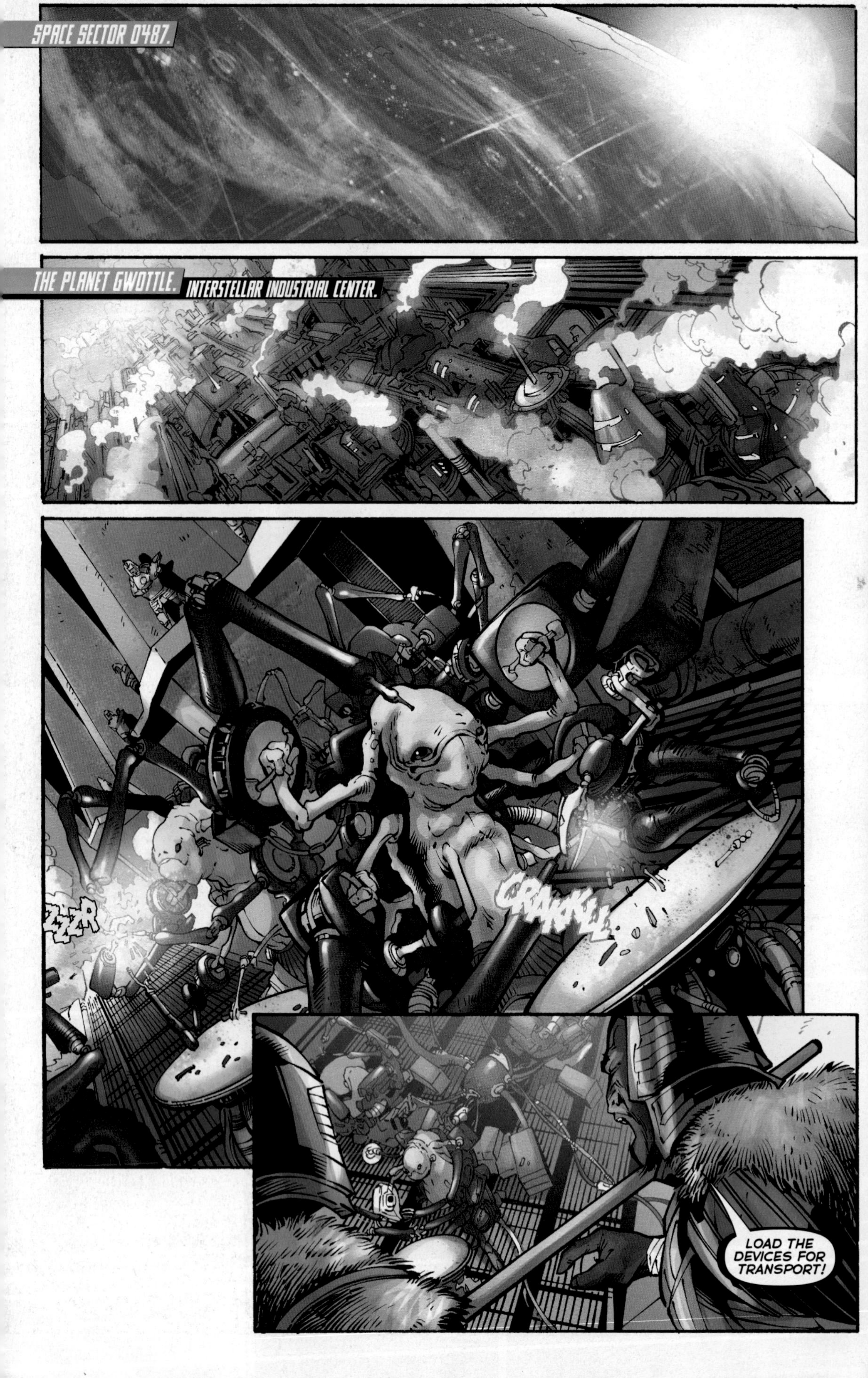
SPACE SECTOR 0487.
THE PLANET GWOTTLE.
INTERSTELLAR INDUSTRIAL CENTER.
CRAKKLL
LOAD THE DEVICES FOR TRANSPORT!

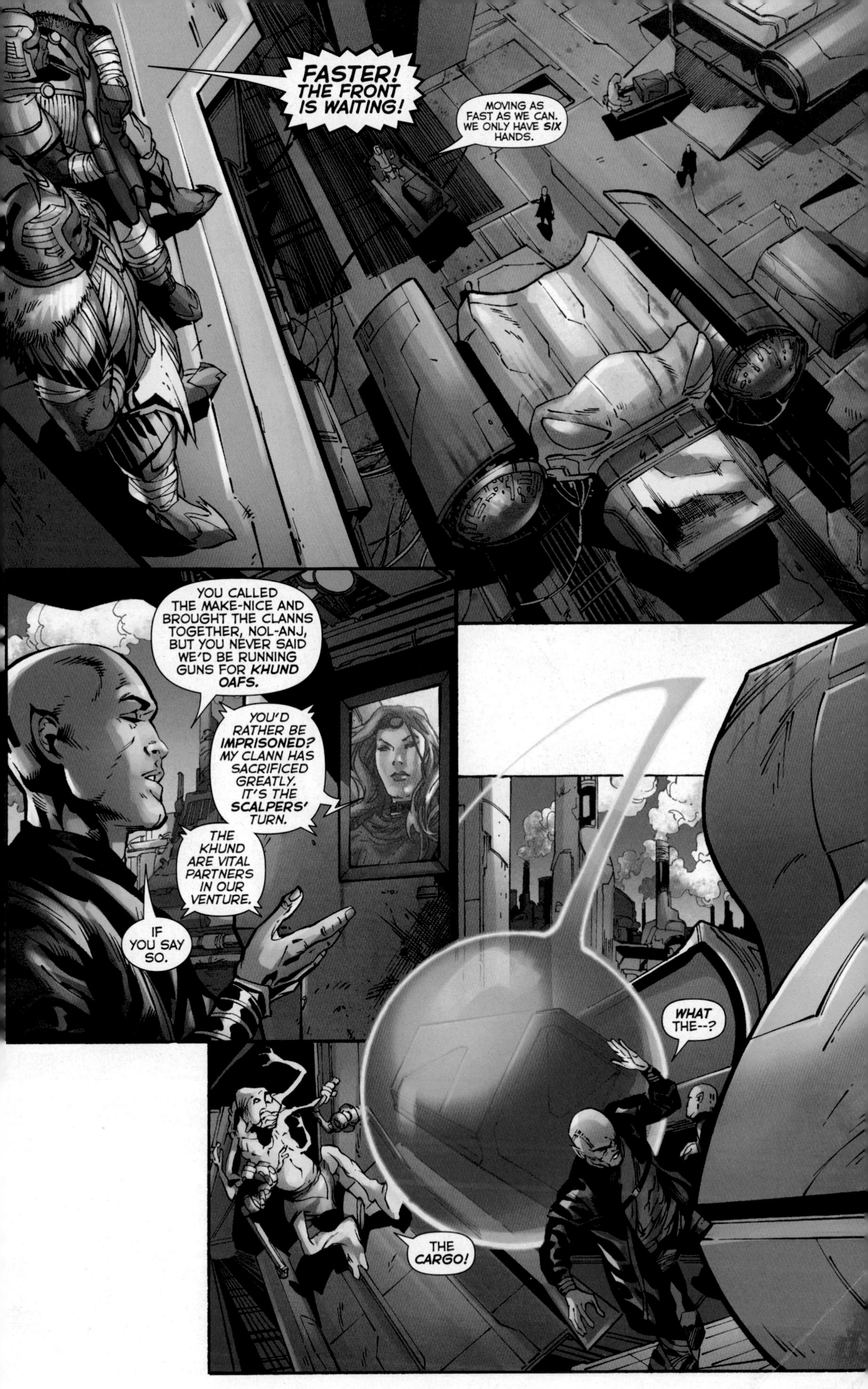
FASTER! THE FRONT IS WAITING!
MOVING AS FAST AS WE CAN. WE ONLY HAVE SIX HANDS.
YOU CALLED THE MAKE-NICE AND BROUGHT THE CLANNS TOGETHER, NOL-ANJ, BUT YOU NEVER SAID WE'D BE RUNNING GUNS FOR KHUND OAFS.
YOU'D RATHER BE IMPRISONED? MY CLANN HAS SACRIFICED GREATLY. IT'S THE SCALPERS' TURN.
THE KHUND ARE VITAL PARTNERS IN OUR VENTURE.
IF YOU SAY SO.
WHAT THE--?
THE CARGO!

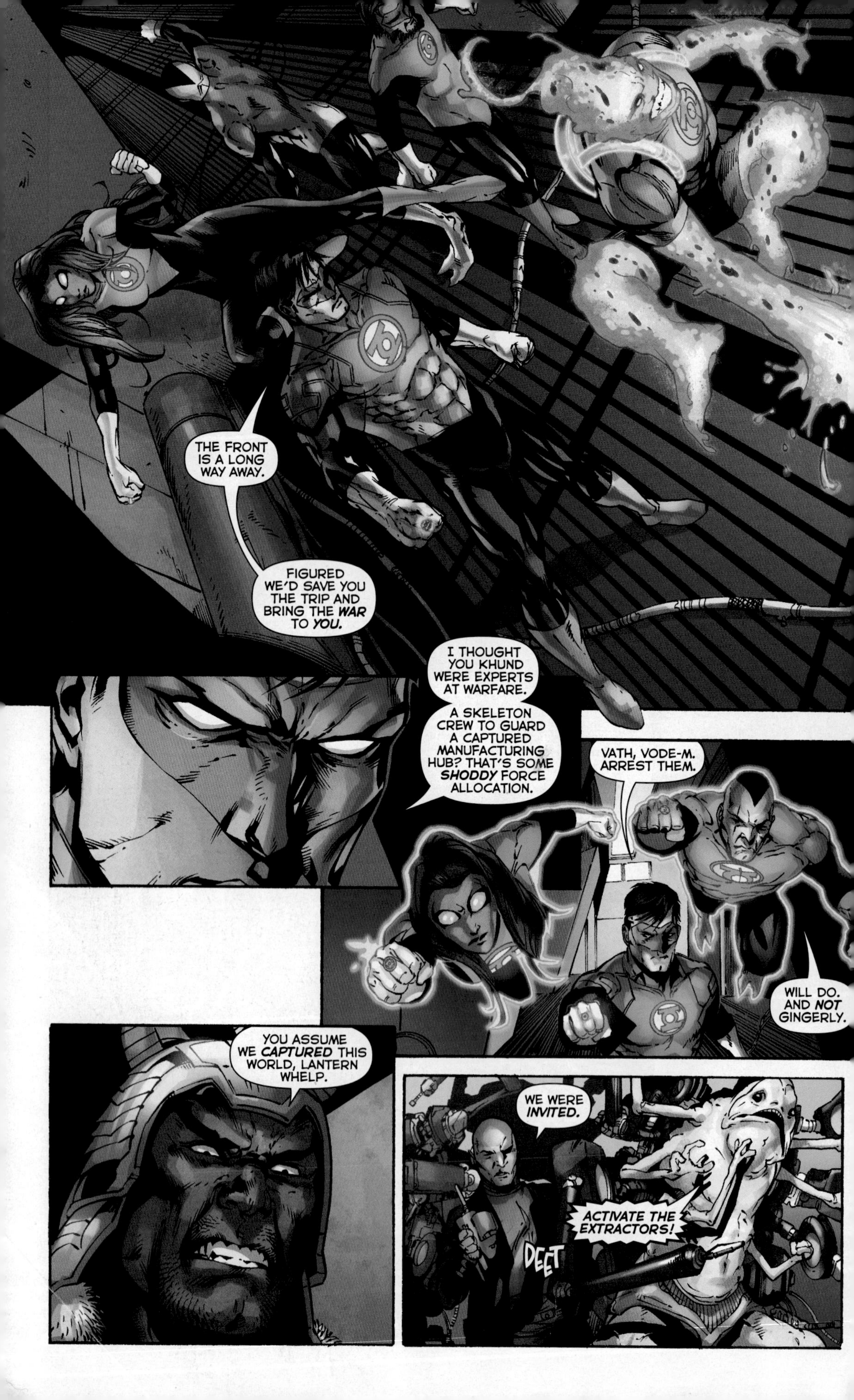
THE FRONT IS A LONG WAY AWAY.
FIGURED WE'D SAVE YOU THE TRIP AND BRING THE *WAR* TO *YOU.*
I THOUGHT YOU KHUND WERE EXPERTS AT WARFARE.
A SKELETON CREW TO GUARD A CAPTURED MANUFACTURING HUB? THAT'S SOME *SHODDY* FORCE ALLOCATION.
VATH, VODE-M. ARREST THEM.
WILL DO. AND *NOT* GINGERLY.
YOU ASSUME WE *CAPTURED* THIS WORLD, LANTERN WHELP.
WE WERE *INVITED.*
ACTIVATE THE EXTRACTORS!
DEET

VVVVMMMMMMMMZZZZZZZ

VMMMMMZZ

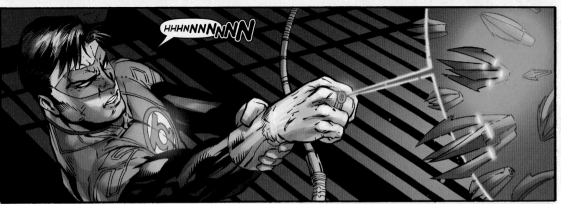

HHHNNNNNNN

GAH!

RAARGH!

HOW'RE THEY ⇒NNG⇐ CONTROLLING THESE THINGS?

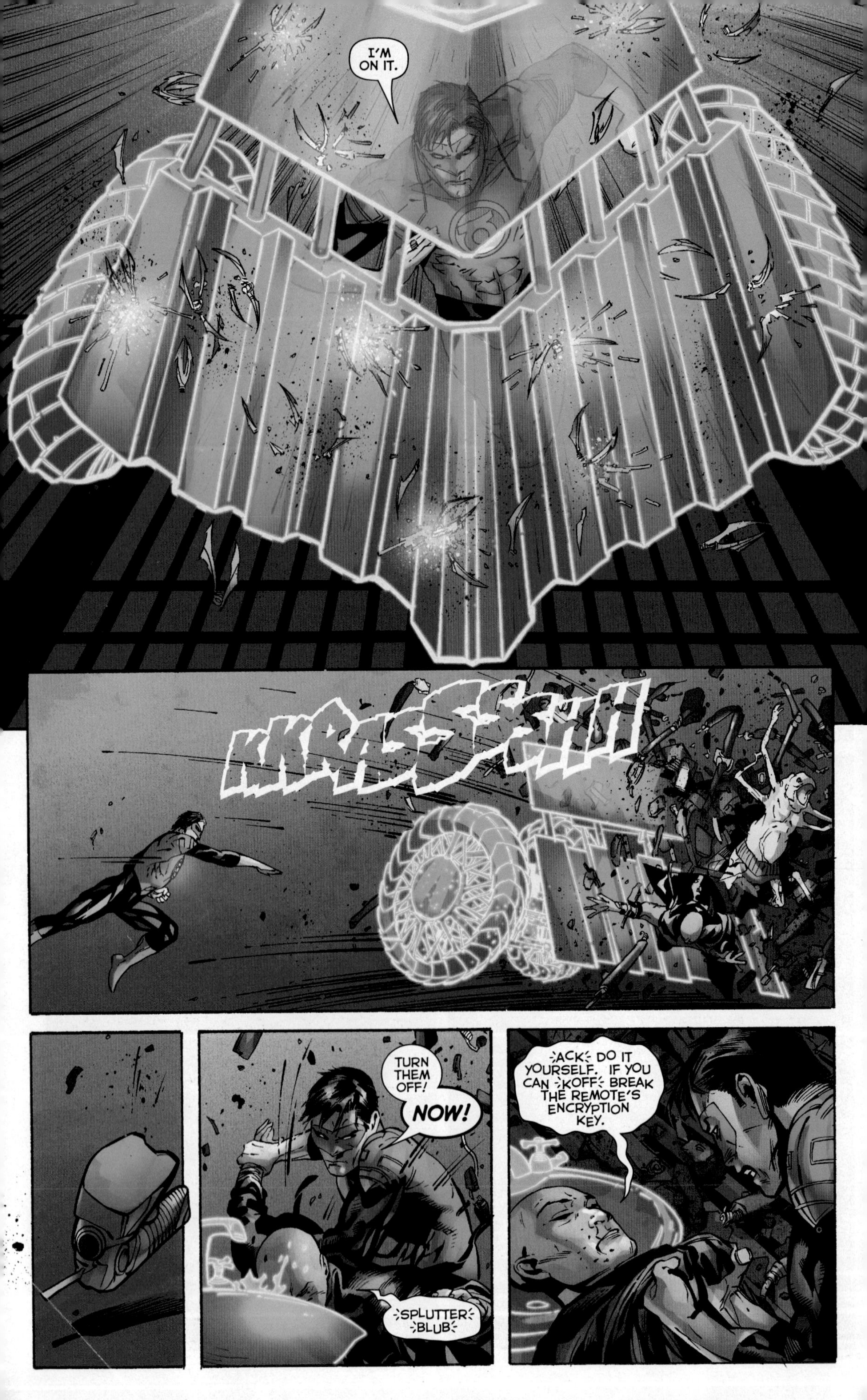
I'M ON IT.
TURN THEM OFF!
NOW!
SPLUTTER BLUB
ACK DO IT YOURSELF. IF YOU CAN KOFF BREAK THE REMOTE'S ENCRYPTION KEY.

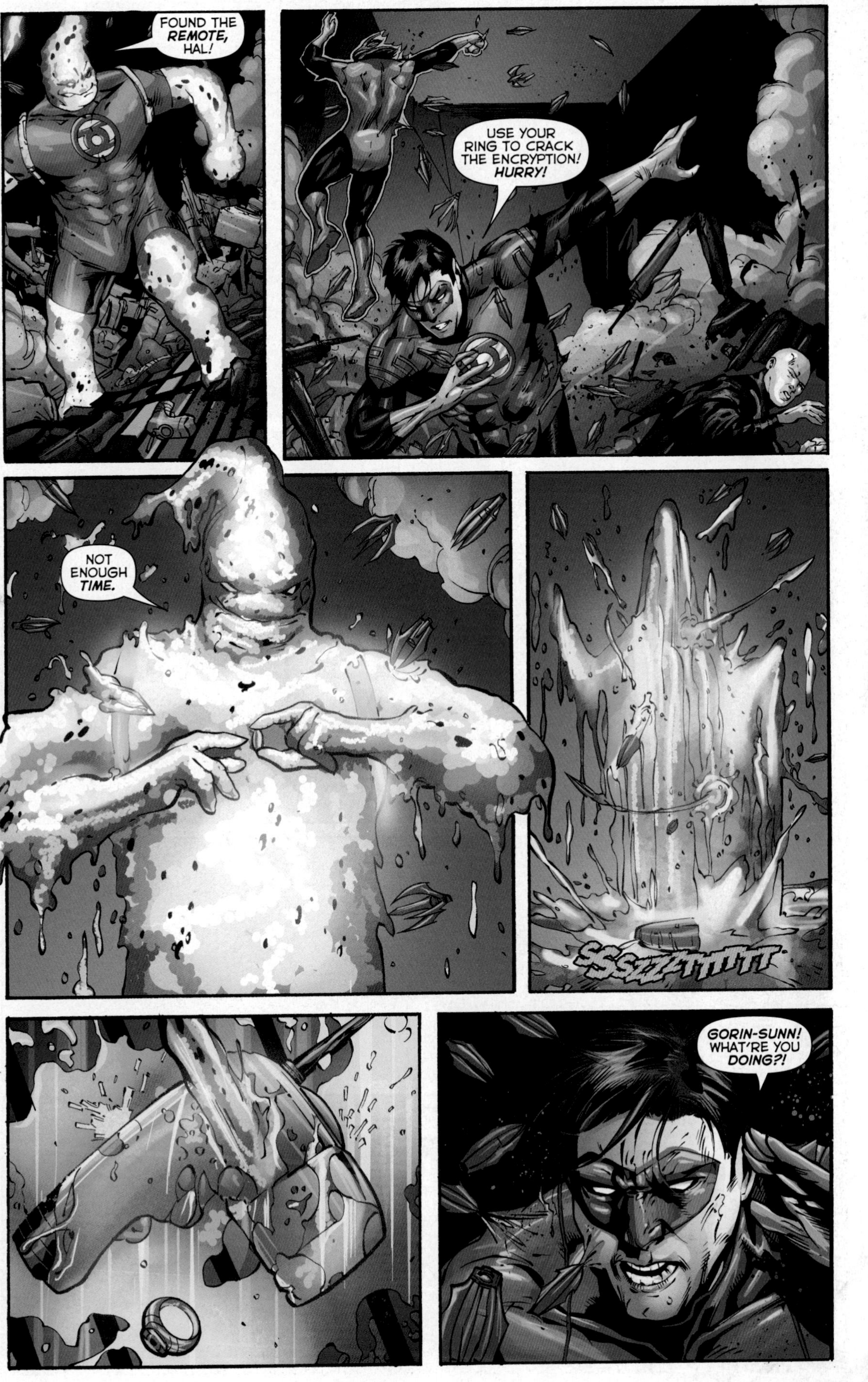
FOUND THE *REMOTE,* HAL!
USE YOUR RING TO CRACK THE ENCRYPTION! *HURRY!*
NOT ENOUGH *TIME.*
SSSZZZTTTTTT
GORIN-SUNN! WHAT'RE YOU *DOING?!*

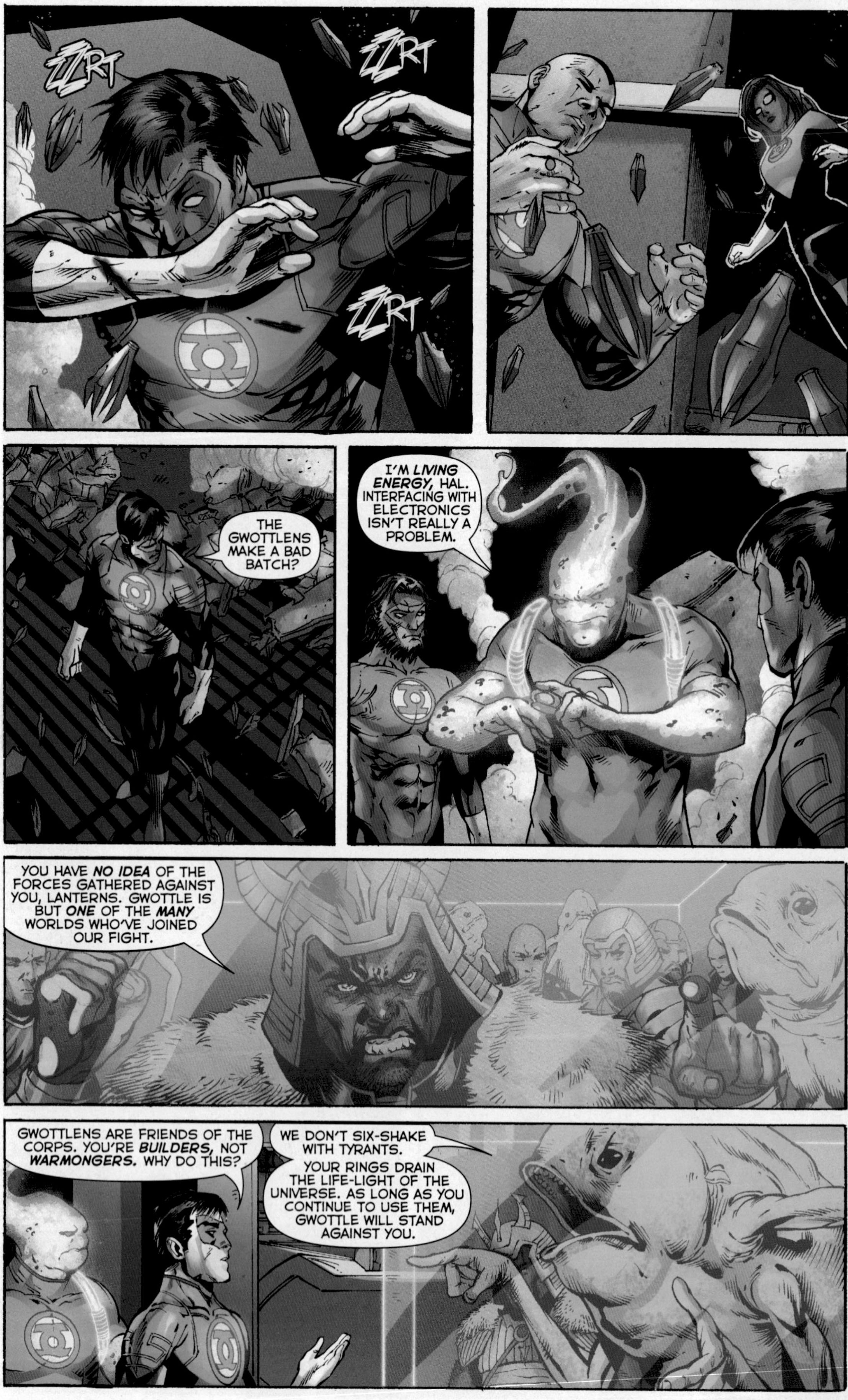
ZZRT
ZZRT
ZZRT
THE GWOTTLENS MAKE A BAD BATCH?
I'M LIVING ENERGY, HAL. INTERFACING WITH ELECTRONICS ISN'T REALLY A PROBLEM.
YOU HAVE NO IDEA OF THE FORCES GATHERED AGAINST YOU, LANTERNS. GWOTTLE IS BUT ONE OF THE MANY WORLDS WHO'VE JOINED OUR FIGHT.
GWOTTLENS ARE FRIENDS OF THE CORPS. YOU'RE BUILDERS, NOT WARMONGERS. WHY DO THIS?
WE DON'T SIX-SHAKE WITH TYRANTS.
YOUR RINGS DRAIN THE LIFE-LIGHT OF THE UNIVERSE. AS LONG AS YOU CONTINUE TO USE THEM, GWOTTLE WILL STAND AGAINST YOU.

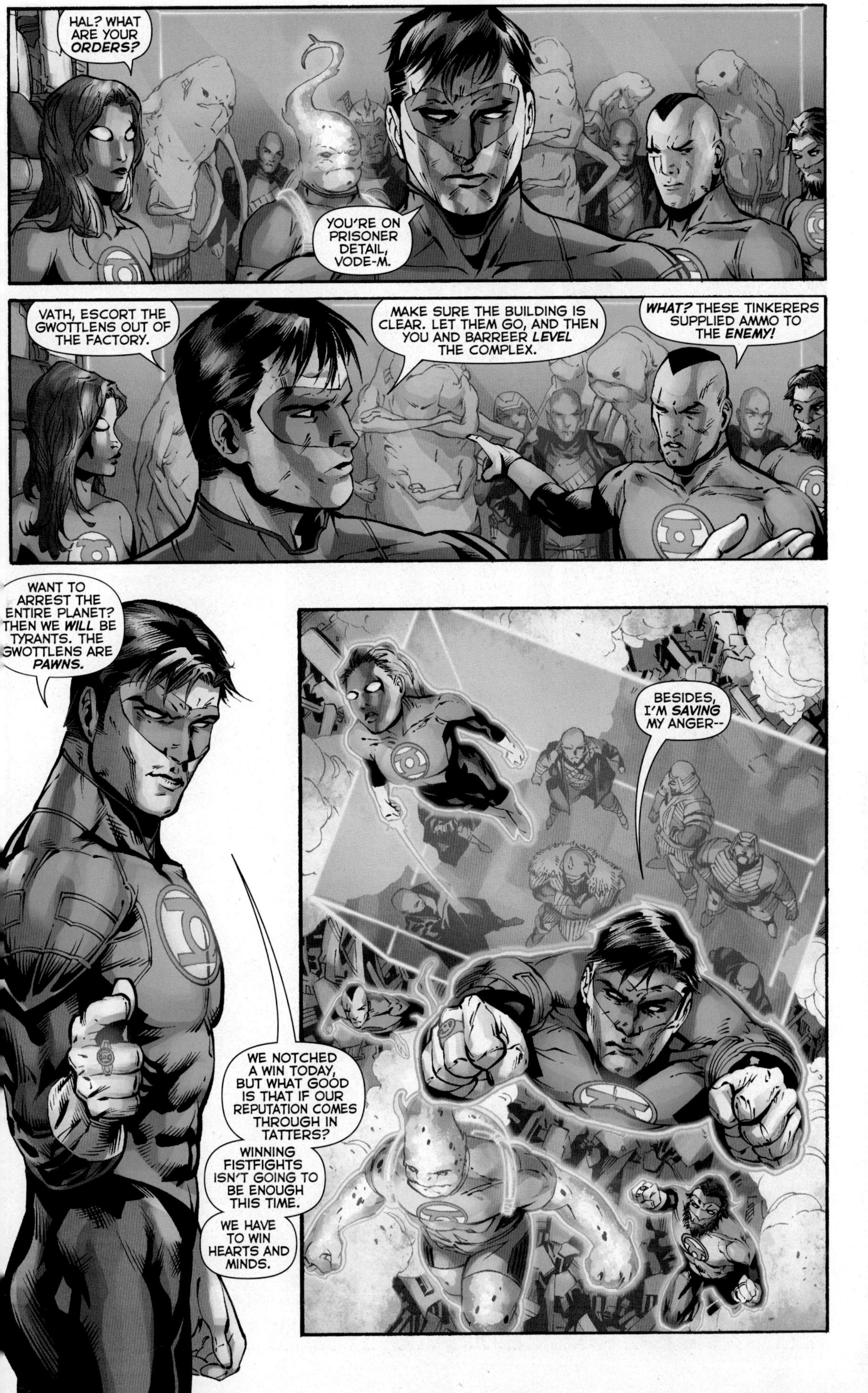
HAL? WHAT ARE YOUR ORDERS?
YOU'RE ON PRISONER DETAIL, VODE-M.
VATH, ESCORT THE GWOTTLENS OUT OF THE FACTORY.
MAKE SURE THE BUILDING IS CLEAR. LET THEM GO, AND THEN YOU AND BARREER LEVEL THE COMPLEX.
WHAT? THESE TINKERERS SUPPLIED AMMO TO THE ENEMY!
WANT TO ARREST THE ENTIRE PLANET? THEN WE WILL BE TYRANTS. THE GWOTTLENS ARE PAWNS.
BESIDES, I'M SAVING MY ANGER--
WE NOTCHED A WIN TODAY, BUT WHAT GOOD IS THAT IF OUR REPUTATION COMES THROUGH IN TATTERS?
WINNING FISTFIGHTS ISN'T GOING TO BE ENOUGH THIS TIME.
WE HAVE TO WIN HEARTS AND MINDS.

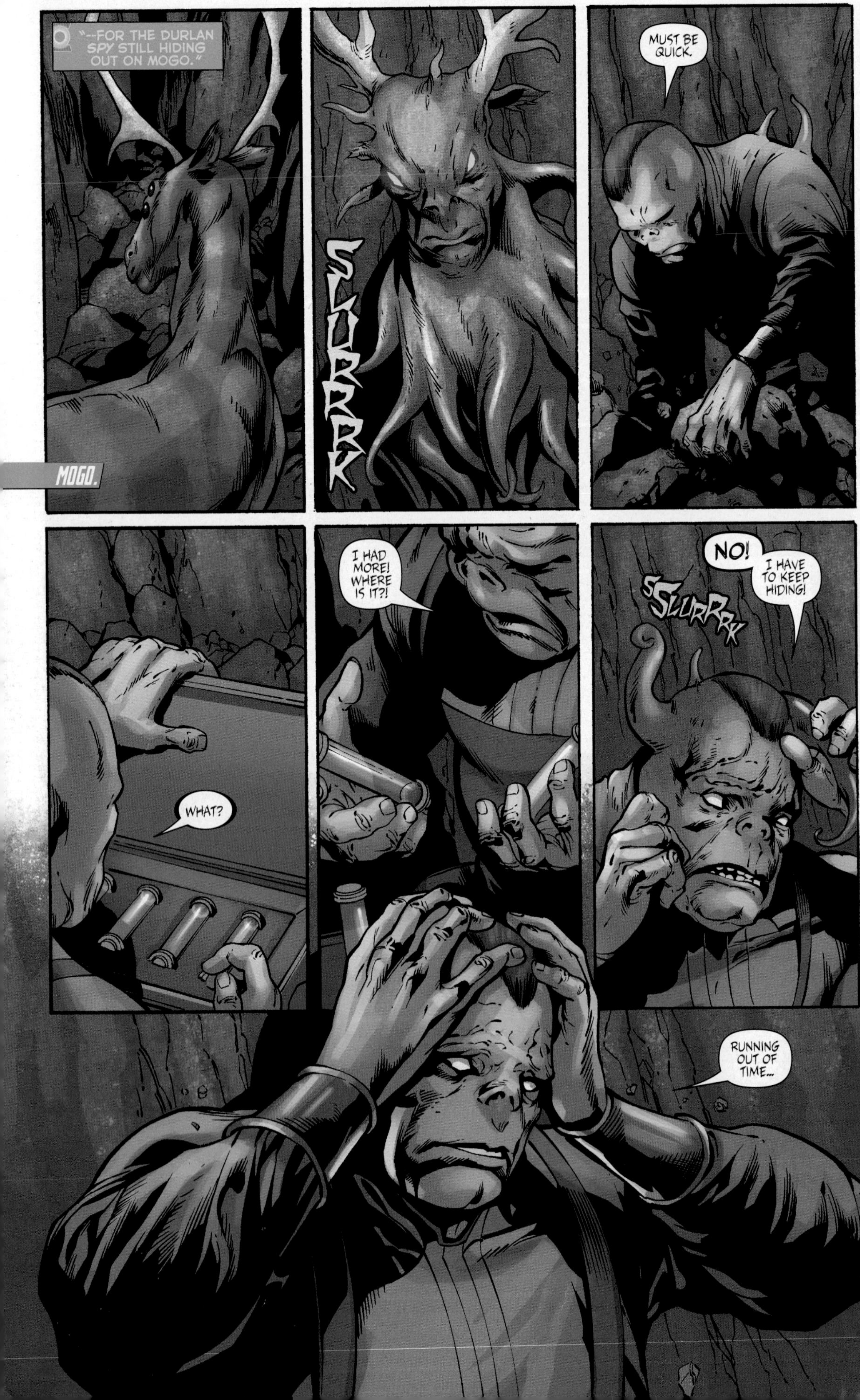
"--FOR THE DURLAN SPY STILL HIDING OUT ON MOGO."
MOGO.
SLURRRK
MUST BE QUICK.
WHAT?
I HAD MORE! WHERE IS IT?!
NO!
I HAVE TO KEEP HIDING!
SSLURRRK
RUNNING OUT OF TIME...

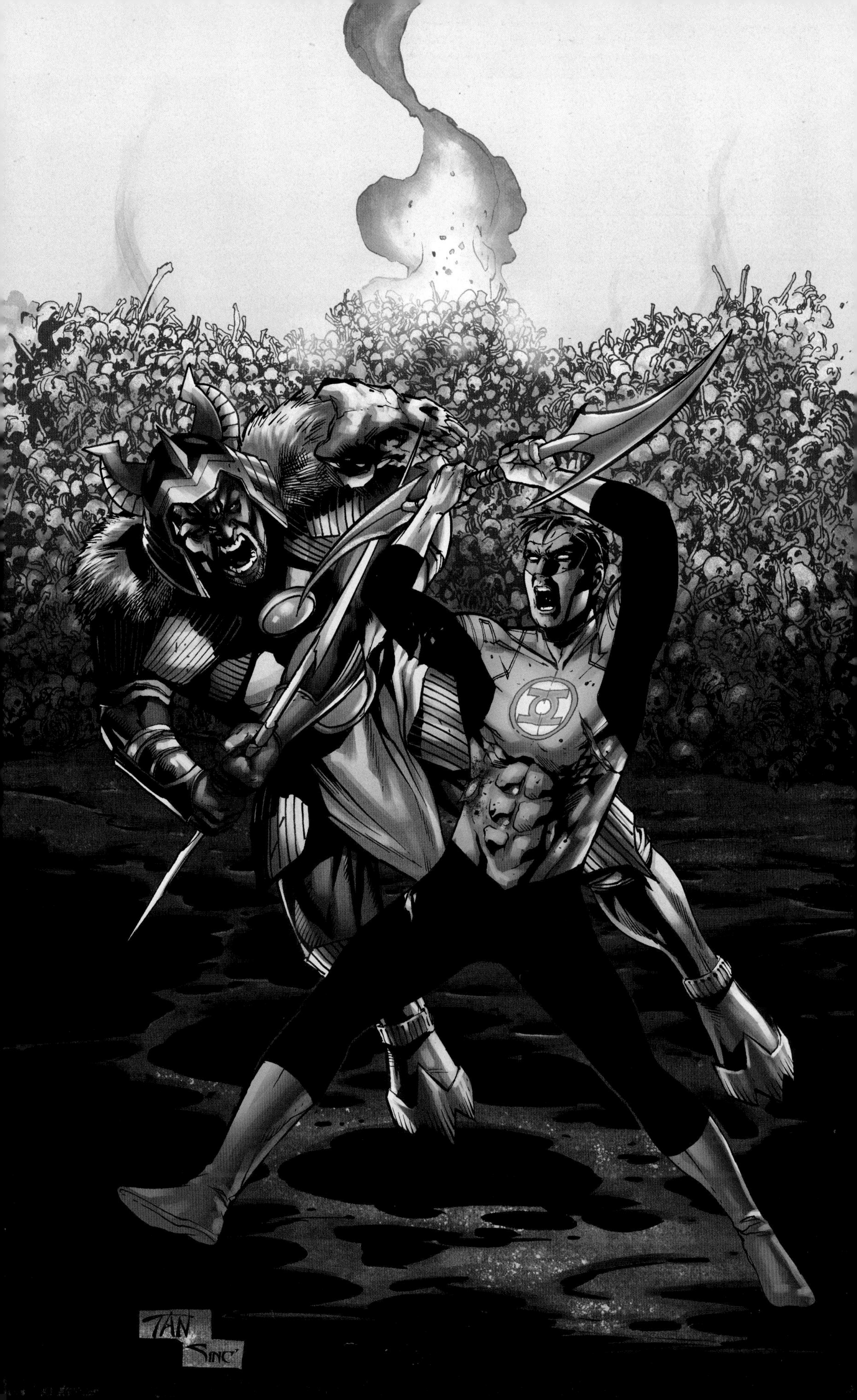
TAN
SINC'

DEATH AND LIFE

ROBERT VENDITTI writer **MARTIN COCCOLO** artist **TONY AVIÑA** & **ALEX SINCLAIR** colorists
cover art by **BILLY TAN** & **ALEX SINCLAIR** MAD variant cover by **RICHARD WILLIAMS**

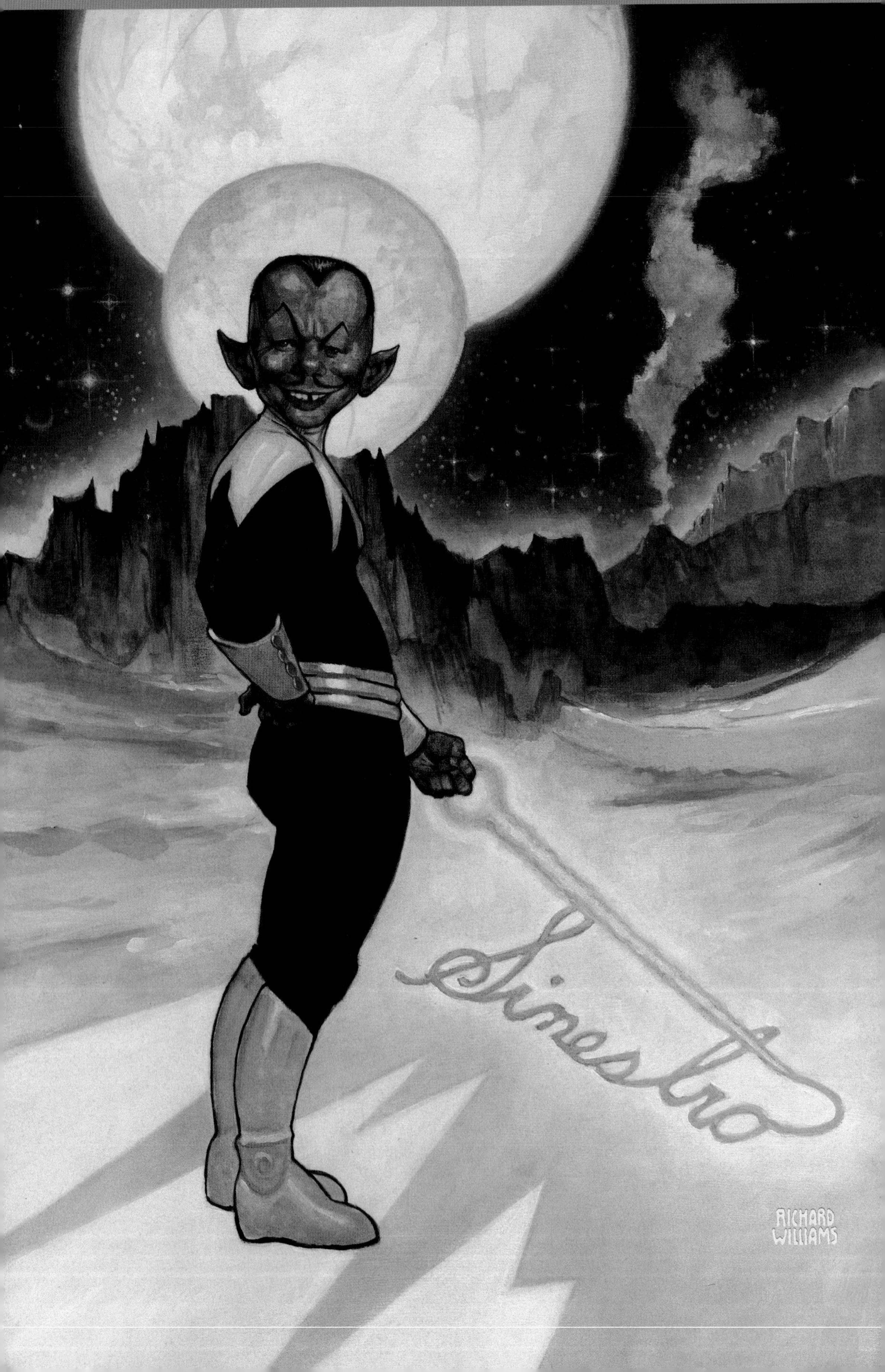
Sinestro
RICHARD WILLIAMS

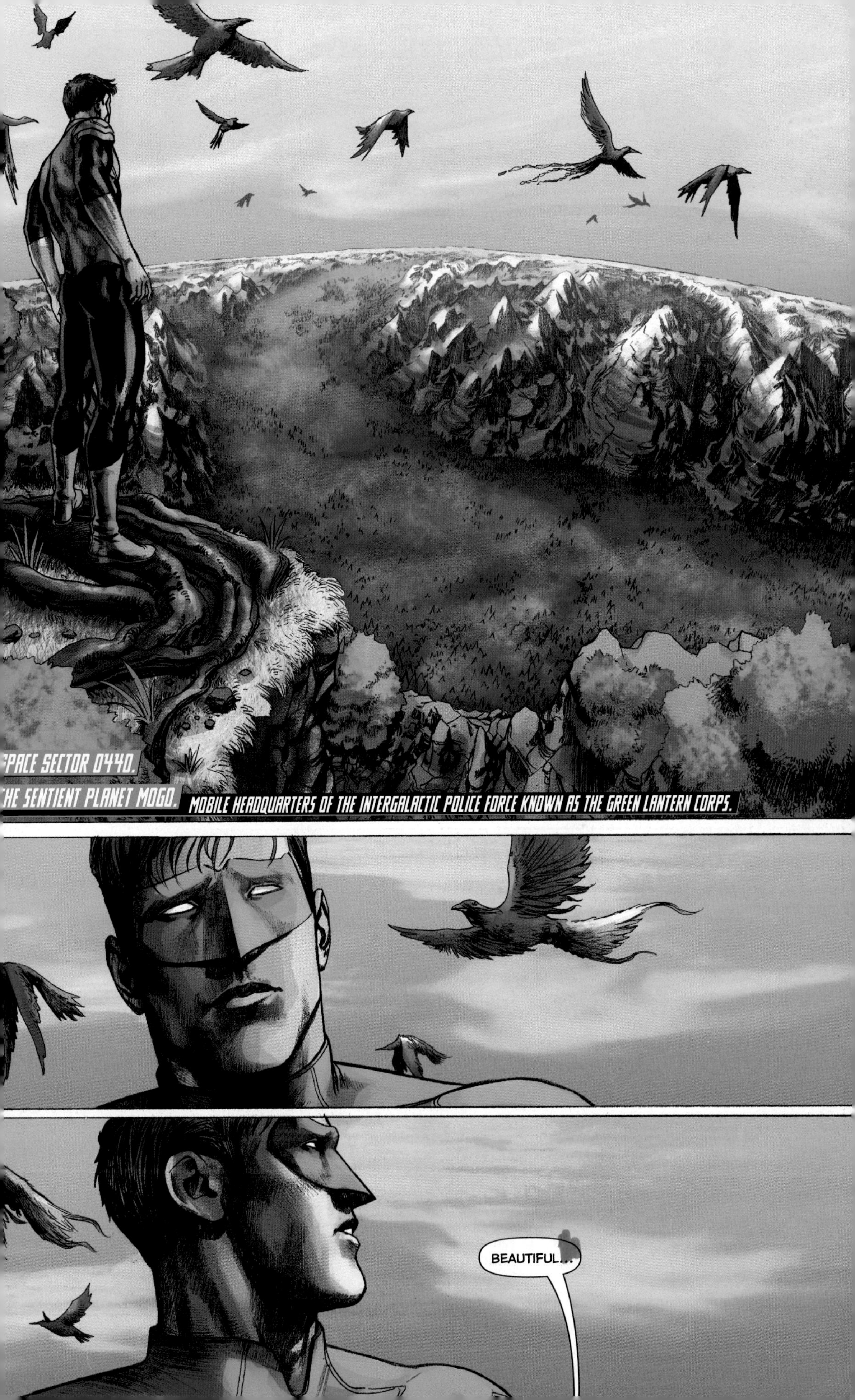
SPACE SECTOR 0440.
THE SENTIENT PLANET MOGO.
MOBILE HEADQUARTERS OF THE INTERGALACTIC POLICE FORCE KNOWN AS THE GREEN LANTERN CORPS.
BEAUTIFUL...

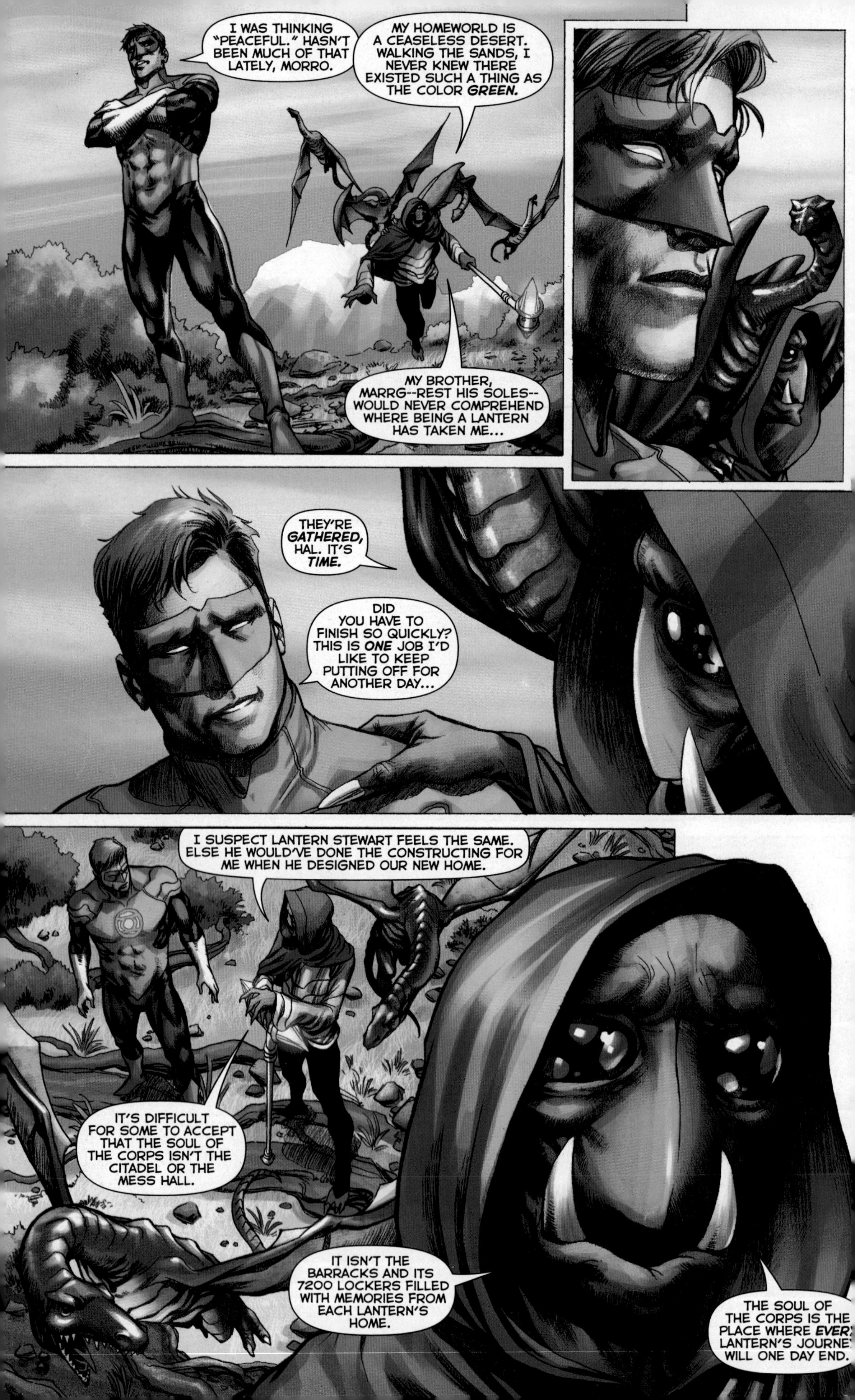
I WAS THINKING "PEACEFUL." HASN'T BEEN MUCH OF THAT LATELY, MORRO.
MY HOMEWORLD IS A CEASELESS DESERT. WALKING THE SANDS, I NEVER KNEW THERE EXISTED SUCH A THING AS THE COLOR *GREEN.*
MY BROTHER, MARRG--REST HIS SOLES--WOULD NEVER COMPREHEND WHERE BEING A LANTERN HAS TAKEN ME...
THEY'RE *GATHERED,* HAL. IT'S *TIME.*
DID YOU HAVE TO FINISH SO QUICKLY? THIS IS *ONE* JOB I'D LIKE TO KEEP PUTTING OFF FOR ANOTHER DAY...
I SUSPECT LANTERN STEWART FEELS THE SAME. ELSE HE WOULD'VE DONE THE CONSTRUCTING FOR ME WHEN HE DESIGNED OUR NEW HOME.
IT'S DIFFICULT FOR SOME TO ACCEPT THAT THE SOUL OF THE CORPS ISN'T THE CITADEL OR THE MESS HALL.
IT ISN'T THE BARRACKS AND ITS 7200 LOCKERS FILLED WITH MEMORIES FROM EACH LANTERN'S HOME.
THE SOUL OF THE CORPS IS THE PLACE WHERE *EVERY* LANTERN'S JOURNEY WILL ONE DAY END.

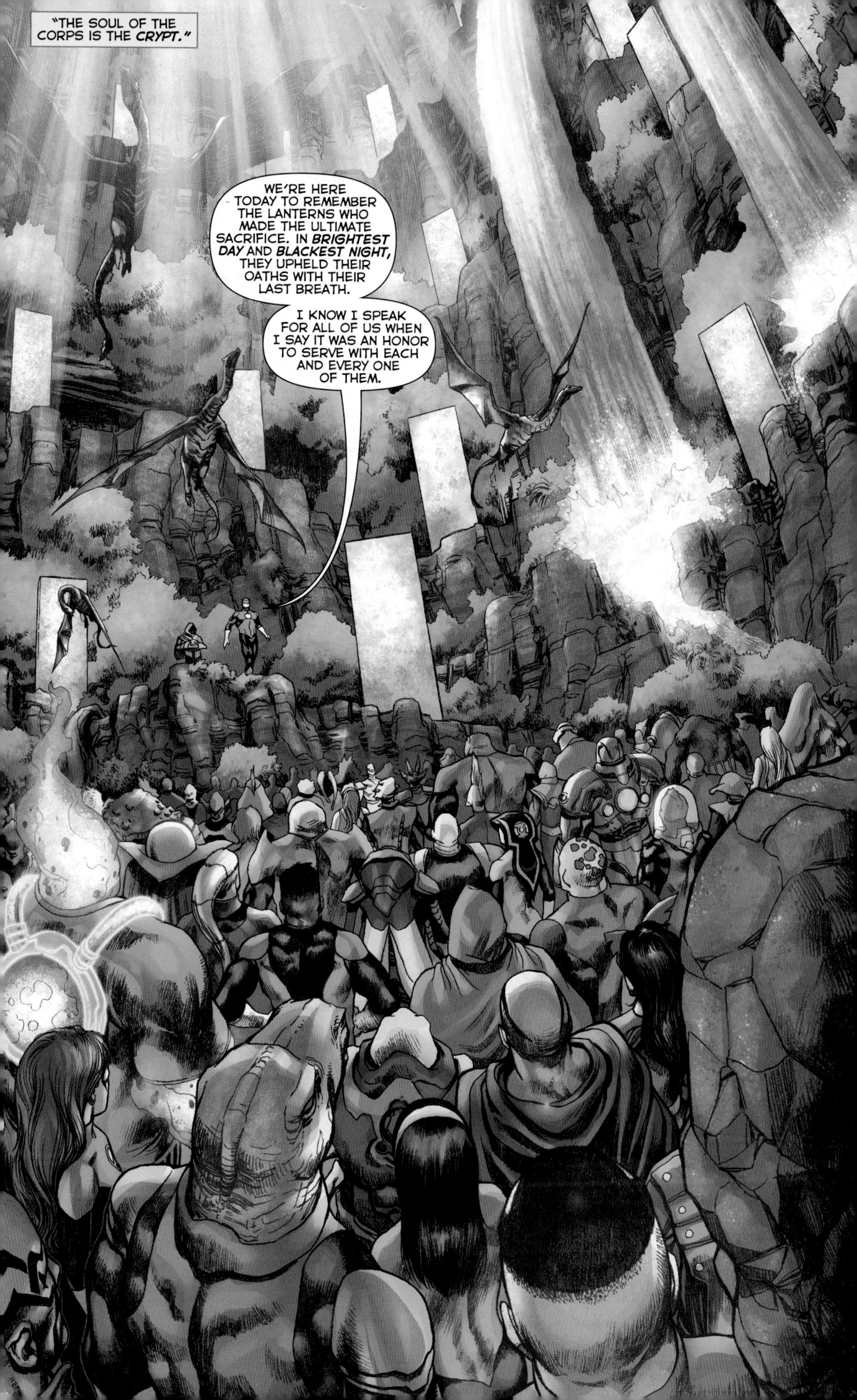
"THE SOUL OF THE CORPS IS THE *CRYPT.*"
WE'RE HERE TODAY TO REMEMBER THE LANTERNS WHO MADE THE ULTIMATE SACRIFICE. IN *BRIGHTEST DAY* AND *BLACKEST NIGHT,* THEY UPHELD THEIR OATHS WITH THEIR LAST BREATH.
I KNOW I SPEAK FOR ALL OF US WHEN I SAY IT WAS AN HONOR TO SERVE WITH EACH AND EVERY ONE OF THEM.

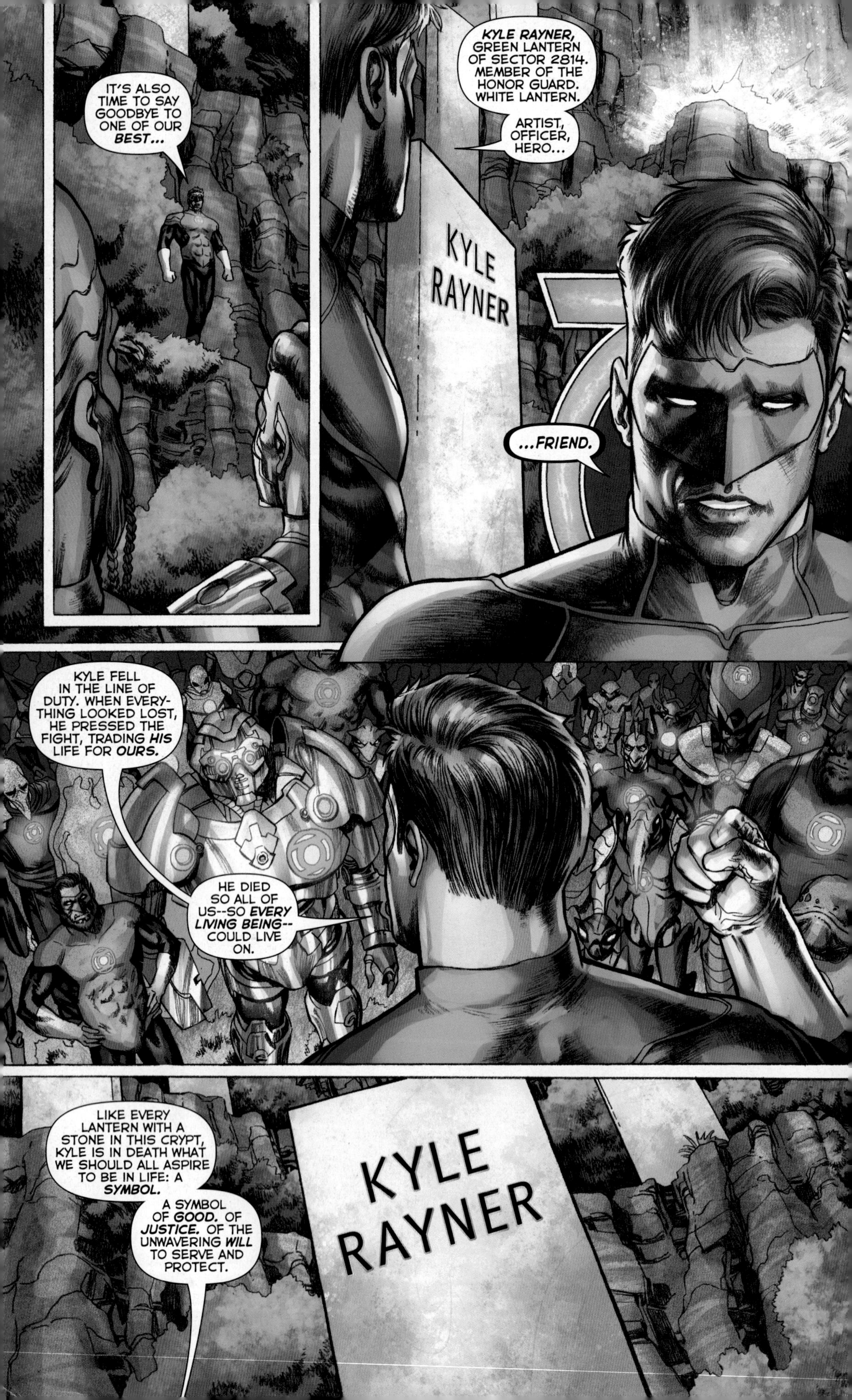

IT'S ALSO TIME TO SAY GOODBYE TO ONE OF OUR BEST...
KYLE RAYNER, GREEN LANTERN OF SECTOR 2814. MEMBER OF THE HONOR GUARD. WHITE LANTERN.
ARTIST, OFFICER, HERO...
KYLE RAYNER
...FRIEND.
KYLE FELL IN THE LINE OF DUTY. WHEN EVERY-THING LOOKED LOST, HE PRESSED THE FIGHT, TRADING HIS LIFE FOR OURS.
HE DIED SO ALL OF US--SO EVERY LIVING BEING--COULD LIVE ON.
LIKE EVERY LANTERN WITH A STONE IN THIS CRYPT, KYLE IS IN DEATH WHAT WE SHOULD ALL ASPIRE TO BE IN LIFE: A SYMBOL.
A SYMBOL OF GOOD. OF JUSTICE. OF THE UNWAVERING WILL TO SERVE AND PROTECT.
KYLE RAYNER

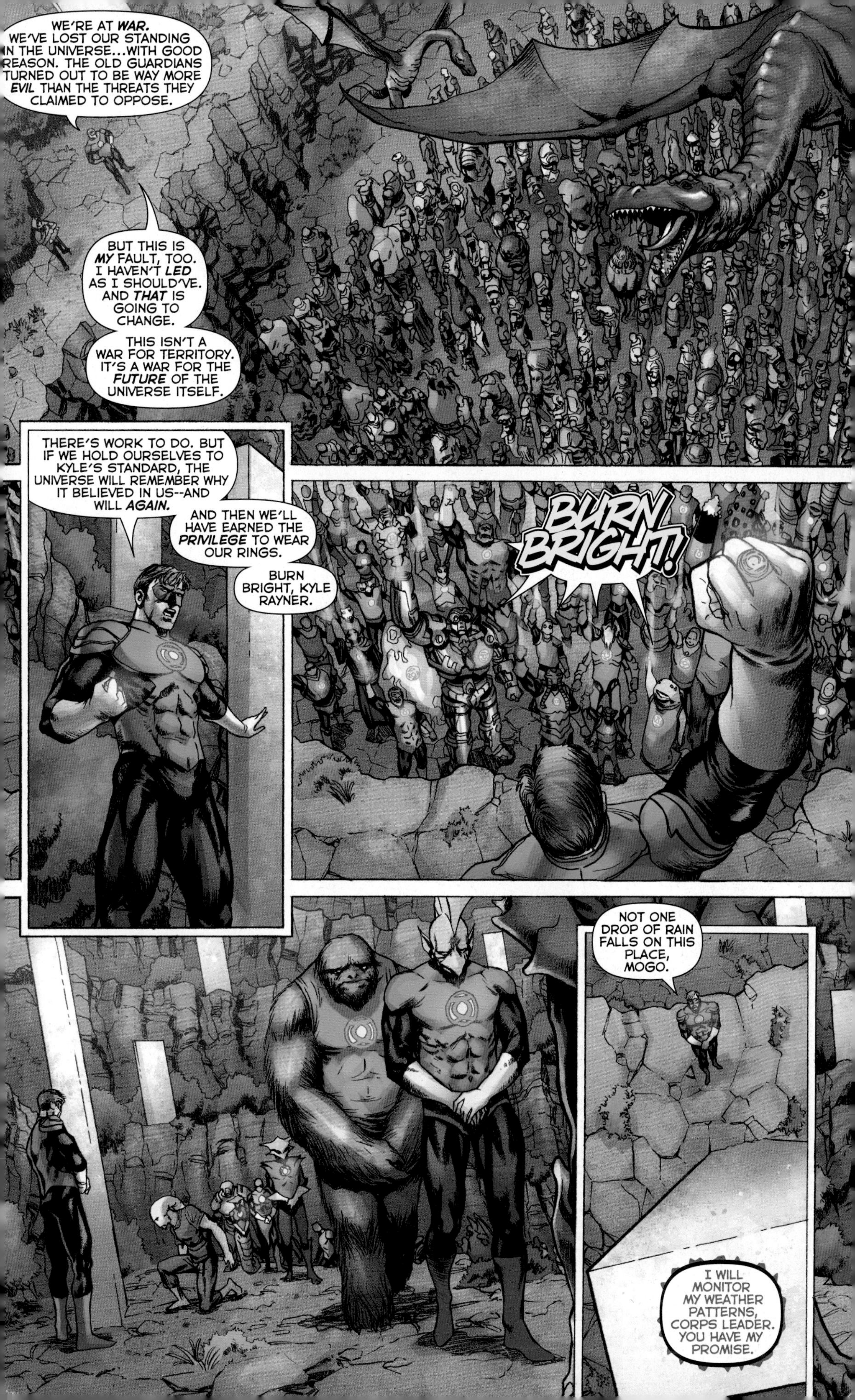
WE'RE AT WAR. WE'VE LOST OUR STANDING IN THE UNIVERSE...WITH GOOD REASON. THE OLD GUARDIANS TURNED OUT TO BE WAY MORE EVIL THAN THE THREATS THEY CLAIMED TO OPPOSE.
BUT THIS IS MY FAULT, TOO. I HAVEN'T LED AS I SHOULD'VE. AND THAT IS GOING TO CHANGE.
THIS ISN'T A WAR FOR TERRITORY. IT'S A WAR FOR THE FUTURE OF THE UNIVERSE ITSELF.
THERE'S WORK TO DO. BUT IF WE HOLD OURSELVES TO KYLE'S STANDARD, THE UNIVERSE WILL REMEMBER WHY IT BELIEVED IN US--AND WILL AGAIN.
AND THEN WE'LL HAVE EARNED THE PRIVILEGE TO WEAR OUR RINGS.
BURN BRIGHT, KYLE RAYNER.
BURN BRIGHT!
NOT ONE DROP OF RAIN FALLS ON THIS PLACE, MOGO.
I WILL MONITOR MY WEATHER PATTERNS, CORPS LEADER. YOU HAVE MY PROMISE.

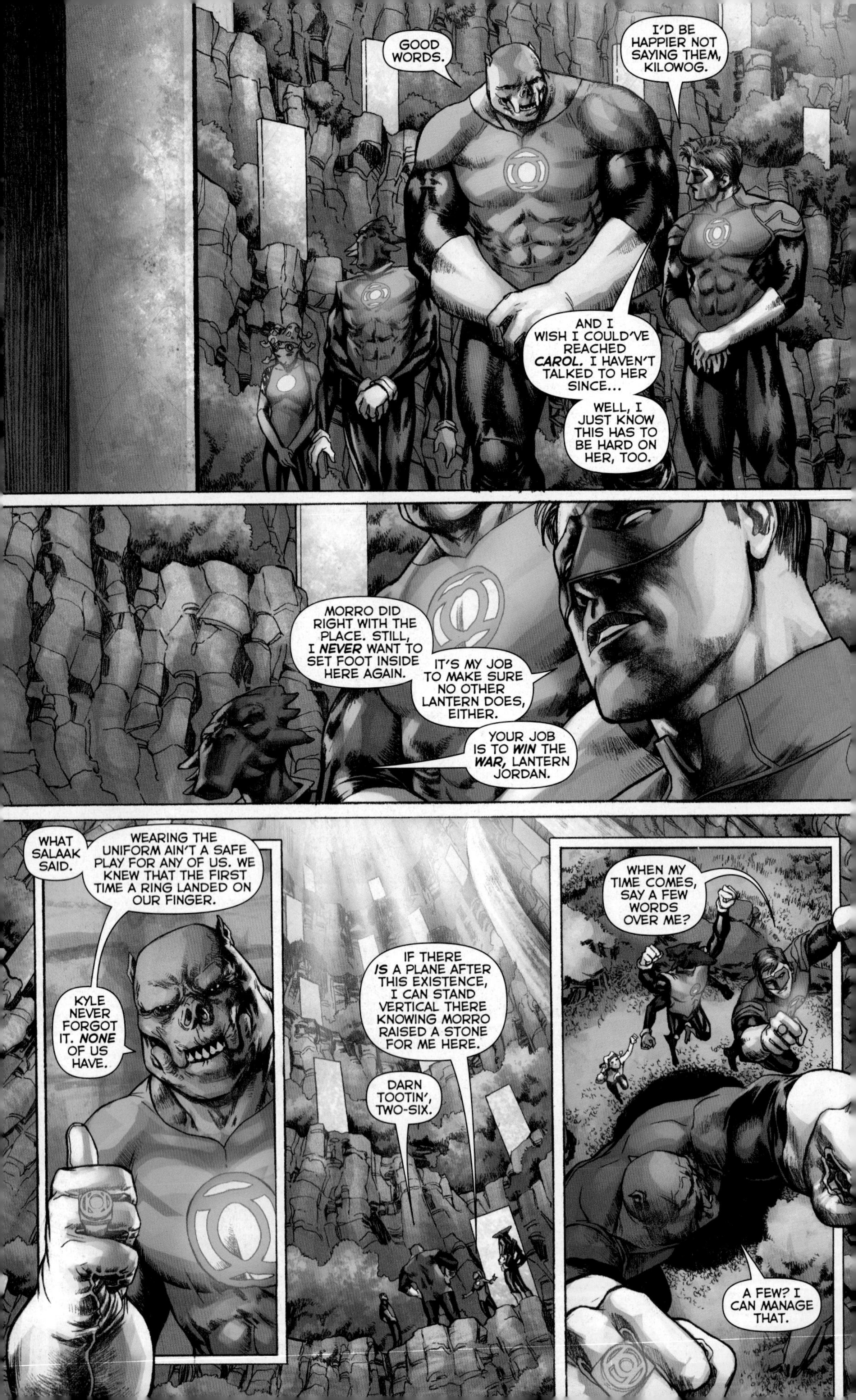
GOOD WORDS.
I'D BE HAPPIER NOT SAYING THEM, KILOWOG.
AND I WISH I COULD'VE REACHED **CAROL.** I HAVEN'T TALKED TO HER SINCE...
WELL, I JUST KNOW THIS HAS TO BE HARD ON HER, TOO.
MORRO DID RIGHT WITH THE PLACE. STILL, I **NEVER** WANT TO SET FOOT INSIDE HERE AGAIN.
IT'S MY JOB TO MAKE SURE NO OTHER LANTERN DOES, EITHER.
YOUR JOB IS TO **WIN** THE **WAR,** LANTERN JORDAN.
WHAT SALAAK SAID.
WEARING THE UNIFORM AIN'T A SAFE PLAY FOR ANY OF US. WE KNEW THAT THE FIRST TIME A RING LANDED ON OUR FINGER.
KYLE NEVER FORGOT IT. **NONE** OF US HAVE.
IF THERE **IS** A PLANE AFTER THIS EXISTENCE, I CAN STAND VERTICAL THERE KNOWING MORRO RAISED A STONE FOR ME HERE.
DARN TOOTIN', TWO-SIX.
WHEN MY TIME COMES, SAY A FEW WORDS OVER ME?
A FEW? I CAN MANAGE THAT.

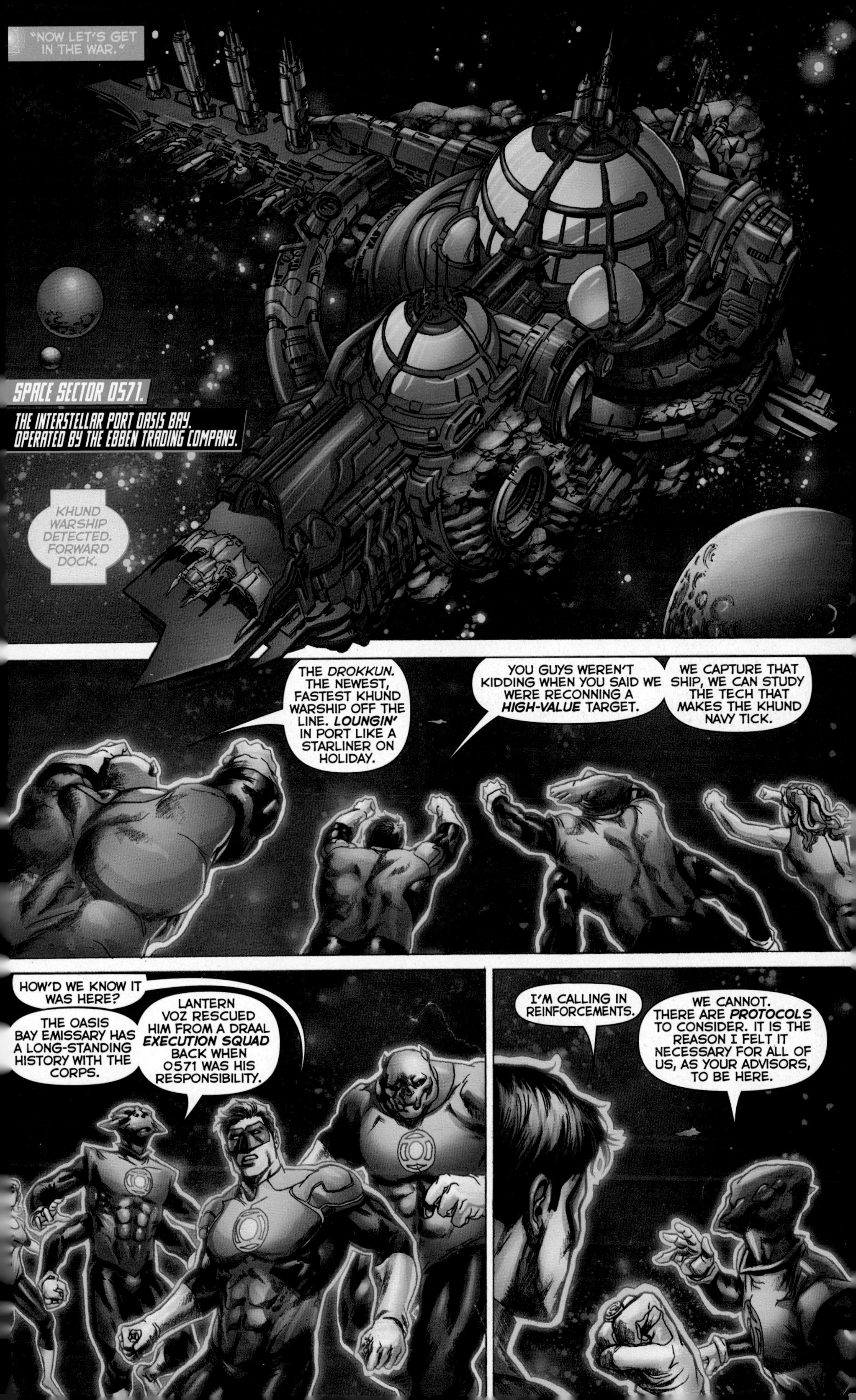

"NOW LET'S GET IN THE WAR."
SPACE SECTOR 0571.
THE INTERSTELLAR PORT OASIS BAY. OPERATED BY THE EBBEN TRADING COMPANY.
KHUND WARSHIP DETECTED. FORWARD DOCK.
THE DROKKUN. THE NEWEST, FASTEST KHUND WARSHIP OFF THE LINE. LOUNGIN' IN PORT LIKE A STARLINER ON HOLIDAY.
YOU GUYS WEREN'T KIDDING WHEN YOU SAID WE WERE RECONNING A HIGH-VALUE TARGET.
WE CAPTURE THAT SHIP, WE CAN STUDY THE TECH THAT MAKES THE KHUND NAVY TICK.
HOW'D WE KNOW IT WAS HERE?
THE OASIS BAY EMISSARY HAS A LONG-STANDING HISTORY WITH THE CORPS.
LANTERN VOZ RESCUED HIM FROM A DRAAL EXECUTION SQUAD BACK WHEN 0571 WAS HIS RESPONSIBILITY.
I'M CALLING IN REINFORCEMENTS.
WE CANNOT. THERE ARE PROTOCOLS TO CONSIDER. IT IS THE REASON I FELT IT NECESSARY FOR ALL OF US, AS YOUR ADVISORS, TO BE HERE.

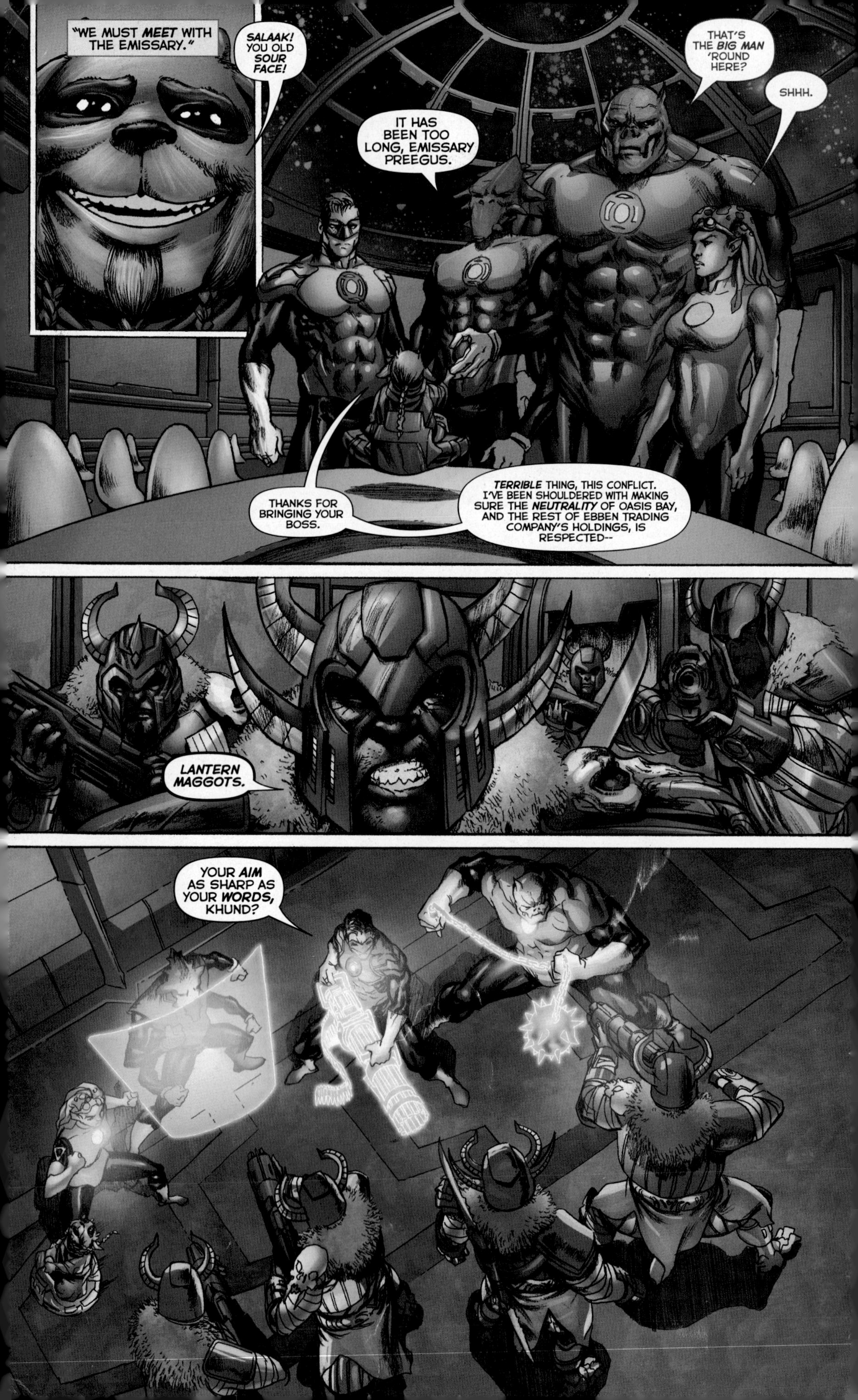
"WE MUST *MEET* WITH THE EMISSARY."
SALAAK! YOU OLD *SOUR FACE!*
IT HAS BEEN TOO LONG, EMISSARY PREEGUS.
THAT'S THE *BIG MAN* 'ROUND HERE?
SHHH.
THANKS FOR BRINGING YOUR BOSS.
TERRIBLE THING, THIS CONFLICT. I'VE BEEN SHOULDERED WITH MAKING SURE THE *NEUTRALITY* OF OASIS BAY, AND THE REST OF EBBEN TRADING COMPANY'S HOLDINGS, IS RESPECTED--
LANTERN MAGGOTS.
YOUR *AIM* AS SHARP AS YOUR *WORDS,* KHUND?

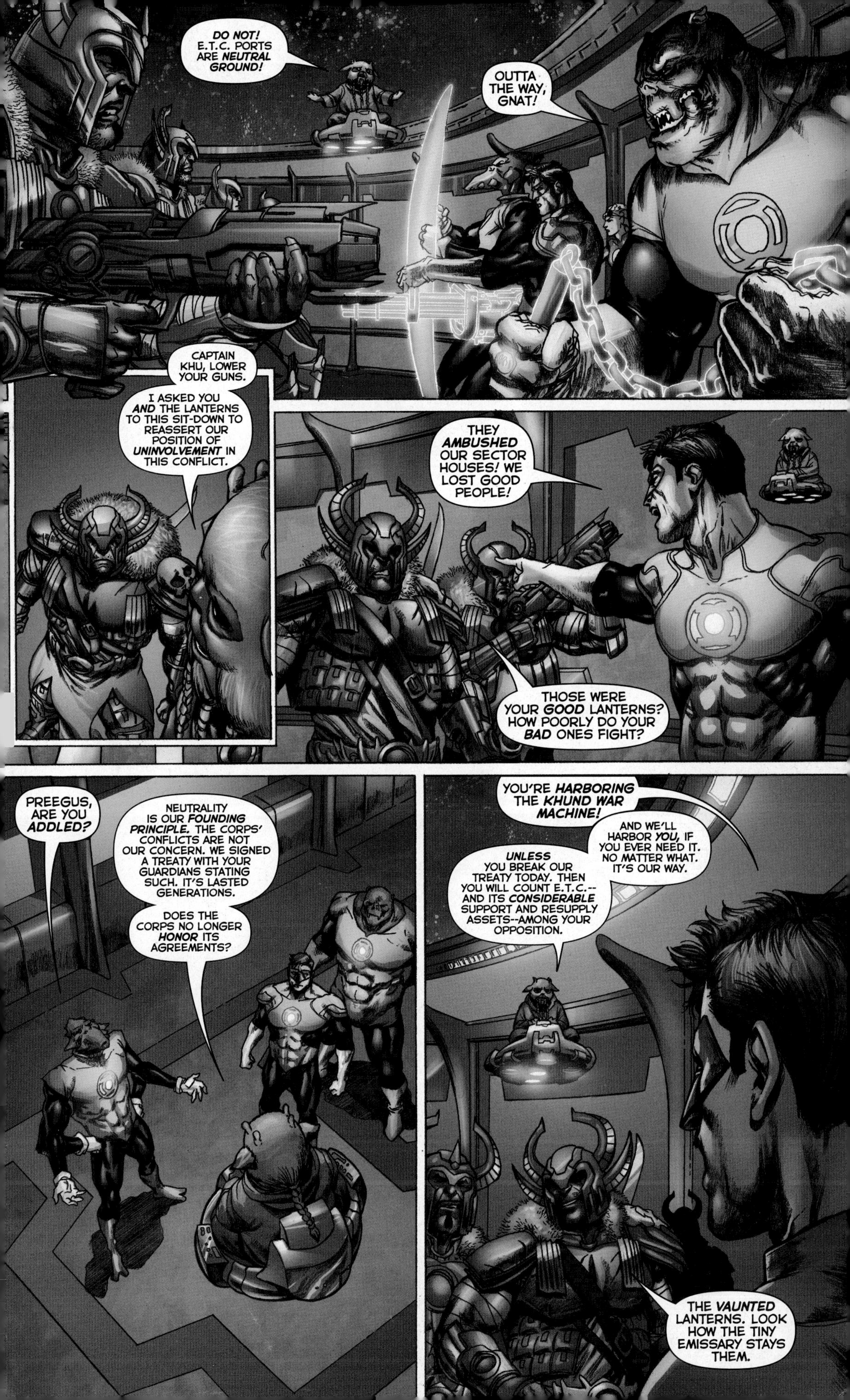
DO NOT! E.T.C. PORTS ARE NEUTRAL GROUND!
OUTTA THE WAY, GNAT!
CAPTAIN KHU, LOWER YOUR GUNS.
I ASKED YOU AND THE LANTERNS TO THIS SIT-DOWN TO REASSERT OUR POSITION OF UNINVOLVEMENT IN THIS CONFLICT.
THEY AMBUSHED OUR SECTOR HOUSES! WE LOST GOOD PEOPLE!
THOSE WERE YOUR GOOD LANTERNS? HOW POORLY DO YOUR BAD ONES FIGHT?
PREEGUS, ARE YOU ADDLED?
NEUTRALITY IS OUR FOUNDING PRINCIPLE. THE CORPS' CONFLICTS ARE NOT OUR CONCERN. WE SIGNED A TREATY WITH YOUR GUARDIANS STATING SUCH. IT'S LASTED GENERATIONS.
DOES THE CORPS NO LONGER HONOR ITS AGREEMENTS?
YOU'RE HARBORING THE KHUND WAR MACHINE!
AND WE'LL HARBOR YOU, IF YOU EVER NEED IT. NO MATTER WHAT. IT'S OUR WAY.
UNLESS YOU BREAK OUR TREATY TODAY. THEN YOU WILL COUNT E.T.C.-- AND ITS CONSIDERABLE SUPPORT AND RESUPPLY ASSETS--AMONG YOUR OPPOSITION.
THE VAUNTED LANTERNS. LOOK HOW THE TINY EMISSARY STAYS THEM.

THE SAME HOLDS TRUE FOR YOU, CAPTAIN. IF YOU *INSIST* ON SETTLING YOUR DISPUTE IN *OUR* PORT, THEN YOU'LL DO SO ACCORDING TO OUR LAWS.

A REPRESENTATIVE FROM EACH GROUP WILL *ARGUE* FOR THE OUTCOME.

FINE BY ME.

LANTERN JORDAN, A WORD--

I'M NO LAWYER, BUT I'LL MATCH WITS WITH *NECKLESS* OVER THERE. POINT ME TOWARD THE PANEL OF JUDGES.

JUDICIARIES RARELY REMAIN AS NEUTRAL AS THEY PROMISE...

YOU'LL *FIGHT* FOR IT.

YOU WIN, THE *DROKKUN* IS YOURS TO DO WITH AS YOU WISH. THE KHUND WIN, THEY GET THE LANTERNS, WITH WHICH THEY CAN DO LIKEWISE.

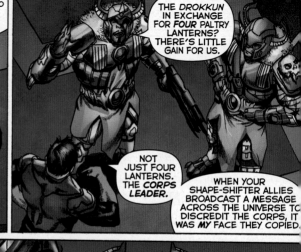

THE *DROKKUN* IN EXCHANGE FOR *FOUR* PALTRY LANTERNS? THERE'S LITTLE GAIN FOR US.

NOT JUST FOUR LANTERNS. THE *CORPS LEADER.*

WHEN YOUR SHAPE-SHIFTER ALLIES BROADCAST A MESSAGE ACROSS THE UNIVERSE TO DISCREDIT THE CORPS, IT WAS *MY* FACE THEY COPIED.

WHEN A CITIZEN SEES A LANTERN AND RUNS THE OTHER WAY, IT'S BECAUSE OF WHAT THEY'VE BEEN MADE TO BELIEVE ABOUT *ME.*

I'LL FIGHT UNTIL MY *LAST DAY* TO WIN BACK THE CORPS' GOOD NAME. BEAT ME, AND THE CORPS WILL BE HUMILIATED. THAT'S WORTH A *THOUSAND* SHIPS.

YOU SEE, LIEUTENANT? COMBAT *ALWAYS* BRINGS REWARD.

CAPTAIN KHU WAS FIRST IN PORT.

ACCORDING TO STATUTE, THE CHOICE OF WEAPON IS HIS.

CEREMONIAL KHUND THROAT KNIFE.

VERY WELL.

LANTERN JORDAN, YOU'RE FORBIDDEN FROM USING YOUR RING. ARGUMENT BEGINS IN TWO HOURS. UNTIL THEN--

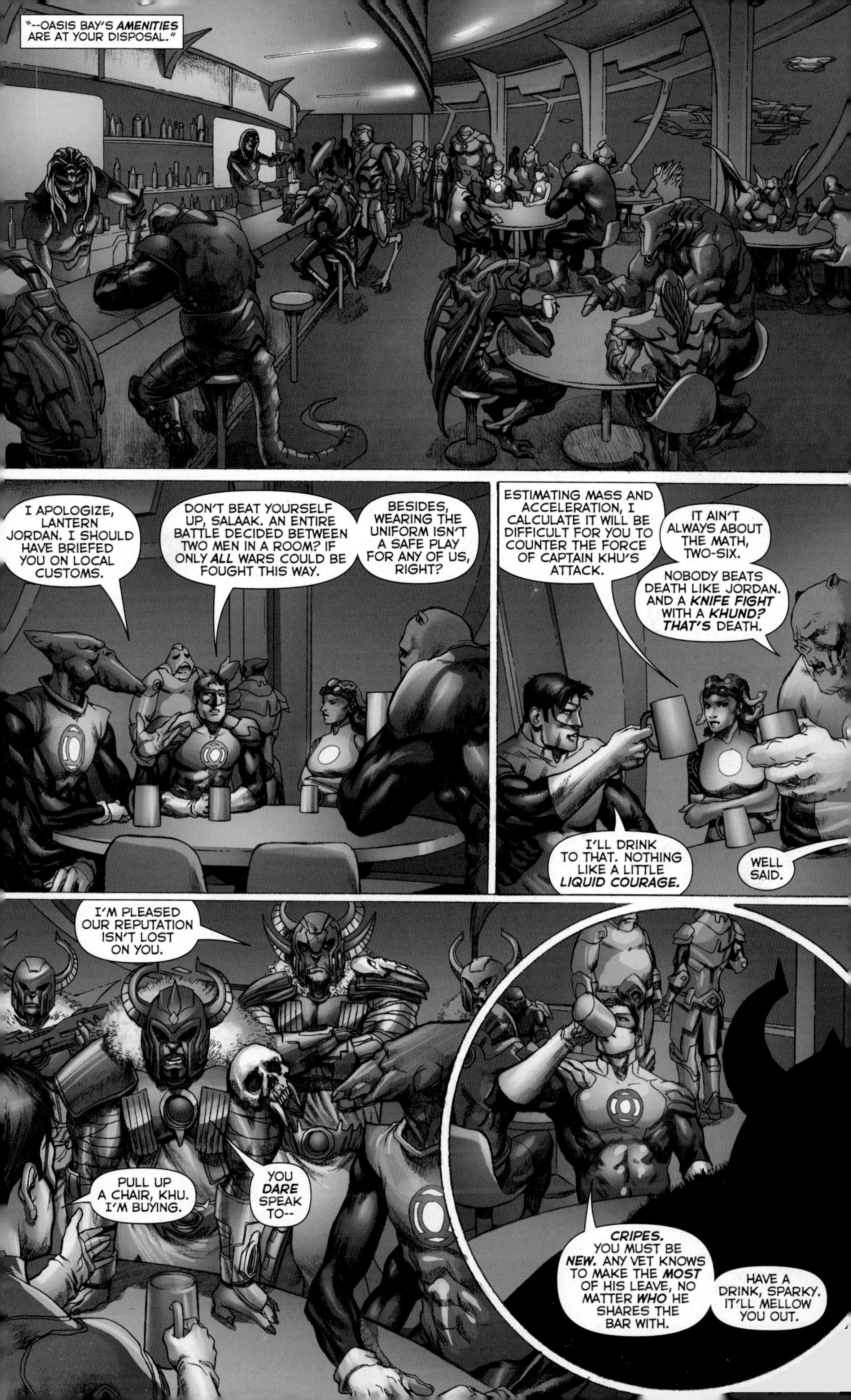
"--OASIS BAY'S AMENITIES ARE AT YOUR DISPOSAL."
I APOLOGIZE, LANTERN JORDAN. I SHOULD HAVE BRIEFED YOU ON LOCAL CUSTOMS.
DON'T BEAT YOURSELF UP, SALAAK. AN ENTIRE BATTLE DECIDED BETWEEN TWO MEN IN A ROOM? IF ONLY ALL WARS COULD BE FOUGHT THIS WAY.
BESIDES, WEARING THE UNIFORM ISN'T A SAFE PLAY FOR ANY OF US, RIGHT?
ESTIMATING MASS AND ACCELERATION, I CALCULATE IT WILL BE DIFFICULT FOR YOU TO COUNTER THE FORCE OF CAPTAIN KHU'S ATTACK.
IT AIN'T ALWAYS ABOUT THE MATH, TWO-SIX.
NOBODY BEATS DEATH LIKE JORDAN. AND A KNIFE FIGHT WITH A KHUND? THAT'S DEATH.
I'LL DRINK TO THAT. NOTHING LIKE A LITTLE LIQUID COURAGE.
WELL SAID.
I'M PLEASED OUR REPUTATION ISN'T LOST ON YOU.
PULL UP A CHAIR, KHU. I'M BUYING.
YOU DARE SPEAK TO--
CRIPES. YOU MUST BE NEW. ANY VET KNOWS TO MAKE THE MOST OF HIS LEAVE, NO MATTER WHO HE SHARES THE BAR WITH.
HAVE A DRINK, SPARKY. IT'LL MELLOW YOU OUT.

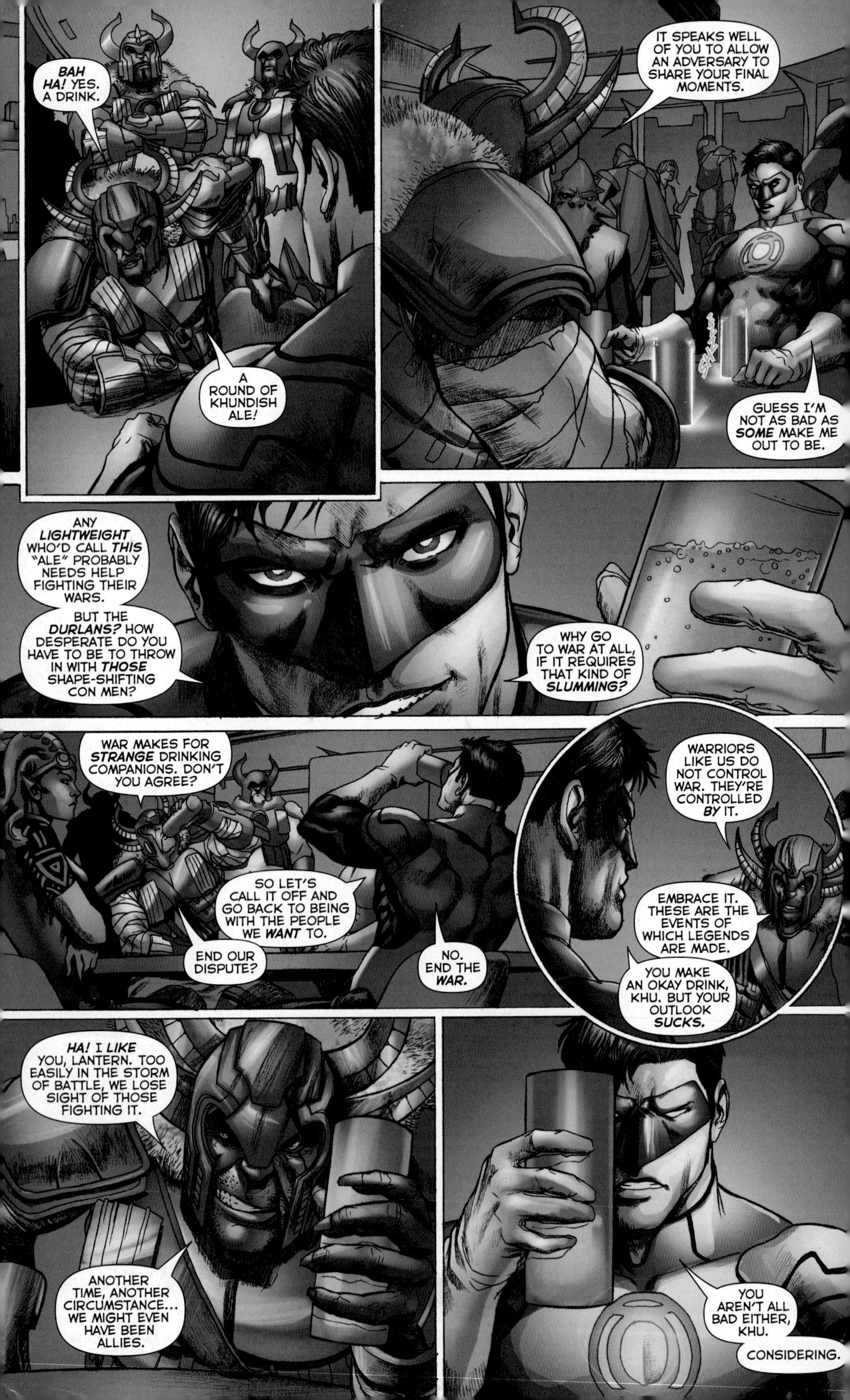
BAH HA! YES. A DRINK.
A ROUND OF KHUNDISH ALE!
IT SPEAKS WELL OF YOU TO ALLOW AN ADVERSARY TO SHARE YOUR FINAL MOMENTS.
GUESS I'M NOT AS BAD AS SOME MAKE ME OUT TO BE.
ANY LIGHTWEIGHT WHO'D CALL THIS "ALE" PROBABLY NEEDS HELP FIGHTING THEIR WARS.
BUT THE DURLANS? HOW DESPERATE DO YOU HAVE TO BE TO THROW IN WITH THOSE SHAPE-SHIFTING CON MEN?
WHY GO TO WAR AT ALL, IF IT REQUIRES THAT KIND OF SLUMMING?
WAR MAKES FOR STRANGE DRINKING COMPANIONS. DON'T YOU AGREE?
SO LET'S CALL IT OFF AND GO BACK TO BEING WITH THE PEOPLE WE WANT TO.
END OUR DISPUTE?
NO. END THE WAR.
WARRIORS LIKE US DO NOT CONTROL WAR. THEY'RE CONTROLLED BY IT.
EMBRACE IT. THESE ARE THE EVENTS OF WHICH LEGENDS ARE MADE.
YOU MAKE AN OKAY DRINK, KHU. BUT YOUR OUTLOOK SUCKS.
HA! I LIKE YOU, LANTERN. TOO EASILY IN THE STORM OF BATTLE, WE LOSE SIGHT OF THOSE FIGHTING IT.
ANOTHER TIME, ANOTHER CIRCUMSTANCE... WE MIGHT EVEN HAVE BEEN ALLIES.
YOU AREN'T ALL BAD EITHER, KHU.
CONSIDERING.

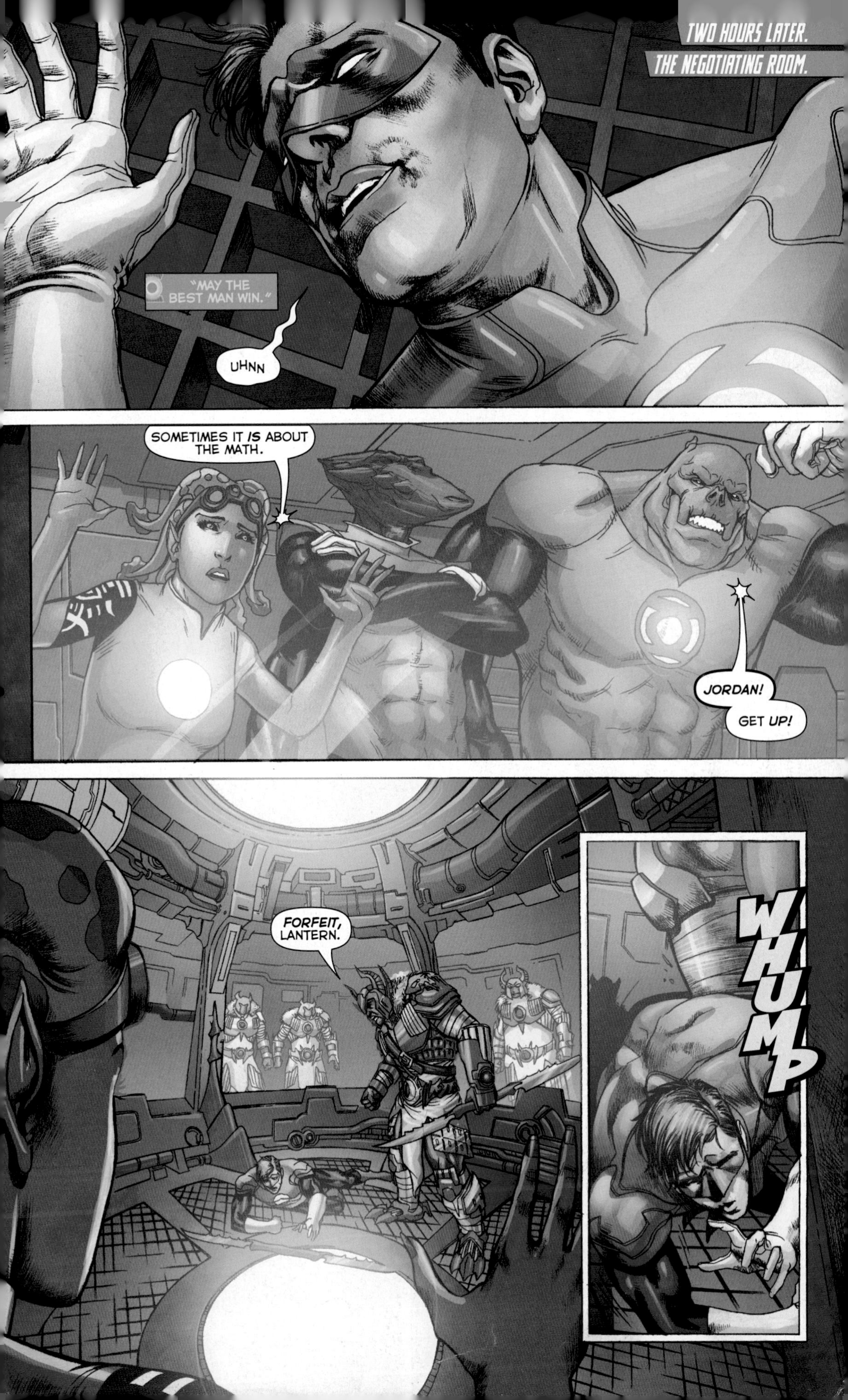

TWO HOURS LATER.
THE NEGOTIATING ROOM.
"MAY THE BEST MAN WIN."
UHNN
SOMETIMES IT IS ABOUT THE MATH.
JORDAN!
GET UP!
FORFEIT, LANTERN.
WHUMP

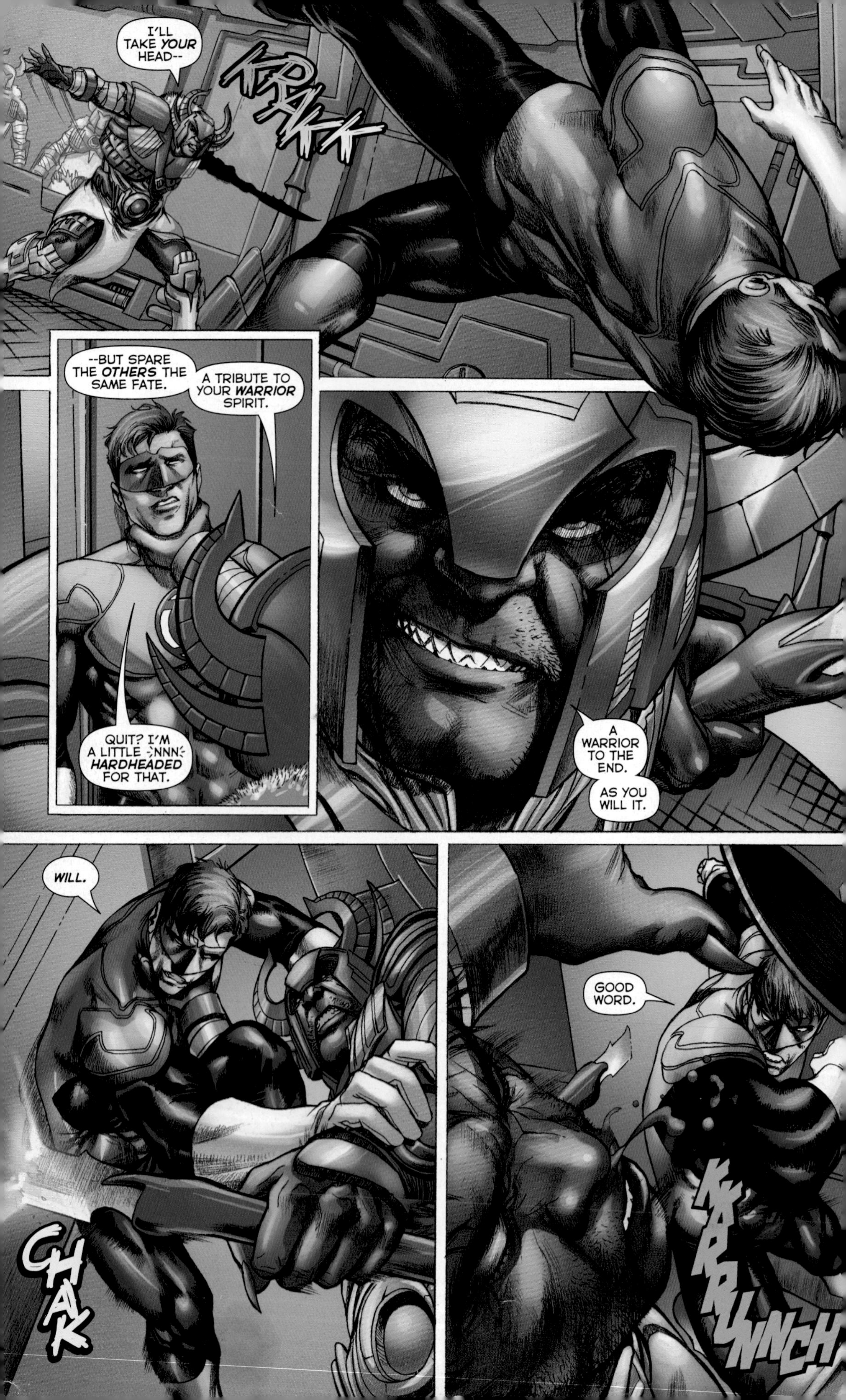
I'LL TAKE YOUR HEAD--
KRAKK
--BUT SPARE THE OTHERS THE SAME FATE.
A TRIBUTE TO YOUR WARRIOR SPIRIT.
QUIT? I'M A LITTLE -NNN- HARDHEADED FOR THAT.
A WARRIOR TO THE END.
AS YOU WILL IT.
WILL.
CHAK
GOOD WORD.
KKRUNNCH

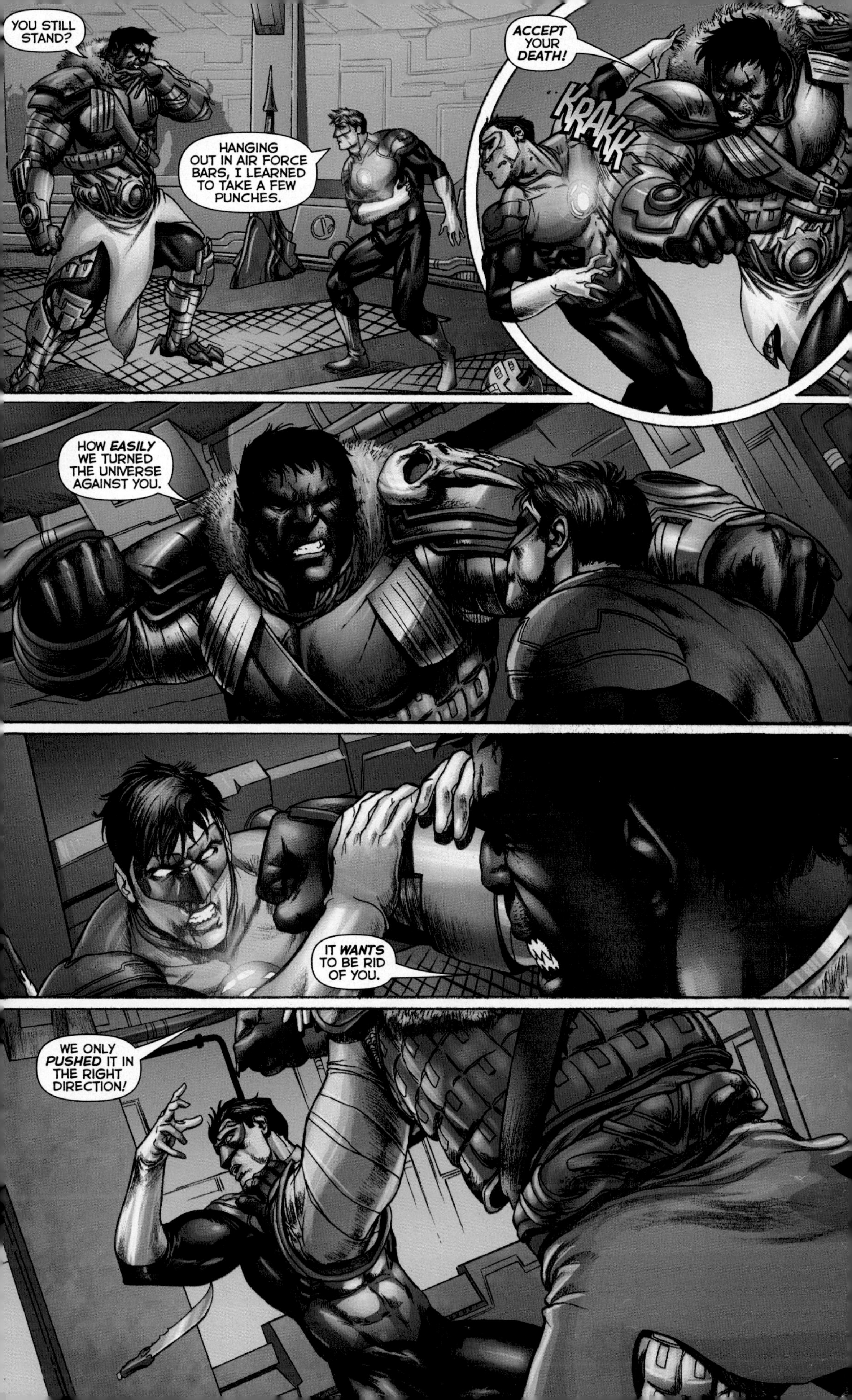
YOU STILL STAND?
HANGING OUT IN AIR FORCE BARS, I LEARNED TO TAKE A FEW PUNCHES.
ACCEPT YOUR DEATH!
KRAKK
HOW EASILY WE TURNED THE UNIVERSE AGAINST YOU.
IT WANTS TO BE RID OF YOU.
WE ONLY PUSHED IT IN THE RIGHT DIRECTION!

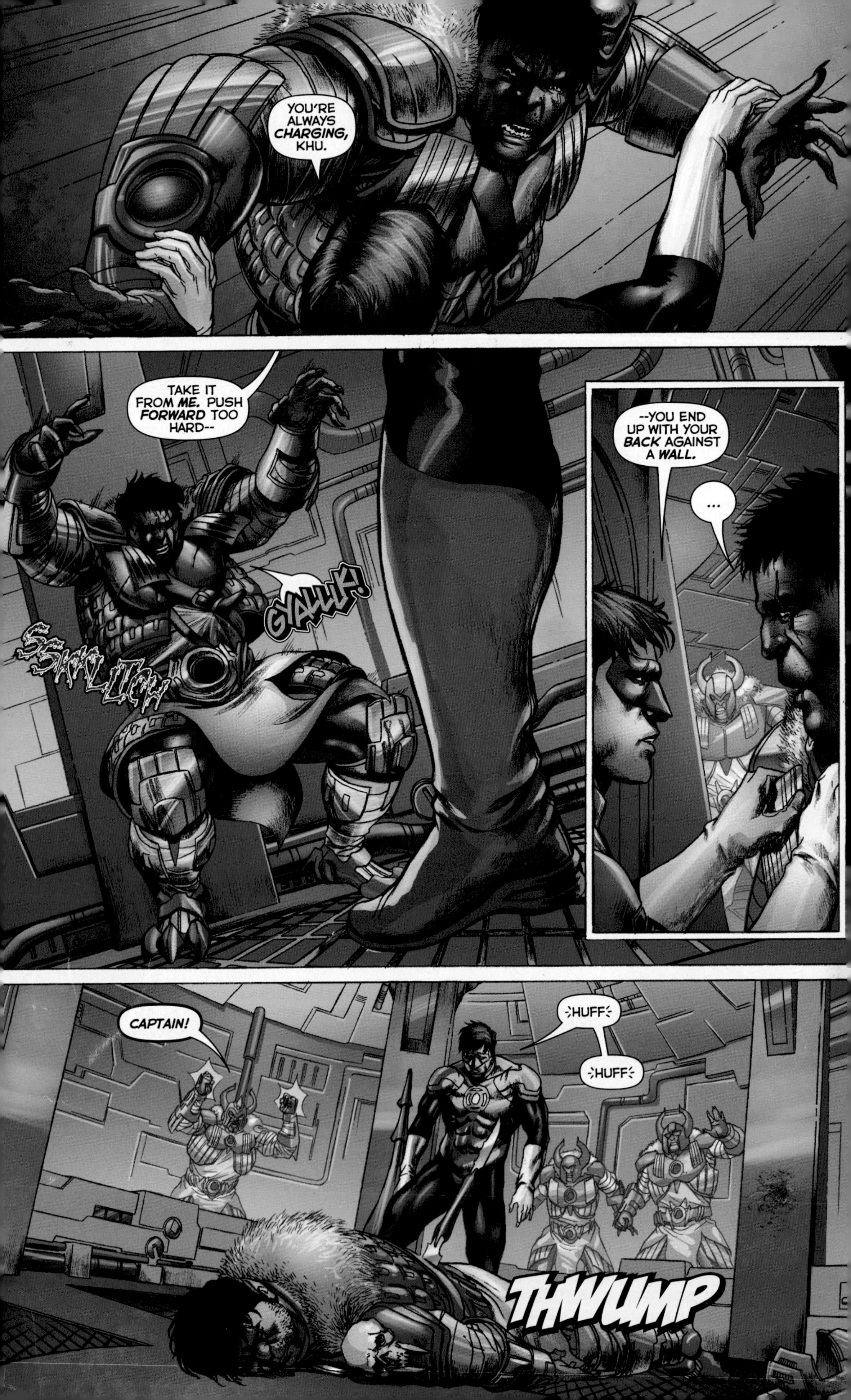
YOU'RE ALWAYS CHARGING, KHU.
TAKE IT FROM ME. PUSH FORWARD TOO HARD--
GYALLK!
SSKWLTCH
--YOU END UP WITH YOUR BACK AGAINST A WALL.
...
CAPTAIN!
HUFF
HUFF
THWUMP

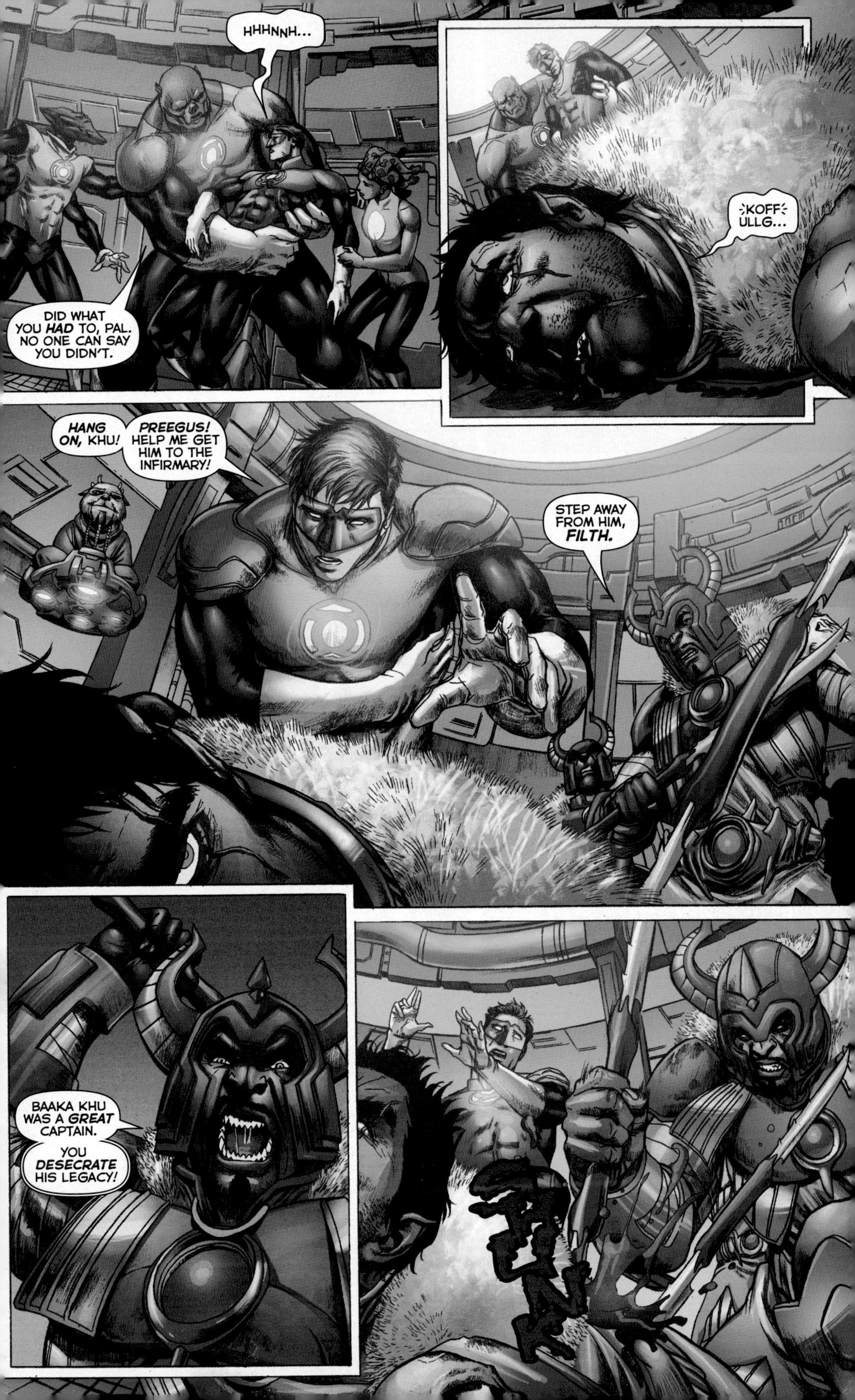
HHHNNH...
DID WHAT YOU HAD TO, PAL. NO ONE CAN SAY YOU DIDN'T.
KOFF ULLG...
HANG ON, KHU!
PREEGUS! HELP ME GET HIM TO THE INFIRMARY!
STEP AWAY FROM HIM, FILTH.
BAAKA KHU WAS A GREAT CAPTAIN.
YOU DESECRATE HIS LEGACY!

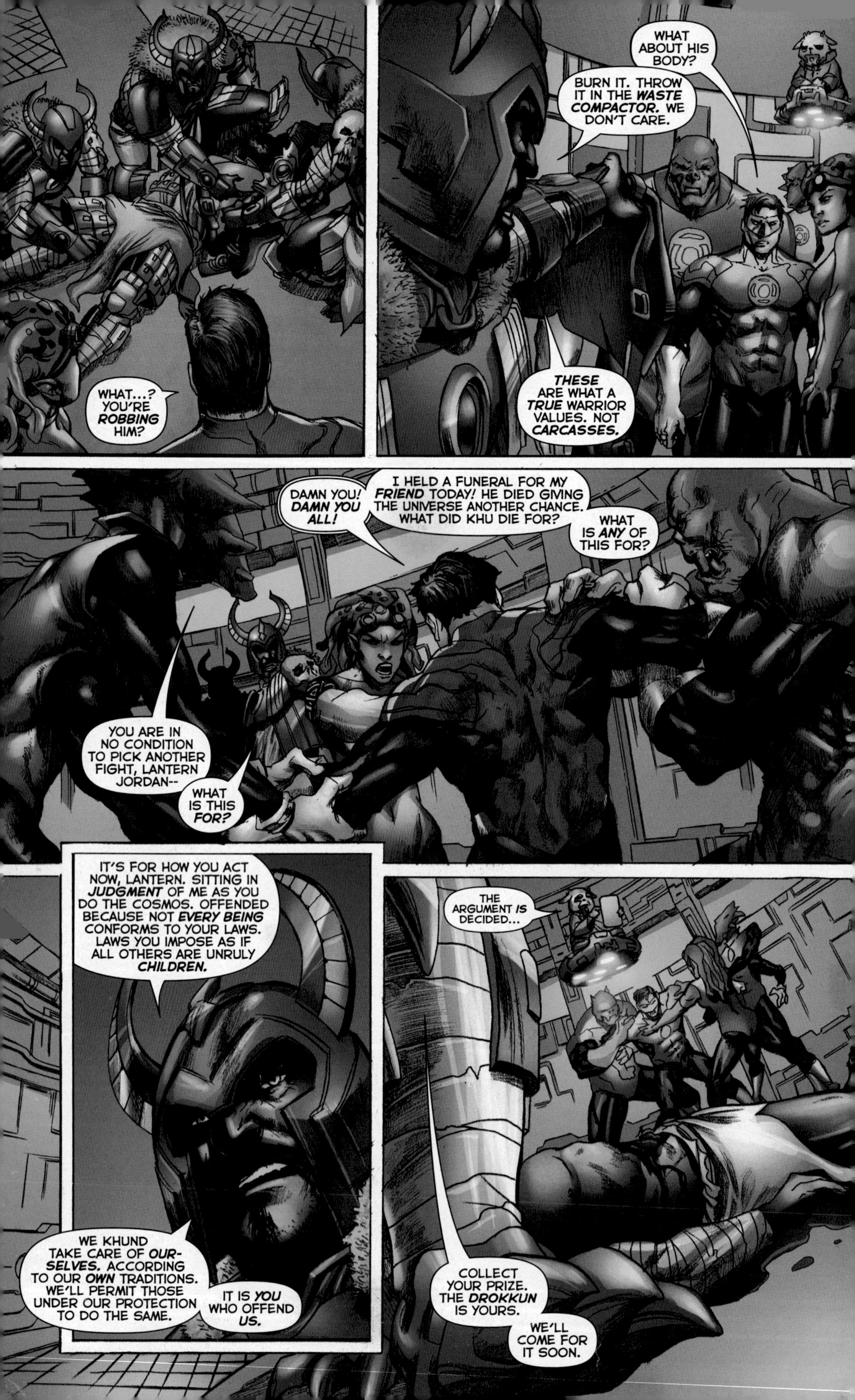
WHAT...? YOU'RE ROBBING HIM?
WHAT ABOUT HIS BODY?
BURN IT. THROW IT IN THE WASTE COMPACTOR. WE DON'T CARE.
THESE ARE WHAT A TRUE WARRIOR VALUES. NOT CARCASSES.
DAMN YOU! DAMN YOU ALL!
I HELD A FUNERAL FOR MY FRIEND TODAY! HE DIED GIVING THE UNIVERSE ANOTHER CHANCE. WHAT DID KHU DIE FOR?
WHAT IS ANY OF THIS FOR?
YOU ARE IN NO CONDITION TO PICK ANOTHER FIGHT, LANTERN JORDAN--
WHAT IS THIS FOR?
IT'S FOR HOW YOU ACT NOW, LANTERN. SITTING IN JUDGMENT OF ME AS YOU DO THE COSMOS. OFFENDED BECAUSE NOT EVERY BEING CONFORMS TO YOUR LAWS. LAWS YOU IMPOSE AS IF ALL OTHERS ARE UNRULY CHILDREN.
WE KHUND TAKE CARE OF OURSELVES. ACCORDING TO OUR OWN TRADITIONS. WE'LL PERMIT THOSE UNDER OUR PROTECTION TO DO THE SAME.
IT IS YOU WHO OFFEND US.
THE ARGUMENT IS DECIDED...
COLLECT YOUR PRIZE. THE DROKKUN IS YOURS.
WE'LL COME FOR IT SOON.

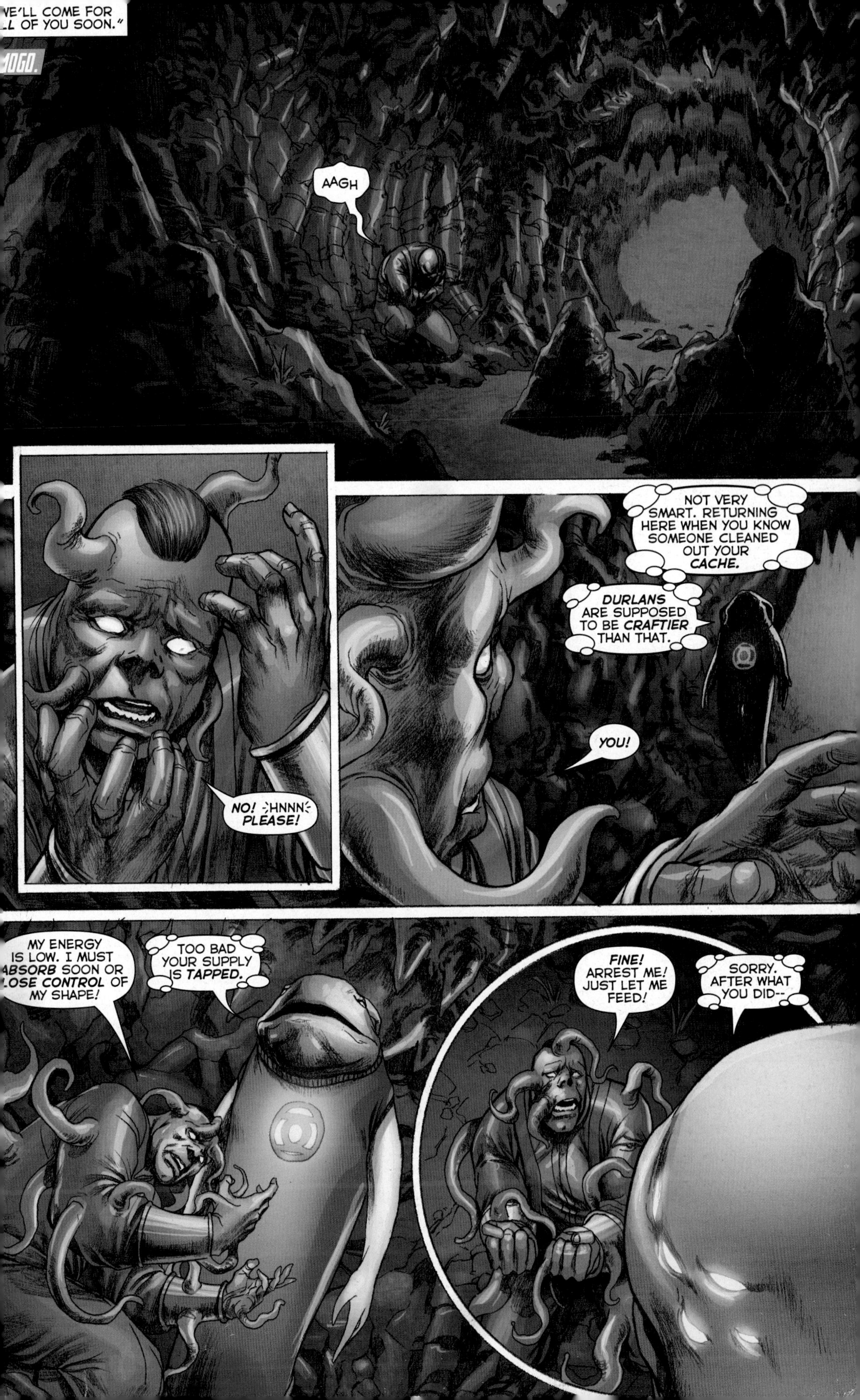
WE'LL COME FOR
LL OF YOU SOON."
MOGO.
AAGH
NO! HNNN PLEASE!
NOT VERY SMART. RETURNING HERE WHEN YOU KNOW SOMEONE CLEANED OUT YOUR CACHE.
DURLANS ARE SUPPOSED TO BE CRAFTIER THAN THAT.
YOU!
MY ENERGY IS LOW. I MUST ABSORB SOON OR LOSE CONTROL OF MY SHAPE!
TOO BAD YOUR SUPPLY IS TAPPED.
FINE! ARREST ME! JUST LET ME FEED!
SORRY. AFTER WHAT YOU DID--

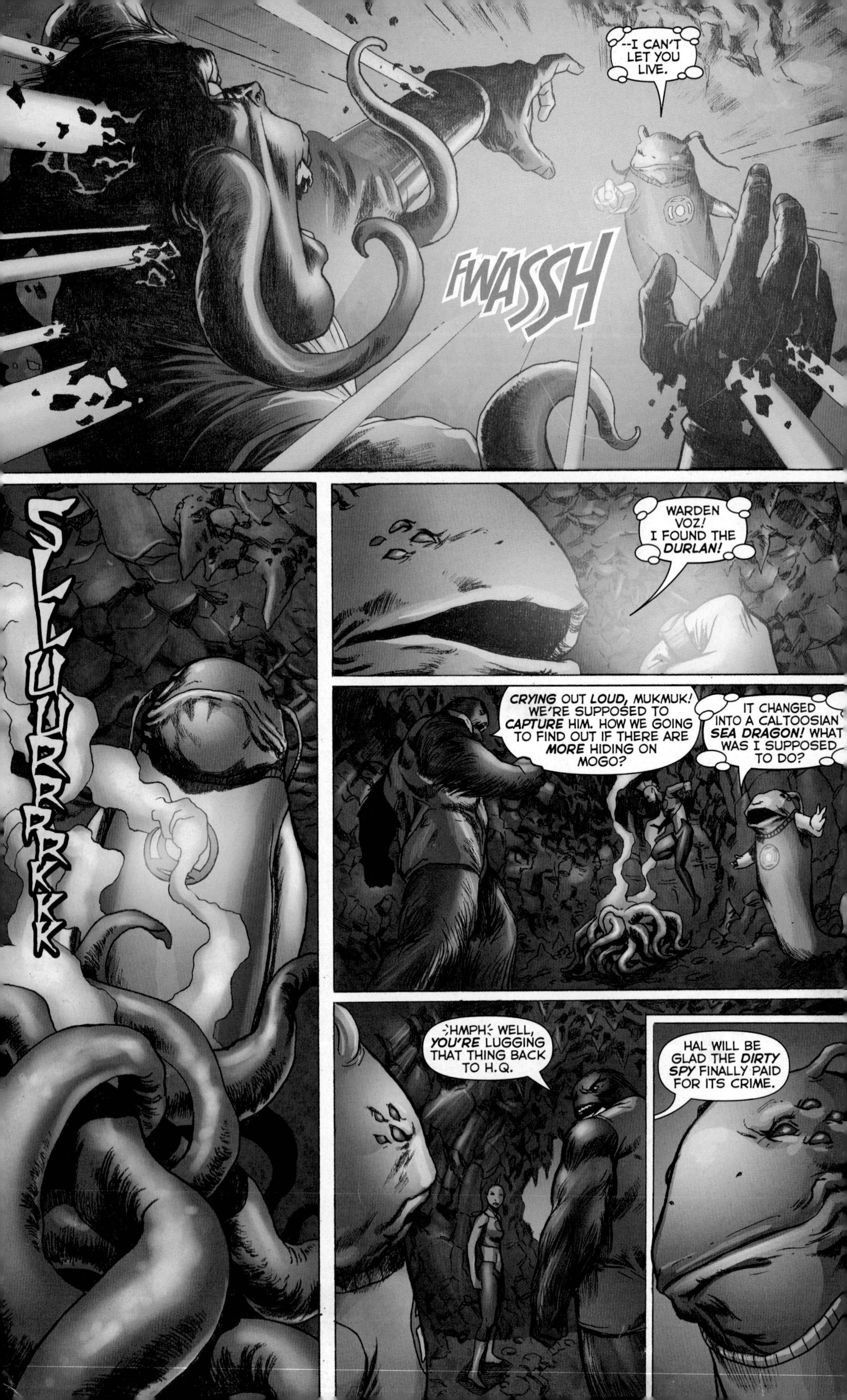
--I CAN'T LET YOU LIVE.
FWASSH
SLLURRRRKKK
WARDEN VOZ! I FOUND THE DURLAN!
CRYING OUT LOUD, MUKMUK! WE'RE SUPPOSED TO CAPTURE HIM. HOW WE GOING TO FIND OUT IF THERE ARE MORE HIDING ON MOGO?
IT CHANGED INTO A CALTOOSIAN SEA DRAGON! WHAT WAS I SUPPOSED TO DO?
HMPH. WELL, YOU'RE LUGGING THAT THING BACK TO H.Q.
HAL WILL BE GLAD THE DIRTY SPY FINALLY PAID FOR ITS CRIME.

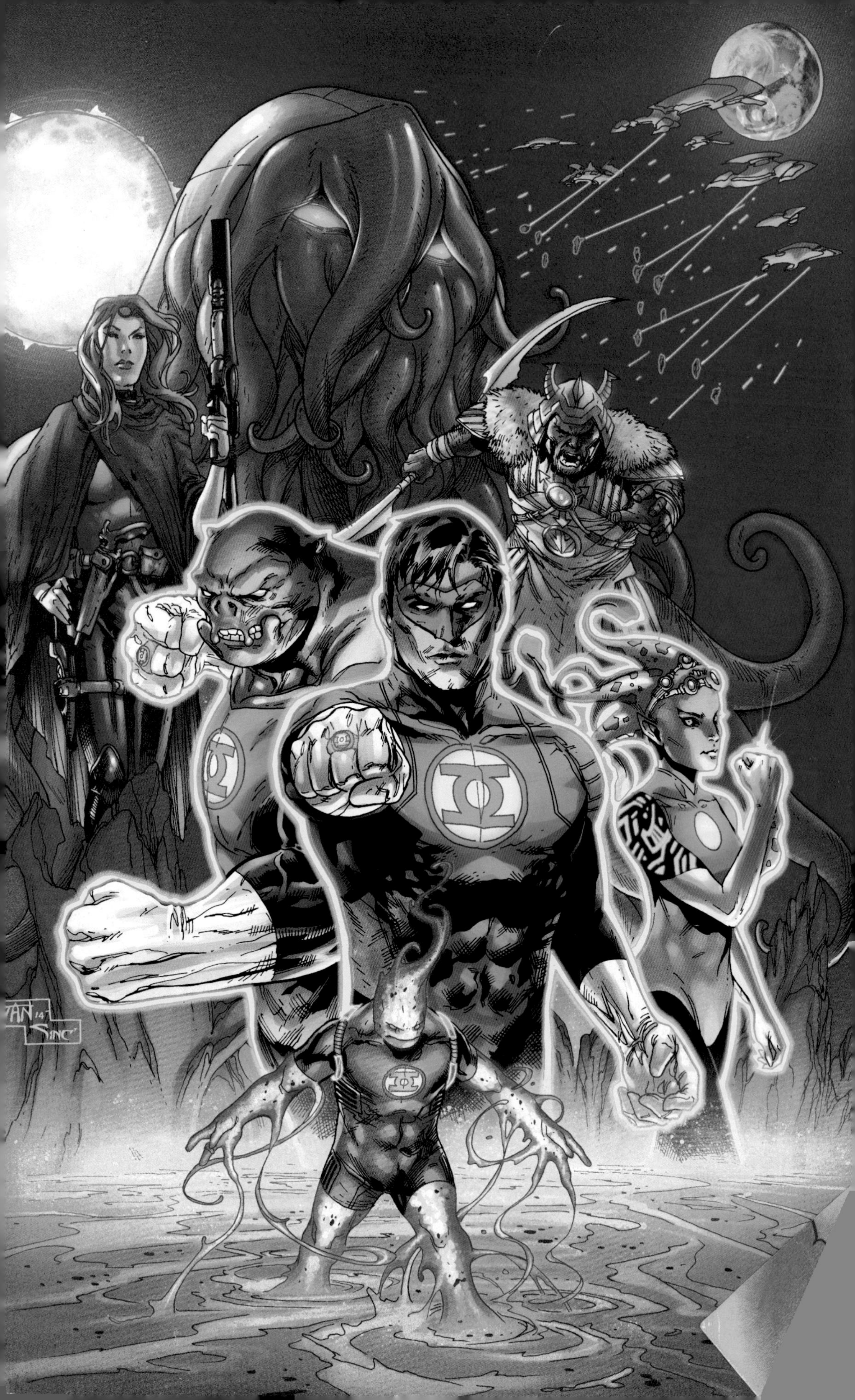

UPRISING PART 1: BATTLE OF WILLS

ROBERT VENDITTI writer **BILLY TAN** penciller **ROB HUNTER** inker **ALEX SINCLAIR** colorist

cover art by **BILLY TAN & ALEX SINCLAIR** BATMAN '66 variant cover by **MIKE & LAURA ALLRED**

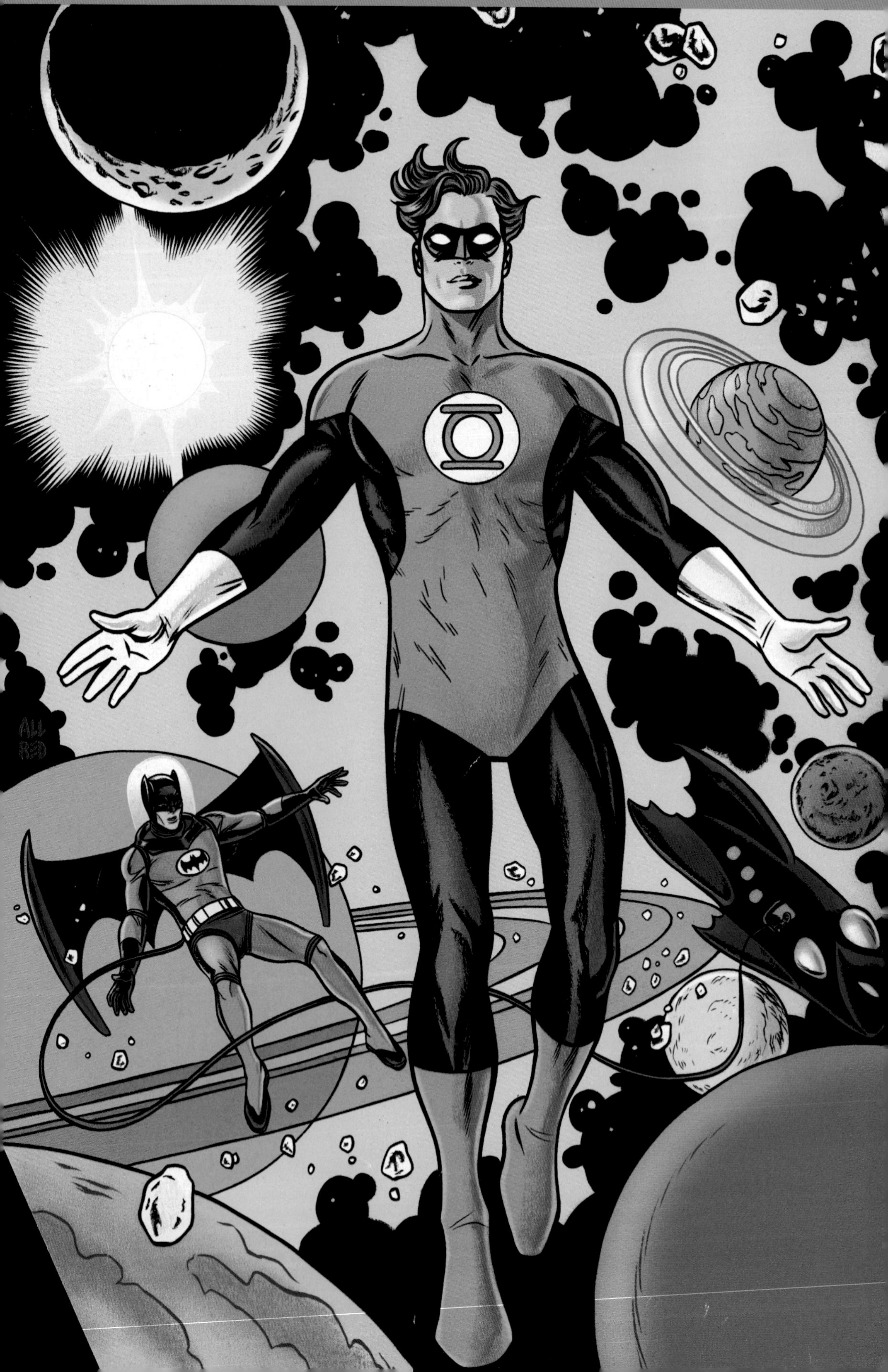

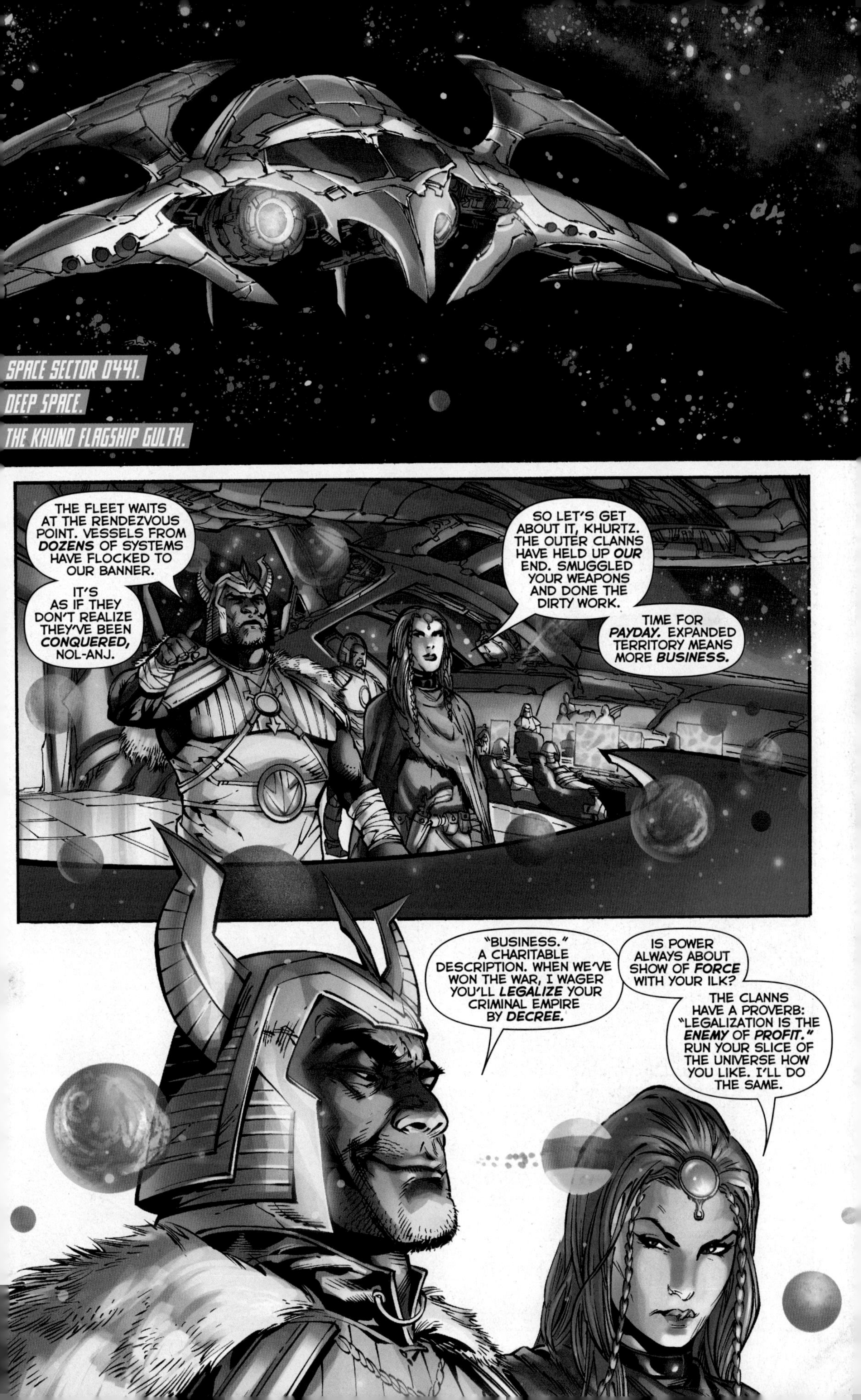
SPACE SECTOR 0441.
DEEP SPACE.
THE KHUND FLAGSHIP GULTH.
THE FLEET WAITS AT THE RENDEZVOUS POINT. VESSELS FROM DOZENS OF SYSTEMS HAVE FLOCKED TO OUR BANNER.
IT'S AS IF THEY DON'T REALIZE THEY'VE BEEN CONQUERED, NOL-ANJ.
SO LET'S GET ABOUT IT, KHURTZ. THE OUTER CLANNS HAVE HELD UP OUR END. SMUGGLED YOUR WEAPONS AND DONE THE DIRTY WORK.
TIME FOR PAYDAY. EXPANDED TERRITORY MEANS MORE BUSINESS.
"BUSINESS." A CHARITABLE DESCRIPTION. WHEN WE'VE WON THE WAR, I WAGER YOU'LL LEGALIZE YOUR CRIMINAL EMPIRE BY DECREE.
IS POWER ALWAYS ABOUT SHOW OF FORCE WITH YOUR ILK?
THE CLANNS HAVE A PROVERB: "LEGALIZATION IS THE ENEMY OF PROFIT." RUN YOUR SLICE OF THE UNIVERSE HOW YOU LIKE. I'LL DO THE SAME.

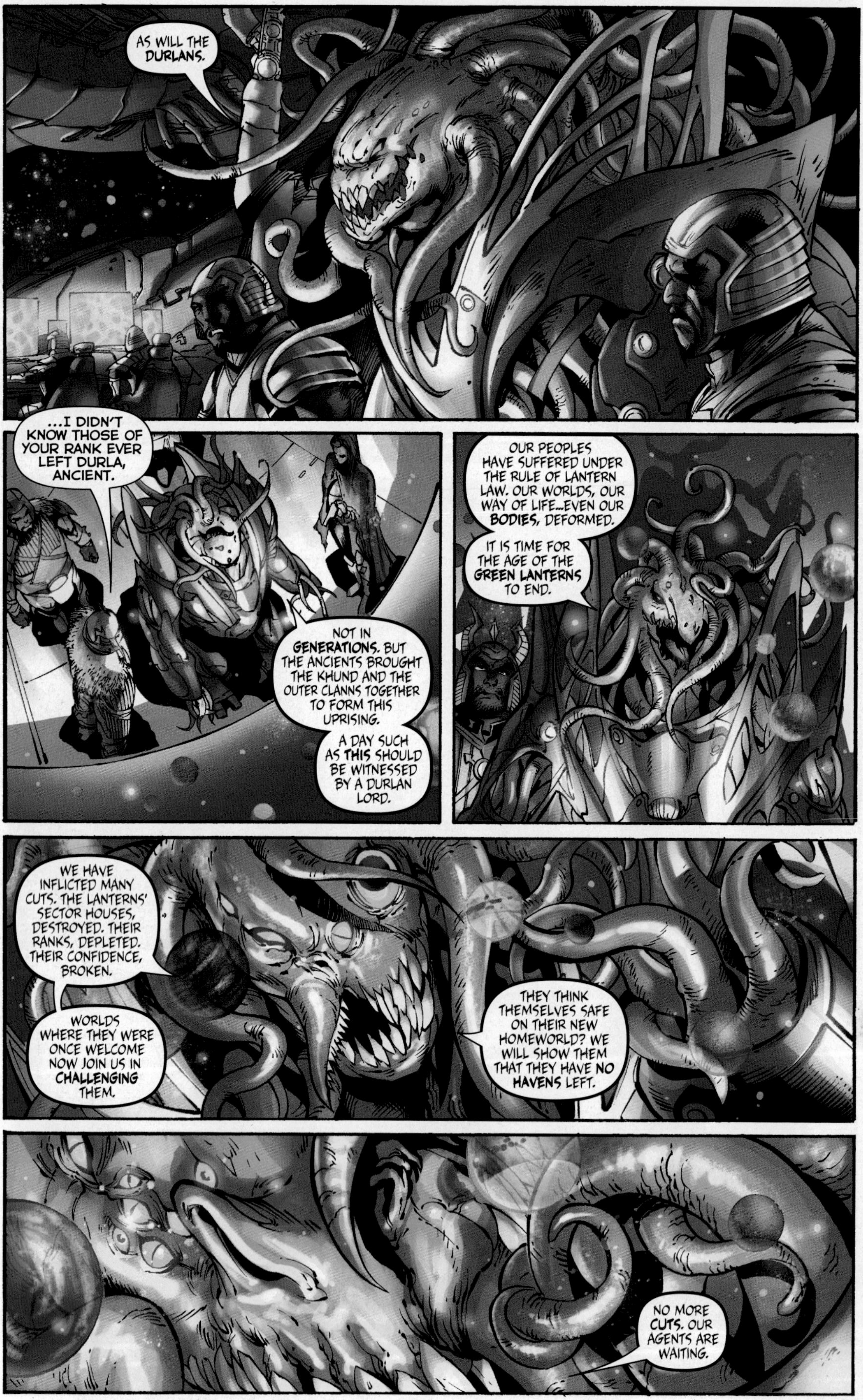
AS WILL THE DURLANS.
...I DIDN'T KNOW THOSE OF YOUR RANK EVER LEFT DURLA, ANCIENT.
NOT IN GENERATIONS. BUT THE ANCIENTS BROUGHT THE KHUND AND THE OUTER CLANNS TOGETHER TO FORM THIS UPRISING.
A DAY SUCH AS THIS SHOULD BE WITNESSED BY A DURLAN LORD.
OUR PEOPLES HAVE SUFFERED UNDER THE RULE OF LANTERN LAW. OUR WORLDS, OUR WAY OF LIFE...EVEN OUR BODIES, DEFORMED.
IT IS TIME FOR THE AGE OF THE GREEN LANTERNS TO END.
WE HAVE INFLICTED MANY CUTS. THE LANTERNS' SECTOR HOUSES, DESTROYED. THEIR RANKS, DEPLETED. THEIR CONFIDENCE, BROKEN.
WORLDS WHERE THEY WERE ONCE WELCOME NOW JOIN US IN CHALLENGING THEM.
THEY THINK THEMSELVES SAFE ON THEIR NEW HOMEWORLD? WE WILL SHOW THEM THAT THEY HAVE NO HAVENS LEFT.
NO MORE CUTS. OUR AGENTS ARE WAITING.

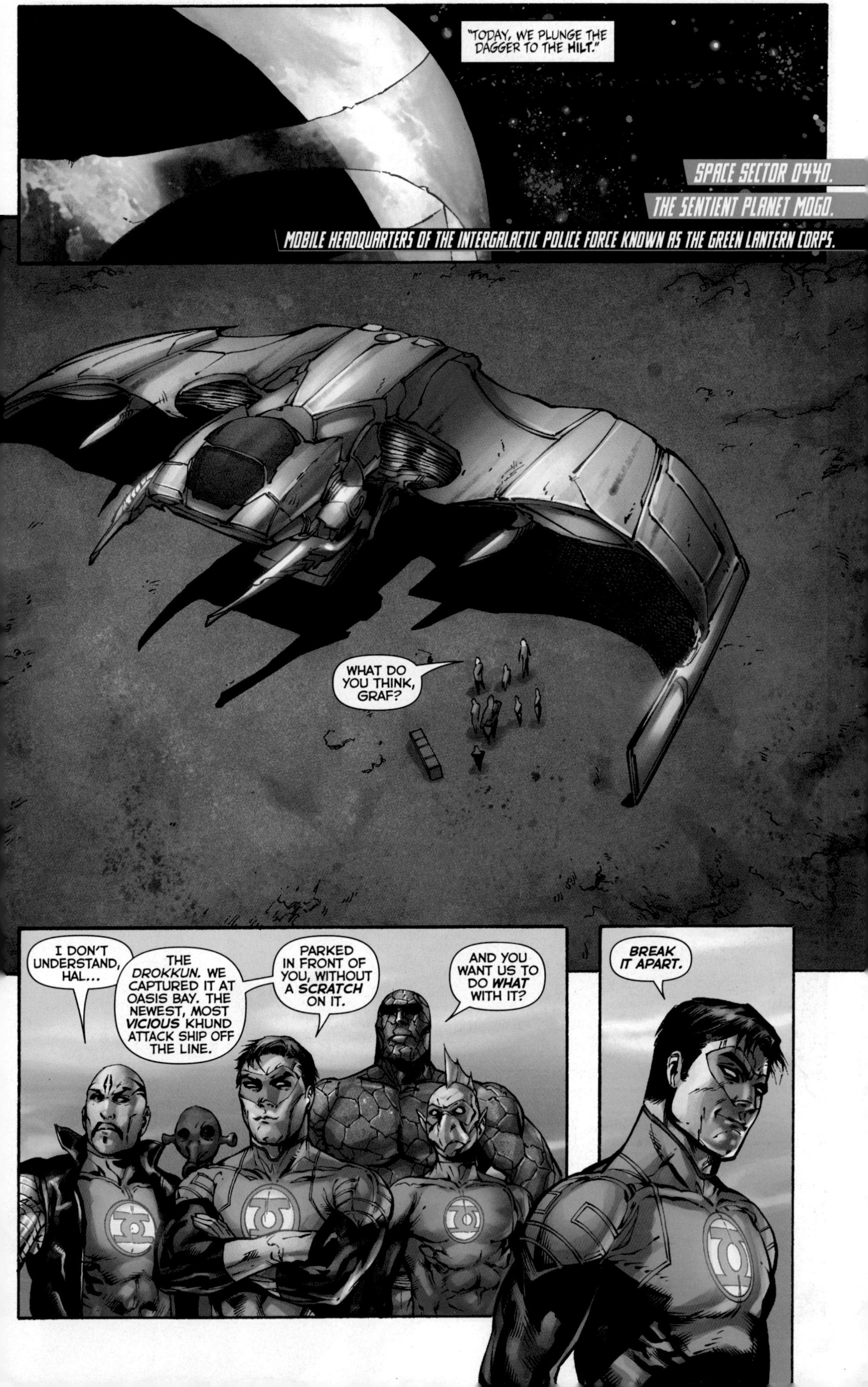
"TODAY, WE PLUNGE THE DAGGER TO THE HILT."
SPACE SECTOR 0440.
THE SENTIENT PLANET MOGO.
MOBILE HEADQUARTERS OF THE INTERGALACTIC POLICE FORCE KNOWN AS THE GREEN LANTERN CORPS.
WHAT DO YOU THINK, GRAF?
I DON'T UNDERSTAND, HAL...
THE DROKKUN. WE CAPTURED IT AT OASIS BAY. THE NEWEST, MOST VICIOUS KHUND ATTACK SHIP OFF THE LINE.
PARKED IN FRONT OF YOU, WITHOUT A SCRATCH ON IT.
AND YOU WANT US TO DO WHAT WITH IT?
BREAK IT APART.

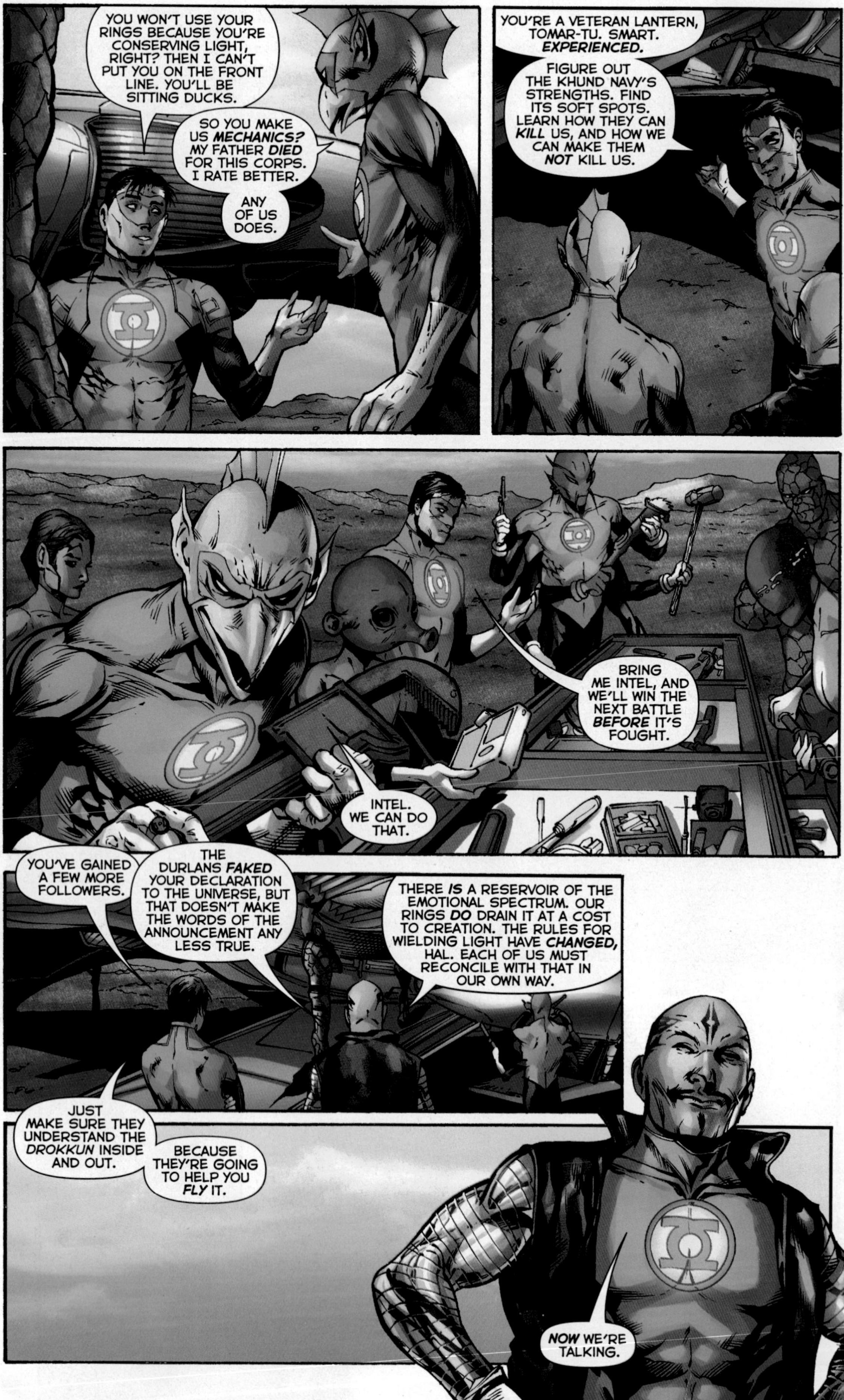

YOU WON'T USE YOUR RINGS BECAUSE YOU'RE CONSERVING LIGHT, RIGHT? THEN I CAN'T PUT YOU ON THE FRONT LINE. YOU'LL BE SITTING DUCKS.
SO YOU MAKE US *MECHANICS?* MY FATHER *DIED* FOR THIS CORPS. I RATE BETTER.
ANY OF US DOES.
YOU'RE A VETERAN LANTERN, TOMAR-TU. SMART. *EXPERIENCED.*
FIGURE OUT THE KHUND NAVY'S STRENGTHS. FIND ITS SOFT SPOTS. LEARN HOW THEY CAN *KILL* US, AND HOW WE CAN MAKE THEM *NOT* KILL US.
BRING ME INTEL, AND WE'LL WIN THE NEXT BATTLE *BEFORE* IT'S FOUGHT.
INTEL. WE CAN DO THAT.
YOU'VE GAINED A FEW MORE FOLLOWERS.
THE DURLANS *FAKED* YOUR DECLARATION TO THE UNIVERSE, BUT THAT DOESN'T MAKE THE WORDS OF THE ANNOUNCEMENT ANY LESS TRUE.
THERE *IS* A RESERVOIR OF THE EMOTIONAL SPECTRUM. OUR RINGS *DO* DRAIN IT AT A COST TO CREATION. THE RULES FOR WIELDING LIGHT HAVE *CHANGED,* HAL. EACH OF US MUST RECONCILE WITH THAT IN OUR OWN WAY.
JUST MAKE SURE THEY UNDERSTAND THE *DROKKUN* INSIDE AND OUT.
BECAUSE THEY'RE GOING TO HELP YOU *FLY* IT.
NOW WE'RE TALKING.

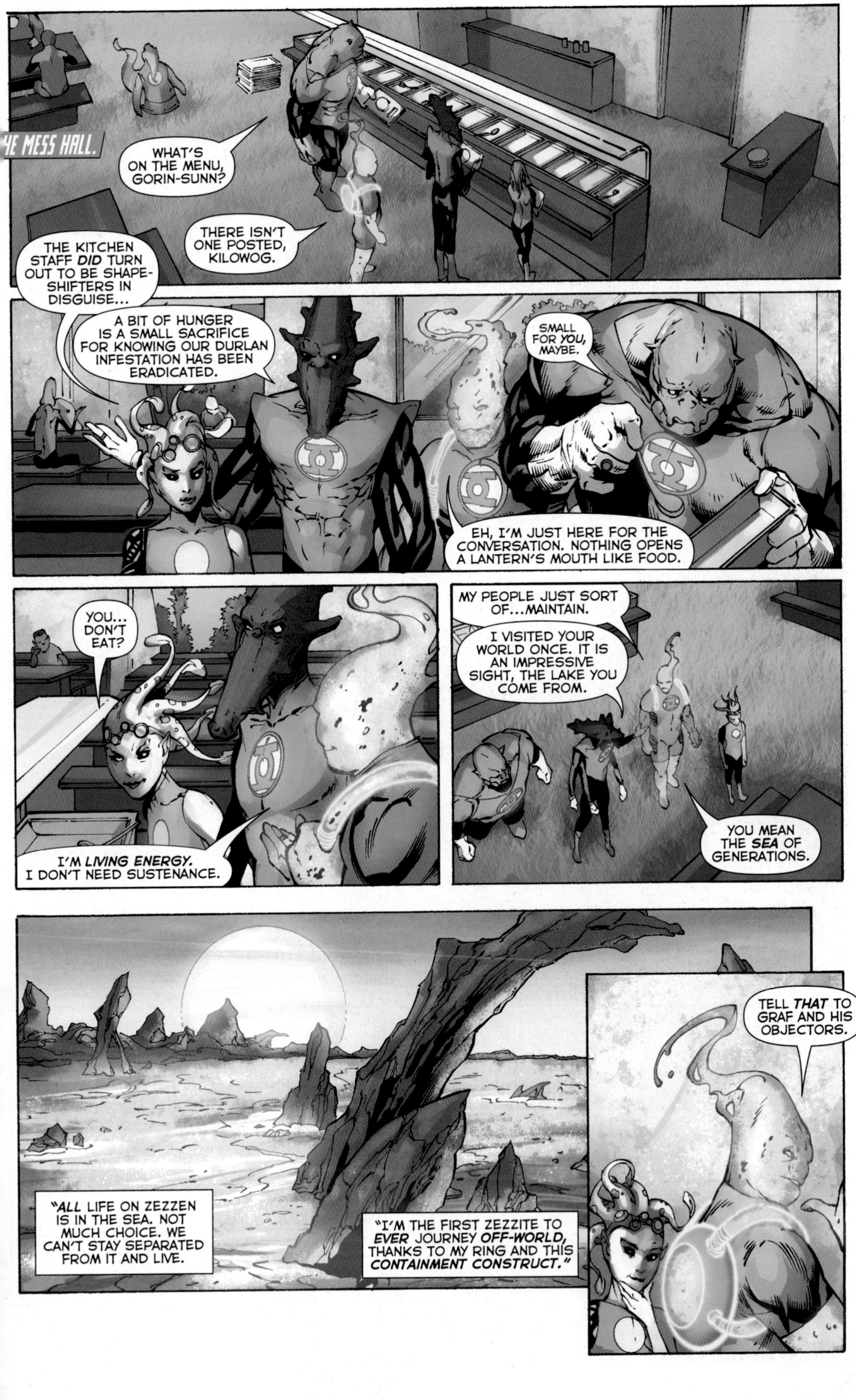
HE MESS HALL.
WHAT'S ON THE MENU, GORIN-SUNN?
THERE ISN'T ONE POSTED, KILOWOG.
THE KITCHEN STAFF DID TURN OUT TO BE SHAPE-SHIFTERS IN DISGUISE...
A BIT OF HUNGER IS A SMALL SACRIFICE FOR KNOWING OUR DURLAN INFESTATION HAS BEEN ERADICATED.
SMALL FOR YOU, MAYBE.
EH, I'M JUST HERE FOR THE CONVERSATION. NOTHING OPENS A LANTERN'S MOUTH LIKE FOOD.
YOU... DON'T EAT?
I'M LIVING ENERGY. I DON'T NEED SUSTENANCE.
MY PEOPLE JUST SORT OF...MAINTAIN.
I VISITED YOUR WORLD ONCE. IT IS AN IMPRESSIVE SIGHT, THE LAKE YOU COME FROM.
YOU MEAN THE SEA OF GENERATIONS.
"ALL LIFE ON ZEZZEN IS IN THE SEA. NOT MUCH CHOICE. WE CAN'T STAY SEPARATED FROM IT AND LIVE.
"I'M THE FIRST ZEZZITE TO EVER JOURNEY OFF-WORLD, THANKS TO MY RING AND THIS CONTAINMENT CONSTRUCT."
TELL THAT TO GRAF AND HIS OBJECTORS.

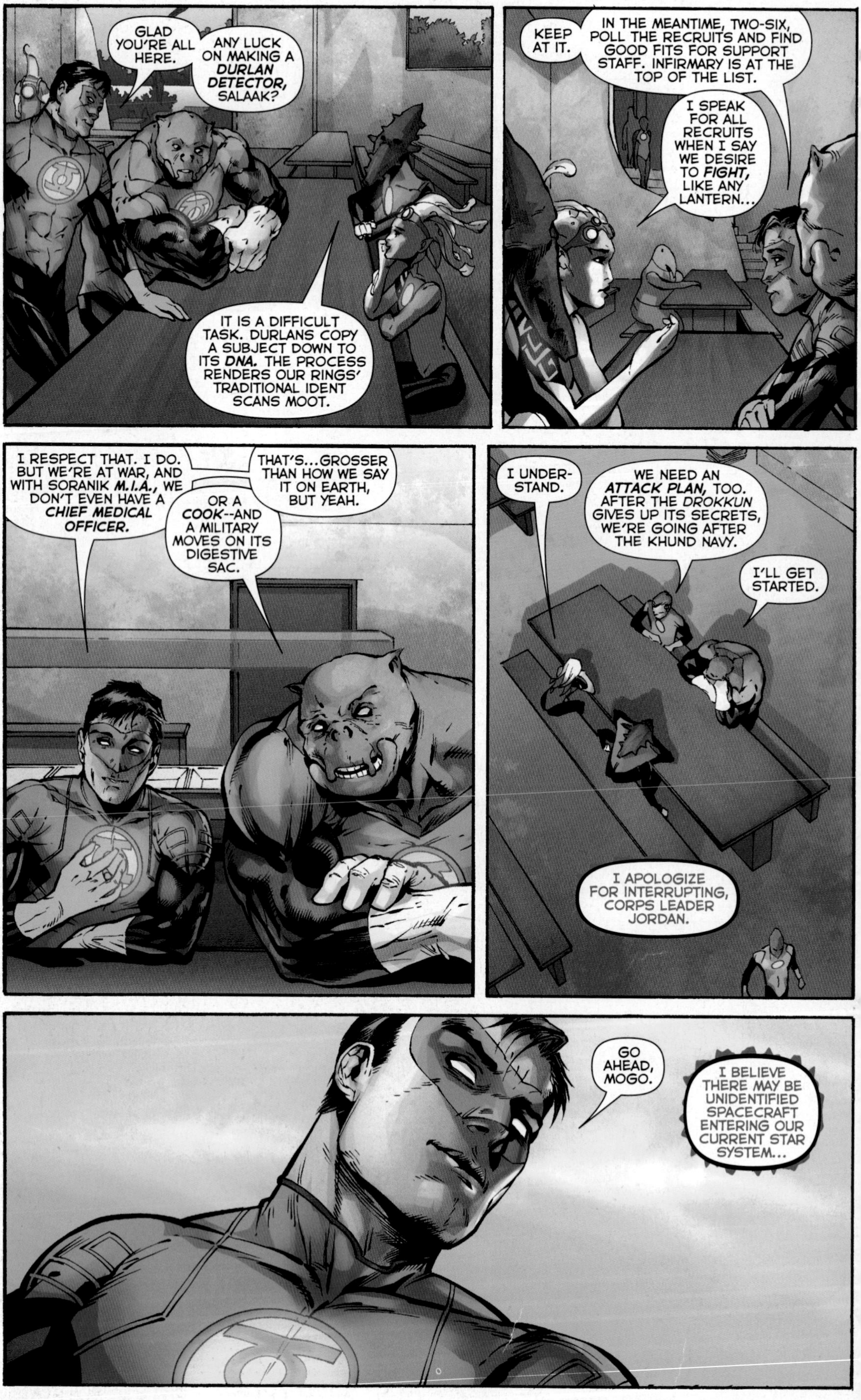
GLAD YOU'RE ALL HERE.
ANY LUCK ON MAKING A DURLAN DETECTOR, SALAAK?
IT IS A DIFFICULT TASK. DURLANS COPY A SUBJECT DOWN TO ITS DNA. THE PROCESS RENDERS OUR RINGS' TRADITIONAL IDENT SCANS MOOT.
KEEP AT IT.
IN THE MEANTIME, TWO-SIX, POLL THE RECRUITS AND FIND GOOD FITS FOR SUPPORT STAFF. INFIRMARY IS AT THE TOP OF THE LIST.
I SPEAK FOR ALL RECRUITS WHEN I SAY WE DESIRE TO FIGHT, LIKE ANY LANTERN...
I RESPECT THAT. I DO. BUT WE'RE AT WAR, AND WITH SORANIK M.I.A., WE DON'T EVEN HAVE A CHIEF MEDICAL OFFICER.
OR A COOK--AND A MILITARY MOVES ON ITS DIGESTIVE SAC.
THAT'S...GROSSER THAN HOW WE SAY IT ON EARTH, BUT YEAH.
I UNDER-STAND.
WE NEED AN ATTACK PLAN, TOO. AFTER THE DROKKUN GIVES UP ITS SECRETS, WE'RE GOING AFTER THE KHUND NAVY.
I'LL GET STARTED.
I APOLOGIZE FOR INTERRUPTING, CORPS LEADER JORDAN.
GO AHEAD, MOGO.
I BELIEVE THERE MAY BE UNIDENTIFIED SPACECRAFT ENTERING OUR CURRENT STAR SYSTEM...

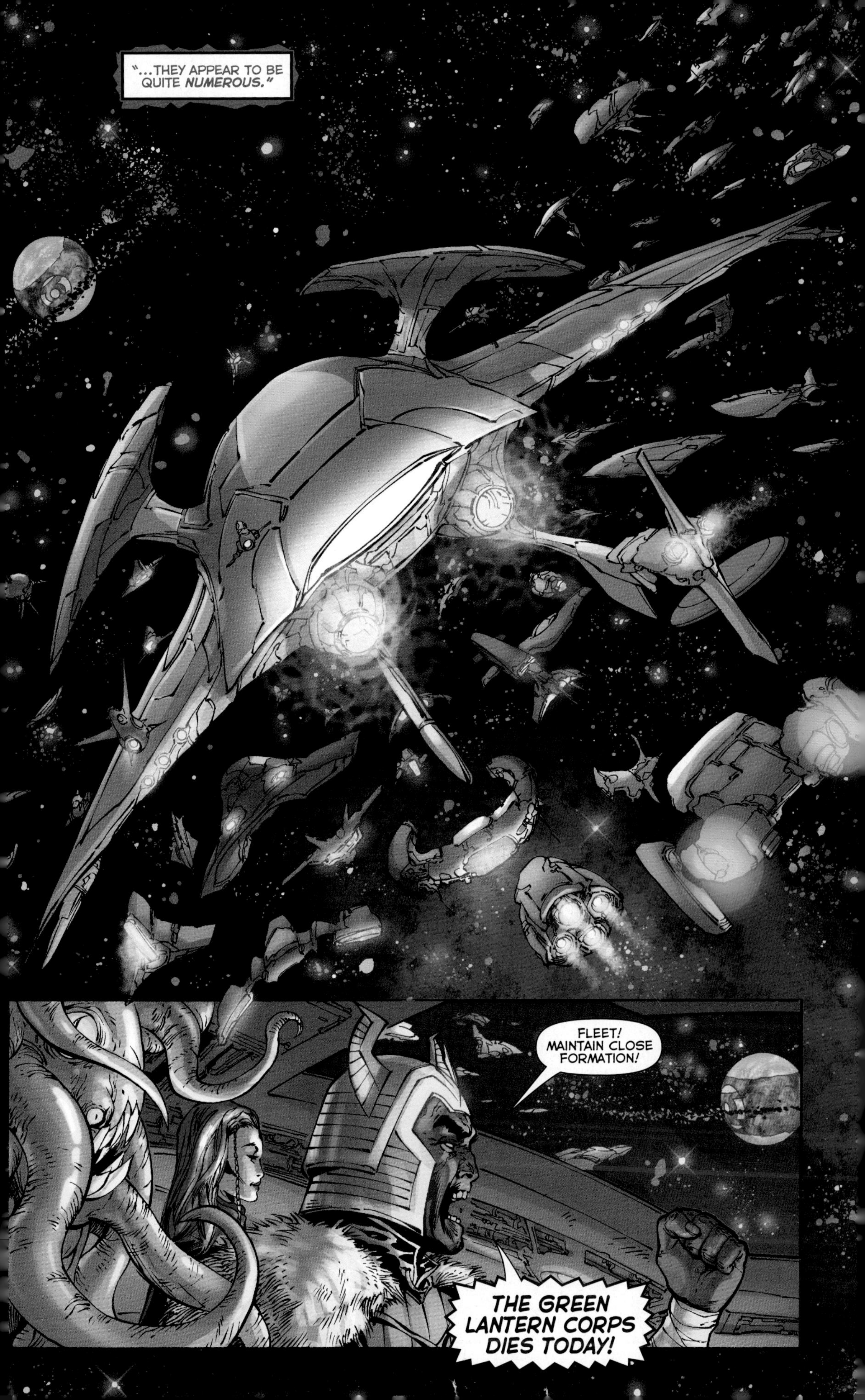
"...THEY APPEAR TO BE QUITE NUMEROUS."
FLEET! MAINTAIN CLOSE FORMATION!
THE GREEN LANTERN CORPS DIES TODAY!

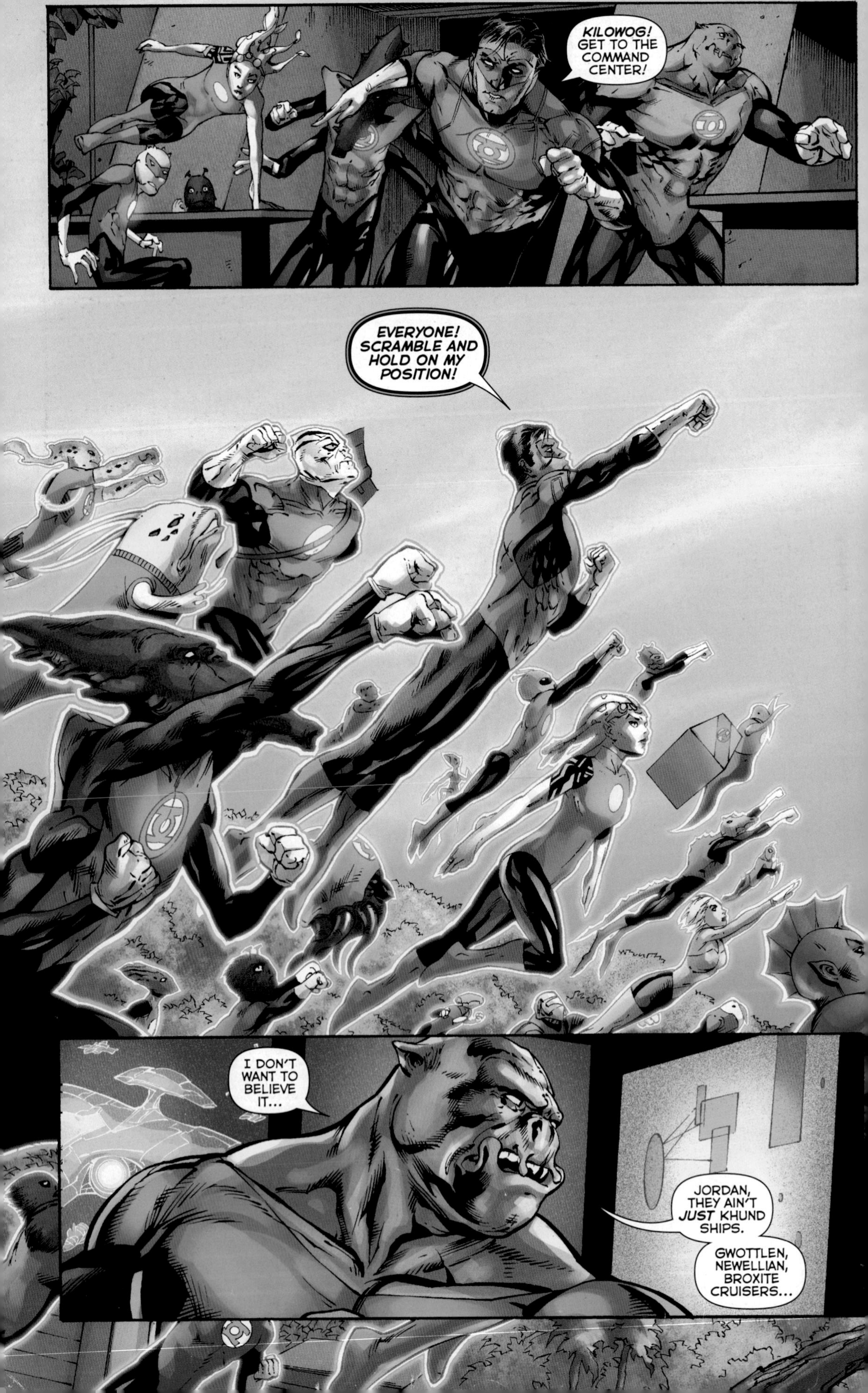
KILOWOG! GET TO THE COMMAND CENTER!
EVERYONE! SCRAMBLE AND HOLD ON MY POSITION!
I DON'T WANT TO BELIEVE IT...
JORDAN, THEY AIN'T JUST KHUND SHIPS.
GWOTTLEN, NEWELLIAN, BROXITE CRUISERS...

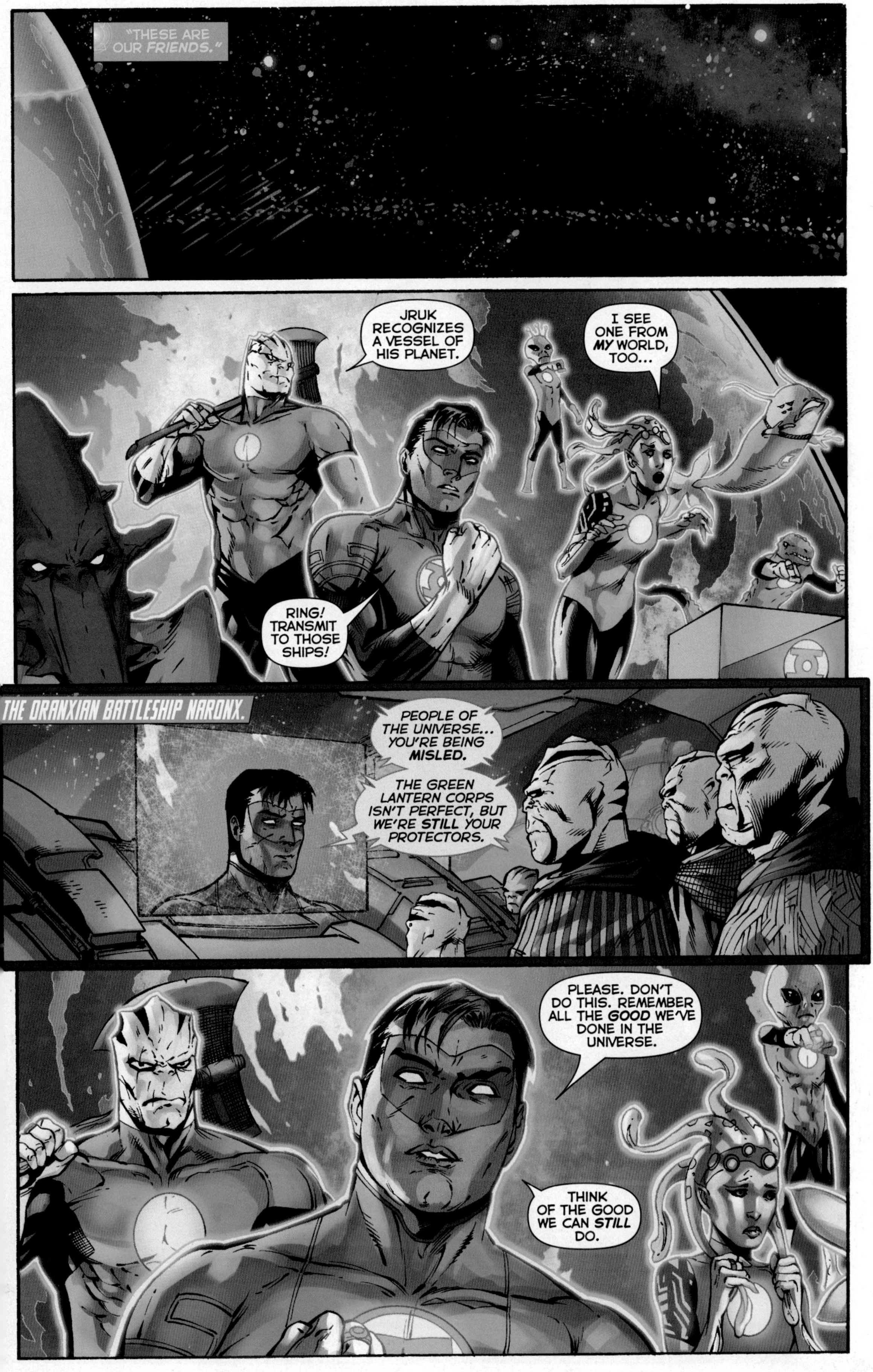

"THESE ARE OUR FRIENDS."
JRUK RECOGNIZES A VESSEL OF HIS PLANET.
I SEE ONE FROM MY WORLD, TOO...
RING! TRANSMIT TO THOSE SHIPS!
THE ORANXIAN BATTLESHIP NARONX.
PEOPLE OF THE UNIVERSE... YOU'RE BEING MISLED.
THE GREEN LANTERN CORPS ISN'T PERFECT, BUT WE'RE STILL YOUR PROTECTORS.
PLEASE. DON'T DO THIS. REMEMBER ALL THE GOOD WE'VE DONE IN THE UNIVERSE.
THINK OF THE GOOD WE CAN STILL DO.

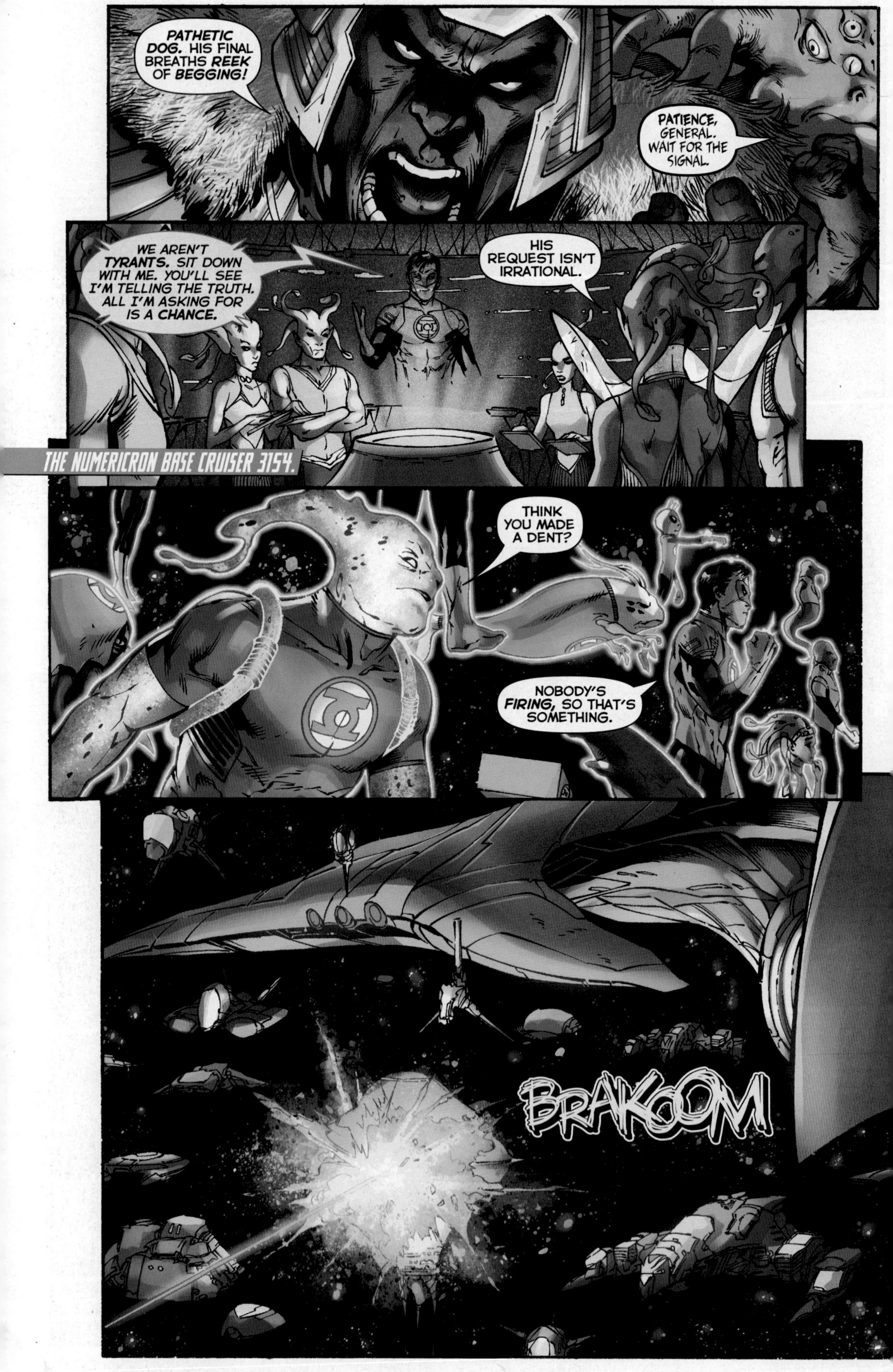
PATHETIC DOG. HIS FINAL BREATHS REEK OF BEGGING!
PATIENCE, GENERAL. WAIT FOR THE SIGNAL.
WE AREN'T TYRANTS. SIT DOWN WITH ME. YOU'LL SEE I'M TELLING THE TRUTH. ALL I'M ASKING FOR IS A CHANCE.
HIS REQUEST ISN'T IRRATIONAL.
THE NUMERICRON BASE CRUISER 3154.
THINK YOU MADE A DENT?
NOBODY'S FIRING, SO THAT'S SOMETHING.
BRAKOOM

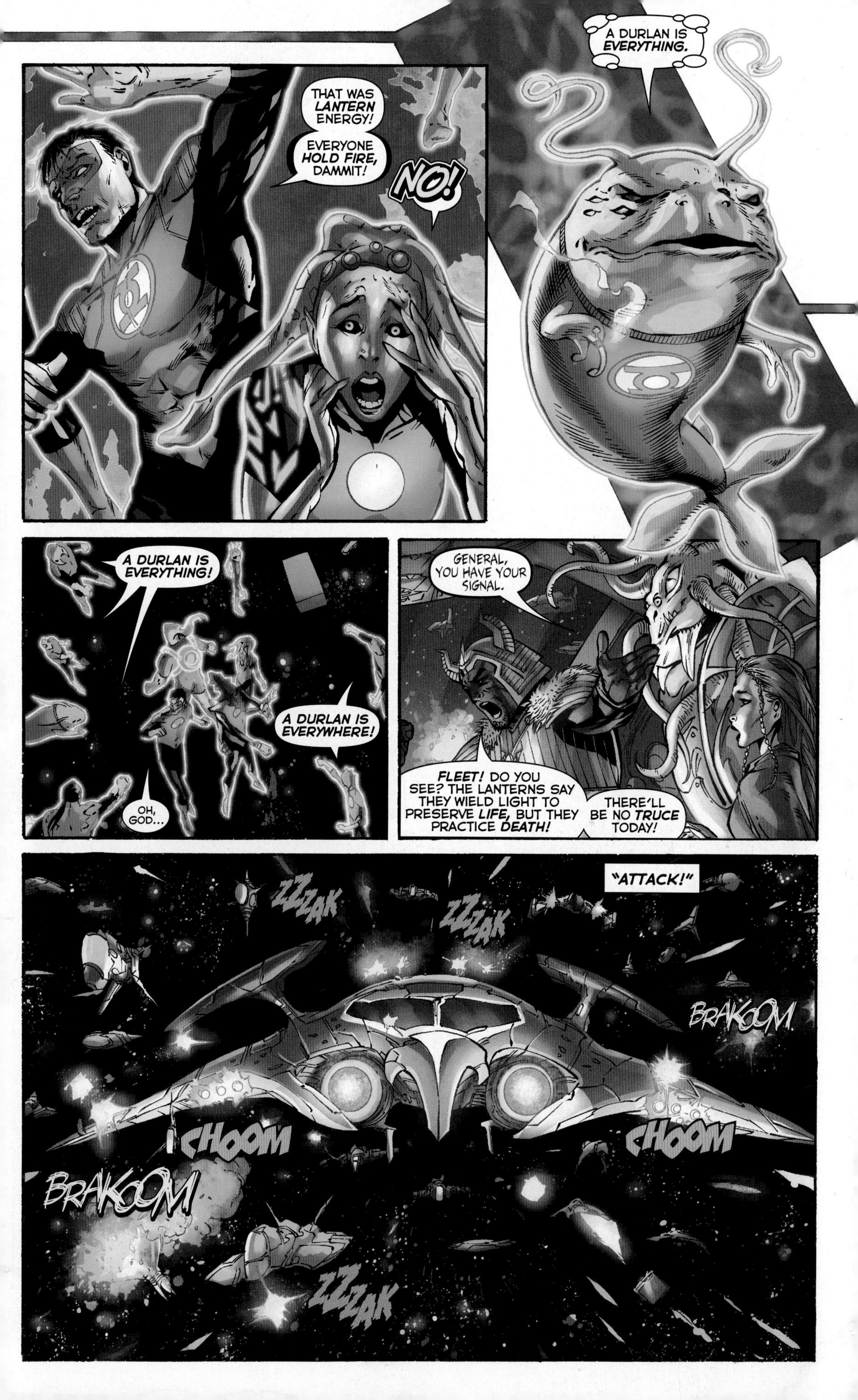
THAT WAS LANTERN ENERGY!
EVERYONE HOLD FIRE, DAMMIT!
NO!
A DURLAN IS EVERYTHING.
A DURLAN IS EVERYTHING!
A DURLAN IS EVERYWHERE!
OH, GOD...
GENERAL, YOU HAVE YOUR SIGNAL.
FLEET! DO YOU SEE? THE LANTERNS SAY THEY WIELD LIGHT TO PRESERVE LIFE, BUT THEY PRACTICE DEATH!
THERE'LL BE NO TRUCE TODAY!
"ATTACK!"
ZZZAK
ZZZAK
BRAKOOM
CHOOM
CHOOM
BRAKOOM
ZZZAK

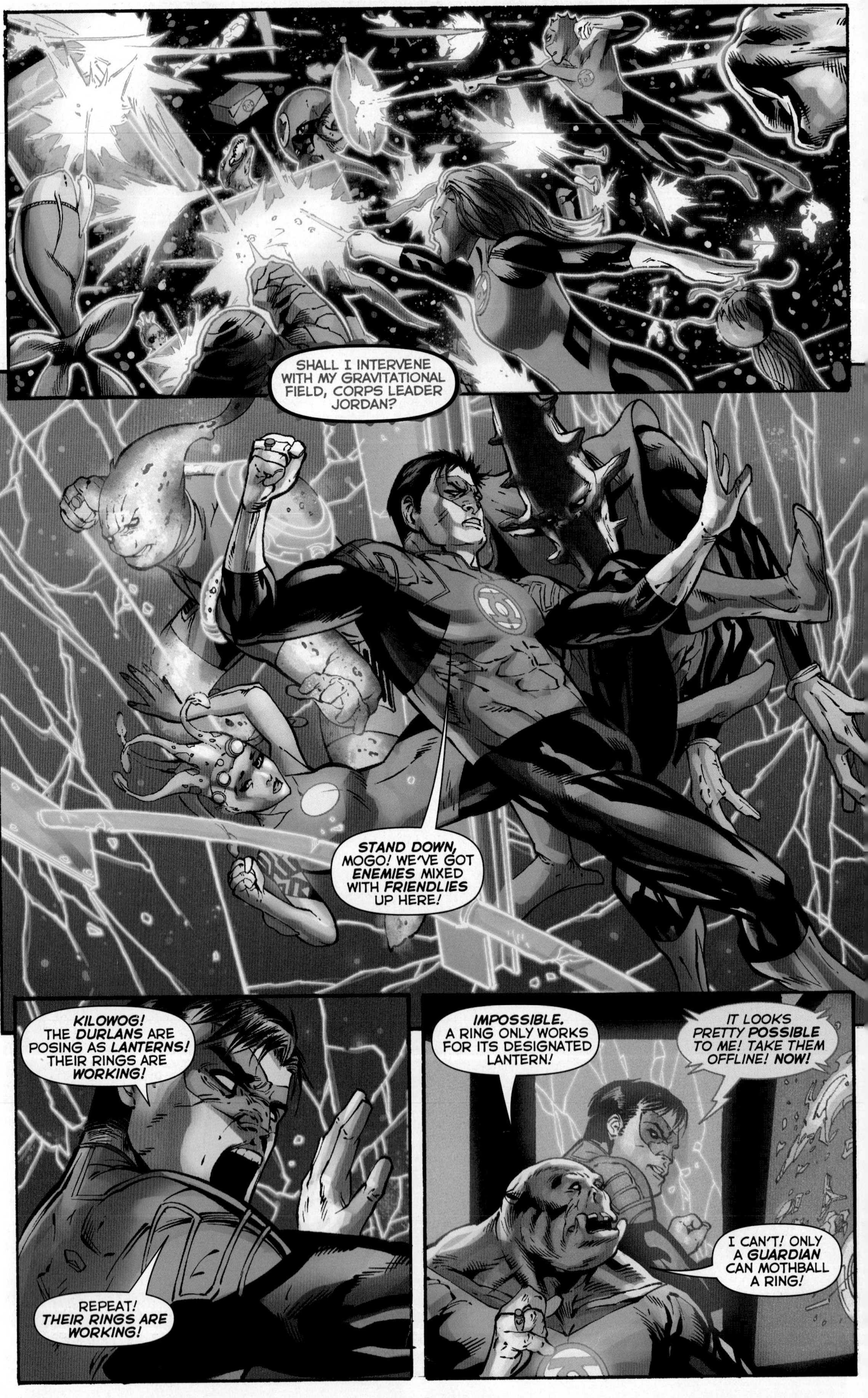
SHALL I INTERVENE WITH MY GRAVITATIONAL FIELD, CORPS LEADER JORDAN?
STAND DOWN, MOGO! WE'VE GOT ENEMIES MIXED WITH FRIENDLIES UP HERE!
KILOWOG! THE DURLANS ARE POSING AS LANTERNS! THEIR RINGS ARE WORKING!
REPEAT! THEIR RINGS ARE WORKING!
IMPOSSIBLE. A RING ONLY WORKS FOR ITS DESIGNATED LANTERN!
IT LOOKS PRETTY POSSIBLE TO ME! TAKE THEM OFFLINE! NOW!
I CAN'T! ONLY A GUARDIAN CAN MOTHBALL A RING!

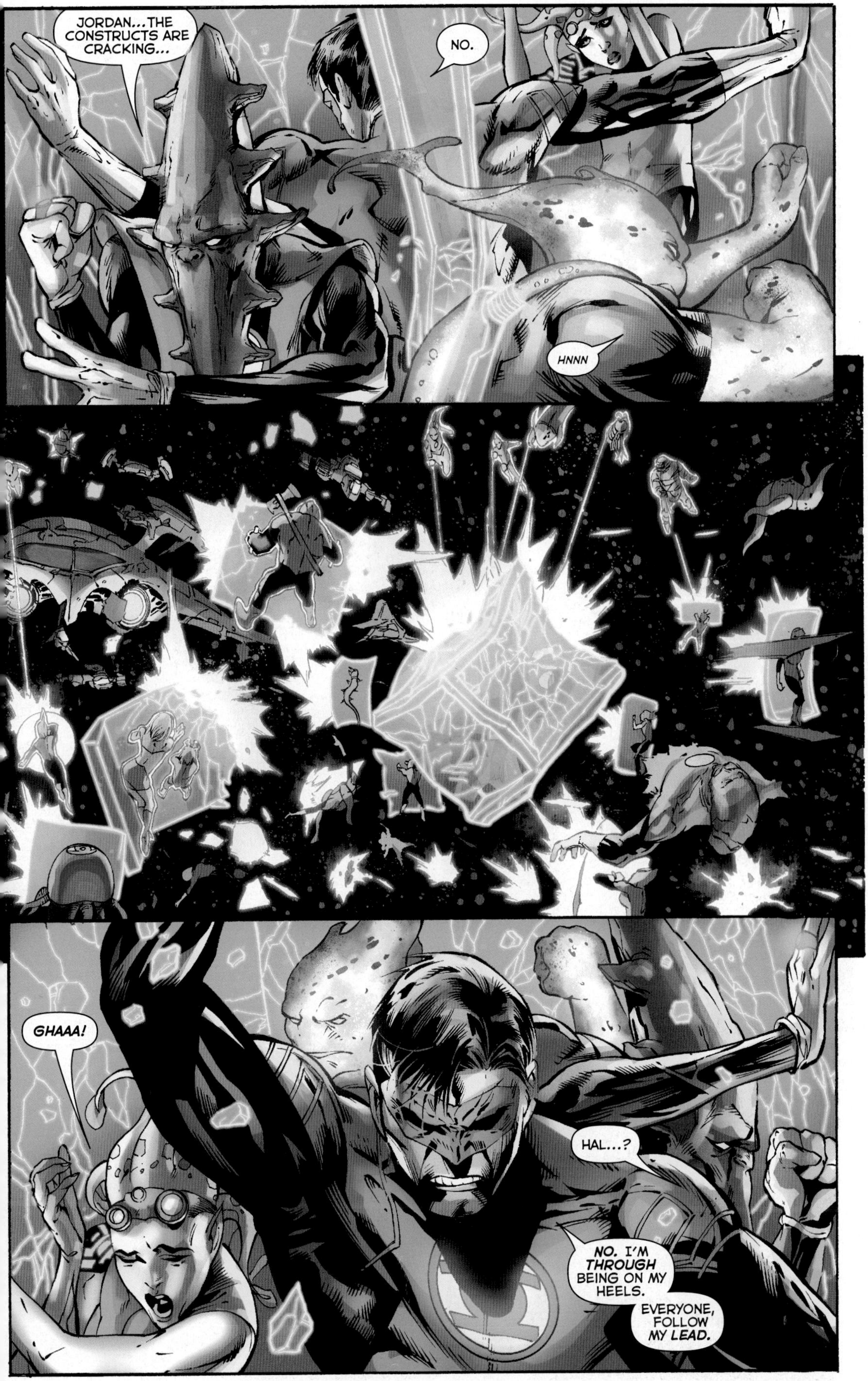

JORDAN...THE CONSTRUCTS ARE CRACKING...
NO.
HNNN
GHAAA!
HAL...?
NO. I'M THROUGH BEING ON MY HEELS.
EVERYONE, FOLLOW MY LEAD.

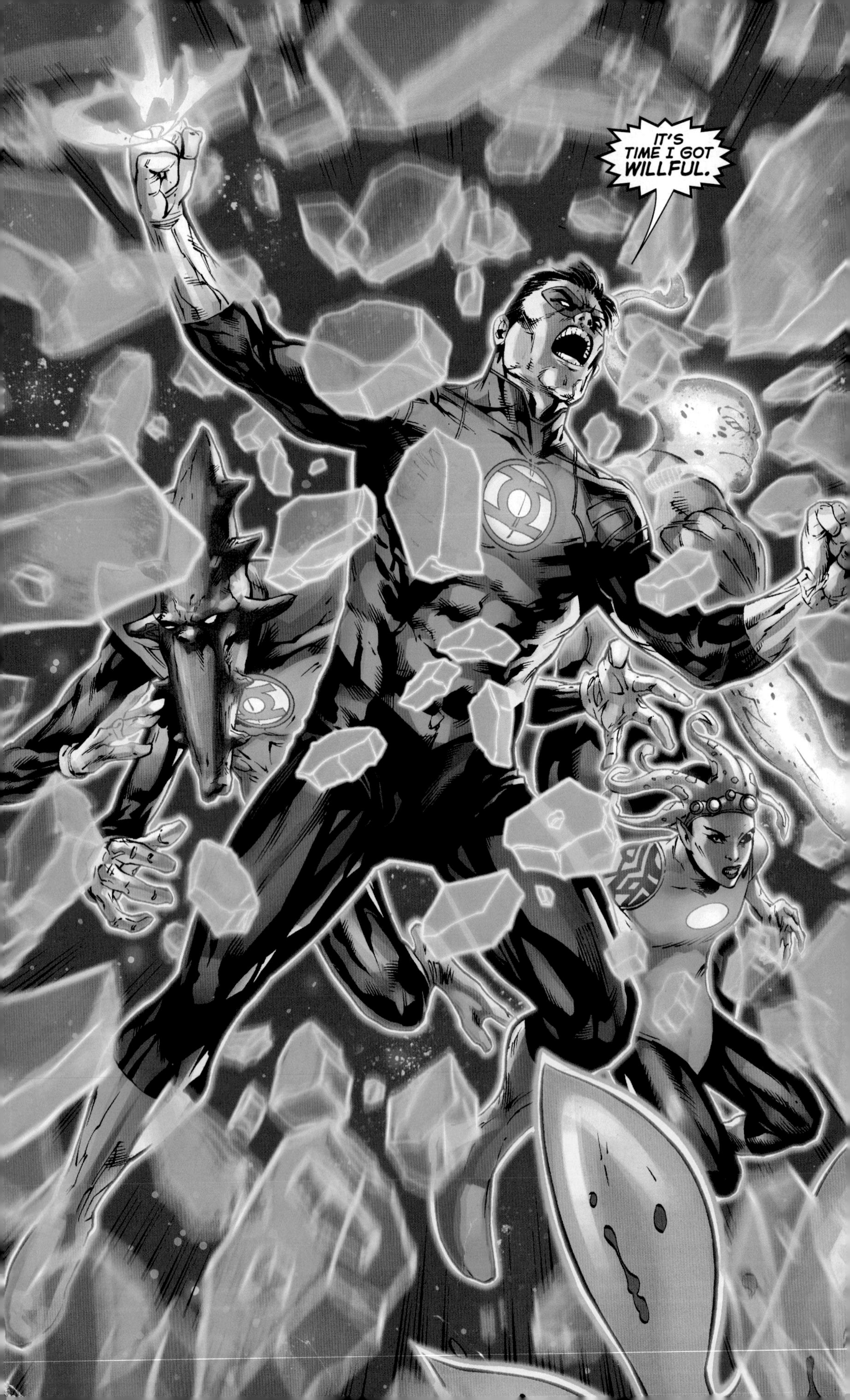
IT'S TIME I GOT WILLFUL.

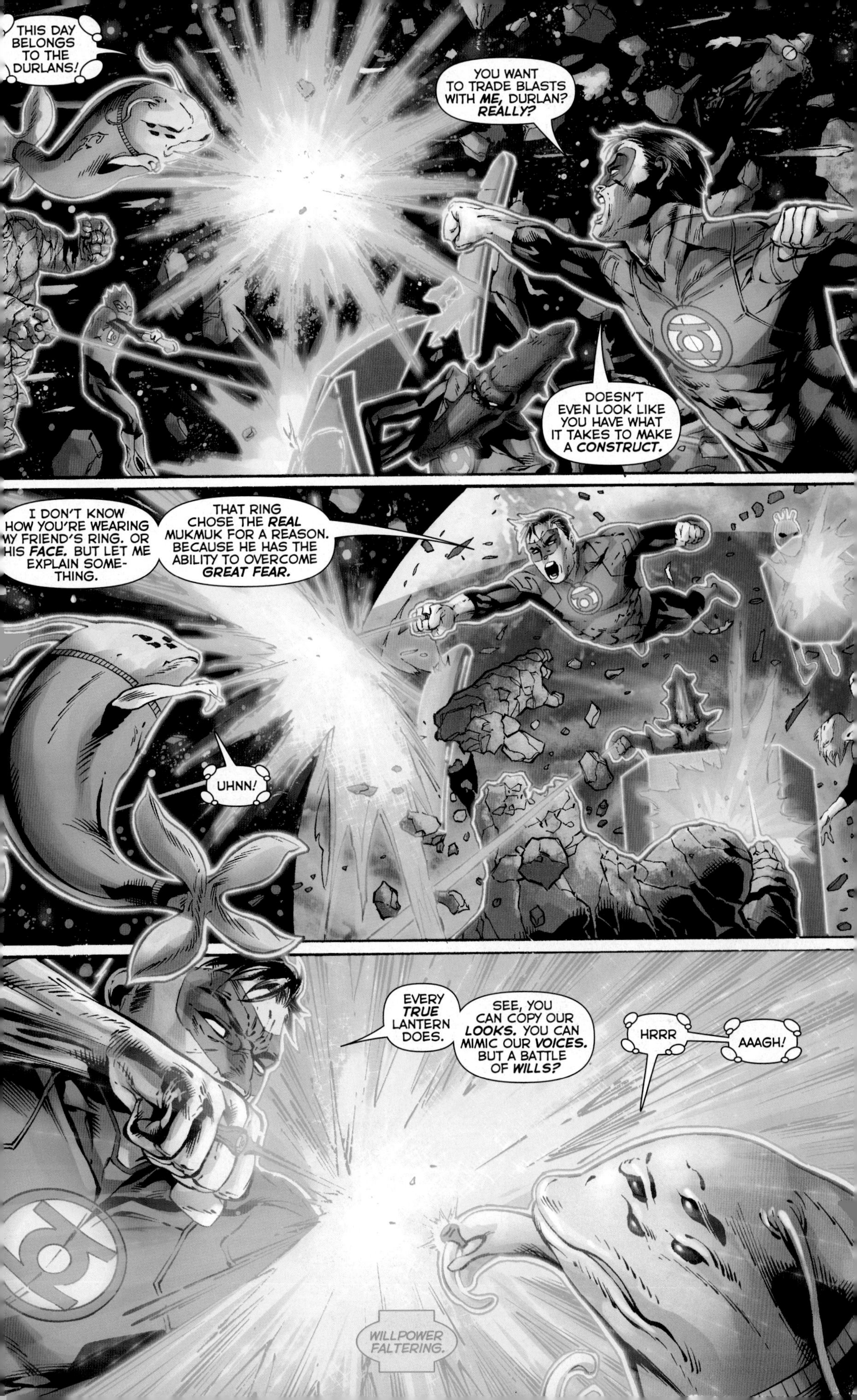
THIS DAY BELONGS TO THE DURLANS!
YOU WANT TO TRADE BLASTS WITH ME, DURLAN? REALLY?
DOESN'T EVEN LOOK LIKE YOU HAVE WHAT IT TAKES TO MAKE A CONSTRUCT.
I DON'T KNOW HOW YOU'RE WEARING MY FRIEND'S RING. OR HIS FACE. BUT LET ME EXPLAIN SOMETHING.
THAT RING CHOSE THE REAL MUKMUK FOR A REASON. BECAUSE HE HAS THE ABILITY TO OVERCOME GREAT FEAR.
UHNN!
EVERY TRUE LANTERN DOES.
SEE, YOU CAN COPY OUR LOOKS. YOU CAN MIMIC OUR VOICES. BUT A BATTLE OF WILLS?
HRRR
AAAGH!
WILLPOWER FALTERING.

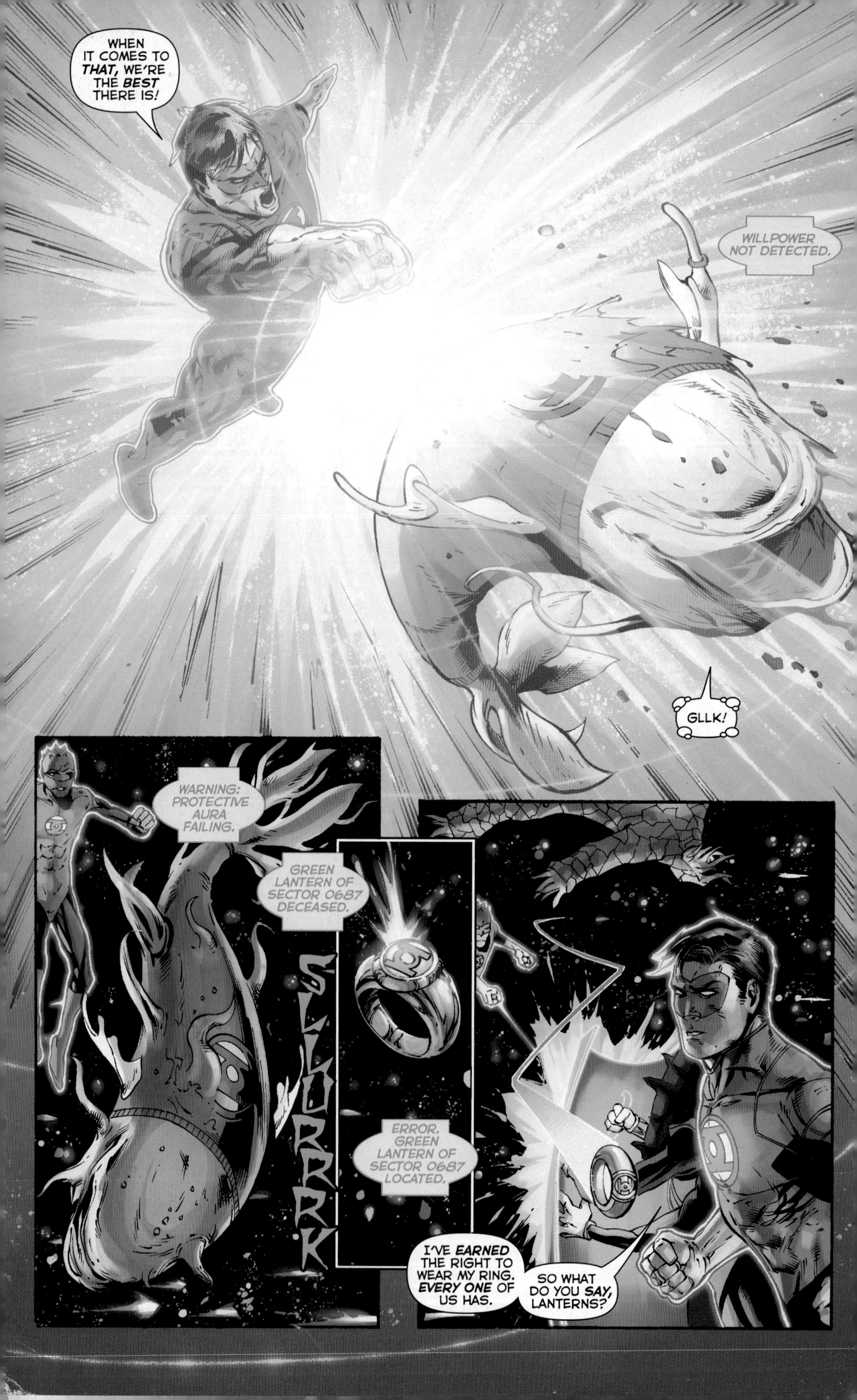

WHEN IT COMES TO *THAT,* WE'RE THE *BEST* THERE IS!
WILLPOWER NOT DETECTED.
GLLK!
WARNING: PROTECTIVE AURA FAILING.
GREEN LANTERN OF SECTOR 0687 DECEASED.
SLLURRRK
ERROR. GREEN LANTERN OF SECTOR 0687 LOCATED.
I'VE *EARNED* THE RIGHT TO WEAR MY RING. *EVERY ONE* OF US HAS.
SO WHAT DO YOU *SAY,* LANTERNS?

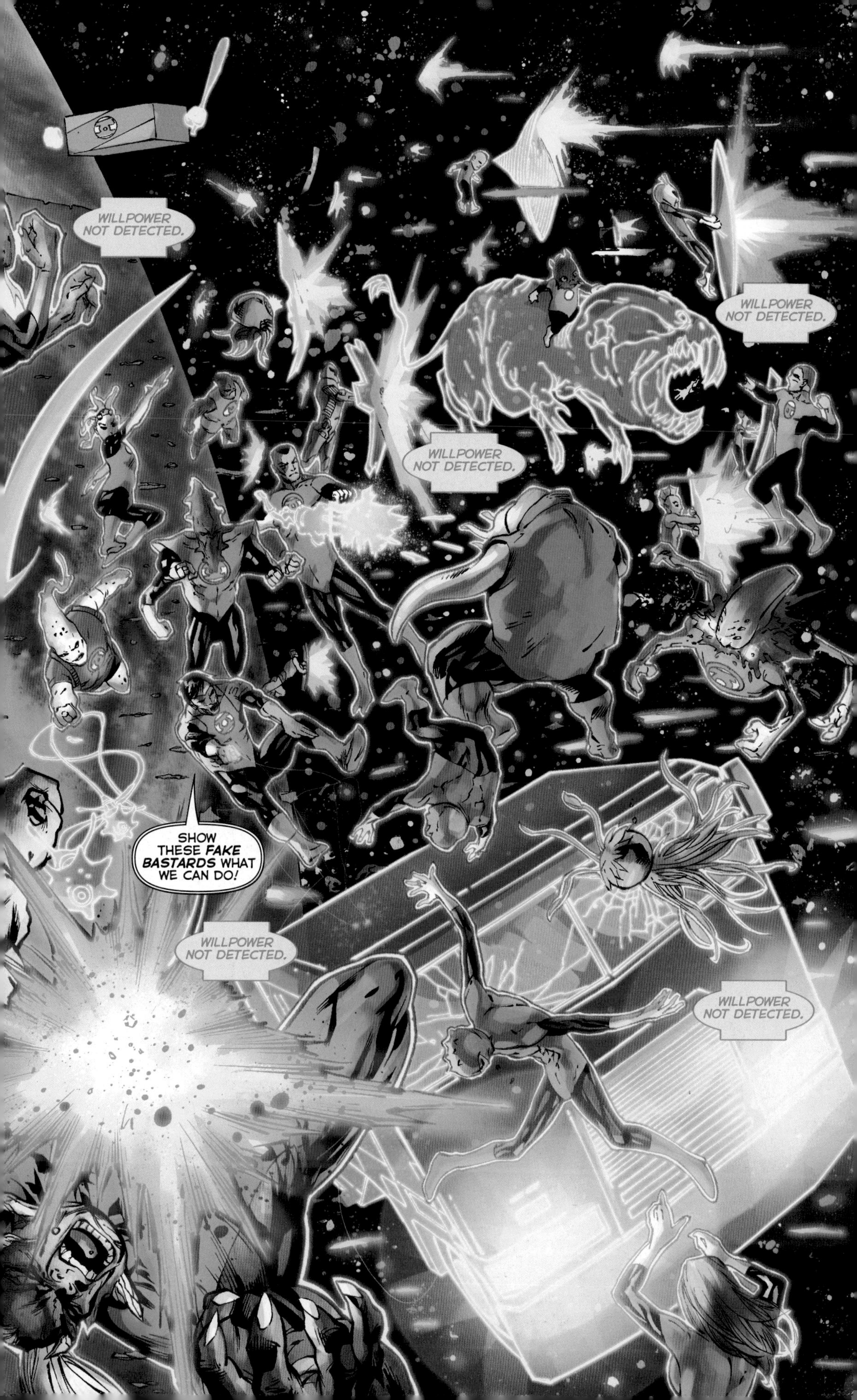
WILLPOWER NOT DETECTED.
WILLPOWER NOT DETECTED.
WILLPOWER NOT DETECTED.
SHOW THESE *FAKE BASTARDS* WHAT WE CAN DO!
WILLPOWER NOT DETECTED.
WILLPOWER NOT DETECTED.

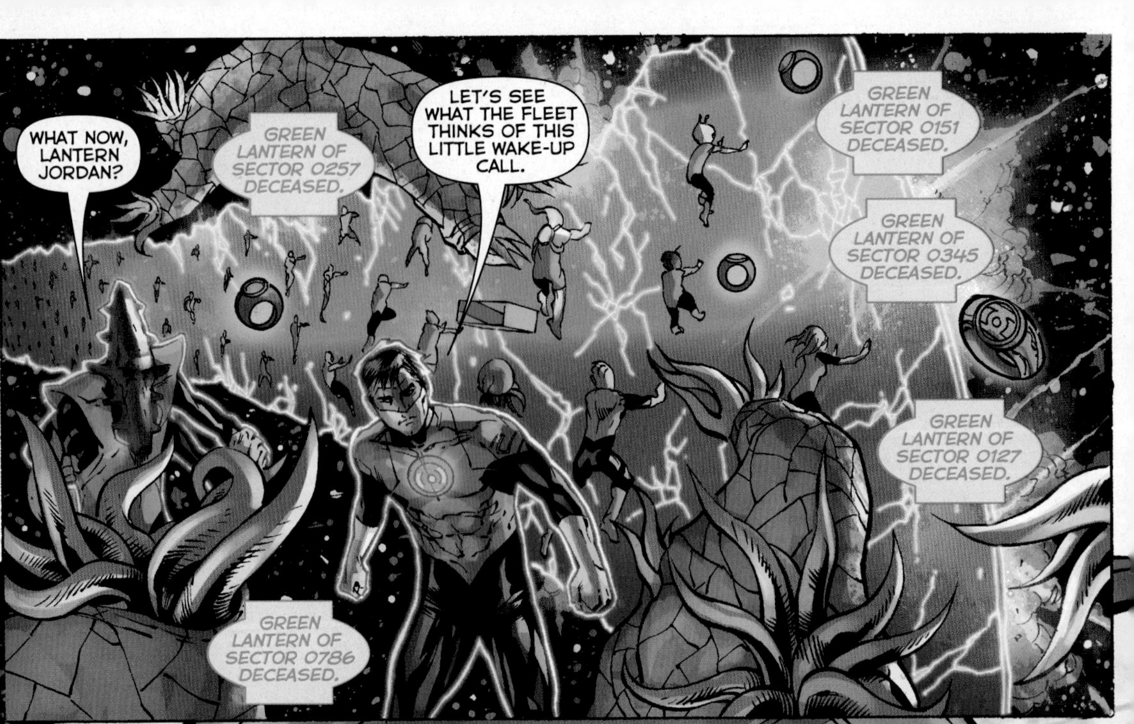
WHAT NOW, LANTERN JORDAN?
GREEN LANTERN OF SECTOR 0257 DECEASED.
LET'S SEE WHAT THE FLEET THINKS OF THIS LITTLE WAKE-UP CALL.
GREEN LANTERN OF SECTOR 0151 DECEASED.
GREEN LANTERN OF SECTOR 0345 DECEASED.
GREEN LANTERN OF SECTOR 0127 DECEASED.
GREEN LANTERN OF SECTOR 0786 DECEASED.

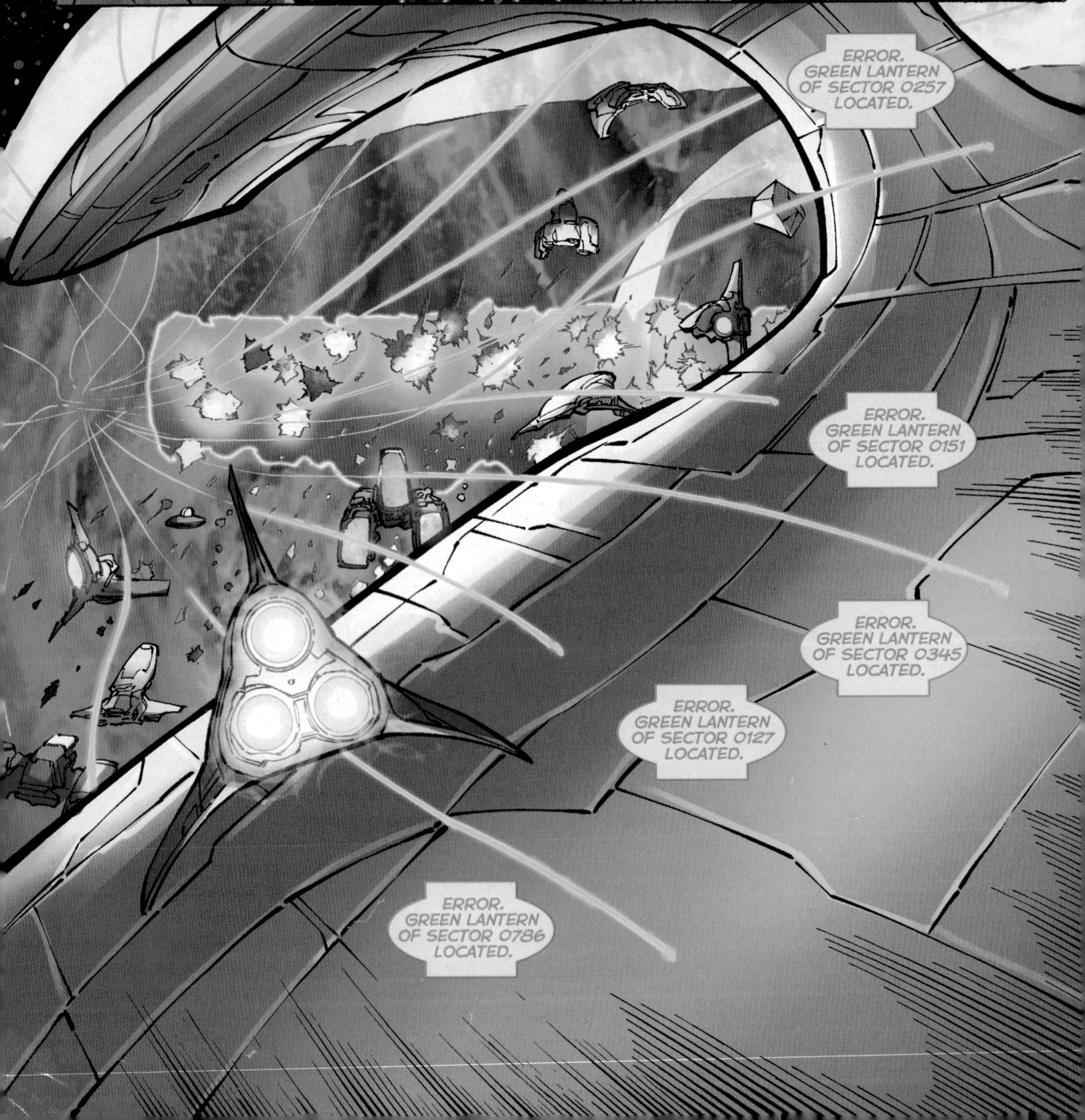
ERROR. GREEN LANTERN OF SECTOR 0257 LOCATED.
ERROR. GREEN LANTERN OF SECTOR 0151 LOCATED.
ERROR. GREEN LANTERN OF SECTOR 0345 LOCATED.
ERROR. GREEN LANTERN OF SECTOR 0127 LOCATED.
ERROR. GREEN LANTERN OF SECTOR 0786 LOCATED.

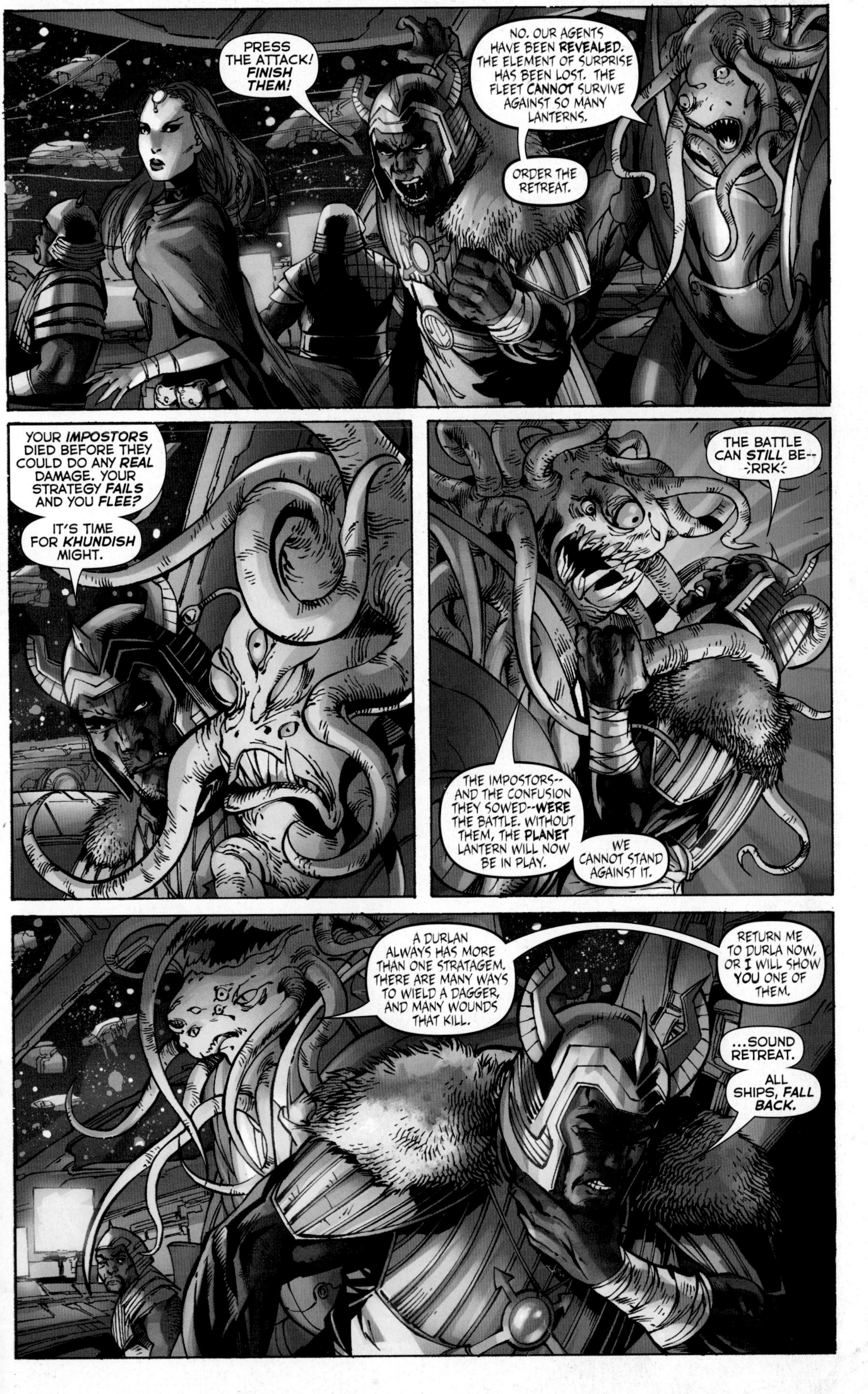

PRESS THE ATTACK! FINISH THEM!
NO. OUR AGENTS HAVE BEEN REVEALED. THE ELEMENT OF SURPRISE HAS BEEN LOST. THE FLEET CANNOT SURVIVE AGAINST SO MANY LANTERNS.
ORDER THE RETREAT.
YOUR IMPOSTORS DIED BEFORE THEY COULD DO ANY REAL DAMAGE. YOUR STRATEGY FAILS AND YOU FLEE?
IT'S TIME FOR KHUNDISH MIGHT.
THE BATTLE CAN STILL BE-- -RRK-
THE IMPOSTORS--AND THE CONFUSION THEY SOWED--WERE THE BATTLE. WITHOUT THEM, THE PLANET LANTERN WILL NOW BE IN PLAY.
WE CANNOT STAND AGAINST IT.
A DURLAN ALWAYS HAS MORE THAN ONE STRATAGEM. THERE ARE MANY WAYS TO WIELD A DAGGER, AND MANY WOUNDS THAT KILL.
RETURN ME TO DURLA NOW, OR I WILL SHOW YOU ONE OF THEM.
...SOUND RETREAT.
ALL SHIPS, FALL BACK.

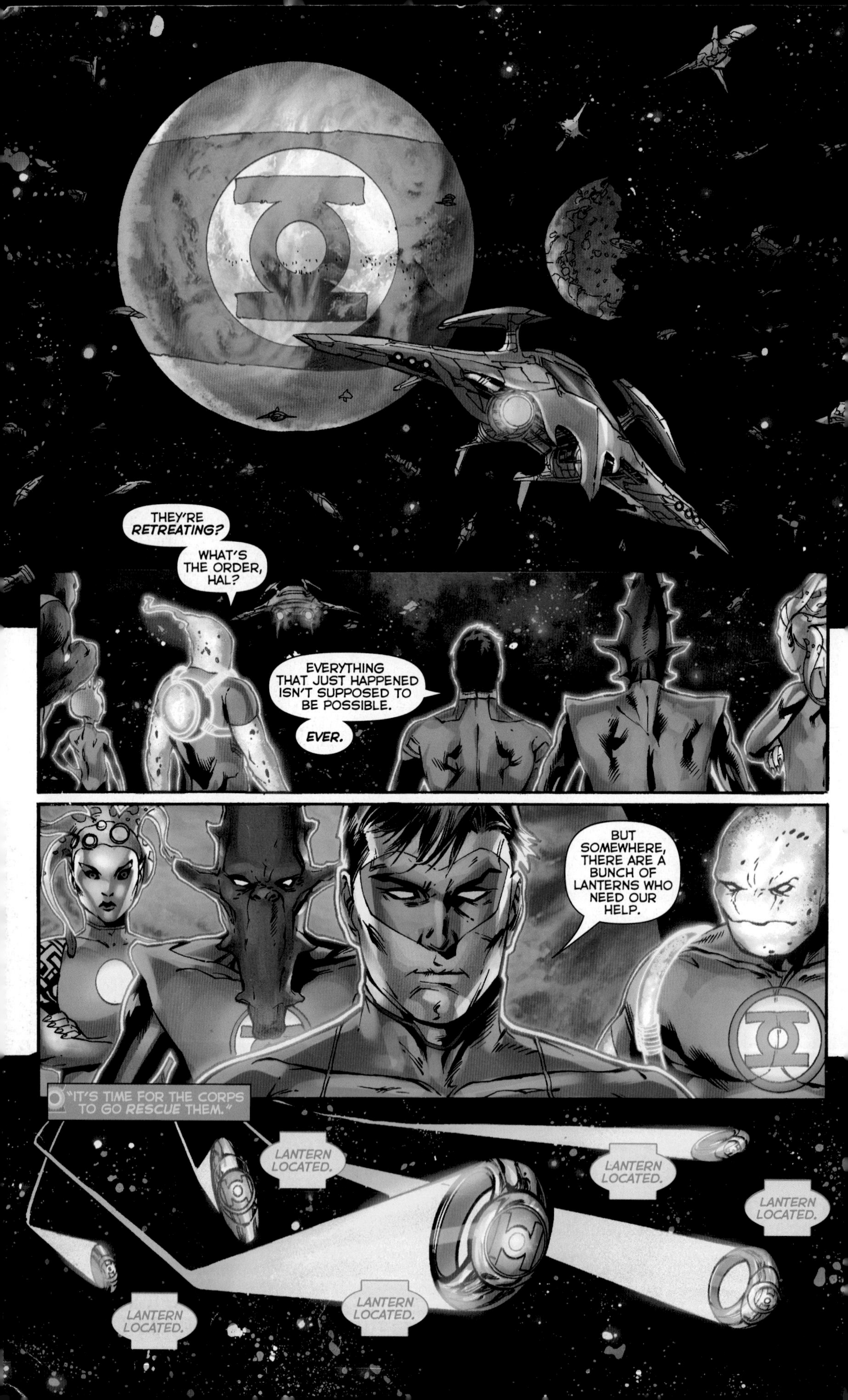
THEY'RE RETREATING?
WHAT'S THE ORDER, HAL?
EVERYTHING THAT JUST HAPPENED ISN'T SUPPOSED TO BE POSSIBLE.
EVER.
BUT SOMEWHERE, THERE ARE A BUNCH OF LANTERNS WHO NEED OUR HELP.
"IT'S TIME FOR THE CORPS TO GO RESCUE THEM."
LANTERN LOCATED.
LANTERN LOCATED.
LANTERN LOCATED.
LANTERN LOCATED.
LANTERN LOCATED.

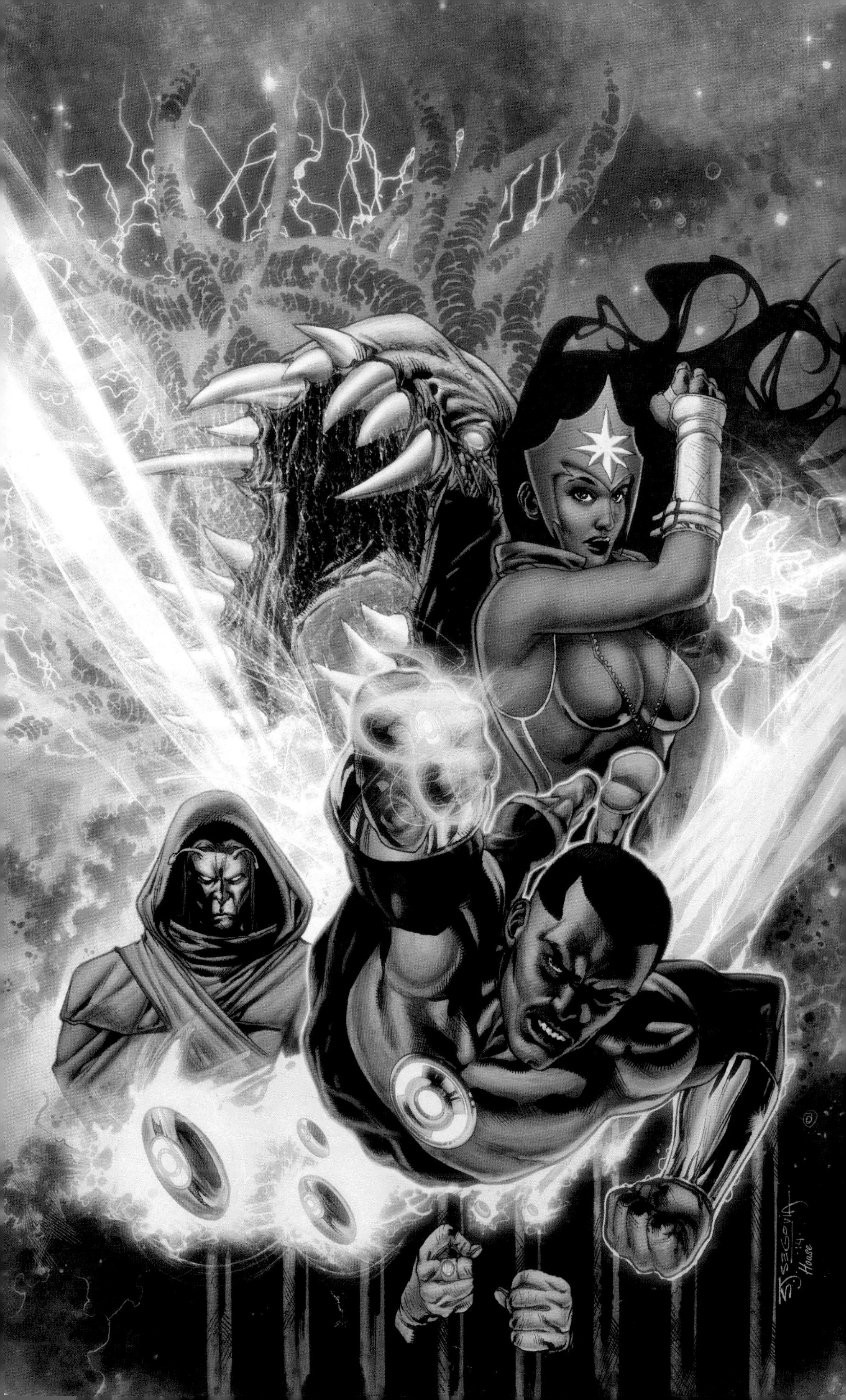

UPRISING PART 2: PRISON BREAK

VAN JENSEN writer BERNARD CHANG artist MARCELO MAIOLO colorist
cover art by STEPHEN SEGOVIA & ANDREW DALHOUSE BATMAN '66 variant cover by MIKE & LAURA ALLRED

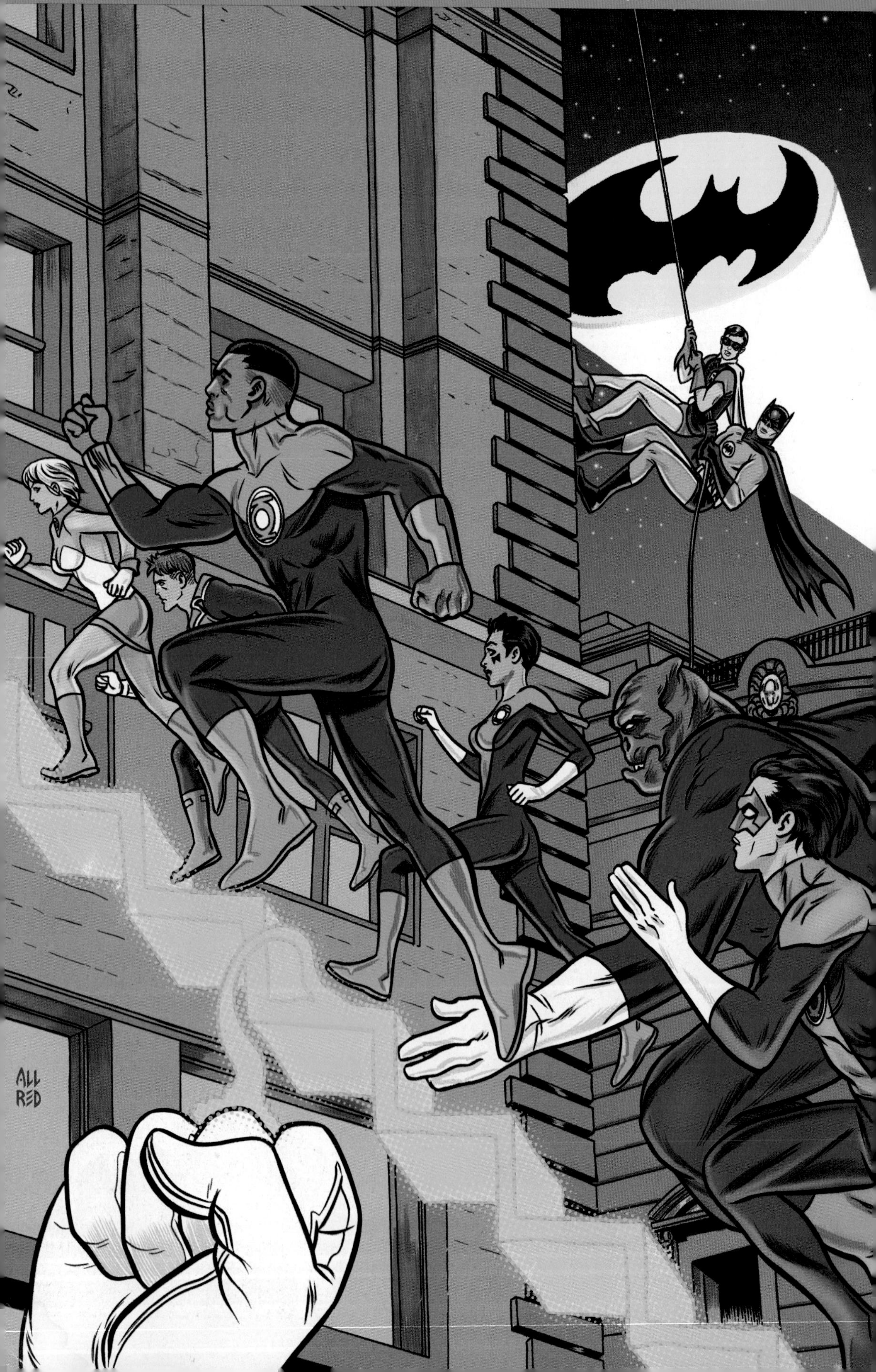
ALL RED

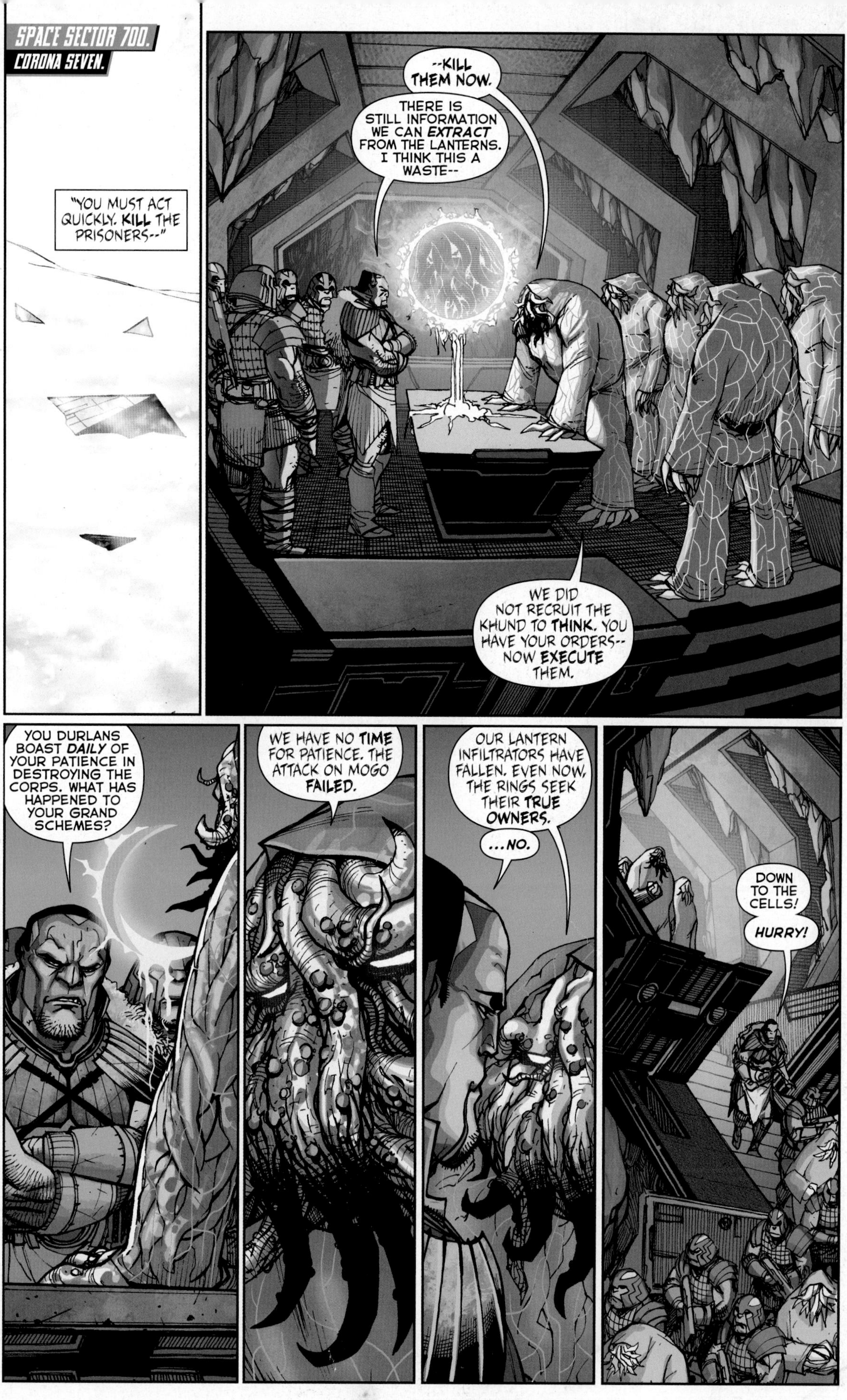
SPACE SECTOR 700.
CORONA SEVEN.
"YOU MUST ACT QUICKLY. KILL THE PRISONERS--"
--KILL THEM NOW.
THERE IS STILL INFORMATION WE CAN EXTRACT FROM THE LANTERNS. I THINK THIS A WASTE--
WE DID NOT RECRUIT THE KHUND TO THINK. YOU HAVE YOUR ORDERS-- NOW EXECUTE THEM.
YOU DURLANS BOAST DAILY OF YOUR PATIENCE IN DESTROYING THE CORPS. WHAT HAS HAPPENED TO YOUR GRAND SCHEMES?
WE HAVE NO TIME FOR PATIENCE. THE ATTACK ON MOGO FAILED.
OUR LANTERN INFILTRATORS HAVE FALLEN. EVEN NOW, THE RINGS SEEK THEIR TRUE OWNERS.
...NO.
DOWN TO THE CELLS!
HURRY!

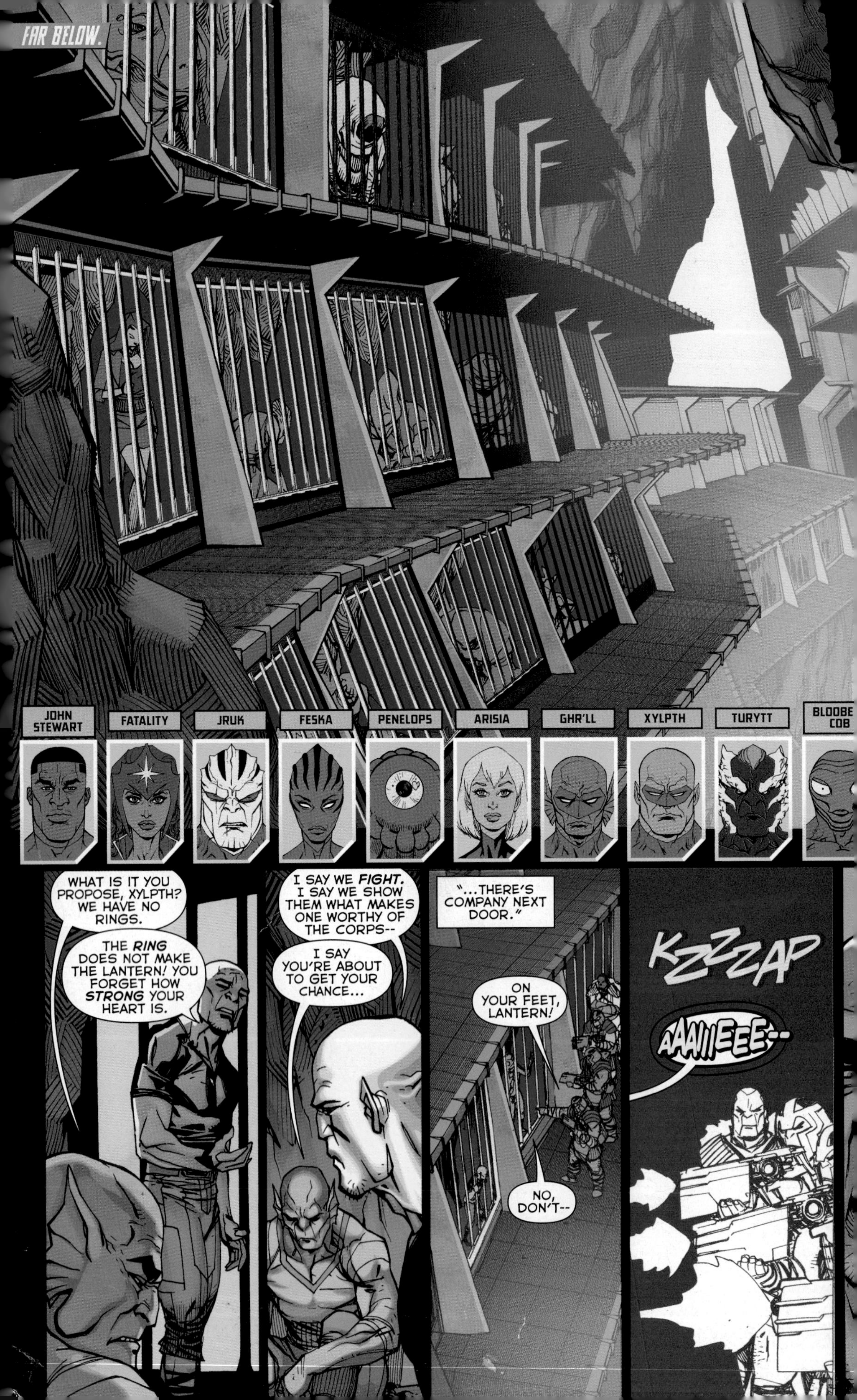
FAR BELOW.
JOHN STEWART
FATALITY
JRUK
FESKA
PENELOPS
ARISIA
GHR'LL
XYLPTH
TURYTT
BLOOBE COB
WHAT IS IT YOU PROPOSE, XYLPTH? WE HAVE NO RINGS.
THE RING DOES NOT MAKE THE LANTERN! YOU FORGET HOW STRONG YOUR HEART IS.
I SAY WE FIGHT. I SAY WE SHOW THEM WHAT MAKES ONE WORTHY OF THE CORPS--
I SAY YOU'RE ABOUT TO GET YOUR CHANCE...
"...THERE'S COMPANY NEXT DOOR."
ON YOUR FEET, LANTERN!
NO, DON'T--
KZZZAP
AAAIIIEEE--

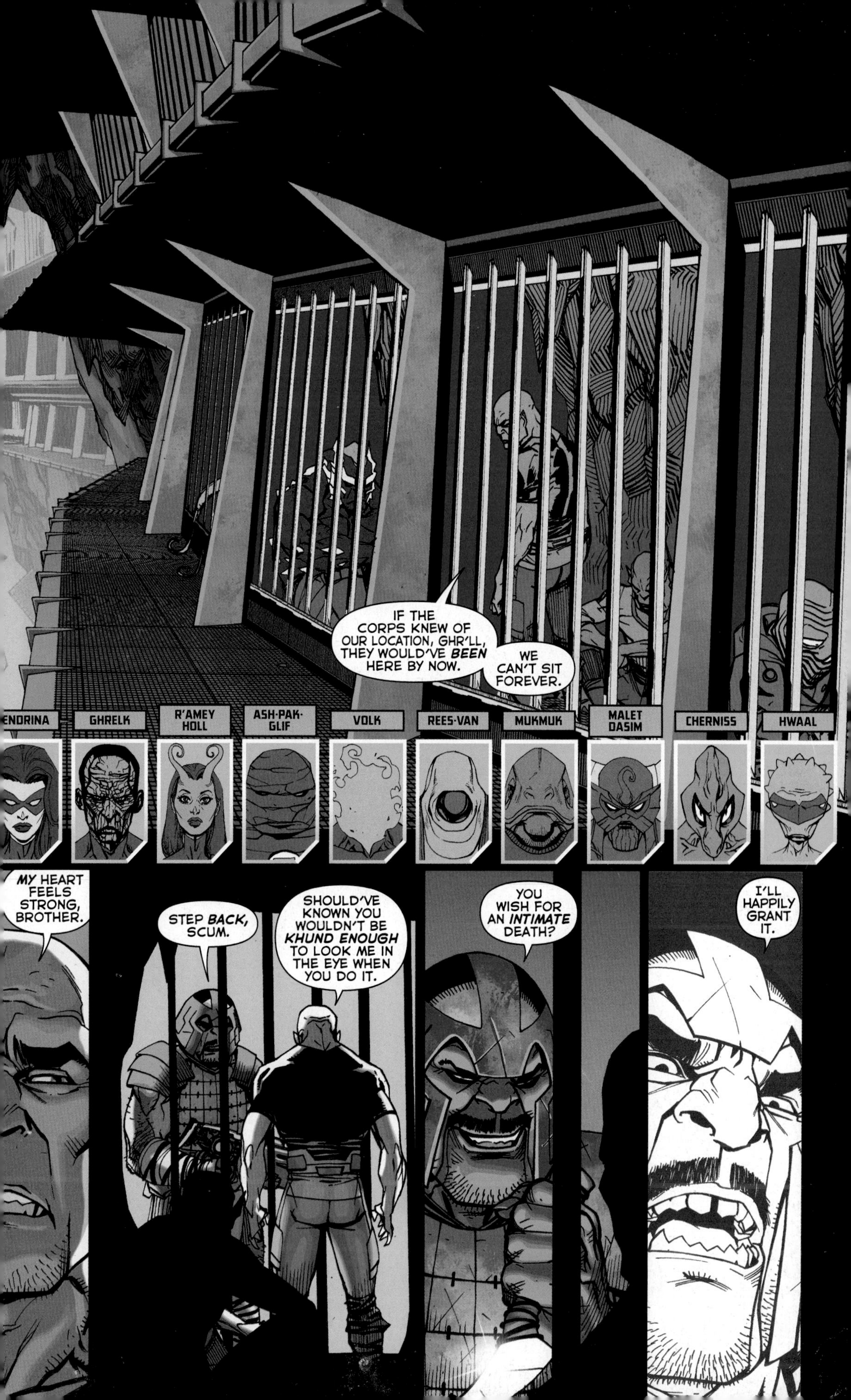
IF THE CORPS KNEW OF OUR LOCATION, GHR'LL, THEY WOULD'VE *BEEN* HERE BY NOW.
WE CAN'T SIT FOREVER.
ENDRINA
GHRELK
R'AMEY HOLL
ASH-PAK-GLIF
VOLK
REES-VAN
MUKMUK
MALET DASIM
CHERNISS
HWAAL
MY HEART FEELS STRONG, BROTHER.
STEP *BACK,* SCUM.
SHOULD'VE KNOWN YOU WOULDN'T BE *KHUND ENOUGH* TO LOOK ME IN THE EYE WHEN YOU DO IT.
YOU WISH FOR AN *INTIMATE* DEATH?
I'LL HAPPILY GRANT IT.

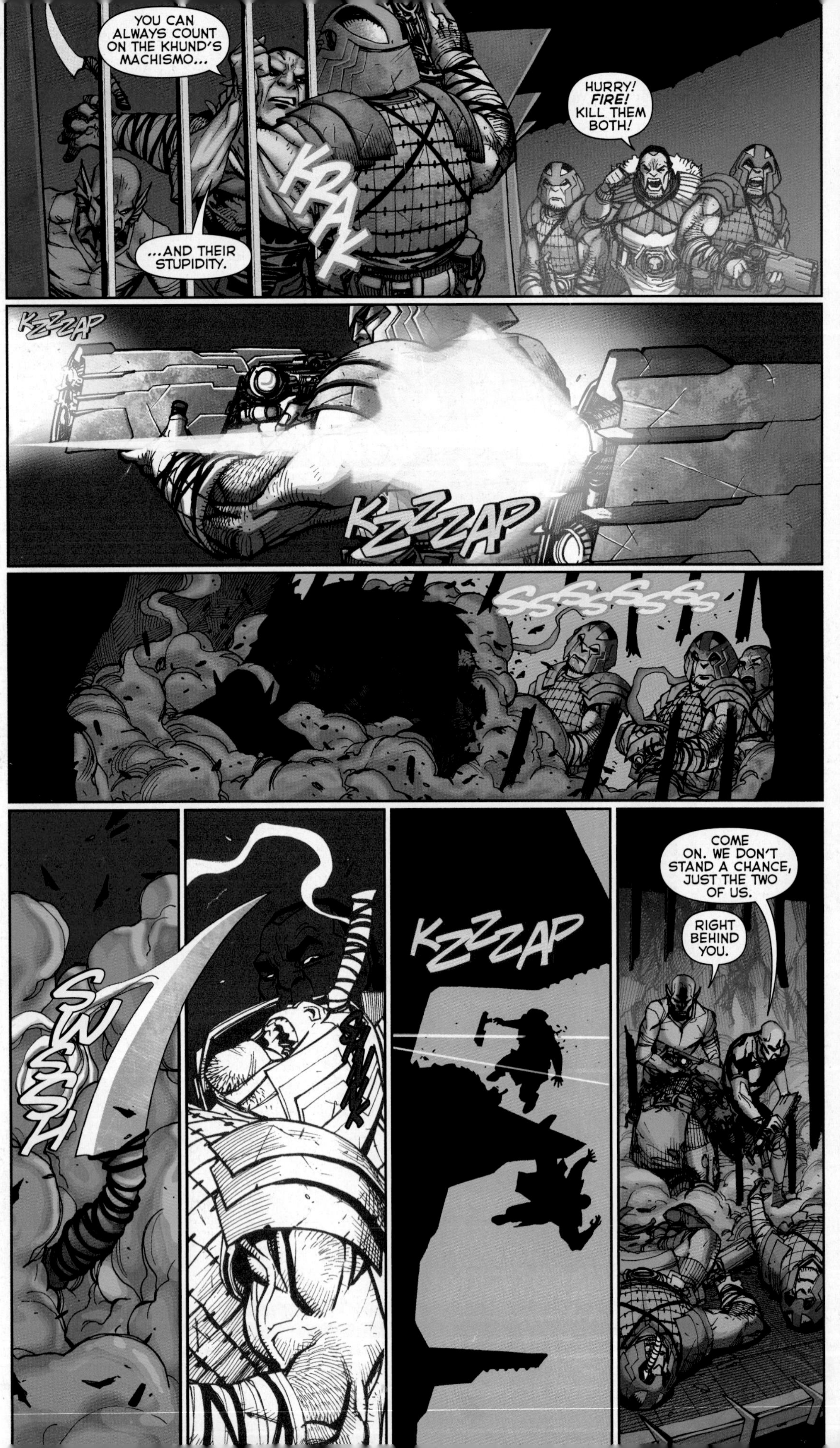
YOU CAN ALWAYS COUNT ON THE KHUND'S MACHISMO...
KRAK
...AND THEIR STUPIDITY.
HURRY! *FIRE!* KILL THEM BOTH!
KZZZAP
KZZZAP
SSSSSSSS
SWSSH
KZZZAP
COME ON. WE DON'T STAND A CHANCE, JUST THE TWO OF US.
RIGHT BEHIND YOU.

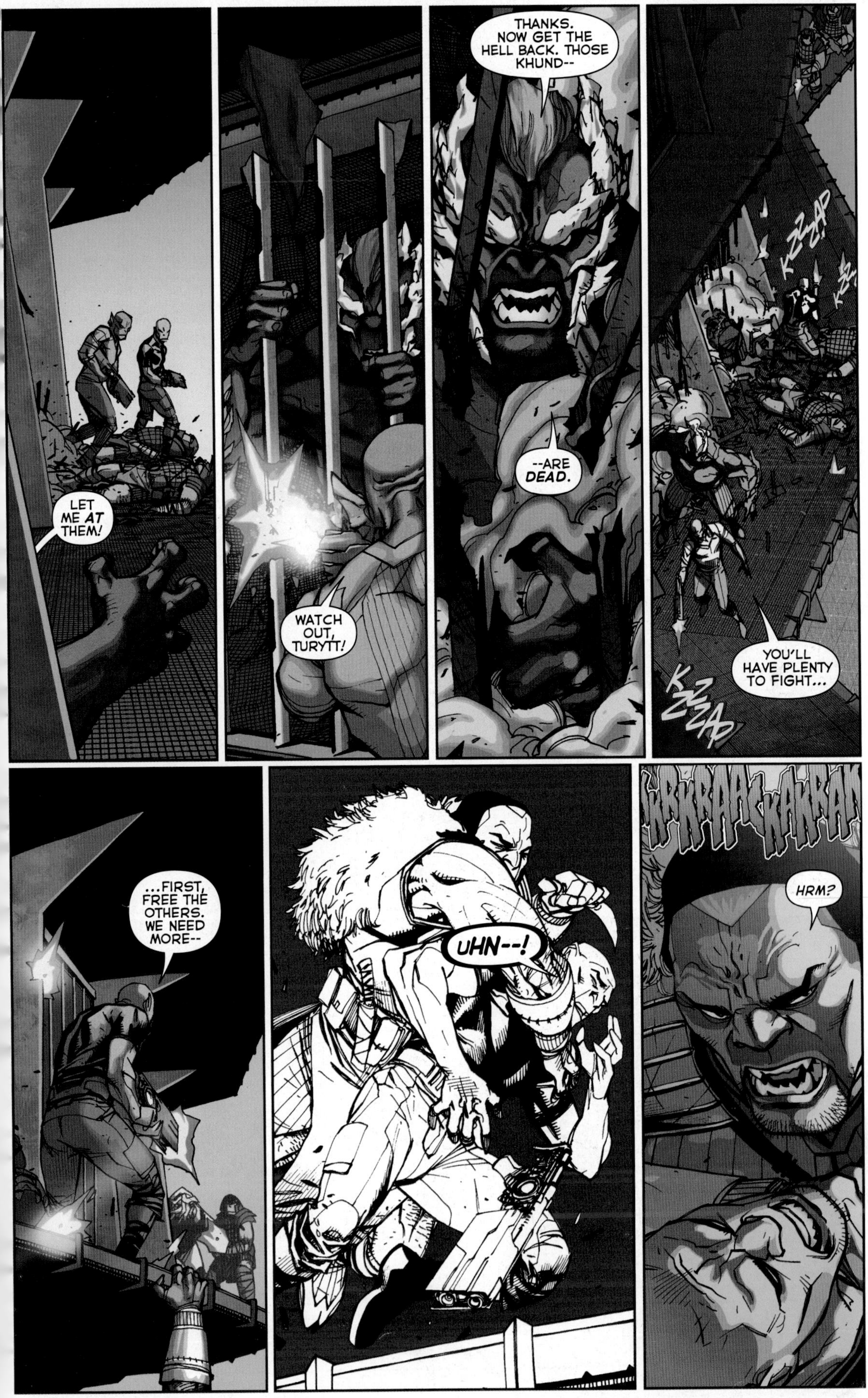
LET ME AT THEM!
WATCH OUT, TURYTT!
THANKS. NOW GET THE HELL BACK. THOSE KHUND--
--ARE DEAD.
KZZZAP
KZZAP
KZZZAP
YOU'LL HAVE PLENTY TO FIGHT...
...FIRST, FREE THE OTHERS. WE NEED MORE--
UHN--!
KRKRAK KRKRAK
HRM?

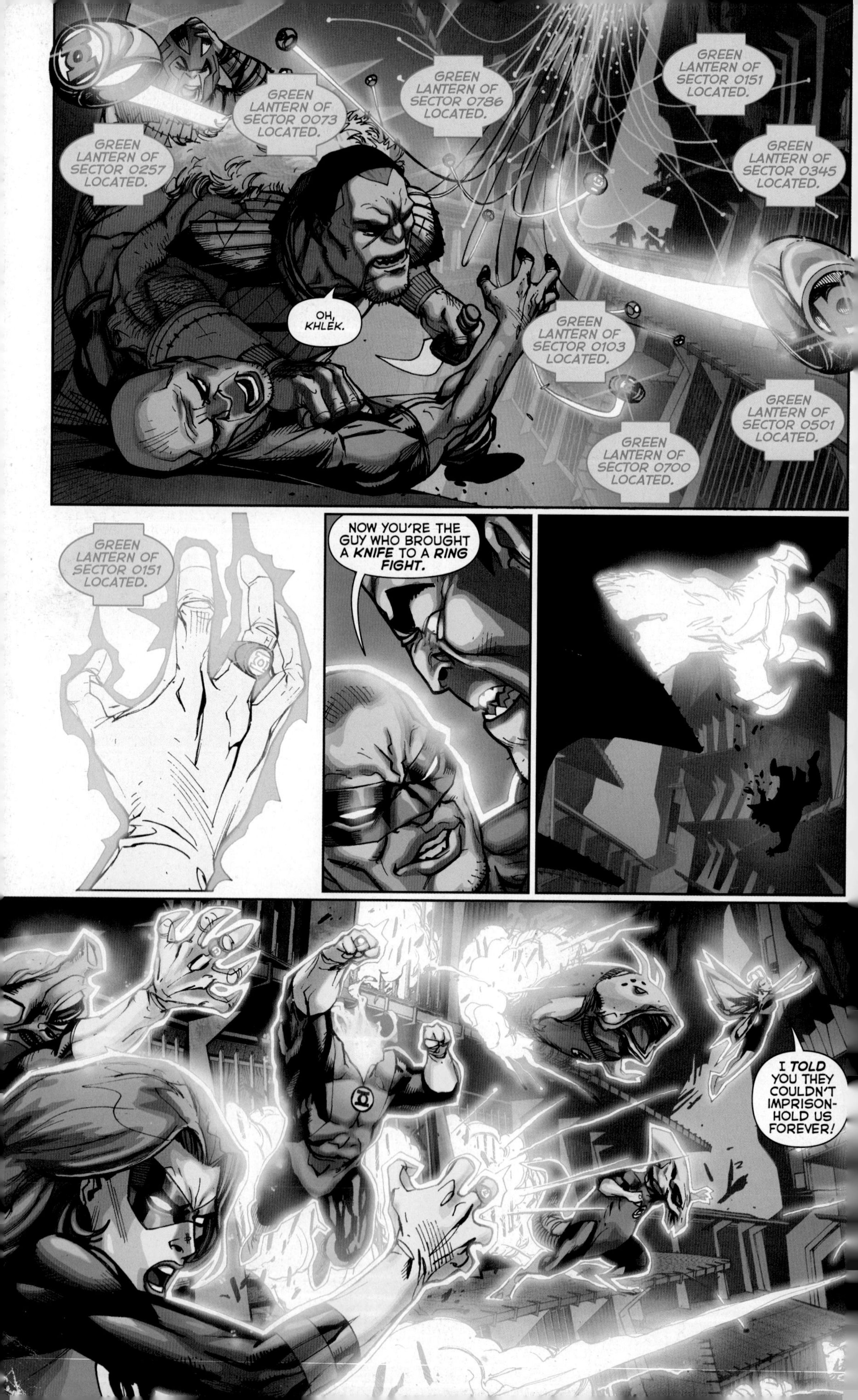
GREEN LANTERN OF SECTOR 0073 LOCATED.
GREEN LANTERN OF SECTOR 0257 LOCATED.
GREEN LANTERN OF SECTOR 0786 LOCATED.
GREEN LANTERN OF SECTOR 0151 LOCATED.
GREEN LANTERN OF SECTOR 0345 LOCATED.
OH, KHLEK.
GREEN LANTERN OF SECTOR 0103 LOCATED.
GREEN LANTERN OF SECTOR 0501 LOCATED.
GREEN LANTERN OF SECTOR 0700 LOCATED.
GREEN LANTERN OF SECTOR 0151 LOCATED.
NOW YOU'RE THE GUY WHO BROUGHT A KNIFE TO A RING FIGHT.
I TOLD YOU THEY COULDN'T IMPRISON-HOLD US FOREVER!

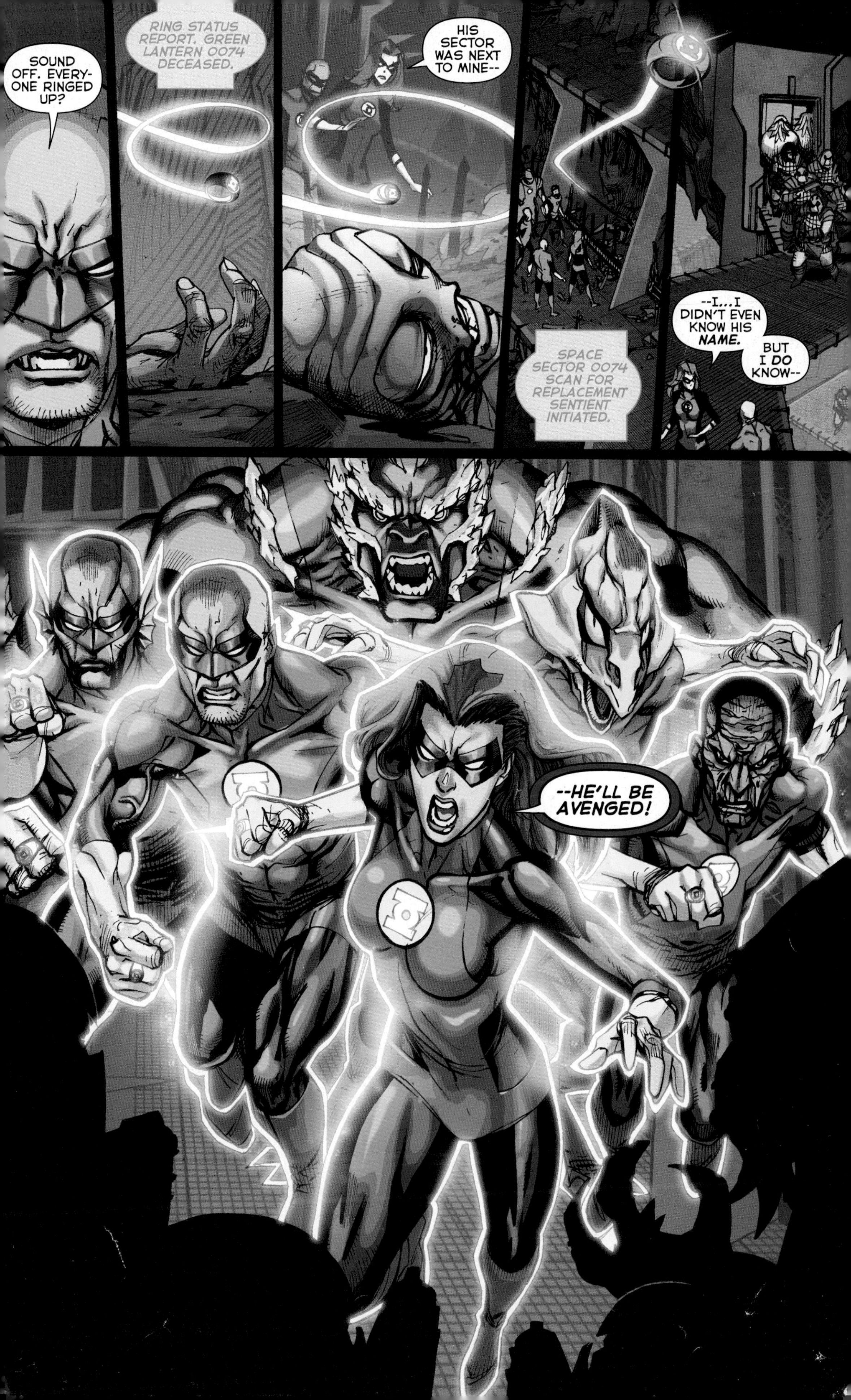
SOUND OFF. EVERY-ONE RINGED UP?
RING STATUS REPORT. GREEN LANTERN 0074 DECEASED.
HIS SECTOR WAS NEXT TO MINE--
SPACE SECTOR 0074 SCAN FOR REPLACEMENT SENTIENT INITIATED.
--I...I DIDN'T EVEN KNOW HIS NAME.
BUT I DO KNOW--
--HE'LL BE AVENGED!

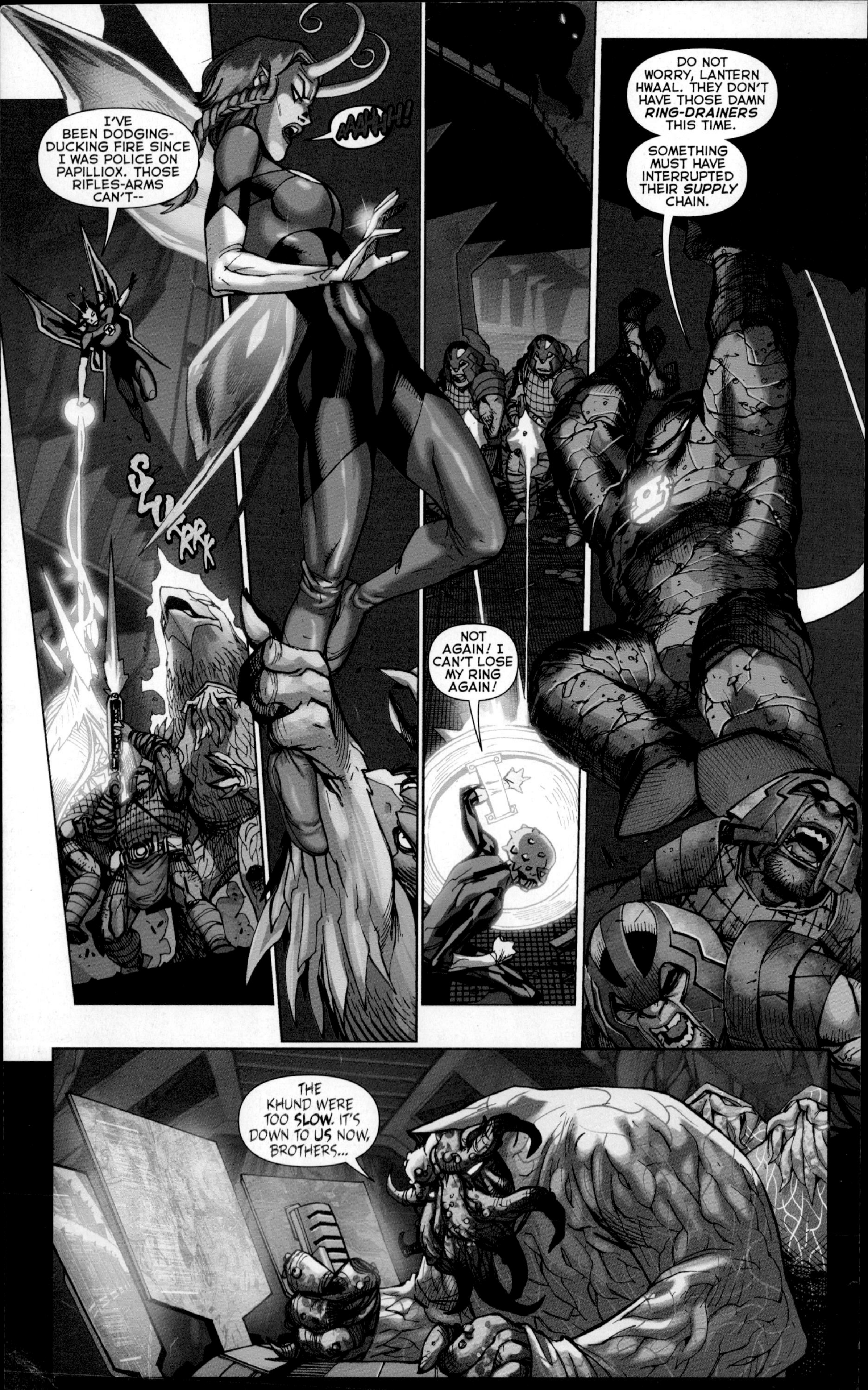

I'VE BEEN DODGING-DUCKING FIRE SINCE I WAS POLICE ON PAPILLIOX. THOSE RIFLES-ARMS CAN'T--
AAAHHH!
SLURRRK
DO NOT WORRY, LANTERN HWAAL. THEY DON'T HAVE THOSE DAMN RING-DRAINERS THIS TIME.
SOMETHING MUST HAVE INTERRUPTED THEIR SUPPLY CHAIN.
NOT AGAIN! I CAN'T LOSE MY RING AGAIN!
THE KHUND WERE TOO SLOW. IT'S DOWN TO US NOW, BROTHERS...

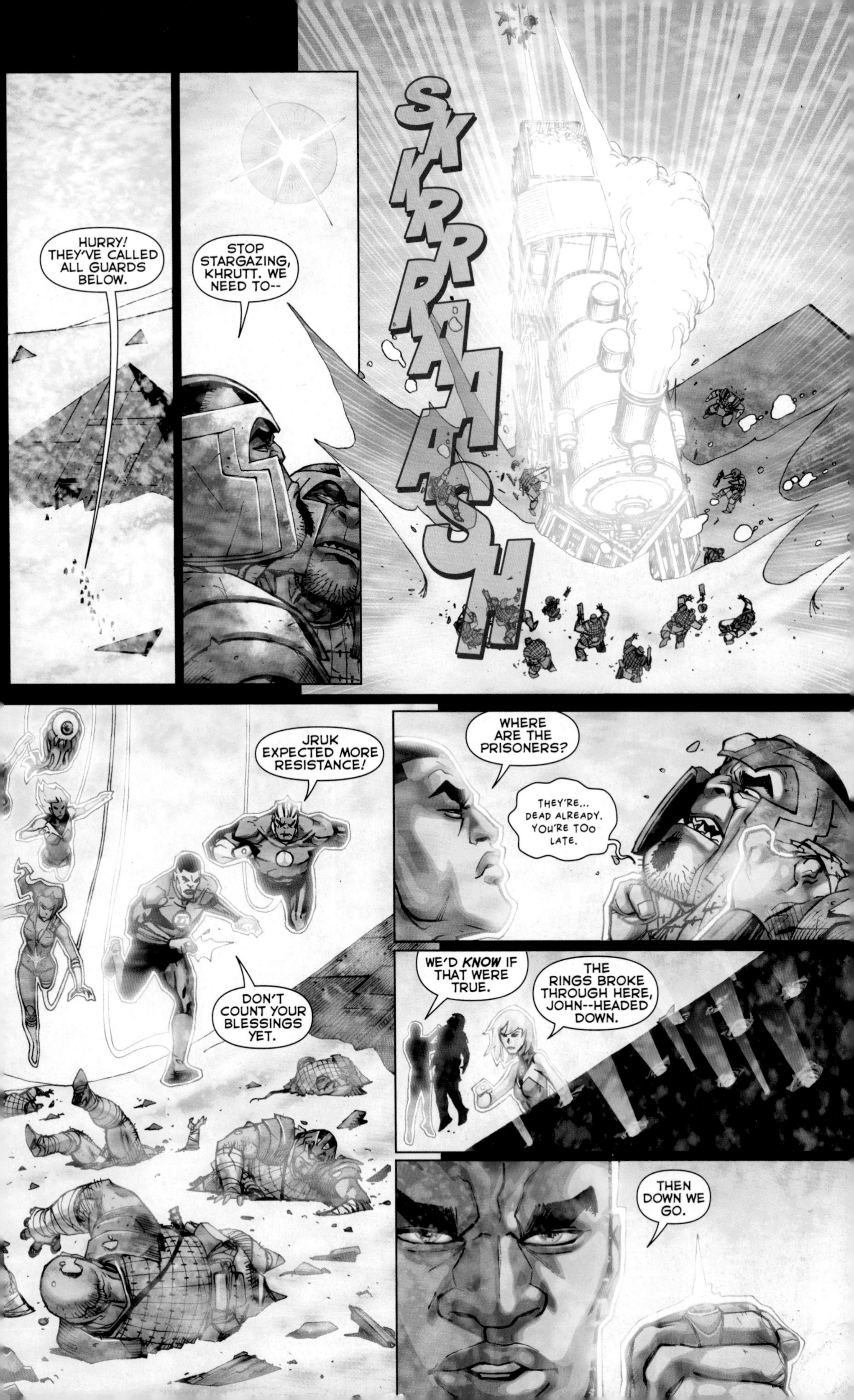
HURRY! THEY'VE CALLED ALL GUARDS BELOW.
STOP STARGAZING, KHRUTT. WE NEED TO--
SKKRRRAASH
JRUK EXPECTED MORE RESISTANCE!
DON'T COUNT YOUR BLESSINGS YET.
WHERE ARE THE PRISONERS?
THEY'RE... DEAD ALREADY. YOU'RE TOO LATE.
WE'D KNOW IF THAT WERE TRUE.
THE RINGS BROKE THROUGH HERE, JOHN--HEADED DOWN.
THEN DOWN WE GO.

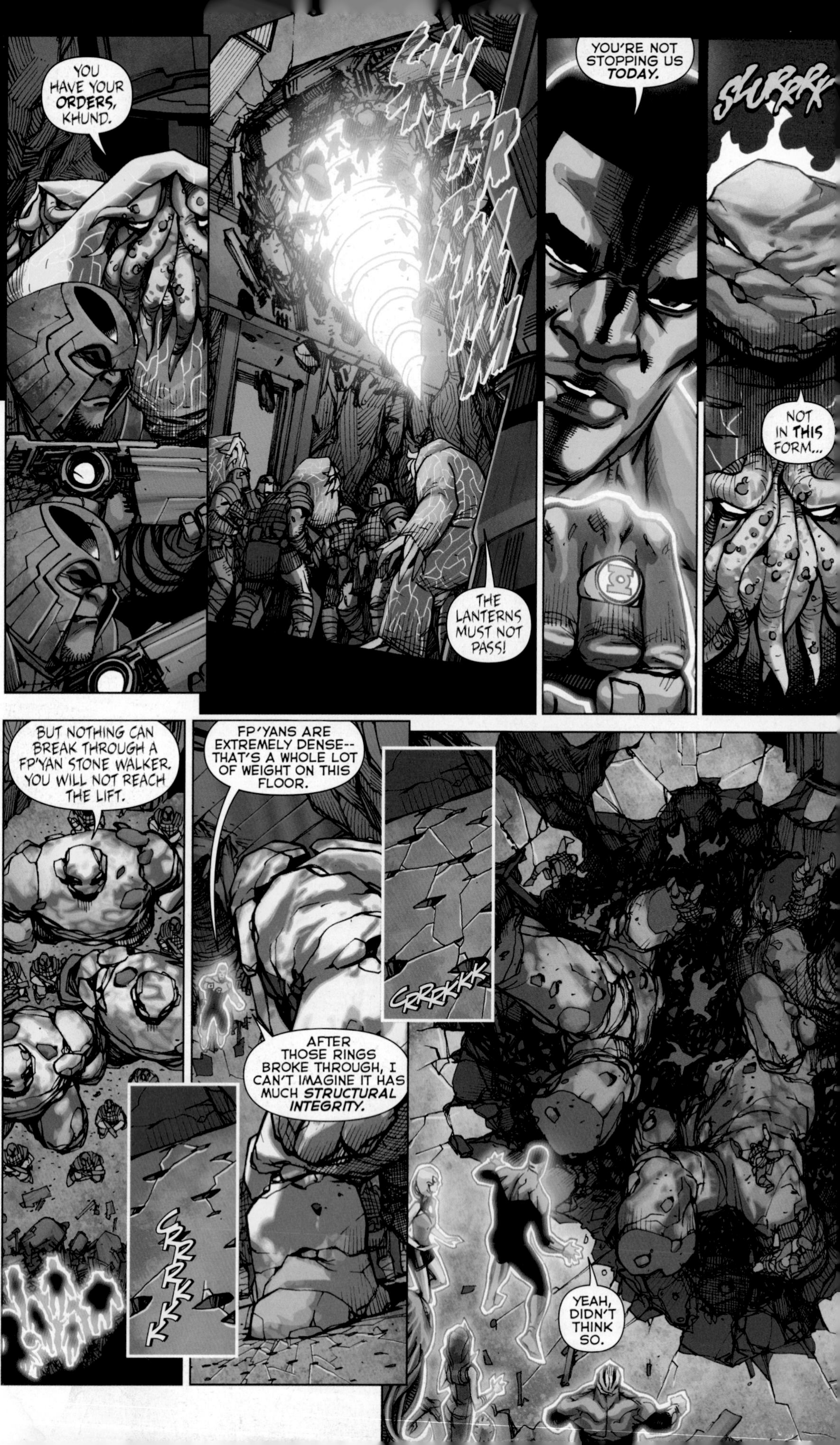
YOU HAVE YOUR ORDERS, KHUND.
SHHRRRMMM
THE LANTERNS MUST NOT PASS!
YOU'RE NOT STOPPING US TODAY.
SLURRK
NOT IN THIS FORM...
BUT NOTHING CAN BREAK THROUGH A FP'YAN STONE WALKER. YOU WILL NOT REACH THE LIFT.
FP'YANS ARE EXTREMELY DENSE-- THAT'S A WHOLE LOT OF WEIGHT ON THIS FLOOR.
CRRRKKK
AFTER THOSE RINGS BROKE THROUGH, I CAN'T IMAGINE IT HAS MUCH STRUCTURAL INTEGRITY.
CRRRKKK
YEAH, DIDN'T THINK SO.

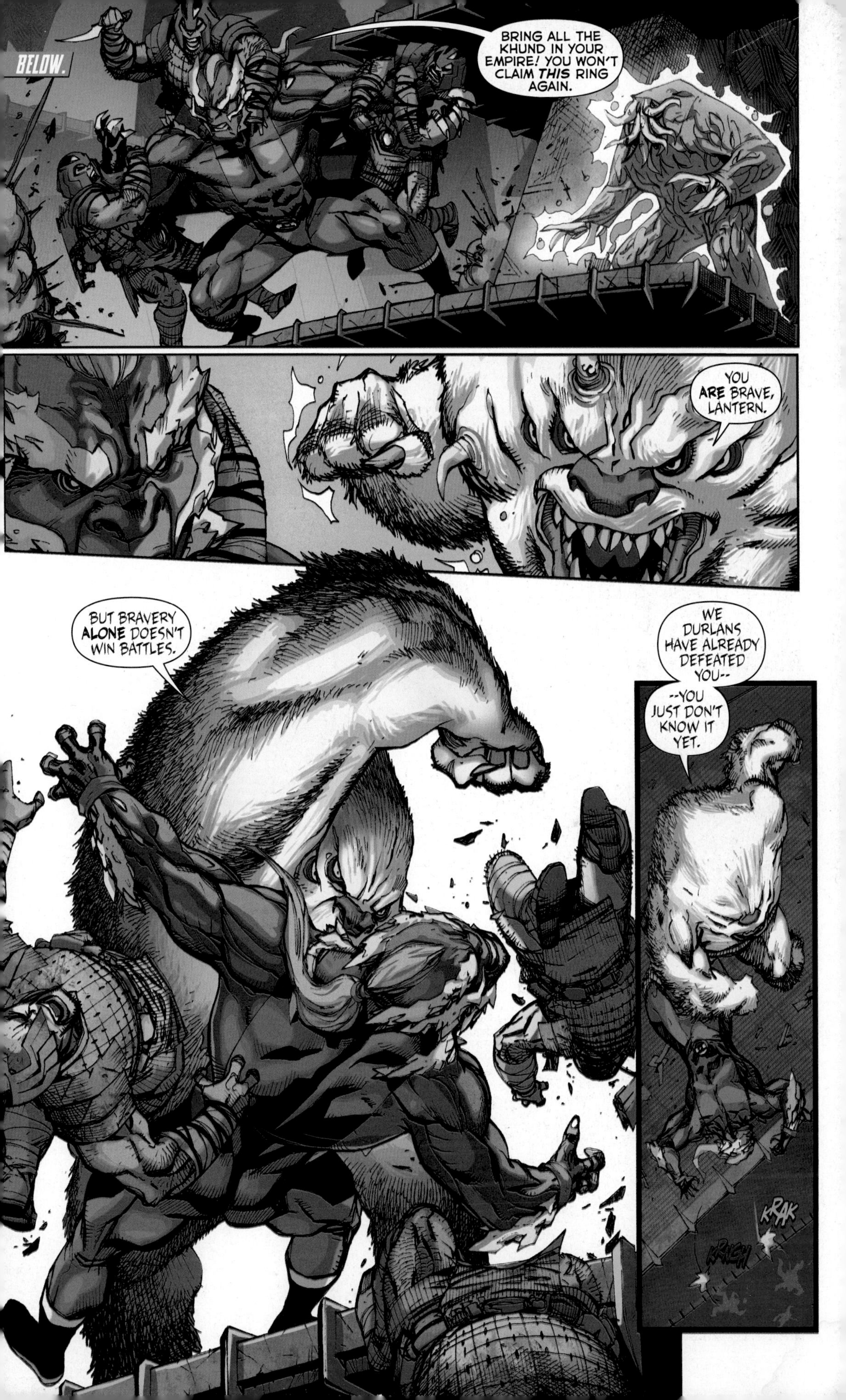
BELOW.
BRING ALL THE KHUND IN YOUR EMPIRE! YOU WON'T CLAIM THIS RING AGAIN.
YOU ARE BRAVE, LANTERN.
BUT BRAVERY ALONE DOESN'T WIN BATTLES.
WE DURLANS HAVE ALREADY DEFEATED YOU--
--YOU JUST DON'T KNOW IT YET.
KRAK
KRASH

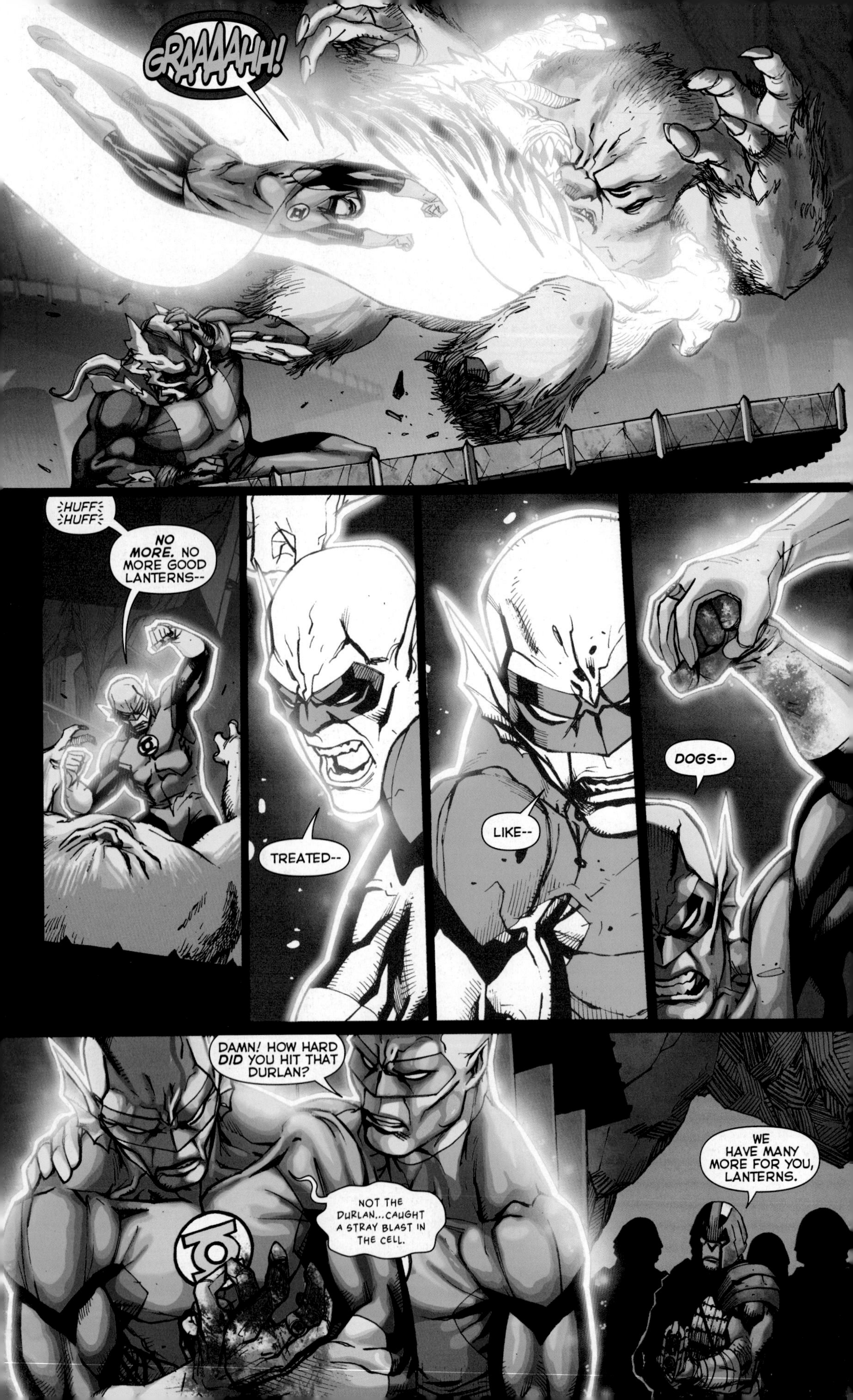
GRAAAAHH!
HUFF HUFF
NO MORE. NO MORE GOOD LANTERNS--
TREATED--
LIKE--
DOGS--
DAMN! HOW HARD DID YOU HIT THAT DURLAN?
NOT THE DURLAN...CAUGHT A STRAY BLAST IN THE CELL.
WE HAVE MANY MORE FOR YOU, LANTERNS.

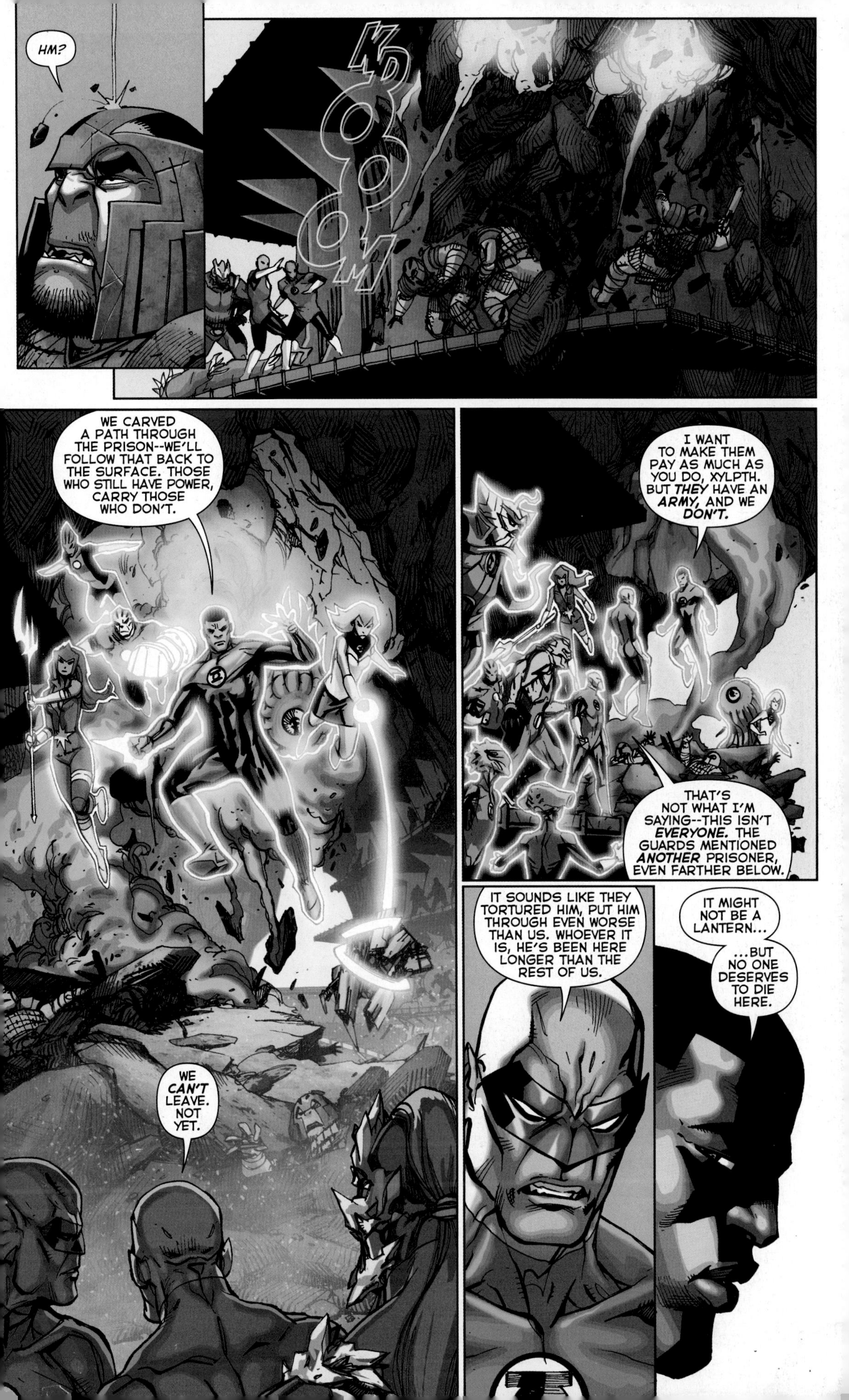
HM?
KDOOOOM
WE CARVED A PATH THROUGH THE PRISON--WE'LL FOLLOW THAT BACK TO THE SURFACE. THOSE WHO STILL HAVE POWER, CARRY THOSE WHO DON'T.
I WANT TO MAKE THEM PAY AS MUCH AS YOU DO, XYLPTH. BUT THEY HAVE AN ARMY, AND WE DON'T.
THAT'S NOT WHAT I'M SAYING--THIS ISN'T EVERYONE. THE GUARDS MENTIONED ANOTHER PRISONER, EVEN FARTHER BELOW.
WE CAN'T LEAVE. NOT YET.
IT SOUNDS LIKE THEY TORTURED HIM, PUT HIM THROUGH EVEN WORSE THAN US. WHOEVER IT IS, HE'S BEEN HERE LONGER THAN THE REST OF US.
IT MIGHT NOT BE A LANTERN...
...BUT NO ONE DESERVES TO DIE HERE.

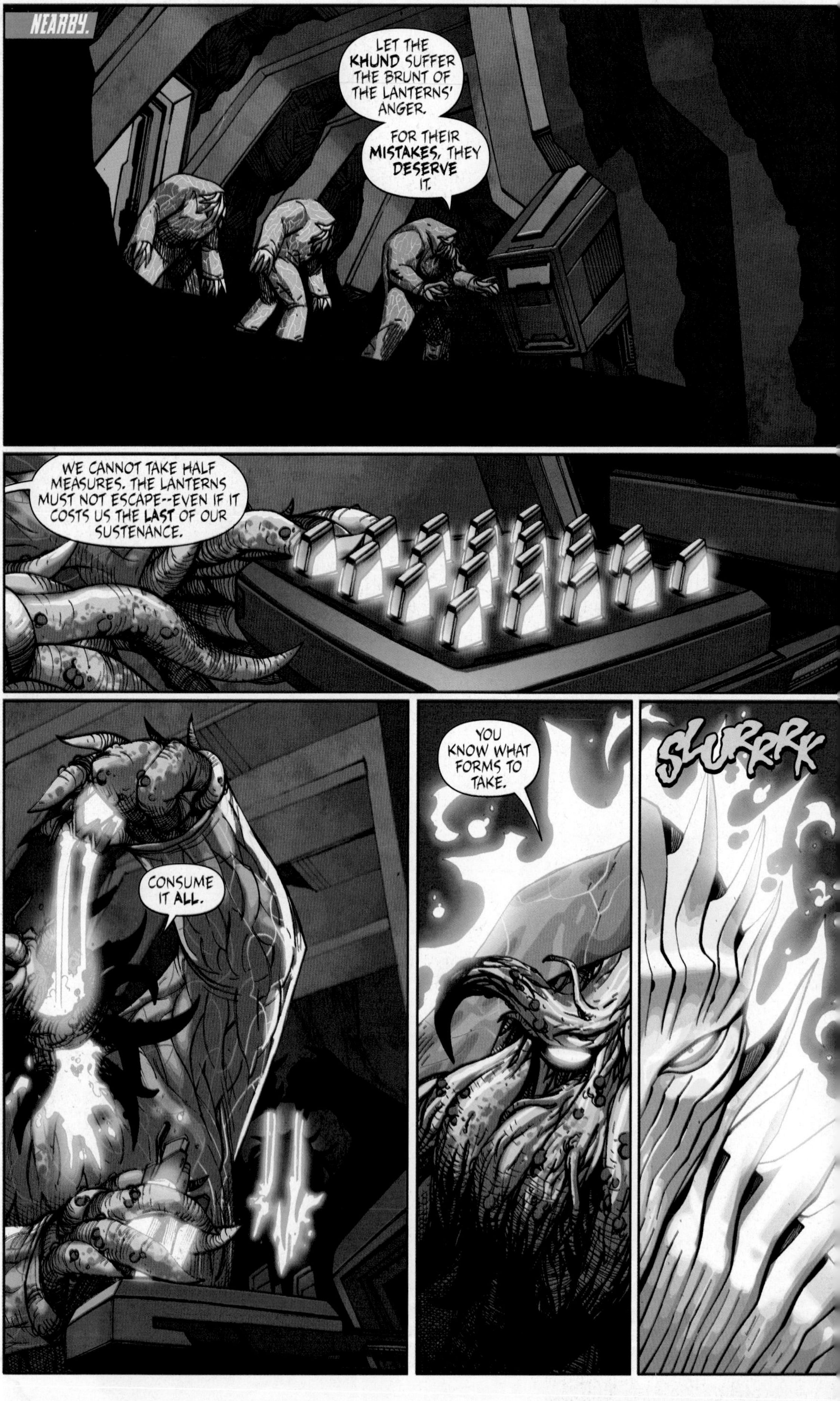
NEARBY.
LET THE KHUND SUFFER THE BRUNT OF THE LANTERNS' ANGER.
FOR THEIR MISTAKES, THEY DESERVE IT.
WE CANNOT TAKE HALF MEASURES. THE LANTERNS MUST NOT ESCAPE--EVEN IF IT COSTS US THE LAST OF OUR SUSTENANCE.
CONSUME IT ALL.
YOU KNOW WHAT FORMS TO TAKE.
SLURRRK

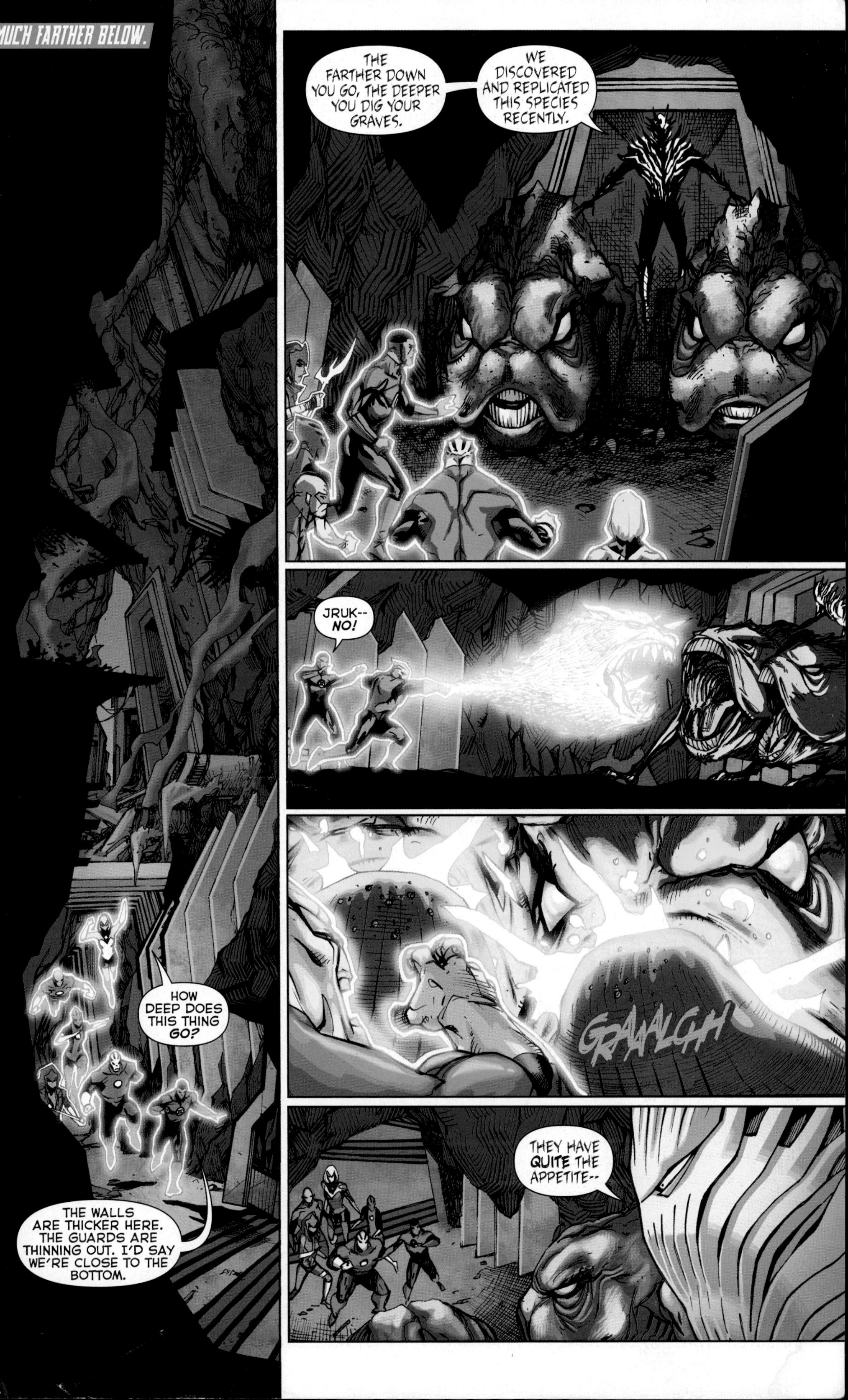
MUCH FARTHER BELOW.
HOW DEEP DOES THIS THING GO?
THE WALLS ARE THICKER HERE. THE GUARDS ARE THINNING OUT. I'D SAY WE'RE CLOSE TO THE BOTTOM.
THE FARTHER DOWN YOU GO, THE DEEPER YOU DIG YOUR GRAVES.
WE DISCOVERED AND REPLICATED THIS SPECIES RECENTLY.
JRUK-- NO!
GRAAALGH
THEY HAVE QUITE THE APPETITE--

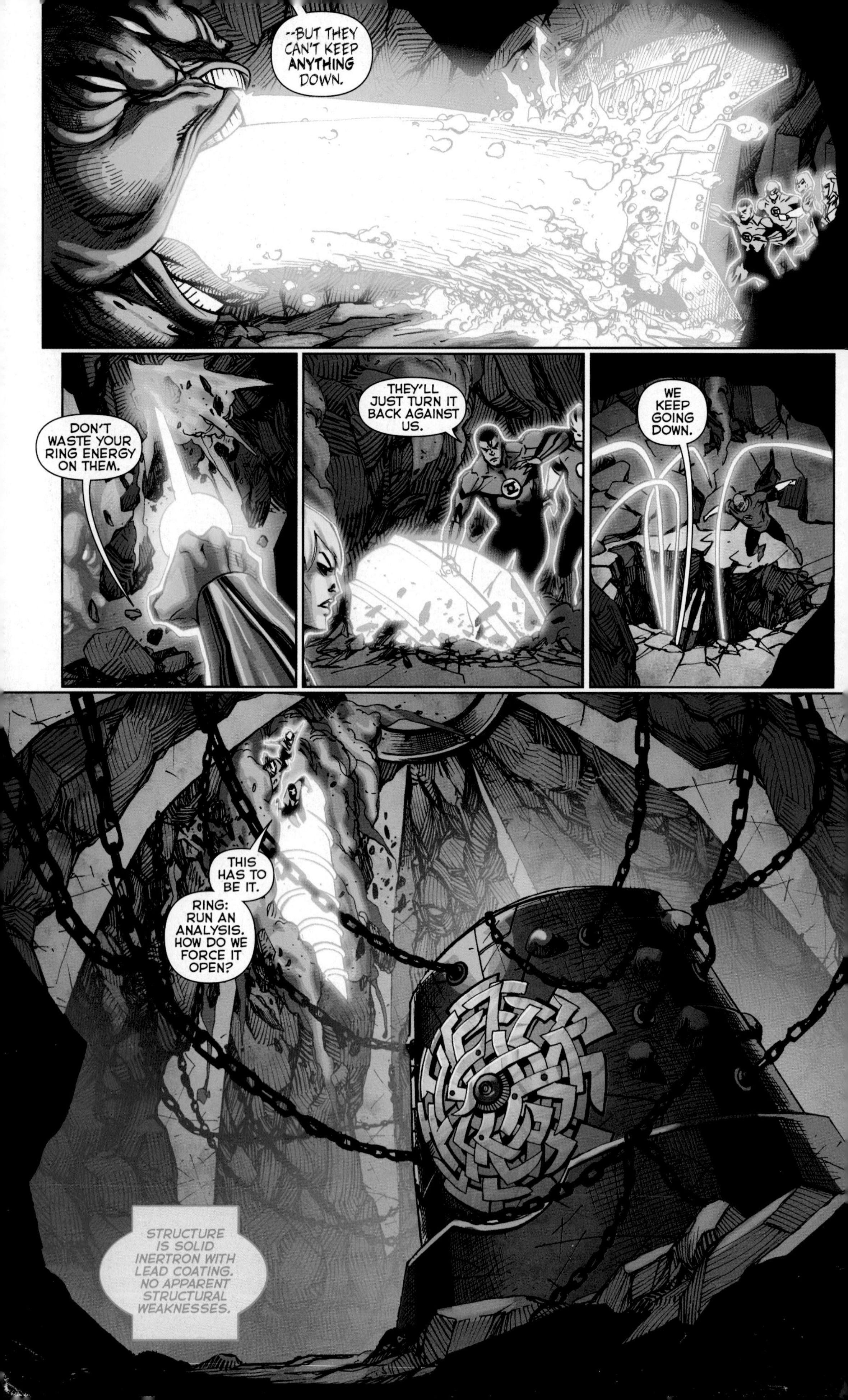
--BUT THEY CAN'T KEEP ANYTHING DOWN.
DON'T WASTE YOUR RING ENERGY ON THEM.
THEY'LL JUST TURN IT BACK AGAINST US.
WE KEEP GOING DOWN.
THIS HAS TO BE IT.
RING: RUN AN ANALYSIS. HOW DO WE FORCE IT OPEN?
STRUCTURE IS SOLID INERTRON WITH LEAD COATING. NO APPARENT STRUCTURAL WEAKNESSES.

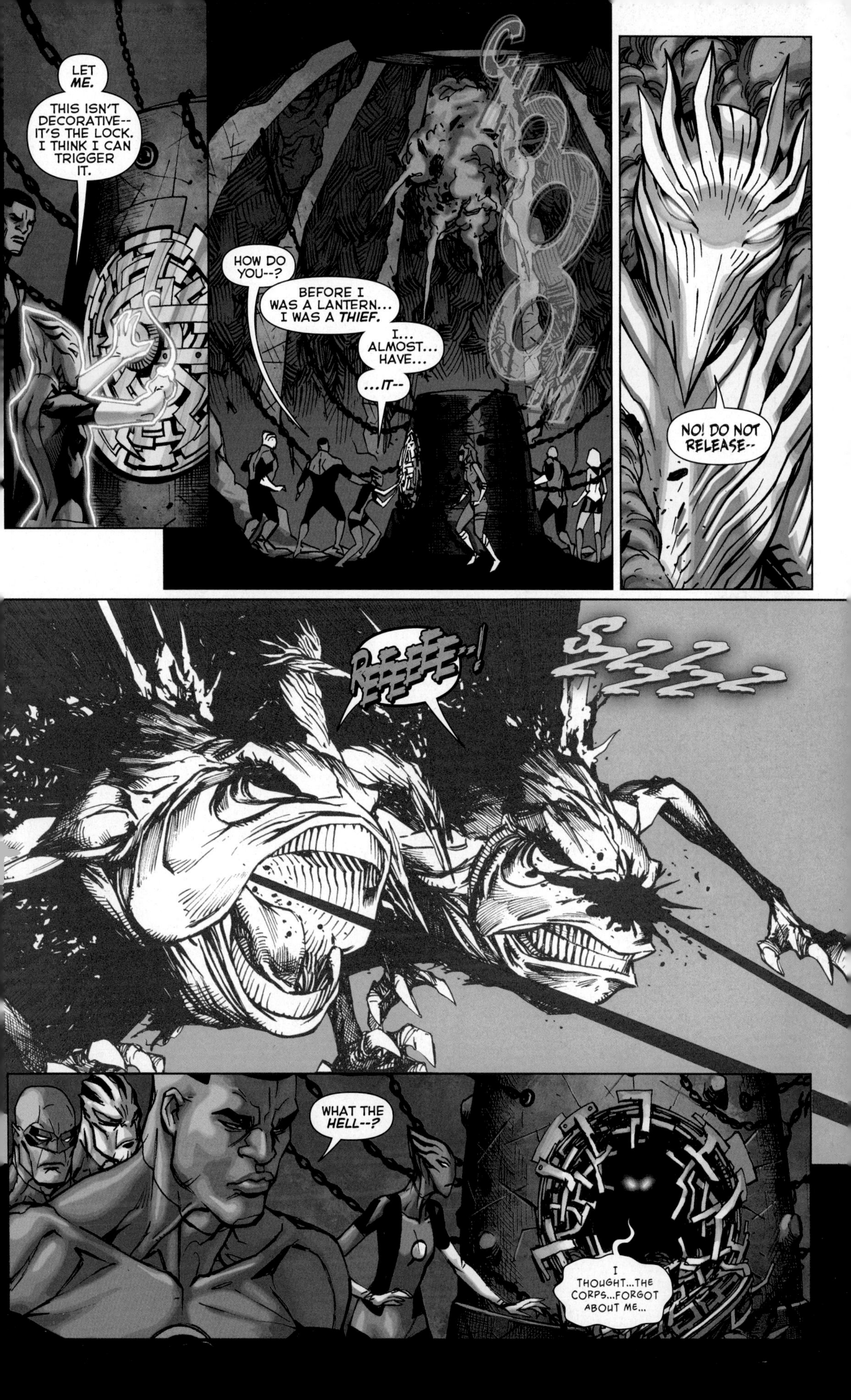
LET ME.
THIS ISN'T DECORATIVE-- IT'S THE LOCK. I THINK I CAN TRIGGER IT.
HOW DO YOU--?
BEFORE I WAS A LANTERN... I WAS A THIEF.
I... ALMOST... HAVE...
...IT--
NO! DO NOT RELEASE--
REEEEE--!
SZZZZZ
WHAT THE HELL--?
I THOUGHT...THE CORPS...FORGOT ABOUT ME...

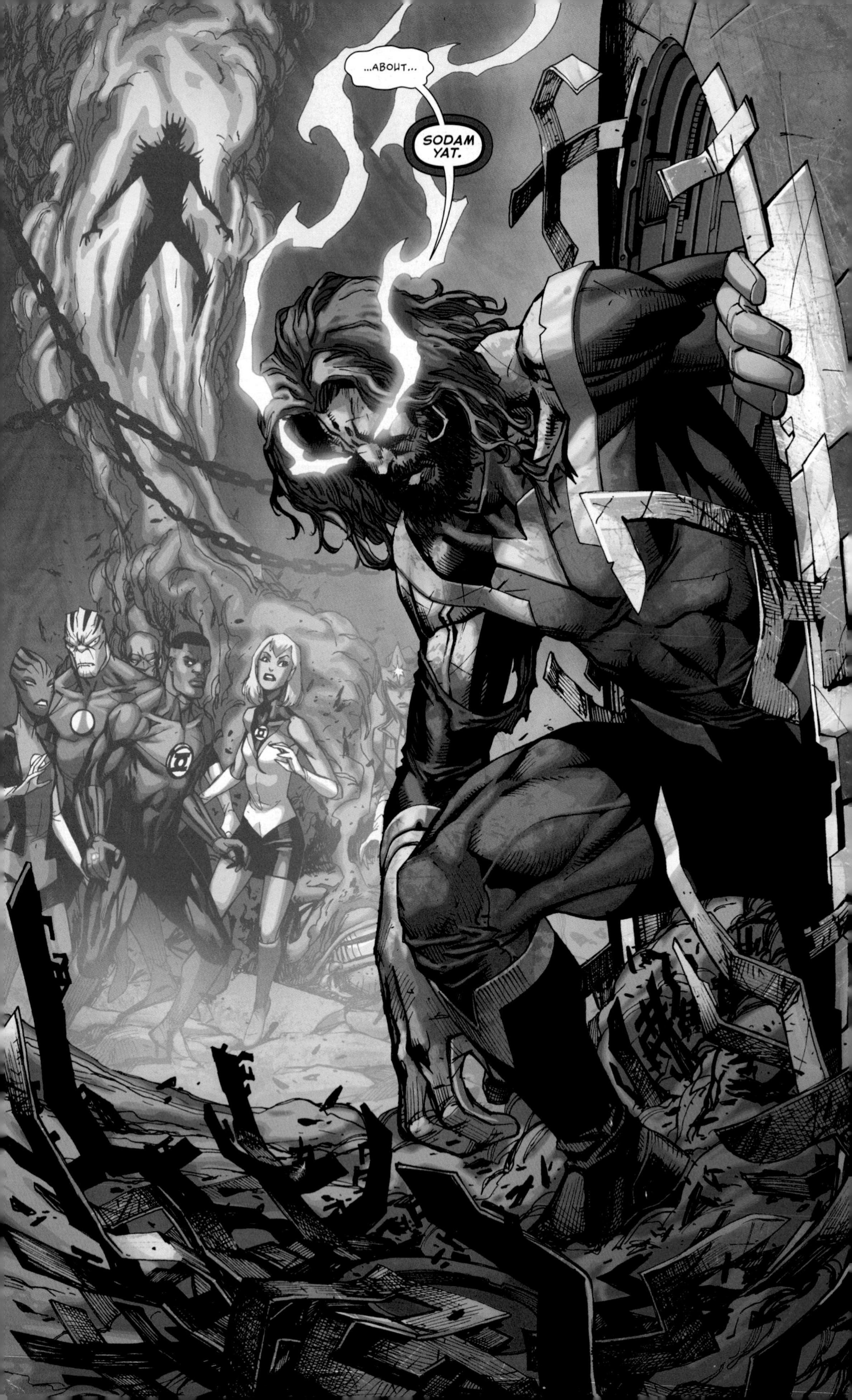
...ABOUT...
SODAM YAT.

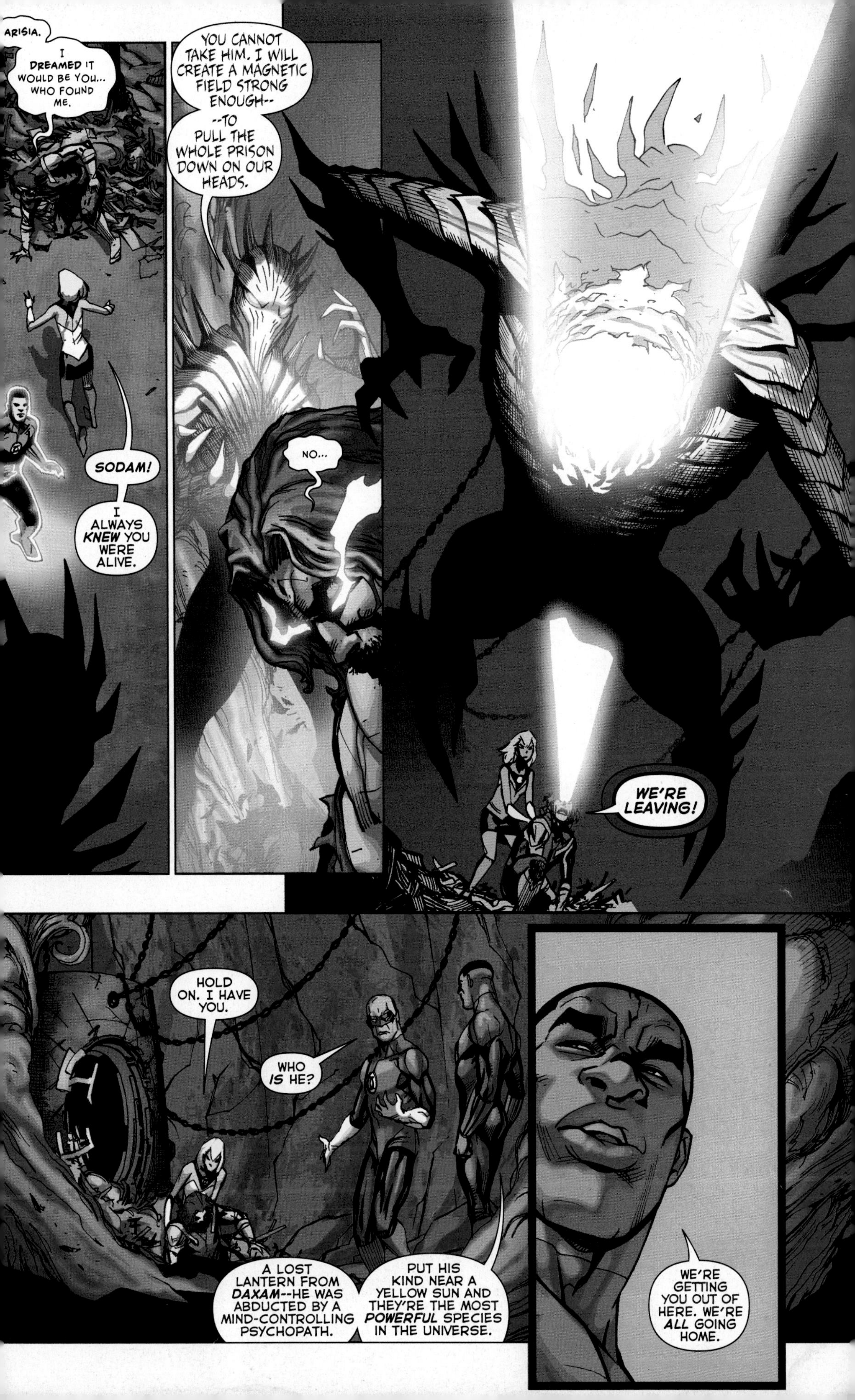

ARISIA.
I DREAMED IT WOULD BE YOU... WHO FOUND ME.
SODAM!
I ALWAYS KNEW YOU WERE ALIVE.
YOU CANNOT TAKE HIM. I WILL CREATE A MAGNETIC FIELD STRONG ENOUGH--
--TO PULL THE WHOLE PRISON DOWN ON OUR HEADS.
NO...
WE'RE LEAVING!
HOLD ON. I HAVE YOU.
WHO IS HE?
A LOST LANTERN FROM DAXAM--HE WAS ABDUCTED BY A MIND-CONTROLLING PSYCHOPATH.
PUT HIS KIND NEAR A YELLOW SUN AND THEY'RE THE MOST POWERFUL SPECIES IN THE UNIVERSE.
WE'RE GETTING YOU OUT OF HERE. WE'RE ALL GOING HOME.

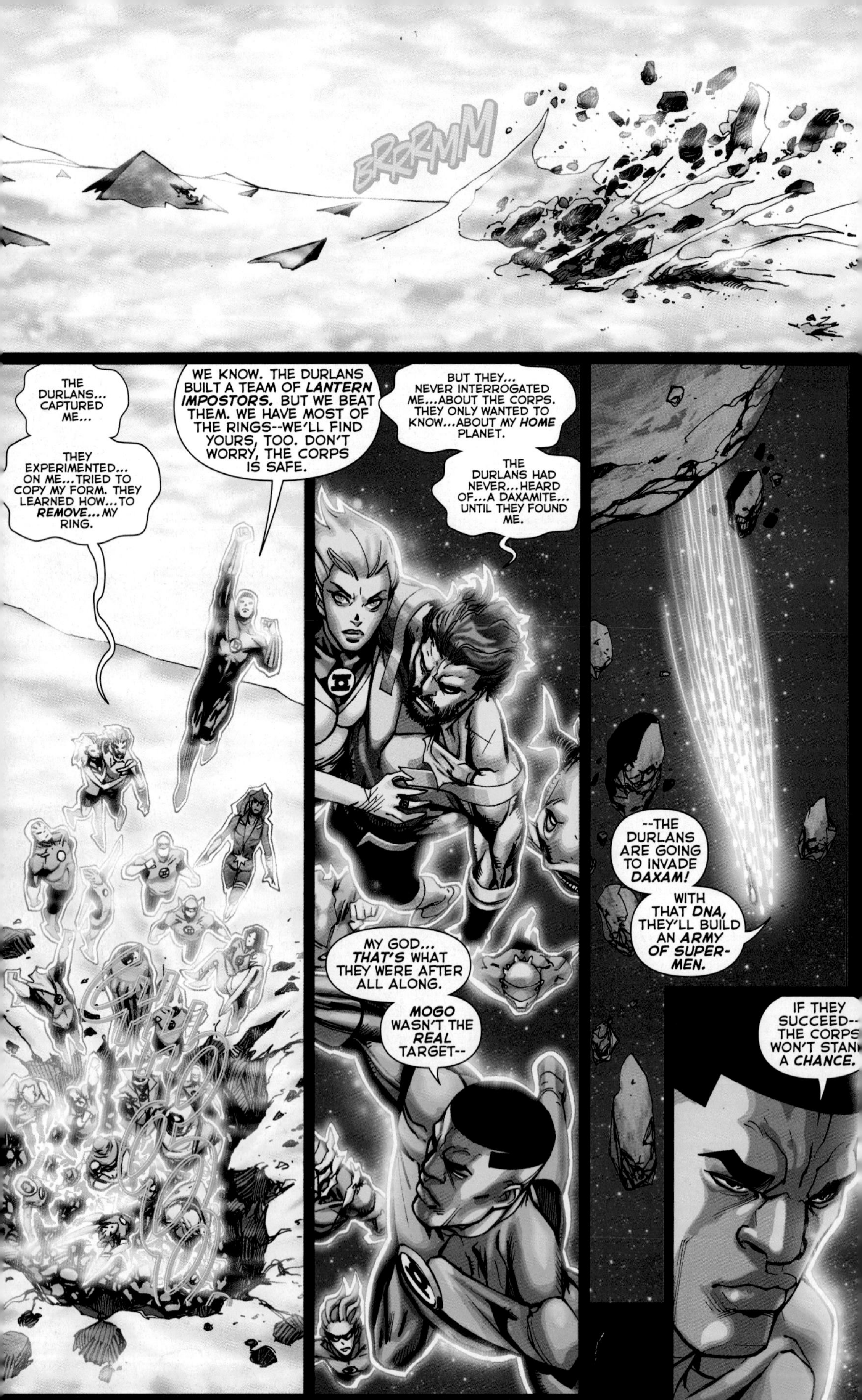
BRRRMMM
THE DURLANS... CAPTURED ME...
THEY EXPERIMENTED... ON ME...TRIED TO COPY MY FORM. THEY LEARNED HOW...TO REMOVE...MY RING.
WE KNOW. THE DURLANS BUILT A TEAM OF LANTERN IMPOSTORS. BUT WE BEAT THEM. WE HAVE MOST OF THE RINGS--WE'LL FIND YOURS, TOO. DON'T WORRY, THE CORPS IS SAFE.
BUT THEY... NEVER INTERROGATED ME...ABOUT THE CORPS. THEY ONLY WANTED TO KNOW...ABOUT MY HOME PLANET.
THE DURLANS HAD NEVER...HEARD OF...A DAXAMITE... UNTIL THEY FOUND ME.
MY GOD... THAT'S WHAT THEY WERE AFTER ALL ALONG.
MOGO WASN'T THE REAL TARGET--
--THE DURLANS ARE GOING TO INVADE DAXAM!
WITH THAT DNA, THEY'LL BUILD AN ARMY OF SUPER-MEN.
IF THEY SUCCEED-- THE CORPS WON'T STAN A CHANCE.

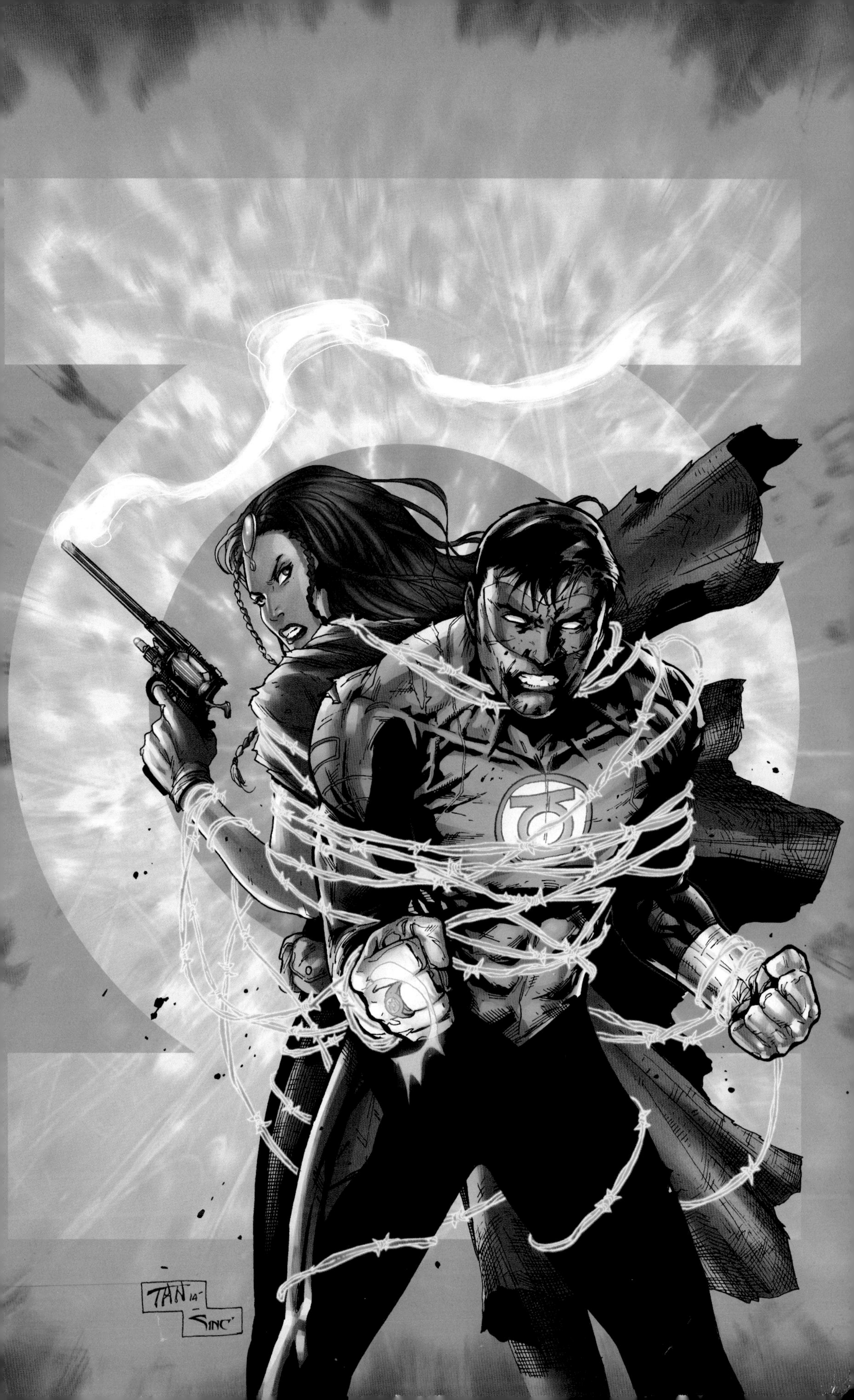

UPRISING PART 3: SEA CHANGE

ROBERT VENDITTI writer **BILLY TAN** penciller **ROB HUNTER** & **JAIME MENDOZA** inkers **TONY AVIÑA** colorist
cover art by **BILLY TAN** & **ALEX SINCLAIR** BOMBSHELL variant cover by **J.G JONES** & **ALEX SINCLAIR**

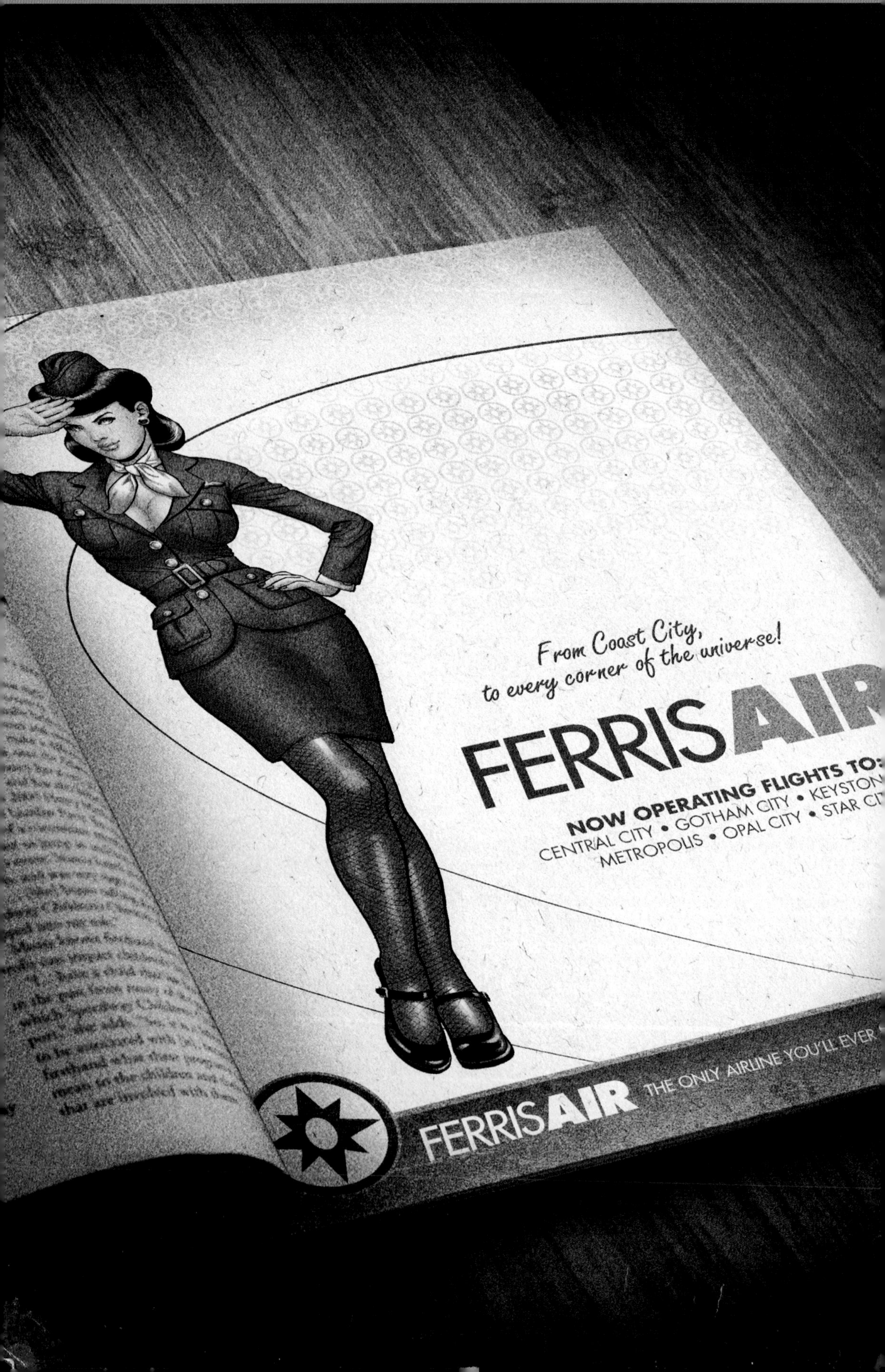

From Coast City,
to every corner of the universe!
FERRISAIR
NOW OPERATING FLIGHTS TO:
CENTRAL CITY • GOTHAM CITY • KEYSTON
METROPOLIS • OPAL CITY • STAR CI
FERRISAIR THE ONLY AIRLINE YOU'LL EVER

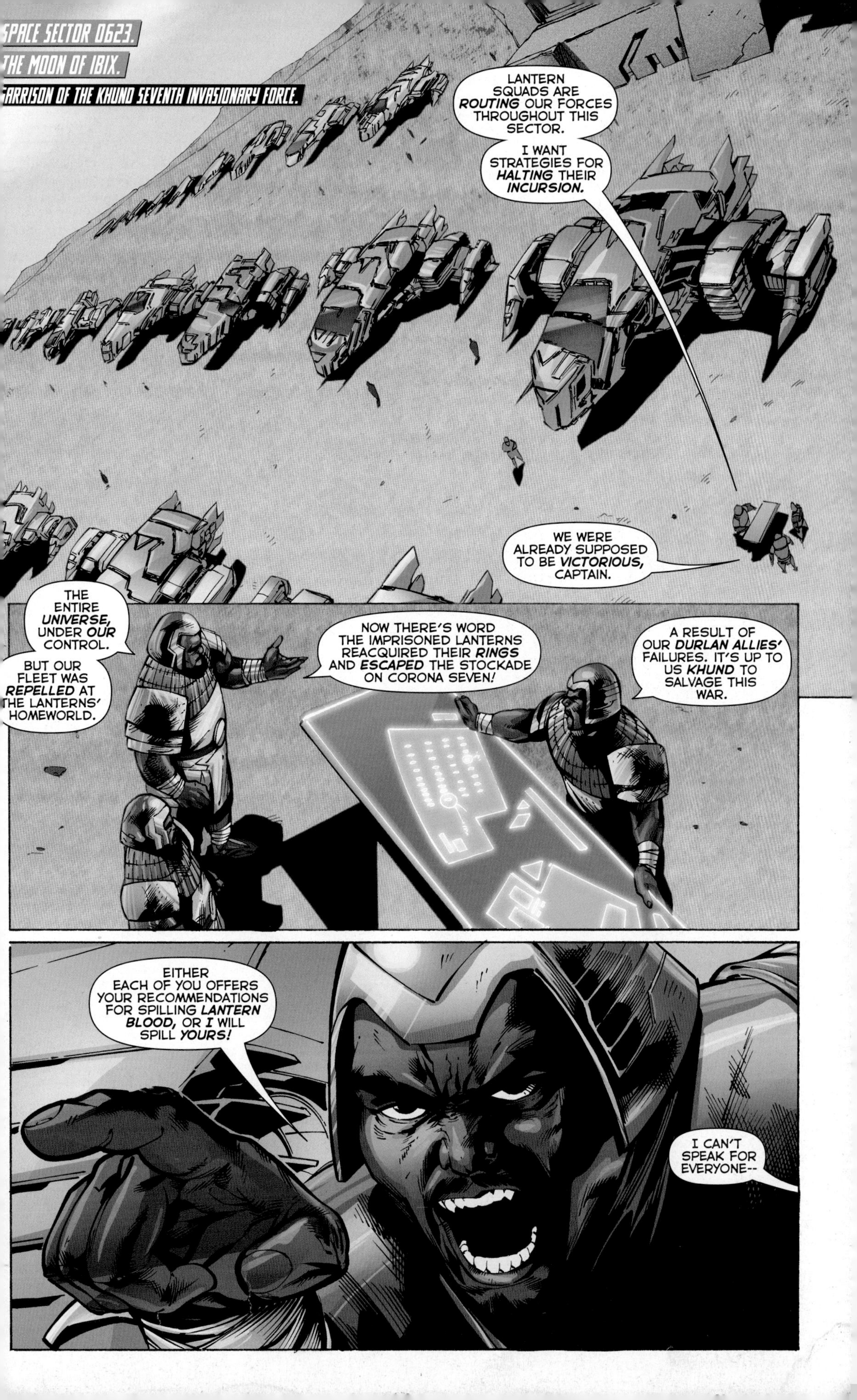
SPACE SECTOR 0623.
THE MOON OF IBIX.
GARRISON OF THE KHUND SEVENTH INVASIONARY FORCE.
LANTERN SQUADS ARE ROUTING OUR FORCES THROUGHOUT THIS SECTOR.
I WANT STRATEGIES FOR HALTING THEIR INCURSION.
WE WERE ALREADY SUPPOSED TO BE VICTORIOUS, CAPTAIN.
THE ENTIRE UNIVERSE, UNDER OUR CONTROL.
BUT OUR FLEET WAS REPELLED AT THE LANTERNS' HOMEWORLD.
NOW THERE'S WORD THE IMPRISONED LANTERNS REACQUIRED THEIR RINGS AND ESCAPED THE STOCKADE ON CORONA SEVEN!
A RESULT OF OUR DURLAN ALLIES' FAILURES. IT'S UP TO US KHUND TO SALVAGE THIS WAR.
EITHER EACH OF YOU OFFERS YOUR RECOMMENDATIONS FOR SPILLING LANTERN BLOOD, OR I WILL SPILL YOURS!
I CAN'T SPEAK FOR EVERYONE--

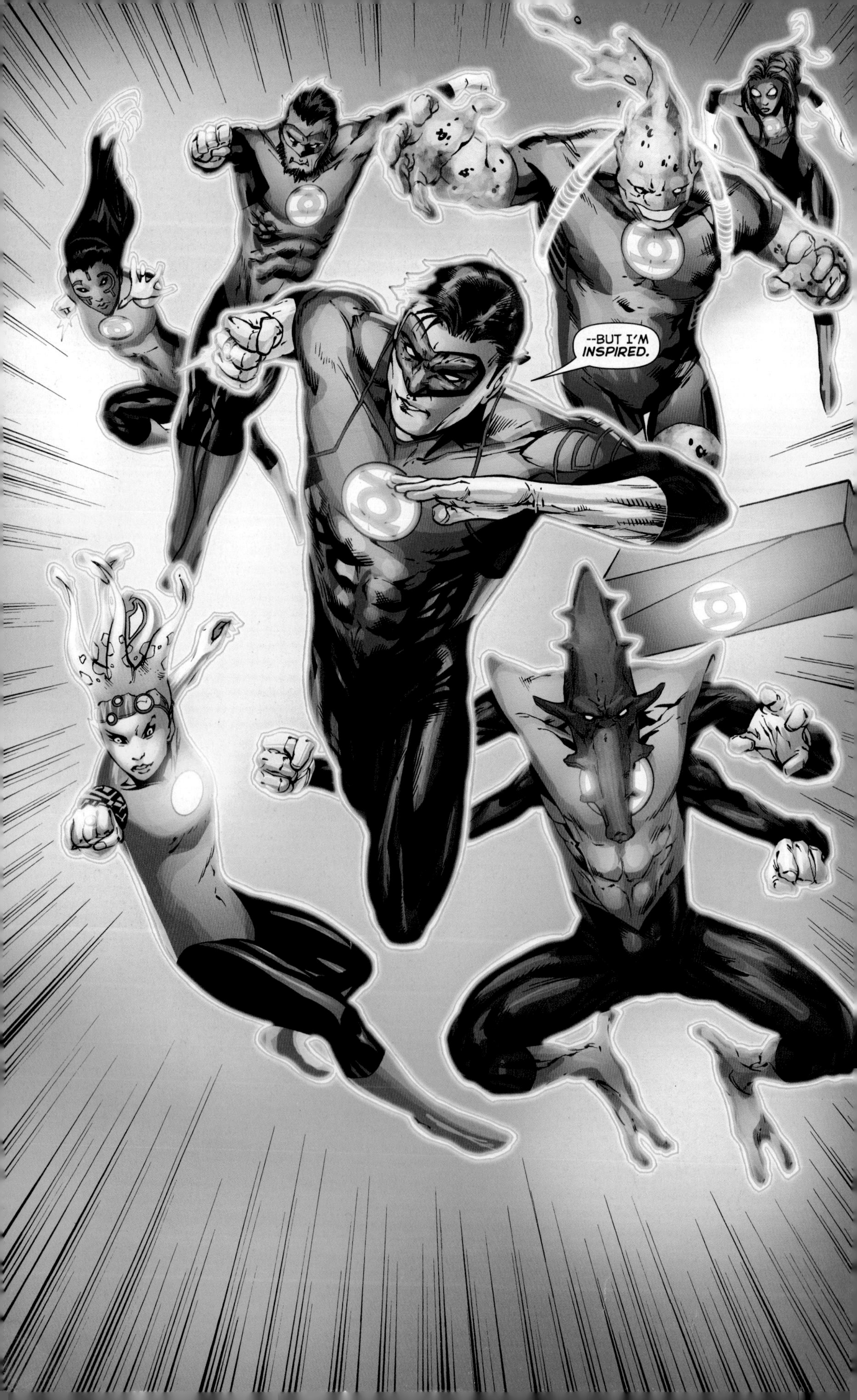
--BUT I'M INSPIRED.

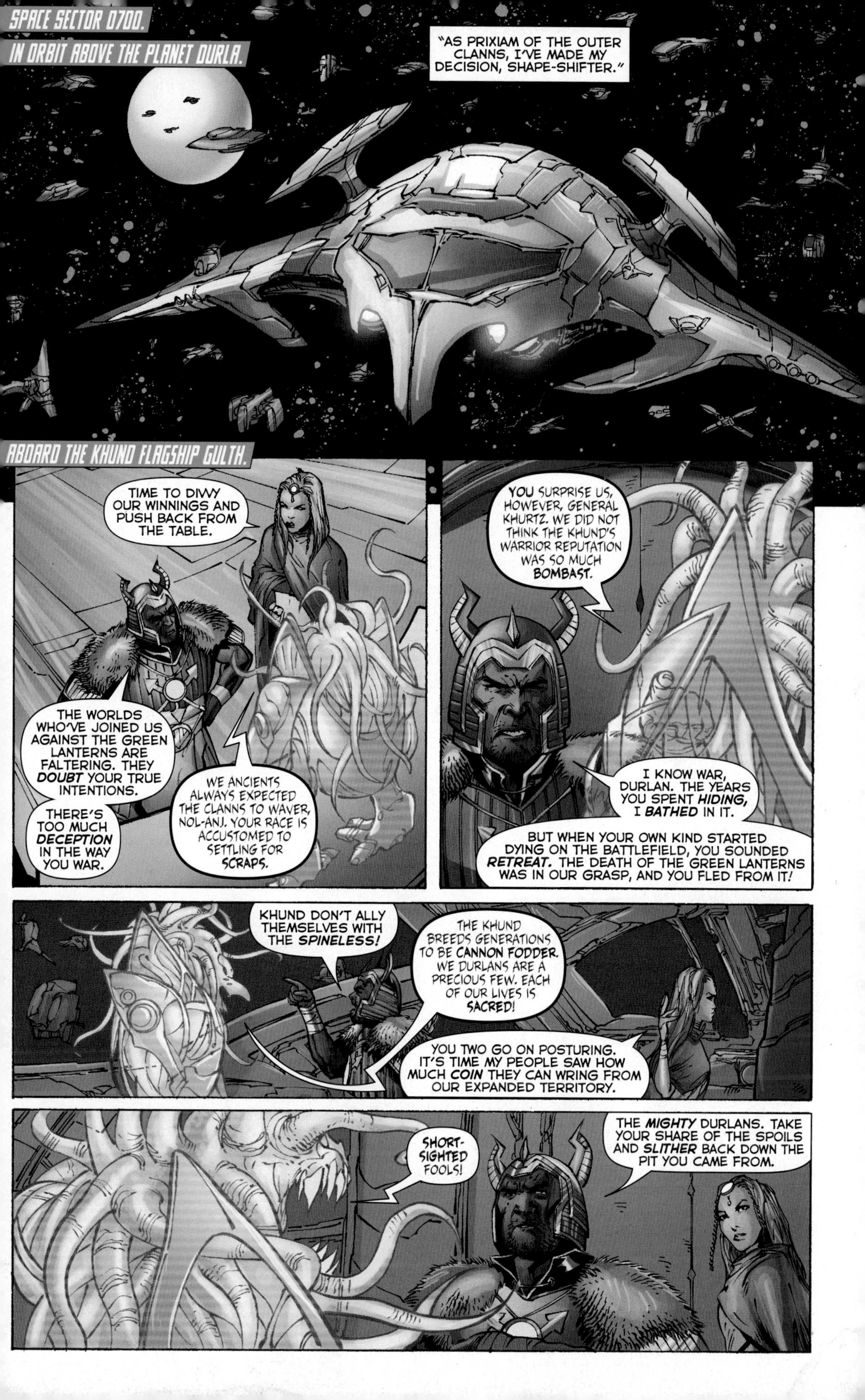

SPACE SECTOR 0700.
IN ORBIT ABOVE THE PLANET DURLA.
"AS PRIXIAM OF THE OUTER CLANNS, I'VE MADE MY DECISION, SHAPE-SHIFTER."
ABOARD THE KHUND FLAGSHIP GULTH.
TIME TO DIVVY OUR WINNINGS AND PUSH BACK FROM THE TABLE.
THE WORLDS WHO'VE JOINED US AGAINST THE GREEN LANTERNS ARE FALTERING. THEY DOUBT YOUR TRUE INTENTIONS.
THERE'S TOO MUCH DECEPTION IN THE WAY YOU WAR.
WE ANCIENTS ALWAYS EXPECTED THE CLANNS TO WAVER, NOL-ANJ. YOUR RACE IS ACCUSTOMED TO SETTLING FOR SCRAPS.
YOU SURPRISE US, HOWEVER, GENERAL KHURTZ. WE DID NOT THINK THE KHUND'S WARRIOR REPUTATION WAS SO MUCH BOMBAST.
I KNOW WAR, DURLAN. THE YEARS YOU SPENT HIDING, I BATHED IN IT.
BUT WHEN YOUR OWN KIND STARTED DYING ON THE BATTLEFIELD, YOU SOUNDED RETREAT. THE DEATH OF THE GREEN LANTERNS WAS IN OUR GRASP, AND YOU FLED FROM IT!
KHUND DON'T ALLY THEMSELVES WITH THE SPINELESS!
THE KHUND BREEDS GENERATIONS TO BE CANNON FODDER. WE DURLANS ARE A PRECIOUS FEW. EACH OF OUR LIVES IS SACRED!
YOU TWO GO ON POSTURING. IT'S TIME MY PEOPLE SAW HOW MUCH COIN THEY CAN WRING FROM OUR EXPANDED TERRITORY.
SHORT-SIGHTED FOOLS!
THE MIGHTY DURLANS. TAKE YOUR SHARE OF THE SPOILS AND SLITHER BACK DOWN THE PIT YOU CAME FROM.

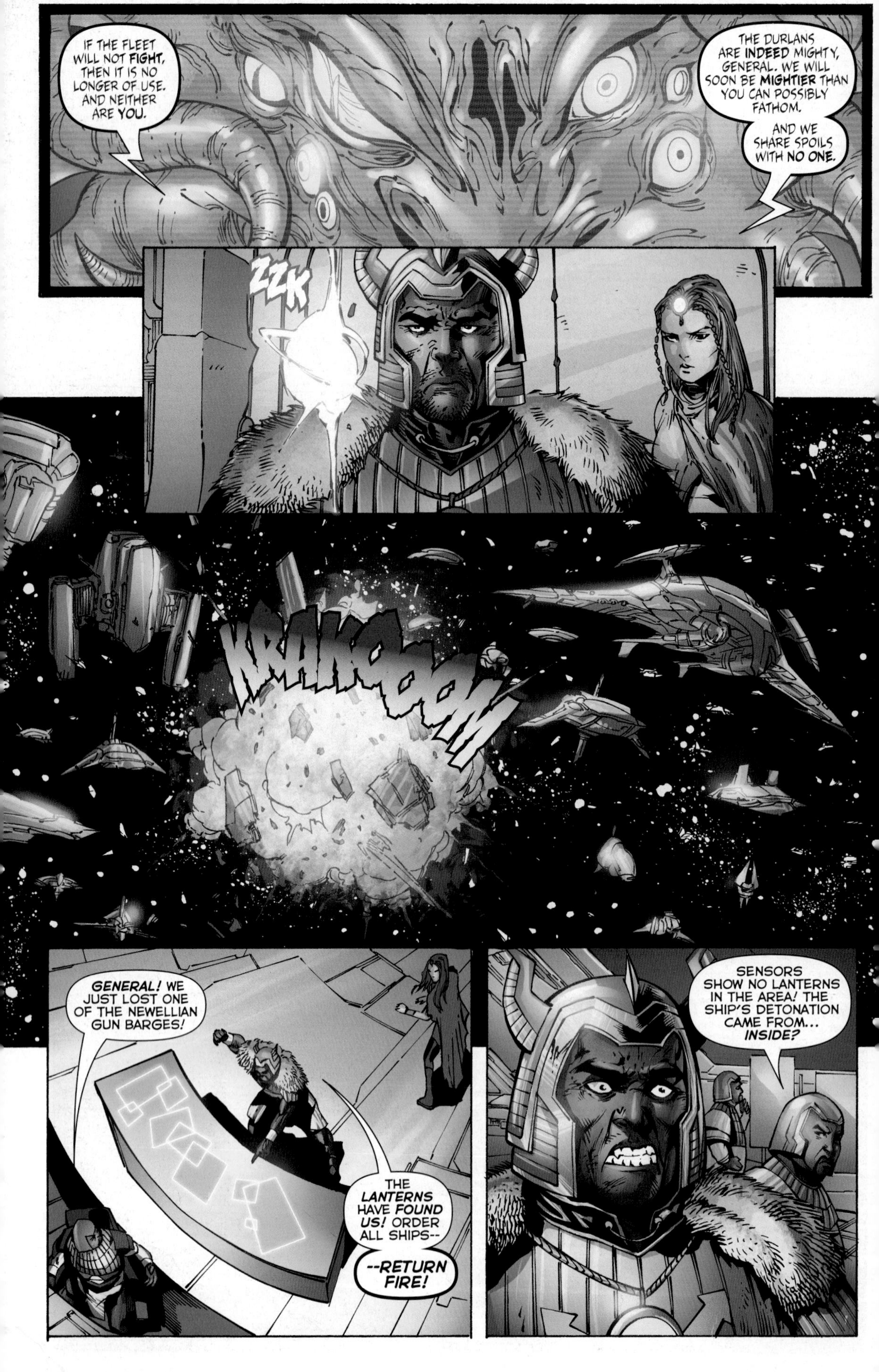
IF THE FLEET WILL NOT FIGHT, THEN IT IS NO LONGER OF USE. AND NEITHER ARE YOU.
THE DURLANS ARE INDEED MIGHTY, GENERAL. WE WILL SOON BE MIGHTIER THAN YOU CAN POSSIBLY FATHOM.
AND WE SHARE SPOILS WITH NO ONE.
ZZK
KRAKOOOM
GENERAL! WE JUST LOST ONE OF THE NEWELLIAN GUN BARGES!
THE LANTERNS HAVE FOUND US! ORDER ALL SHIPS--
--RETURN FIRE!
SENSORS SHOW NO LANTERNS IN THE AREA! THE SHIP'S DETONATION CAME FROM... INSIDE?

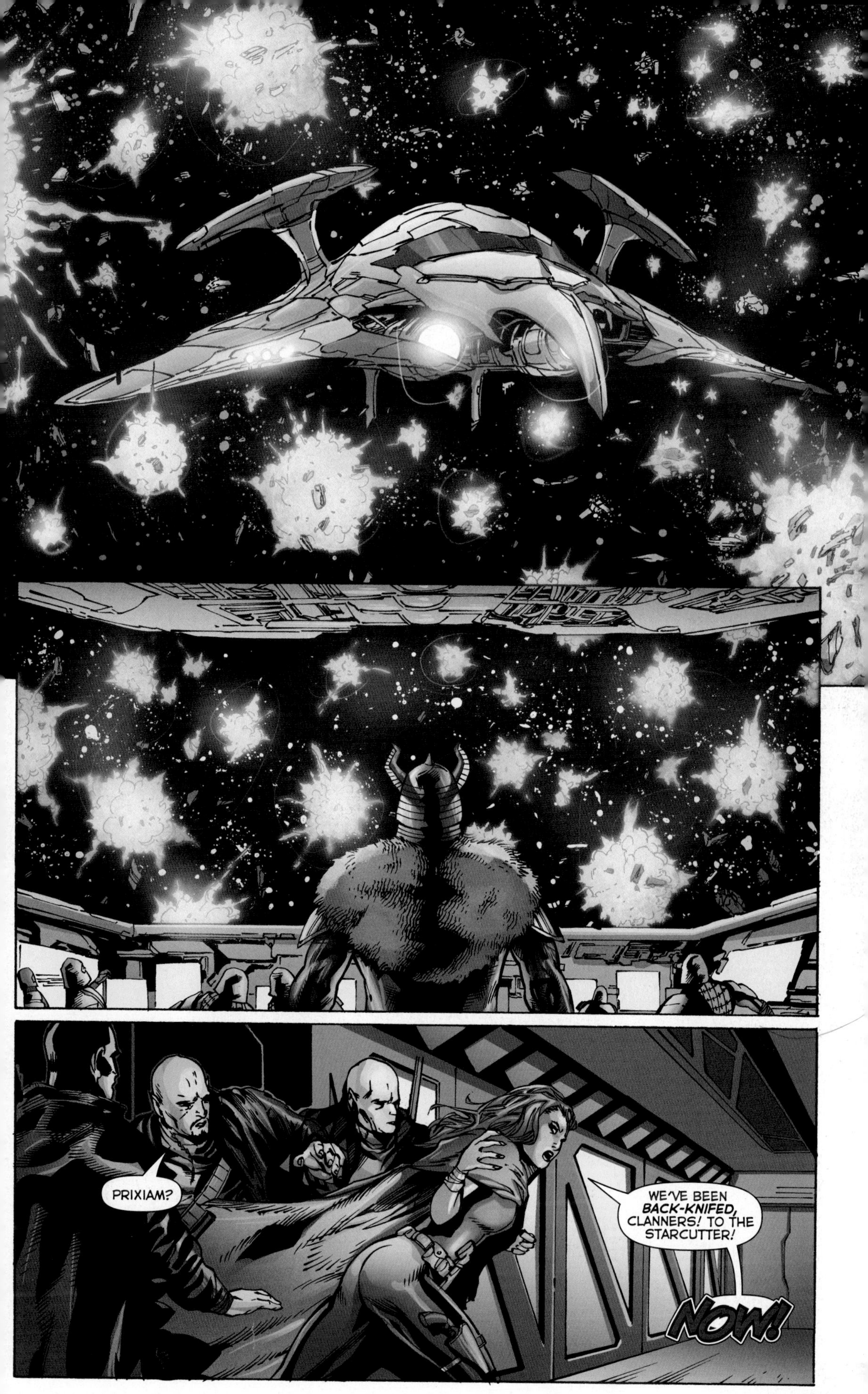
PRIXIAM?
WE'VE BEEN BACK-KNIFED, CLANNERS! TO THE STARCUTTER!
NOW!

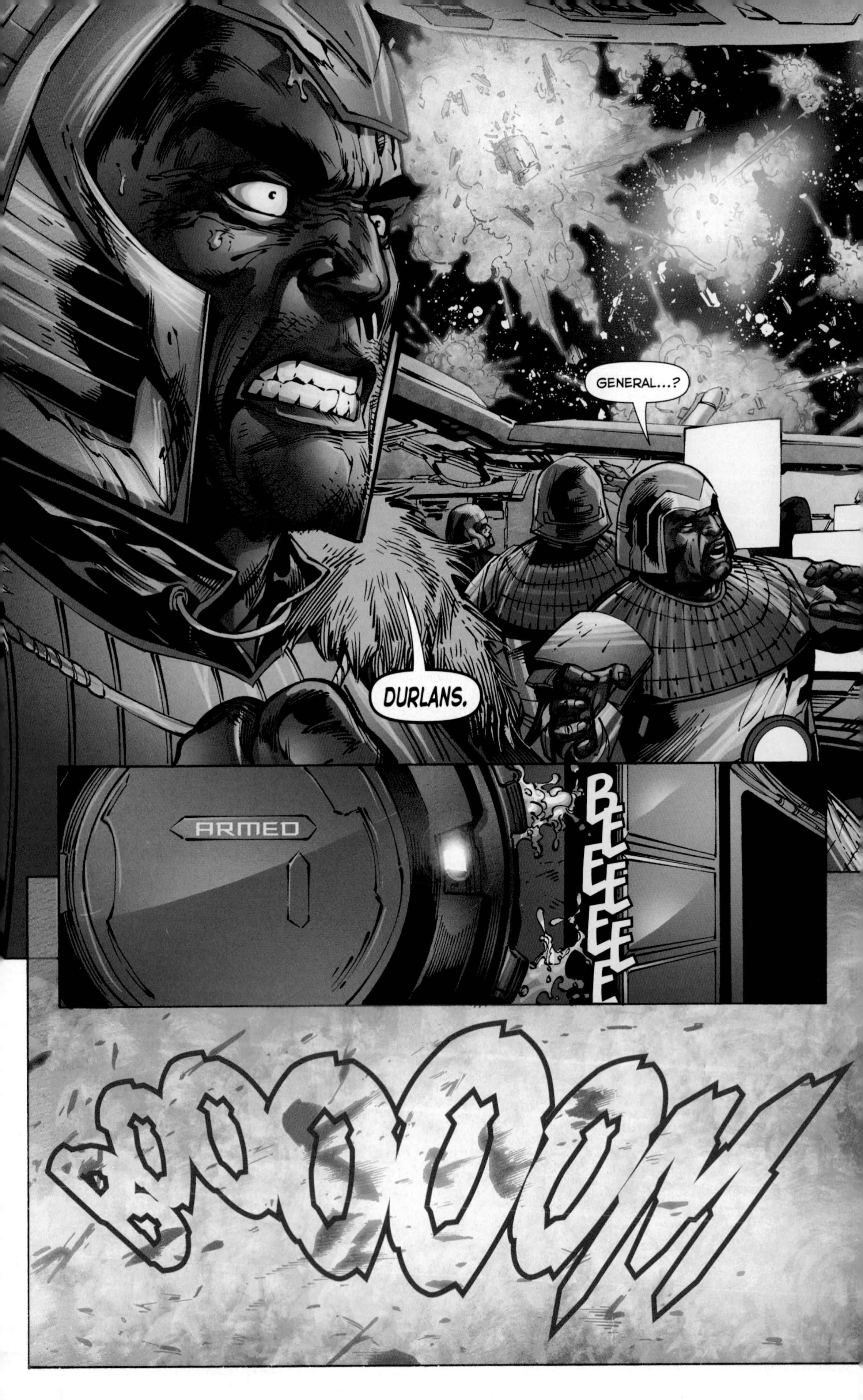
GENERAL...?
DURLANS.
ARMED
BEEEEEE
BOOOOM

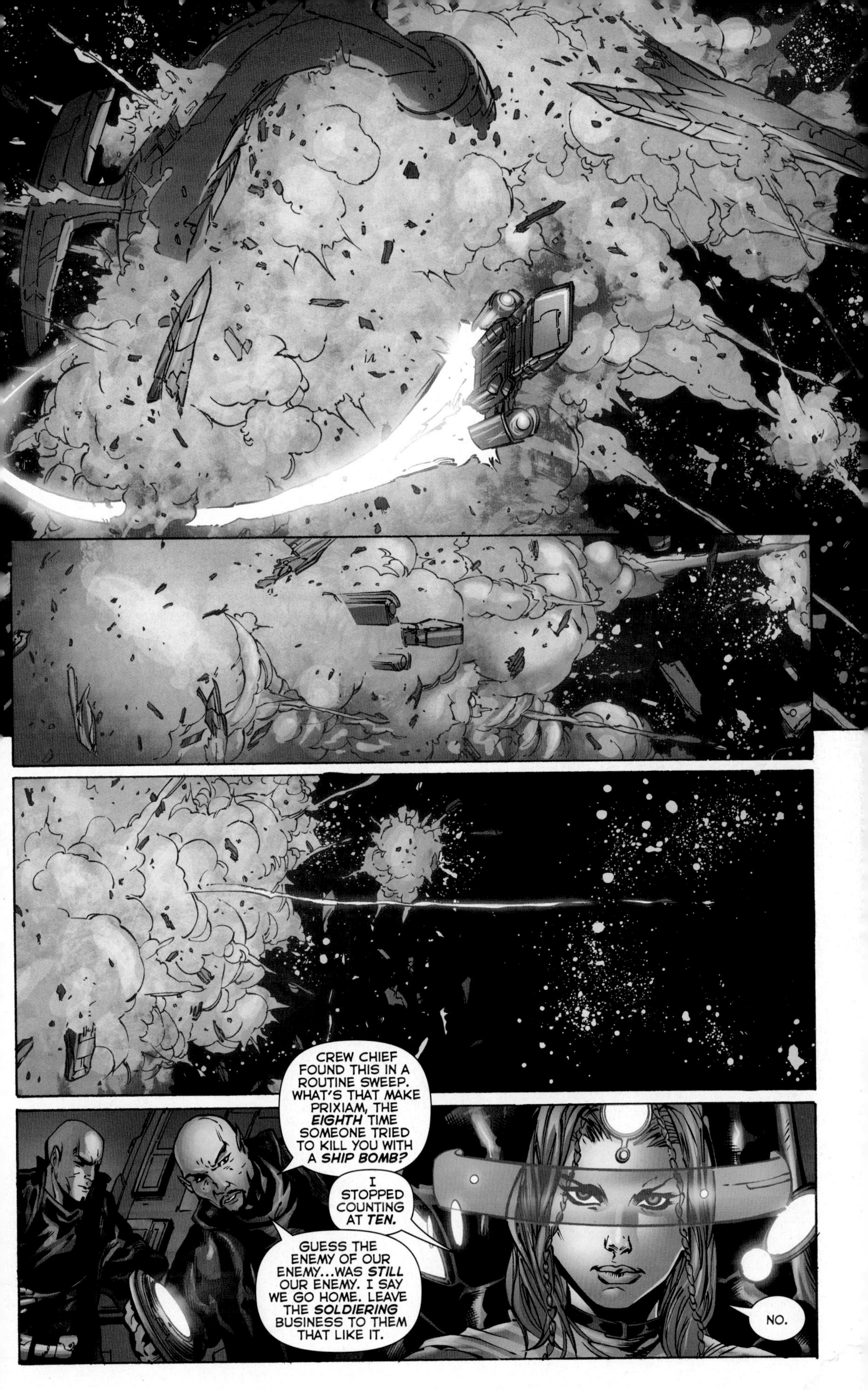
CREW CHIEF FOUND THIS IN A ROUTINE SWEEP. WHAT'S THAT MAKE PRIXIAM, THE EIGHTH TIME SOMEONE TRIED TO KILL YOU WITH A SHIP BOMB?
I STOPPED COUNTING AT TEN.
GUESS THE ENEMY OF OUR ENEMY...WAS STILL OUR ENEMY. I SAY WE GO HOME. LEAVE THE SOLDIERING BUSINESS TO THEM THAT LIKE IT.
NO.

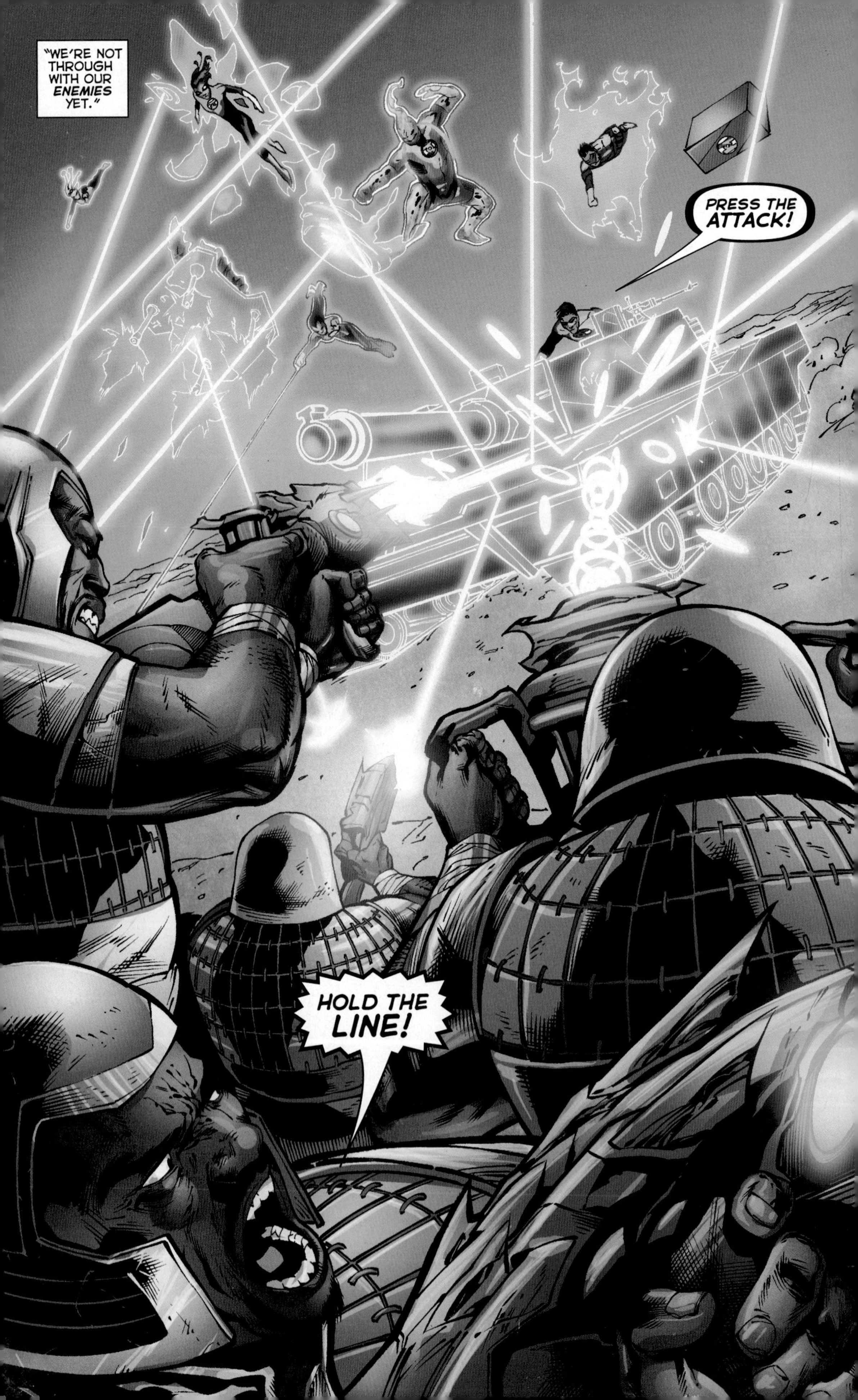
"WE'RE NOT THROUGH WITH OUR ENEMIES YET."
PRESS THE ATTACK!
HOLD THE LINE!

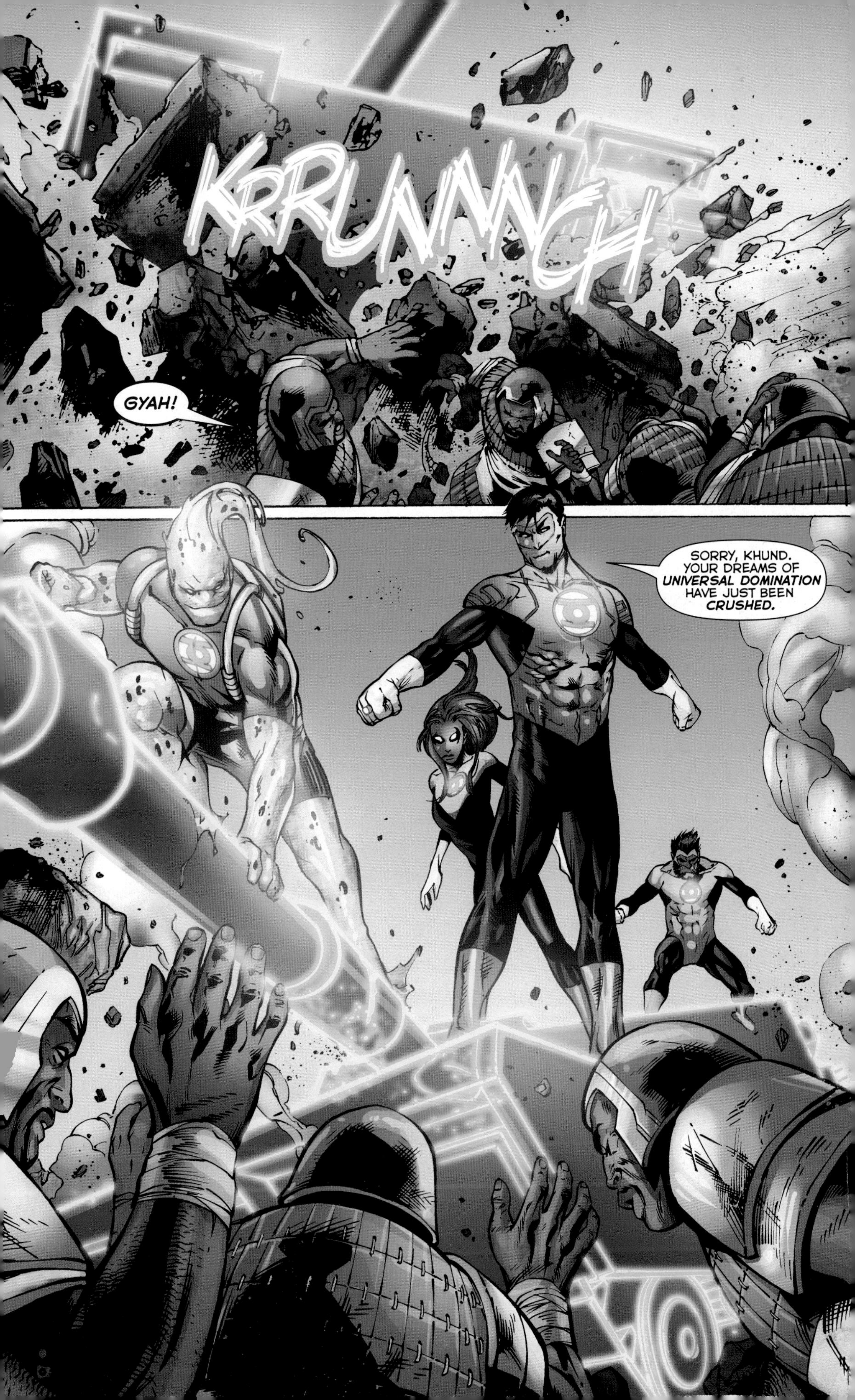
KRRUNNNCH
GYAH!
SORRY, KHUND. YOUR DREAMS OF UNIVERSAL DOMINATION HAVE JUST BEEN CRUSHED.

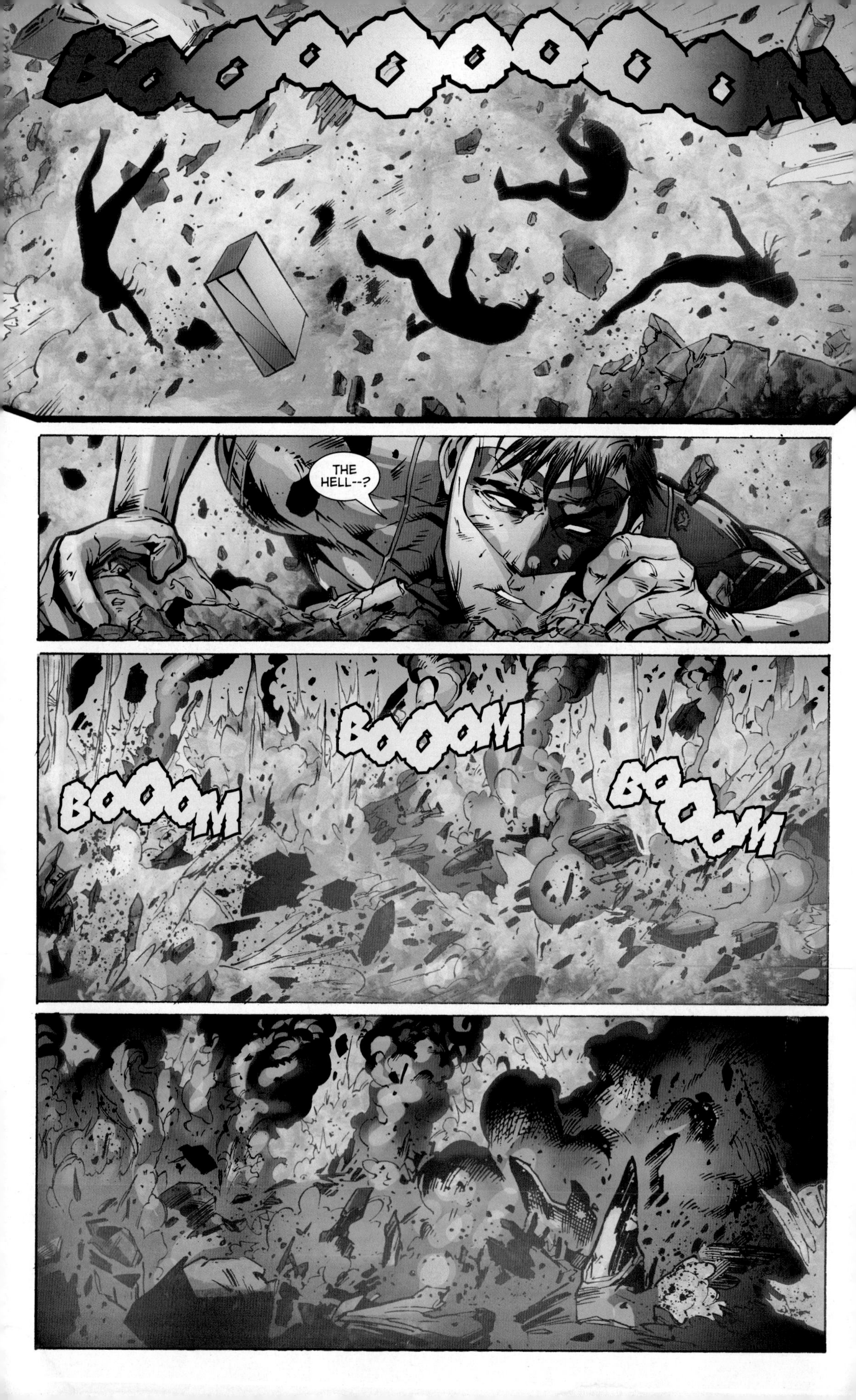
BOOOOOOOOOM
THE HELL--?
BOOOM
BOOOM
BOOOOM

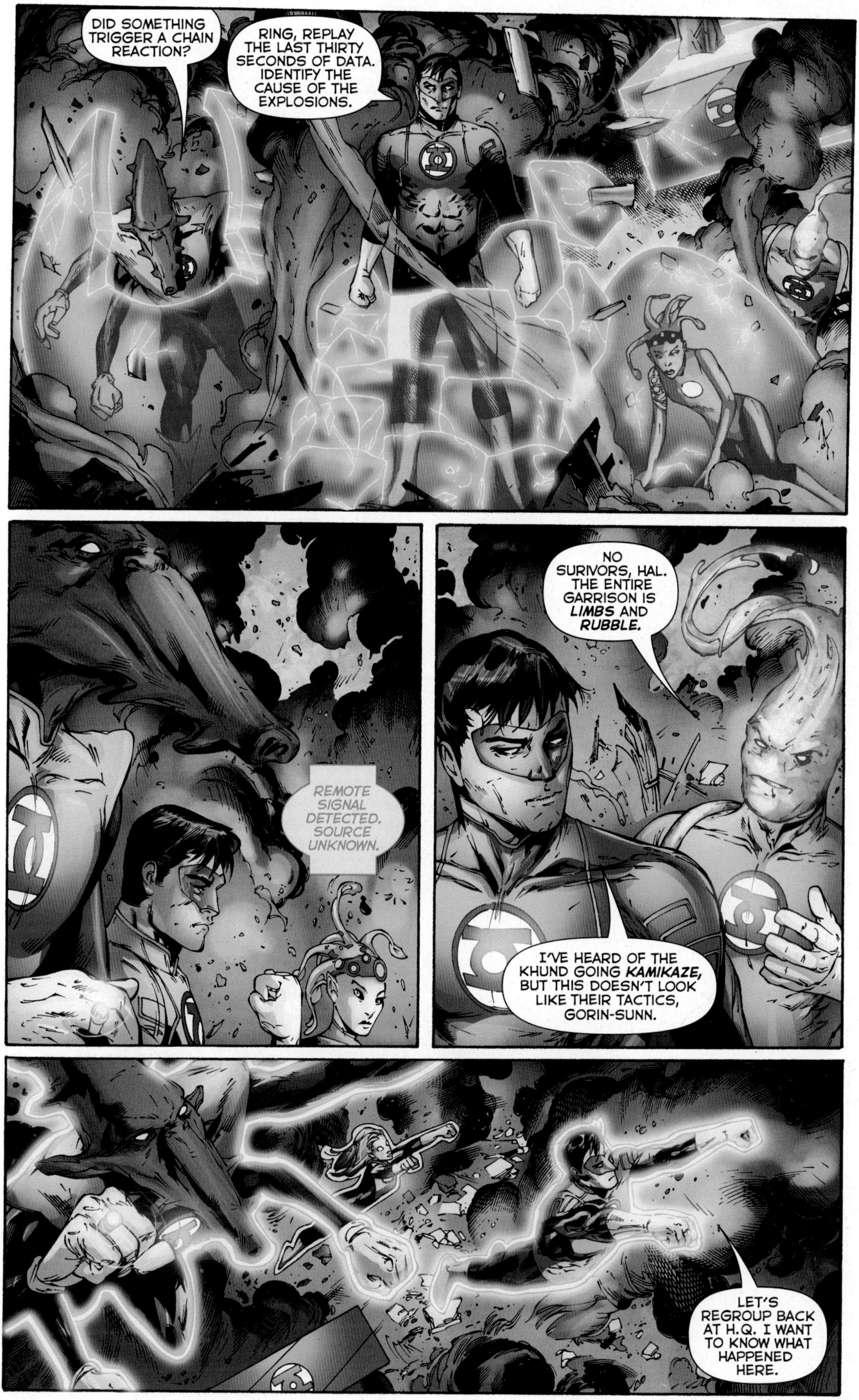
DID SOMETHING TRIGGER A CHAIN REACTION?
RING, REPLAY THE LAST THIRTY SECONDS OF DATA. IDENTIFY THE CAUSE OF THE EXPLOSIONS.
REMOTE SIGNAL DETECTED. SOURCE UNKNOWN.
NO SURIVORS, HAL. THE ENTIRE GARRISON IS *LIMBS* AND *RUBBLE.*
I'VE HEARD OF THE KHUND GOING *KAMIKAZE,* BUT THIS DOESN'T LOOK LIKE THEIR TACTICS, GORIN-SUNN.
LET'S REGROUP BACK AT H.Q. I WANT TO KNOW WHAT HAPPENED HERE.

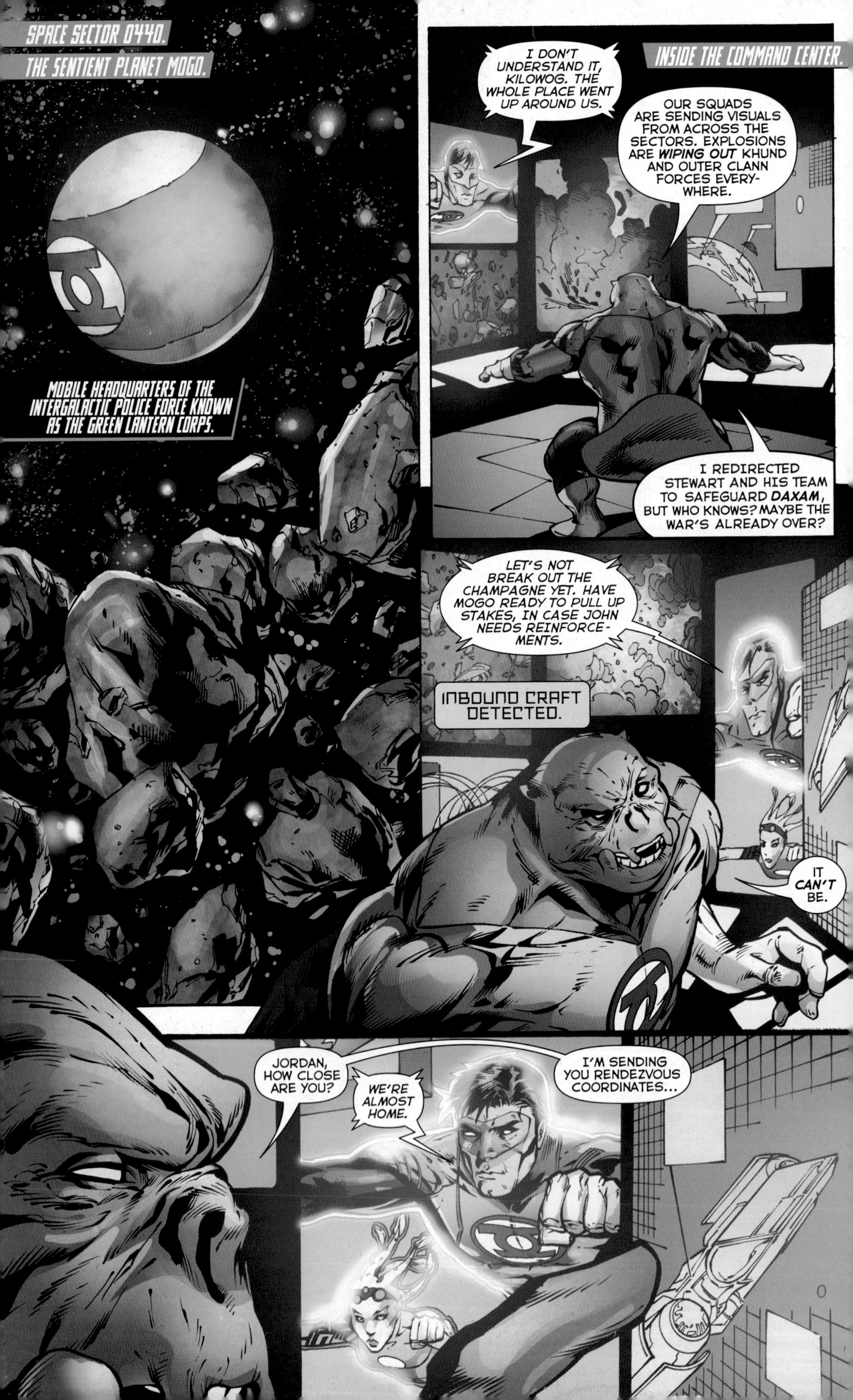
SPACE SECTOR 0440.
THE SENTIENT PLANET MOGO.
MOBILE HEADQUARTERS OF THE INTERGALACTIC POLICE FORCE KNOWN AS THE GREEN LANTERN CORPS.
INSIDE THE COMMAND CENTER.
I DON'T UNDERSTAND IT, KILOWOG. THE WHOLE PLACE WENT UP AROUND US.
OUR SQUADS ARE SENDING VISUALS FROM ACROSS THE SECTORS. EXPLOSIONS ARE WIPING OUT KHUND AND OUTER CLANN FORCES EVERY-WHERE.
I REDIRECTED STEWART AND HIS TEAM TO SAFEGUARD DAXAM, BUT WHO KNOWS? MAYBE THE WAR'S ALREADY OVER?
LET'S NOT BREAK OUT THE CHAMPAGNE YET. HAVE MOGO READY TO PULL UP STAKES, IN CASE JOHN NEEDS REINFORCE-MENTS.
INBOUND CRAFT DETECTED.
IT CAN'T BE.
JORDAN, HOW CLOSE ARE YOU?
WE'RE ALMOST HOME.
I'M SENDING YOU RENDEZVOUS COORDINATES...

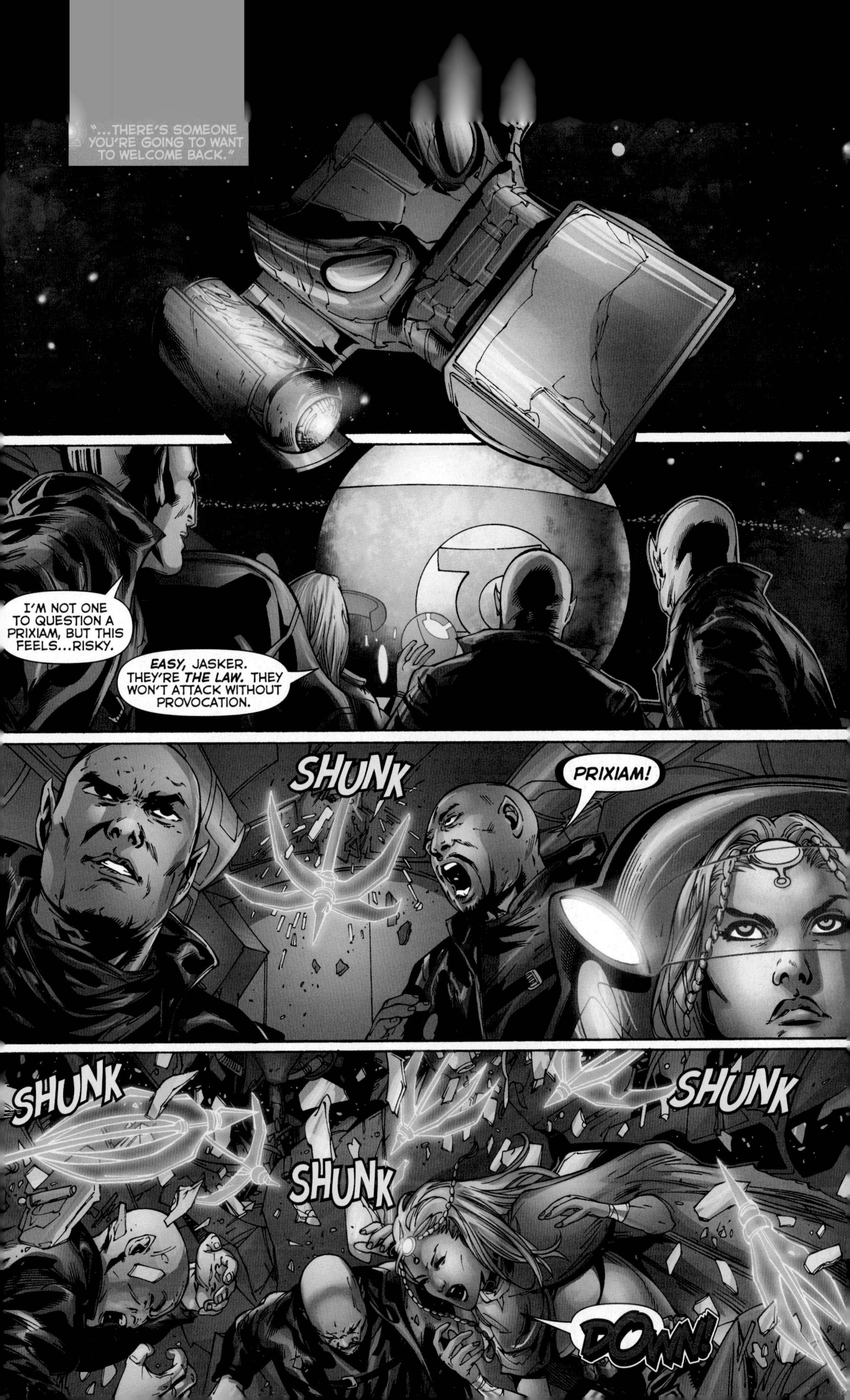
"...THERE'S SOMEONE YOU'RE GOING TO WANT TO WELCOME BACK."
I'M NOT ONE TO QUESTION A PRIXIAM, BUT THIS FEELS...RISKY.
EASY, JASKER. THEY'RE THE LAW. THEY WON'T ATTACK WITHOUT PROVOCATION.
SHUNK
PRIXIAM!
SHUNK
SHUNK
SHUNK
DOWN!

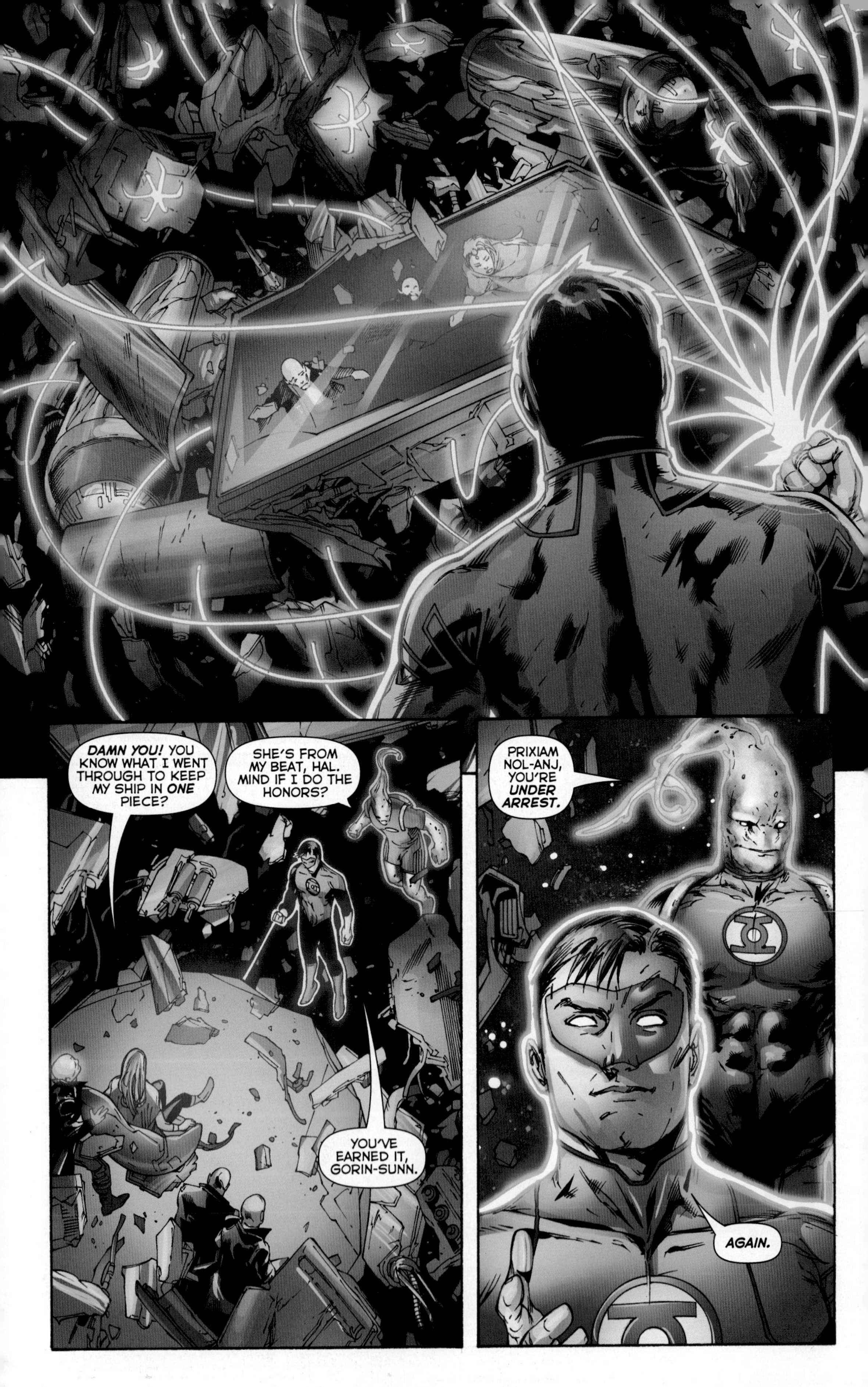

DAMN YOU! YOU KNOW WHAT I WENT THROUGH TO KEEP MY SHIP IN ONE PIECE?
SHE'S FROM MY BEAT, HAL. MIND IF I DO THE HONORS?
YOU'VE EARNED IT, GORIN-SUNN.
PRIXIAM NOL-ANJ, YOU'RE UNDER ARREST.
AGAIN.

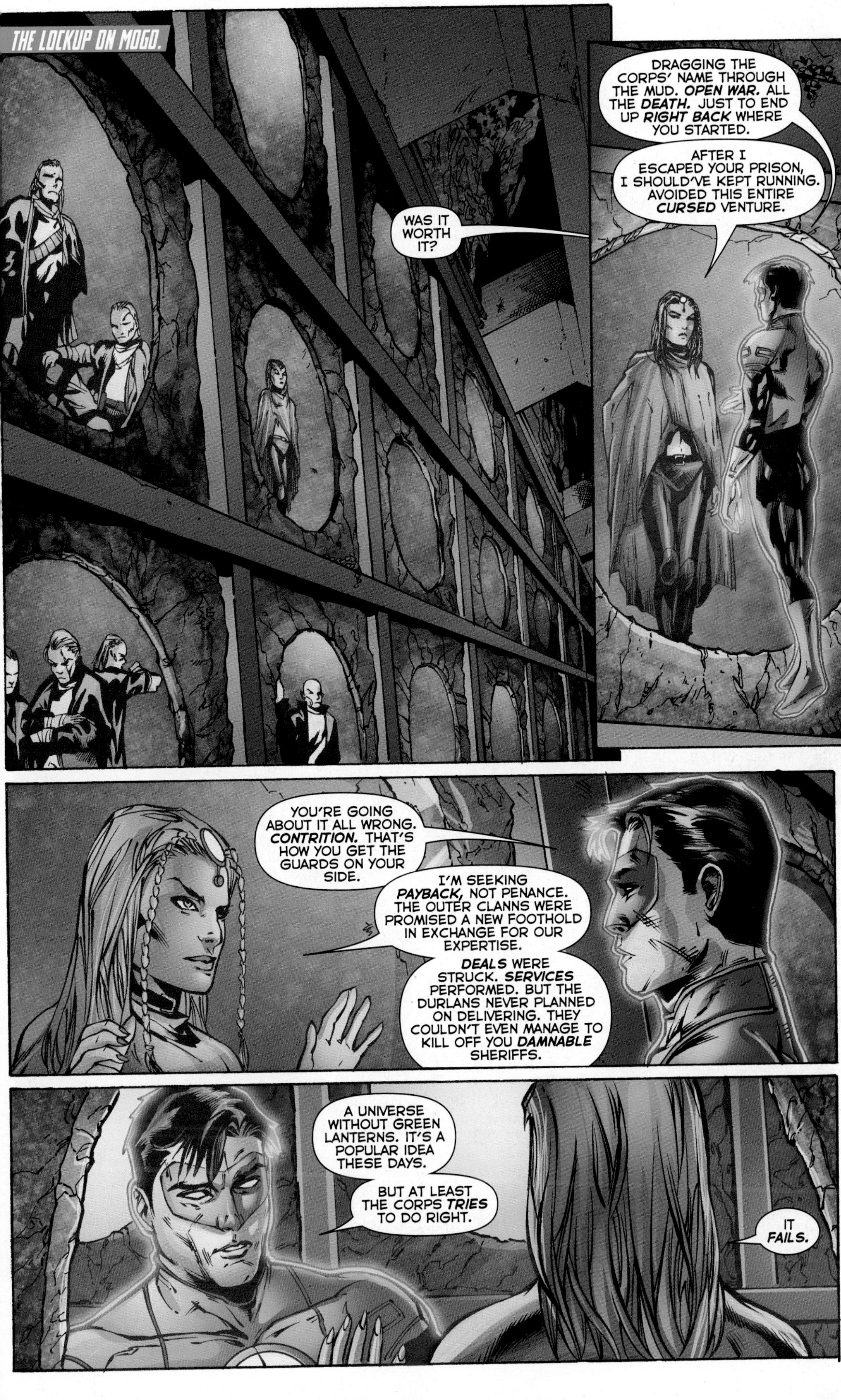
THE LOCKUP ON MOGO.
WAS IT WORTH IT?
DRAGGING THE CORPS' NAME THROUGH THE MUD. OPEN WAR. ALL THE DEATH. JUST TO END UP RIGHT BACK WHERE YOU STARTED.
AFTER I ESCAPED YOUR PRISON, I SHOULD'VE KEPT RUNNING. AVOIDED THIS ENTIRE CURSED VENTURE.
YOU'RE GOING ABOUT IT ALL WRONG. CONTRITION. THAT'S HOW YOU GET THE GUARDS ON YOUR SIDE.
I'M SEEKING PAYBACK, NOT PENANCE. THE OUTER CLANNS WERE PROMISED A NEW FOOTHOLD IN EXCHANGE FOR OUR EXPERTISE.
DEALS WERE STRUCK. SERVICES PERFORMED. BUT THE DURLANS NEVER PLANNED ON DELIVERING. THEY COULDN'T EVEN MANAGE TO KILL OFF YOU DAMNABLE SHERIFFS.
A UNIVERSE WITHOUT GREEN LANTERNS. IT'S A POPULAR IDEA THESE DAYS.
BUT AT LEAST THE CORPS TRIES TO DO RIGHT.
IT FAILS.

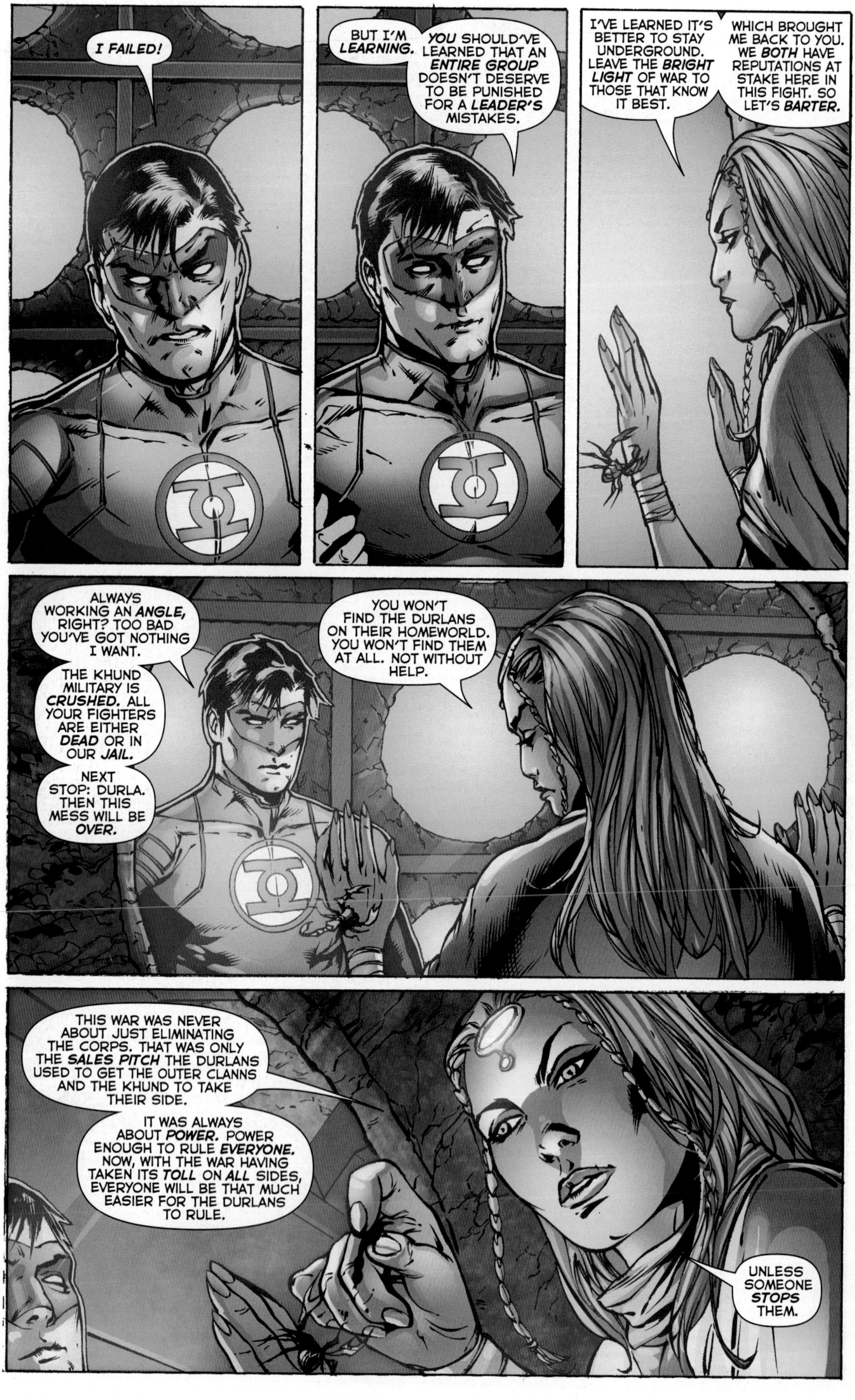
I FAILED!
BUT I'M LEARNING.
YOU SHOULD'VE LEARNED THAT AN ENTIRE GROUP DOESN'T DESERVE TO BE PUNISHED FOR A LEADER'S MISTAKES.
I'VE LEARNED IT'S BETTER TO STAY UNDERGROUND. LEAVE THE BRIGHT LIGHT OF WAR TO THOSE THAT KNOW IT BEST.
WHICH BROUGHT ME BACK TO YOU. WE BOTH HAVE REPUTATIONS AT STAKE HERE IN THIS FIGHT. SO LET'S BARTER.
ALWAYS WORKING AN ANGLE, RIGHT? TOO BAD YOU'VE GOT NOTHING I WANT.
THE KHUND MILITARY IS CRUSHED. ALL YOUR FIGHTERS ARE EITHER DEAD OR IN OUR JAIL.
NEXT STOP: DURLA. THEN THIS MESS WILL BE OVER.
YOU WON'T FIND THE DURLANS ON THEIR HOMEWORLD. YOU WON'T FIND THEM AT ALL. NOT WITHOUT HELP.
THIS WAR WAS NEVER ABOUT JUST ELIMINATING THE CORPS. THAT WAS ONLY THE SALES PITCH THE DURLANS USED TO GET THE OUTER CLANNS AND THE KHUND TO TAKE THEIR SIDE.
IT WAS ALWAYS ABOUT POWER. POWER ENOUGH TO RULE EVERYONE. NOW, WITH THE WAR HAVING TAKEN ITS TOLL ON ALL SIDES, EVERYONE WILL BE THAT MUCH EASIER FOR THE DURLANS TO RULE.
UNLESS SOMEONE STOPS THEM.

SEE, DURLAN PHYSIOLOGY IS *UNSTABLE*. IT TAKES *ENERGY* FOR THEM TO CHANGE FORM. CONSUME ENOUGH, THEY CAN *LOCK* THEIR FORM.

THIS RACE OF BEINGS THEY FOUND-- THESE *DAXAMITES*, WHOEVER THEY ARE-- THE DURLANS WANT TO BECOME THEM. *PERMANENTLY*.

AFTER THE WAY THEY *DOUBLE-CROSSED* ME TODAY, I'M STARTING TO WONDER IF THAT MIGHT NOT BE A GOOD THING.

LUCKILY, THEY CAN'T DO IT WITHOUT *A LOT* OF ENERGY.

A *VAST* SUPPLY OF *CONSUMABLE* POWER. *POTENT*, TOO. NOT EASY TO COME BY.

YOU KNOW WHERE THE *ENERGY SOURCE* IS, DON'T YOU.

DO I DETECT A CRACK IN YOUR CONFIDENCE? A FEAR THAT MAYBE--JUST *MAYBE*--YOU HAVEN'T PLANNED FOR EVERY CONTINGENCY?

I TACKED ON A HEFTY *FINDER'S FEE* BEFORE GIVING THE DURLANS THAT INFORMATION.

NATURALLY YOU DIDN'T CONSIDER FINDING OUT *WHY* THEY WERE WILLING TO PAY SO MUCH.

LIKE, MAYBE BECAUSE IF THEY CAN BECOME DAXAMITES, THEY'LL BE DAMN NEAR *INVINCIBLE*.

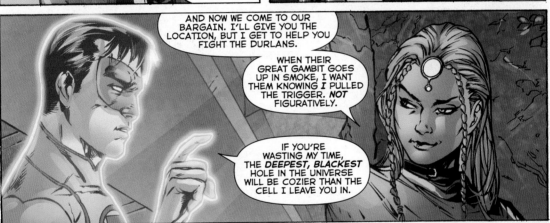

AND NOW WE COME TO OUR BARGAIN. I'LL GIVE YOU THE LOCATION, BUT I GET TO HELP YOU FIGHT THE DURLANS.

WHEN THEIR GREAT GAMBIT GOES UP IN SMOKE, I WANT THEM KNOWING *I* PULLED THE TRIGGER. *NOT* FIGURATIVELY.

IF YOU'RE WASTING MY TIME, THE *DEEPEST, BLACKEST* HOLE IN THE UNIVERSE WILL BE COZIER THAN THE CELL I LEAVE YOU IN.

THE ANSWER'S BEEN IN FRONT OF YOU ALL ALONG.

HOW MANY OF MY *CLANN* HAS HE LOCKED UP? HOW MUCH *BUSINESS* HAS *HE* COST US?

A BEING OF LIVING ENERGY, FROM AN *OCEAN* OF THE SAME.

GORIN-SUNN...

THE DURLANS ARE HEADED FOR *ZEZZEN*...

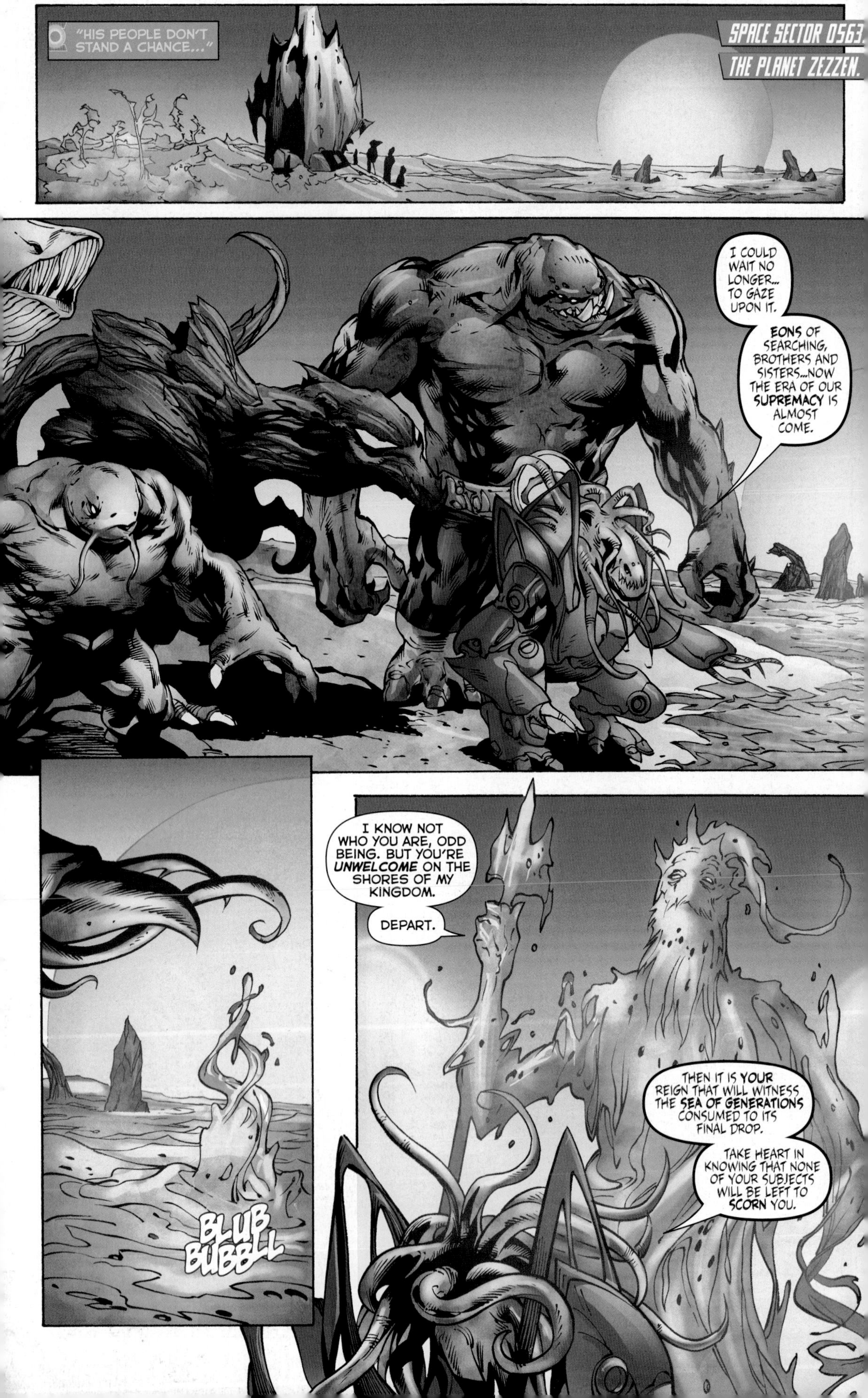
"HIS PEOPLE DON'T STAND A CHANCE..."
SPACE SECTOR 0563.
THE PLANET ZEZZEN.
I COULD WAIT NO LONGER... TO GAZE UPON IT.
EONS OF SEARCHING, BROTHERS AND SISTERS...NOW THE ERA OF OUR SUPREMACY IS ALMOST COME.
BLUB BUBBLL
I KNOW NOT WHO YOU ARE, ODD BEING. BUT YOU'RE UNWELCOME ON THE SHORES OF MY KINGDOM.
DEPART.
THEN IT IS YOUR REIGN THAT WILL WITNESS THE SEA OF GENERATIONS CONSUMED TO ITS FINAL DROP.
TAKE HEART IN KNOWING THAT NONE OF YOUR SUBJECTS WILL BE LEFT TO SCORN YOU.

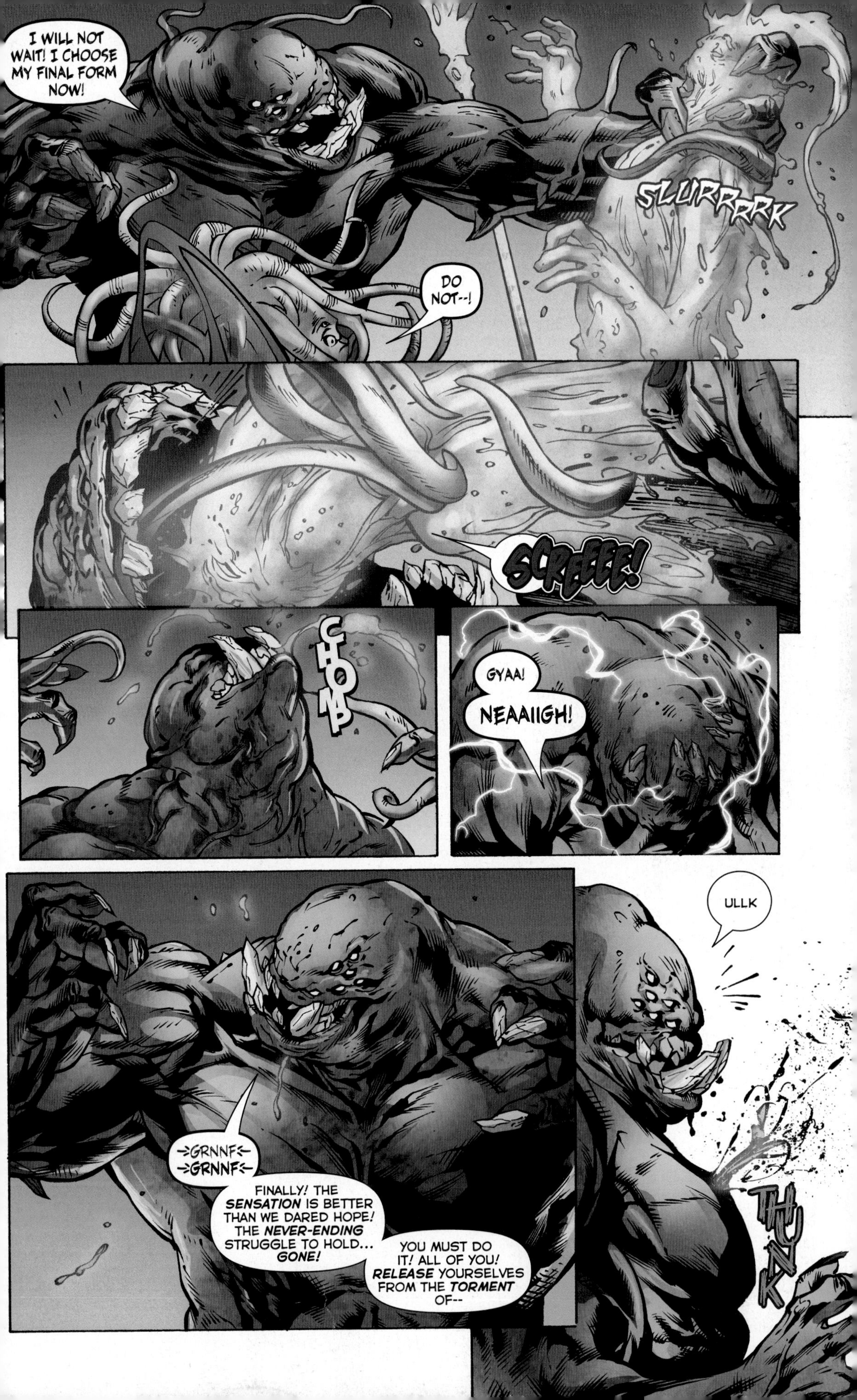
I WILL NOT WAIT! I CHOOSE MY FINAL FORM NOW!
SLURRRRK
DO NOT--!
SCREEEE!
CHOMP
GYAA!
NEAAIIGH!
-GRNNF-
-GRNNF-
FINALLY! THE SENSATION IS BETTER THAN WE DARED HOPE! THE NEVER-ENDING STRUGGLE TO HOLD... GONE!
YOU MUST DO IT! ALL OF YOU! RELEASE YOURSELVES FROM THE TORMENT OF--
ULLK
THUNK

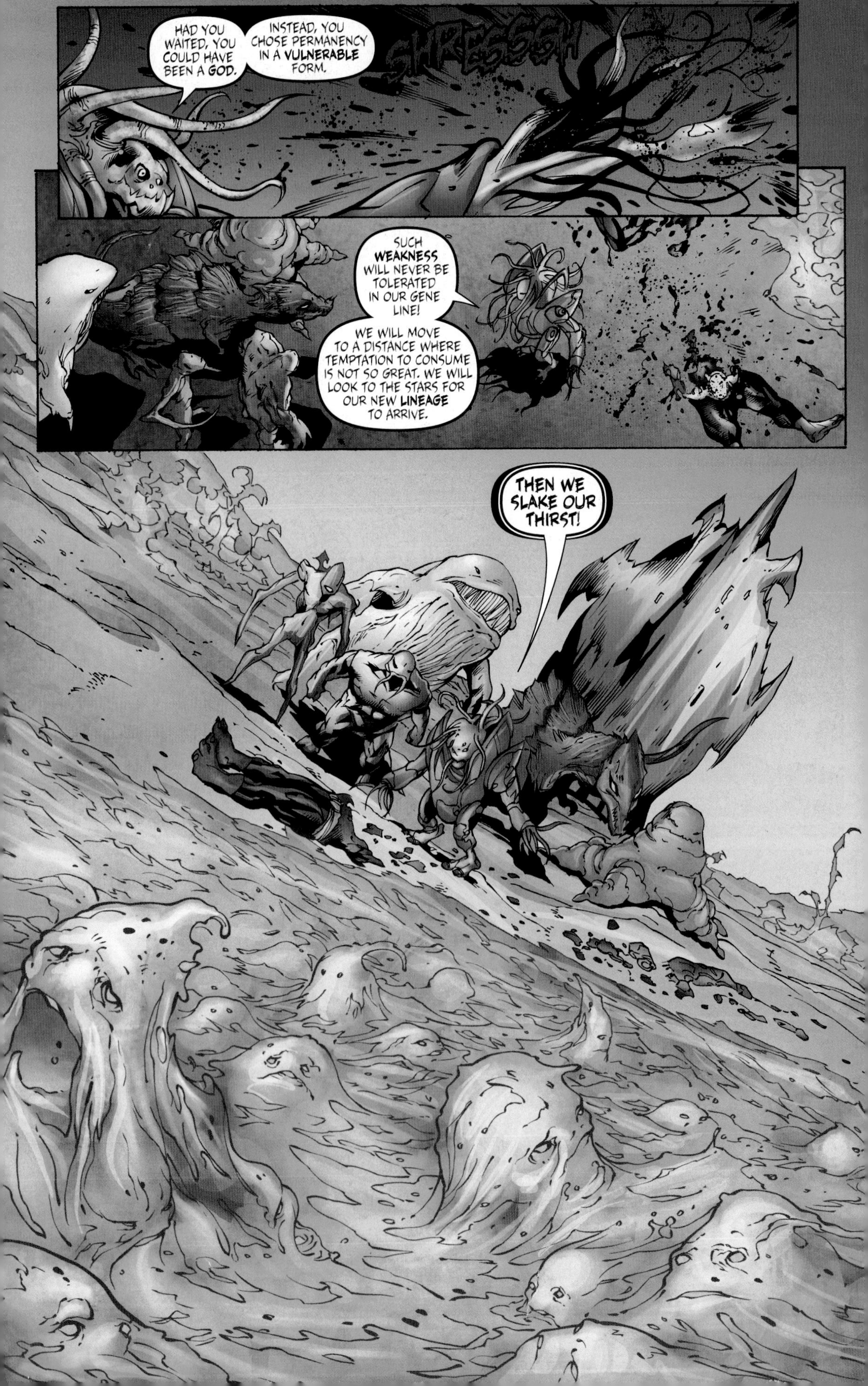
HAD YOU WAITED, YOU COULD HAVE BEEN A GOD.
INSTEAD, YOU CHOSE PERMANENCY IN A VULNERABLE FORM.
SHRSSSH
SUCH WEAKNESS WILL NEVER BE TOLERATED IN OUR GENE LINE!
WE WILL MOVE TO A DISTANCE WHERE TEMPTATION TO CONSUME IS NOT SO GREAT. WE WILL LOOK TO THE STARS FOR OUR NEW LINEAGE TO ARRIVE.
THEN WE SLAKE OUR THIRST!

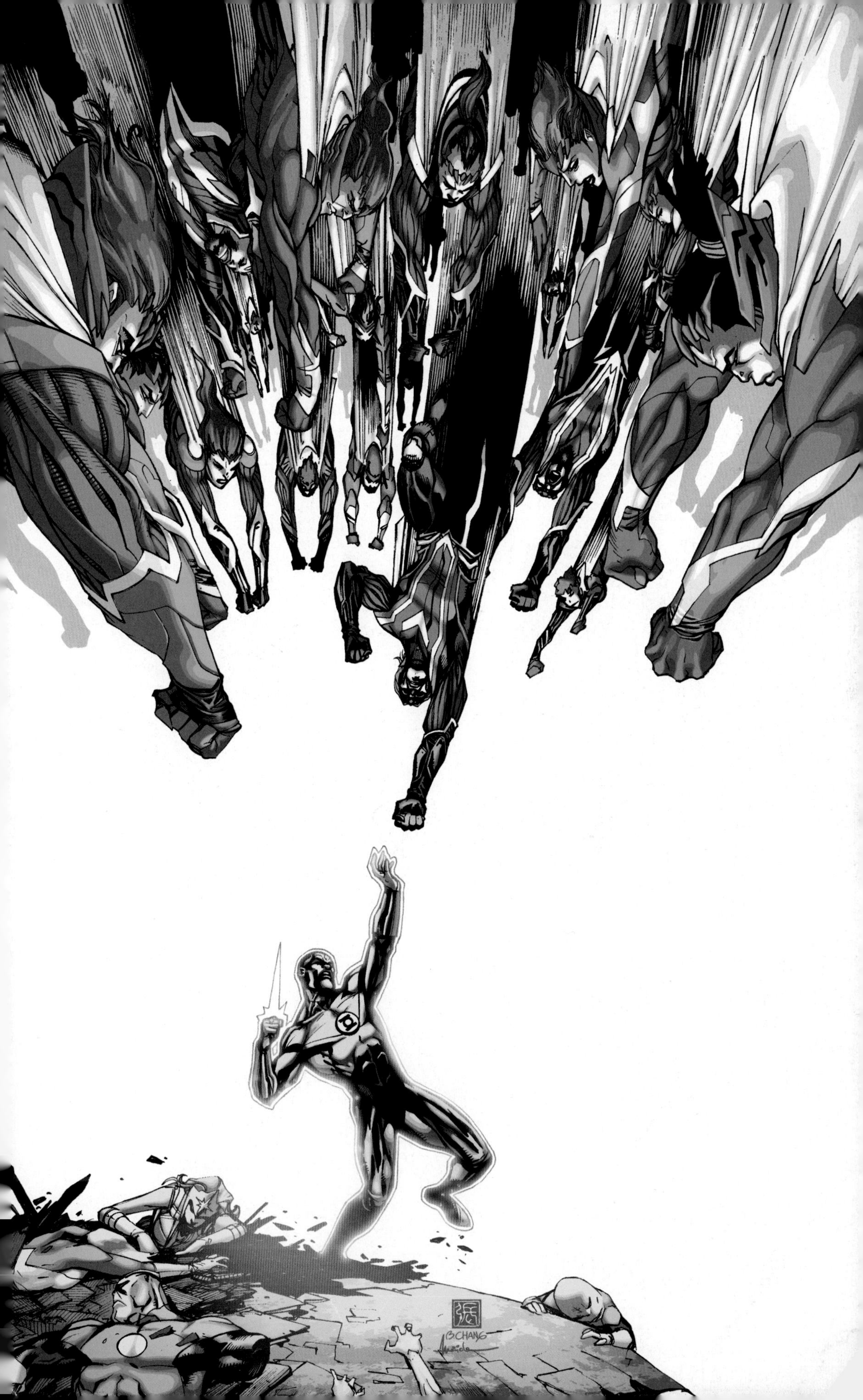
BCHANG

UPRISING PART 4: INSIDIOUS

VAN JENSEN writer **BERNARD CHANG** & **MORITAT** artists **MARCELO MAIOLO** colorist
cover art by **BERNARD CHANG** & **MARCELO MAIOLO** **BOMBSHELL** variant cover by **ANT LUCIA**

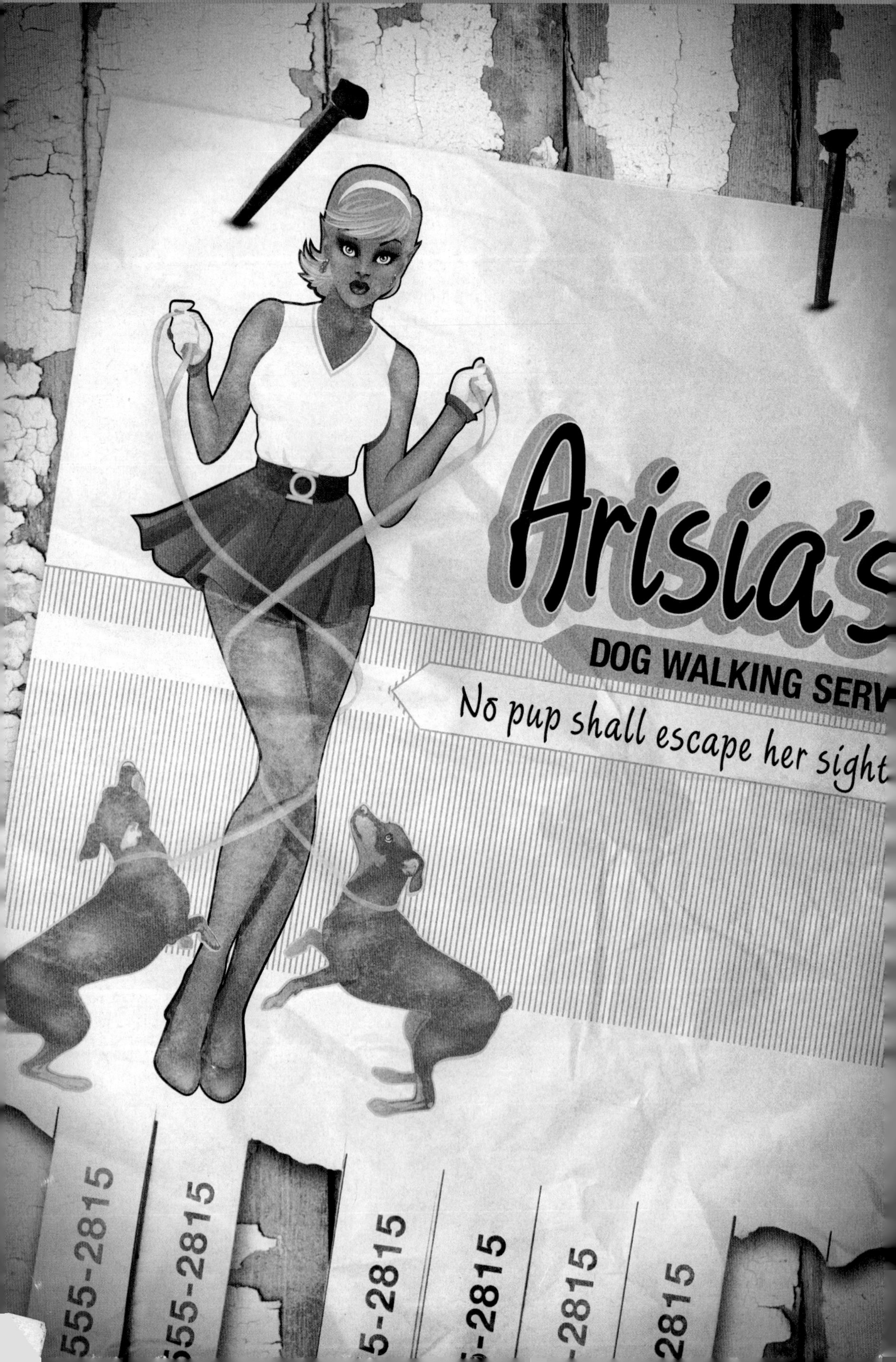

Arisia's
DOG WALKING SERV
No pup shall escape her sight
555-2815
555-2815
5-2815
-2815
-2815
2815

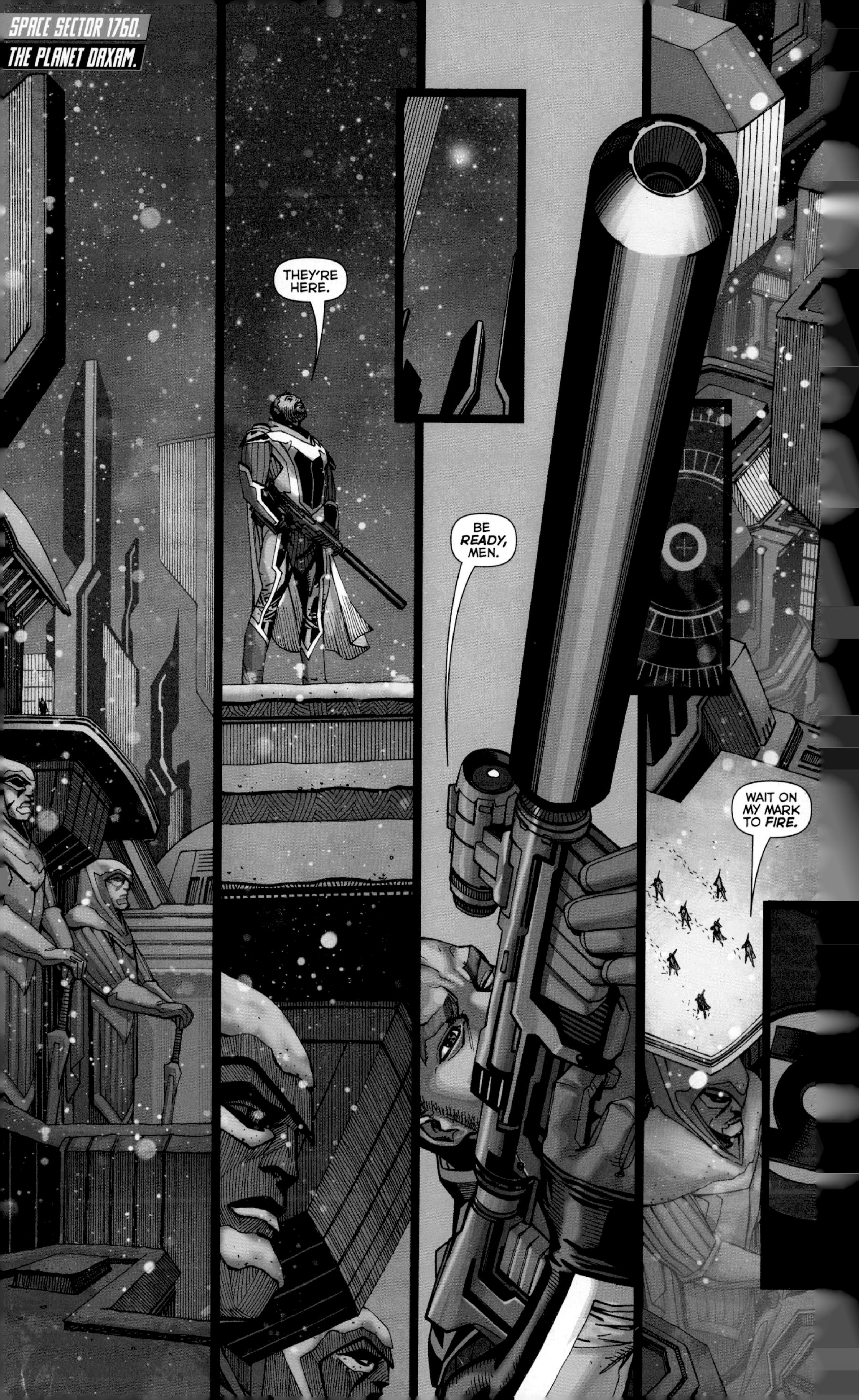
SPACE SECTOR 1760.
THE PLANET DAXAM.
THEY'RE HERE.
BE READY, MEN.
WAIT ON MY MARK TO FIRE.

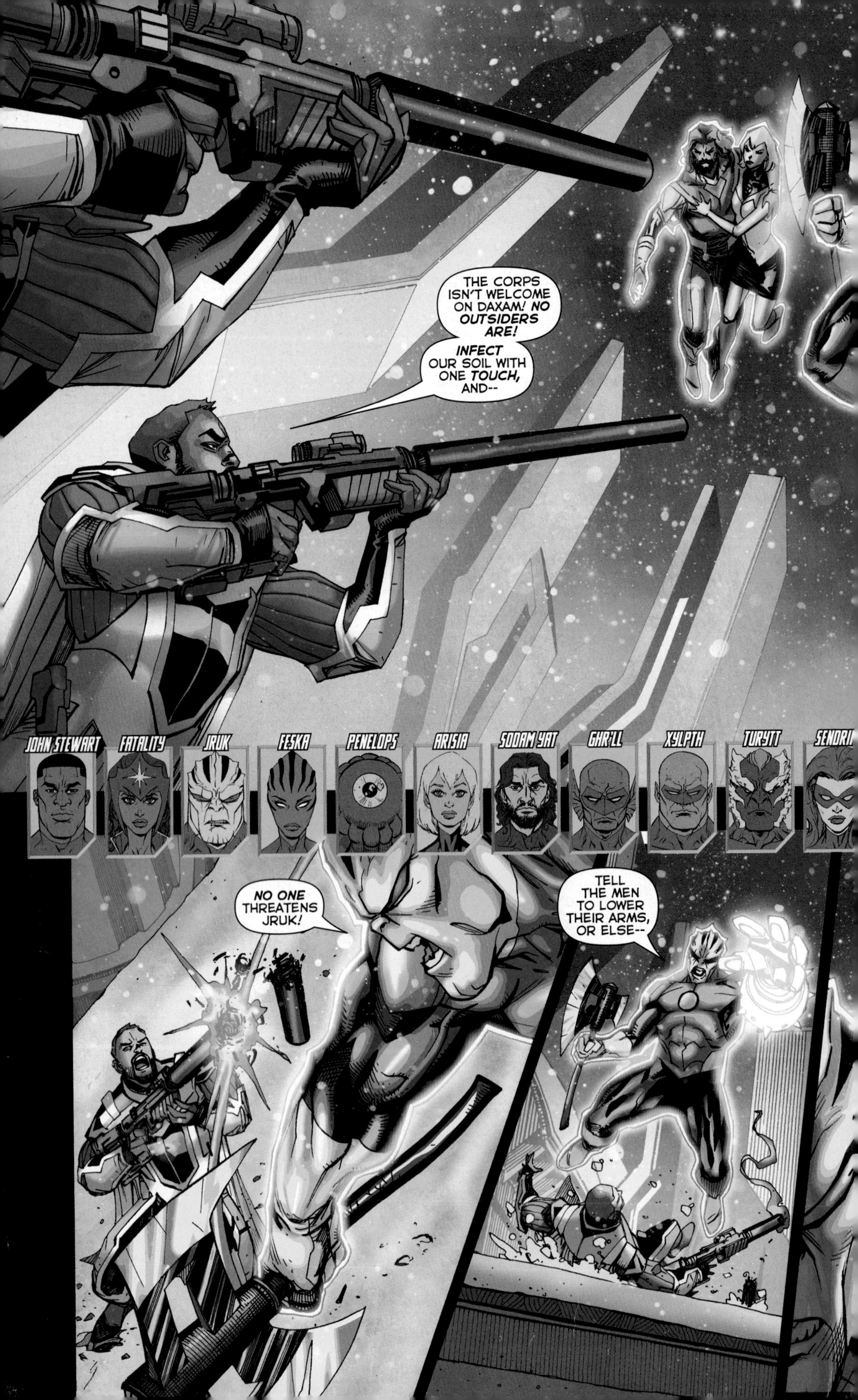
THE CORPS ISN'T WELCOME ON DAXAM! NO OUTSIDERS ARE!
INFECT OUR SOIL WITH ONE TOUCH, AND--
JOHN STEWART
FATALITY
JRUK
FESKA
PENELOPS
ARISIA
SODAM YAT
GHR'LL
XYLPTH
TURYTT
SENDRII
NO ONE THREATENS JRUK!
TELL THE MEN TO LOWER THEIR ARMS, OR ELSE--

PEOPLE OF DAXAM, YOU'RE IN *GRAVE* DANGER...

R'AMEY HOLL | ASH-PAK-GLIF | VOLK | REES-VAN | MUKMUK | MALET DASIM | CHERNISS | HWAAL | VON DAGGLE | SALAAK

STAND DOWN, JRUK.

YOU DAXAMITES ARE AMONG THE MOST POWERFUL BEINGS IN THE UNIVERSE WHEN EXPOSED TO A YELLOW SUN. BUT YOUR SUN IS RED. WE CAME TO PROTECT YOU.

TELL HIM, PROLLET. WE NEED NO HELP.

AS HE SAID, WE DAXAMITES HAVE LEARNED TO PROTECT *OURSELVES*. YOU LANTERNS HAVE CAUSED ENOUGH DAMAGE HERE.

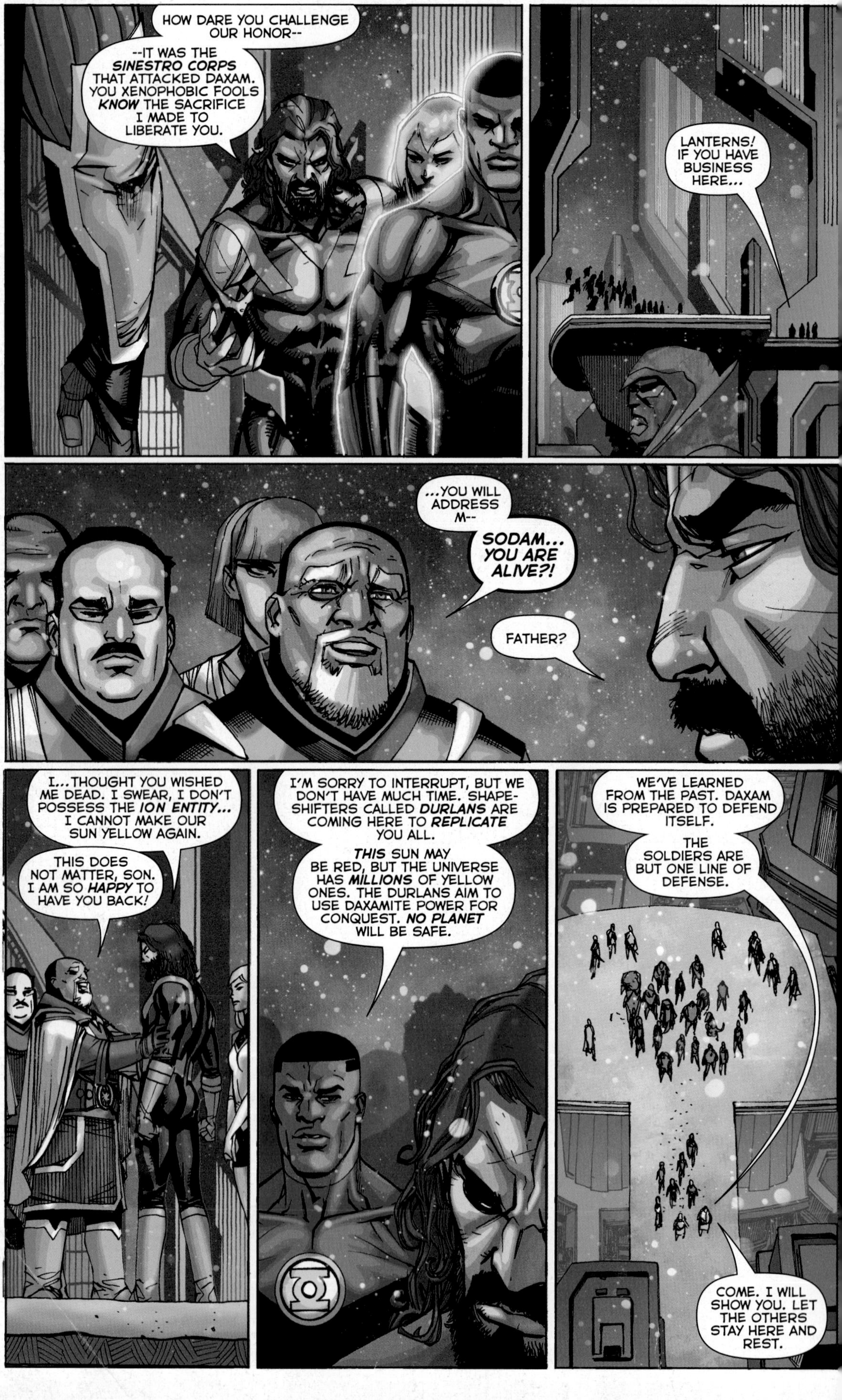
HOW DARE YOU CHALLENGE OUR HONOR--
--IT WAS THE SINESTRO CORPS THAT ATTACKED DAXAM. YOU XENOPHOBIC FOOLS KNOW THE SACRIFICE I MADE TO LIBERATE YOU.
LANTERNS! IF YOU HAVE BUSINESS HERE...
...YOU WILL ADDRESS M--
SODAM... YOU ARE ALIVE?!
FATHER?
I...THOUGHT YOU WISHED ME DEAD. I SWEAR, I DON'T POSSESS THE ION ENTITY... I CANNOT MAKE OUR SUN YELLOW AGAIN.
THIS DOES NOT MATTER, SON. I AM SO HAPPY TO HAVE YOU BACK!
I'M SORRY TO INTERRUPT, BUT WE DON'T HAVE MUCH TIME. SHAPE-SHIFTERS CALLED DURLANS ARE COMING HERE TO REPLICATE YOU ALL.
THIS SUN MAY BE RED, BUT THE UNIVERSE HAS MILLIONS OF YELLOW ONES. THE DURLANS AIM TO USE DAXAMITE POWER FOR CONQUEST. NO PLANET WILL BE SAFE.
WE'VE LEARNED FROM THE PAST. DAXAM IS PREPARED TO DEFEND ITSELF.
THE SOLDIERS ARE BUT ONE LINE OF DEFENSE.
COME. I WILL SHOW YOU. LET THE OTHERS STAY HERE AND REST.

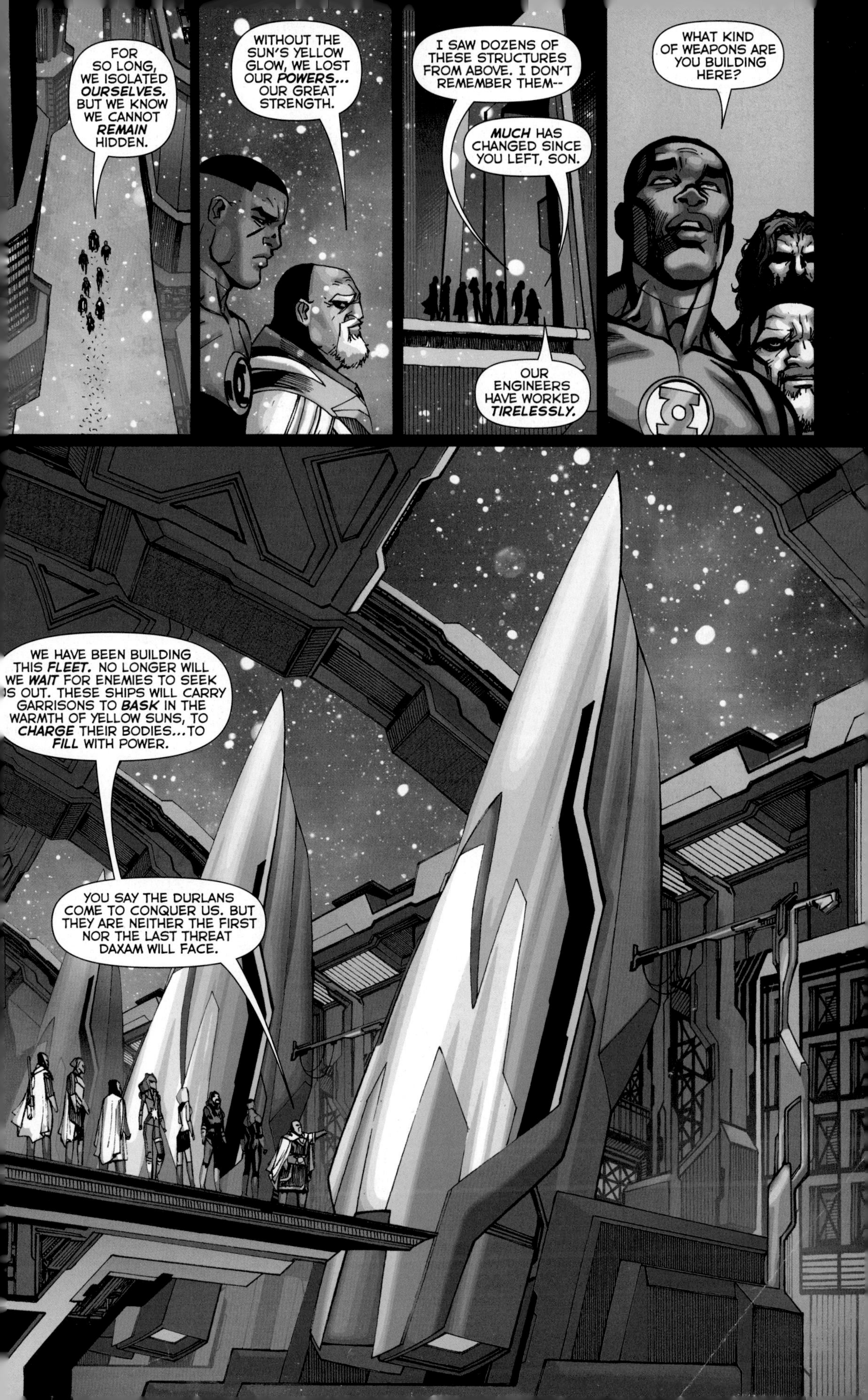

FOR SO LONG, WE ISOLATED OURSELVES. BUT WE KNOW WE CANNOT REMAIN HIDDEN.
WITHOUT THE SUN'S YELLOW GLOW, WE LOST OUR POWERS... OUR GREAT STRENGTH.
I SAW DOZENS OF THESE STRUCTURES FROM ABOVE. I DON'T REMEMBER THEM--
MUCH HAS CHANGED SINCE YOU LEFT, SON.
OUR ENGINEERS HAVE WORKED TIRELESSLY.
WHAT KIND OF WEAPONS ARE YOU BUILDING HERE?
WE HAVE BEEN BUILDING THIS FLEET. NO LONGER WILL WE WAIT FOR ENEMIES TO SEEK US OUT. THESE SHIPS WILL CARRY GARRISONS TO BASK IN THE WARMTH OF YELLOW SUNS, TO CHARGE THEIR BODIES...TO FILL WITH POWER.
YOU SAY THE DURLANS COME TO CONQUER US. BUT THEY ARE NEITHER THE FIRST NOR THE LAST THREAT DAXAM WILL FACE.

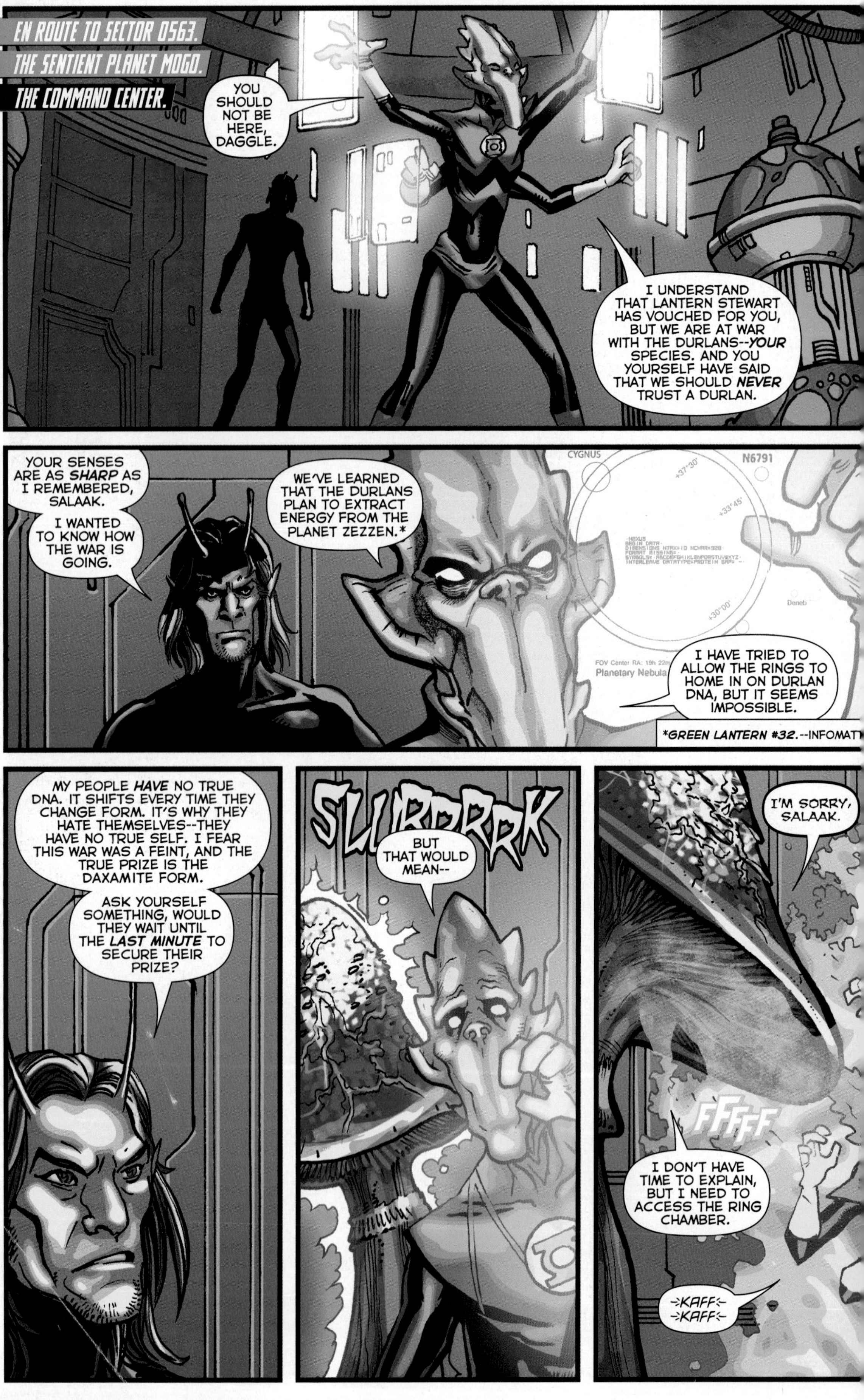
EN ROUTE TO SECTOR 0563.
THE SENTIENT PLANET MOGO.
THE COMMAND CENTER.
YOU SHOULD NOT BE HERE, DAGGLE.
I UNDERSTAND THAT LANTERN STEWART HAS VOUCHED FOR YOU, BUT WE ARE AT WAR WITH THE DURLANS--YOUR SPECIES. AND YOU YOURSELF HAVE SAID THAT WE SHOULD NEVER TRUST A DURLAN.
YOUR SENSES ARE AS SHARP AS I REMEMBERED, SALAAK.
I WANTED TO KNOW HOW THE WAR IS GOING.
WE'VE LEARNED THAT THE DURLANS PLAN TO EXTRACT ENERGY FROM THE PLANET ZEZZEN.*
CYGNUS
N6791
Deneb
Planetary Nebula
I HAVE TRIED TO ALLOW THE RINGS TO HOME IN ON DURLAN DNA, BUT IT SEEMS IMPOSSIBLE.
*GREEN LANTERN #32.--INFOMAT
MY PEOPLE HAVE NO TRUE DNA. IT SHIFTS EVERY TIME THEY CHANGE FORM. IT'S WHY THEY HATE THEMSELVES--THEY HAVE NO TRUE SELF. I FEAR THIS WAR WAS A FEINT, AND THE TRUE PRIZE IS THE DAXAMITE FORM.
ASK YOURSELF SOMETHING, WOULD THEY WAIT UNTIL THE LAST MINUTE TO SECURE THEIR PRIZE?
SLIRRRRK
BUT THAT WOULD MEAN--
I'M SORRY, SALAAK.
FFFFF
I DON'T HAVE TIME TO EXPLAIN, BUT I NEED TO ACCESS THE RING CHAMBER.
KAFF
KAFF

SLURRRK

SWORE I'D NEVER WEAR THIS AGAIN.

·GHKK·

GREEN LANTERN OF SECTOR 700 RECOGNIZED.

SYSTEM OVERRIDE CONFIRMED. RING PROGRAMMING INTERFACE ONLINE.

EXTRACTION SEQUENCE INITIATED. COMMAND EXECUTE IN 3...2...

SORRY, SALAAK. I WISH IT DIDN'T HAVE TO BE THIS WAY.

EXTRACTION BEGUN.

SSKKRRL

AAAAGGGHHHH-!

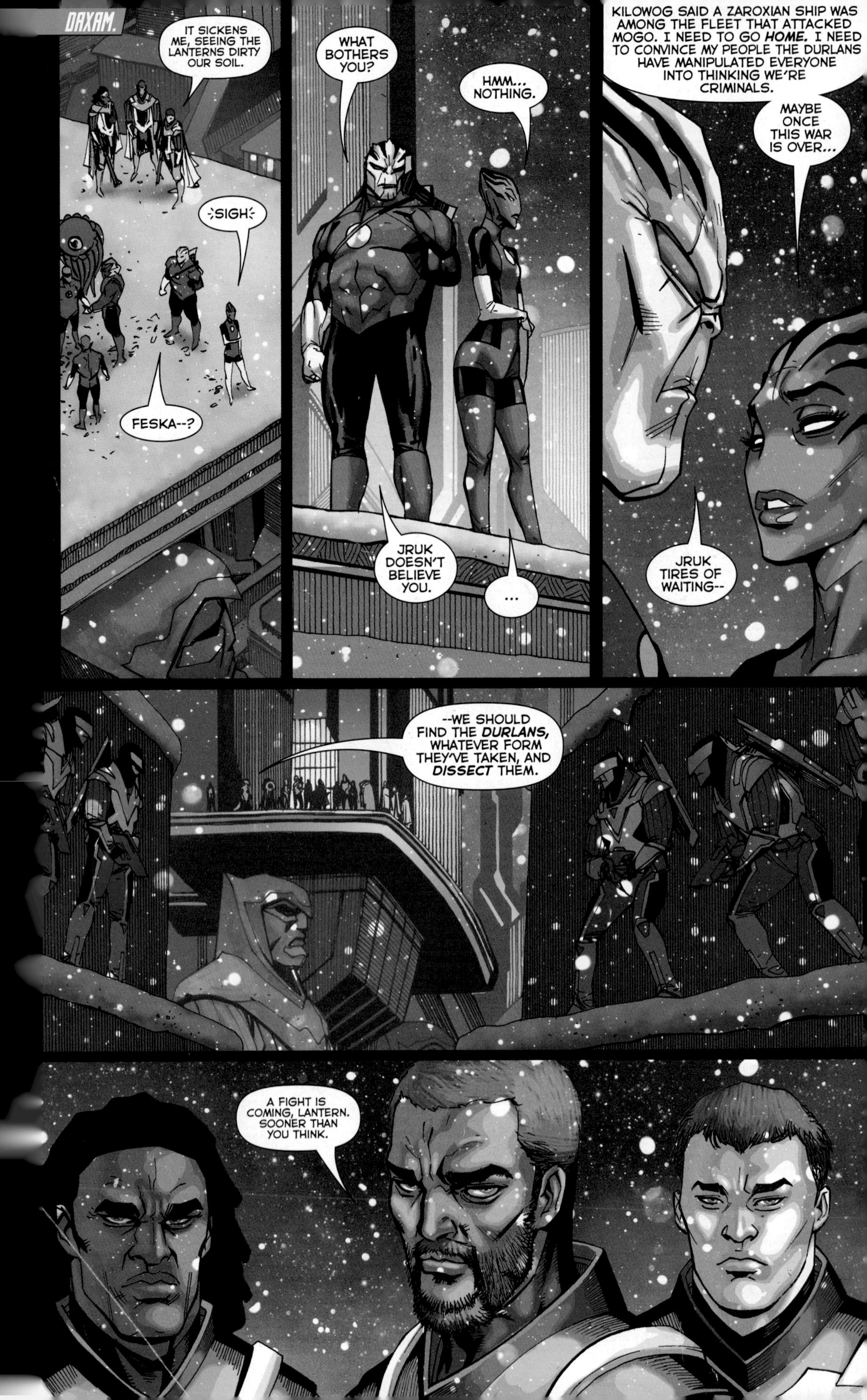
DAXAM.
IT SICKENS ME, SEEING THE LANTERNS DIRTY OUR SOIL.
·SIGH·
FESKA--?
WHAT BOTHERS YOU?
HMM... NOTHING.
JRUK DOESN'T BELIEVE YOU.
...
KILOWOG SAID A ZAROXIAN SHIP WAS AMONG THE FLEET THAT ATTACKED MOGO. I NEED TO GO HOME. I NEED TO CONVINCE MY PEOPLE THE DURLANS HAVE MANIPULATED EVERYONE INTO THINKING WE'RE CRIMINALS.
MAYBE ONCE THIS WAR IS OVER...
JRUK TIRES OF WAITING--
--WE SHOULD FIND THE DURLANS, WHATEVER FORM THEY'VE TAKEN, AND DISSECT THEM.
A FIGHT IS COMING, LANTERN. SOONER THAN YOU THINK.

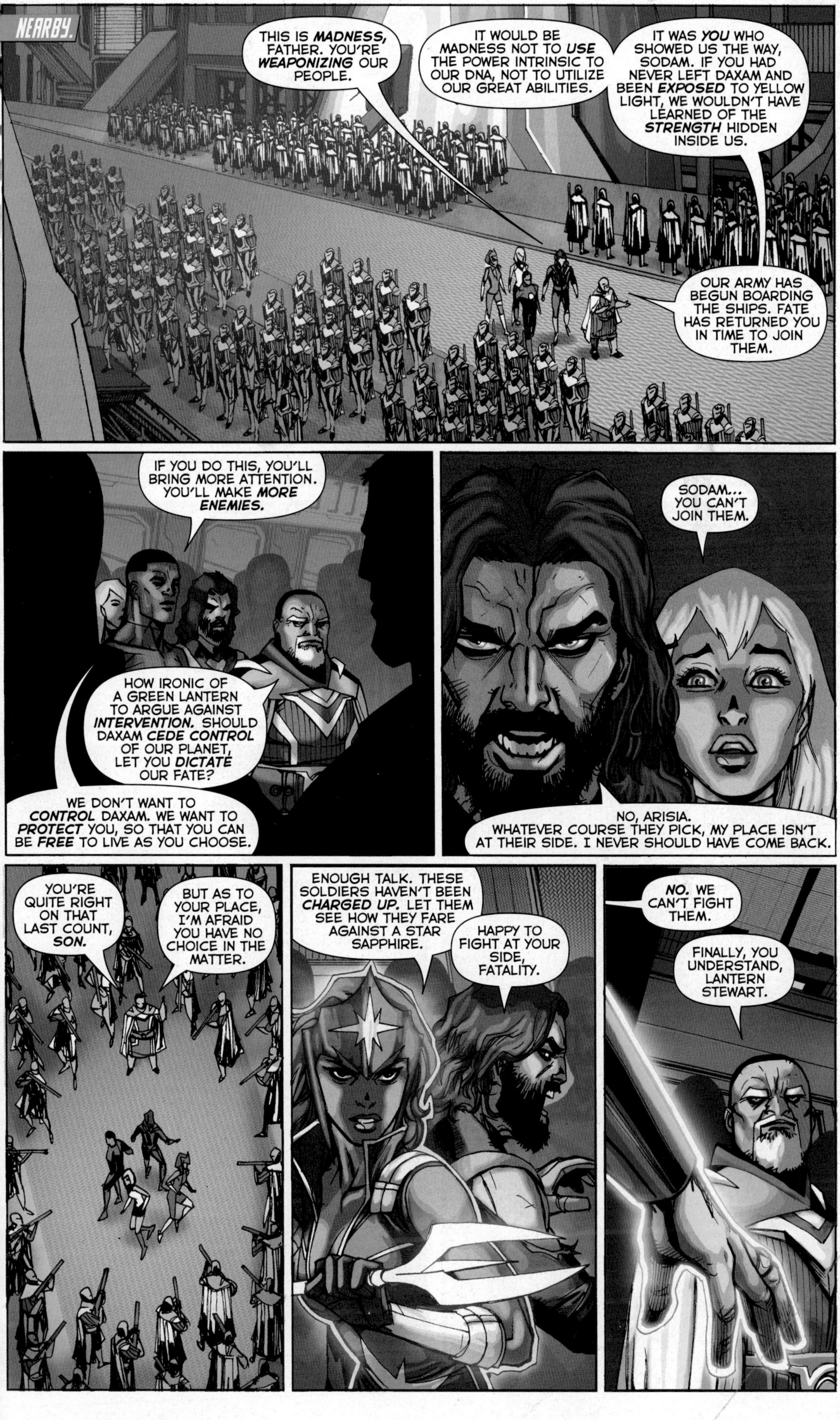
NEARBY.
THIS IS MADNESS, FATHER. YOU'RE WEAPONIZING OUR PEOPLE.
IT WOULD BE MADNESS NOT TO USE THE POWER INTRINSIC TO OUR DNA, NOT TO UTILIZE OUR GREAT ABILITIES.
IT WAS YOU WHO SHOWED US THE WAY, SODAM. IF YOU HAD NEVER LEFT DAXAM AND BEEN EXPOSED TO YELLOW LIGHT, WE WOULDN'T HAVE LEARNED OF THE STRENGTH HIDDEN INSIDE US.
OUR ARMY HAS BEGUN BOARDING THE SHIPS. FATE HAS RETURNED YOU IN TIME TO JOIN THEM.
IF YOU DO THIS, YOU'LL BRING MORE ATTENTION. YOU'LL MAKE MORE ENEMIES.
HOW IRONIC OF A GREEN LANTERN TO ARGUE AGAINST INTERVENTION. SHOULD DAXAM CEDE CONTROL OF OUR PLANET, LET YOU DICTATE OUR FATE?
WE DON'T WANT TO CONTROL DAXAM. WE WANT TO PROTECT YOU, SO THAT YOU CAN BE FREE TO LIVE AS YOU CHOOSE.
SODAM... YOU CAN'T JOIN THEM.
NO, ARISIA. WHATEVER COURSE THEY PICK, MY PLACE ISN'T AT THEIR SIDE. I NEVER SHOULD HAVE COME BACK.
YOU'RE QUITE RIGHT ON THAT LAST COUNT, SON.
BUT AS TO YOUR PLACE, I'M AFRAID YOU HAVE NO CHOICE IN THE MATTER.
ENOUGH TALK. THESE SOLDIERS HAVEN'T BEEN CHARGED UP. LET THEM SEE HOW THEY FARE AGAINST A STAR SAPPHIRE.
HAPPY TO FIGHT AT YOUR SIDE, FATALITY.
NO. WE CAN'T FIGHT THEM.
FINALLY, YOU UNDERSTAND, LANTERN STEWART.

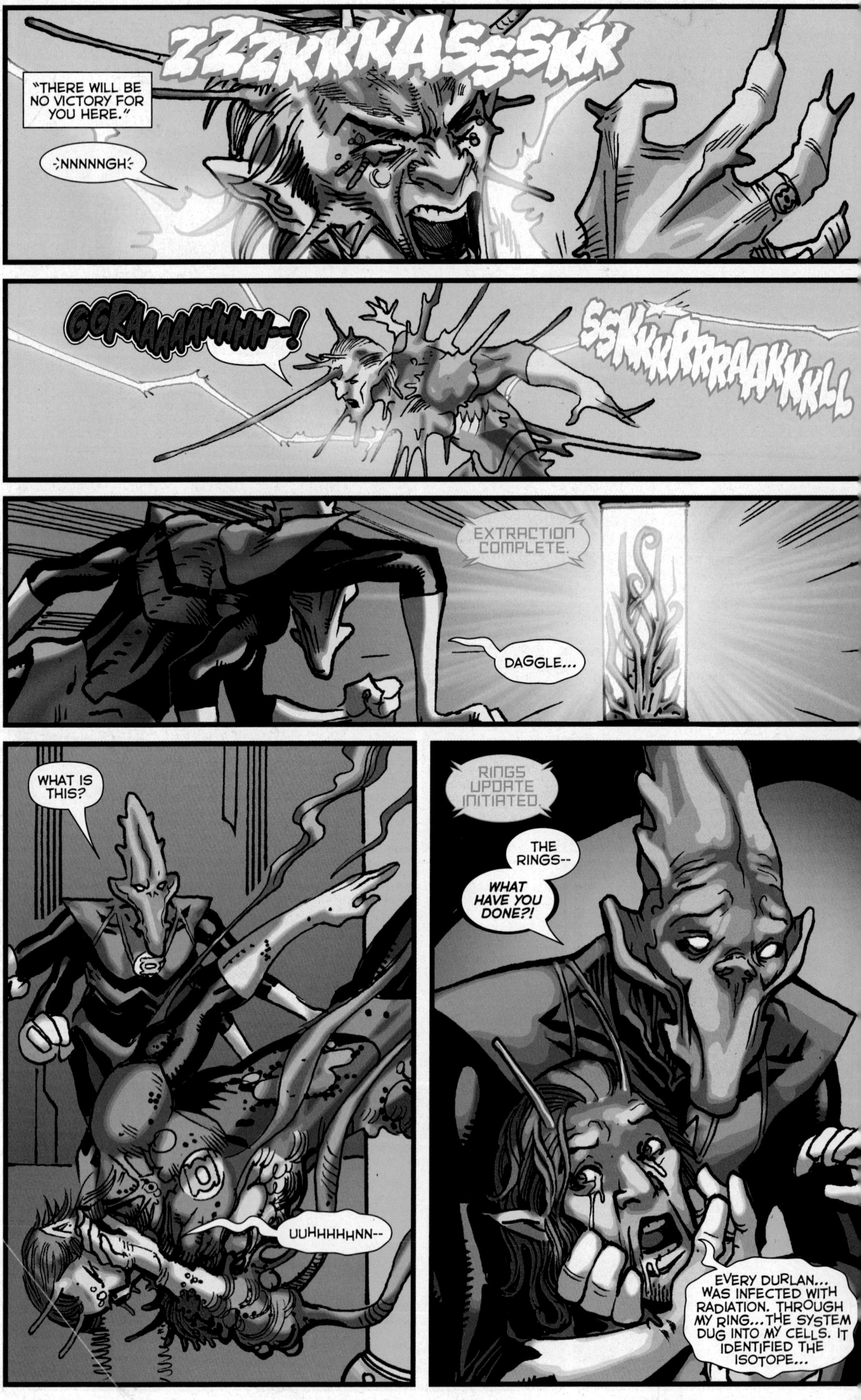
ZZZKKKASSSKK
"THERE WILL BE NO VICTORY FOR YOU HERE."
NNNNNGH
GGRAAAAAAHHHH--!
SSKKKRRRAAKKKLL
EXTRACTION COMPLETE.
DAGGLE...
WHAT IS THIS?
UUHHHHHNN--
RINGS UPDATE INITIATED.
THE RINGS--
WHAT HAVE YOU DONE?!
EVERY DURLAN... WAS INFECTED WITH RADIATION. THROUGH MY RING... THE SYSTEM DUG INTO MY CELLS. IT IDENTIFIED THE ISOTOPE...

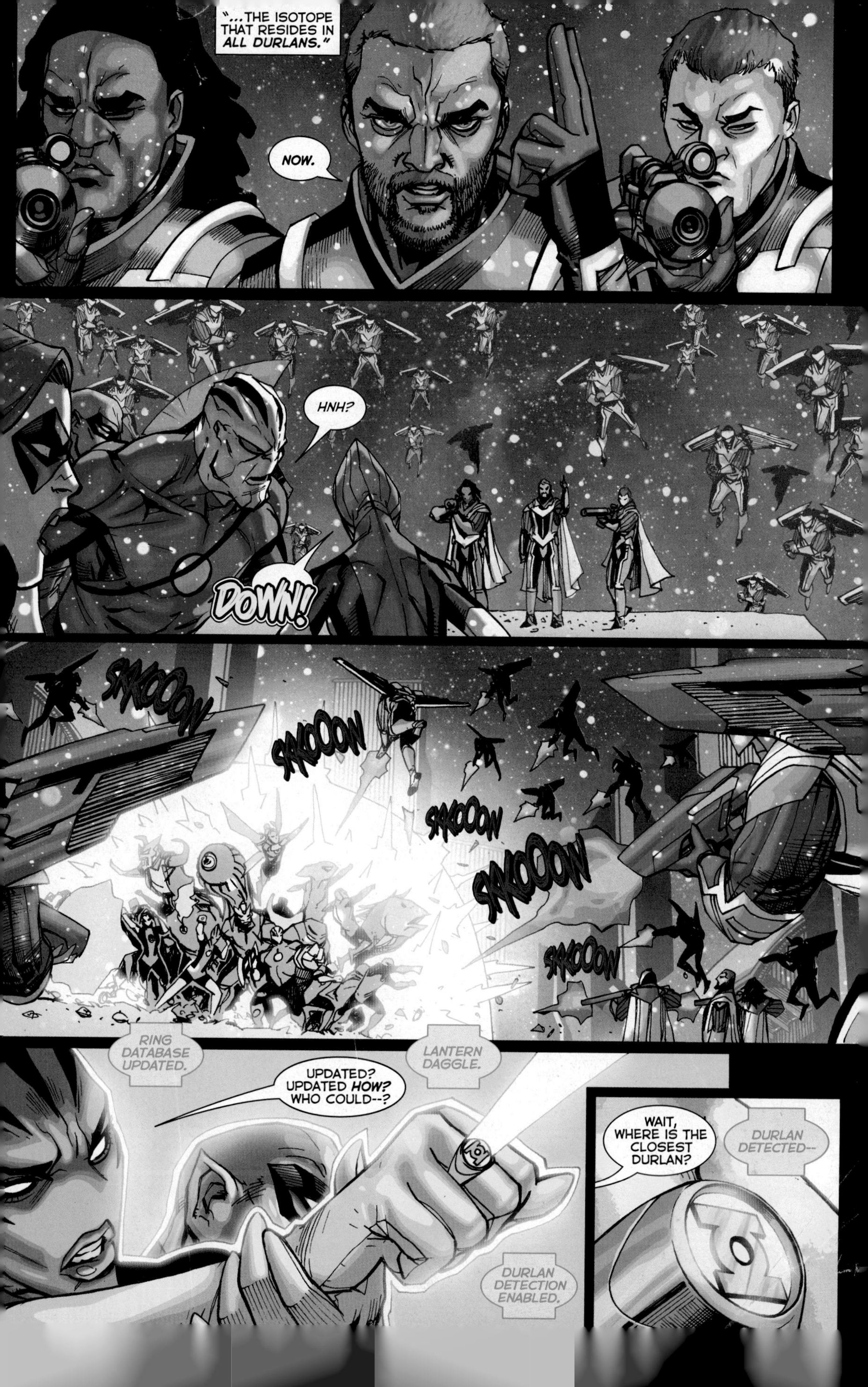
"...THE ISOTOPE THAT RESIDES IN ALL DURLANS."
NOW.
HNH?
DOWN!
SKKOOOOM
SKKOOOM
SKKOOOM
SKKOOOM
SKKOOOM
RING DATABASE UPDATED.
LANTERN DAGGLE.
UPDATED? UPDATED HOW? WHO COULD--?
DURLAN DETECTION ENABLED.
WAIT, WHERE IS THE CLOSEST DURLAN?
DURLAN DETECTED--

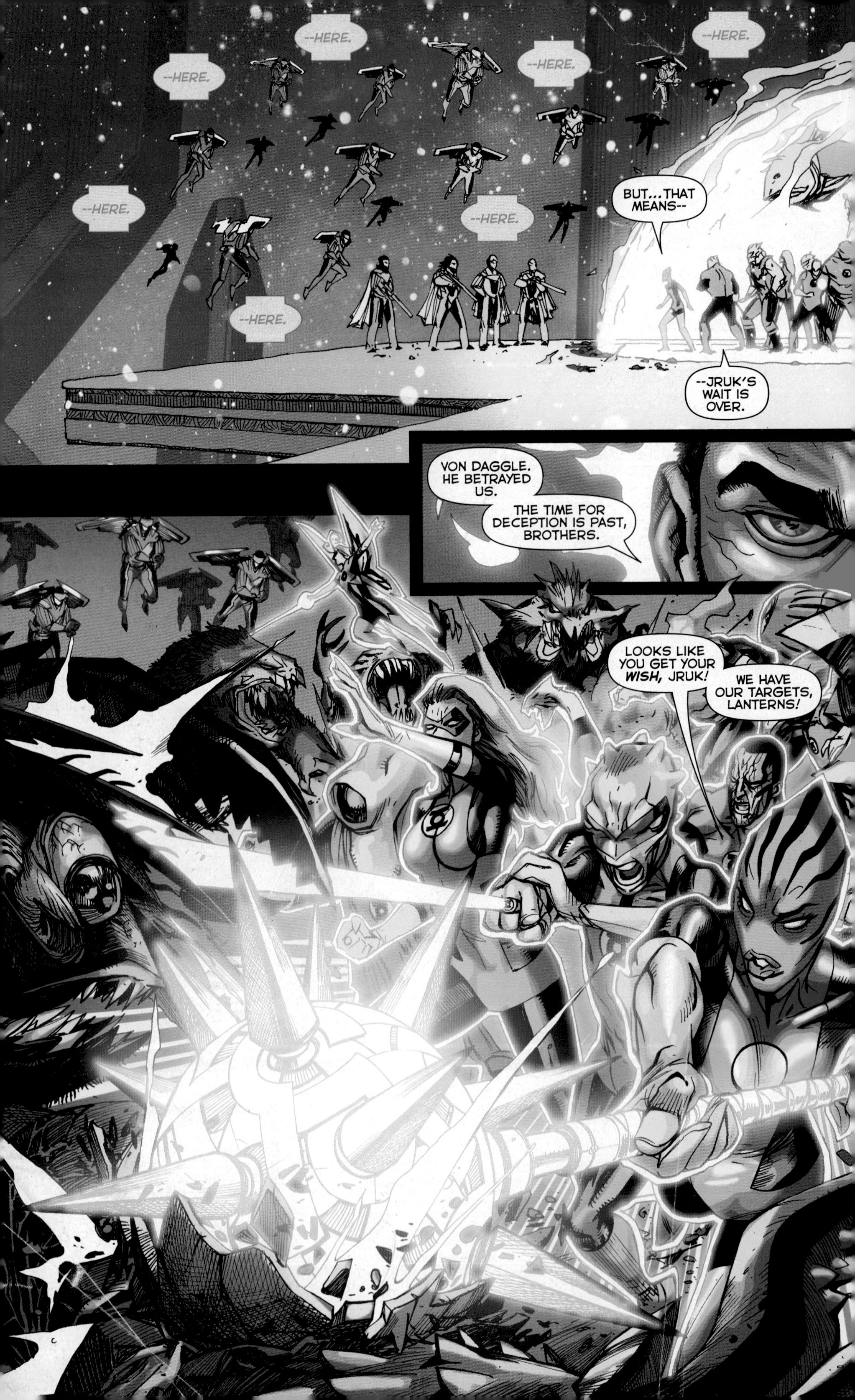
--HERE.
--HERE.
--HERE.
--HERE.
--HERE.
--HERE.
--HERE.
BUT...THAT MEANS--
--JRUK'S WAIT IS OVER.
VON DAGGLE. HE BETRAYED US.
THE TIME FOR DECEPTION IS PAST, BROTHERS.
LOOKS LIKE YOU GET YOUR *WISH,* JRUK!
WE HAVE OUR TARGETS, LANTERNS!

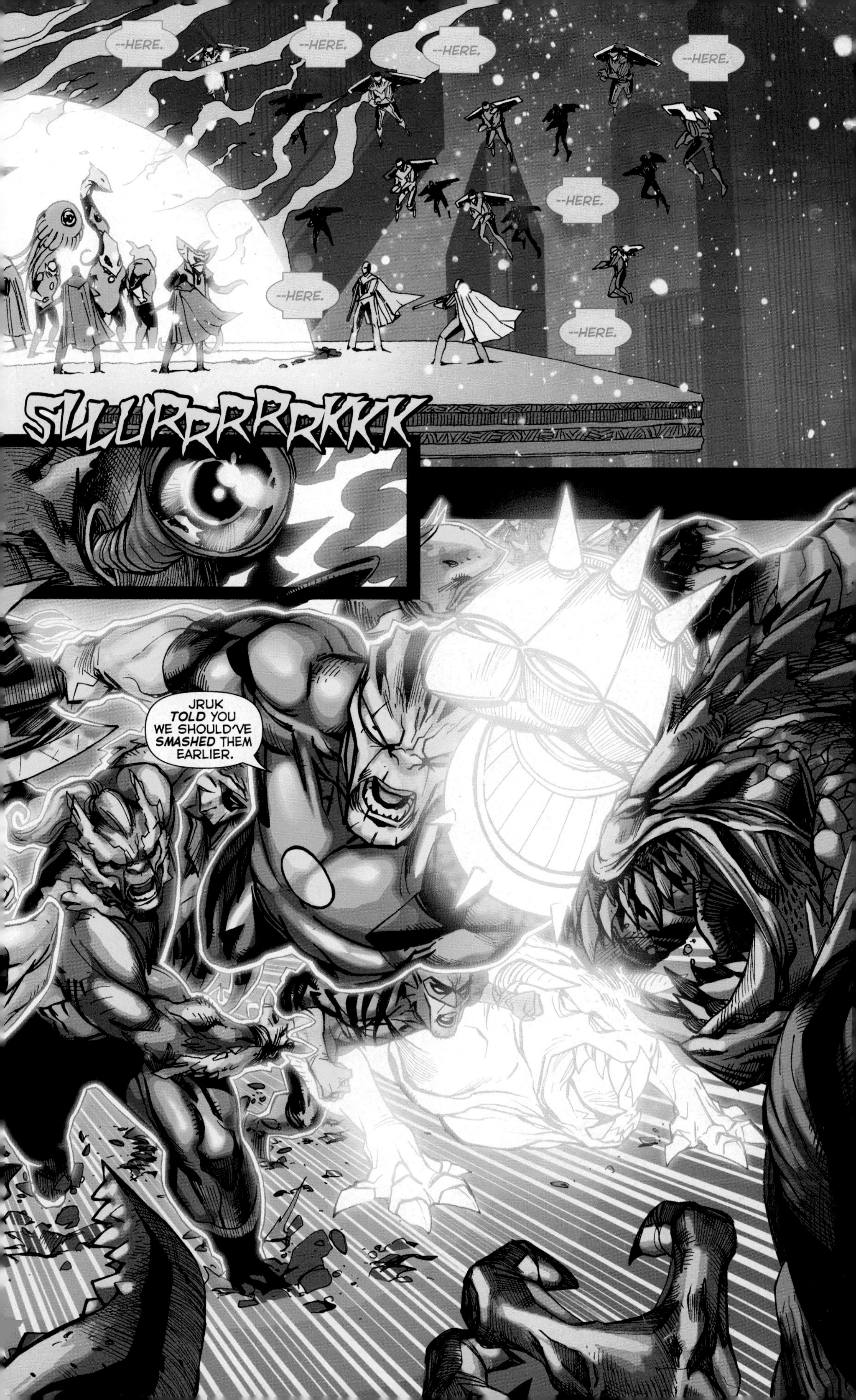
--HERE.
--HERE.
--HERE.
--HERE.
--HERE.
--HERE.
--HERE.
SLLURRRRRKKK
JRUK TOLD YOU WE SHOULD'VE SMASHED THEM EARLIER.

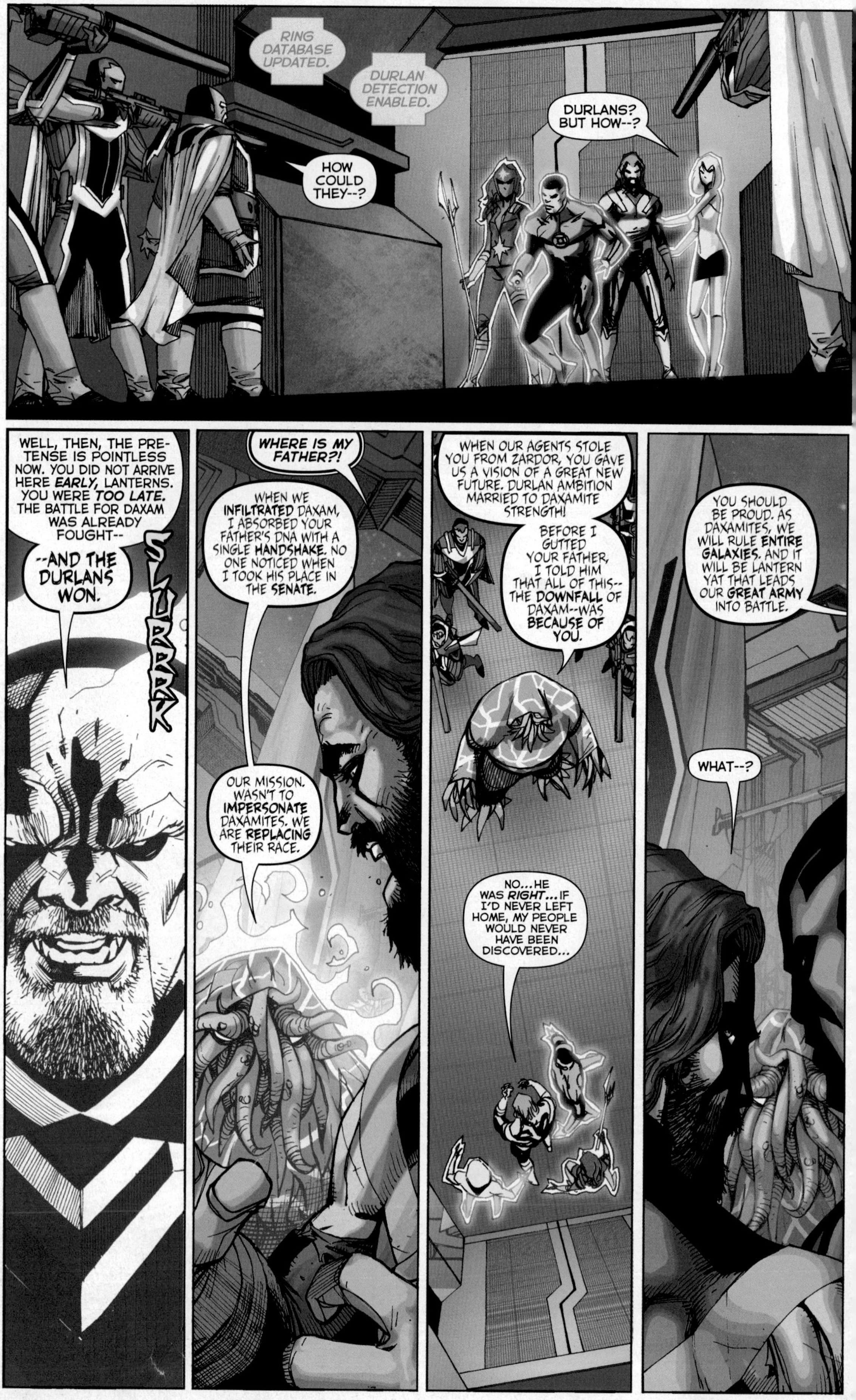
RING DATABASE UPDATED.
DURLAN DETECTION ENABLED.
HOW COULD THEY--?
DURLANS? BUT HOW--?
WELL, THEN, THE PRETENSE IS POINTLESS NOW. YOU DID NOT ARRIVE HERE EARLY, LANTERNS. YOU WERE TOO LATE. THE BATTLE FOR DAXAM WAS ALREADY FOUGHT--
--AND THE DURLANS WON.
SLURRRK
WHERE IS MY FATHER?!
WHEN WE INFILTRATED DAXAM, I ABSORBED YOUR FATHER'S DNA WITH A SINGLE HANDSHAKE. NO ONE NOTICED WHEN I TOOK HIS PLACE IN THE SENATE.
OUR MISSION. WASN'T TO IMPERSONATE DAXAMITES. WE ARE REPLACING THEIR RACE.
WHEN OUR AGENTS STOLE YOU FROM ZARDOR, YOU GAVE US A VISION OF A GREAT NEW FUTURE. DURLAN AMBITION MARRIED TO DAXAMITE STRENGTH!
BEFORE I GUTTED YOUR FATHER, I TOLD HIM THAT ALL OF THIS--THE DOWNFALL OF DAXAM--WAS BECAUSE OF YOU.
NO...HE WAS RIGHT...IF I'D NEVER LEFT HOME, MY PEOPLE WOULD NEVER HAVE BEEN DISCOVERED...
YOU SHOULD BE PROUD. AS DAXAMITES, WE WILL RULE ENTIRE GALAXIES. AND IT WILL BE LANTERN YAT THAT LEADS OUR GREAT ARMY INTO BATTLE.
WHAT--?

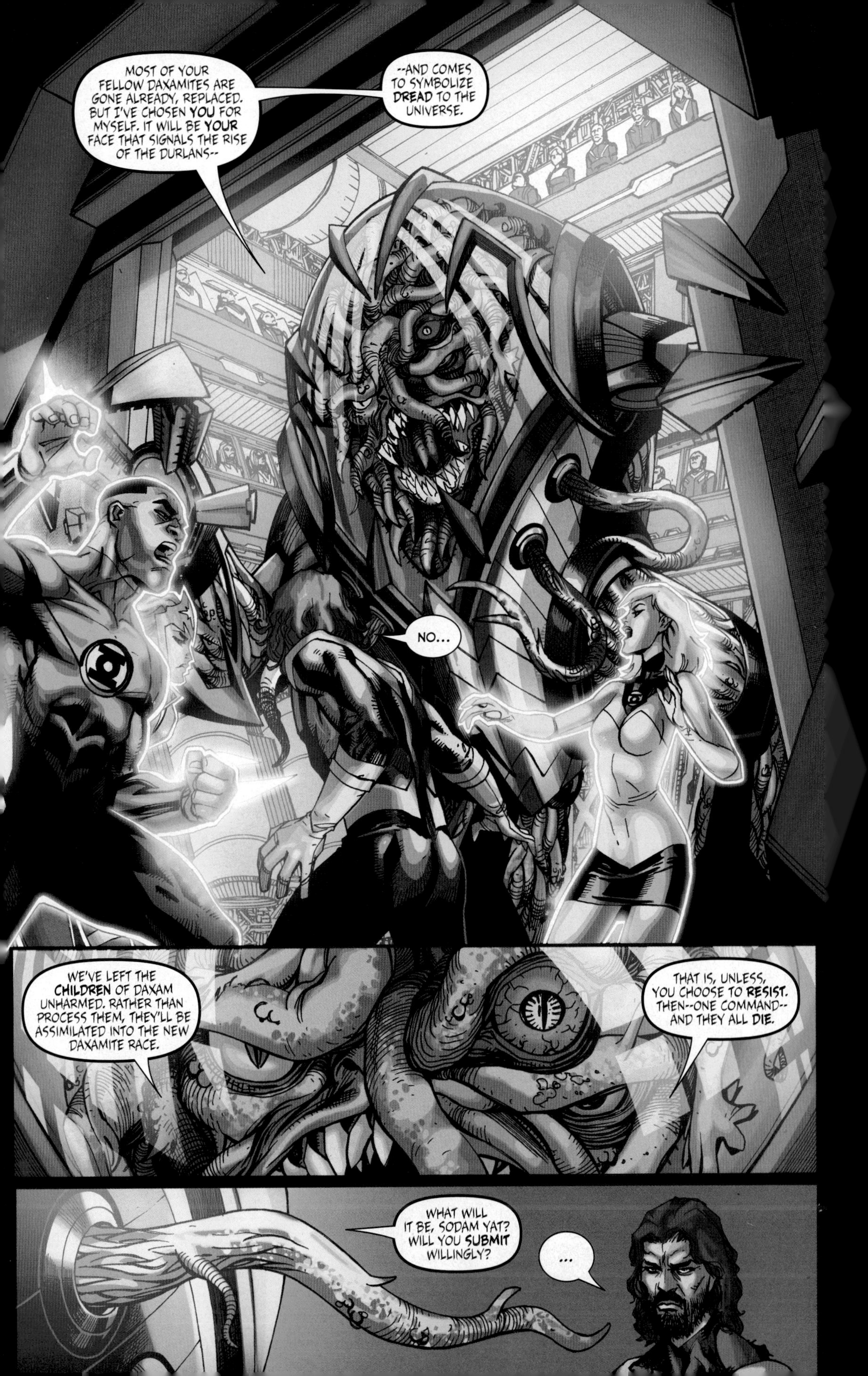
MOST OF YOUR FELLOW DAXAMITES ARE GONE ALREADY, REPLACED. BUT I'VE CHOSEN YOU FOR MYSELF. IT WILL BE YOUR FACE THAT SIGNALS THE RISE OF THE DURLANS--
--AND COMES TO SYMBOLIZE DREAD TO THE UNIVERSE.
NO...
WE'VE LEFT THE CHILDREN OF DAXAM UNHARMED. RATHER THAN PROCESS THEM, THEY'LL BE ASSIMILATED INTO THE NEW DAXAMITE RACE.
THAT IS, UNLESS, YOU CHOOSE TO RESIST. THEN--ONE COMMAND--AND THEY ALL DIE.
WHAT WILL IT BE, SODAM YAT? WILL YOU SUBMIT WILLINGLY?
...

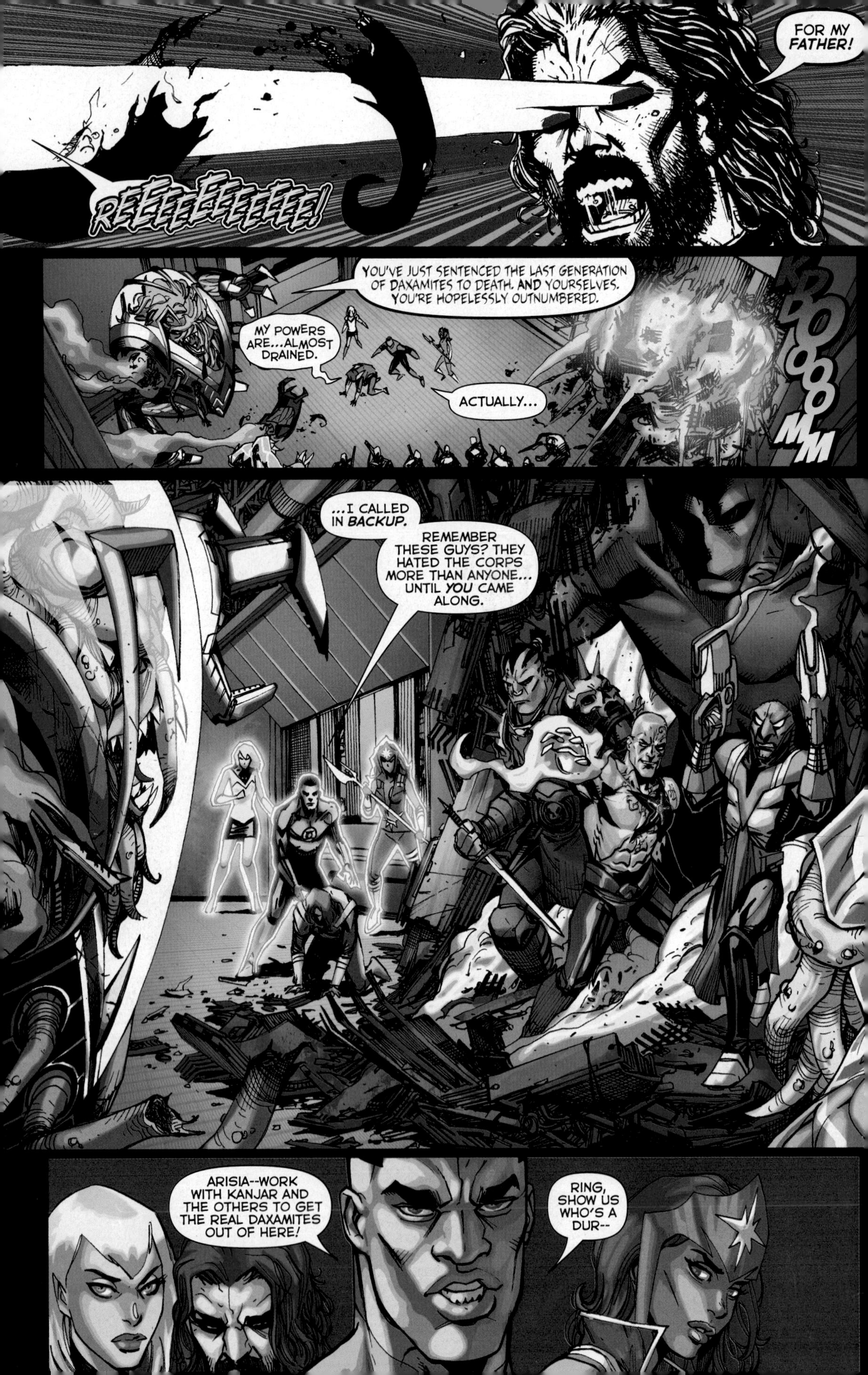
FOR MY FATHER!
REEEEEEEEEEEE!
YOU'VE JUST SENTENCED THE LAST GENERATION OF DAXAMITES TO DEATH. AND YOURSELVES. YOU'RE HOPELESSLY OUTNUMBERED.
KBOOOOMM
MY POWERS ARE...ALMOST DRAINED.
ACTUALLY...
...I CALLED IN BACKUP.
REMEMBER THESE GUYS? THEY HATED THE CORPS MORE THAN ANYONE... UNTIL YOU CAME ALONG.
ARISIA--WORK WITH KANJAR AND THE OTHERS TO GET THE REAL DAXAMITES OUT OF HERE!
RING, SHOW US WHO'S A DUR--

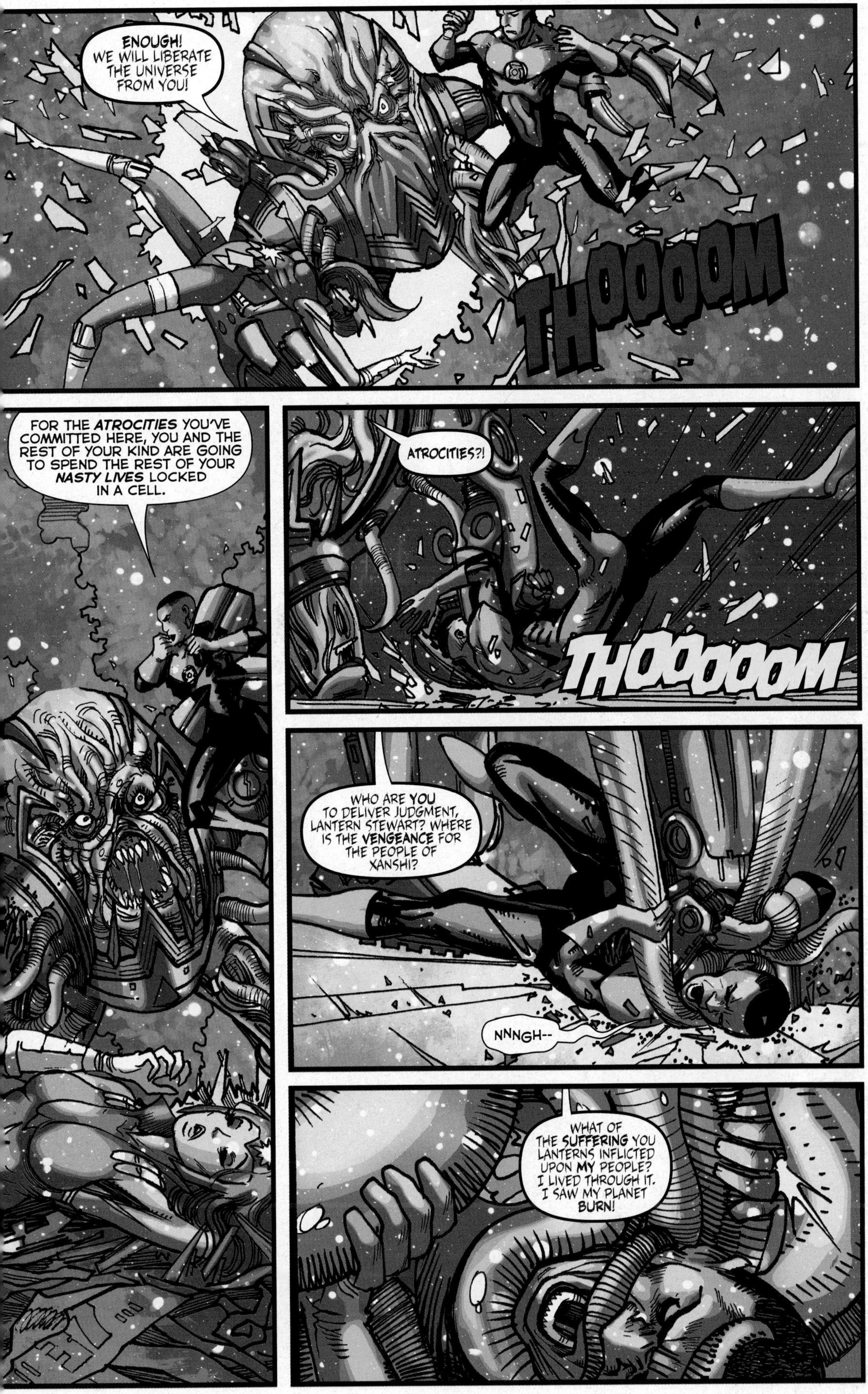

ENOUGH! WE WILL LIBERATE THE UNIVERSE FROM YOU!
THOOOOM
FOR THE ATROCITIES YOU'VE COMMITTED HERE, YOU AND THE REST OF YOUR KIND ARE GOING TO SPEND THE REST OF YOUR NASTY LIVES LOCKED IN A CELL.
ATROCITIES?!
THOOOOOM
WHO ARE YOU TO DELIVER JUDGMENT, LANTERN STEWART? WHERE IS THE VENGEANCE FOR THE PEOPLE OF XANSHI?
NNNGH--
WHAT OF THE SUFFERING YOU LANTERNS INFLICTED UPON MY PEOPLE? I LIVED THROUGH IT. I SAW MY PLANET BURN!

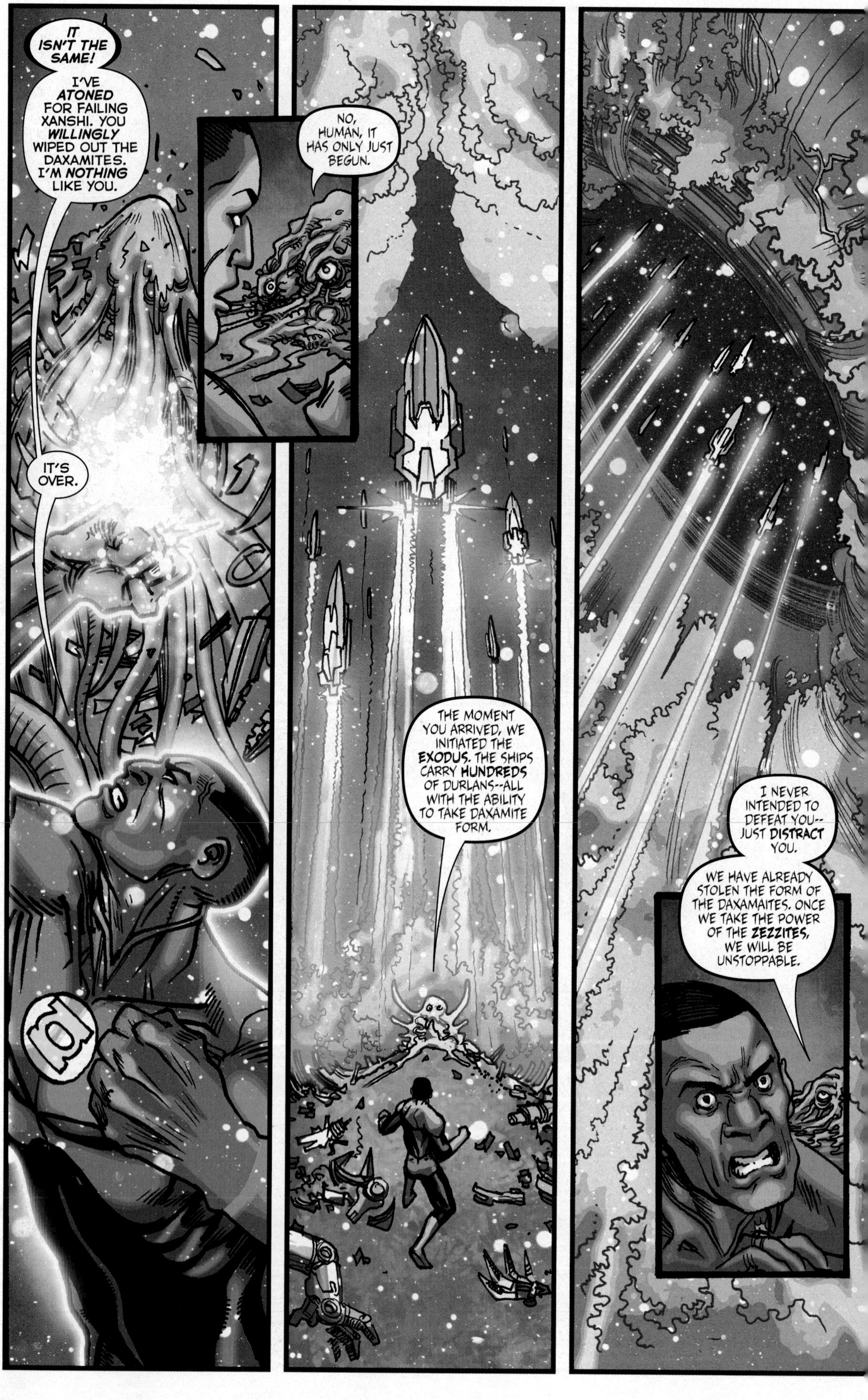
IT ISN'T THE SAME!
I'VE ATONED FOR FAILING XANSHI. YOU WILLINGLY WIPED OUT THE DAXAMITES. I'M NOTHING LIKE YOU.
NO, HUMAN, IT HAS ONLY JUST BEGUN.
IT'S OVER.
THE MOMENT YOU ARRIVED, WE INITIATED THE EXODUS. THE SHIPS CARRY HUNDREDS OF DURLANS--ALL WITH THE ABILITY TO TAKE DAXAMITE FORM.
I NEVER INTENDED TO DEFEAT YOU--JUST DISTRACT YOU.
WE HAVE ALREADY STOLEN THE FORM OF THE DAXAMAITES. ONCE WE TAKE THE POWER OF THE ZEZZITES, WE WILL BE UNSTOPPABLE.

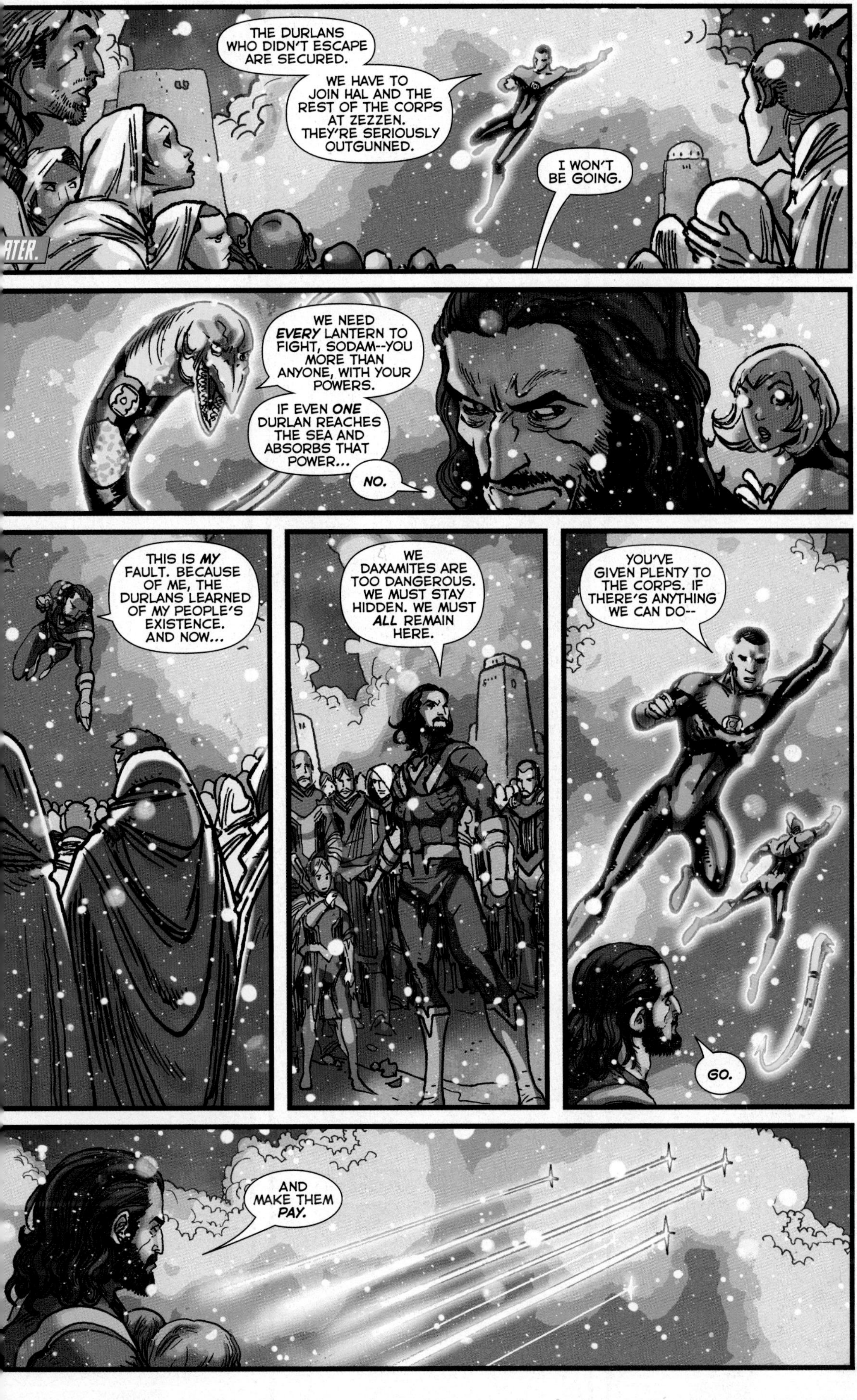
ATER.
THE DURLANS WHO DIDN'T ESCAPE ARE SECURED.
WE HAVE TO JOIN HAL AND THE REST OF THE CORPS AT ZEZZEN. THEY'RE SERIOUSLY OUTGUNNED.
I WON'T BE GOING.
WE NEED *EVERY* LANTERN TO FIGHT, SODAM--YOU MORE THAN ANYONE, WITH YOUR POWERS.
IF EVEN *ONE* DURLAN REACHES THE SEA AND ABSORBS THAT POWER...
NO.
THIS IS *MY* FAULT. BECAUSE OF ME, THE DURLANS LEARNED OF MY PEOPLE'S EXISTENCE. AND NOW...
WE DAXAMITES ARE TOO DANGEROUS. WE MUST STAY HIDDEN. WE MUST *ALL* REMAIN HERE.
YOU'VE GIVEN PLENTY TO THE CORPS. IF THERE'S ANYTHING WE CAN DO--
GO.
AND MAKE THEM *PAY.*

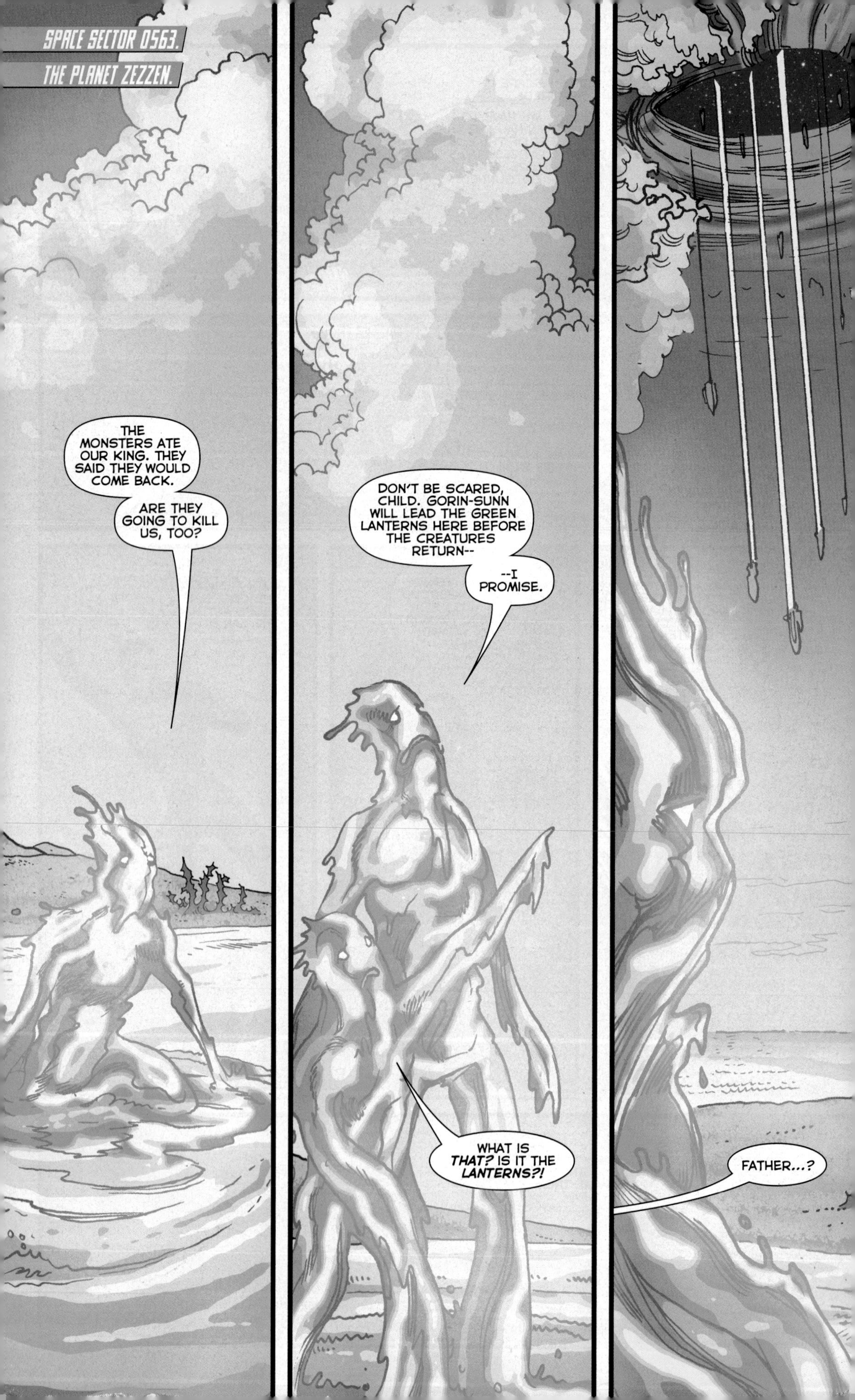
SPACE SECTOR 0563.
THE PLANET ZEZZEN.
THE MONSTERS ATE OUR KING. THEY SAID THEY WOULD COME BACK.
ARE THEY GOING TO KILL US, TOO?
DON'T BE SCARED, CHILD. GORIN-SUNN WILL LEAD THE GREEN LANTERNS HERE BEFORE THE CREATURES RETURN--
--I PROMISE.
WHAT IS *THAT?* IS IT THE *LANTERNS?!*
FATHER...?

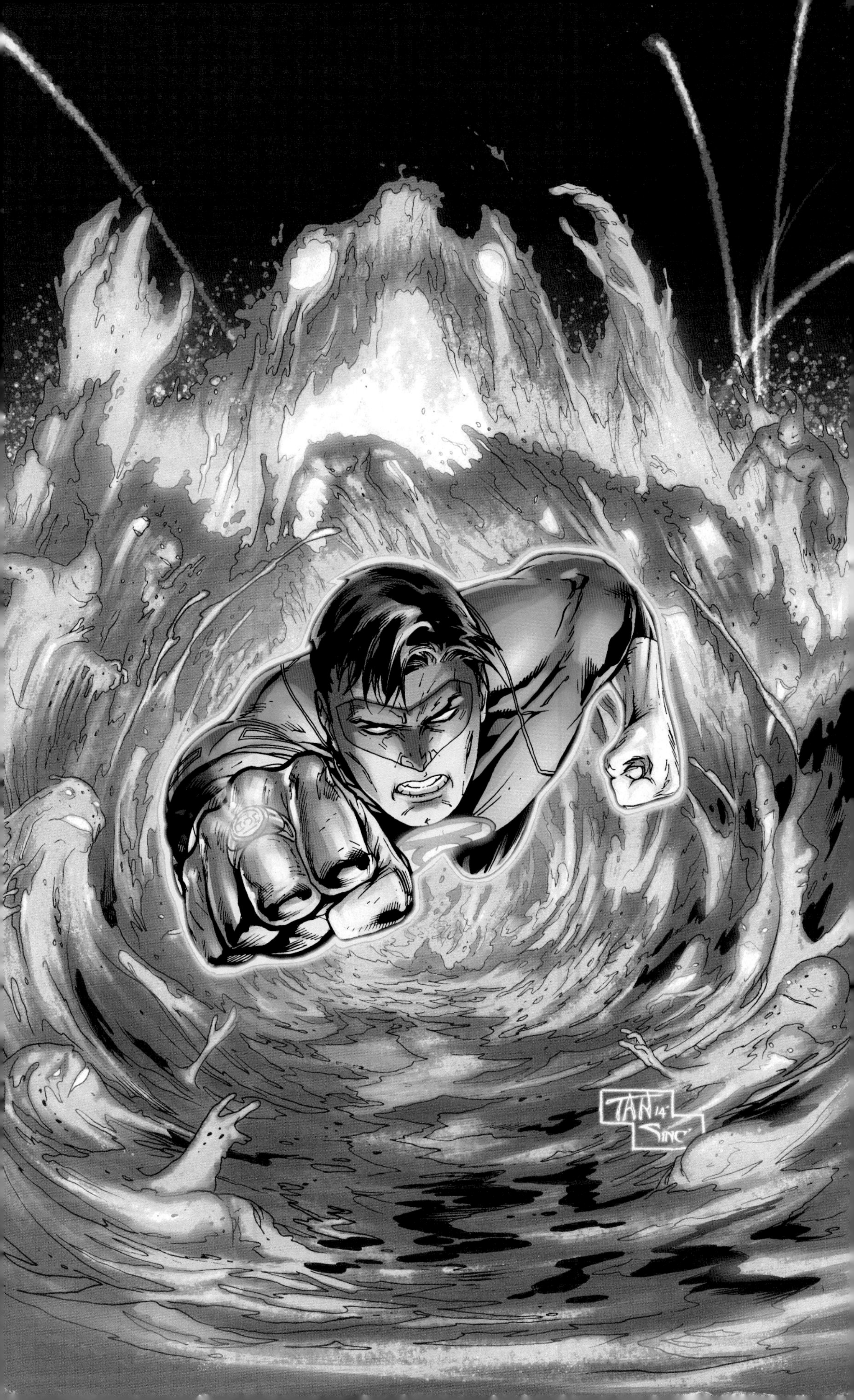
TAN '14
SINC

UPRISING PART 5: LAST STAND OF THE LANTERNS

ROBERT VENDITTI writer **BILLY TAN** penciller **MATT BANNING, ROB HUNTER** and **JAIME MENDOZA** inkers **ALEX SINCLAIR** colorist
cover art by **BILLY TAN & ALEX SINCLAIR** BATMAN 75TH ANNIVERSARY variant cover by **ETHAN VAN SCIVER & ALEX SINCLAIR**

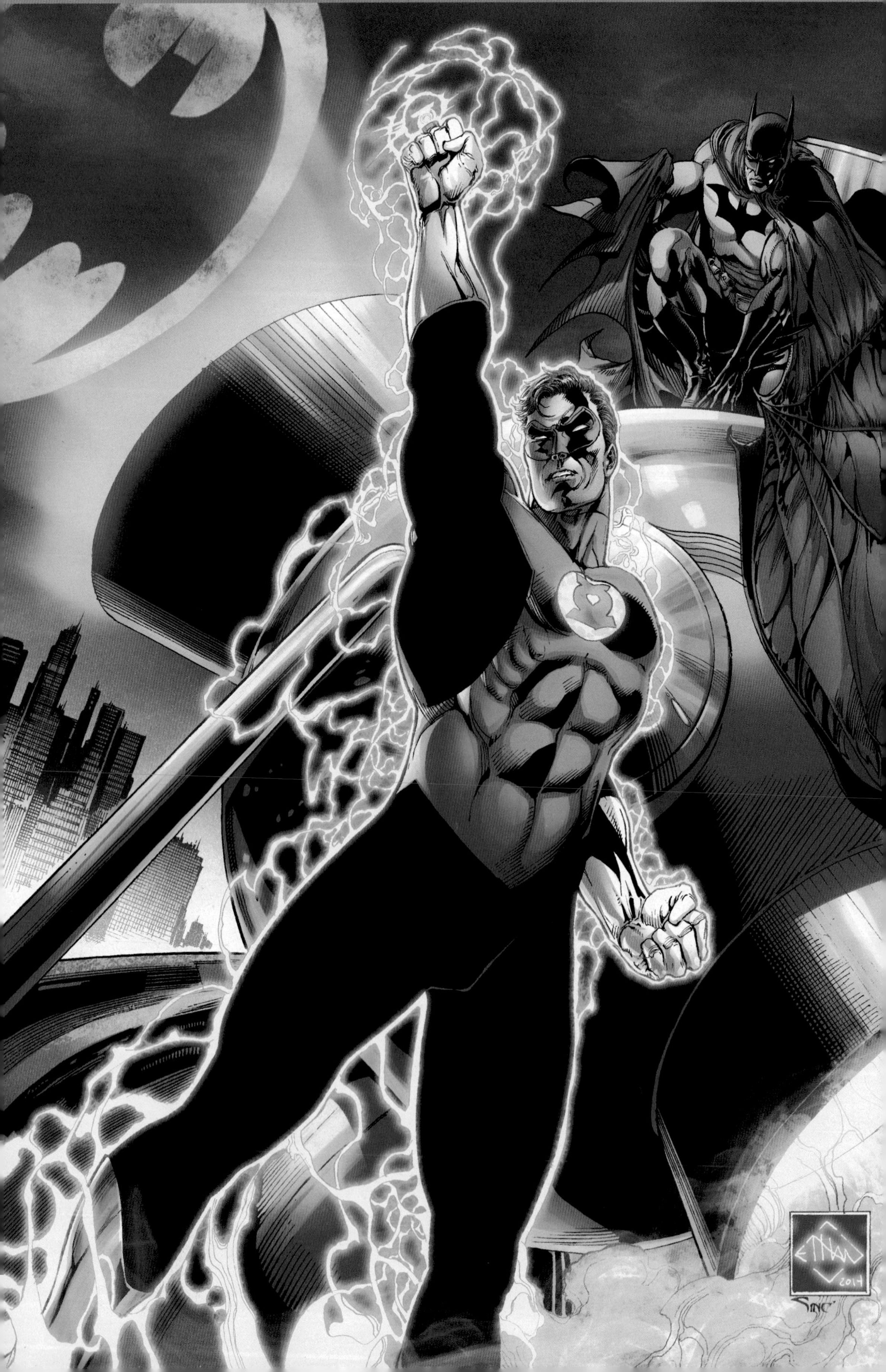

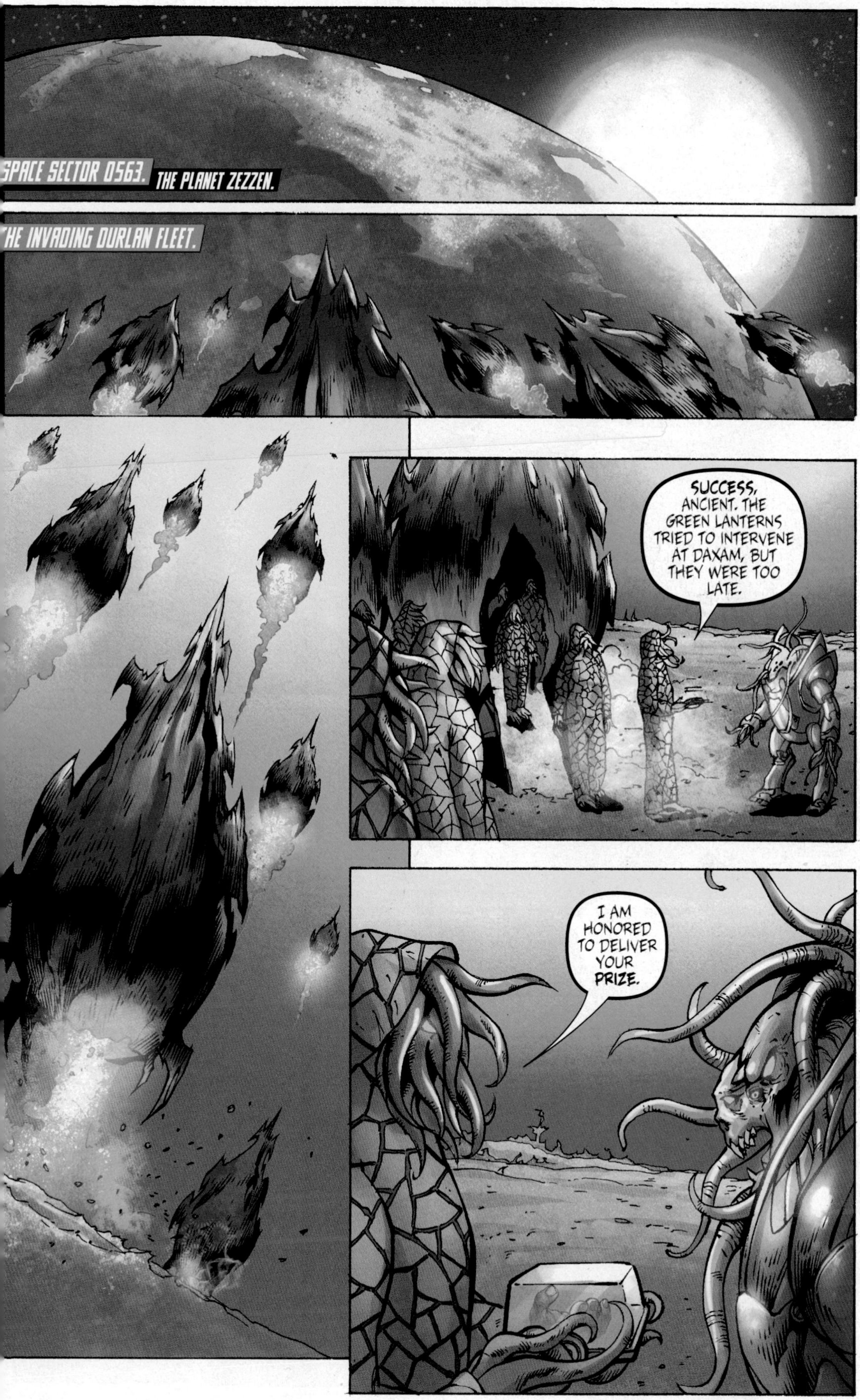
SPACE SECTOR 0563.
THE PLANET ZEZZEN.
THE INVADING DURLAN FLEET.
SUCCESS, ANCIENT. THE GREEN LANTERNS TRIED TO INTERVENE AT DAXAM, BUT THEY WERE TOO LATE.
I AM HONORED TO DELIVER YOUR PRIZE.

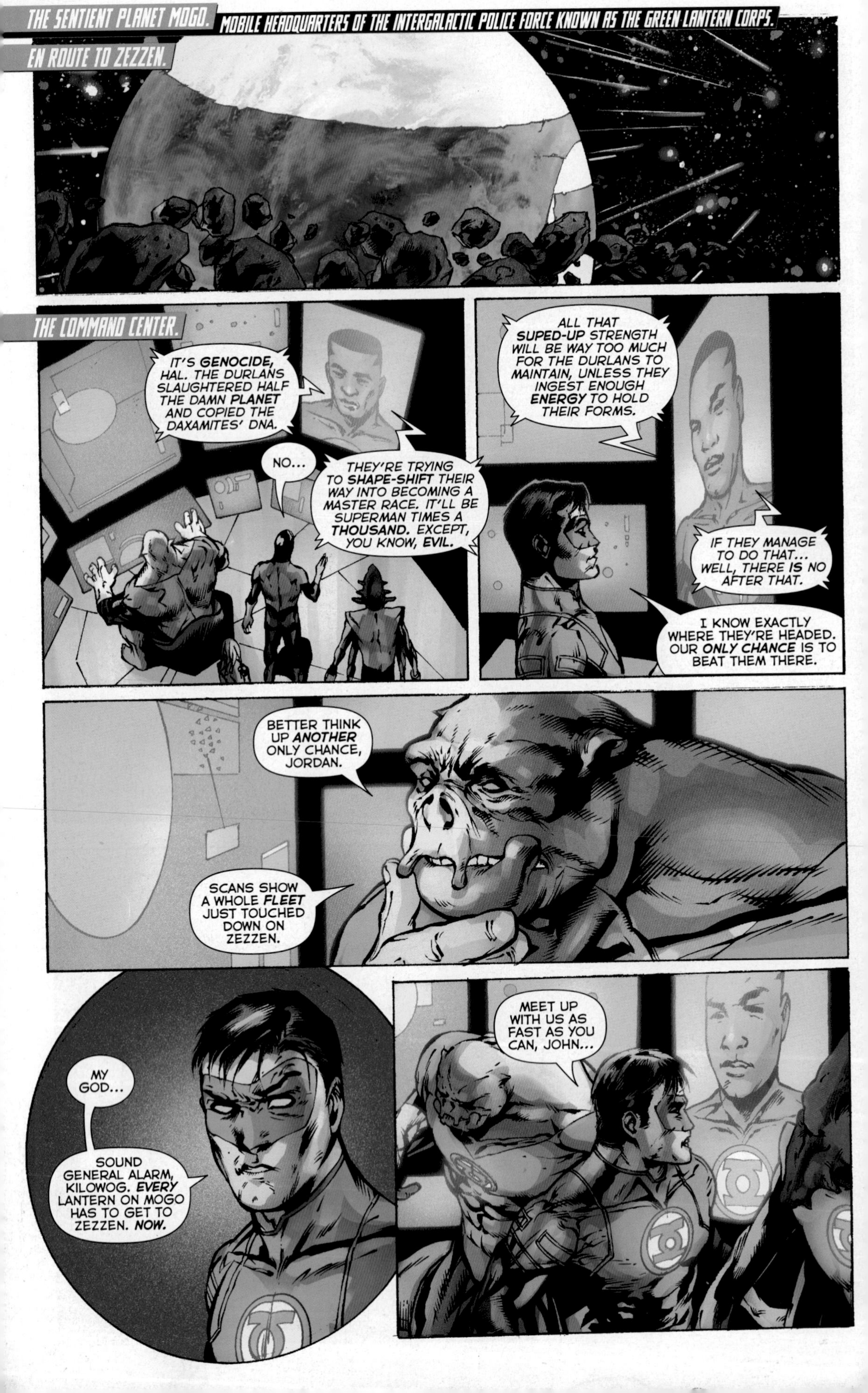
THE SENTIENT PLANET MOGO.
MOBILE HEADQUARTERS OF THE INTERGALACTIC POLICE FORCE KNOWN AS THE GREEN LANTERN CORPS.
EN ROUTE TO ZEZZEN.
THE COMMAND CENTER.
IT'S GENOCIDE, HAL. THE DURLANS SLAUGHTERED HALF THE DAMN PLANET AND COPIED THE DAXAMITES' DNA.
NO...
THEY'RE TRYING TO SHAPE-SHIFT THEIR WAY INTO BECOMING A MASTER RACE. IT'LL BE SUPERMAN TIMES A THOUSAND. EXCEPT, YOU KNOW, EVIL.
ALL THAT SUPED-UP STRENGTH WILL BE WAY TOO MUCH FOR THE DURLANS TO MAINTAIN, UNLESS THEY INGEST ENOUGH ENERGY TO HOLD THEIR FORMS.
IF THEY MANAGE TO DO THAT... WELL, THERE IS NO AFTER THAT.
I KNOW EXACTLY WHERE THEY'RE HEADED. OUR ONLY CHANCE IS TO BEAT THEM THERE.
BETTER THINK UP ANOTHER ONLY CHANCE, JORDAN.
SCANS SHOW A WHOLE FLEET JUST TOUCHED DOWN ON ZEZZEN.
MY GOD...
SOUND GENERAL ALARM, KILOWOG. EVERY LANTERN ON MOGO HAS TO GET TO ZEZZEN. NOW.
MEET UP WITH US AS FAST AS YOU CAN, JOHN...

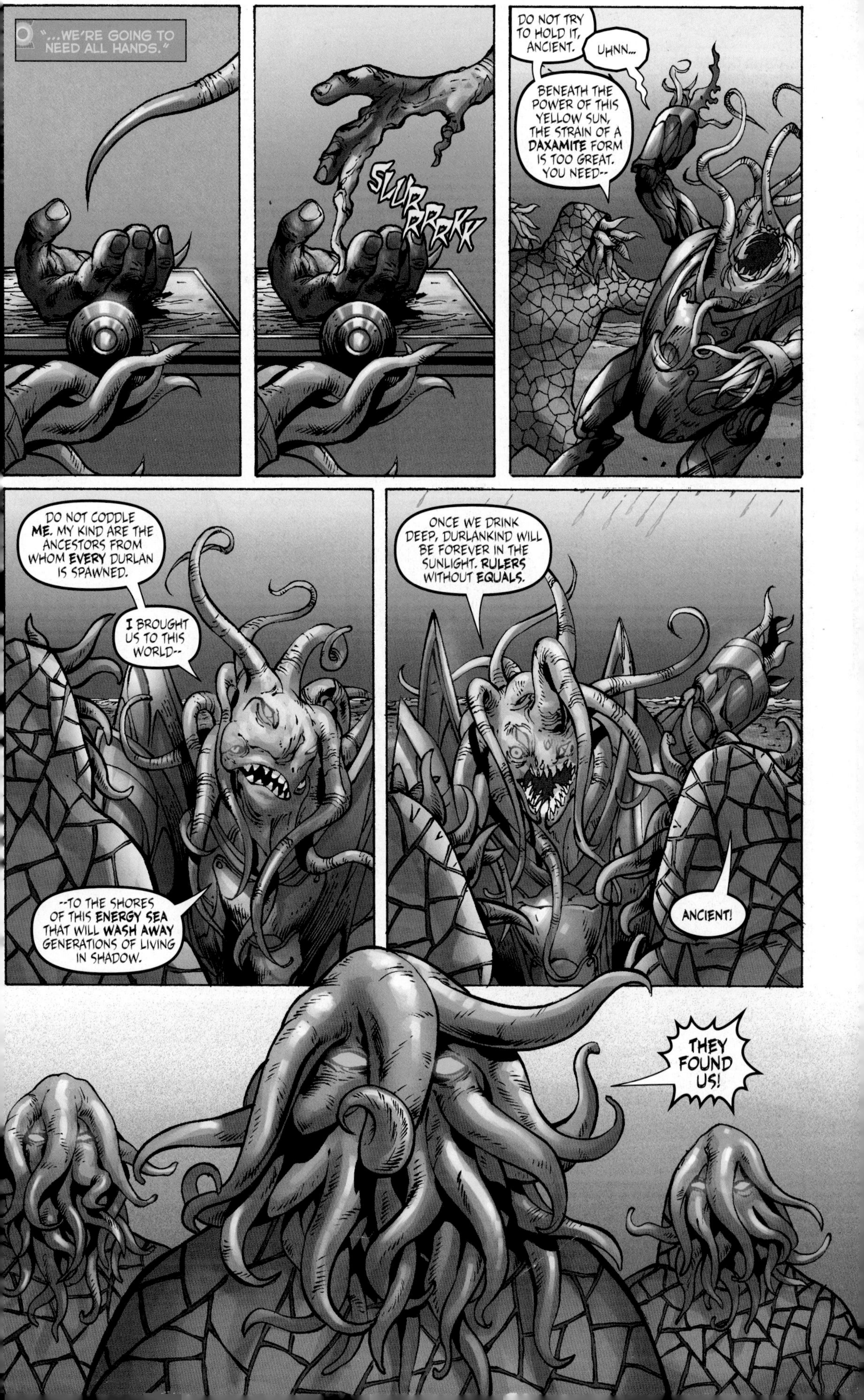

"...WE'RE GOING TO NEED ALL HANDS."
SLURRRKK
DO NOT TRY TO HOLD IT, ANCIENT.
UHNN...
BENEATH THE POWER OF THIS YELLOW SUN, THE STRAIN OF A DAXAMITE FORM IS TOO GREAT. YOU NEED--
DO NOT CODDLE ME. MY KIND ARE THE ANCESTORS FROM WHOM EVERY DURLAN IS SPAWNED.
I BROUGHT US TO THIS WORLD--
--TO THE SHORES OF THIS ENERGY SEA THAT WILL WASH AWAY GENERATIONS OF LIVING IN SHADOW.
ONCE WE DRINK DEEP, DURLANKIND WILL BE FOREVER IN THE SUNLIGHT. RULERS WITHOUT EQUALS.
ANCIENT!
THEY FOUND US!

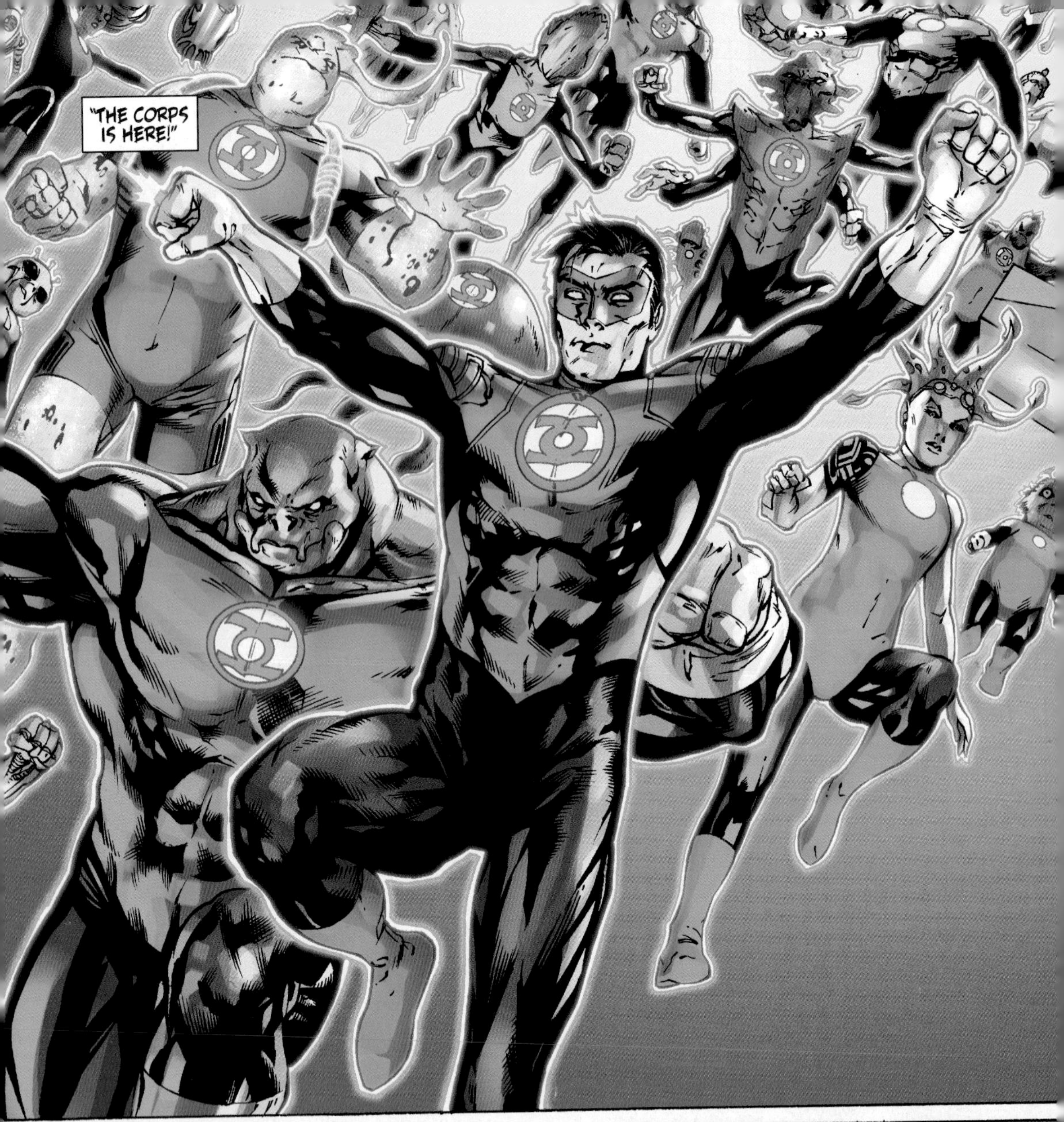
"THE CORPS IS HERE!"
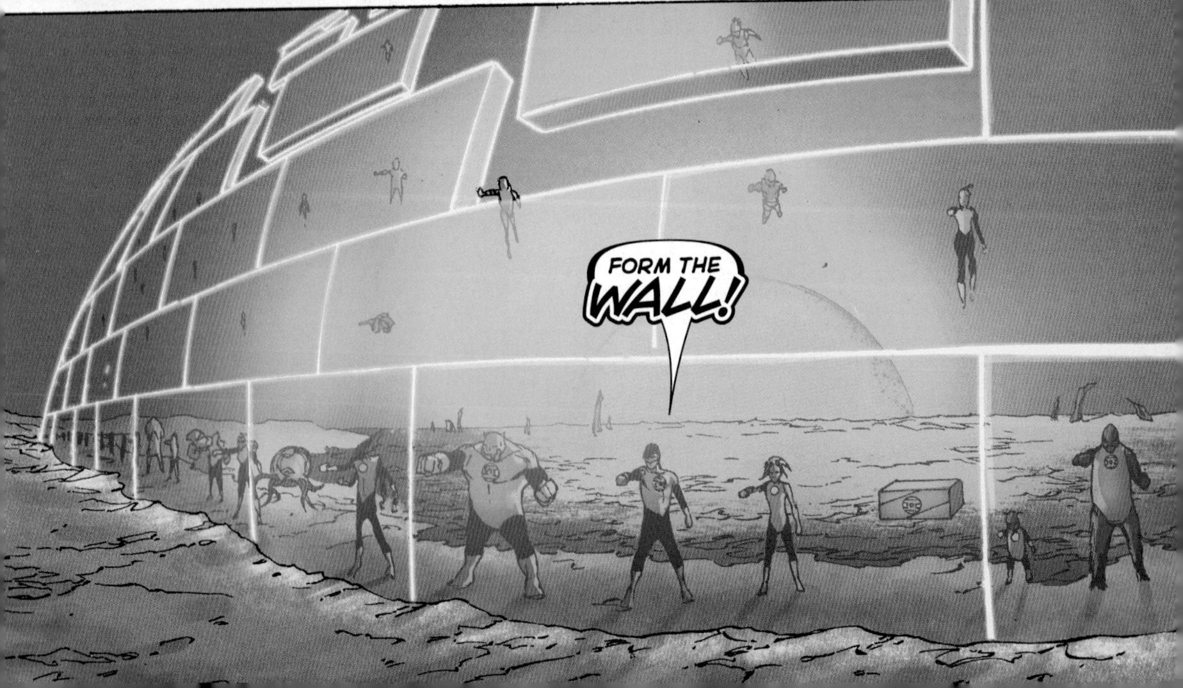
FORM THE WALL!

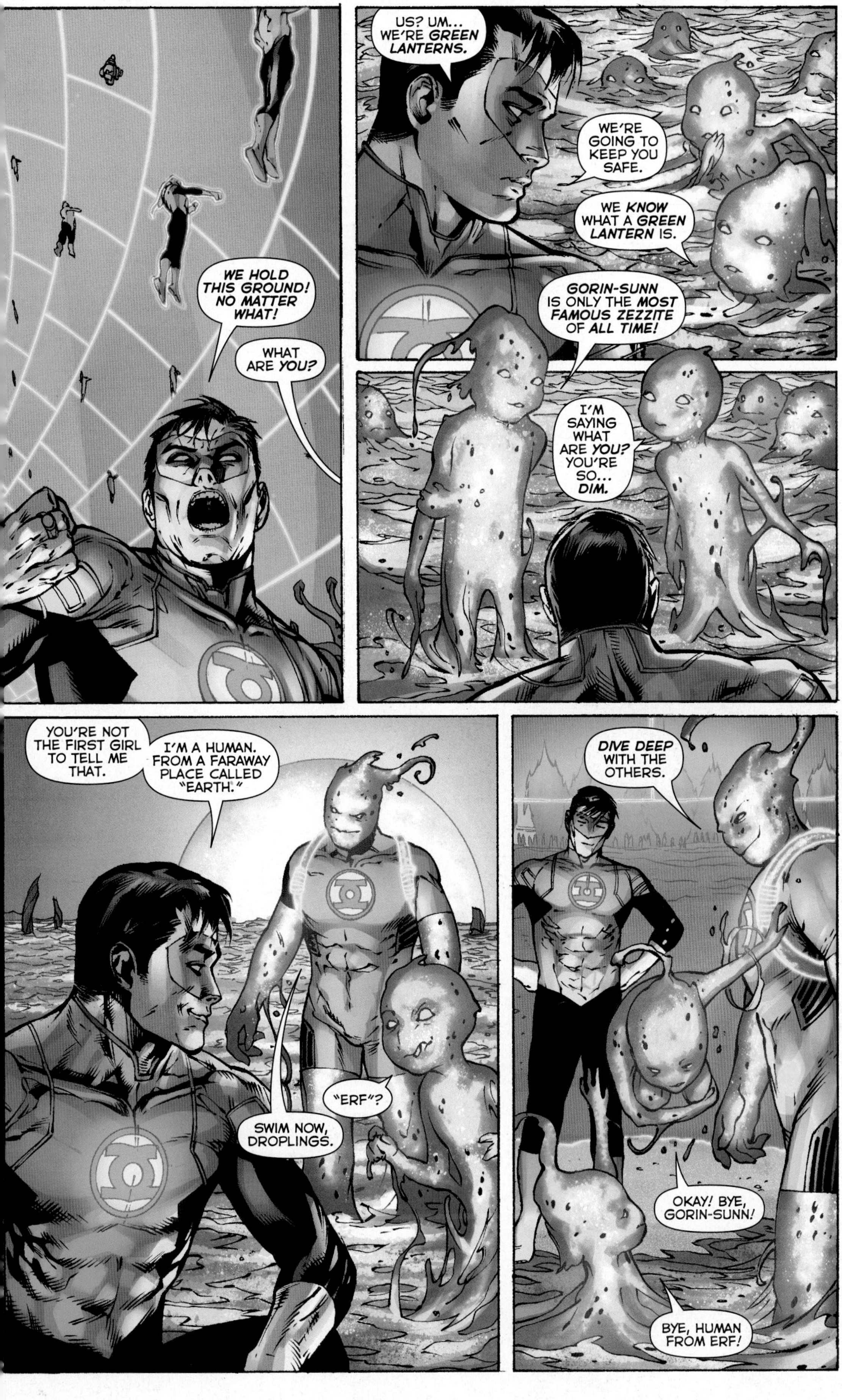
WE HOLD THIS GROUND! NO MATTER WHAT!
WHAT ARE YOU?
US? UM... WE'RE GREEN LANTERNS.
WE'RE GOING TO KEEP YOU SAFE.
WE KNOW WHAT A GREEN LANTERN IS.
GORIN-SUNN IS ONLY THE MOST FAMOUS ZEZZITE OF ALL TIME!
I'M SAYING WHAT ARE YOU? YOU'RE SO... DIM.
YOU'RE NOT THE FIRST GIRL TO TELL ME THAT.
I'M A HUMAN. FROM A FARAWAY PLACE CALLED "EARTH."
"ERF"?
SWIM NOW, DROPLINGS.
DIVE DEEP WITH THE OTHERS.
OKAY! BYE, GORIN-SUNN!
BYE, HUMAN FROM ERF!

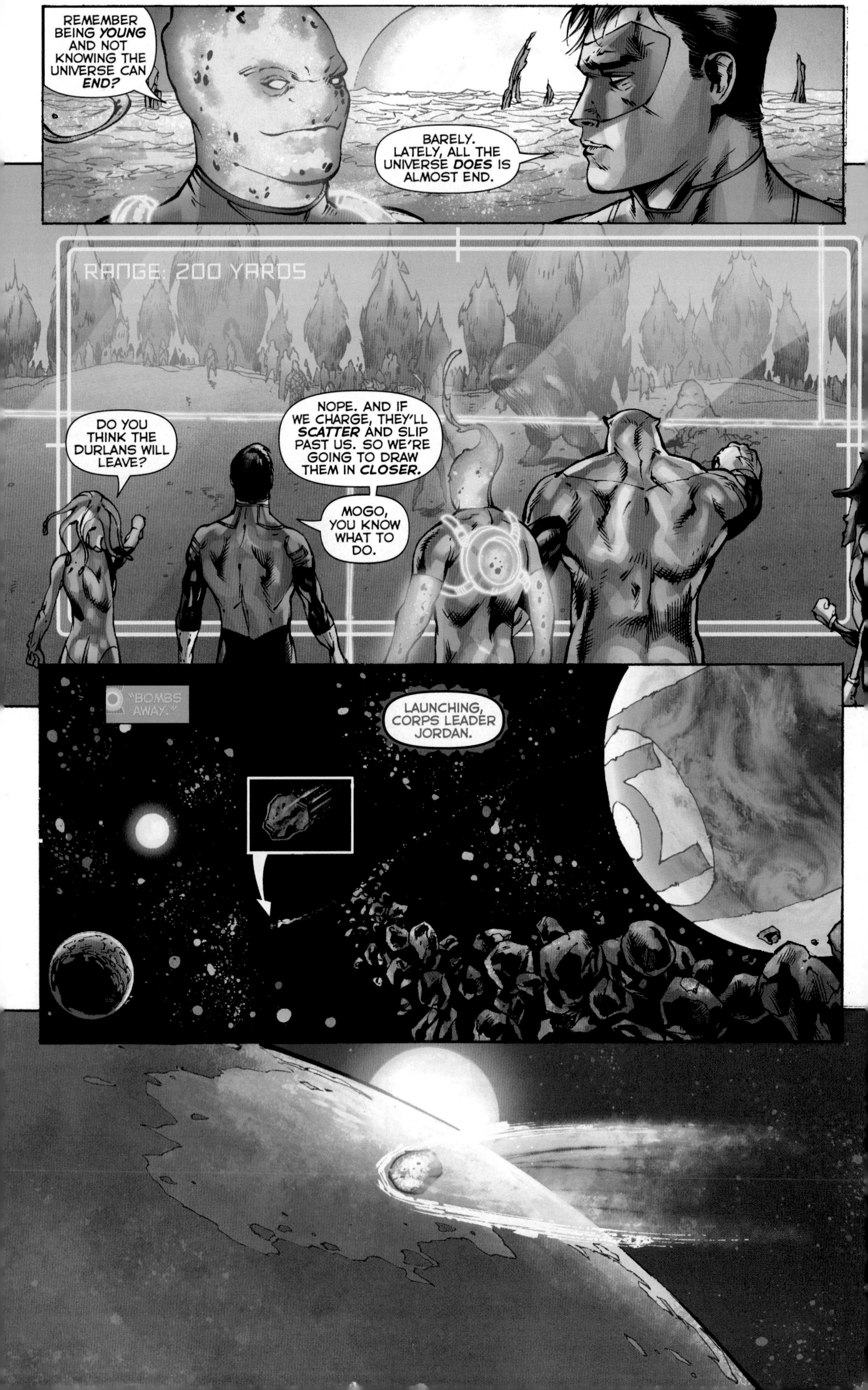

REMEMBER BEING *YOUNG* AND NOT KNOWING THE UNIVERSE CAN *END?*
BARELY. LATELY, ALL THE UNIVERSE *DOES* IS ALMOST END.
RANGE: 200 YARDS
DO YOU THINK THE DURLANS WILL LEAVE?
NOPE. AND IF WE CHARGE, THEY'LL *SCATTER* AND SLIP PAST US. SO WE'RE GOING TO DRAW THEM IN *CLOSER.*
MOGO, YOU KNOW WHAT TO DO.
"BOMBS AWAY."
LAUNCHING, CORPS LEADER JORDAN.

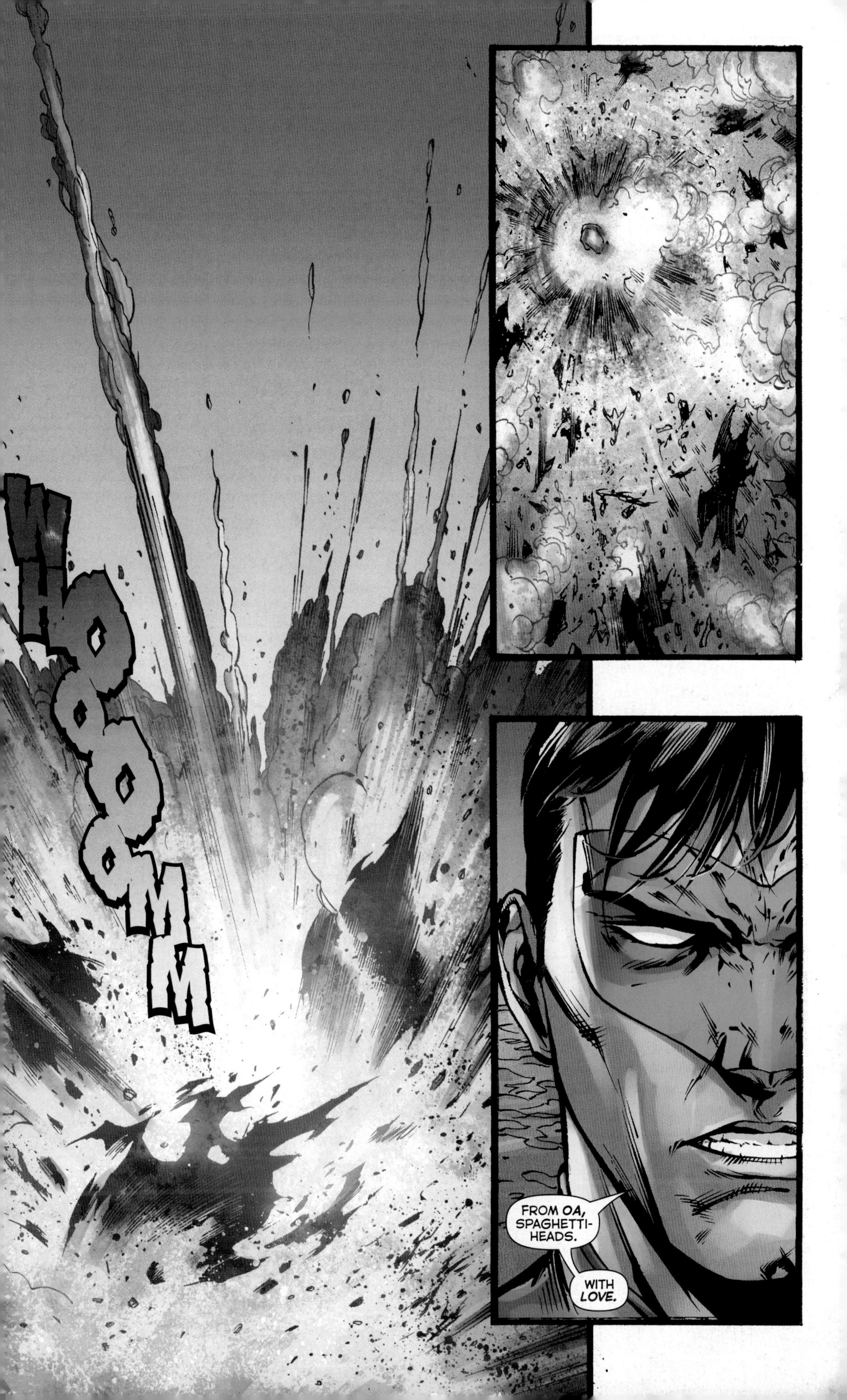
WHOOOMM
FROM OA, SPAGHETTI-HEADS.
WITH LOVE.

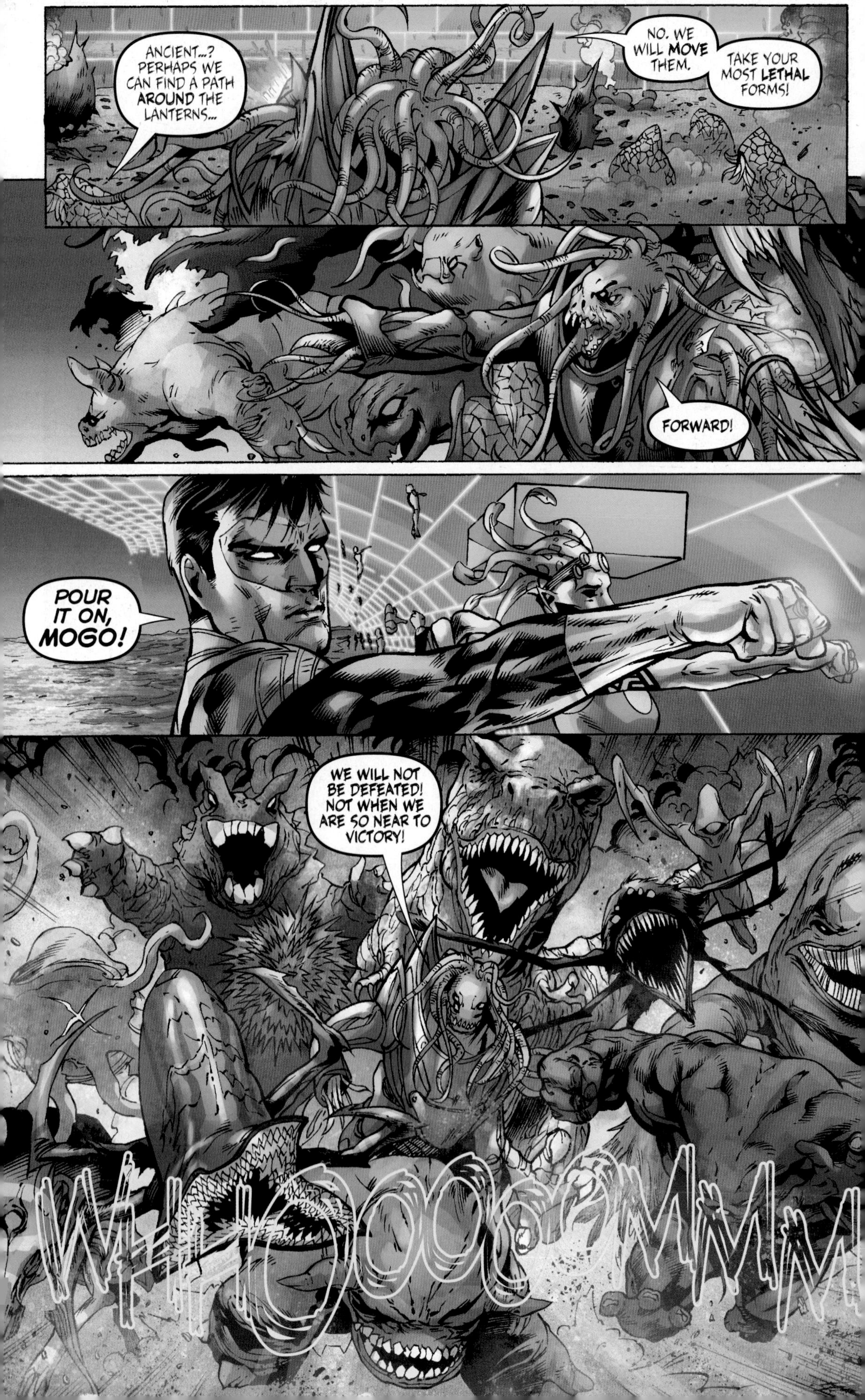
ANCIENT...? PERHAPS WE CAN FIND A PATH AROUND THE LANTERNS...
NO. WE WILL MOVE THEM.
TAKE YOUR MOST LETHAL FORMS!
FORWARD!
POUR IT ON, MOGO!
WE WILL NOT BE DEFEATED! NOT WHEN WE ARE SO NEAR TO VICTORY!
WHOOOOOMMM

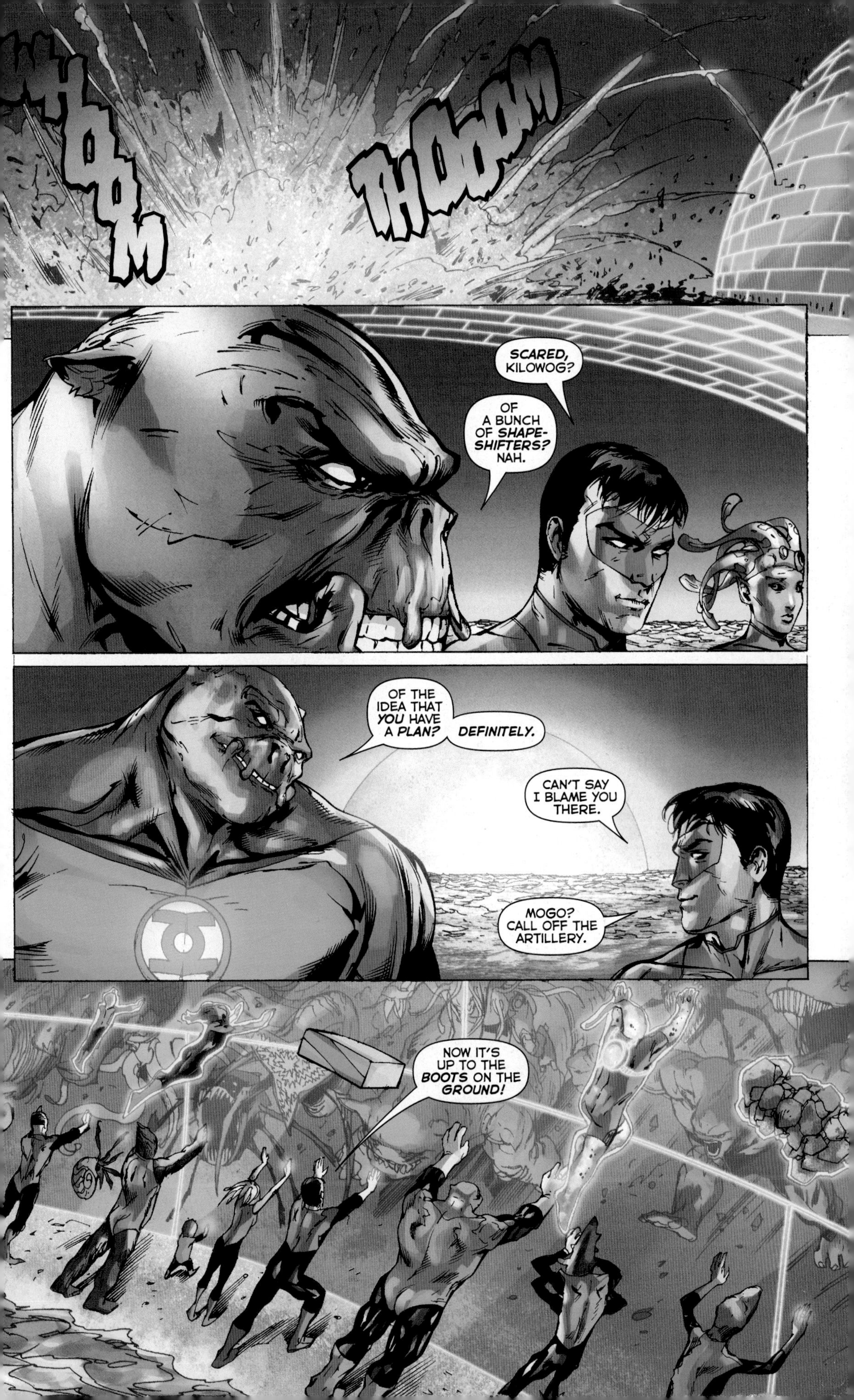
THOOOM
THOOOM
SCARED, KILOWOG?
OF A BUNCH OF SHAPE-SHIFTERS? NAH.
OF THE IDEA THAT YOU HAVE A PLAN?
DEFINITELY.
CAN'T SAY I BLAME YOU THERE.
MOGO? CALL OFF THE ARTILLERY.
NOW IT'S UP TO THE BOOTS ON THE GROUND!

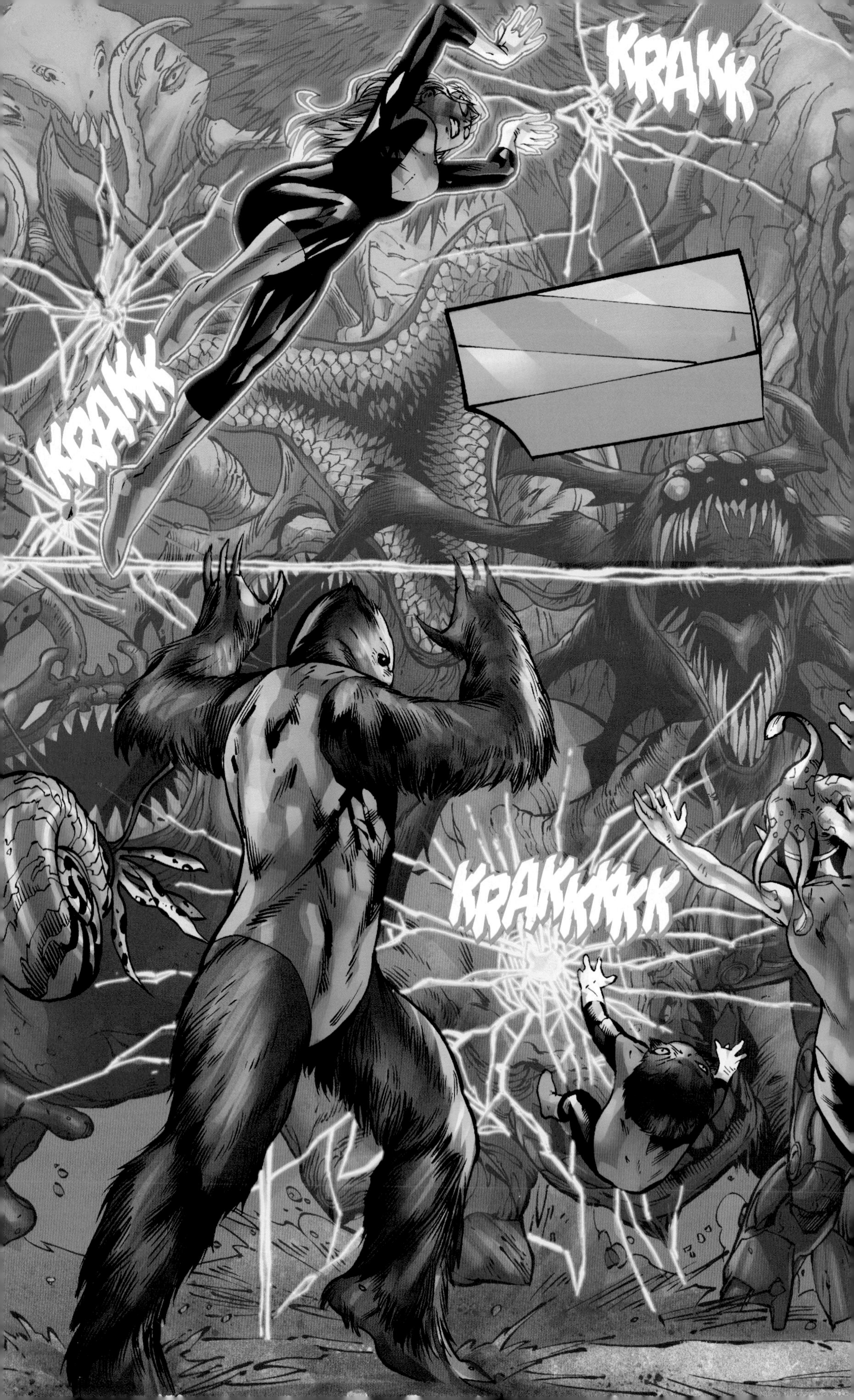
KRAKK
KRAKK
KRAKKKKK

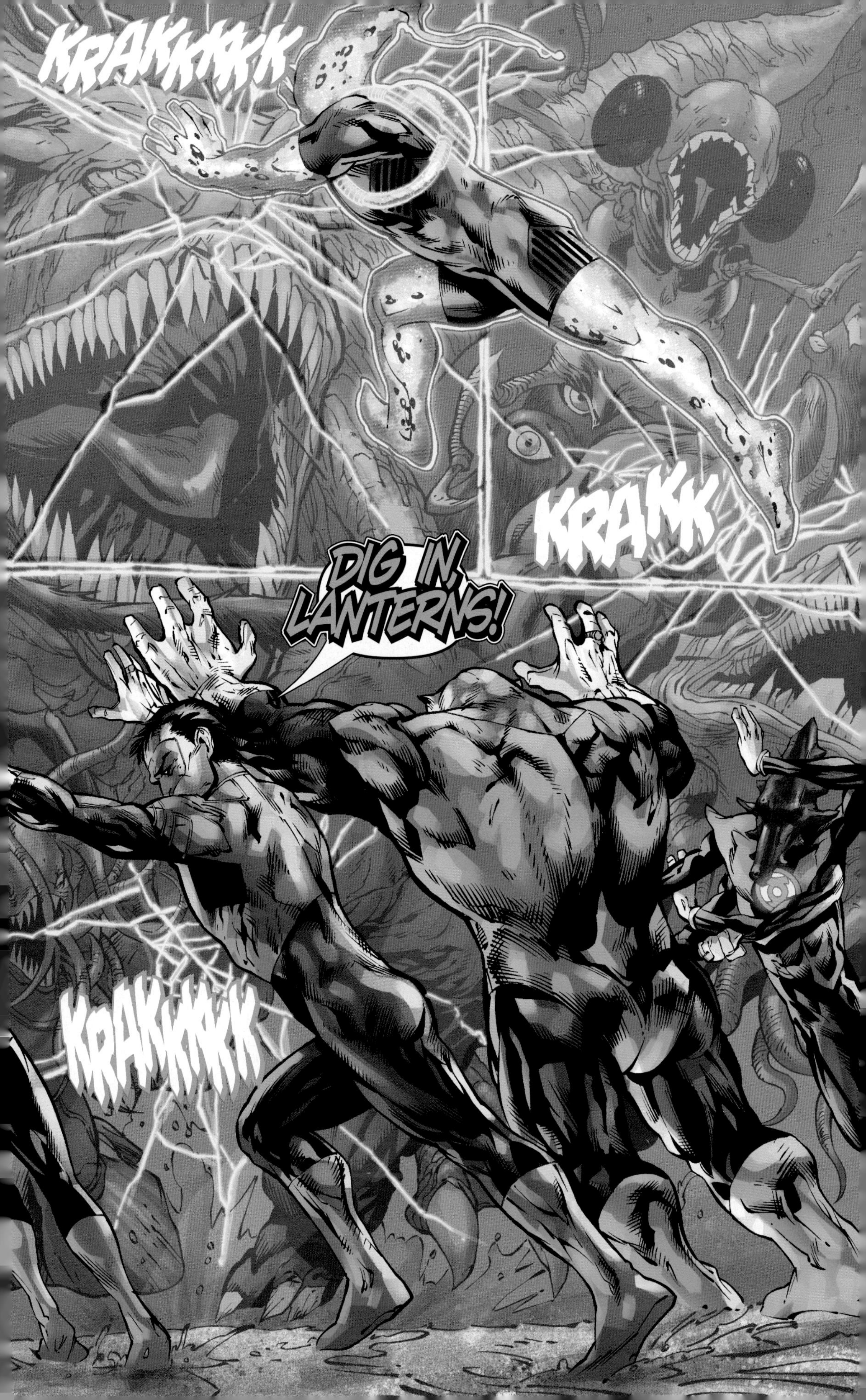
KRAKKKKK
KRAKK
DIG IN, LANTERNS!
KRAKKKKK

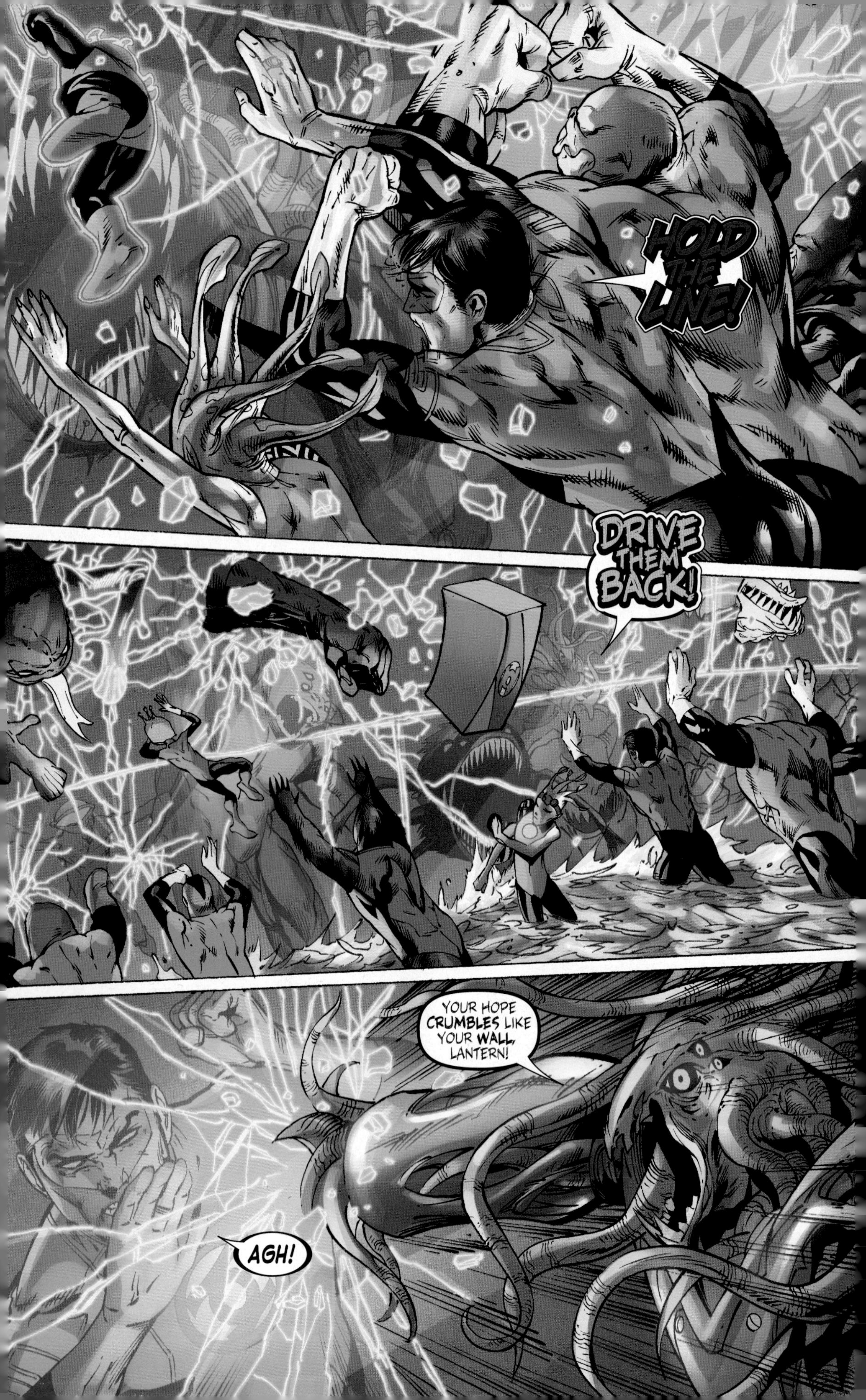
HOLD THE LINE!
DRIVE THEM BACK!
YOUR HOPE CRUMBLES LIKE YOUR WALL, LANTERN!
AGH!

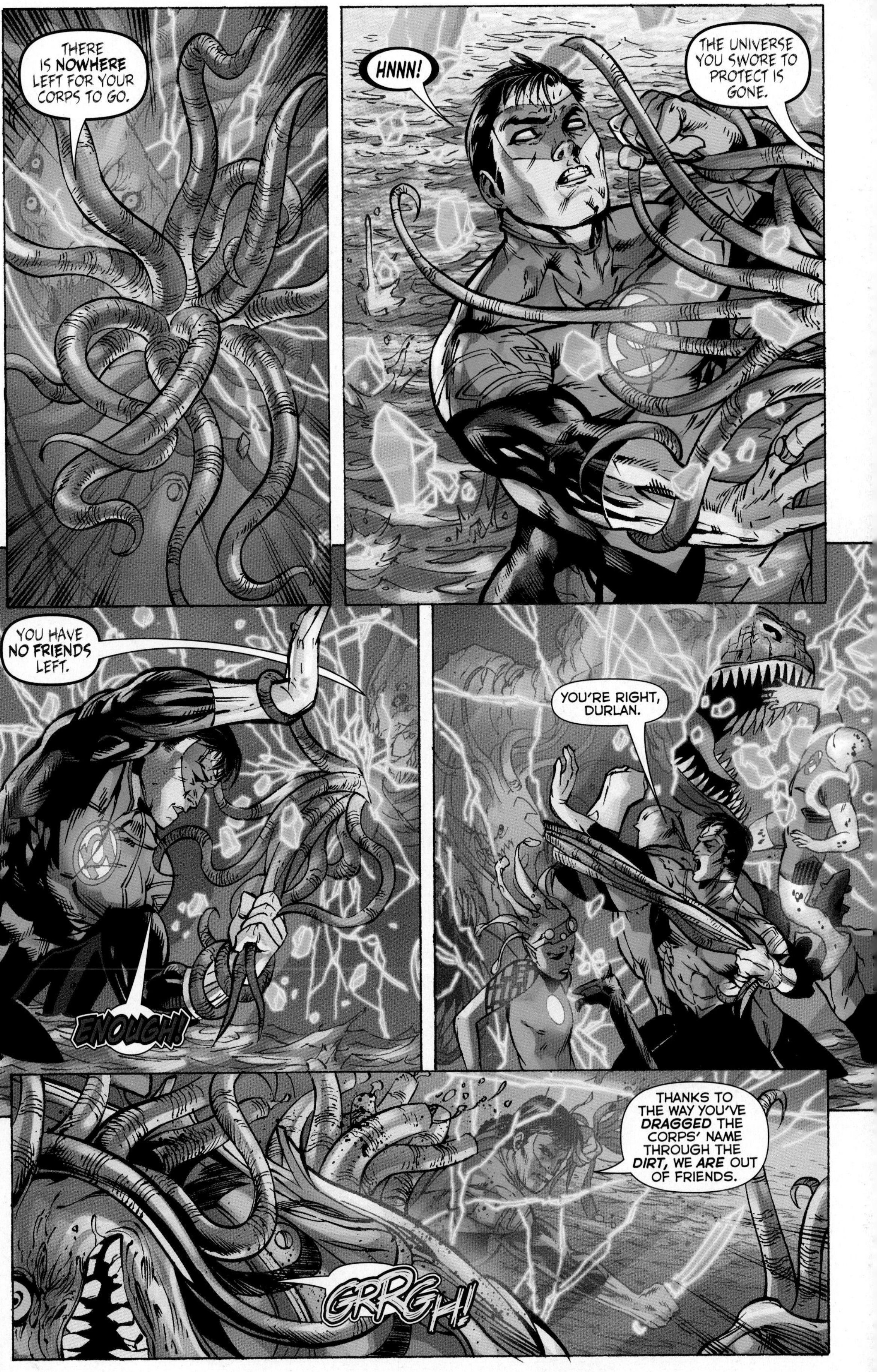

THERE IS NOWHERE LEFT FOR YOUR CORPS TO GO.
HNNN!
THE UNIVERSE YOU SWORE TO PROTECT IS GONE.
YOU HAVE NO FRIENDS LEFT.
ENOUGH!
YOU'RE RIGHT, DURLAN.
THANKS TO THE WAY YOU'VE DRAGGED THE CORPS' NAME THROUGH THE DIRT, WE ARE OUT OF FRIENDS.
GRRGH!

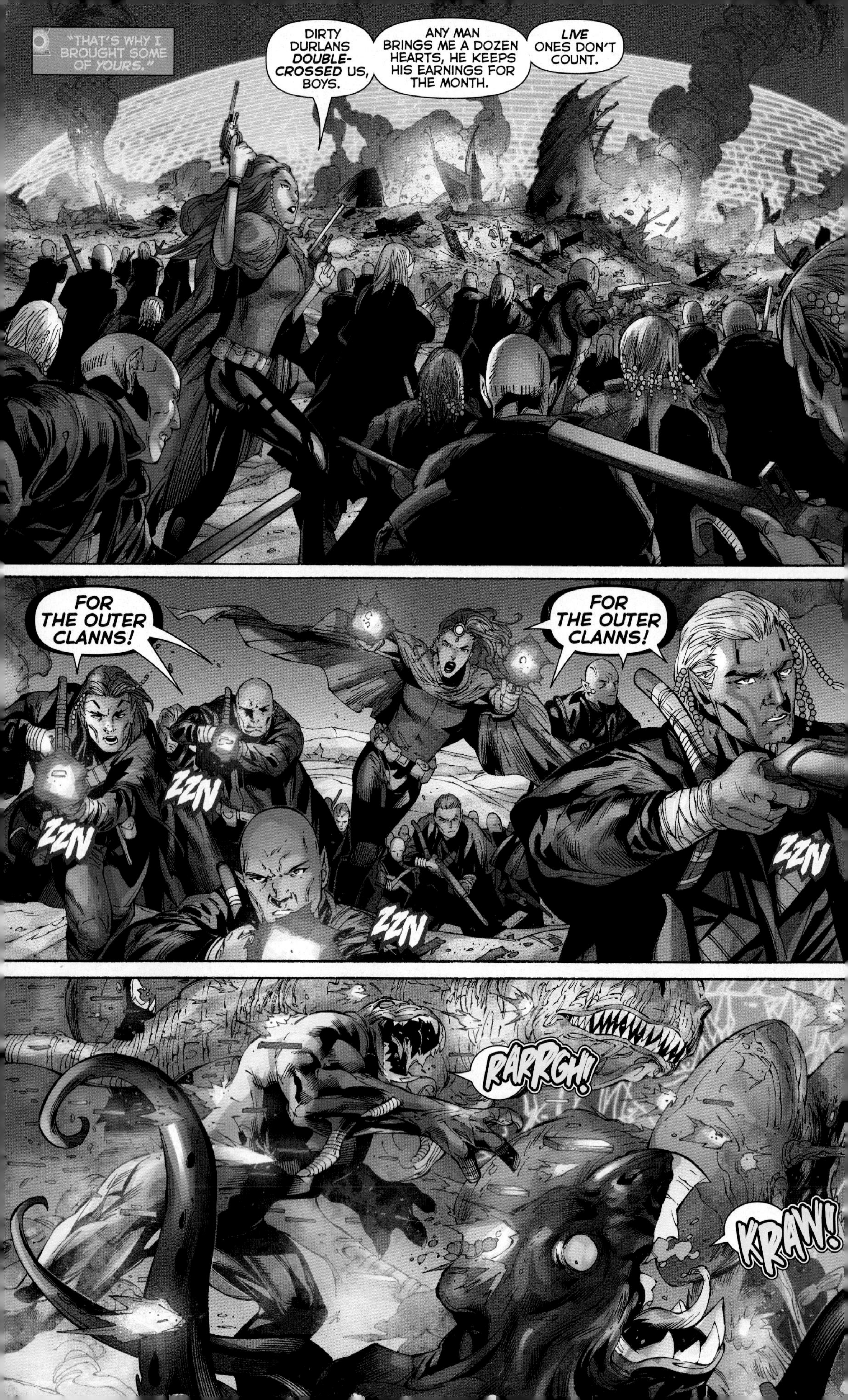
"THAT'S WHY I BROUGHT SOME OF *YOURS*."
DIRTY DURLANS *DOUBLE-CROSSED* US, BOYS.
ANY MAN BRINGS ME A DOZEN HEARTS, HE KEEPS HIS EARNINGS FOR THE MONTH.
LIVE ONES DON'T COUNT.
FOR THE OUTER CLANNS!
FOR THE OUTER CLANNS!
ZZN
ZZN
ZZN
ZZN
RARRGH!
KRAW!

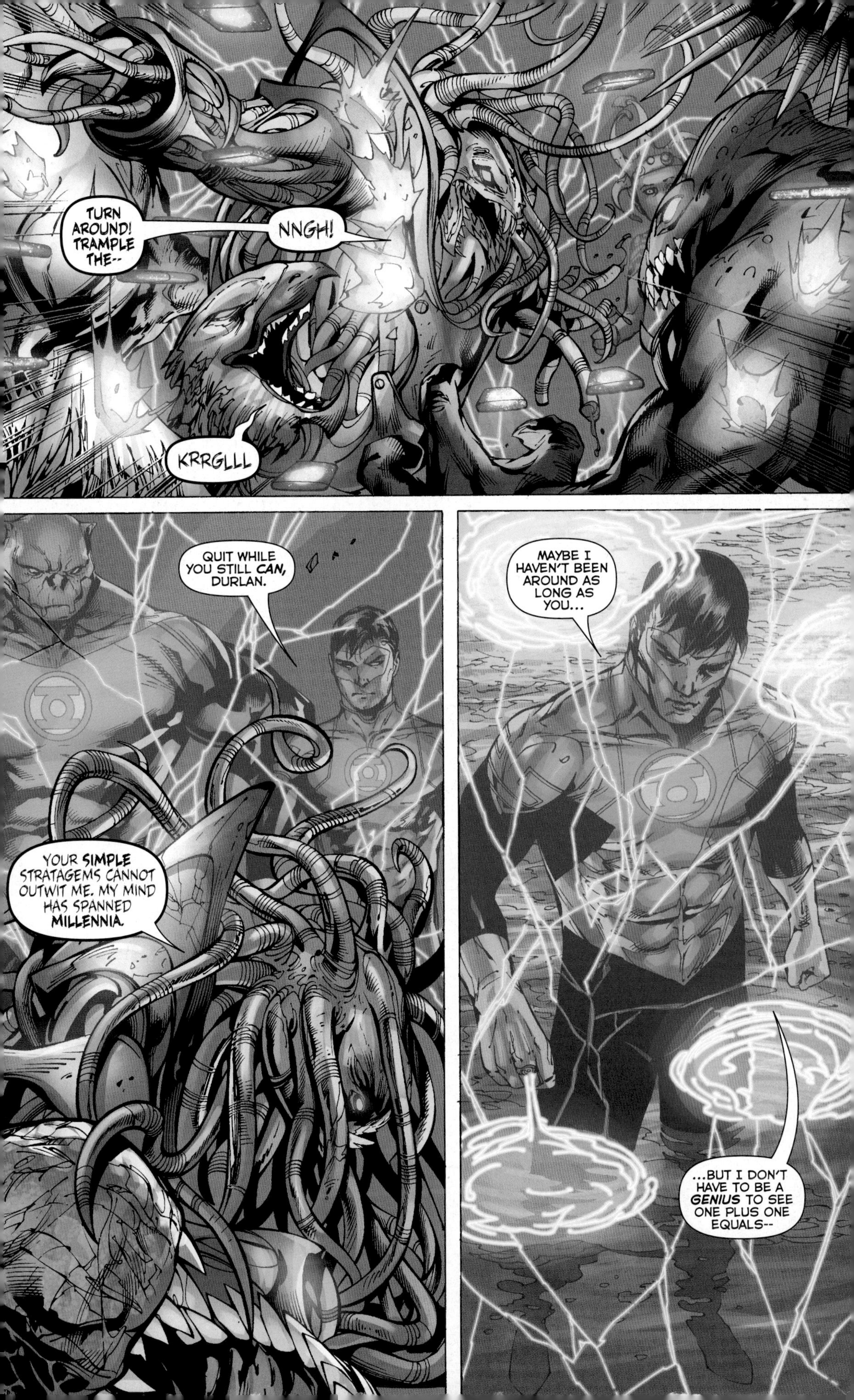
TURN AROUND! TRAMPLE THE--
NNGH!
KRRGLLL
QUIT WHILE YOU STILL CAN, DURLAN.
YOUR SIMPLE STRATAGEMS CANNOT OUTWIT ME. MY MIND HAS SPANNED MILLENNIA.
MAYBE I HAVEN'T BEEN AROUND AS LONG AS YOU...
...BUT I DON'T HAVE TO BE A GENIUS TO SEE ONE PLUS ONE EQUALS--

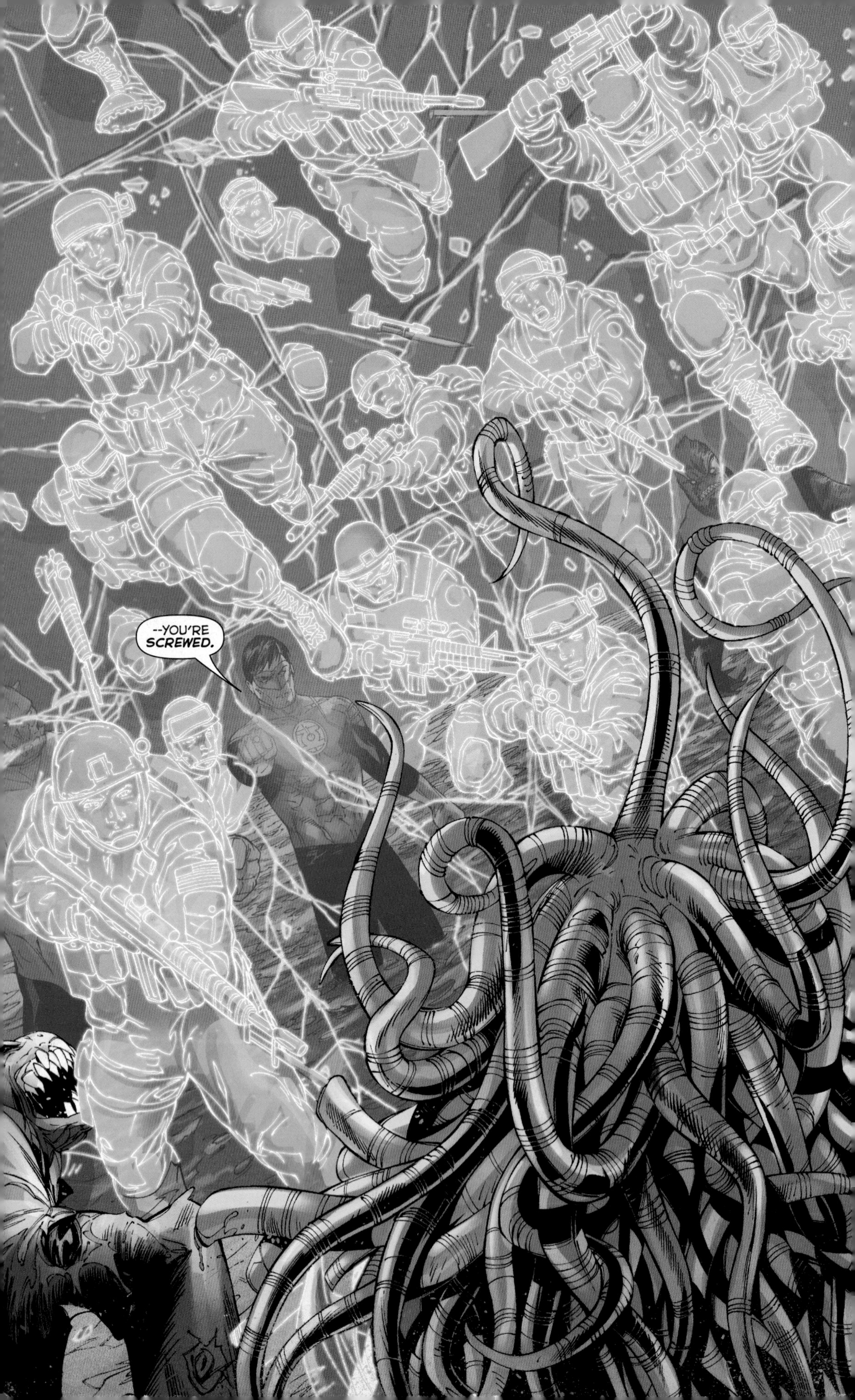
--YOU'RE SCREWED.

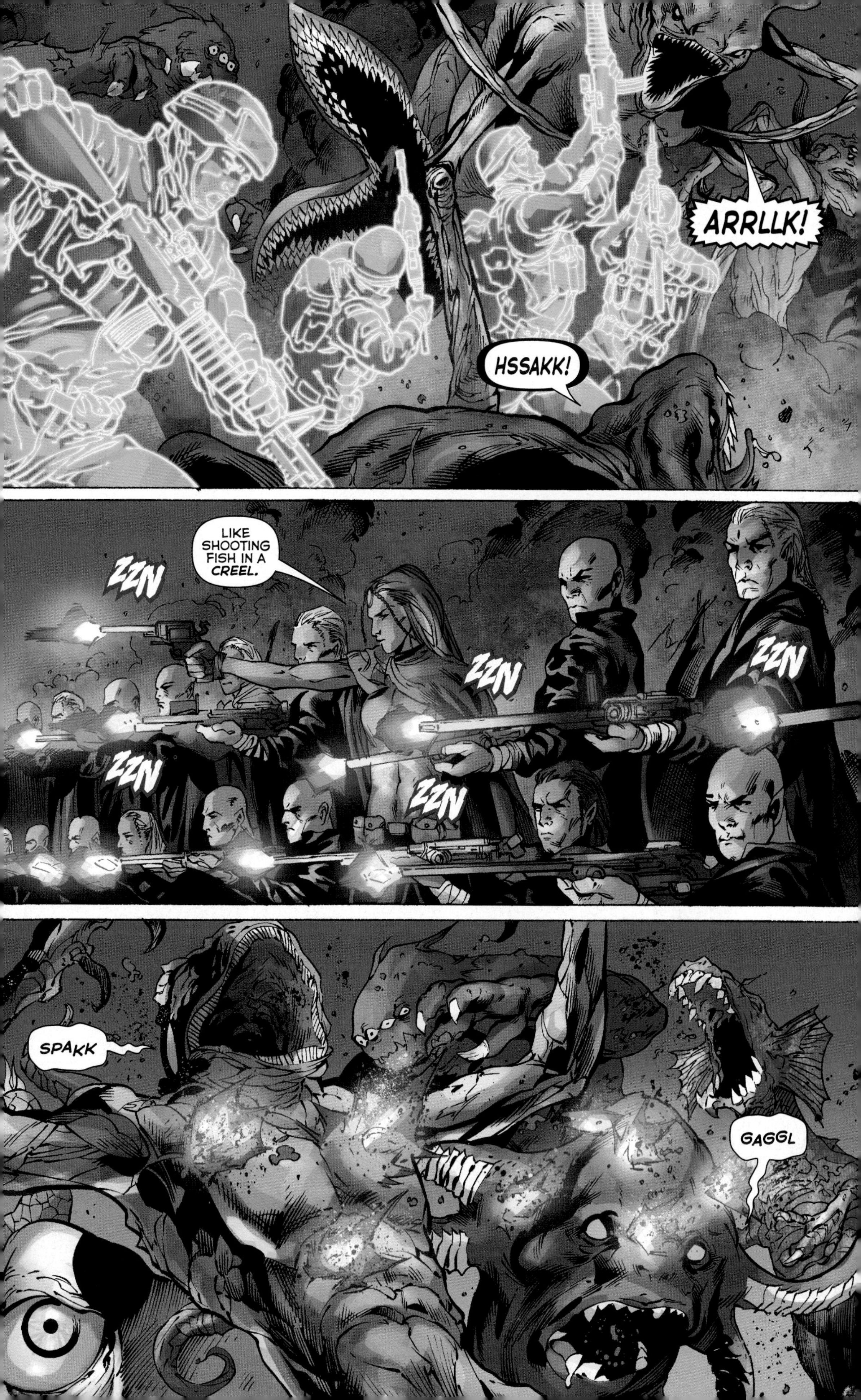
ARRLLK!
HSSAKK!
LIKE SHOOTING FISH IN A CREEL.
ZZN
ZZN
ZZN
ZZN
ZZN
SPAKK
GAGGL

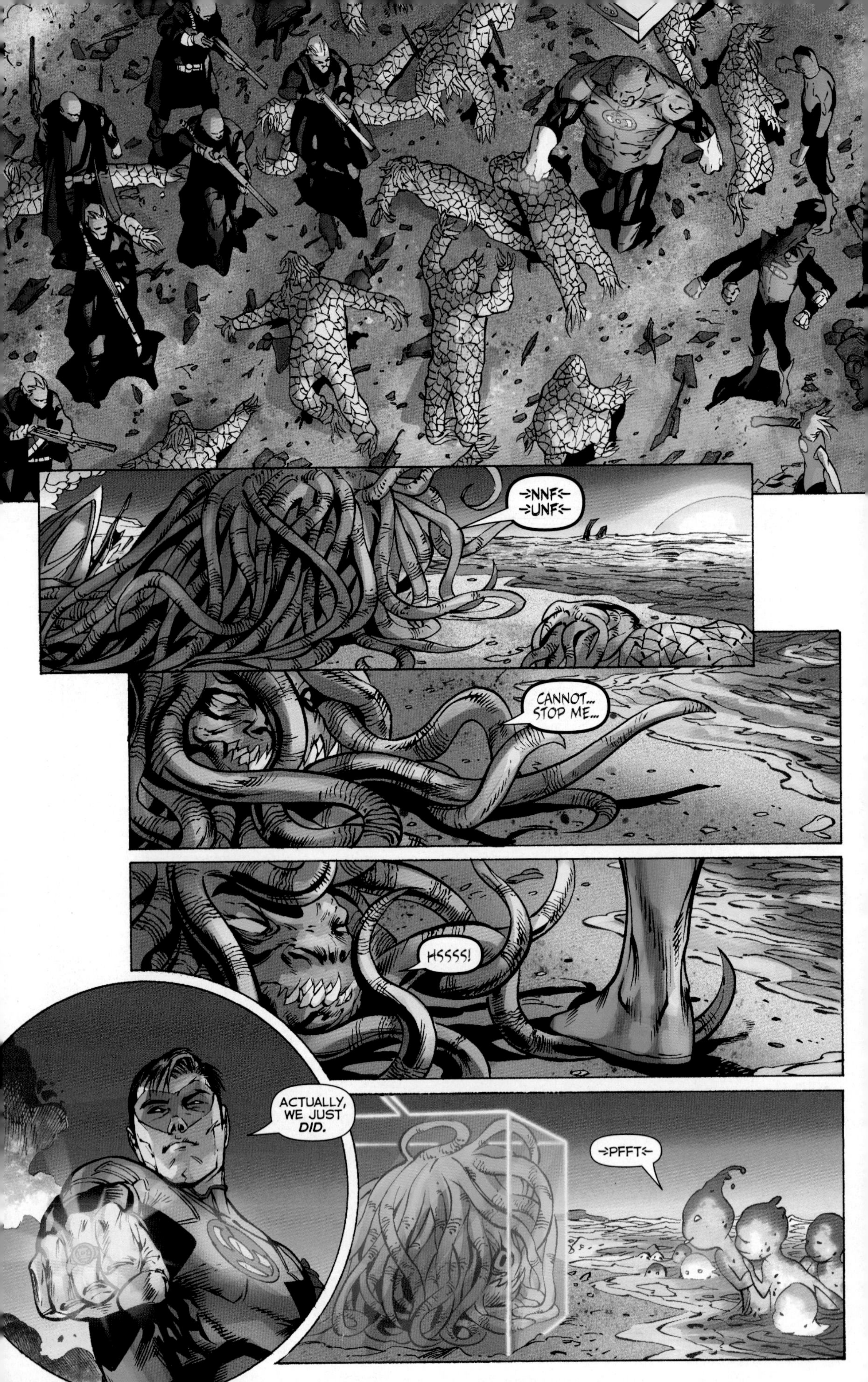

NNF UNF
CANNOT... STOP ME...
HSSSS!
ACTUALLY, WE JUST DID.
PFFT

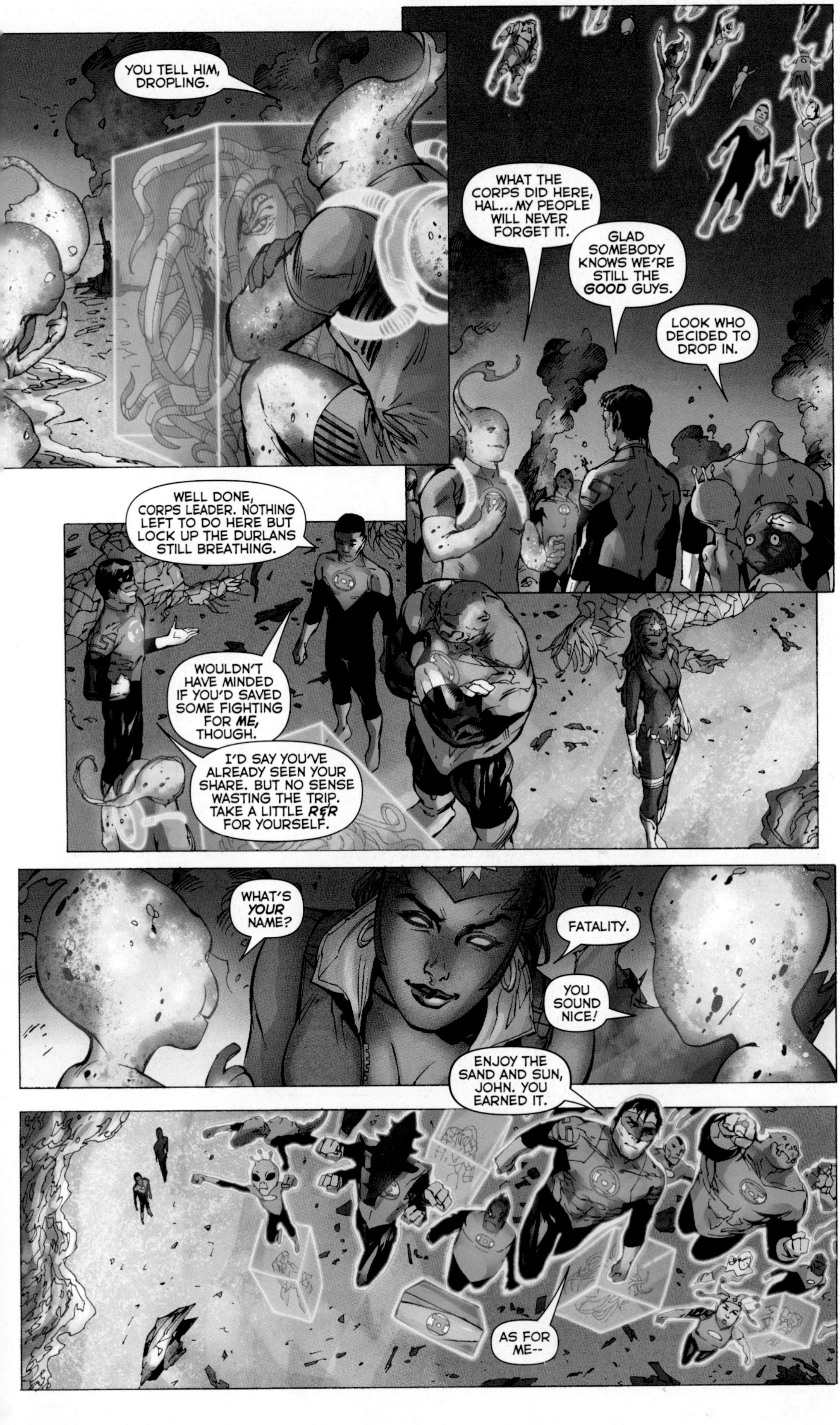

YOU TELL HIM, DROPLING.
WHAT THE CORPS DID HERE, HAL...MY PEOPLE WILL NEVER FORGET IT.
GLAD SOMEBODY KNOWS WE'RE STILL THE GOOD GUYS.
LOOK WHO DECIDED TO DROP IN.
WELL DONE, CORPS LEADER. NOTHING LEFT TO DO HERE BUT LOCK UP THE DURLANS STILL BREATHING.
WOULDN'T HAVE MINDED IF YOU'D SAVED SOME FIGHTING FOR ME, THOUGH.
I'D SAY YOU'VE ALREADY SEEN YOUR SHARE. BUT NO SENSE WASTING THE TRIP. TAKE A LITTLE R&R FOR YOURSELF.
WHAT'S YOUR NAME?
FATALITY.
YOU SOUND NICE!
ENJOY THE SAND AND SUN, JOHN. YOU EARNED IT.
AS FOR ME--

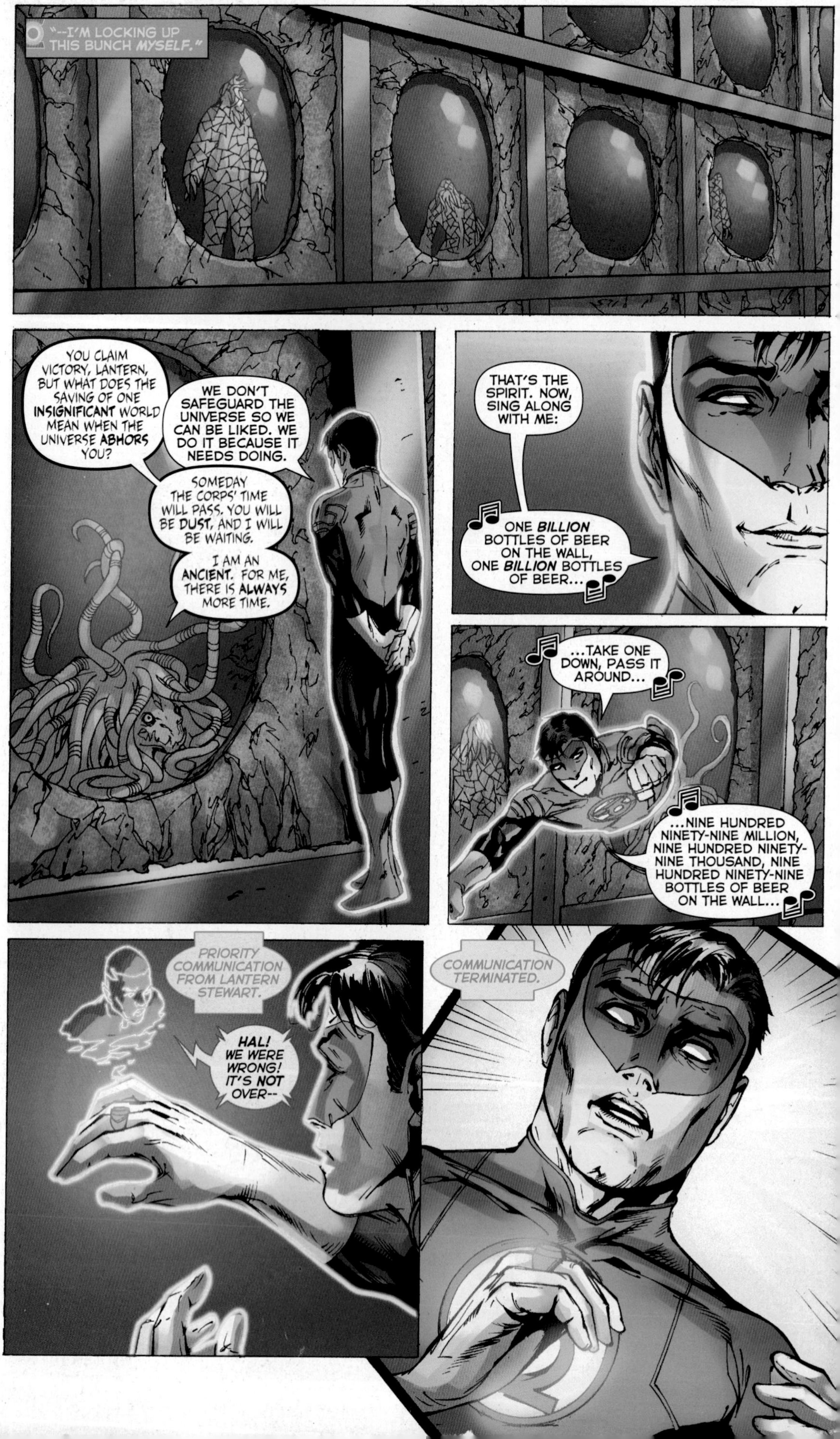
"--I'M LOCKING UP THIS BUNCH MYSELF."
YOU CLAIM VICTORY, LANTERN, BUT WHAT DOES THE SAVING OF ONE INSIGNIFICANT WORLD MEAN WHEN THE UNIVERSE ABHORS YOU?
WE DON'T SAFEGUARD THE UNIVERSE SO WE CAN BE LIKED. WE DO IT BECAUSE IT NEEDS DOING.
SOMEDAY THE CORPS' TIME WILL PASS. YOU WILL BE DUST, AND I WILL BE WAITING.
I AM AN ANCIENT. FOR ME, THERE IS ALWAYS MORE TIME.
THAT'S THE SPIRIT. NOW, SING ALONG WITH ME:
ONE BILLION BOTTLES OF BEER ON THE WALL, ONE BILLION BOTTLES OF BEER...
...TAKE ONE DOWN, PASS IT AROUND...
...NINE HUNDRED NINETY-NINE MILLION, NINE HUNDRED NINETY-NINE THOUSAND, NINE HUNDRED NINETY-NINE BOTTLES OF BEER ON THE WALL...
PRIORITY COMMUNICATION FROM LANTERN STEWART.
HAL! WE WERE WRONG! IT'S NOT OVER--
COMMUNICATION TERMINATED.

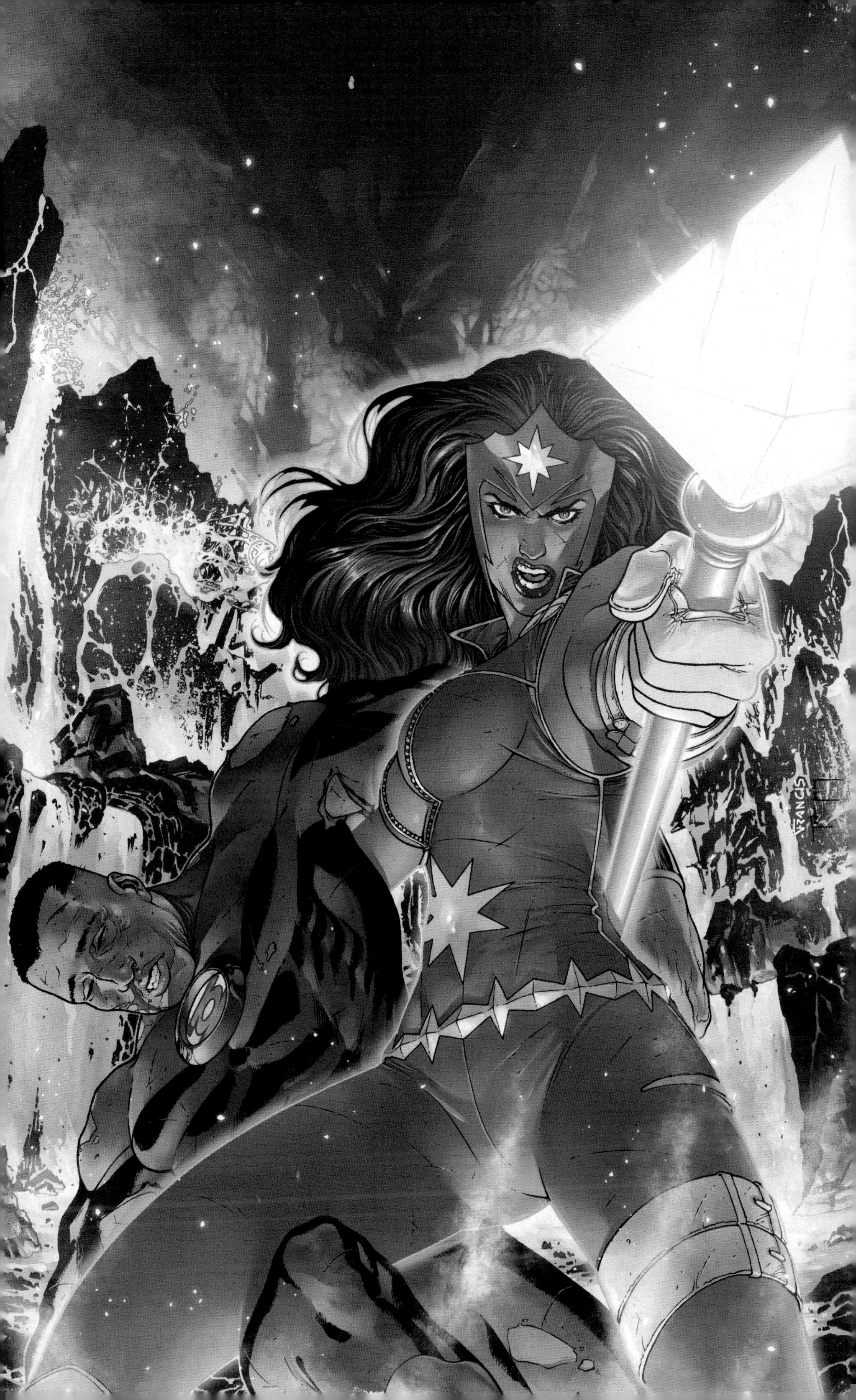

UPRISING PART 6: FATALE

VAN JENSEN writer **BERNARD CHANG** artist **MARCELO MAIOLO** colorist

cover art by **FRANCIS PORTELA & TOMEU MOREY** BATMAN 75TH ANNIVERSARY variant cover by **SEAN CHEN & ALEX SINCLAIR**

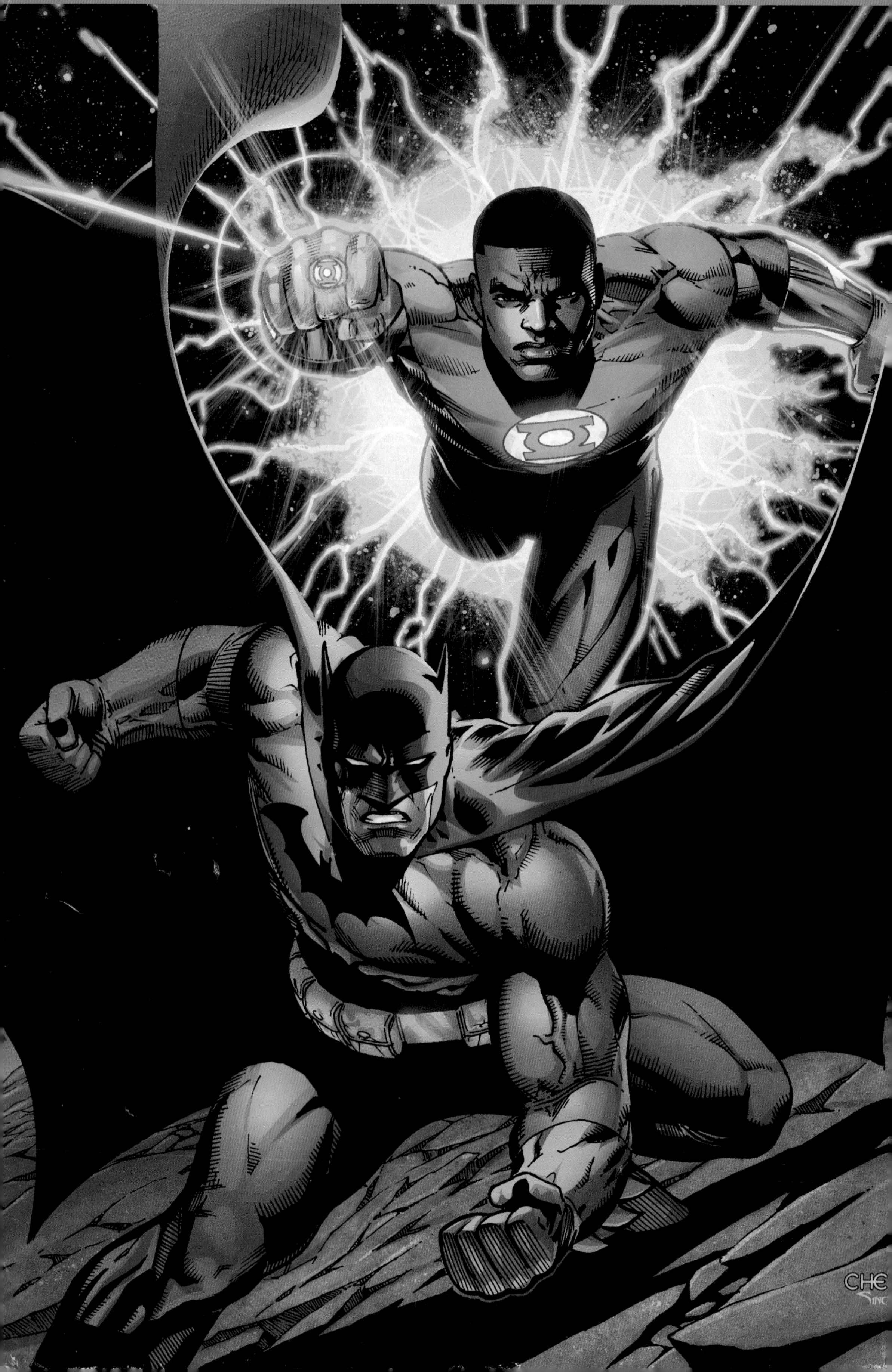

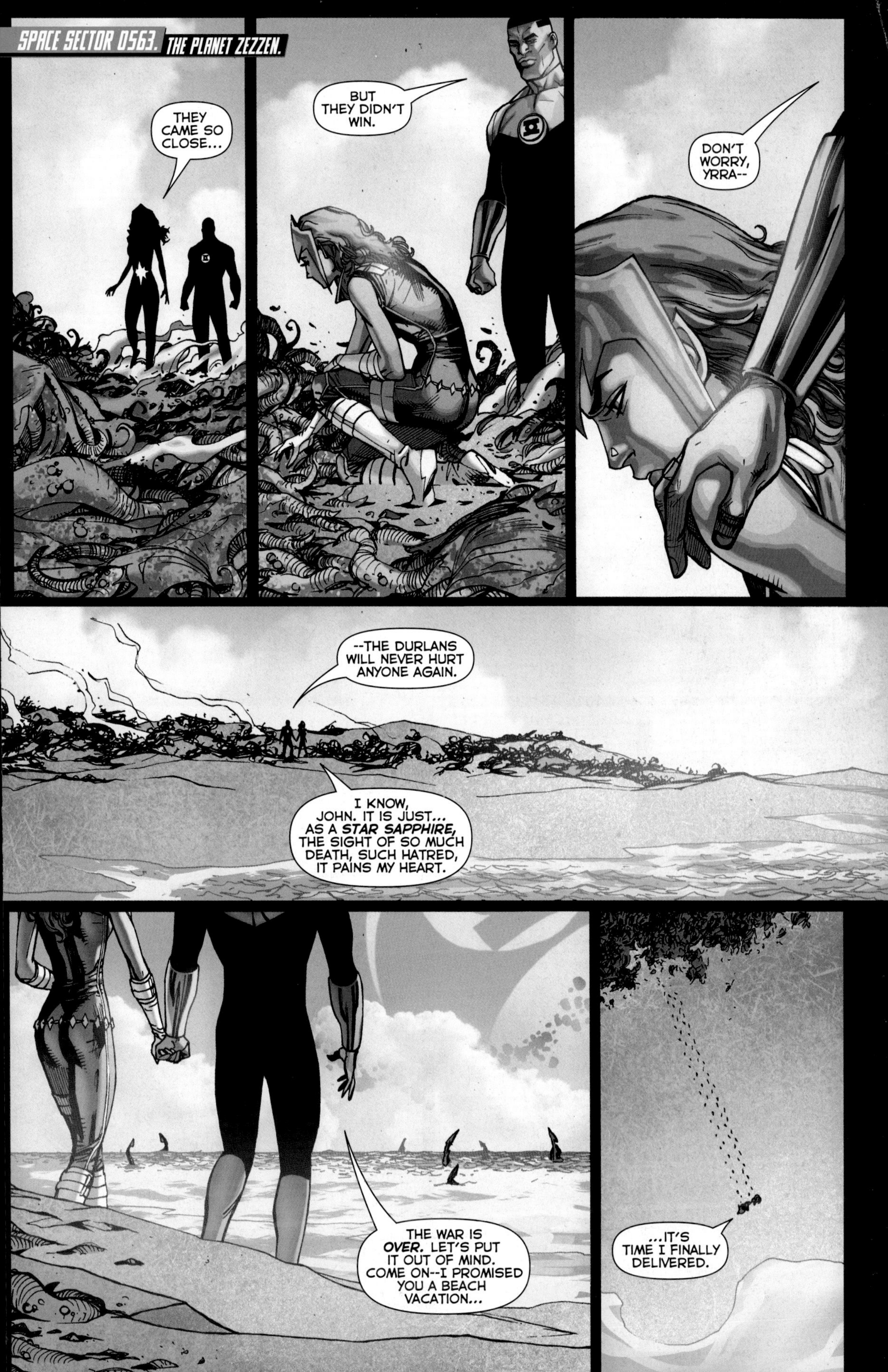
SPACE SECTOR 0563. THE PLANET ZEZZEN.
THEY CAME SO CLOSE...
BUT THEY DIDN'T WIN.
DON'T WORRY, YRRA--
--THE DURLANS WILL NEVER HURT ANYONE AGAIN.
I KNOW, JOHN. IT IS JUST... AS A STAR SAPPHIRE, THE SIGHT OF SO MUCH DEATH, SUCH HATRED, IT PAINS MY HEART.
THE WAR IS OVER. LET'S PUT IT OUT OF MIND. COME ON--I PROMISED YOU A BEACH VACATION...
...IT'S TIME I FINALLY DELIVERED.

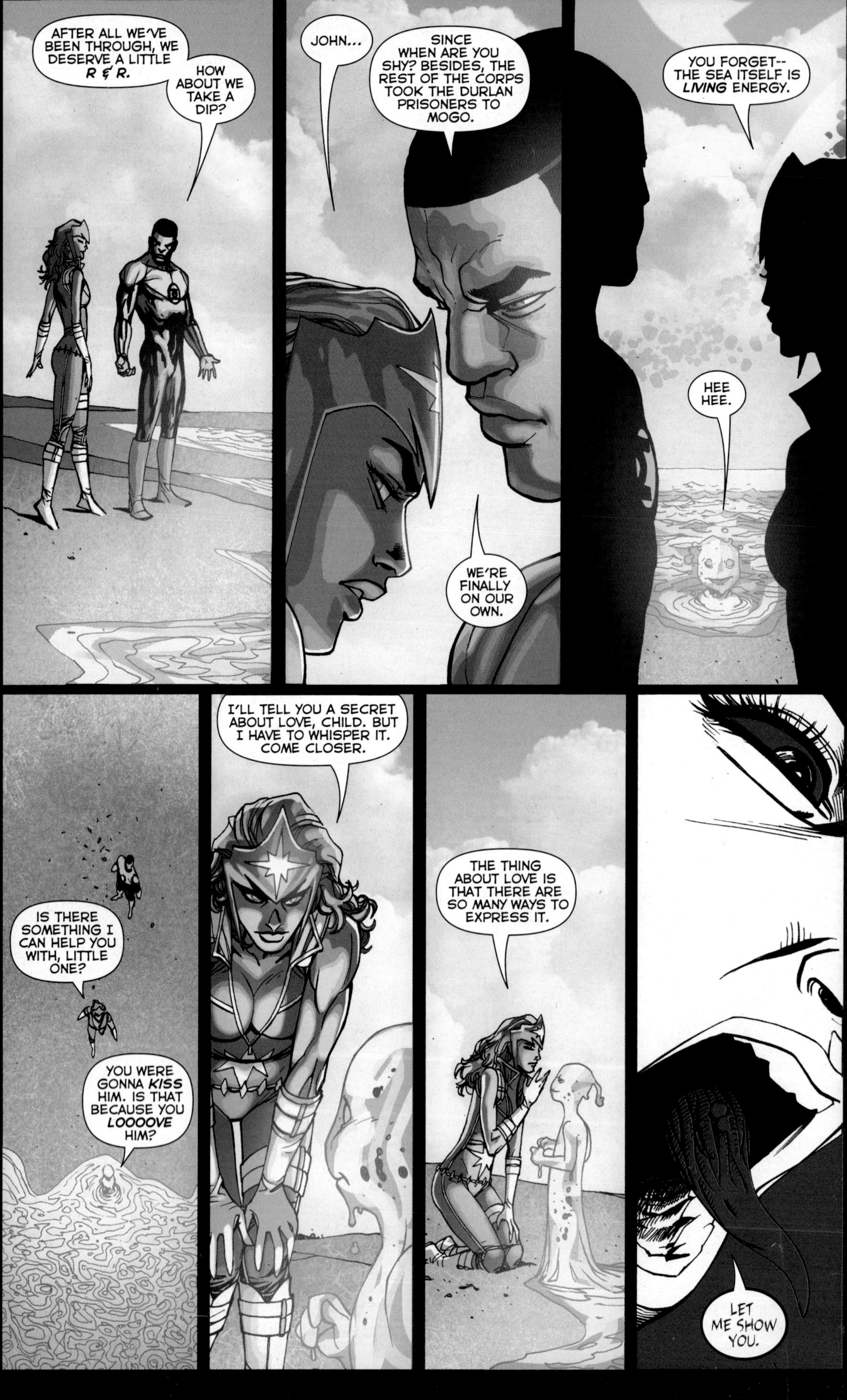
AFTER ALL WE'VE BEEN THROUGH, WE DESERVE A LITTLE R & R.
HOW ABOUT WE TAKE A DIP?
JOHN...
SINCE WHEN ARE YOU SHY? BESIDES, THE REST OF THE CORPS TOOK THE DURLAN PRISONERS TO MOGO.
WE'RE FINALLY ON OUR OWN.
YOU FORGET-- THE SEA ITSELF IS LIVING ENERGY.
HEE HEE.
IS THERE SOMETHING I CAN HELP YOU WITH, LITTLE ONE?
YOU WERE GONNA KISS HIM. IS THAT BECAUSE YOU LOOOOVE HIM?
I'LL TELL YOU A SECRET ABOUT LOVE, CHILD. BUT I HAVE TO WHISPER IT. COME CLOSER.
THE THING ABOUT LOVE IS THAT THERE ARE SO MANY WAYS TO EXPRESS IT.
LET ME SHOW YOU.

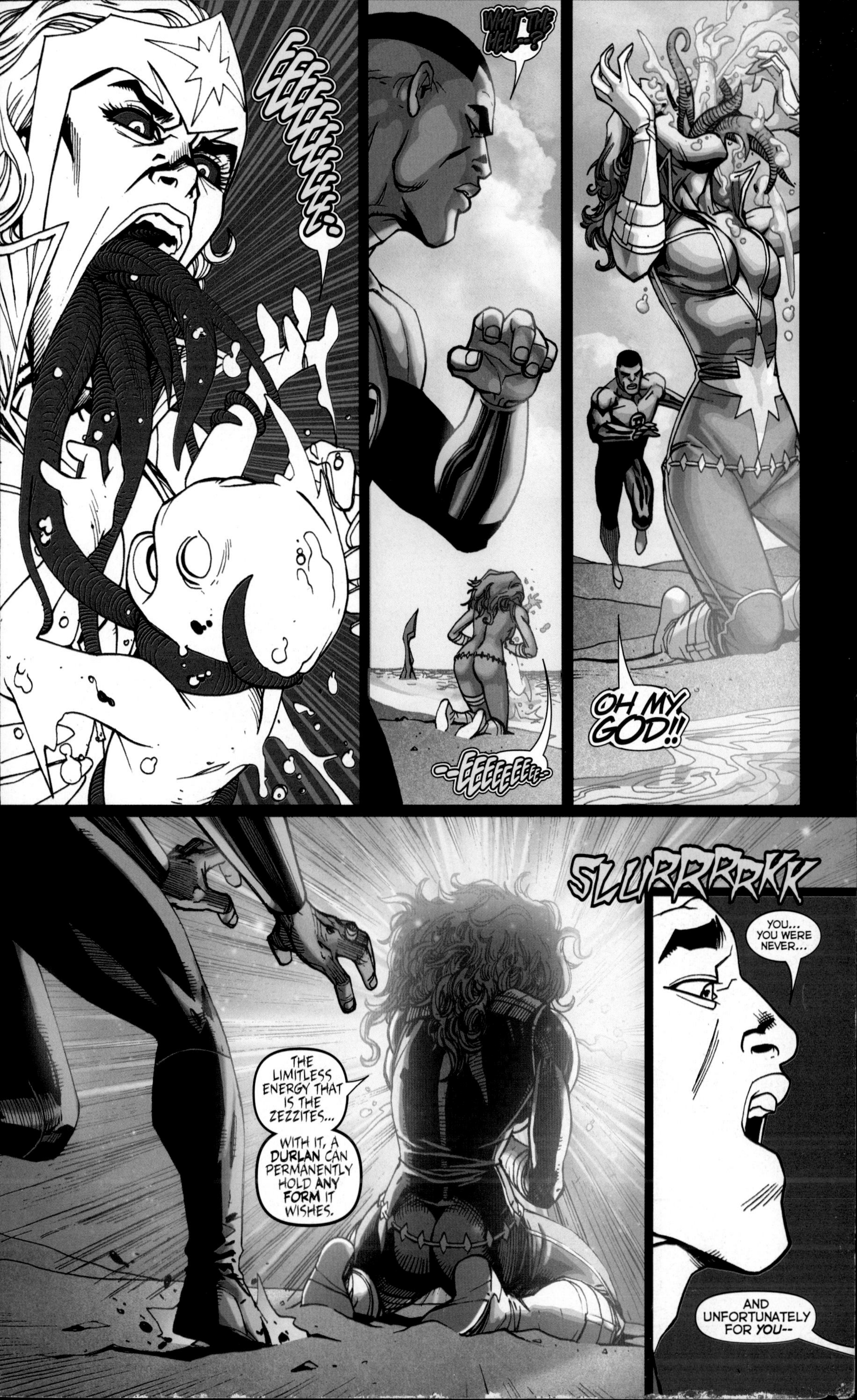

EEEEEEEEEEEEE...
WHAT THE HELL--?
--EEEEEEEEEE--
OH MY GOD!!
SLURRRRKK
THE LIMITLESS ENERGY THAT IS THE ZEZZITES...
WITH IT, A DURLAN CAN PERMANENTLY HOLD ANY FORM IT WISHES.
YOU... YOU WERE NEVER...
AND UNFORTUNATELY FOR YOU--

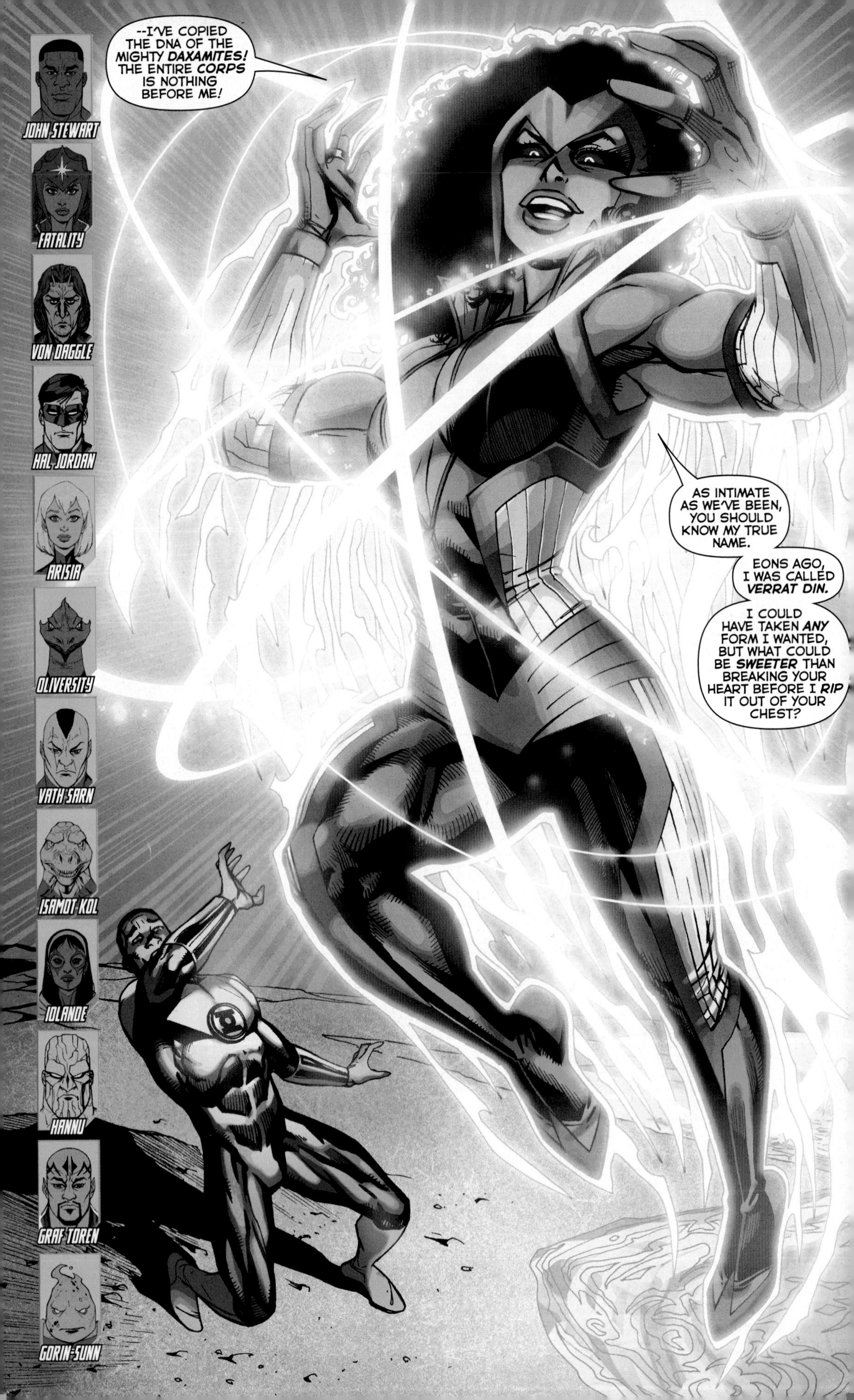
JOHN STEWART
FATALITY
VON DAGGLE
HAL JORDAN
ARISIA
OLIVERSITY
VATH SARN
ISAMOT KOL
IOLANDE
HANNU
GRAF TOREN
GORIN-SUNN
--I'VE COPIED THE DNA OF THE MIGHTY DAXAMITES! THE ENTIRE CORPS IS NOTHING BEFORE ME!
AS INTIMATE AS WE'VE BEEN, YOU SHOULD KNOW MY TRUE NAME.
EONS AGO, I WAS CALLED VERRAT DIN.
I COULD HAVE TAKEN ANY FORM I WANTED, BUT WHAT COULD BE SWEETER THAN BREAKING YOUR HEART BEFORE I RIP IT OUT OF YOUR CHEST?

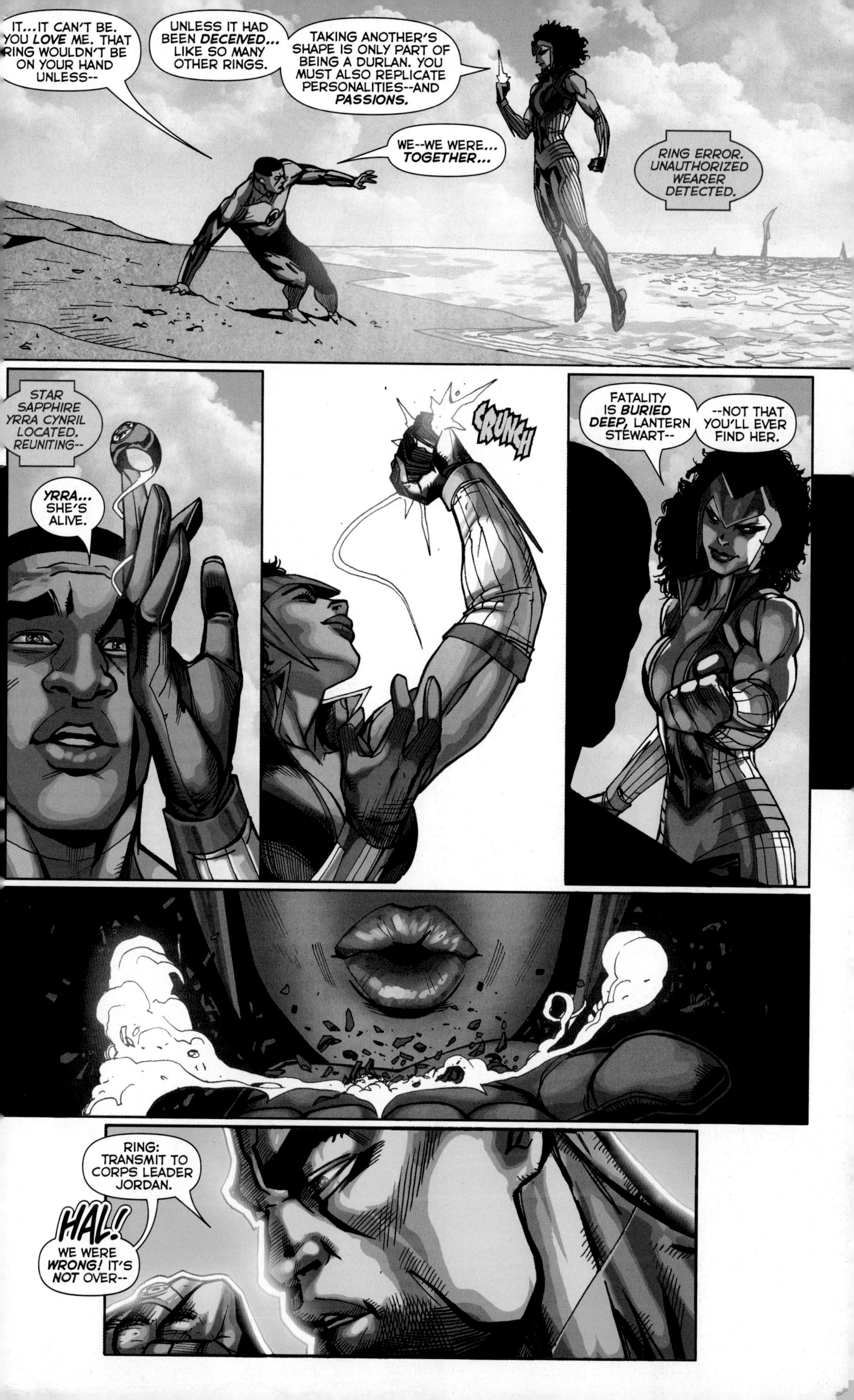
IT...IT CAN'T BE. YOU LOVE ME. THAT RING WOULDN'T BE ON YOUR HAND UNLESS--
UNLESS IT HAD BEEN DECEIVED... LIKE SO MANY OTHER RINGS.
TAKING ANOTHER'S SHAPE IS ONLY PART OF BEING A DURLAN. YOU MUST ALSO REPLICATE PERSONALITIES--AND PASSIONS.
WE--WE WERE... TOGETHER...
RING ERROR. UNAUTHORIZED WEARER DETECTED.
STAR SAPPHIRE YRRA CYNRIL LOCATED. REUNITING--
YRRA... SHE'S ALIVE.
CRUNCH
FATALITY IS BURIED DEEP, LANTERN STEWART--
--NOT THAT YOU'LL EVER FIND HER.
RING: TRANSMIT TO CORPS LEADER JORDAN.
HAL!
WE WERE WRONG! IT'S NOT OVER--

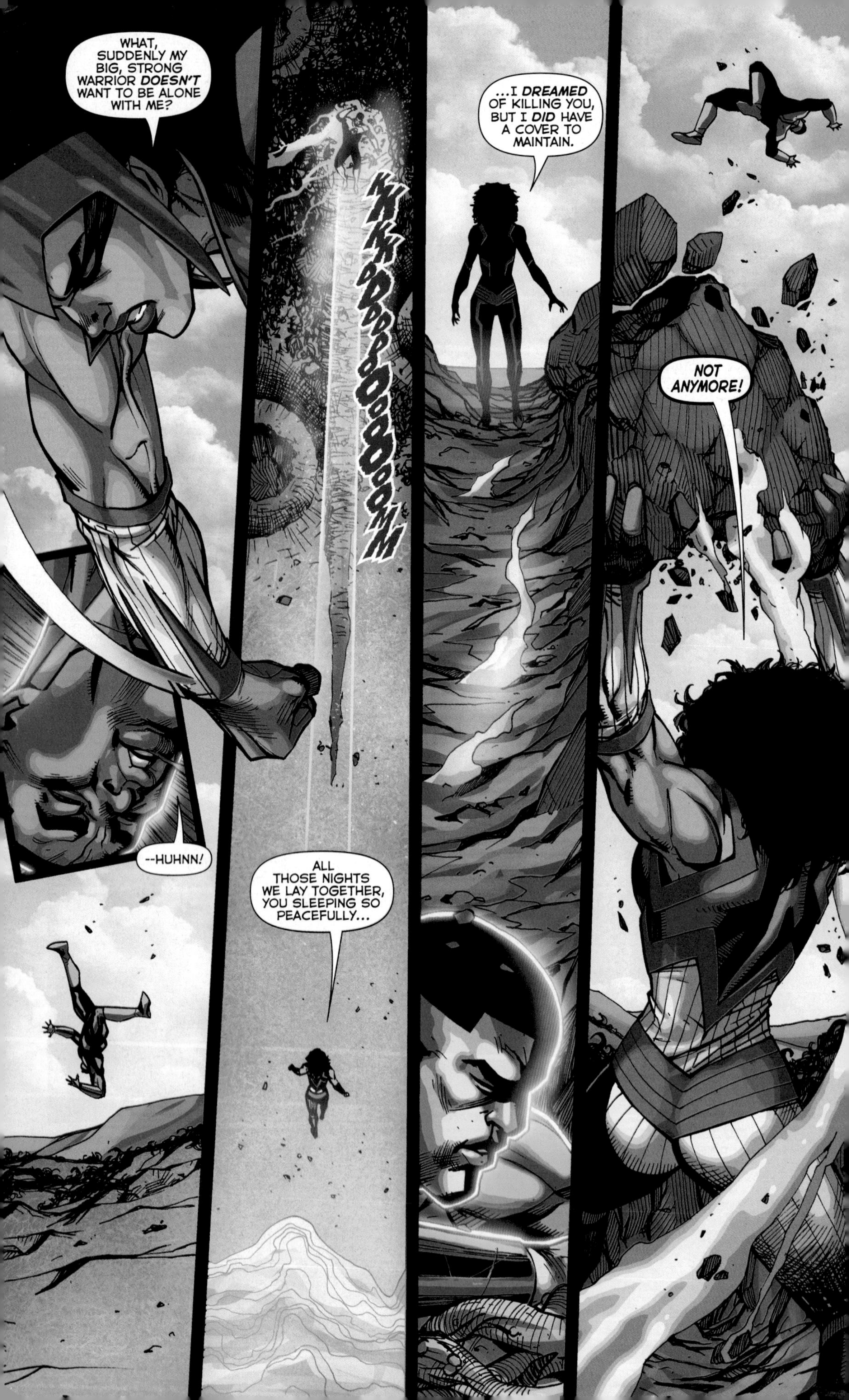
WHAT, SUDDENLY MY BIG, STRONG WARRIOR DOESN'T WANT TO BE ALONE WITH ME?
--HUHNN!
KKKROOOOOOOOOOOOOOOOMM
ALL THOSE NIGHTS WE LAY TOGETHER, YOU SLEEPING SO PEACEFULLY...
...I DREAMED OF KILLING YOU, BUT I DID HAVE A COVER TO MAINTAIN.
NOT ANYMORE!

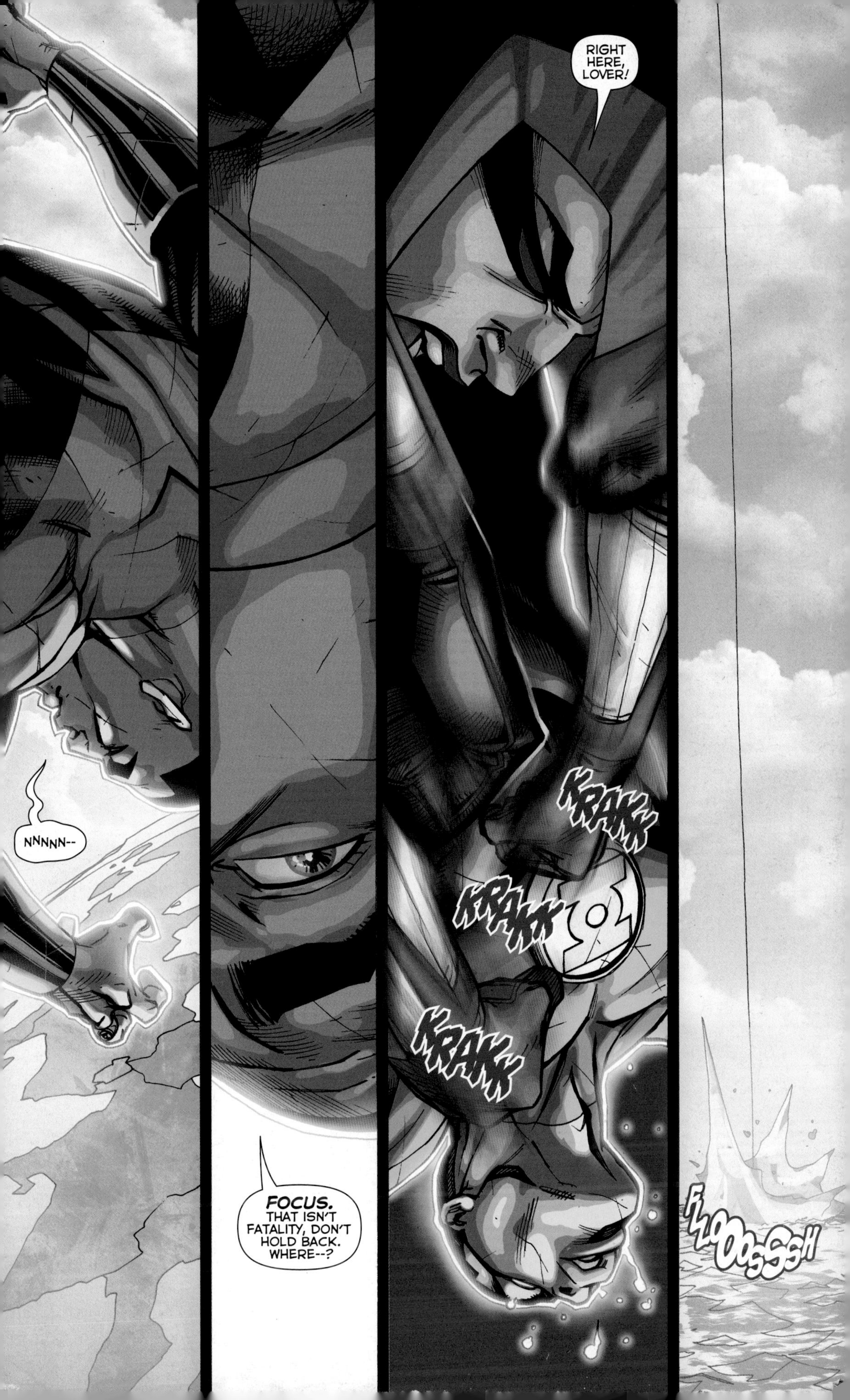
NNNNN--
FOCUS. THAT ISN'T FATALITY, DON'T HOLD BACK. WHERE--?
RIGHT HERE, LOVER!
KRAKK
KRAKK
KRAKK
FLOOOSSSH

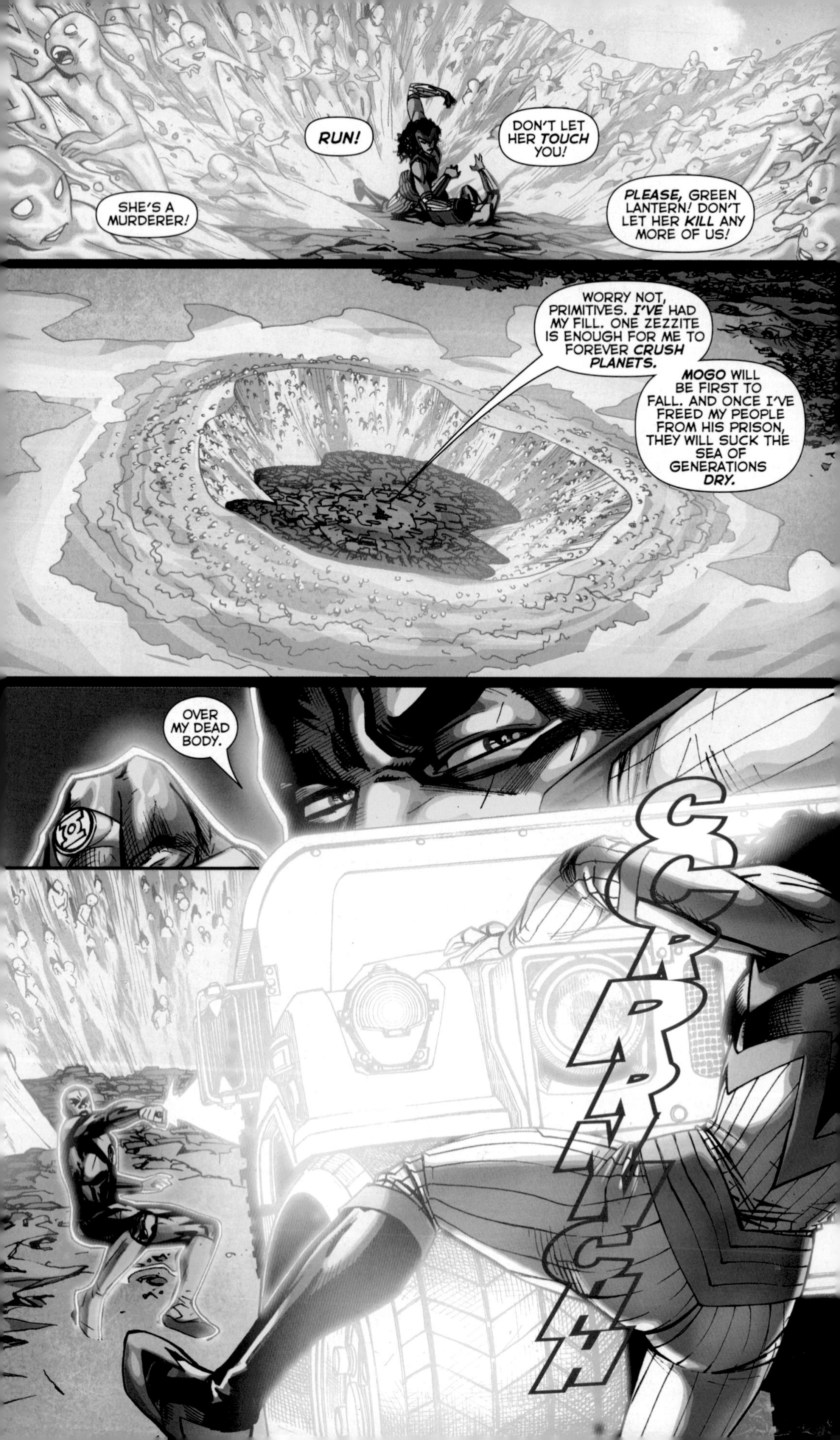
RUN!
DON'T LET HER TOUCH YOU!
SHE'S A MURDERER!
PLEASE, GREEN LANTERN! DON'T LET HER KILL ANY MORE OF US!
WORRY NOT, PRIMITIVES. I'VE HAD MY FILL. ONE ZEZZITE IS ENOUGH FOR ME TO FOREVER CRUSH PLANETS.
MOGO WILL BE FIRST TO FALL. AND ONCE I'VE FREED MY PEOPLE FROM HIS PRISON, THEY WILL SUCK THE SEA OF GENERATIONS DRY.
OVER MY DEAD BODY.
CRRNCH

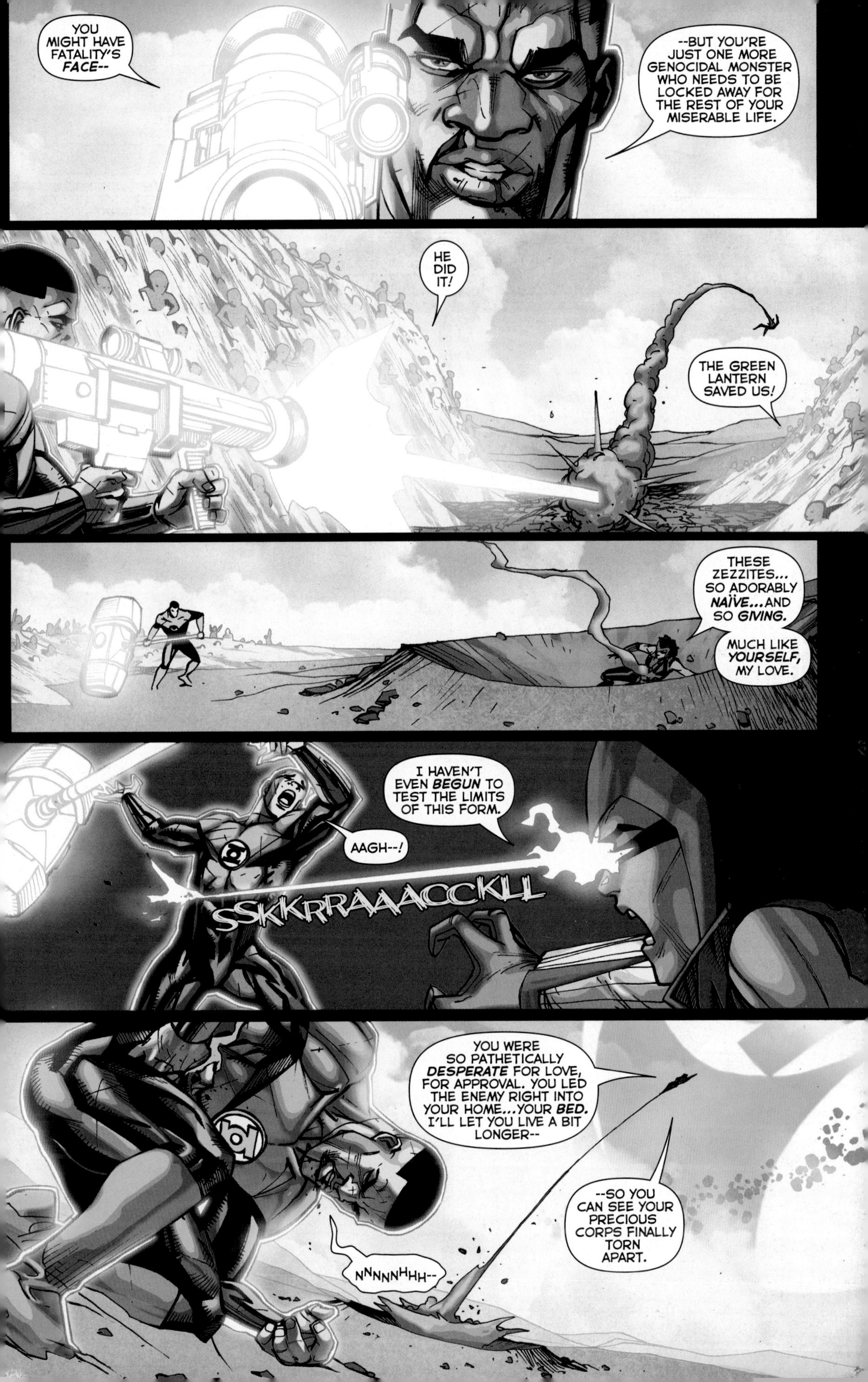
YOU MIGHT HAVE FATALITY'S *FACE*--
--BUT YOU'RE JUST ONE MORE GENOCIDAL MONSTER WHO NEEDS TO BE LOCKED AWAY FOR THE REST OF YOUR MISERABLE LIFE.
HE DID IT!
THE GREEN LANTERN SAVED US!
THESE ZEZZITES... SO ADORABLY *NAÏVE*...AND SO *GIVING.*
MUCH LIKE *YOURSELF,* MY LOVE.
I HAVEN'T EVEN *BEGUN* TO TEST THE LIMITS OF THIS FORM.
AAGH--!
SSKKRRAAACCKLL
YOU WERE SO PATHETICALLY *DESPERATE* FOR LOVE, FOR APPROVAL. YOU LED THE ENEMY RIGHT INTO YOUR HOME...YOUR *BED.* I'LL LET YOU LIVE A BIT LONGER--
--SO YOU CAN SEE YOUR PRECIOUS CORPS FINALLY TORN APART.
NNNNNHHH--

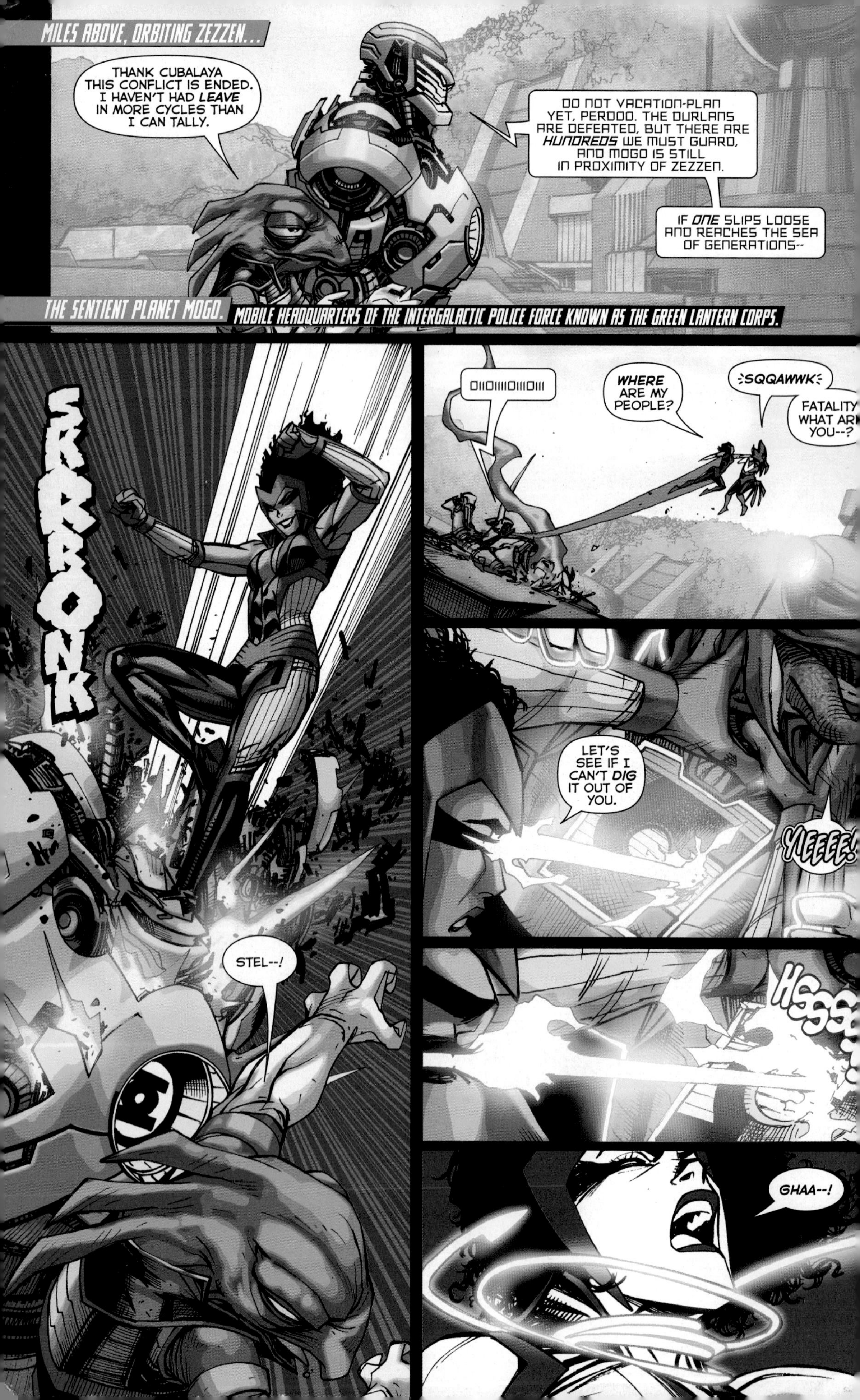
MILES ABOVE, ORBITING ZEZZEN...
THANK CUBALAYA THIS CONFLICT IS ENDED. I HAVEN'T HAD LEAVE IN MORE CYCLES THAN I CAN TALLY.
DO NOT VACATION-PLAN YET, PERDOO. THE DURLANS ARE DEFEATED, BUT THERE ARE HUNDREDS WE MUST GUARD, AND MOGO IS STILL IN PROXIMITY OF ZEZZEN.
IF ONE SLIPS LOOSE AND REACHES THE SEA OF GENERATIONS--
THE SENTIENT PLANET MOGO.
MOBILE HEADQUARTERS OF THE INTERGALACTIC POLICE FORCE KNOWN AS THE GREEN LANTERN CORPS.
SKRRONK
STEL--!
0110111011011
WHERE ARE MY PEOPLE?
SQQAWWK
FATALITY WHAT AR YOU--?
LET'S SEE IF I CAN'T DIG IT OUT OF YOU.
YIEEEE!
HSSS
GHAA--!

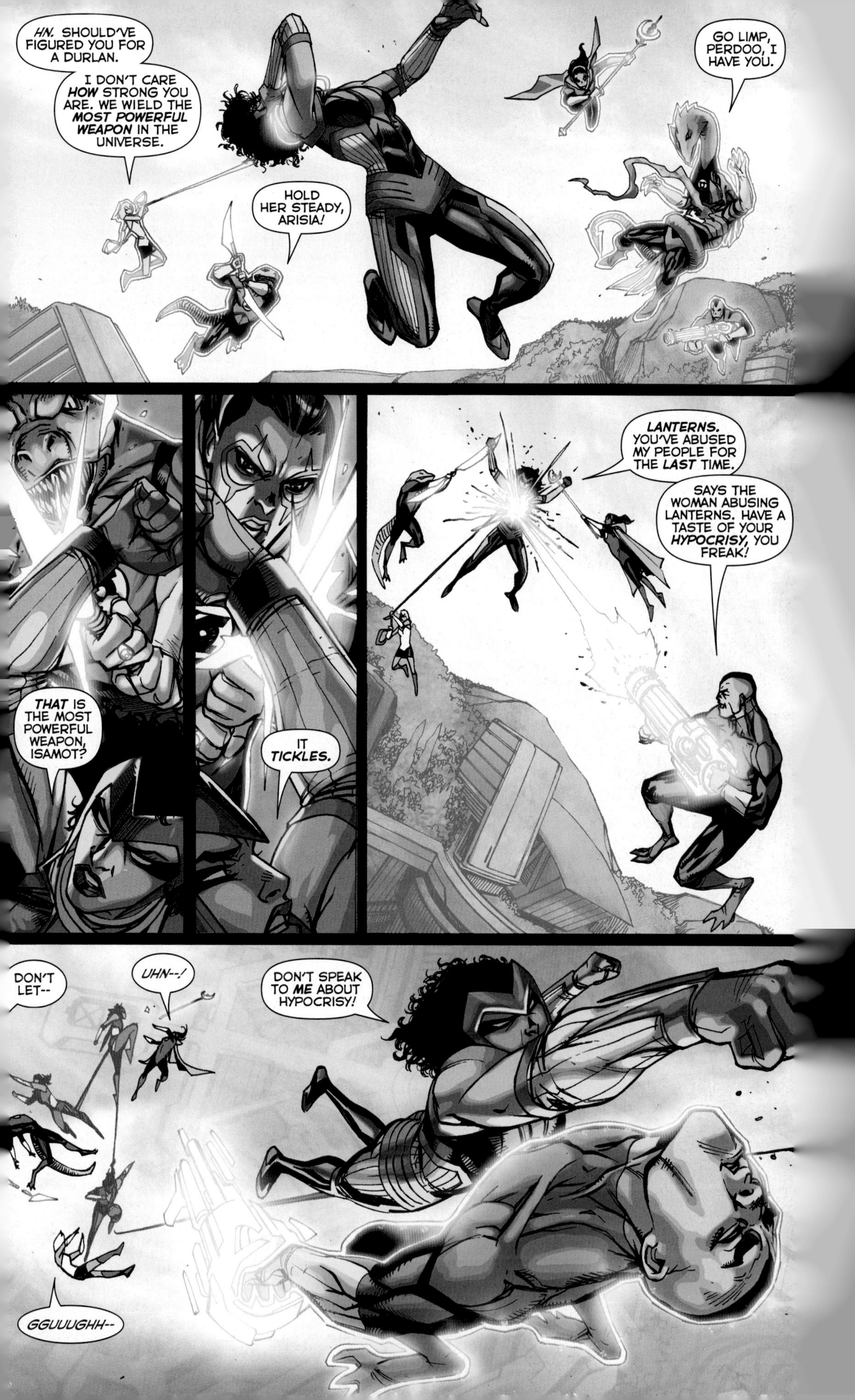
HN. SHOULD'VE FIGURED YOU FOR A DURLAN.
I DON'T CARE HOW STRONG YOU ARE. WE WIELD THE MOST POWERFUL WEAPON IN THE UNIVERSE.
HOLD HER STEADY, ARISIA!
GO LIMP, PERDOO, I HAVE YOU.
THAT IS THE MOST POWERFUL WEAPON, ISAMOT?
IT TICKLES.
LANTERNS. YOU'VE ABUSED MY PEOPLE FOR THE LAST TIME.
SAYS THE WOMAN ABUSING LANTERNS. HAVE A TASTE OF YOUR HYPOCRISY, YOU FREAK!
DON'T LET--
UHN--!
DON'T SPEAK TO ME ABOUT HYPOCRISY!
GGUUUGHH--

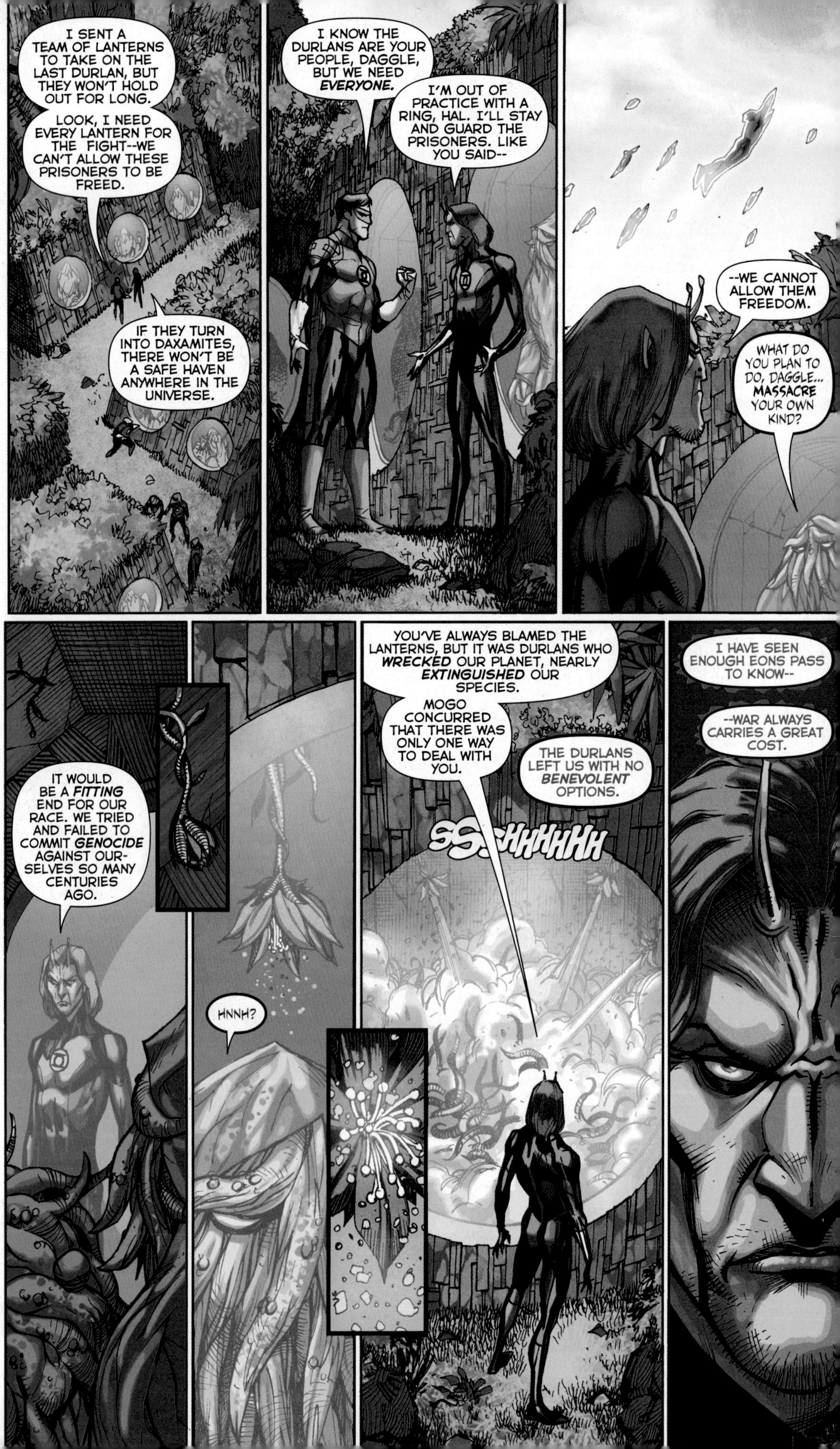
I SENT A TEAM OF LANTERNS TO TAKE ON THE LAST DURLAN, BUT THEY WON'T HOLD OUT FOR LONG.
LOOK, I NEED EVERY LANTERN FOR THE FIGHT--WE CAN'T ALLOW THESE PRISONERS TO BE FREED.
IF THEY TURN INTO DAXAMITES, THERE WON'T BE A SAFE HAVEN ANYWHERE IN THE UNIVERSE.
I KNOW THE DURLANS ARE YOUR PEOPLE, DAGGLE, BUT WE NEED EVERYONE.
I'M OUT OF PRACTICE WITH A RING, HAL. I'LL STAY AND GUARD THE PRISONERS. LIKE YOU SAID--
--WE CANNOT ALLOW THEM FREEDOM.
WHAT DO YOU PLAN TO DO, DAGGLE... MASSACRE YOUR OWN KIND?
IT WOULD BE A FITTING END FOR OUR RACE. WE TRIED AND FAILED TO COMMIT GENOCIDE AGAINST OURSELVES SO MANY CENTURIES AGO.
HNNH?
YOU'VE ALWAYS BLAMED THE LANTERNS, BUT IT WAS DURLANS WHO WRECKED OUR PLANET, NEARLY EXTINGUISHED OUR SPECIES.
MOGO CONCURRED THAT THERE WAS ONLY ONE WAY TO DEAL WITH YOU.
THE DURLANS LEFT US WITH NO BENEVOLENT OPTIONS.
SSSHHHHHH
I HAVE SEEN ENOUGH EONS PASS TO KNOW--
--WAR ALWAYS CARRIES A GREAT COST.

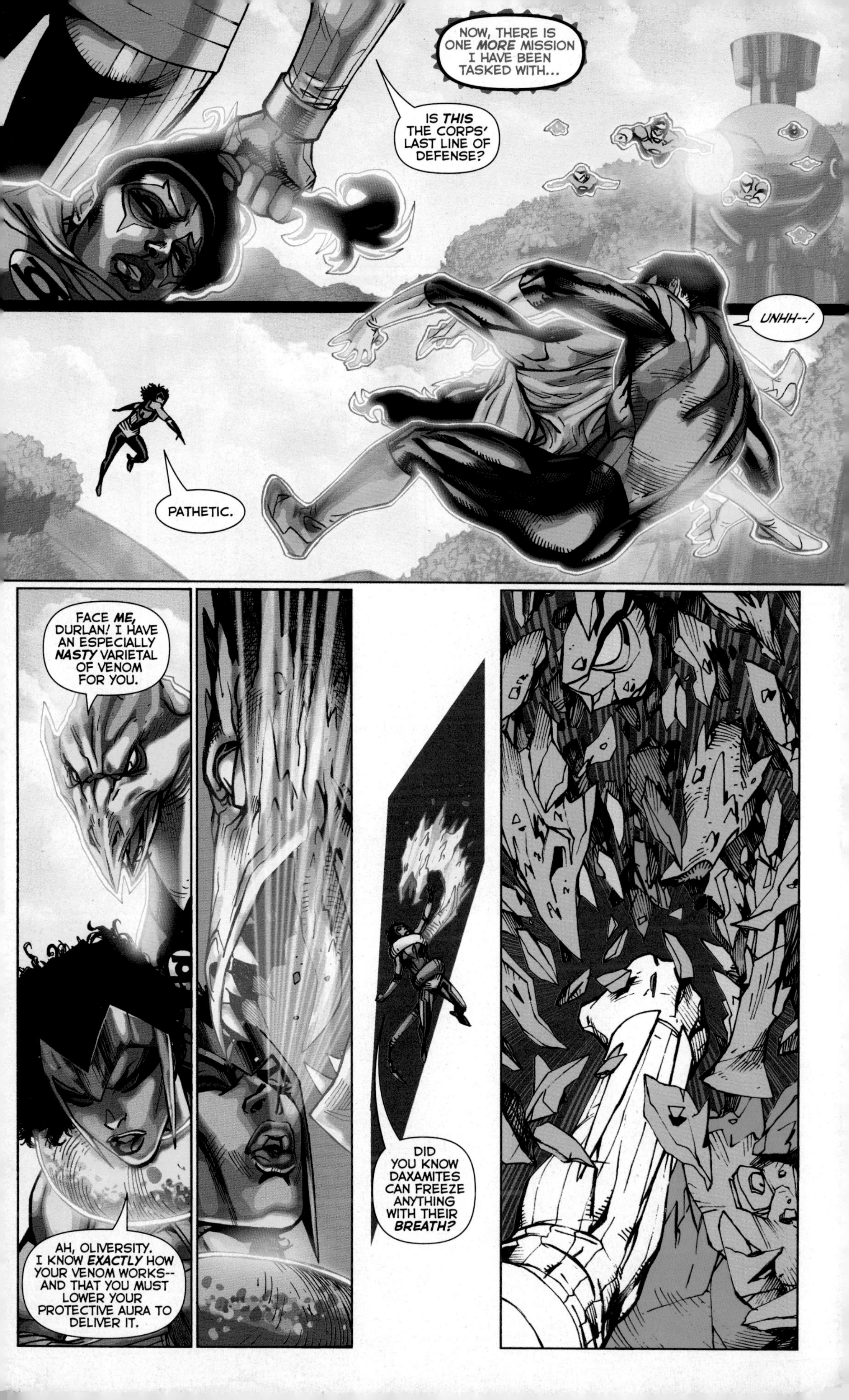

NOW, THERE IS ONE MORE MISSION I HAVE BEEN TASKED WITH...
IS THIS THE CORPS' LAST LINE OF DEFENSE?
UNHH--!
PATHETIC.
FACE ME, DURLAN! I HAVE AN ESPECIALLY NASTY VARIETAL OF VENOM FOR YOU.
AH, OLIVERSITY. I KNOW EXACTLY HOW YOUR VENOM WORKS-- AND THAT YOU MUST LOWER YOUR PROTECTIVE AURA TO DELIVER IT.
DID YOU KNOW DAXAMITES CAN FREEZE ANYTHING WITH THEIR BREATH?

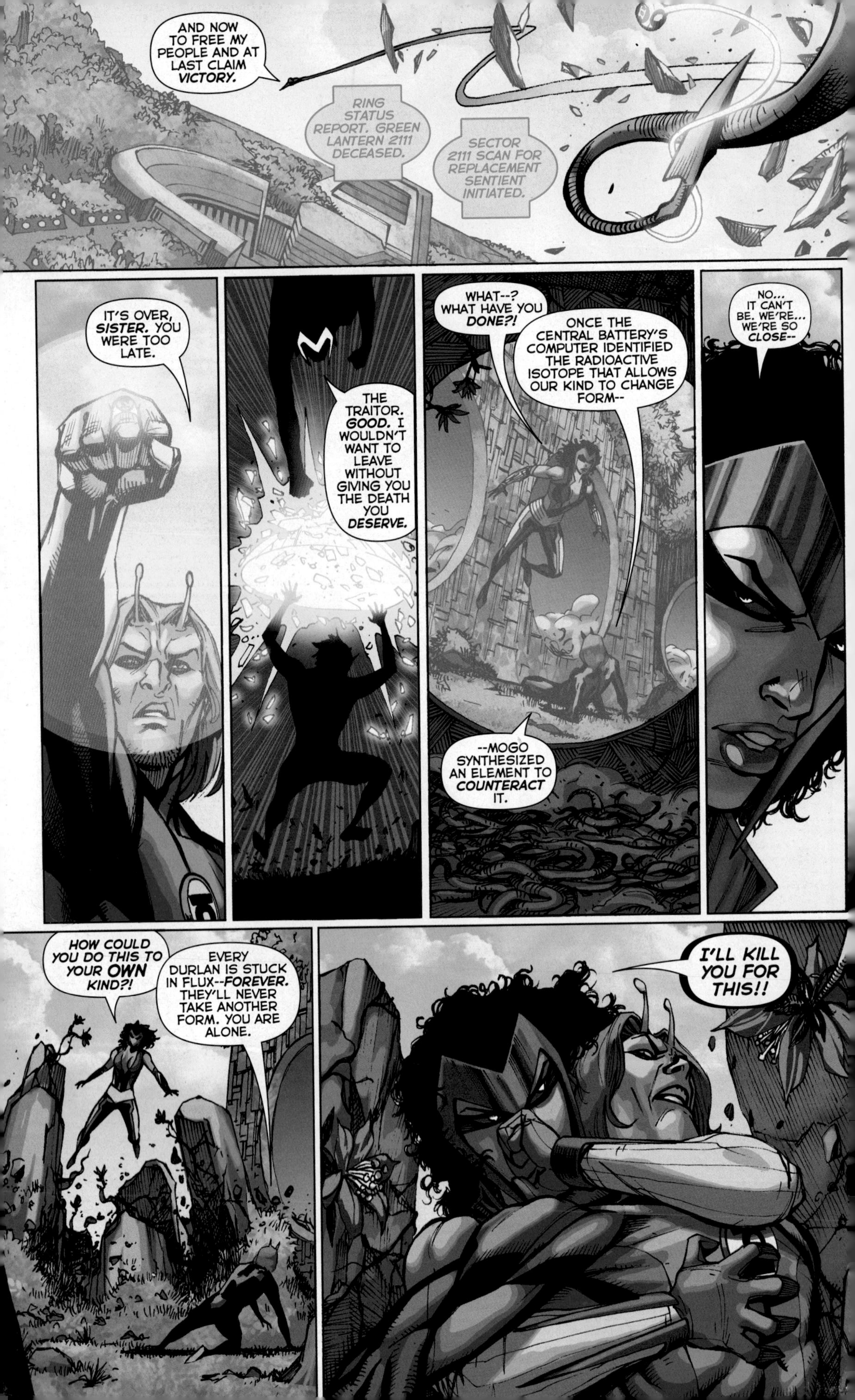

AND NOW TO FREE MY PEOPLE AND AT LAST CLAIM VICTORY.
RING STATUS REPORT. GREEN LANTERN 2111 DECEASED.
SECTOR 2111 SCAN FOR REPLACEMENT SENTIENT INITIATED.
IT'S OVER, SISTER. YOU WERE TOO LATE.
THE TRAITOR. GOOD. I WOULDN'T WANT TO LEAVE WITHOUT GIVING YOU THE DEATH YOU DESERVE.
WHAT--? WHAT HAVE YOU DONE?!
ONCE THE CENTRAL BATTERY'S COMPUTER IDENTIFIED THE RADIOACTIVE ISOTOPE THAT ALLOWS OUR KIND TO CHANGE FORM--
--MOGO SYNTHESIZED AN ELEMENT TO COUNTERACT IT.
NO... IT CAN'T BE. WE'RE... WE'RE SO CLOSE--
HOW COULD YOU DO THIS TO YOUR OWN KIND?!
EVERY DURLAN IS STUCK IN FLUX--FOREVER. THEY'LL NEVER TAKE ANOTHER FORM. YOU ARE ALONE.
I'LL KILL YOU FOR THIS!!

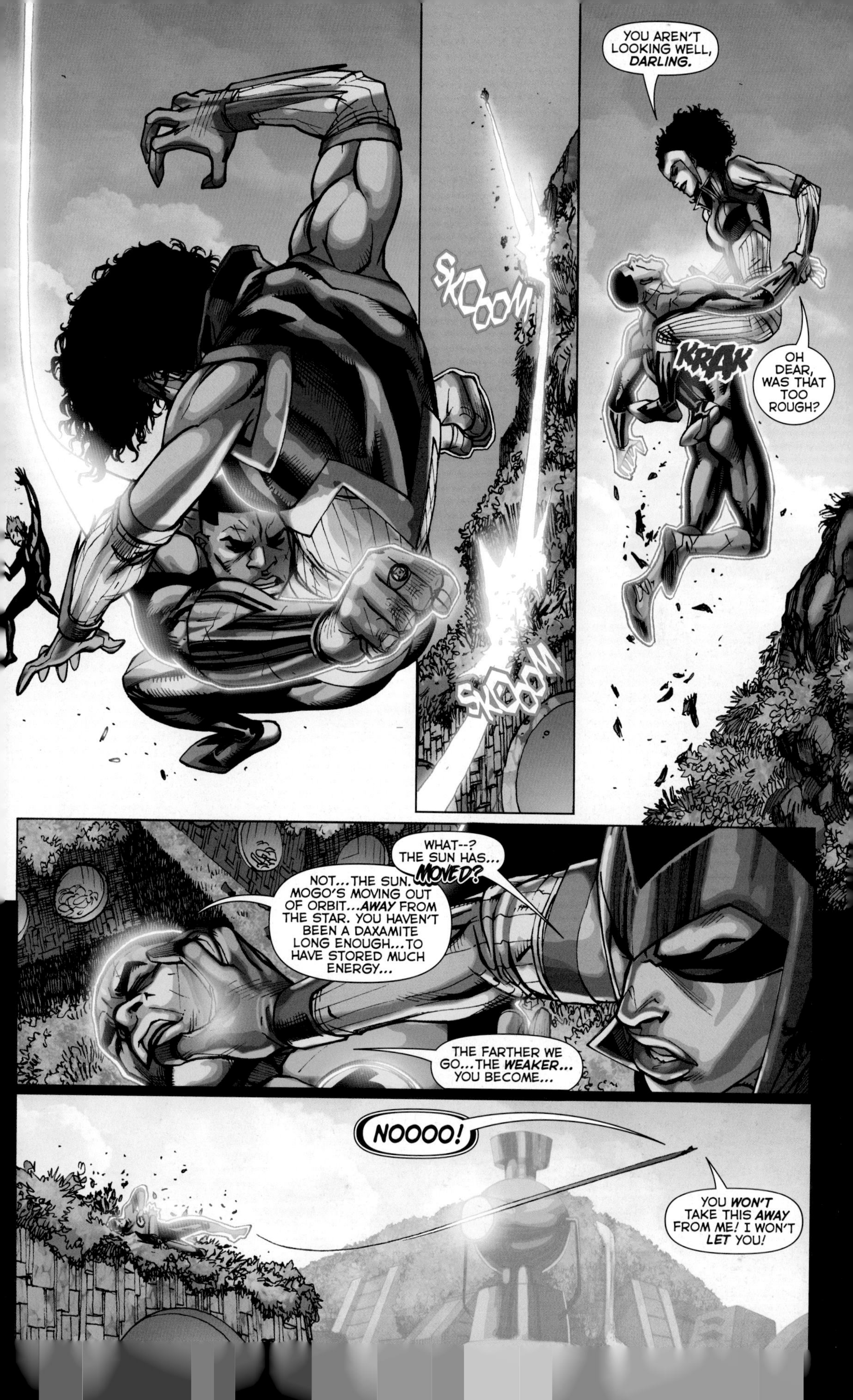
SKOOOM
SKOOOM
YOU AREN'T LOOKING WELL, *DARLING.*
KRAK
OH DEAR, WAS THAT TOO ROUGH?
WHAT--? THE SUN HAS... *MOVED?*
NOT... THE SUN. MOGO'S MOVING OUT OF ORBIT... *AWAY* FROM THE STAR. YOU HAVEN'T BEEN A DAXAMITE LONG ENOUGH... TO HAVE STORED MUCH ENERGY...
THE FARTHER WE GO... THE *WEAKER*... YOU BECOME...
NOOOO!
YOU *WON'T* TAKE THIS *AWAY* FROM ME! I WON'T *LET* YOU!

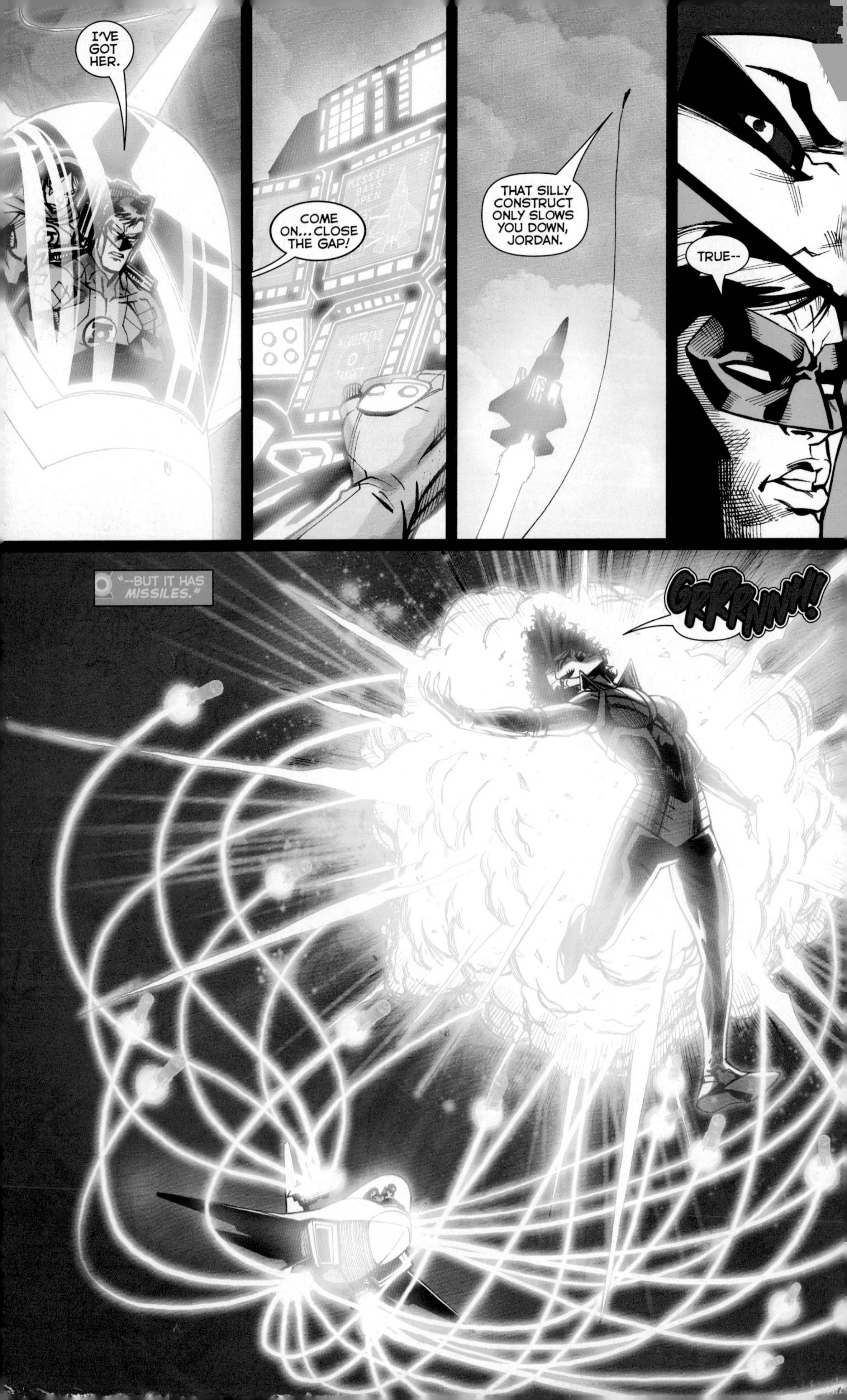
I'VE GOT HER.
COME ON...CLOSE THE GAP!
MISSILE BAYS OPEN
ACQUIRING TARGET
THAT SILLY CONSTRUCT ONLY SLOWS YOU DOWN, JORDAN.
TRUE--
"--BUT IT HAS *MISSILES.*"
GRRRNNNH!

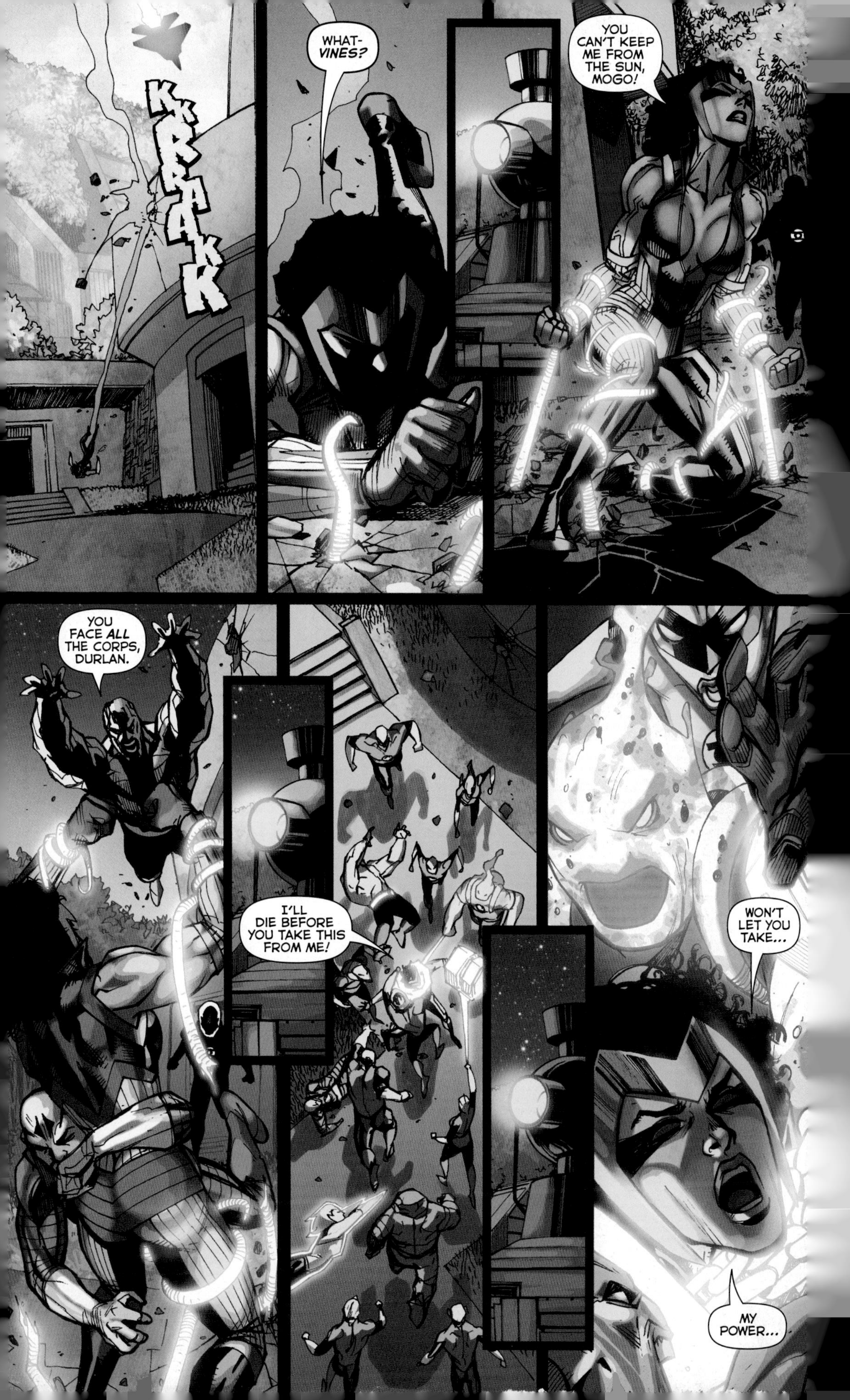
KKRAKK
WHAT- VINES?
YOU CAN'T KEEP ME FROM THE SUN, MOGO!
YOU FACE ALL THE CORPS, DURLAN.
I'LL DIE BEFORE YOU TAKE THIS FROM ME!
WON'T LET YOU TAKE...
MY POWER...

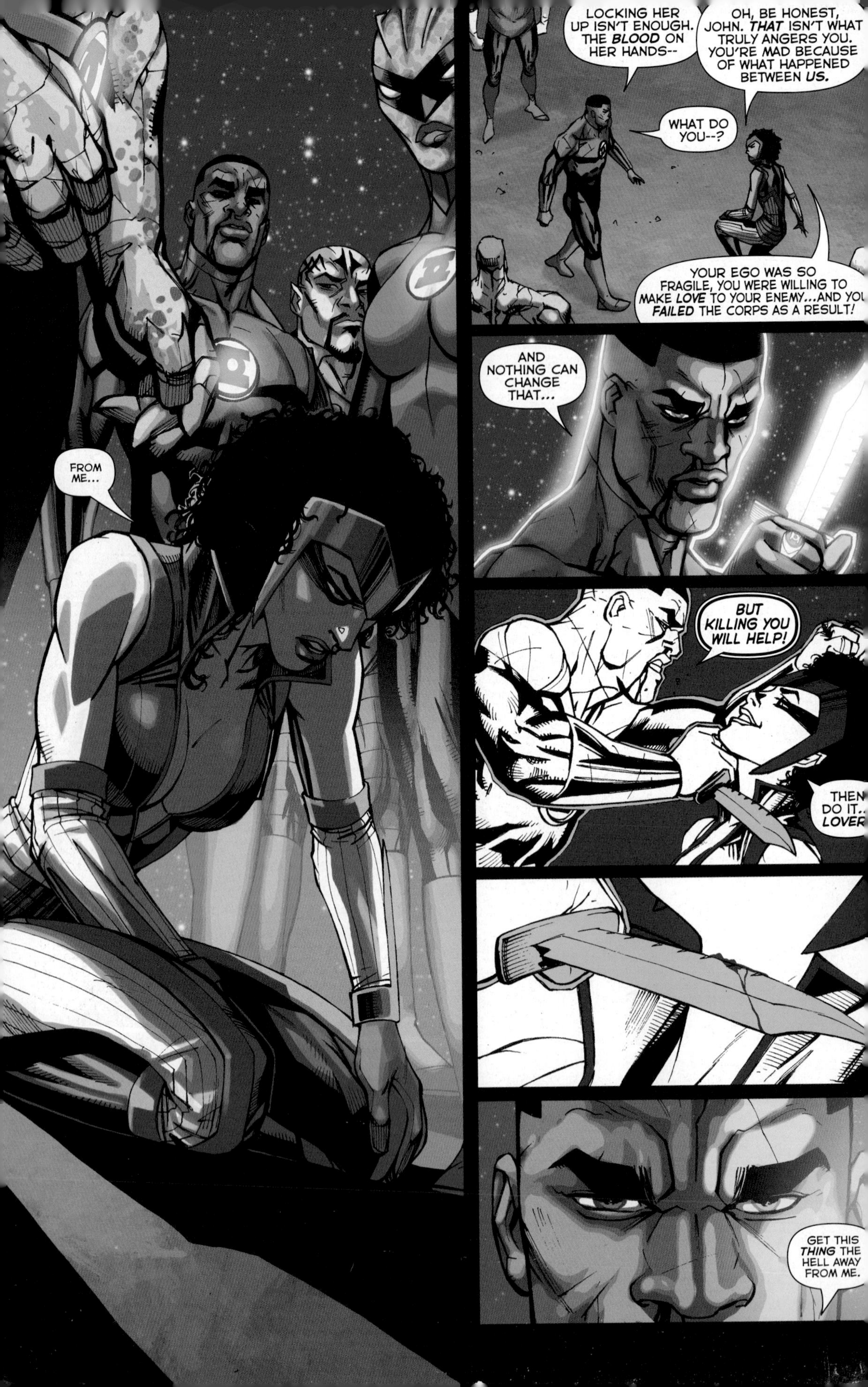
FROM ME...
LOCKING HER UP ISN'T ENOUGH. THE BLOOD ON HER HANDS--
OH, BE HONEST, JOHN. THAT ISN'T WHAT TRULY ANGERS YOU. YOU'RE MAD BECAUSE OF WHAT HAPPENED BETWEEN US.
WHAT DO YOU--?
YOUR EGO WAS SO FRAGILE, YOU WERE WILLING TO MAKE LOVE TO YOUR ENEMY...AND YOU FAILED THE CORPS AS A RESULT!
AND NOTHING CAN CHANGE THAT...
BUT KILLING YOU WILL HELP!
THEN DO IT... LOVER
GET THIS THING THE HELL AWAY FROM ME.

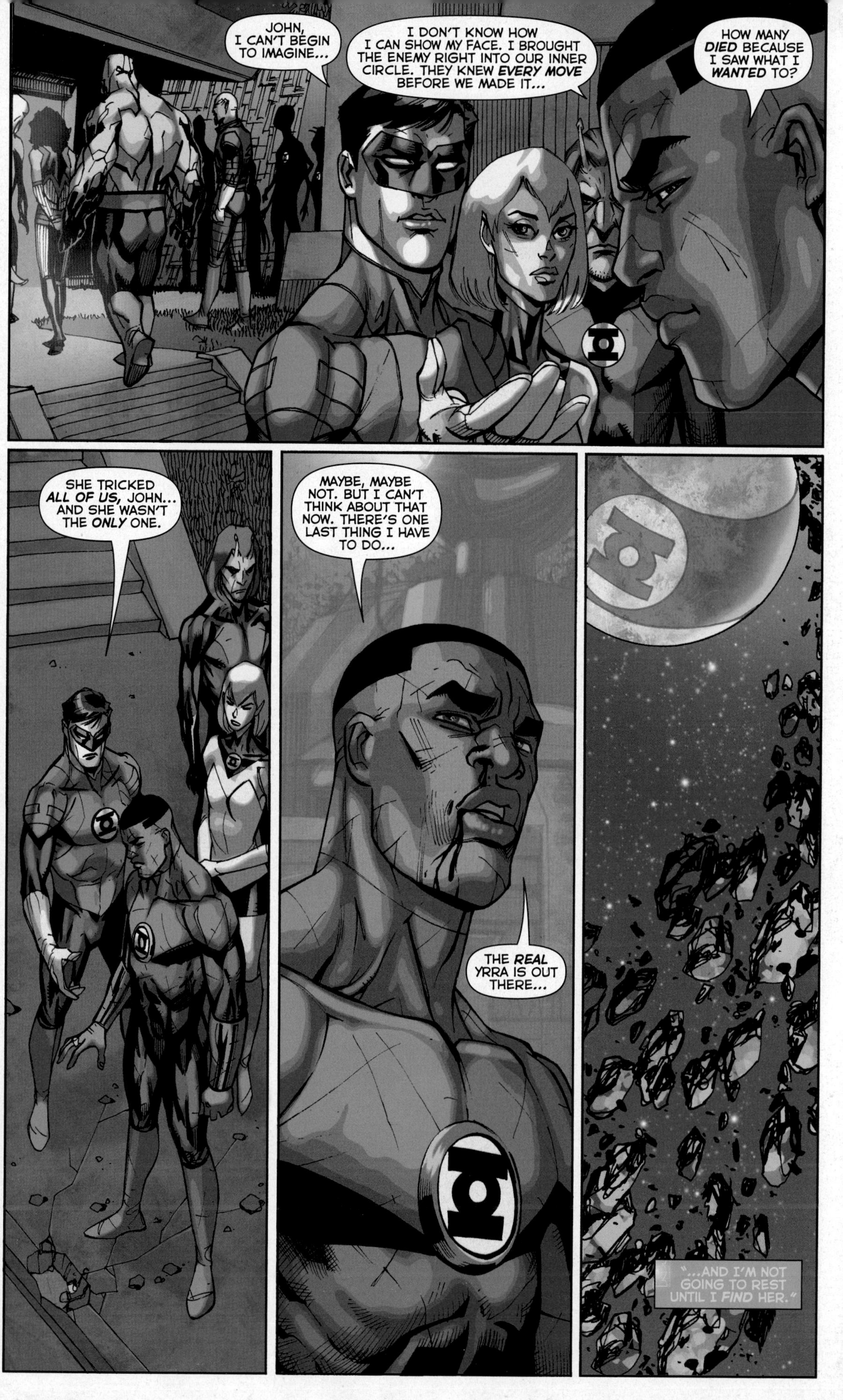
JOHN, I CAN'T BEGIN TO IMAGINE...
I DON'T KNOW HOW I CAN SHOW MY FACE. I BROUGHT THE ENEMY RIGHT INTO OUR INNER CIRCLE. THEY KNEW EVERY MOVE BEFORE WE MADE IT...
HOW MANY DIED BECAUSE I SAW WHAT I WANTED TO?
SHE TRICKED ALL OF US, JOHN... AND SHE WASN'T THE ONLY ONE.
MAYBE, MAYBE NOT. BUT I CAN'T THINK ABOUT THAT NOW. THERE'S ONE LAST THING I HAVE TO DO...
THE REAL YRRA IS OUT THERE...
"...AND I'M NOT GOING TO REST UNTIL I FIND HER."

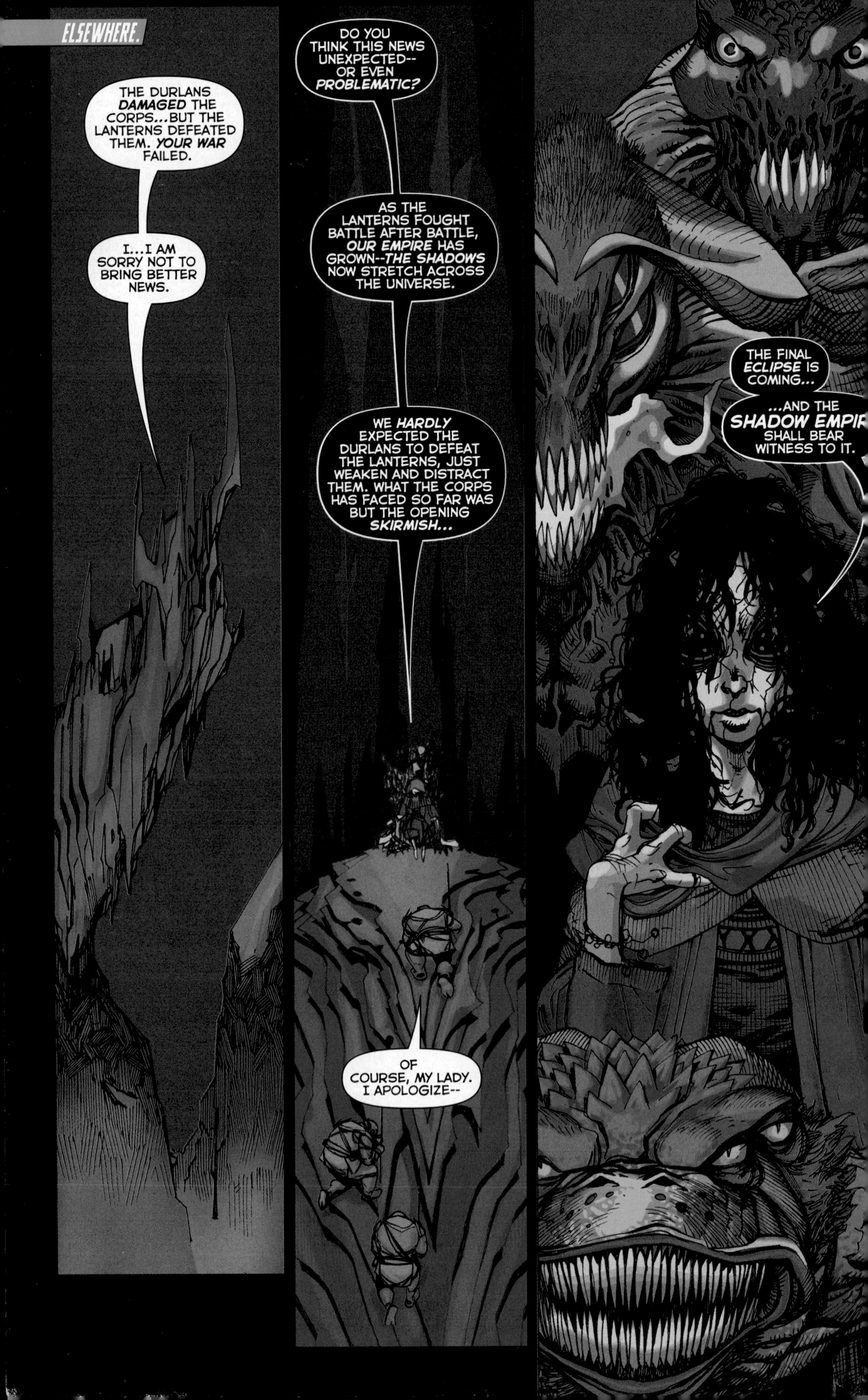
ELSEWHERE.
THE DURLANS DAMAGED THE CORPS...BUT THE LANTERNS DEFEATED THEM. YOUR WAR FAILED.
I...I AM SORRY NOT TO BRING BETTER NEWS.
DO YOU THINK THIS NEWS UNEXPECTED-- OR EVEN PROBLEMATIC?
AS THE LANTERNS FOUGHT BATTLE AFTER BATTLE, OUR EMPIRE HAS GROWN--THE SHADOWS NOW STRETCH ACROSS THE UNIVERSE.
WE HARDLY EXPECTED THE DURLANS TO DEFEAT THE LANTERNS, JUST WEAKEN AND DISTRACT THEM. WHAT THE CORPS HAS FACED SO FAR WAS BUT THE OPENING SKIRMISH...
OF COURSE, MY LADY. I APOLOGIZE--
THE FINAL ECLIPSE IS COMING...
...AND THE SHADOW EMPIR
SHALL BEAR WITNESS TO IT.

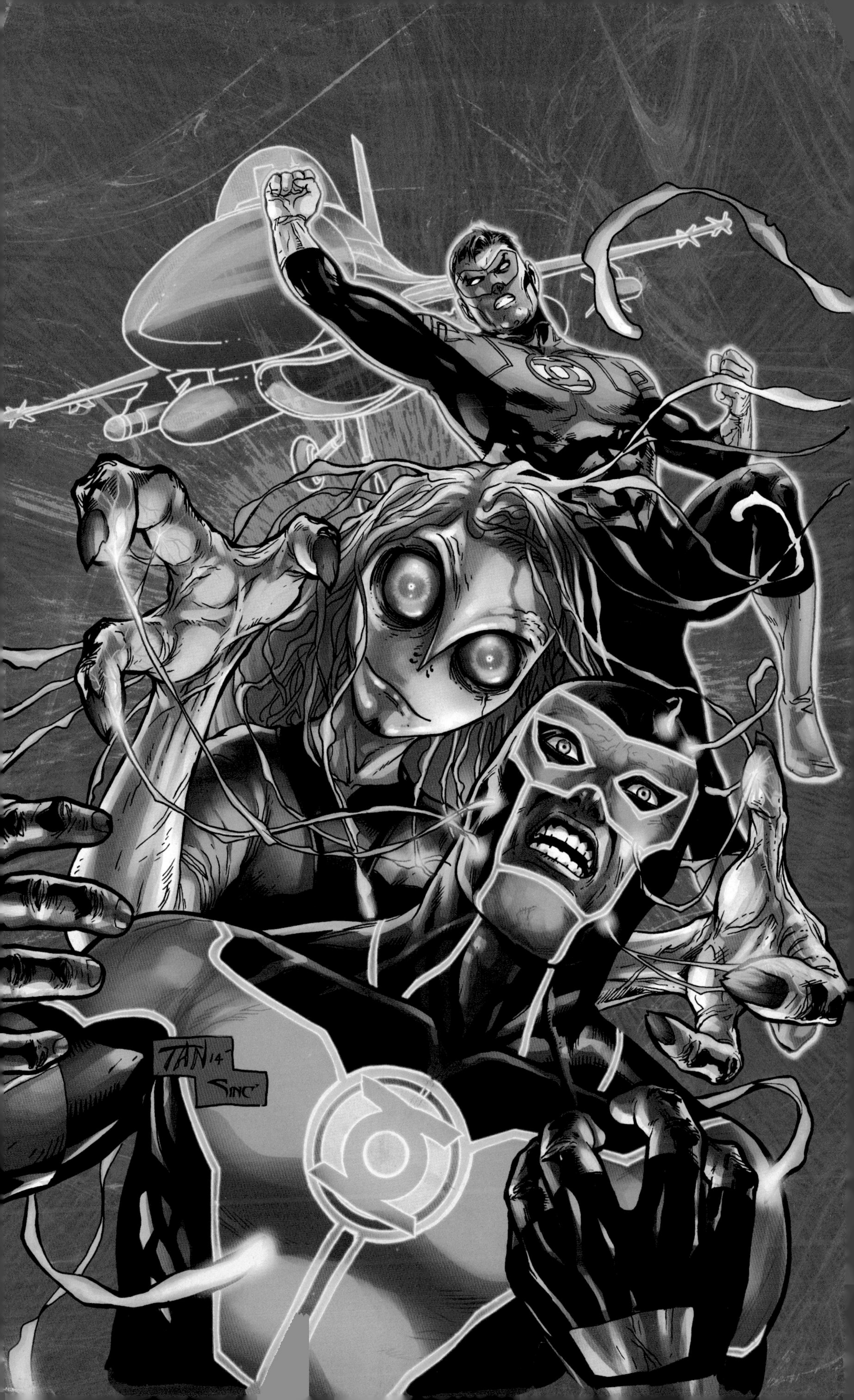
TAN '14
SINC

INCURSION

ROBERT VENDITTI writer **BILLY TAN** & **MARTIN COCCOLO** pencillers **MARTIN COCCOLO** & **ROB HUNTER** inkers **ALEX SINCLAIR** colorist
cover art by **BILLY TAN** & **ALEX SINCLAIR** **SELFIE** variant cover by **CRAIG ROUSSEAU** & **DAVE McCAIG**

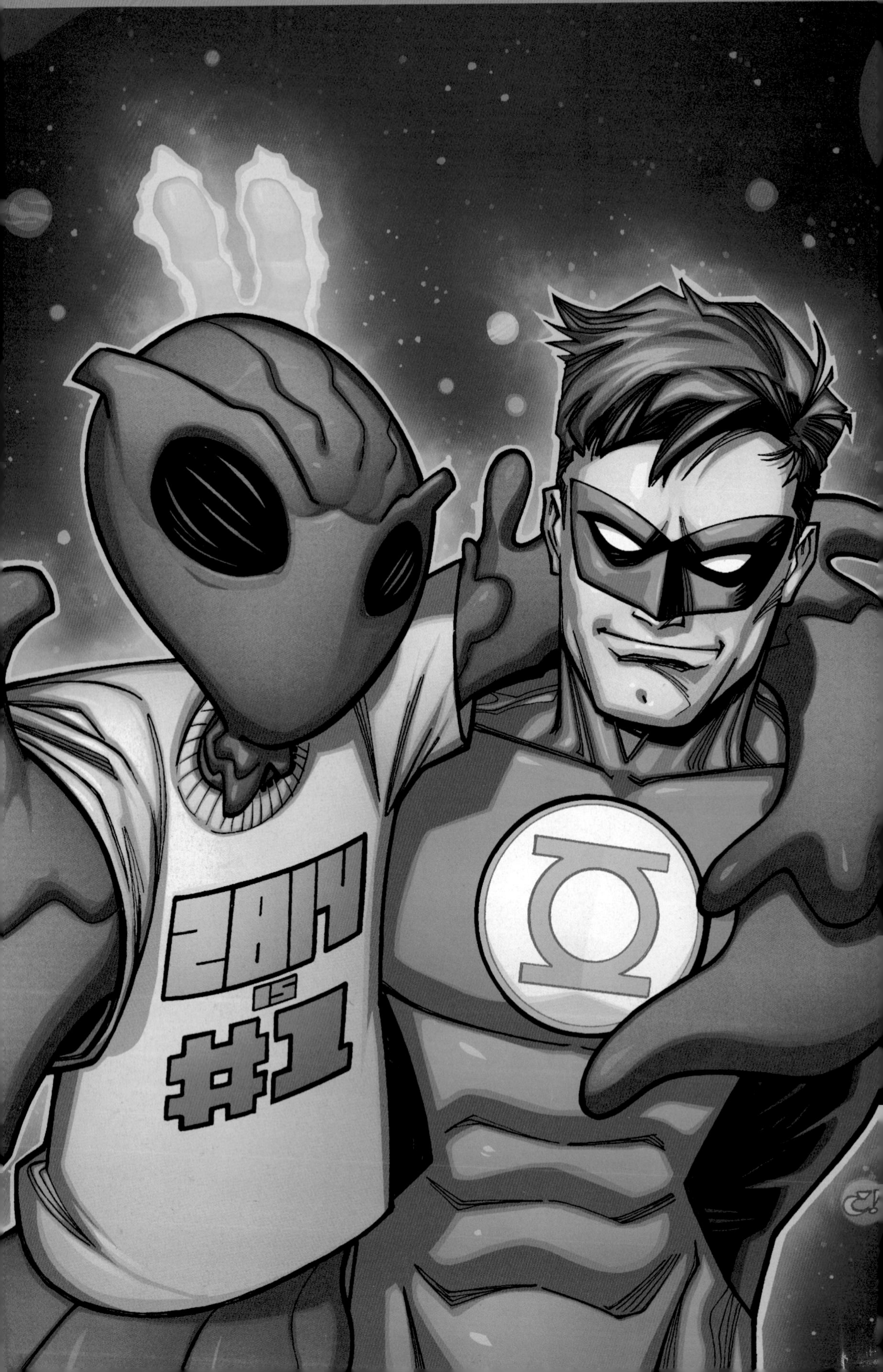

ZAIN IS #1

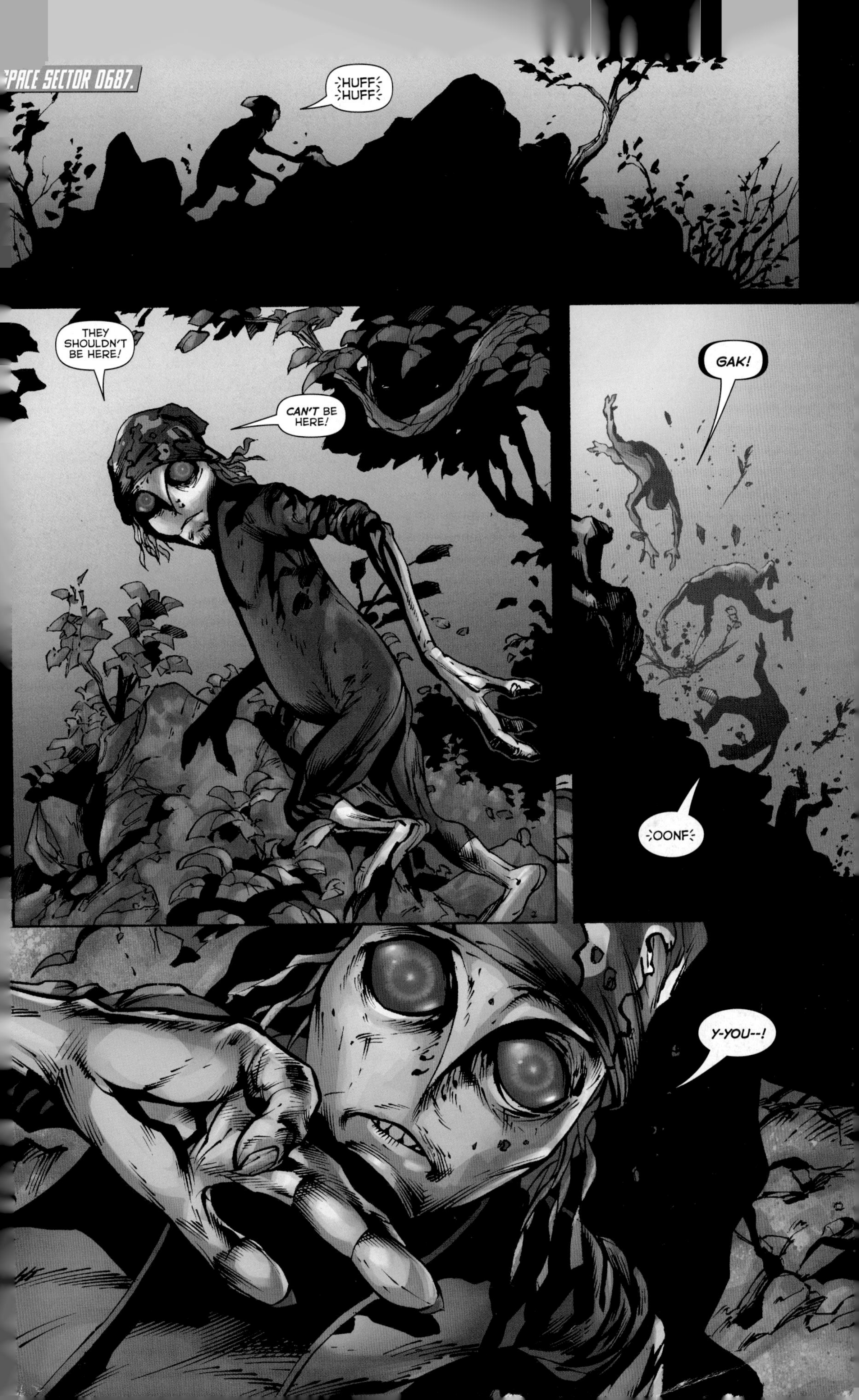
PACE SECTOR 0687.
HUFF HUFF
THEY SHOULDN'T BE HERE!
CAN'T BE HERE!
GAK!
OONF
Y-YOU--!

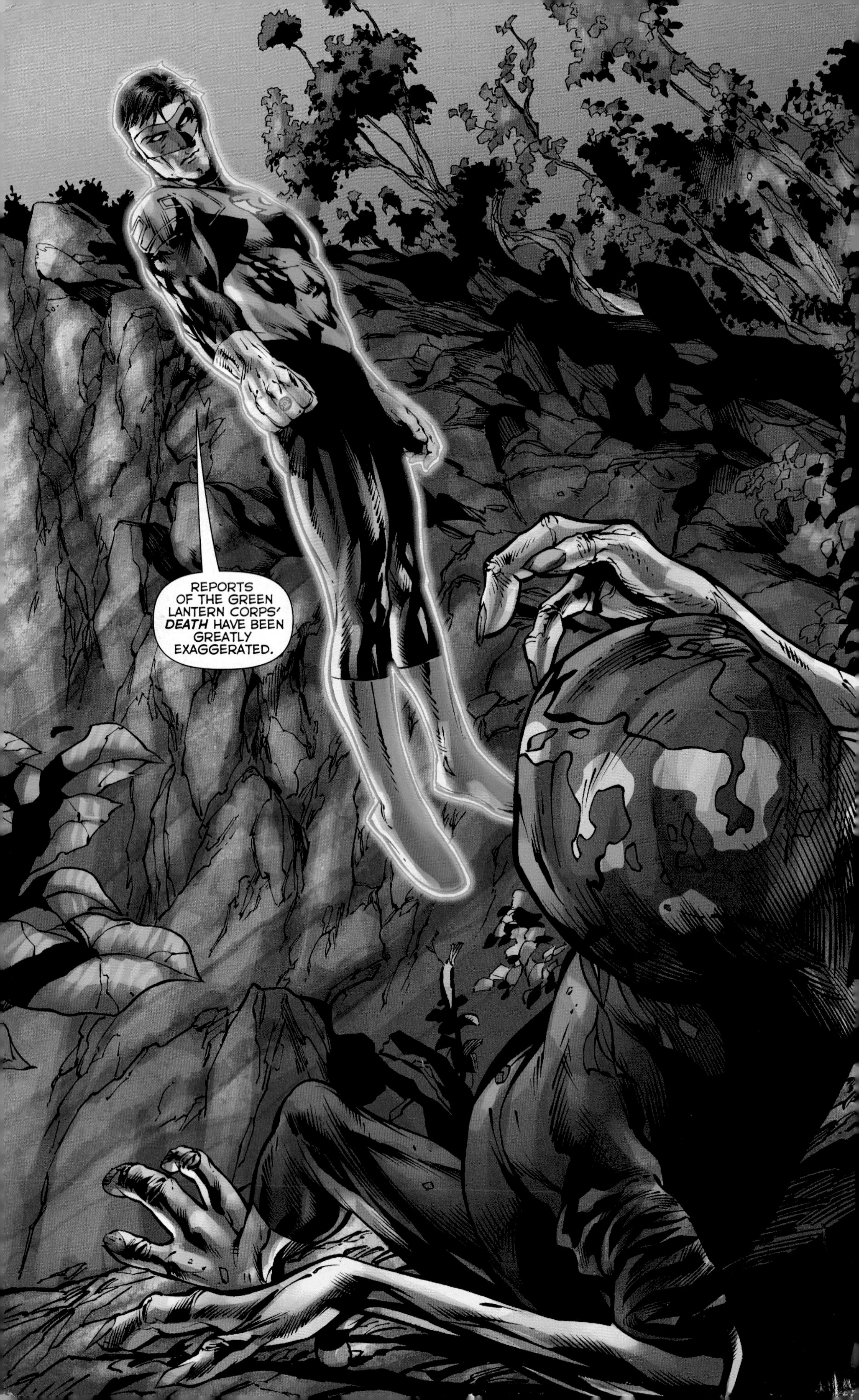
REPORTS OF THE GREEN LANTERN CORPS' *DEATH* HAVE BEEN GREATLY EXAGGERATED.

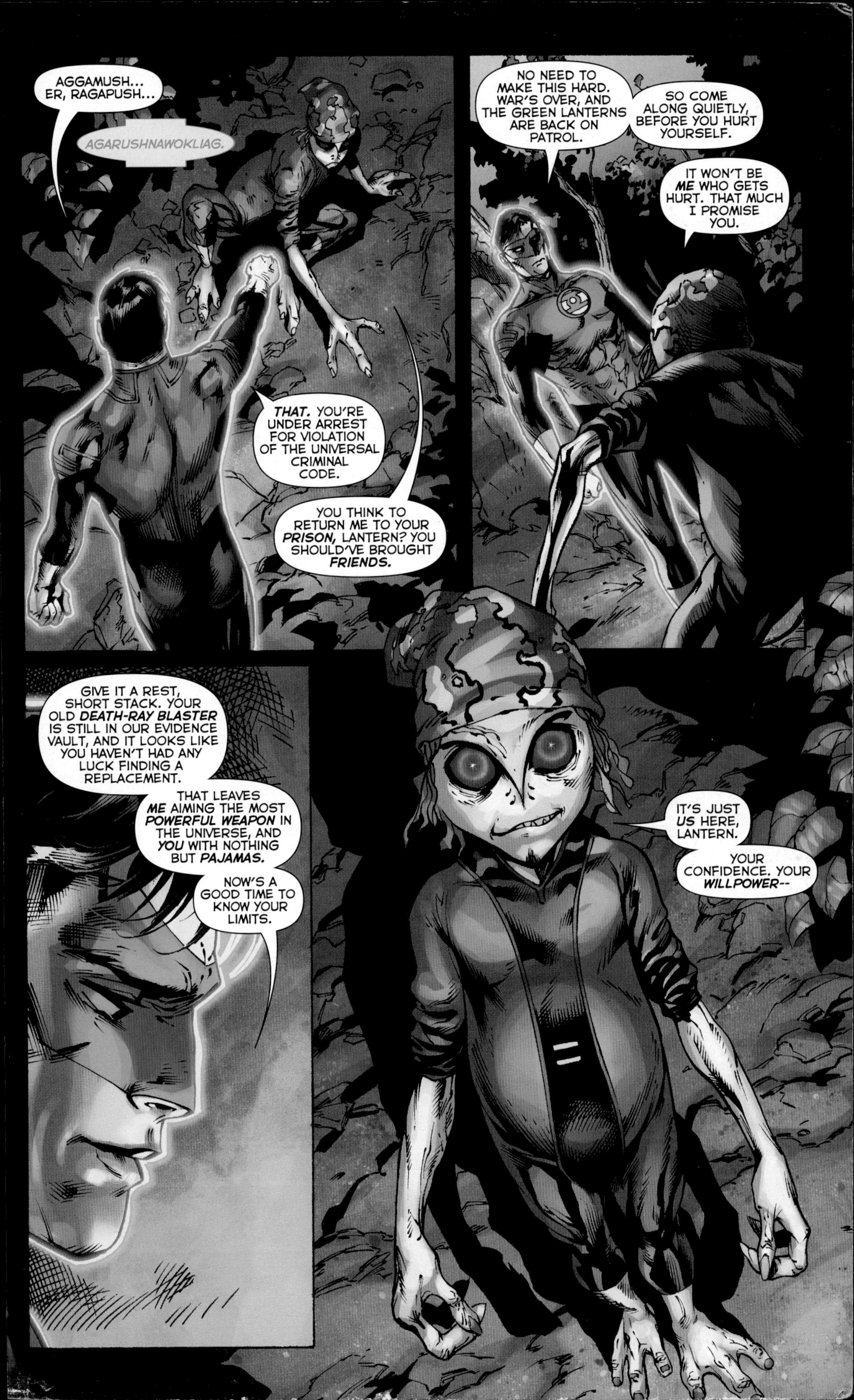
AGGAMUSH... ER, RAGAPUSH...
AGARUSHNAWOKLIAG.
THAT. YOU'RE UNDER ARREST FOR VIOLATION OF THE UNIVERSAL CRIMINAL CODE.
YOU THINK TO RETURN ME TO YOUR PRISON, LANTERN? YOU SHOULD'VE BROUGHT FRIENDS.
NO NEED TO MAKE THIS HARD. WAR'S OVER, AND THE GREEN LANTERNS ARE BACK ON PATROL.
SO COME ALONG QUIETLY, BEFORE YOU HURT YOURSELF.
IT WON'T BE ME WHO GETS HURT. THAT MUCH I PROMISE YOU.
GIVE IT A REST, SHORT STACK. YOUR OLD DEATH-RAY BLASTER IS STILL IN OUR EVIDENCE VAULT, AND IT LOOKS LIKE YOU HAVEN'T HAD ANY LUCK FINDING A REPLACEMENT.
THAT LEAVES ME AIMING THE MOST POWERFUL WEAPON IN THE UNIVERSE, AND YOU WITH NOTHING BUT PAJAMAS.
NOW'S A GOOD TIME TO KNOW YOUR LIMITS.
IT'S JUST US HERE, LANTERN.
YOUR CONFIDENCE. YOUR WILLPOWER--

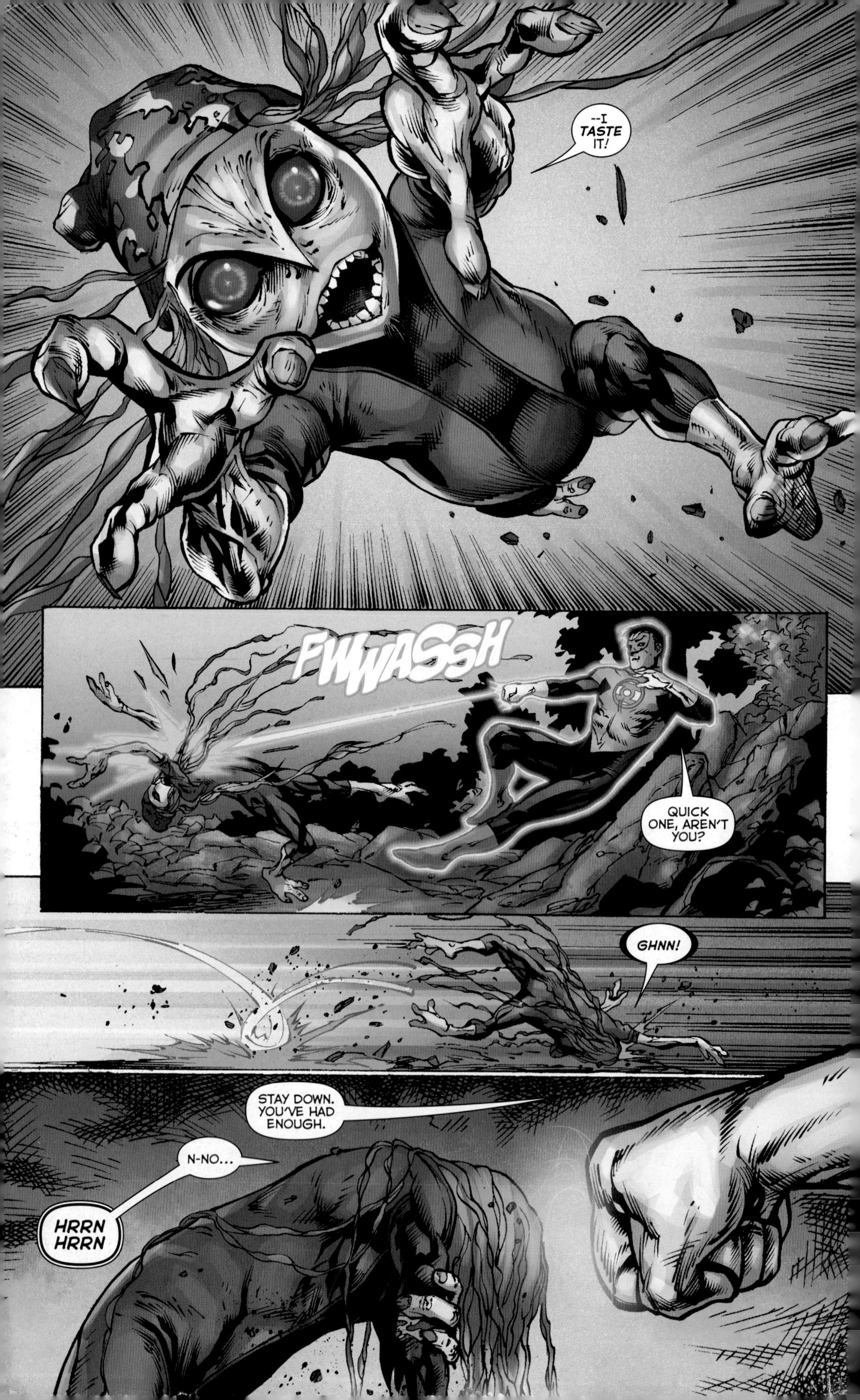
--I TASTE IT!
FWWASSH
QUICK ONE, AREN'T YOU?
GHNN!
STAY DOWN. YOU'VE HAD ENOUGH.
N-NO...
HRRN HRRN

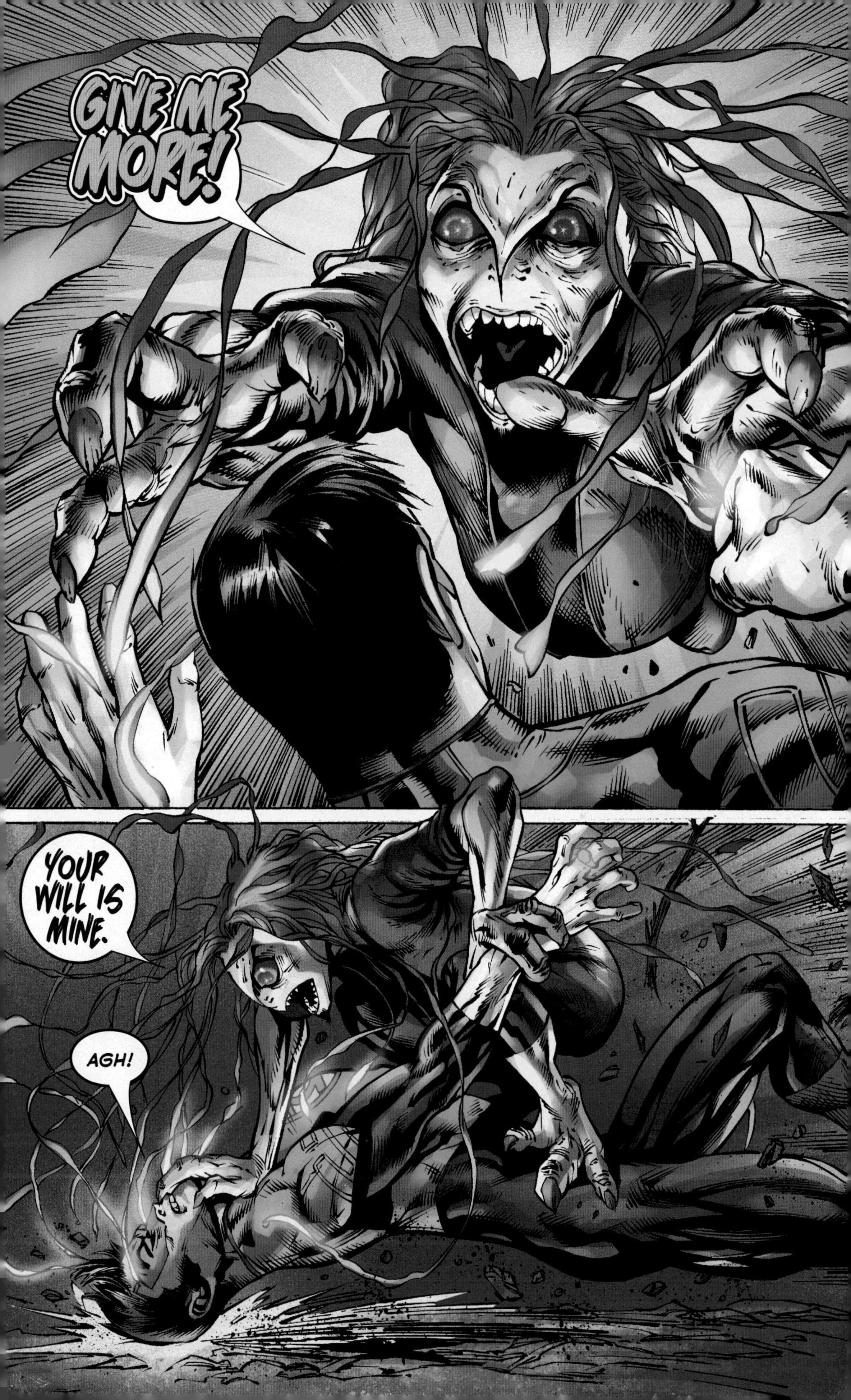
GIVE ME MORE!
YOUR WILL IS MINE.
AGH!

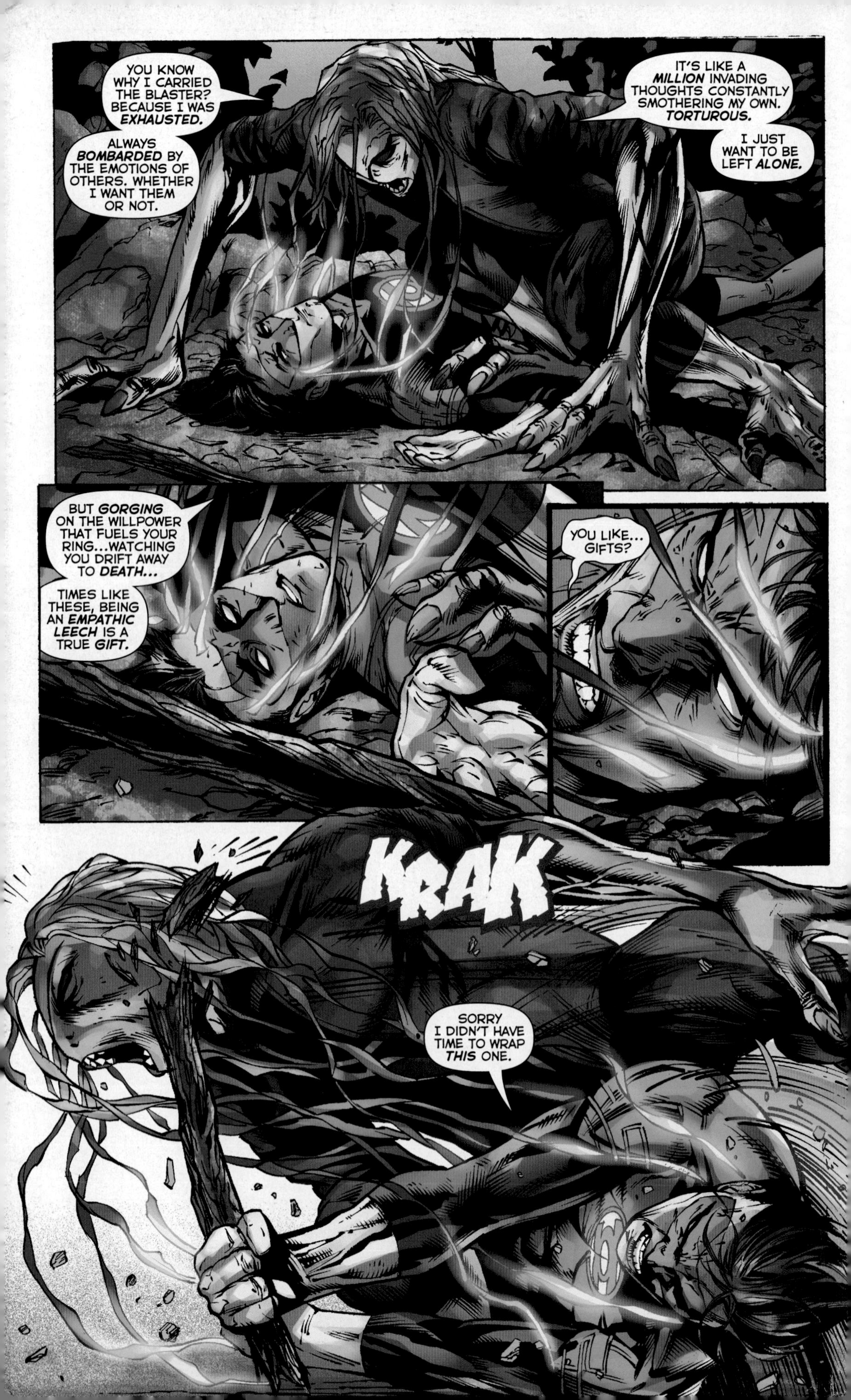
YOU KNOW WHY I CARRIED THE BLASTER? BECAUSE I WAS EXHAUSTED.
ALWAYS BOMBARDED BY THE EMOTIONS OF OTHERS. WHETHER I WANT THEM OR NOT.
IT'S LIKE A MILLION INVADING THOUGHTS CONSTANTLY SMOTHERING MY OWN. TORTUROUS.
I JUST WANT TO BE LEFT ALONE.
BUT GORGING ON THE WILLPOWER THAT FUELS YOUR RING...WATCHING YOU DRIFT AWAY TO DEATH...
TIMES LIKE THESE, BEING AN EMPATHIC LEECH IS A TRUE GIFT.
YOU LIKE... GIFTS?
KRAK
SORRY I DIDN'T HAVE TIME TO WRAP THIS ONE.

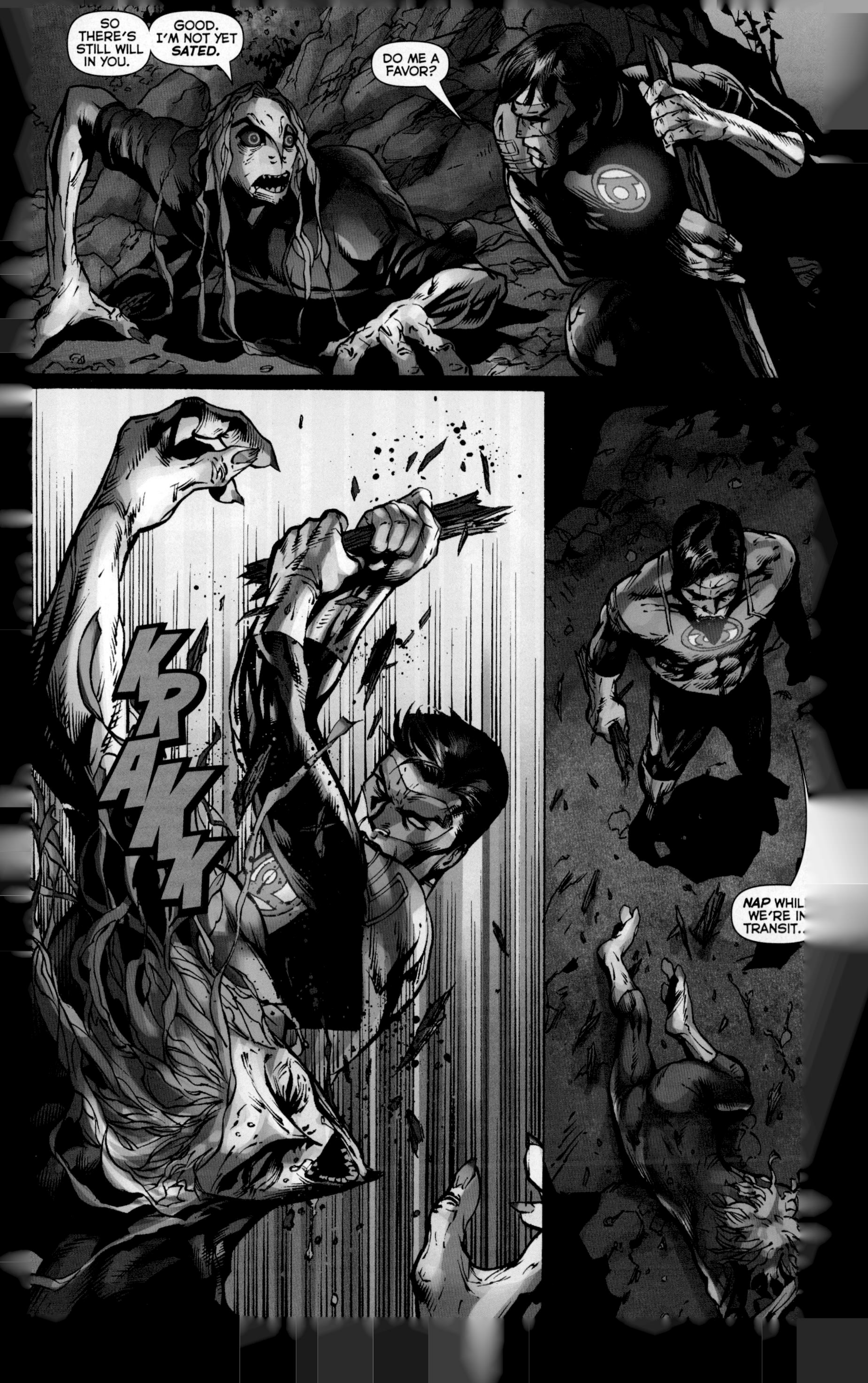
SO THERE'S STILL WILL IN YOU.
GOOD. I'M NOT YET SATED.
DO ME A FAVOR?
KRAKK
NAP WHIL WE'RE IN TRANSIT...

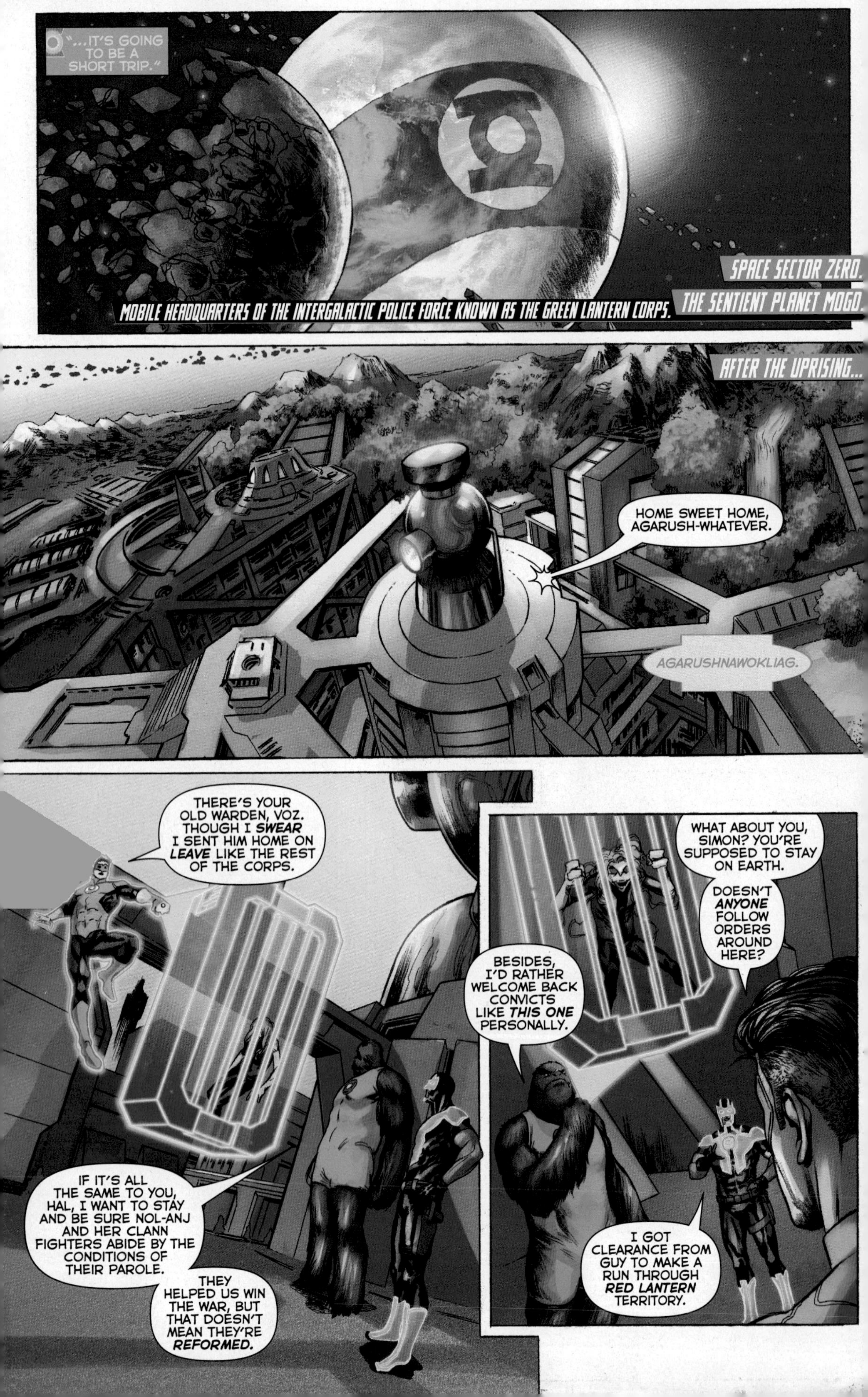
"...IT'S GOING TO BE A SHORT TRIP."
SPACE SECTOR ZERO.
THE SENTIENT PLANET MOGO.
MOBILE HEADQUARTERS OF THE INTERGALACTIC POLICE FORCE KNOWN AS THE GREEN LANTERN CORPS.
AFTER THE UPRISING...
HOME SWEET HOME, AGARUSH-WHATEVER.
AGARUSHNAWOKLIAG.
THERE'S YOUR OLD WARDEN, VOZ. THOUGH I SWEAR I SENT HIM HOME ON LEAVE LIKE THE REST OF THE CORPS.
IF IT'S ALL THE SAME TO YOU, HAL, I WANT TO STAY AND BE SURE NOL-ANJ AND HER CLANN FIGHTERS ABIDE BY THE CONDITIONS OF THEIR PAROLE.
THEY HELPED US WIN THE WAR, BUT THAT DOESN'T MEAN THEY'RE REFORMED.
BESIDES, I'D RATHER WELCOME BACK CONVICTS LIKE THIS ONE PERSONALLY.
WHAT ABOUT YOU, SIMON? YOU'RE SUPPOSED TO STAY ON EARTH.
DOESN'T ANYONE FOLLOW ORDERS AROUND HERE?
I GOT CLEARANCE FROM GUY TO MAKE A RUN THROUGH RED LANTERN TERRITORY.

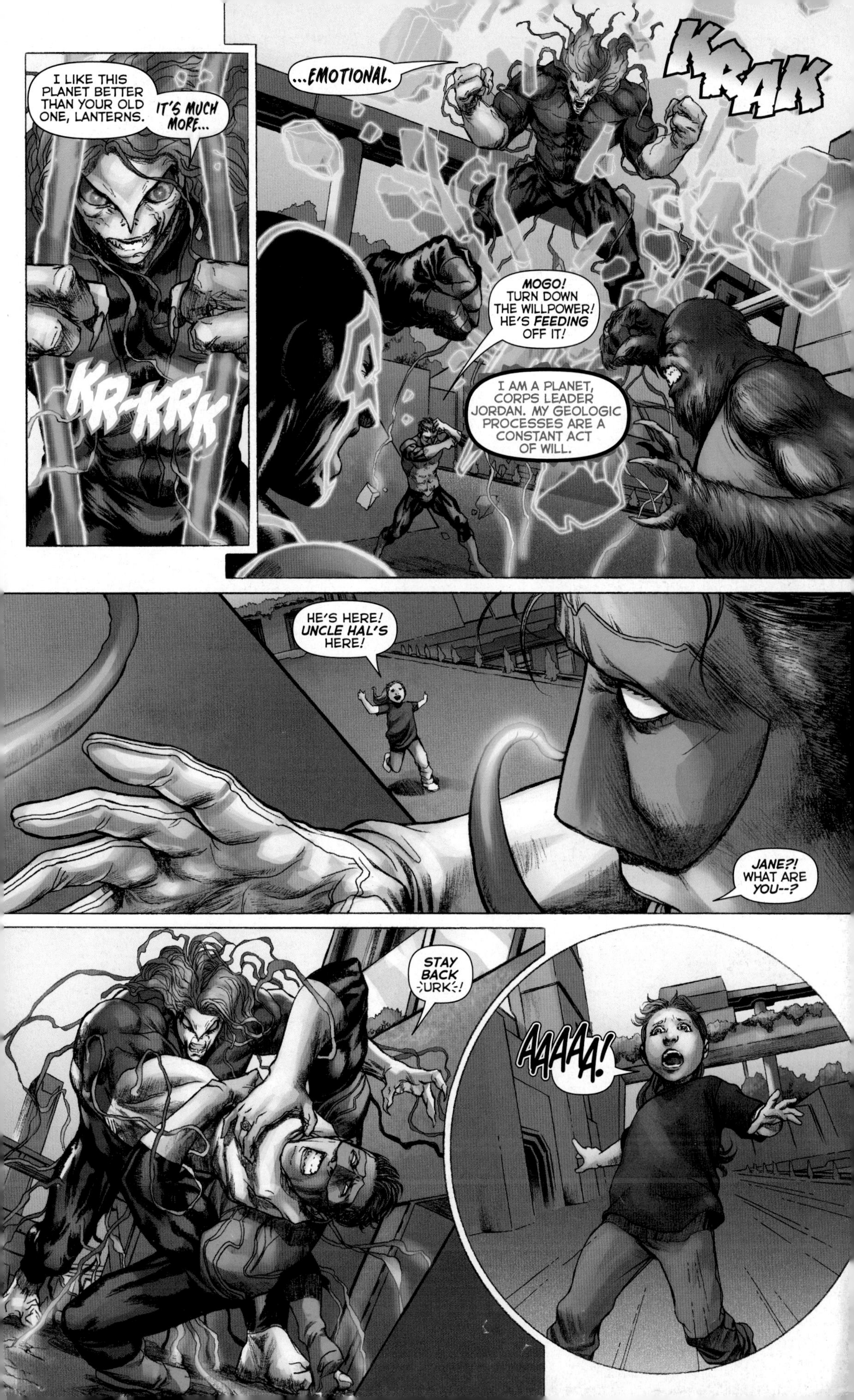
I LIKE THIS PLANET BETTER THAN YOUR OLD ONE, LANTERNS.
IT'S MUCH MORE...
KR-KRK
...EMOTIONAL.
KRAK
MOGO! TURN DOWN THE WILLPOWER! HE'S FEEDING OFF IT!
I AM A PLANET, CORPS LEADER JORDAN. MY GEOLOGIC PROCESSES ARE A CONSTANT ACT OF WILL.
HE'S HERE! UNCLE HAL'S HERE!
JANE?! WHAT ARE YOU--?
STAY BACK -URK-!
AAAAA!

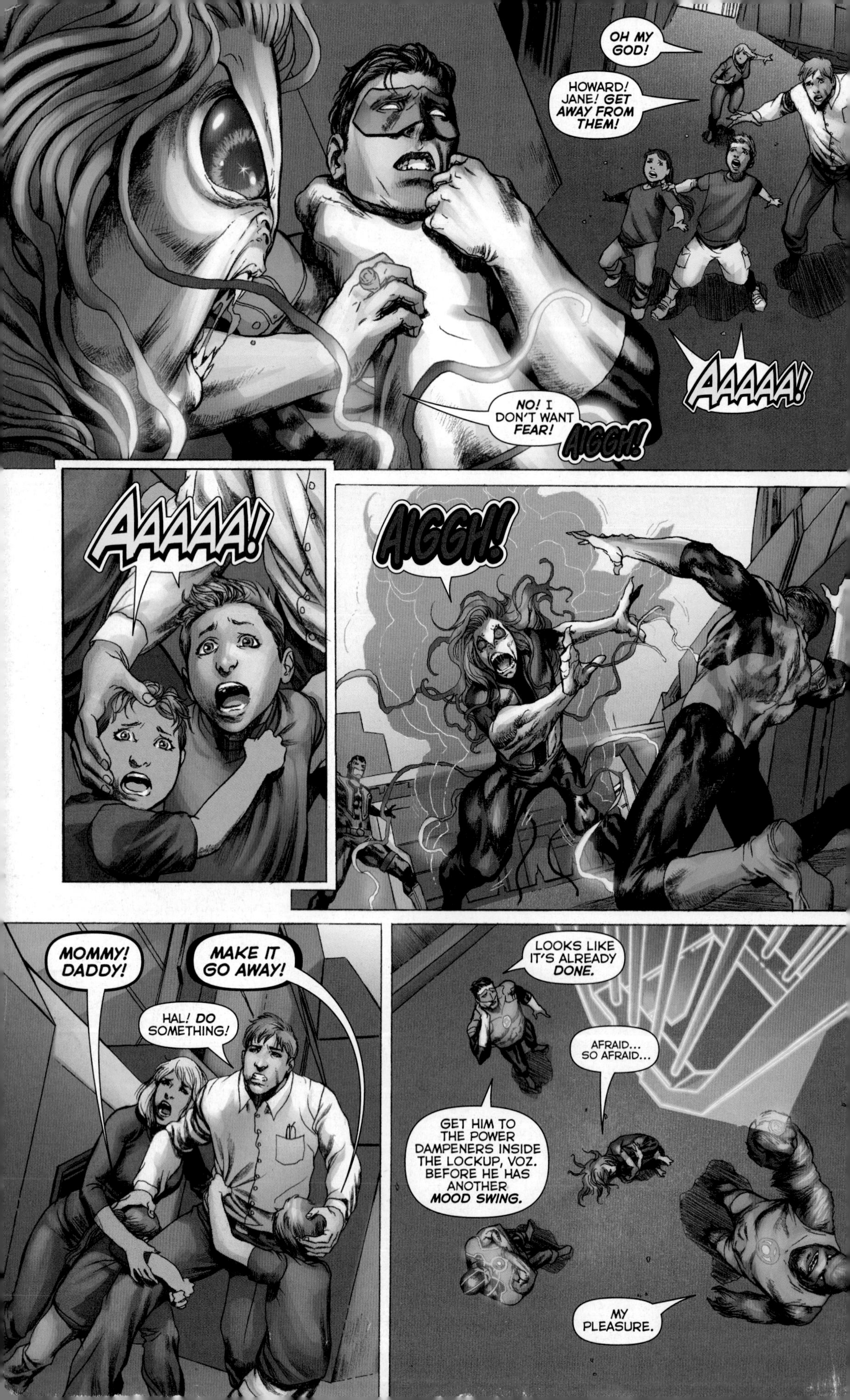

OH MY GOD!
HOWARD! JANE! GET AWAY FROM THEM!
AAAAA!
NO! I DON'T WANT FEAR!
AIGGH!
AAAAA!
AIGGH!
MOMMY! DADDY!
MAKE IT GO AWAY!
HAL! DO SOMETHING!
LOOKS LIKE IT'S ALREADY DONE.
AFRAID... SO AFRAID...
GET HIM TO THE POWER DAMPENERS INSIDE THE LOCKUP, VOZ. BEFORE HE HAS ANOTHER MOOD SWING.
MY PLEASURE.

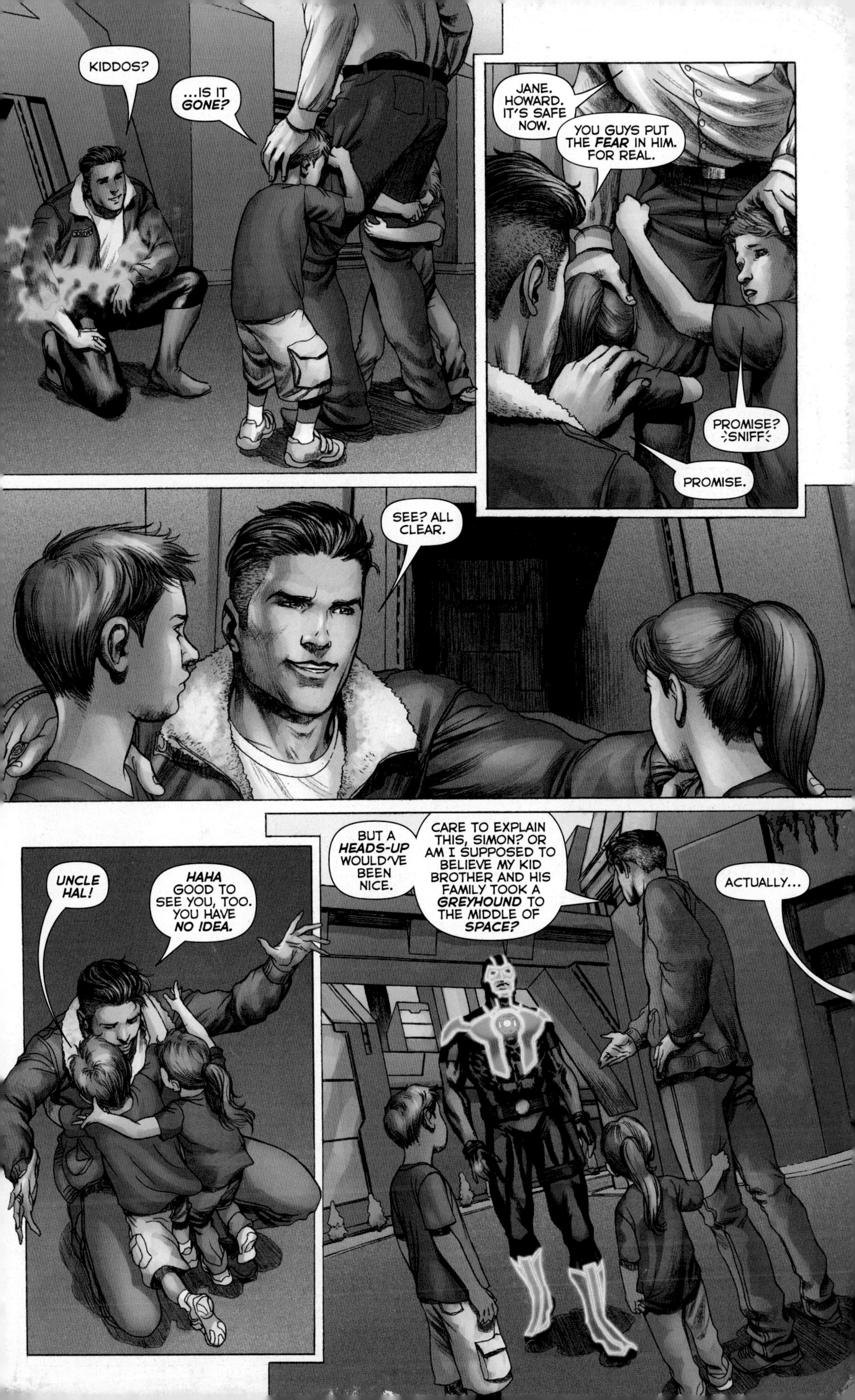
KIDDOS?
...IS IT *GONE?*
JANE. HOWARD. IT'S SAFE NOW.
YOU GUYS PUT THE *FEAR* IN HIM. FOR REAL.
PROMISE? *SNIFF*
PROMISE.
SEE? ALL CLEAR.
UNCLE HAL!
HAHA GOOD TO SEE YOU, TOO. YOU HAVE *NO IDEA.*
BUT A *HEADS-UP* WOULD'VE BEEN NICE.
CARE TO EXPLAIN THIS, SIMON? OR AM I SUPPOSED TO BELIEVE MY KID BROTHER AND HIS FAMILY TOOK A *GREYHOUND* TO THE MIDDLE OF *SPACE?*
ACTUALLY...

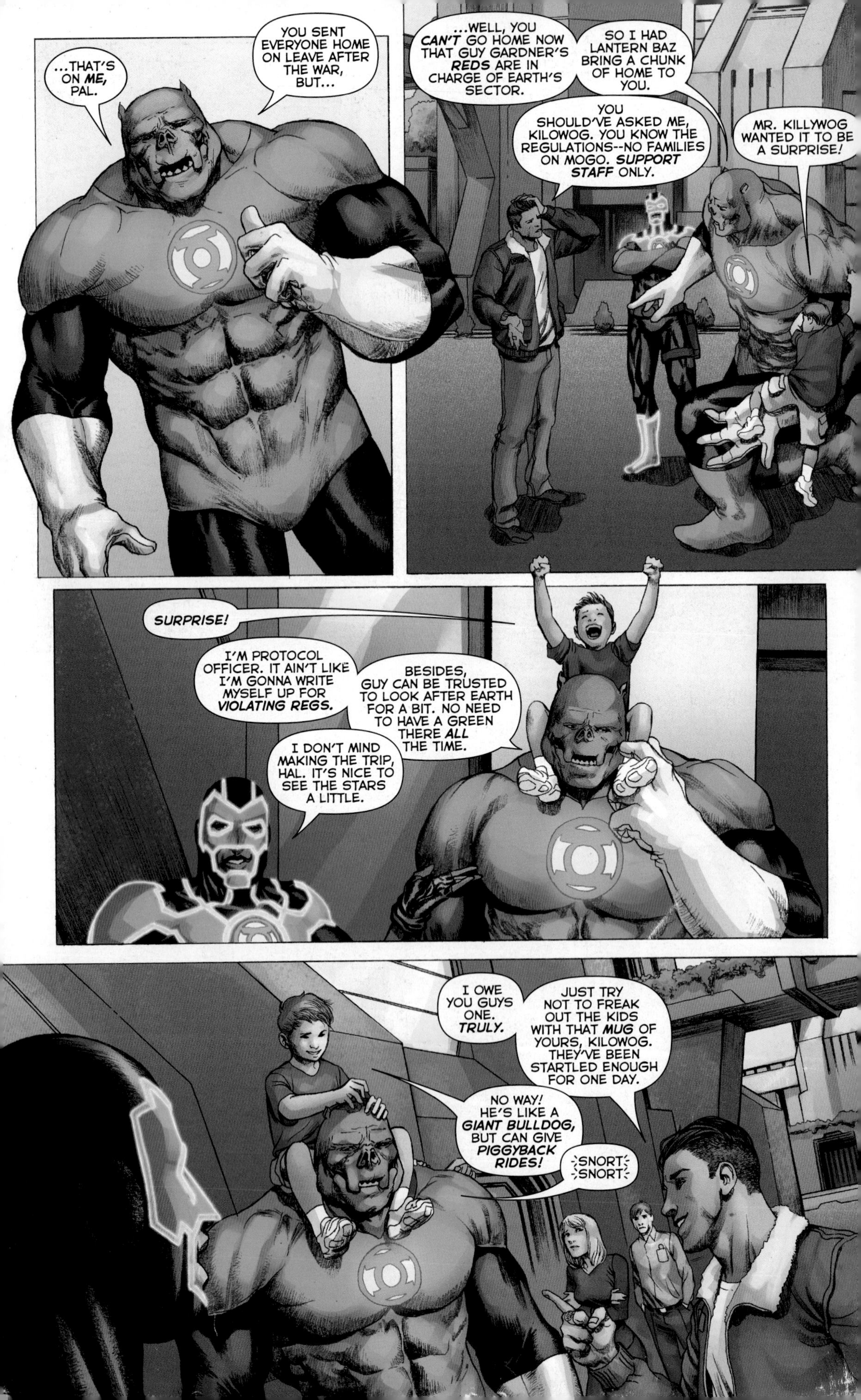
...THAT'S ON *ME*, PAL.
YOU SENT EVERYONE HOME ON LEAVE AFTER THE WAR, BUT...
...WELL, YOU *CAN'T* GO HOME NOW THAT GUY GARDNER'S *REDS* ARE IN CHARGE OF EARTH'S SECTOR.
SO I HAD LANTERN BAZ BRING A CHUNK OF HOME TO YOU.
YOU SHOULD'VE ASKED ME, KILOWOG. YOU KNOW THE REGULATIONS--NO FAMILIES ON MOGO. *SUPPORT STAFF* ONLY.
MR. KILLYWOG WANTED IT TO BE A SURPRISE!
SURPRISE!
I'M PROTOCOL OFFICER. IT AIN'T LIKE I'M GONNA WRITE MYSELF UP FOR *VIOLATING REGS.*
BESIDES, GUY CAN BE TRUSTED TO LOOK AFTER EARTH FOR A BIT. NO NEED TO HAVE A GREEN THERE *ALL* THE TIME.
I DON'T MIND MAKING THE TRIP, HAL. IT'S NICE TO SEE THE STARS A LITTLE.
I OWE YOU GUYS ONE. *TRULY.*
JUST TRY NOT TO FREAK OUT THE KIDS WITH THAT *MUG* OF YOURS, KILOWOG. THEY'VE BEEN STARTLED ENOUGH FOR ONE DAY.
NO WAY! HE'S LIKE A *GIANT BULLDOG,* BUT CAN GIVE *PIGGYBACK RIDES!*
SNORT SNORT

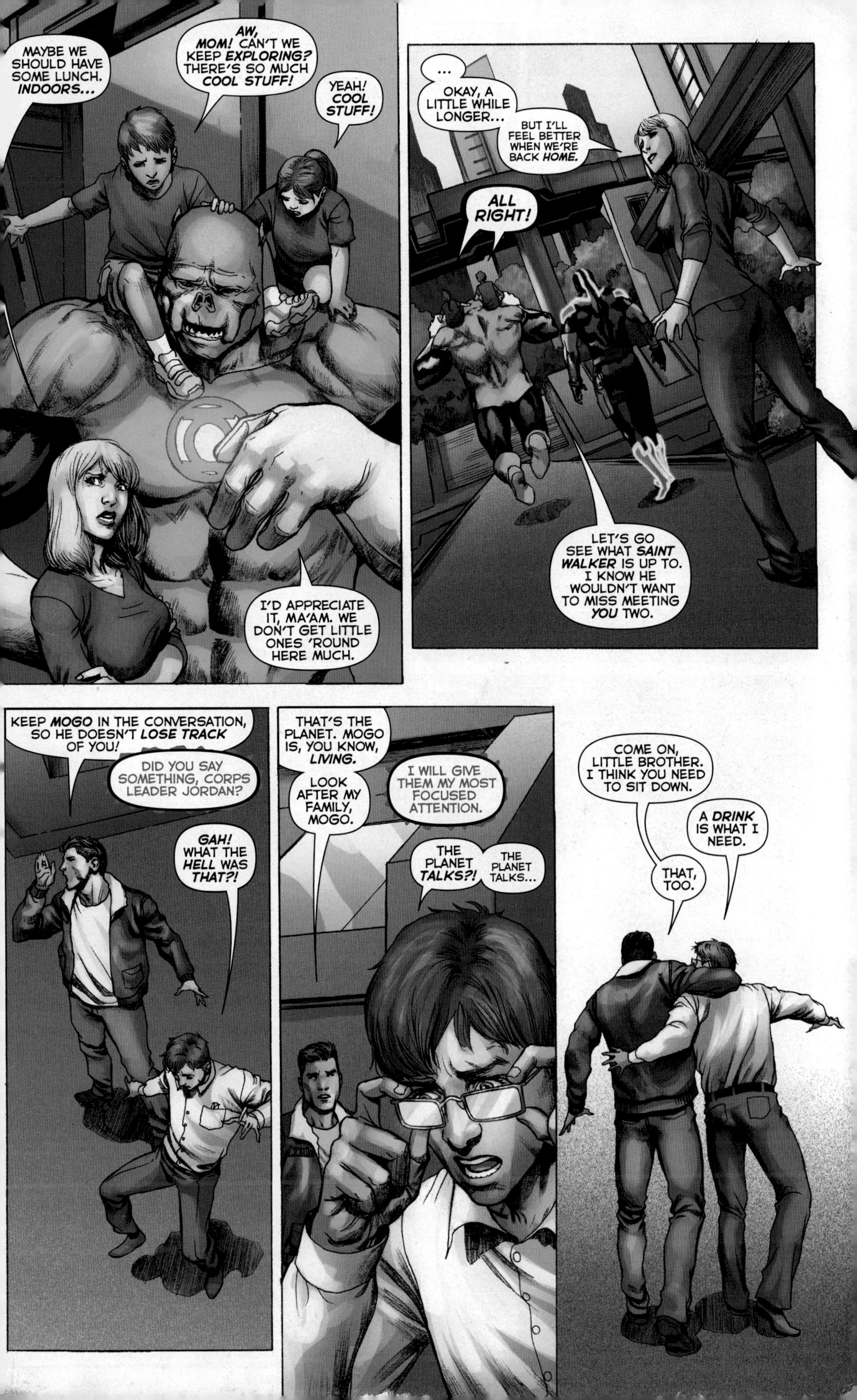
MAYBE WE SHOULD HAVE SOME LUNCH. *INDOORS...*
AW, MOM! CAN'T WE KEEP *EXPLORING?* THERE'S SO MUCH *COOL STUFF!*
YEAH! *COOL STUFF!*
I'D APPRECIATE IT, MA'AM. WE DON'T GET LITTLE ONES 'ROUND HERE MUCH.
...
OKAY, A LITTLE WHILE LONGER...
BUT I'LL FEEL BETTER WHEN WE'RE BACK *HOME.*
ALL RIGHT!
LET'S GO SEE WHAT *SAINT WALKER* IS UP TO. I KNOW HE WOULDN'T WANT TO MISS MEETING *YOU* TWO.
KEEP *MOGO* IN THE CONVERSATION, SO HE DOESN'T *LOSE TRACK* OF YOU!
DID YOU SAY SOMETHING, CORPS LEADER JORDAN?
GAH! WHAT THE *HELL* WAS *THAT?!*
THAT'S THE PLANET. MOGO IS, YOU KNOW, *LIVING.*
LOOK AFTER MY FAMILY, MOGO.
I WILL GIVE THEM MY MOST FOCUSED ATTENTION.
THE PLANET *TALKS?!*
THE PLANET TALKS...
COME ON, LITTLE BROTHER. I THINK YOU NEED TO SIT DOWN.
A *DRINK* IS WHAT I NEED.
THAT, TOO.

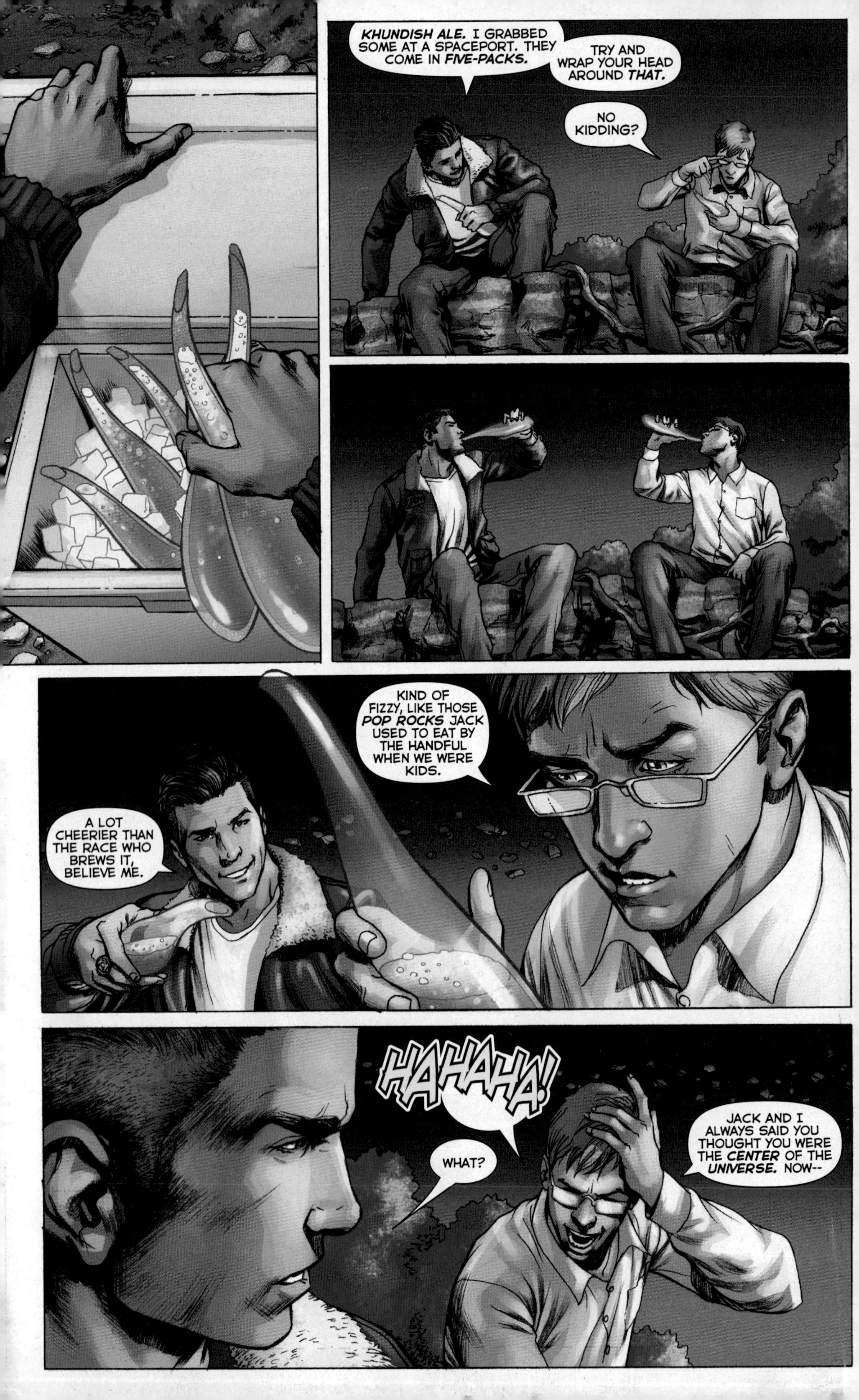
KHUNDISH ALE. I GRABBED SOME AT A SPACEPORT. THEY COME IN FIVE-PACKS.
TRY AND WRAP YOUR HEAD AROUND THAT.
NO KIDDING?
KIND OF FIZZY, LIKE THOSE POP ROCKS JACK USED TO EAT BY THE HANDFUL WHEN WE WERE KIDS.
A LOT CHEERIER THAN THE RACE WHO BREWS IT, BELIEVE ME.
HAHAHA!
WHAT?
JACK AND I ALWAYS SAID YOU THOUGHT YOU WERE THE CENTER OF THE UNIVERSE. NOW--

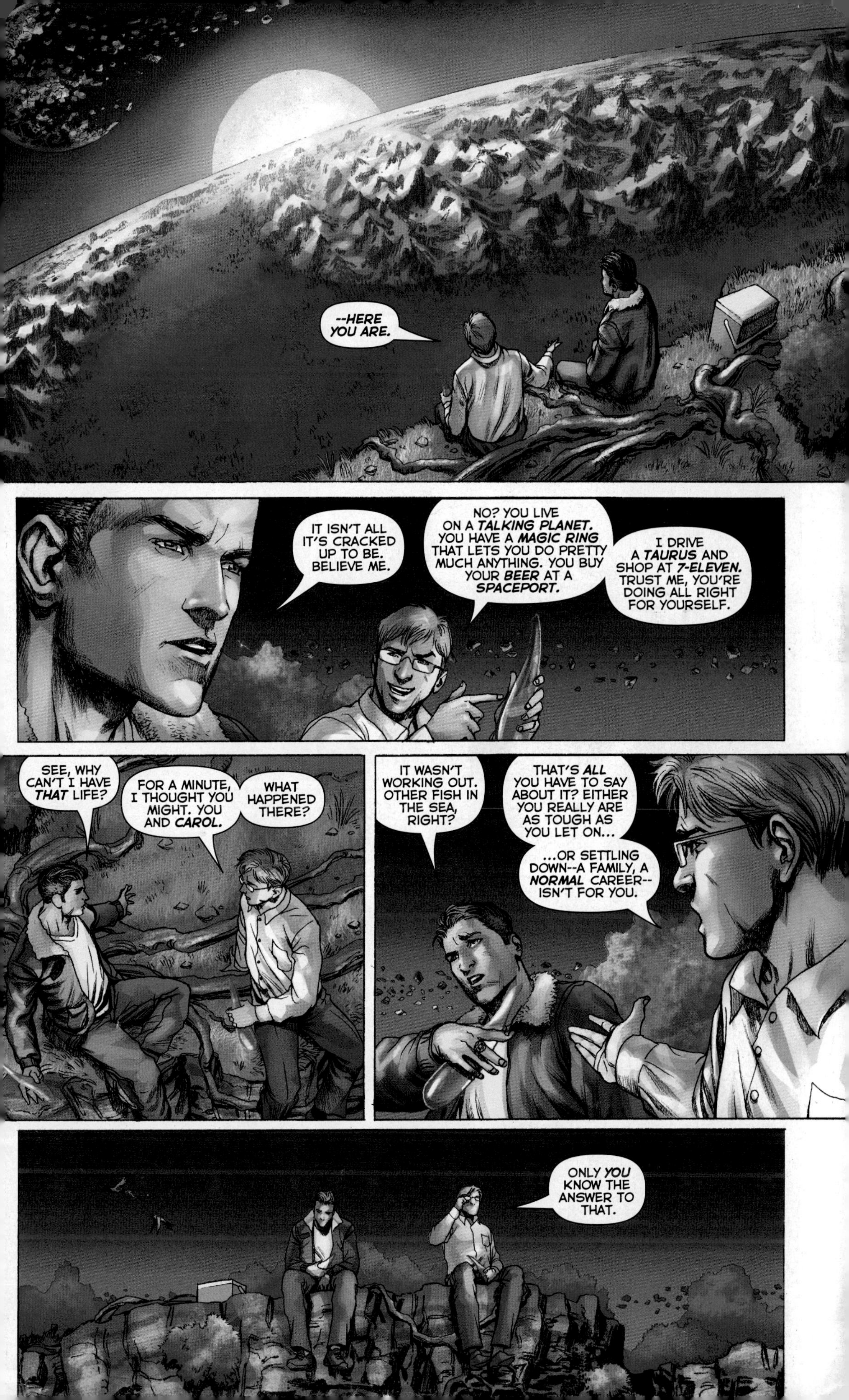
--HERE YOU ARE.
IT ISN'T ALL IT'S CRACKED UP TO BE. BELIEVE ME.
NO? YOU LIVE ON A TALKING PLANET. YOU HAVE A MAGIC RING THAT LETS YOU DO PRETTY MUCH ANYTHING. YOU BUY YOUR BEER AT A SPACEPORT.
I DRIVE A TAURUS AND SHOP AT 7-ELEVEN. TRUST ME, YOU'RE DOING ALL RIGHT FOR YOURSELF.
SEE, WHY CAN'T I HAVE THAT LIFE?
FOR A MINUTE, I THOUGHT YOU MIGHT. YOU AND CAROL.
WHAT HAPPENED THERE?
IT WASN'T WORKING OUT. OTHER FISH IN THE SEA, RIGHT?
THAT'S ALL YOU HAVE TO SAY ABOUT IT? EITHER YOU REALLY ARE AS TOUGH AS YOU LET ON...
...OR SETTLING DOWN--A FAMILY, A NORMAL CAREER--ISN'T FOR YOU.
ONLY YOU KNOW THE ANSWER TO THAT.

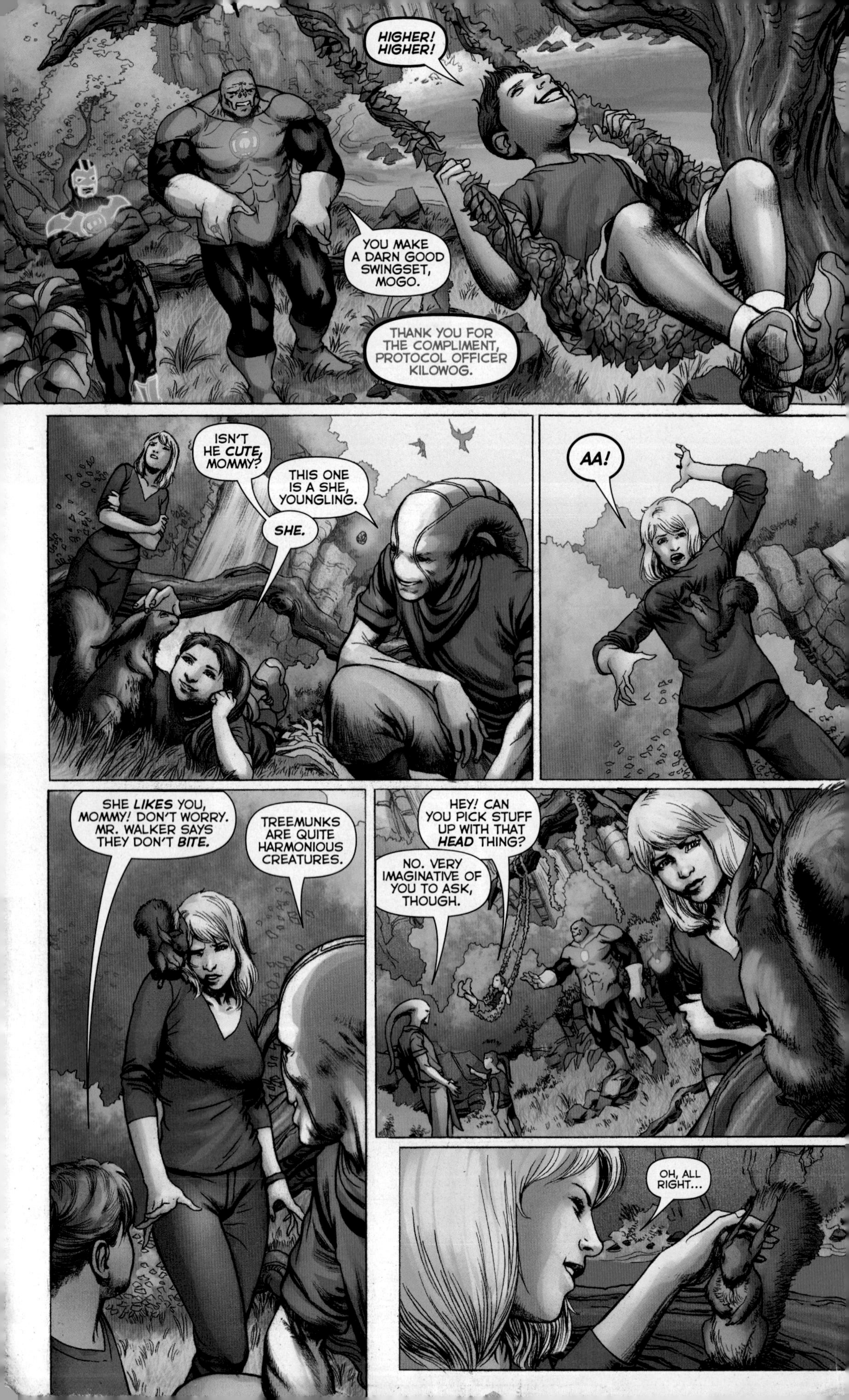
HIGHER! HIGHER!
YOU MAKE A DARN GOOD SWINGSET, MOGO.
THANK YOU FOR THE COMPLIMENT, PROTOCOL OFFICER KILOWOG.
ISN'T HE CUTE, MOMMY?
THIS ONE IS A SHE, YOUNGLING.
SHE.
AA!
SHE LIKES YOU, MOMMY! DON'T WORRY. MR. WALKER SAYS THEY DON'T BITE.
TREEMUNKS ARE QUITE HARMONIOUS CREATURES.
HEY! CAN YOU PICK STUFF UP WITH THAT HEAD THING?
NO. VERY IMAGINATIVE OF YOU TO ASK, THOUGH.
OH, ALL RIGHT...

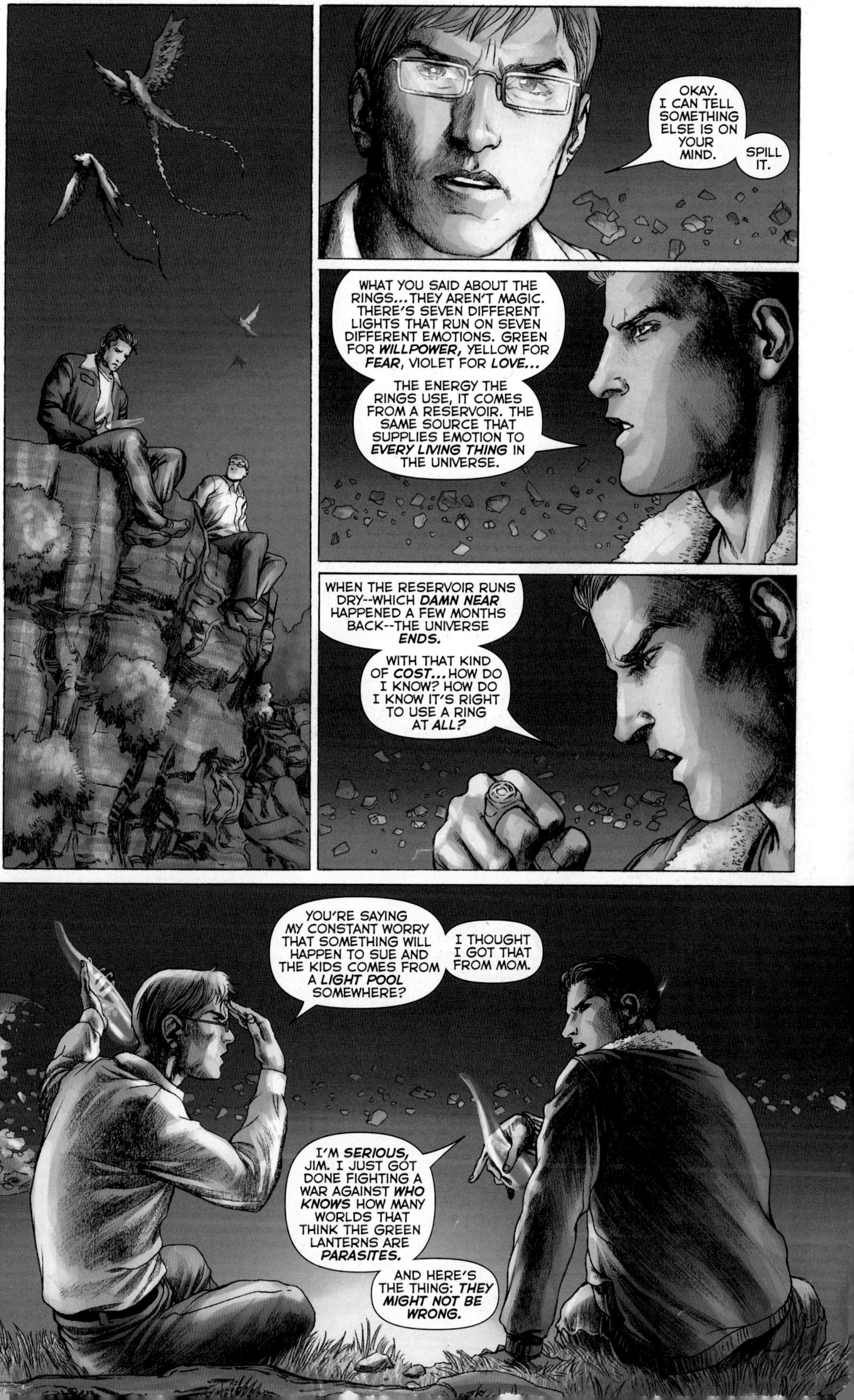
OKAY. I CAN TELL SOMETHING ELSE IS ON YOUR MIND.
SPILL IT.
WHAT YOU SAID ABOUT THE RINGS... THEY AREN'T MAGIC. THERE'S SEVEN DIFFERENT LIGHTS THAT RUN ON SEVEN DIFFERENT EMOTIONS. GREEN FOR *WILLPOWER*, YELLOW FOR *FEAR*, VIOLET FOR *LOVE*...
THE ENERGY THE RINGS USE, IT COMES FROM A RESERVOIR. THE SAME SOURCE THAT SUPPLIES EMOTION TO *EVERY LIVING THING* IN THE UNIVERSE.
WHEN THE RESERVOIR RUNS DRY--WHICH *DAMN NEAR* HAPPENED A FEW MONTHS BACK--THE UNIVERSE *ENDS*.
WITH THAT KIND OF *COST*... HOW DO I KNOW? HOW DO I KNOW IT'S RIGHT TO USE A RING AT *ALL?*
YOU'RE SAYING MY CONSTANT WORRY THAT SOMETHING WILL HAPPEN TO SUE AND THE KIDS COMES FROM A *LIGHT POOL* SOMEWHERE?
I THOUGHT I GOT THAT FROM MOM.
I'M *SERIOUS*, JIM. I JUST GOT DONE FIGHTING A WAR AGAINST *WHO KNOWS* HOW MANY WORLDS THAT THINK THE GREEN LANTERNS ARE *PARASITES*.
AND HERE'S THE THING: *THEY MIGHT NOT BE WRONG.*

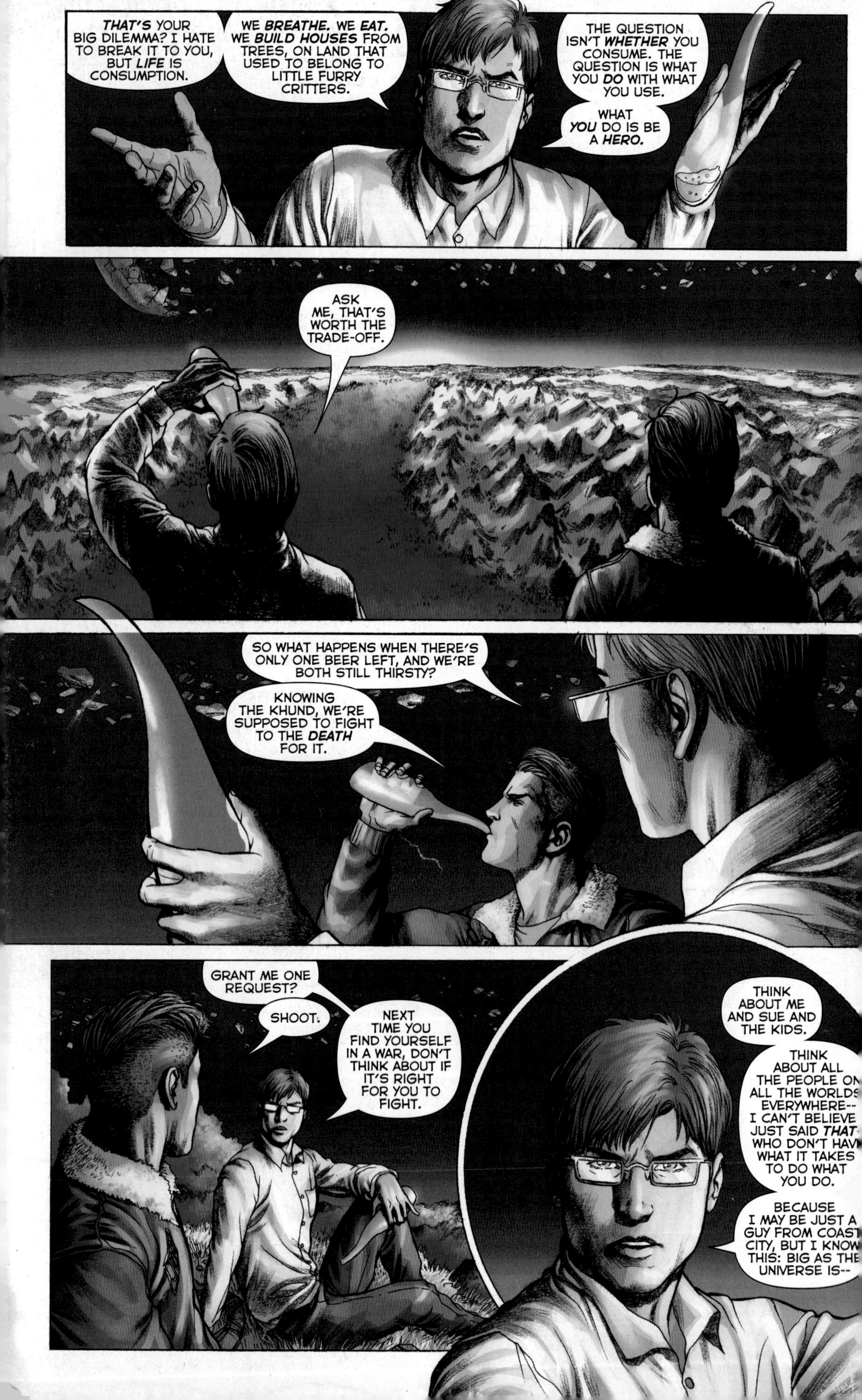
THAT'S YOUR BIG DILEMMA? I HATE TO BREAK IT TO YOU, BUT LIFE IS CONSUMPTION.
WE BREATHE. WE EAT. WE BUILD HOUSES FROM TREES, ON LAND THAT USED TO BELONG TO LITTLE FURRY CRITTERS.
THE QUESTION ISN'T WHETHER YOU CONSUME. THE QUESTION IS WHAT YOU DO WITH WHAT YOU USE.
WHAT YOU DO IS BE A HERO.
ASK ME, THAT'S WORTH THE TRADE-OFF.
SO WHAT HAPPENS WHEN THERE'S ONLY ONE BEER LEFT, AND WE'RE BOTH STILL THIRSTY?
KNOWING THE KHUND, WE'RE SUPPOSED TO FIGHT TO THE DEATH FOR IT.
GRANT ME ONE REQUEST?
SHOOT.
NEXT TIME YOU FIND YOURSELF IN A WAR, DON'T THINK ABOUT IF IT'S RIGHT FOR YOU TO FIGHT.
THINK ABOUT ME AND SUE AND THE KIDS.
THINK ABOUT ALL THE PEOPLE O ALL THE WORLDS EVERYWHERE-- I CAN'T BELIEVE JUST SAID THAT- WHO DON'T HAV WHAT IT TAKES TO DO WHAT YOU DO.
BECAUSE I MAY BE JUST A GUY FROM COAST CITY, BUT I KNOW THIS: BIG AS THE UNIVERSE IS--

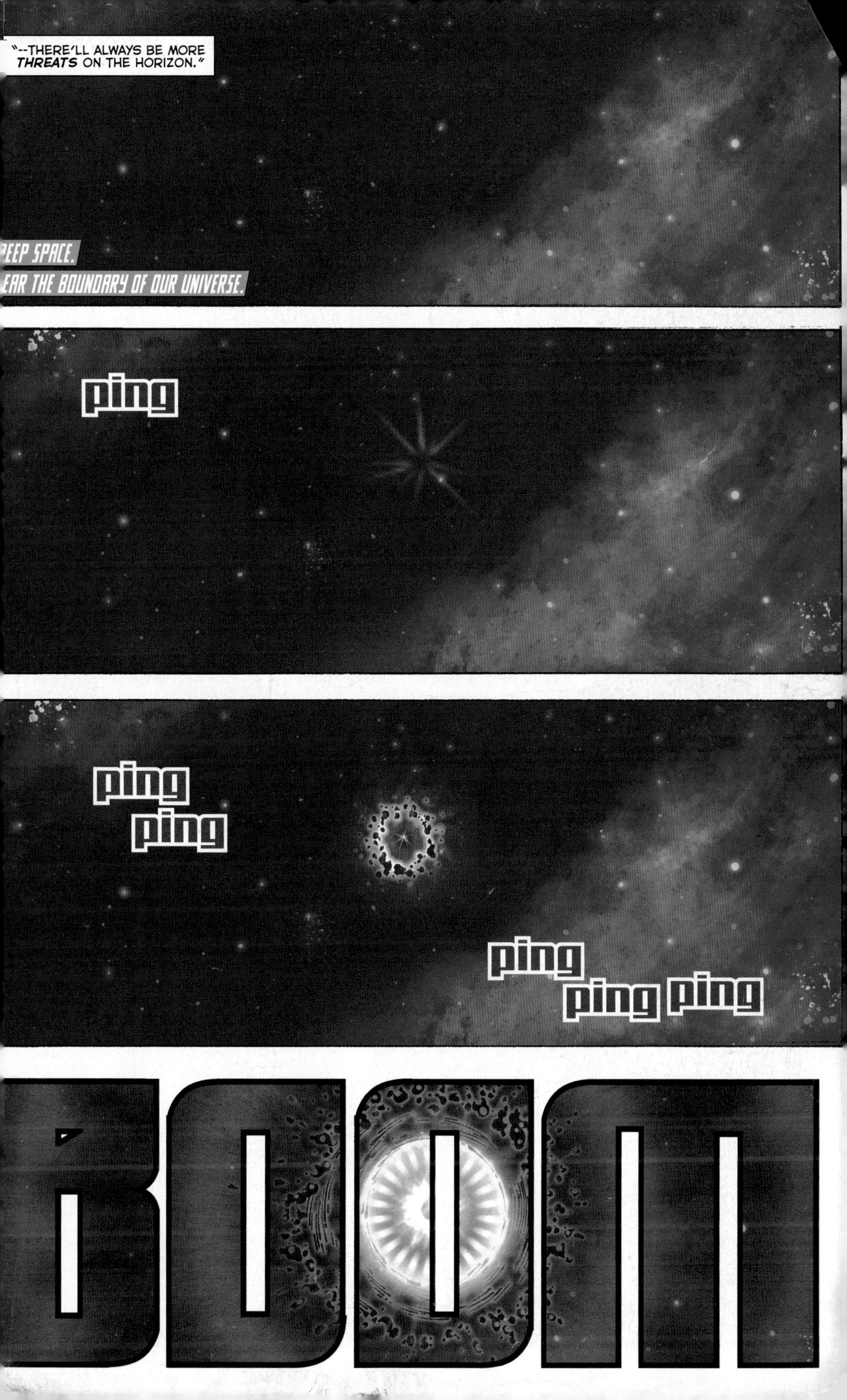
"--THERE'LL ALWAYS BE MORE THREATS ON THE HORIZON."
EEP SPACE.
EAR THE BOUNDARY OF OUR UNIVERSE.
ping
ping
ping
ping
ping ping
BOOM

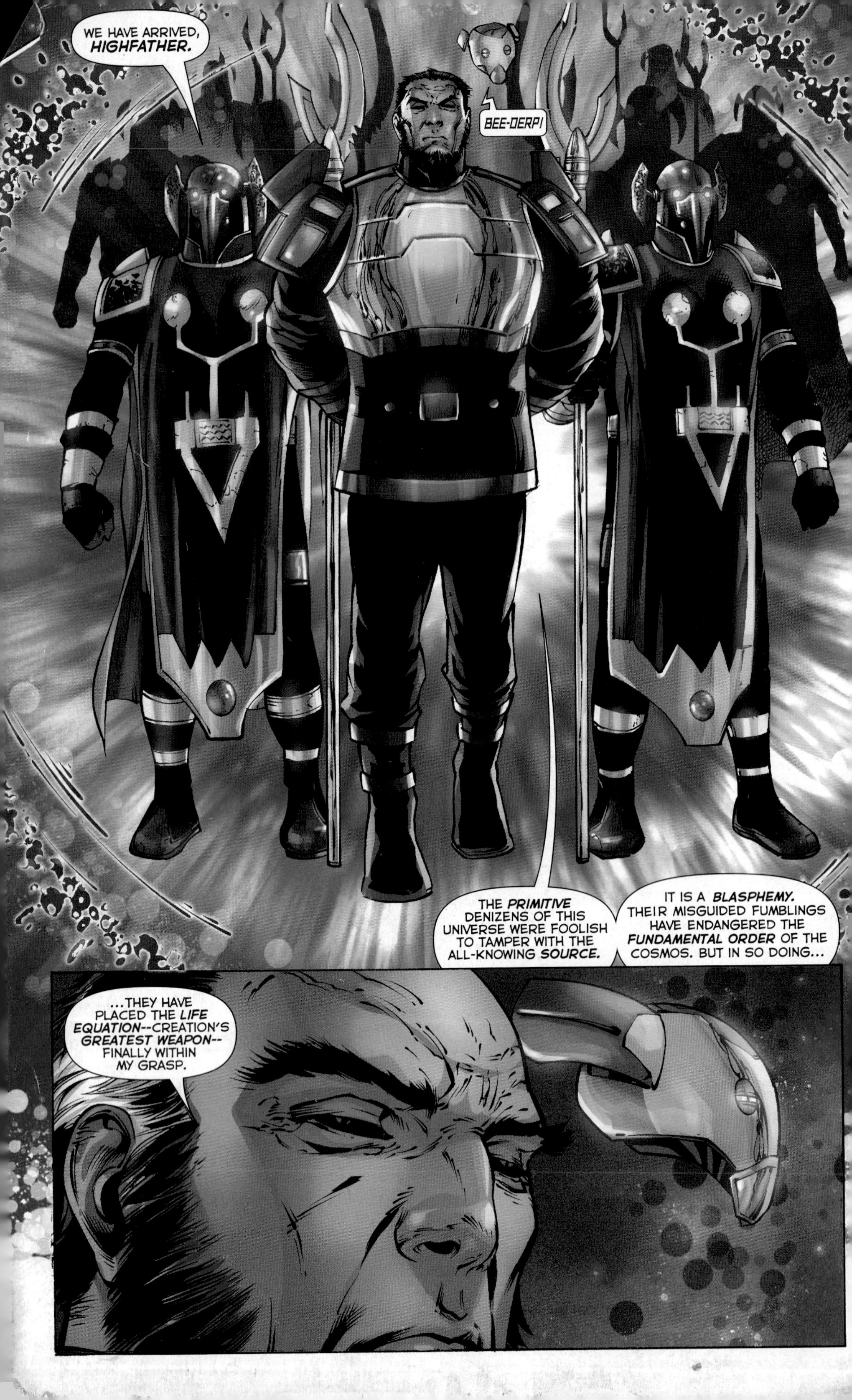
WE HAVE ARRIVED, HIGHFATHER.
BEE-DERP!
THE PRIMITIVE DENIZENS OF THIS UNIVERSE WERE FOOLISH TO TAMPER WITH THE ALL-KNOWING SOURCE.
IT IS A BLASPHEMY. THEIR MISGUIDED FUMBLINGS HAVE ENDANGERED THE FUNDAMENTAL ORDER OF THE COSMOS. BUT IN SO DOING...
...THEY HAVE PLACED THE LIFE EQUATION--CREATION'S GREATEST WEAPON--FINALLY WITHIN MY GRASP.